W9-DIM-951

BUILDING THE NATION

Building the Nation

Americans Write About Their Architecture,
Their Cities, and Their Landscape

Edited by
STEVEN CONN and MAX PAGE

PENN

UNIVERSITY OF PENNSYLVANIA PRESS
Philadelphia

Publication of this volume was assisted by grants from the Graham Foundation for Advanced Studies in the Fine Arts and from Furthermore: a program of the J. M. Kaplan Fund

10   9   8   7   6   5   4   3   2   1

Published by
University of Pennsylvania Press
Philadelphia, Pennsylvania 19104-4011

Library of Congress Cataloging-in-Publication Data
Building the nation : Americans write about their architecture, their cities, and their landscape /
    edited by Steven Conn and Max Page.
        p. cm.
    Includes bibliographical references and index.
    ISBN 0-8122-3734-X (cloth : alk. paper)—ISBN 0-8122-1852-3 (pbk. : alk. paper)
        1. Architecture—United States.   2. Cities and towns—United States   I. Conn, Steven.
II. Page, Max.

NA705.B759 2003
720'.973—dc21
                                                                                    2003048413

To Jonah and Olivia
and to
Aviva and Zachary,
who slowed this book down
in all the right ways

CONTENTS

CHAPTER 1. INTRODUCTION: AMERICAN ARCHITECTURE?   1

1. Anonymous, excerpt from "On the Architecture of America," 1790   9

2. Anonymous, excerpt from "On the Arts," 1815   10

3. R. C. Long, "Architecture: Its Alleged Degeneracy," 1842   12

4. Horatio Greenough, excerpt from "American Architecture," 1843   14

5. Anonymous, excerpt from "A Public Building," 1869   17

6. Frederick Jackson Turner, "Architecture Through Oppression," 1884   22

7. Montgomery Schuyler, "The Point of View," 1891   24

8. John Dos Passos, excerpt from *The Big Money*, 1936   26

9. Mary Hornaday, "Melting Pot of Architecture," 1937   27

10. Talbot F. Hamlin, excerpt from "The Architecture of the Future," 1943   30

11. G. E. Kidder Smith, excerpt from "The Tragedy of American Architecture," 1945   33

12. John A. Kouwenhoven, excerpt from "What Is 'American' in Architecture and Design? Notes Toward an Aesthetic of Process," 1961   37

13. Douglas Davis, "Towers of Mammon," 1973   41

14. Vincent Scully, "Tomorrow's Ruins Today," 1999   43

CHAPTER 2. "THEY DO THINGS BETTER IN EUROPE": AMERICANS VIEW THE WORLD   47

15. Thomas Jefferson, Letters from Paris, 1785–1786   53

16. Anonymous, excerpt from "Description of the City of Morocco," 1795   55

17. Anonymous, excerpt from "Sketch of Amsterdam," 1804   57

18. Catherine Maria Sedgwick, excerpt from *Letters from Abroad to Kindred at Home*, 1841   59

19. Constance Fenimore Woolson, excerpt from *Mentone, Cairo, and Corfu*, 1896   61

20. Mark Twain, excerpts from *The Innocents Abroad*, 1869   64

21. Edith Wharton, excerpt from *Italian Villas and Their Gardens*, 1904   66

22. Sylvester Baxter, excerpt from "The German Way of Making Better Cities," 1909   69

23. Malcolm Cowley, excerpt from *Exile's Return: A Literary Odyssey of the 1920s*, 1934   73

24. Frank Lloyd Wright, excerpt from "Architecture and Life in the U.S.S.R.," 1937   76

25. Douglas Haskell, excerpt from "Recent Architecture Abroad," 1940   79

26. George Biddle, excerpt from "Israel: Young Blood and Old," 1949   81

27. Paul Goldberger, excerpt from "The International Style After Half a Century," 1983   84

28. Suzanne Stephens, "Manifest Disney," 1992   87

CHAPTER 3. SO GLORIOUS A LANDSCAPE:
    SHAPING NATURE THE AMERICAN WAY   93

29. C. W. Short, "Antiquities of Ohio," 1817   97

30. Anonymous, "Pine Lands of New Jersey," 1829   99

31. John McPhee, excerpt from *The Pine Barrens*, 1967   100

32. Washington Irving, excerpt from *A Tour on the Prairies*, 1835   102

33. Anonymous, Review of Andrew Jackson Downing, "Landscape Gardening
and Rural Architecture in America," 1845   106

34. H. M. Alden, excerpt from "The Pennsylvania Coal Region," 1863   112

35. Frederick Lewis Allen, "Our National Shabbiness," 1915   114

36. Douglas Haskell, "Architecture of the TVA," 1941   118

37. John D. MacDonald, "Last Chance to Save the Everglades," 1969   120

38. John A. Kouwenhoven, excerpt from "Preliminary Glance at an American
Landscape," 1961   123

39. William F. Buckley, excerpt from "The Politics of Beauty," 1966 125

40. Peter Blake, excerpt from *God's Own Junkyard*, 1964   130

41. Michael Pollan, "Abolish the White House Lawn," 1991   133

42. William Cronon, "The Trouble with Wilderness," 1995   137

CHAPTER 4. ONE NATION, OF MANY PARTS:
    REGIONALISM AND THE BUILT ENVIRONMENT   141

43. Anonymous, excerpt from "Topographical Sketches of the County
of Essex," 1792   147

44. Anonymous, excerpt from "An Account of Moravian Settlements," 1796 149

45. Z, excerpt from "Domestic Architecture," 1832   152

46. W. E. B. Du Bois, excerpt from *The Souls of Black Folk*, 1903   155

47. Clifton Johnson, excerpt from *Highways and Byways of the South*, 1904 159

48. Corra Harris, excerpt from "The Abomination of Cities," 1914   163

49. J. W. Hoover, excerpt from "House and Village Types of the Southwest as
Conditioned by Aridity," 1935; and Talbot Hamlin, excerpt from "What Makes It
American? Architecture in the Southwest and West," 1939   165

50. Phyllis Fenner, excerpt from "Grandfather's Store," 1942   173

51. Carey McWilliams, excerpt from "Look What's Happened to California," 1949 174

52. Charlotte Conway, "Why Is This an American Style House?" 1951   177

53. Thomas Griffith, "Show Me the Way to Go Home," 1974   179

54. John Brinckerhoff Jackson, excerpt from "A Vision of New Fields," 1984 181

55. Steven Conn, "Bulldozing Our Sense of Place," 1999   184

CHAPTER 5. URBANISM, REAL AND IMAGINED   187

56. The Reverend Dr. Duche, "Description of Philadelphia," 1789   193

57. Anonymous, "Description of the City of Washington," 1791   195

58. M. G. Upton, excerpt from "The Plan of San Francisco," 1869   197

59. The Reverend Josiah Strong, excerpt from "The Problem of the Twentieth
Century City," 1888   200

60. Julian Ralph, excerpt from "Colorado and Its Capital," 1893   203

61. John Coleman Adams, excerpt from "What a Great City Might Be—A Lesson
from the White City," 1896   206

62. Anonymous, excerpt from "Art and Railway Stations," 1909   210

63. Charles Mulford Robinson, excerpt from "Improvement in City Life: Aesthetic
Progress," 1899   212

64. W. E. B. Du Bois, excerpt from *The Philadelphia Negro: A Social Study*, 1899   215

65. Louis Sullivan, excerpt from "The Tall Office Building Artistically
Considered," 1896; and Henry James, excerpt from *The American Scene*, 1907   221

66. *Commonweal* Editors, "The Terrible Super-City," 1925   227

67. Norman Bel Geddes, excerpt from *Magic Motorways*, 1940   228

68. E. B. White, excerpt from "Here Is New York," 1949   231

69. Simone de Beauvoir, *America Day by Day* (*L'Amérique au jour le jour*), 1954   236

70. Jane Jacobs, "Downtown Is for People," 1958   237

71. Alfred Kazin, "Fear of the City, 1783 to 1983," 1983   240

72. Camillo Jose Vergara, excerpt from "The New American Ghetto," 1994   243

73. Kurt Andersen, excerpt from "A City on a Hill," 1997   246

74. Richard Todd, excerpt from "Las Vegas, Tis of Thee," 2001   250

75. Max Page, "On Edge, Again," 2001   252

CHAPTER 6. TAMING THE CRABGRASS FRONTIER:
                THE TRIUMPH OF THE SUBURBS   257

76. Anonymous, "Landscape-Gardening: Llewellen Park," 1857; and Anonymous,
"Llewellyn Park," 1871   263

77. Olmsted, Vaux and Co., excerpt from "Letter to the Riverside Improvement
Company," 1868   265

78. Anonymous, excerpt from *Suburban Homes on the West Jersey Railroad*, 1881   268

79. R. Clipston Sturgis, excerpt from "Suburban Homes: A Plea for Privacy in
Home Life," 1896   271

80. Christine Frederick, excerpt from "Is Suburban Living a Delusion?" 1928; and
Ethel Longworth Swift, excerpt from "In Defense of Suburbia," 1928   273

81. Thomas H. and Doris Reed, with Murray Teigh Bloom, excerpt from "Does
Your City Suffer from Suburbanitis?" 1952   279

82. Frederick Lewis Allen, excerpt from "The Big Change in Suburbia," 1954   284

83. William H. Whyte, Jr., excerpt from "Are Cities Un-American?" 1957   289

84. Betty Friedan, excerpt from *The Feminine Mystique*, 1963   292

85. David Guterson, excerpt from "No Place Like Home," 1992   295

86. James Howard Kunstler, excerpt from "Home from Nowhere," 1996   301

CHAPTER 7. BETTER BUILDINGS, BETTER PEOPLE:
      ARCHITECTURE AND SOCIAL REFORM   307

87. Charles Dickens, excerpt from *American Notes*, 1842   311

88. Anonymous, excerpt from "The Shakers at Lebanon," 1851   315

89. Anonymous, excerpt from "College Edifices and Their Relation
to Education," 1847   320

90. Catherine E. Beecher and Harriet Beecher Stowe, excerpt from *The American
Woman's Home*, 1869   324

91. Richard T. Ely, excerpt from "Pullman: A Social Study," 1885   328

92. C. John Hexamer, excerpt from "Mill Architecture," 1885   335

93. Mary Bronson Hartt, excerpt from "Beautifying the Ugly Things," 1905   336

94. Isaac F. Marcosson, excerpt from "Giving Carnegie Libraries," 1905   338

95. Benjamin Marsh, excerpt from "City Planning in Justice to the Working
Population," 1908   342

96. Edith Elmer Wood, excerpt from "That 'One Third of a Nation,' " 1940   345

97. James Bailey, "The Case History of a Failure," 1965   348

98. Vincent Scully, "The Threat and Promise of Urban Redevelopment in
New Haven," 1967   353

99. John Edgar Wideman, "Doing Time, Marking Race," 1995;
and Peter Annin, "Inside the New Alcatraz," 1998   355

CHAPTER 8. MONUMENTS AND MEMORY:
      BUILDING AND PROTECTING THE AMERICAN PAST   361

100. Joseph Sansom, "Description of an Indian Mound," 1822   367

101. S., excerpt from "Church Architecture in New-York," 1847   368

102. Anonymous, "Washington's Examples," 1866   372

103. Charles Eliot Norton, excerpt from "The Lack of Old Homes in America," 1889   373

104. Anonymous, excerpt from "A Great Battle Park," 1895   375

105. Park Pressey, excerpt from "Preserving the Landmarks," 1914   376

106. Helen Burns, excerpt from "Colonial Williamsburg," 1940   378

107. Lewis Mumford, "The Disappearance of Pennsylvania Station," 1958   381

108. Russell Kirk, "Destroying the Past by 'Development,' " 1965   387

109. Herbert J. Gans, excerpt from "Preserving Everyone's Noo Yawk," 1975; and Ada Louise Huxtable, excerpt from "Preserving Noo Yawk Landmarks," 1975   389

110. Paul Goldberger, "The Vietnam Memorial," 1982   392

111. Phil Patton, excerpt from "The House That Ruth's Father Built," 1991   396

112. Ann Carrns, "How a Brand-New Development Came by Its Rich History," 1998   397

113. Tracie Rozhon, excerpt from "Old Baltimore Row Houses Fall Before the Wrecking Ball," 1999   400

114. Herbert Muschamp, "New War Memorial Is Shrine to Sentiment," 2001   404

Thematic Index   409

Acknowledgments   411

1.1. Thomas Cole, *The Architect's Dream*, 1840. Oil on canvas, 53 × 84 ¹⁄₁₆ in. Toledo Museum of Art, Toledo, Ohio. Purchased with funds from the Florence Scott Libbey Bequest in memory of her father, Maurice A. Scott. Thomas Cole painted this fantasy landscape just four years after Ralph Waldo Emerson complained that Americans groped too much among the "dry bones of the past." The architect, Ithiel Town, had requested a view of Athens but gave Cole discretion as to the contents of the picture. (Town ultimately rejected the painting.) The result was a scene of the architect imagining many of the great architectural traditions of the past, from the pyramids of Egypt down to the Gothic church. Squeezed into the foreground lies the American wilderness. For many American architects in the nineteenth century the dream depicted here only underscored how difficult it would be to create a distinctively American architecture.

CHAPTER 1

Introduction: American Architecture?

> Architecture is the best expression of a society, where it is and where
> it hopes to go.
>
> —Vincent Scully

Buildings spoke to Henry James. When James, a towering figure in the world of American letters, returned to the United States in 1904 after an absence of nearly twenty-five years, he toured his old haunts, the places of his growing-up, and the buildings whispered to him. It is not important here what they said. James's record of his visit, published as *The American Scene*, serves as a reminder that buildings, cities, landscapes—the totality of our built environment—speak to all of us.

In this sense, architecture is the one fine art that cannot be escaped. Many Americans go their whole lives without ever reading James, or Edith Wharton or James Baldwin, without ever listening to a symphony orchestra or hearing live jazz. But no one lives a life outside and apart from architecture. Regardless of where we live or what our work might be, we live our lives and do our work within spaces shaped by human imagination and human hands. Architecture thus stands as the one indispensable cultural production.

No less than Egypt, Rome, or the Ottoman Empire, the United States has, since its founding, relied on its buildings and its landscapes to reflect, define, and contest a national identity. Debates over what constitutes an American architecture, and what architecture's role in the nation's life should be, have therefore stood at the center of public life. As Americans have wrestled with issues of architectural form and style, with the nature of their cities, and with their relationship to the natural environment, they have evaluated and reevaluated the state of their democratic experiment and the meaning of participation in it by critiquing the design of their homes, their institutions, their urban spaces, and the landscapes that have surrounded them.

We offer here a window onto some of these debates over America's "built environment." By that term we mean all the ways in which people shape their surroundings—from formal architecture, to informal, vernacular buildings, to town and city planning, to the design of parks and the manipulation of the natural landscape—and the reasons they have done so. *Building the Nation* is a critical anthology of American writings about the built environment from the founding of the nation until the close of the twentieth century.

Our approach is to heed the insight of the old Shaker proverb "Every force evolves a form." Every force in American life—whether the Civil War, the rise of industrial capitalism, the Great Depression or, more locally, the desire of people to live in better homes or of a town to have a public library—has left its mark on the built environment. To the proverb we add, "Every form evolves a force." American buildings and places, once built, become social and cultural actors in their own right, shaping how Americans understand themselves and their place in the world.

Our aims are several. We want to give readers a glimpse into the lively public conversations that have taken place over the course of the nation's history about the built environment. More boldly, we want this anthology to help reimagine American architectural history by tying it to the broader themes in American social, cultural, and intellectual history. Perhaps most important of all, we hope that this collection gives readers the critical tools with which they can not only evaluate the state of their own built environments but also start to change it. Our premise, though it may sound straightforward, is that architecture should serve the needs of a larger society and should advance its ideals—in the words of Ralph Erskine, "The job of buildings is to improve human relations: architecture must ease them, not make them worse." The selections we have made all wrestle in one way or another with that fundamental issue.

We begin late in the eighteenth century with the ratification of the Constitution and the founding of the nation in order to make clear this assertion: The quest to define a unique and distinctively American approach to the built environment has undergirded the designing of homes, the building of cities and towns, and the way nature and human activity have been merged. While the traditions of earlier architectures were not forgotten or abandoned, the political, military, and intellectual acts that culminated in 1789 did create a new context for the discussion of architecture and its meaning. We bring our consideration up to the end of the twentieth century both to chart the ways in which the discussion of architecture has shifted over the course of two centuries and to notice how many of the issues raised at the birth of the republic remain live today.

That there is not now nor has there ever been a final answer to the question "What is an American architecture?" goes almost without saying. What the voices collected here demonstrate, disparate as they are, is that the search for an "American architecture" has been the central idea animating what Americans have built.

To illuminate these questions, we have relied a great deal on newspaper clippings, articles from popular magazines, travelogues, and even the occasional novel. Absent, or nearly so, are pieces written by architects speaking to other architects. It merits remembering that while building is eternal, architecture as a profession is quite young. The vast majority—upwards of 90 percent according to some estimates—of buildings and designed landscapes in the United State have been built without professional assistance. They are the products of pattern books, local builders, and individual imaginations. Since our interest is in the relationship between the built environment and other social issues, we have looked to popular, mass venues of communication. The voices here, many of them, are ordinary, largely unknown, and in some cases anonymous. In this way, we hope we have recreated some of the popular conversations that have taken place around architecture and not merely recapitulated the concerns of professionals. In the course of our researches, we have been struck by just how much writing there has been, in all sorts of places, about the built environment; indeed, we collected far more material for this volume than could ultimately fit! We make no claim that this represents a comprehensive collection, but we do think it will give readers a representative sense of how Americans have discussed their built environment at different moments in our history.

Some readers may be stunned to find that Frank Lloyd Wright's Fallingwater is not discussed here. Nor are most of the buildings we have come to regard as iconic: not Louis Sullivan's Wainwright Building in Chicago or Mies van der Rohe's Seagram Building in New York. Where we present a document about the U. S. Capitol, it is not to delineate the classical references in the friezes or to sort out which architect did what on the building.

Rather it is to discuss how that building in that city proposed to embody the very ideals of the nation itself. In some senses, this book is a documentary history of the nation's built environment that joins some of the more recent histories written by scholars like Vincent Scully, John Stilgoe, Dolores Hayden, Gwendolyn Wright, Daniel Bluestone, and others who have broadened our understanding of the built environment beyond a particular set of architects and a canonical set of buildings. Other areas of American history have benefited in recent years from volumes of primary documents, and while there a few fine volumes of documents on architecture—notably Don Gifford's *Literature and Architecture* (1966), Leland Roth's *America Builds* (1983), and Joan Ockman's *Architecture Culture* (1993)—none takes the comprehensive and historically grounded approach to the built environment that we have provided here.

This book is organized into eight chapters, each dealing with a different theme. Documents within each chapter span both the nineteenth and twentieth centuries. Each chapter begins with our brief introduction, sketching the issues to be considered and tracing their chronological trajectory. These introductions also glance at some larger cultural, social, and intellectual developments relevant to the topic. Readers will find that each document is introduced briefly as well.

We begin, then, in Chapter 1 with a series of writings very broad in their scope, which seek to address the nature of American architecture as a whole. Architecture, perhaps more than any of the fine arts, embodies the values, tastes, and ambitions of a culture: How might one create an architecture that would give physical form to the new nation's aspirations? Sweeping statements, these writings consider American architecture and its relationship to the state of the nation at particular moments—the country's founding, for example, or its crisis in the 1930s. As the nation developed in the late eighteenth and early nineteenth centuries, Americans who wrote about architecture believed that the new nation demanded a new architecture, one commensurate with the boldness of the American political experiment. They asked questions about what a "democratic" architecture should be and about how American cities could avoid the "corruption" of their European counterparts. Americans, especially in the nineteenth century, surveyed the history of architecture trying to figure out what, exactly, from architecture's past could be appropriated to build an American future. Indeed, as architectural critic and historian Joseph Rykwert has pointed out, the most vigorous architectural debates of the nineteenth century revolved around the meanings and appropriateness of different styles. American architects and builders who tried to create buildings to reflect the new nation found themselves relying, perhaps inevitably, on the styles of the past. Later in the nineteenth century, facing a variety of crises—secession and war, chaotic urban growth, the social traumas associated with industrialization—writers continued to talk about architecture as a curative for an ailing nation. In the twentieth century, faced with both the challenges and opportunities of growing national diversity and an increasingly prominent international presence, writers reconsidered how American buildings would reflect the changing populace and democratic ideals.

Americans have always had a strained cultural relationship with Europe, and Chapter 2 provides a window through which to view that. Travel writings of Europeans who visited the United States and wrote, often disparagingly, about their findings have become familiar to readers. Less well known are the writings of Americans who went back across the Atlantic looking for sources of cultural inspiration, hoping to bring European design ideas back to the United States. The essays included in this chapter reveal how, through the nineteenth and much of the twentieth centuries, the cultural traffic went largely in one direction between Europe and the United States, as many Americans felt they lived in Europe's shadow. By the latter half of the twentieth century, however, writers discuss how American ideas and forms began to proliferate around the globe and the rest of the world began to take on a decidedly American cast.

At some level, America exists more powerfully in the imagination as a landscape. Just as Americans debated the proper way to design individual buildings and how to build better cities, they wondered about how to shape the vast natural landscape they saw stretching before them, and Chapter 3 fleshes out these debates. On one hand, Americans viewed the natural world they saw as their birthright, as an almost limitless arena for the development of cities and commerce, as resources to be exploited. On the other hand, they looked to the landscape, almost reverentially, as the reservoir of moral power and as the source of democracy's reinvigoration, and they worried about what would happen to America as the loss of landscape continued apace. By the end of the twentieth century, many lamented that, except in a few preserves, the American landscape had been reduced to a homogenized lowest common denominator, a landscape of banality and sameness.

Too often discussion of American architecture has focused on the buildings of the Northeast, as if this region spoke for the entire nation. Chapter 4 stands as a corrective to this regional bias. Through much of the nation's history, the United States might better be viewed as three regions—North, South, and West—with numbers of smaller regions within these. By shifting the lens through which we examine questions of the built environment to different regions of the country, we hope to broaden and complicate our thinking about the diversity of American architecture and space. The writings included in this chapter also reveal that regional distinctiveness in architecture, like the American landscape itself, had eroded dramatically by the end of the twentieth century.

Chapter 5 focuses on the debates over visions of America as an urban nation. Central to this debate was both the repulsion and attraction Americans felt—and continue to feel—about their cities. Attempts to reconcile this simultaneous enthusiasm and suspicion included efforts to redesign cities with park and parkway plans, utopian settlements in rural areas, and temporary urban fantasies embodied most powerfully in the 1893 World's Columbian Exposition in Chicago and more recently by Disney's theme park cities.

In Chapter 6, we give special attention to the suburbs, which have come to be the dominant type of housing settlement in the United States since the 1950s. In 1980, the federal census announced that the United States had become a suburban nation, with a majority of us living in these "in between" places rather than in cities or in rural areas. Chapter 6 considers the American suburb. Even as America was building its great cities in the nineteenth century, it was also developing the ideology and forms of a new type of settlement. Originally the suburb was conceived of in the nineteenth century as a place where one could have the benefits of both city and country, where carefully planned picturesque natural beauty might be only a brief train ride from the bustle of downtown. In the twentieth century, the automobile changed profoundly how the suburb was built and how it functioned; after the Second World War, suburban sprawl began in earnest, fueled in part by a perception that American cities were in crisis. Postwar suburbanization has transformed the American landscape—both the physical and the political landscape—

more profoundly and more quickly than any other phenomenon in American history. We are only just beginning to tally the consequences.

Chapter 7 looks at the American impulse to reform both individuals and society through architecture. In the nineteenth century, environmental factors replaced essentialist and theological ones as explanations for human behavior, both good and bad. Bad people, once thought to be bad intrinsically, were now believed to be bad because of the circumstances that surrounded them. As a result of this intellectual shift, many Americans became what we might call "architectural determinists." For them bad buildings produced bad people; good buildings would produce good ones. Schools, properly designed, would generate better students; proper houses led to proper families; prisons built according to the right principles would reform criminals. In the twentieth century, the religious roots of this reforming instinct became less overt, but the belief that physical design would create better citizens and foster healthier communities persisted.

We conclude with a chapter dealing with how Americans have preserved the past in the built environment. It was during the nineteenth century that Americans developed a distinctive historical consciousness. This presented something of a paradox because the United States was both celebrated and derided as a nation without history. The nascent movement for historic preservation was driven by an urgency that the physical remains of America's history were disappearing, victim in many cases to the very economic "progress" Americans lauded. This movement grew in the late nineteenth century and exploded into a national phenomenon by the mid-twentieth century. The writings in Chapter 8 illustrate how Americans attempted to embody a sense of the past in the built environment, and how Americans debated which pasts were worthy of saving in the first place.

The issues around which we have organized this volume themselves represent certain choices we have made and issues we want to emphasize. Like any categorization, these chapters focusing on these issues are to some extent artificial; they certainly do not mirror perfectly the writings we have included. As a consequence many of these pieces speak to two or even more of the chapters—an essay we have included in the chapter on landscape, for example, might have much to say about regionalism; issues of urbanism and suburbanization are necessarily intertwined. Drawing connections between chapters and issues is part of what we hope will be fun for readers.

Over the course of many centuries, and perhaps more so than any other cultural production, architecture has prompted some angry, vitriolic polemics, couched often in the language of ethics and morality. And although not all the voices that populate this volume ring out with that kind of invective, this collection does have a point of view. Or several. Ostensibly anthologies are merely collections of other people's work. But in fact every anthology bears the strong imprint of its editors. The selection of documents and the way they are arranged, edited, and introduced all shape an underlying argument the editors want to make. This is as it should and must be. We would like to make the implicit explicit, however, and lay out for readers now some of the motivations that lie behind this book and that prompted us to put it together.

To begin, we are skeptical of the architectural determinism mentioned above if it means that difficult, complicated problems of social justice and inequalities generate only design solutions. We don't believe that architecture can solve social problems without serious attention to the other causes of those problems. At the same time, however, we share a strong belief in the power of architecture to shape people's lives, to destroy or invigorate communities. Good buildings will not cure all of what ails this society, but they are surely part of the solution.

We believe that the varieties of America's natural landscape have been one of the main sources of what is and has been powerful and unique about American life, whether for Henry David Thoreau at the unassuming Walden Pond or John Muir staring at the spectacular Yosemite Valley. The American landscape is closely tied to what it means to be an American, different meanings, needless to say, for different people interacting with different landscapes. We also lament that Americans have been erratic caretakers of that landscape, saving some of the most spectacular places, letting much of the more ordinary but no less important landscapes disappear. We are convinced that when people live within a built environment that inspires us, when we become part of the process of protecting and cherishing the landscapes around us, we understand better what it means not simply to be American, but to be human. Symptomatic of the way we have failed to be good caretakers of the landscape is the wiping away of many of the regional differences that used to make traveling around this great country such an extraordinary cultural revelation. We believe that the forces of architectural homogenization that have left Phoenix and Boston, Atlanta and Seattle virtually indistinguishable have also left us a poorer nation.

Many of the nation's landscapes have been trashed—we can think of no better word—in the past half century as private citizens, private developers, banks, and pliant politicians have pushed headlong into the crabgrass frontier to create the suburban nation we live in today. We see no abatement of this on the horizon. We are relentless critics of the suburbs as an architectural "form" and as a ubiquitous landscape and are deeply suspicious of the faux populism of those who would defend strip malls and racially and economically segregated housing developments as a "democratic" response to market demand. Even if that were true, which it is surely not, a disembodied "market demand" is no excuse for the social and environmental damage done to this country by suburban development. The escape from public life and public responsibilities into the insular isolated spaces of private suburban life would be terrible in any society. In a democratic one, it is downright irresponsible and dangerous.

The term "urban sprawl" is a misnomer and ought to be replaced with the more accurate phrase "suburban sprawl." Most cities, after all, have remained fixed spots on the map, while it is suburbia that continues to metastasize cancerously into the landscape. In making this small, but critical semantic distinction we underscore our great love of cities. We find in American cities endless possibilities—diversity, argument, friction, inspiration. A true public life. American cities have become the warehouses of most of this nation's social problems—if we have any hope of solving them, we will do so in the cities. We agree with the great writer Walter Lippmann when he said years ago: "A great society is simply a big, complicated urban society."

Our training as historians leads us to believe that a nuanced and deep understanding of how Americans have understood their pasts is crucial to building better places in a better future. We believe that the presence of the past in the landscape—not a mummified, Disney-fied past, but a living link to it—is crucial to the health of our society.

We believe that architects and all who shape the built environment practice the most public of the fine arts. Therefore they have a public responsibility greater than novelists, dancers, or musicians. We have been frustrated that too few members of the architectural profession in the twentieth century have made this simple acknowledgment, and we are deeply disappointed by the cataclysmic results of some public architectural acts, such as highways and public buildings of the urban renewal era. More, we are deeply distressed that almost none of the builders, contractors, and developers who do most of the shaping of our built environment talk about their work in these terms. We believe that discussions of architecture need to take place in the public realm.

Perhaps because discussions of architecture have become professionalized and therefore more and more obscure to more and more people, too many Americans ignore the built environment altogether. We also too often ignore our own personal role in creating or destroying spaces, including places of personal, community, or national value. Just as architects and developers have an obligation to talk with the public, we have an obligation to listen and to talk back.

By focusing not only on "great" works of architecture but also on more common and vernacular examples, we insist that each has important things to teach us. As the cultural historian Warren Susman put it some years ago, one does not have to believe that Superman comics and Shakespeare's *Hamlet* are somehow equivalent cultural products to believe that the former might have a great deal to tell us about American culture. Likewise, a Baltimore row house does not represent the same kind of architectural achievement as, say, the Getty Museum, but they are each culturally important and worth our consideration. By treating the extraordinary along with the ordinary, we hope readers will take away a greater appreciation for both.

Finally, and perhaps most radically in this indeterminate age, we believe there is an America—a powerful set of cultural ideals manifest in and shaped by a powerful set of physical symbols. We are, in our way, American exceptionalists, and we have been drawn to the efforts of all those who have sought to find a uniquely American architecture.

Not only does it go without saying that there has never been, is not now, nor will ever be a definitive answer to the question What is an American architecture? it is precisely the point of this volume. What interests us are the attempts, the strivings, the debates more than the results. A city art museum, a shotgun shack, an adobe pueblo—each is a perfect answer to the question, and incompletely so. Like democracy itself, what matters most in evaluating the history of America's built environment is the process of trying to answer that question. Part of what makes that history so extraordinarily rich is the many ways people have responded in their own way to the call to build the nation.

1.2. *The Architect's Dream*. Original painting by Thomas Cole, © Toledo Museum of Art. Augmented by VSBA, © Venturi, Scott Brown and Associates, Inc. In this send-up of Thomas Cole's painting, Robert Venturi and Denise Scott Brown have imagined their own dream of a truly American architecture: a landscape of McDonald's arches, glittering casino signs, and hotdog stands shaped like, well, hotdogs. Venturi and Scott Brown, two of the most influential American architects of the last third of the twentieth century, rejected the cold universality of the International Style and celebrated the gaudy, messy, garish complexity of the contemporary American cityscape. "Less is not more," Venturi wrote in 1966. "Less is a bore."

1

ANONYMOUS, EXCERPT FROM "ON THE ARCHITECTURE
OF AMERICA," 1790

This anonymous author, writing just as the nation had been formed, agrees with Thomas
Jefferson's famous quip about American architecture, and then offers his own explanation.
There are two problems, as this author sees it. First, architecture, more so than any other
art, grows out of an accumulated history of building. The United States, of course, is too
young to have such a tradition. Second, Americans build in wood, which is to say, imperma-
nently. Because they build only to address immediate, short-term needs, and do so with
shoddy materials, they do not reach to create more lasting architectural achievements.
Echoing the hopefulness felt by so many in the early Republic, this author is convinced that
American architecture can become great, once Americans understand its importance.

"The genius of architecture has shed maledictions over our land," says mr. Jefferson. In a
democracy, whoever of the citizens sees a public evil, and does not speak of it, is silently
treacherous to the world: and whoever of them perceives, and yet does not endeavor to
remove, a public inconvenience, is an accessory to it. Impressed with these opinions, on
the score of the duty of all good citizens, and believing that we exceedingly suffer from
the style in which we build our houses, and the materials of which they are erected, I
have devoted one of these humble lubrications to a hasty survey of architecture.

There can be no doubt but our style of building has, within a few years, very considerably improved: but there yet is open to the taste and good sense of the citizens a very
great space, indeed, for their inventions, taste and wealth, to be laudably exerted in. In
this country, we are less confused in our ideas of propriety, in general than are the inhabitants of any other country on the globe. We recur to first principles with ease, because
our customs, tastes and refinements, are less artificial than those of other countries; and
because we act more from the impulse of an enlightened nature, than from the coercion
of the fashions, imposed tyrannically by that immense opulence which in Europe trifles
with nature, and draws its pleasures from the more inaccessible reservoirs of art. Such is
our happiness. In architecture, of which no prototype exists in the vast variety of nature,
and which is the most artificial of all the points to which civilized man proceeds we have
it not in our power to profit by this happy freedom. Architecture comprehends in itself
the collective discoveries in proportion, solidity, strength, harmony, and fitness of parts,
economy of space, and subservience to domestic utility and comfort, which artists of different countries and ages have collected together into the art of building of houses. Different eras have been influenced by different tastes. A peculiar style of building was
adapted to each climate. . . .

The Americans have a taste, not corrupted—but suspended in its progress. The moment they see what is truly beautiful, they acknowledge its ascendancy. Hitherto they
have but little attended to this branch of the fine arts. In reaching perfection, they will
not have to travel through the rubbish of Gothic whim and caprice: the Grecian school is
open to them—and they ought to adopt its models in all their severe and elegant sim-

Originally printed in *The American Museum, or, Universal Magazine* 8 (October 1790): 174–76.

plicity. Their present style is slovenly in the greatest degree: they may step from this situation to the highest attainments at a stride.

The evil in our architecture lies principally in this—that we build of wood. From this custom much immediate, as well as remote inconvenience, is to be expected: and certainly, however suddenly felt may be the comfort arising from celerity and dispatch, the numerous considerations of perishableness, and want of safety, and call for repairs, added to the reflection, that the public [ ] is for the time deprived of one great field of exertion, will very much weigh with an enlightened people, when once they become awakened to their advantages, and proud of the singular novelty of the physical and moral opportunities of the situation. . . .

Bachelors only ought to build of wood—men who have but a life estate in this world, and who care little for those who come after them. Those who have either children or a wife to leave behind them will build of brick, if they wish to leave monuments of kindness, rather than a rent-charge, behind them. . . .

We have this melancholy consolation, that posterity will find few of the deformities of our bad taste existing to mislead their own. But then, again, we ought to reflect, that those who come after us, and who will take up the arts where we left off, will be deprived of any permanent vestige of our refinement, on which we ought to hope they would improve. . . .

The last and highest consideration, that strikes me, is, that emigration would be less easy, and not so common, were a finer spirit of building to prevail. Were the Tartars to build houses instead of waggons and tents . . . they would not rove, and their country might become a land of tillage. The facility with which we *may* move, is a strong incentive to that love of change, which it particularly interests us to repress in our citizens.

2

ANONYMOUS, EXCERPT FROM "ON THE ARTS," 1815

Coming just after the United States had for a second time defeated Great Britain and secured its independence, this essay examines the state of the arts in the nation. The article touches on all the fine arts, and we have excerpted the section on architecture. Characteristically, this author dispenses critique and encouragement, disappointment and hope in equal measure. The author complains both that the state of architecture is still "very far behind" and that Americans continue to import European architecture inappropriate for the American nation. He ends by reminding readers of the importance of grand public buildings for a republic as a way to facilitate a sense of democratic community.

In architecture, it must be confessed, we are still very far behind hand. Our domestic architecture is for the most part copied, and often badly copied too, from the common English books, with but little variety, and no adaptation to our own climate or habits of life.

Originally printed in *Analectic Magazine*, vol. VI, 1815.

Our better sort of country houses, have generally an air of too much pretension for the scale of size and expense on which they are built; while we despise or overlook the humble beauties and snug comforts of the cottage, we but seldom attain to the grandeur of the *chateau* or the *villa*. Our country churches and other rural public edifices, are for the most part mean and slight, and few of our builders have yet learnt the important secret, that good taste and proportion cost nothing. The defects of our rural architecture are the more to be regretted, because it is in the country that architecture appears to the greatest advantage. The contrast of art and nature, is so pleasing, that any tolerably well proportioned and spacious building, surrounded by rich natural scenery, has always a most pleasing effect. The colonnade, the portico, and the tower never appear with half so much grace and majesty, as when half hid from view by a grove, or "bosomed high in tufted trees." But a rapid improvement is going on in this respect; and indeed what is there in the United States in which a rapid improvement is not going on? City architecture too, has taken a sudden start, and has gained much within these few years, both in comfort and in variety; this is especially observable in the city of Philadelphia. But I know not how it has happened, that so many of our finest and most costly public edifices have been vitiated by the predominance of that style of architecture which prevailed in the age of Louis XIV, I mean that corruption of the Grecian, or rather of the Palladian architecture, which delights in great profusion of ornament, in piling one order upon another, and frequently perching the top one upon a narrow cornice where the pillars, or more commonly, the pilasters, look as if they were dancing on the tight rope—in multitudes of small and useless columns and unmeaning pilasters, and in long rows of staring windows, each of them decorated with a heavy periwig of massy stone garlands. . . .

But in its very best estate, this style of architecture can rise to nothing nobler than ponderous stateliness, and cumbrous magnificence; and the effect which it produces with infinite labor, is always poor and contemptible when compared with the grandeur and beauty of Grecian simplicity.

The wings of the unfinished capitol at Washington, were examples of this taste, though it is probable that by the aid of a noble and lofty centre, or a fine portico, they might have been made to harmonise in one majestic mass. The City Hall of New York, is another instance of this manner—a fine building, no doubt, a most excellent piece of masonry, beautiful, in many of its parts, and as a whole, honorable to the city and creditable to the architect. But it wants unity and dignity, and is broken up into elaborate littleness. When the eye is near enough to embrace at once many of the minuter parts, the whole has an air of much richness and even of elegance. But if the spectator retires two or three hundred yards farther back, he must at once perceive the unsuitableness of this style to so fine a situation. With far less expense, how much nobler an effect could have been produced by a grand portico or some regular architectural front composed of few parts, and those large, simple, in unison with each other, and all subordinate to one general character of simple greatness.

There is scarcely any single circumstance which contributes more powerfully towards elevating the reputation of any people, than the grandeur of public edifices; nor is there any way in which a republican government can with so much propriety display its munificence. The tinsel trappings and pageantry of office, which have been affected by some free states, are not only discordant to the general simplicity of republican institutions, but like the show and pomp of private luxury, they are of a selfish nature; they communicate gratification only to the individual who enjoys them, and reflect little lustre on the state by which they are bestowed. But a noble hall for the purposes of legislation or of justice is the immediate property of the people, and forms a portion of the patrimony of every citizen. Love of country should indeed rest upon a far broader ground, yet it is well to have local pride and attachments come in to the aid of patriotism. . . . Nor will a benevolent mind be inclined to overlook the effect which these displays of public magnificence may have in imparting "an hour's importance to the poor man's heart," and enabling him for a time to forget the inferiority of his condition, and feel a community of interest with his wealthy neighbor.

3

R.C. LONG, "ARCHITECTURE: ITS ALLEGED DEGENERACY," 1842

By the 1840s, as R. C. Long indicates, the charge that American architecture had "degenerated" was a commonplace. Taking this head on, Long begs to differ, not so much by defending American architecture but by asking why we think it is bad in the first place. Writing in the middle of an enthusiasm for various revival styles—Greek, Gothic, Palladian, even Egyptian—Long wonders why we should consider these as the height of architectural achievement and the yardstick against which to measure how much American buildings have fallen short. Does every great age and every great society not produce its own forms, he asks? Why do we continue to rely on the "antique" to give architectural expression to our modern age? The essay originally appeared in the *Journal of the Franklin Institute* but apparently hit enough of a nerve to be reprinted.

What do the critics mean by "degeneracy of modern architecture?" It is a stereotyped phrase used by both great and small writers, and, by the frequency of it, we cannot but believe that it means something. When we look, however, into the books, or consult the magazine-articles of said critics, we are puzzled to find out, exactly, what this something is.

If we listen to some of them, we must needs conclude that there never was any architecture but the Gothic, and that there never will be any again until the Gothic is *revived,* thus admitting that Gothic architecture is now dead, in a stupor, or else has fainted away in very weakness.

From another set of essayists, we learn that Palladio first invented that thing called architecture; that, before his time, people built, "every man according to what was right in his own eyes," until Palladio taught them better, and gave such unerring rules for the production of design in architecture, showing so indisputably what is beautiful and what is not, that thence forward the simplest tyro in art need never go astray. . . .

[T]here is one point on which they all agree, and this is, they all equally deplore the

Originally printed in *American Magazine and Repository of Useful Literature* (1842): 43–44.

degeneracy of modern architecture, and cry loudly for the *revival* of some one favorite style, in order to regenerate the defunct art.

But let us inquire what do the critics mean by "the degeneracy of modern architecture." Is it degenerate because it is not Gothic; because it is not Greek, not Palladian, not Elizabethan, not Egyptian? If so, then in truth we say, architecture will never be any thing else but degenerate, unless we either turn Greeks, or Romans, or Egyptians, &c., and assuredly no one believes that such is ever going to be the case.

Yet why are architects taking it for granted that nothing is architectural unless it be either Greek or Gothic, or some other style, and that, if drawing from these sources they did not try to throw into their designs a portico, a pediment, or fasten buttresses and pinnacles to the outside walls, or shape the door and window heads into some particular curve or arch, or indeed apply any other features which can be taken entirely out of books, that all traces of architectural art would vanish from the earth? These are *civilized* times, and men require houses to live in; they worship God and must build temples, if not for His glory, at least for their own comfort, and in ministering to these requirements, this practice of pinning to a building appropriated to either of the above uses, some of the embellishments of another building, held as classic precedents, producing excrescences which architects seem to think are the only things about the structure which have any right to the name of architecture, is, in fact, the great hindrance to the natural growth of architecture. It is *this* practice which is the degeneracy of modern architecture.

Is it to be supposed that Grecian architecture would ever have grown to what it is, if the architects of that land had not given free room for the genius of their country, and its institutions, to manifest itself architecturally? Imagine *them* believing that the Egyptian was the only correct architecture, and insisting on sloping the sides of their buildings, placing their columns within the walls, and hiding their sloping roofs, necessary for the climate, behind an immense horizontal entablature. What a monster would have frowned from the heights of the Acropolis, instead of the ever-living edifice that stood there glowing with the life, the youth, the poetry of Greece.

Why was it that the Romans never attained to an original style of architecture, although they had, to begin with, that emblem of strength and beauty, the arch, as an elemental national feature? Simply because they believed that the Greek was the only architecture in the world. They therefore modestly used the arch as a constructive element, and imprisoned it within an external Greek facade, binding the free curve of their own glorious arch under the dominion of column and entablature. . . .

Thus it was that the arch, with the Romans, never gave birth, as it should have done, to a national style, and yet we see how, in different hands, out of that same arch and its wonderful capabilities, the Norman style was formed, and thence by true artistic treatment, managing this same arch with the buttress, it became the most yielding thing in art-creation, the graceful, the flexible Gothic, coming out of it "as sweetness out of strength," honey indeed "out of the jaws of the lion."

And yet the degeneracy of architecture is now loudly talked of, and no one sees at the present day *how* anything new is ever to be done in that art, except by adherence to the rules, not according to which any greatness in architecture was ever achieved, but according to which you may copy any given production of the art.

According to these same critics, it would be easy to show that modern architecture is not by any means degenerate, if their own rules of perfection are at all good for anything. Is the Parthenon good architecture? What hinders us from building a Parthenon? The money being given we could reproduce that, or any other building that has been re-measured as the Parthenon has been. Is Yorkminister good architecture? Then the front of the new national Scotch church, in London, is assuredly good architecture enough to content one, for it is as near a fac similie of the west front of York cathedral as modern means will allow. Indeed do we not possess already a modern specimen of every conceivable style that has existed in any quarter of the globe? Surely then, according to such views, our architecture is not degenerate. But has this endless repetition of the architecture of the past, any title to be called the architecture of the present? Is this the way to produce any thing new, or good, or great, in architecture, any thing bearing on it the impress of the characteristics of this generation, any thing homogeneous with the advanced state of civilization?

Truly, indeed, modern architecture is degenerate, is utterly dead, we should say, in view of what we have just shown, (for if there is any modern architecture at all, what and where is it?) did we not possess a cheerful faith, which is ever telling us that architecture is too intimately connected with man to perish while there is a man upon the earth. Must *man* progress in goodness and in wisdom? then must *architecture* also! Is man so progressing? then is architecture also, though we may not know it nor see it. Architecture must manifest the changes that are taking place in society, the greater ones, we hope and believe, that are yet to come.

It is as much out of the rule of rationality to think it possible to reinvigorate architecture by forcing it into any antique mould, as to expect that, if disgusted with manhood, we can bring back simplicity and innocence by putting on again the garments of youth. Architecture must grow naturally, its own peculiar tendencies must be observed, and it must be trained accordingly. How is this to be done? let us try to find out, let us all try and see which of us will first produce something in the art peculiar—characteristic—suited to the age—national.

4

HORATIO GREENOUGH, EXCERPT FROM "AMERICAN ARCHITECTURE," 1843

Horatio Greenough stands as the most accomplished American sculptor of the antebellum period, best known, perhaps, for the large seated statue of George Washington dressed in a toga installed in the Capitol. Here the sculptor has turned his attention to architecture, and he offers his complaint that Americans have been too quick to adopt—and badly at that—the styles of the European past. Architecture is rooted more deeply in the national experience and must spring more originally from it. Greenough's complaints

Originally printed in *United States Magazine and Democratic Review* (1843): 206–10.

echoed those of many who saw in transplanting Greek, Gothic, and other styles to the United States a certain architectural slavishness.

The mind of this country has never been seriously applied to the subject of building. Intently engaged in matters of more pressing importance, we have been content to receive our notions of architecture as we have received the fashion of our garments, and the form of our entertainments, from Europe. In our eagerness to appropriate we have neglected to adapt, to distinguish,—nay, to understand. We have built small Gothic temples of wood, and have omitted all ornament for economy, unmindful that size, material, and ornament are the elements of effect in that style of building. Captivated by the classic symmetry of the Athenian models, we have sought to bring the Parthenon into our streets, to make the temple of Theseus work in our towns. We have shorn them of their lateral colonnades, let them down from their dignified platform, pierced their walls for light, and, instead of the storied relief and the eloquent statue which enriched the frieze, and graced the pediment, we have made our chimney tops to peer over the broken profile, and tell by their rising smoke of the traffic and desecration of the interior. Still the model may be recognized, some of the architectural features are entire; like the captive king stripped alike of arms and purple, and drudging amid the Helots of a capital, the Greek temple as seen among us claims pity for its degraded majesty, and attests the barbarian force which has abused its nature, and been blind to its qualities. . . .

We say that the mind of this country has never been seriously applied to architecture. True it is, that the commonwealth, with that desire of public magnificence which has ever been a leading feature of democracy, has called from the vasty deep of the past the spirits of the Greek, the Roman, and the Gothic styles; but they would not come when she did call to them! The vast cathedral with its ever open portals, towering high above the courts of kings, inviting all men to its cool and fragrant twilight, where the voice of the organ stirs the blood, and the dim-seen visions of saints and martyrs bleed and die upon the canvass amid the echoes of hymning voices and the clouds of frankincense, this architectural embodying of the divine and blessed words "come to me, ye who labor and are heavy laden, and I will give you rest!" demands a sacrifice of what we hold dearest. Its corner-stone must be laid upon the right to judge the claims of the church. The style of Greek architecture as seen in the Greek temple, demands the aid of sculpture, insists upon every feature of its original organization, loses its harmony if a note be dropped in the execution, and when so modified as to serve for a custom-house or a bank, departs from its original beauty and propriety as widely as the crippled gelding of a hackney coach differs from the bounding and neighing wild horse of the desert. Even where, in the fervor of our faith in shapes, we have sternly adhered to the dictum of another age, and have actually succeeded in securing the entire exterior which echoes the forms of Athens, the pile stands a stranger among us! and receives a respect akin to what we should feel for a fellow-citizen clothed in the garb of Greece. It is a make-believe! It is not the real thing! We see the marble capitals; we trace the acanthus leaves of a celebrated model—incredulous odi! It is not a temple.

The number and variety of our experiments in building show the dissatisfaction of the public taste with what has been hitherto achieved; the expense at which they have been made proves how strong is the yearning after excellence; the talents and acquirements of the artists whose services have been engaged in them are such as to convince us that the fault lies in the system, not in the men. Is it possible that out of this chaos order can arise? . . . In answering these questions let us remember with humility that all salutary changes are the work of many and of time; but let us encourage experiment at the risk of license, rather than submit to an iron rule that begins by sacrificing reason, dignity and comfort. Let us consult nature, and in the assurance that she will disclose a mine, richer than was ever dreamed of by the Greeks, in art as well as in philosophy. . . .

Let us now turn to a structure of our own, one which from its nature and uses commands us to reject authority, and we shall find the result of the manly use of plain good sense so like that of taste and genius too, as scarce to require a distinctive title. Observe a ship at sea! Mark the majestic form of her hull as she rushes through the water, observe the graceful bend of her body, the gentle transition from round to flat, the grasp of her keel, the leap of her bows, the symmetry and rich tracery of her spars and rigging, and those grand wind muscles, her sails! Behold an organization second only to that of an animal, obedient as the horse, swift as the stag, and bearing the burden of a thousand camels from pole to pole! What Academy of Design, what research of connoisseurship, what imitation of the Greeks produced this marvel of construction? Here is the result of the study of man upon the great deep, where Nature spake of the laws of building, not in the feather and in the flower, but in winds and waves, and he bent all his mind to hear and to obey. Could we carry into our civil architecture the responsibilities that weigh upon our ship-building, we should ere long have edifices as superior to the Parthenon for the purposes that we require, as the Constitution or the Pennsylvania is to the galley of the Argonauts. Could our blunders on terra-firma be put to the same dread test that those of ship-builders are, little would be now left to say on this subject.

Instead of forcing the functions of every sort of building into one general form, adopting an outward shape for the sake of the eye or of association, without reference to the inner distribution, let us begin from the heart as a nucleus and work outward. The most convenient size and arrangement of the rooms that are to constitute the building being fixed, the access of the light that may, of the air that must, be wanted, being provided for, we have the skeleton of our building. Nay, we have all excepting the dress. The connexion and order of parts, juxtaposed for convenience, cannot fail to speak of their relation and uses. As a group of idlers on the quay, if they grasp a rope to haul a vessel to the pier, are united in harmonious action by the cord they seize, as the slowly yielding mass forms a thorough-bass to their livelier movement, so the un-flinching adaptation of a building to its position and use gives, as a sure product of that adaptation, character and expression. . . .

To conclude. The fundamental laws of building found at the basis of every style of architecture, must be the basis of ours. The adaptation of the forms and magnitude of structures to the climate they are exposed to, and the offices for which they are intended, teaches us to study our own varied wants in these respects. The harmony of their ornaments with the nature that the embellished and the institutions from which they sprang, calls on us to do the like justice to our country, our government, and our faith. As a Christian preacher may give weight to truth, and add persuasion to proof, by studying the models of pagan writers, so the American builder, by a truly philosophic investigation of ancient art, will learn of the Greeks to be American. . . .

We are fully aware that many regard all matters of taste as matters of pure caprice and fashion. We are aware that many think our architecture already perfect; but we have chosen, during this sultry weather, to exercise a truly American right—the right of talking. . . .

Each man is free to present his notions on any subject. We have also talked, firm in the be-lief that the development of a nation's taste in art depends on a thousand deep-seated in-fluences beyond the ken of the ignorant present; firm in the belief that freedom and knowledge will bear the fruit of refinement and beauty, we have yet dared to utter a few words of discontent, a few crude thoughts of what might be, and we feel the better for it.

5

ANONYMOUS, EXCERPT FROM "A PUBLIC BUILDING," 1869

President Abraham Lincoln insisted that the work on the Capitol dome continue even in the midst of the Civil War. For Lincoln this building project symbolized the enduring con-tinuity of the Union the war was attempting to preserve. Though Lincoln did not live to see the dome completed, when it was, it refocused the nation's attention on that building as the heart of the American political experiment, the symbol of the "second American revolution." In this sense, the completion of the Capitol dome serves implicitly as a force for national reconciliation and a spur to ongoing reform. With memories of war and Lin-coln's assassination in the background, this author takes us on a tour of the Capitol. He begins with the dome, fittingly enough, and he ends with history—with the ghosts of the great figures who once roamed the hallways. The author can be quite sharp about more modern additions to the Capitol, and especially about the artwork recently installed. The past here seems a more comfortable refuge than the present, where the dust of war still settled.

Few of its owners are aware how stately a structure is the Capitol Building at Washing-ton. Not that it is by any means a perfect thing: far from it—it is full of faults; and though it seems fitting that our central seat of power should represent our riches and re-sources, still there is a trace of something barbaric today in all its lavishly squandered splendor. Yet, with some genius of their own, with the models of all the ages before them, and with the unlimited treasure of the whole country at command to carry out their ideas, it would be strange if all the designers employed upon it since Washington laid its first corner-stone could fail to give it that portion of excellence with which one, who does not fret soul and body apart in search of abstract perfection, can rest well pleased, if not utterly satisfied.

Yet whoever may find much to blame in the body of the building, the architects have their full need of praise in the loveliness and grandeur of the dome. It is something unsurpassed; it springs into the sky as lightly as a bubble—as resplendently; it rests there as easily as a cloud: it seems, as it should, to be only a part of its airy surroundings. Art could do no more in its construction. . . .

[Y]et, though erected on comparatively low ground, go where you will, for miles on

Originally published in *Harper's New Monthly Magazine* 32 (1869): 204–10.

1.3. Abraham Lincoln speaking in front of the Capitol, 1861. Library of Congress. No single building has symbolized the nation's political ideals more than the U.S. Capitol, and at no time was that symbolism more potent than during the Civil War, when the nation itself seemed poised for dissolution. Abraham Lincoln, seen here delivering his first inaugural address in the shadow of the uncompleted Capitol dome, understood that power and insisted that work on the dome continue during the war.

miles, that dome haunts and follows you; now as you see it from the heights of Arlington—while you stand in the midst of the acres of graves there and picture the terrible moment when some trumpet shall call all this army of ghosts from their trenches—rising like a guardian genius still overlooking these white head-stones that stretch away across the rolling land on every side; like the crests of mighty and melancholy waves; now as you cease treading down the purple hyacinths in the grass, and wandering under the magnolia-trees, and between the breast-high hedges of fragrant box at Mount Vernon, and, turning the bend of the river almost twenty miles away, meet its great shadow resting like a film upon the air, opening slowly on the gaze like a vision, with its phantom-like length of lustrous column and setting of wind-tossed greenery. When you behold it thus remote it seems like a dream of the past—too beautiful a thing for the common use of daily life; only men in sweeping Grecian raiment and phylactered purple should move slow and meditative through its halls—never these hurrying black beetles, these rough garments and rude gestures of the modern generations. . . .

The critical aspect which the outline of the edifice presents at a single glance leans, it must be admitted, toward a striking coincidence. Thus seen its proportions are more nearly those of a spread-eagle than any thing else. If the architect had really no design of glorifying the national bird, we must look upon the fact of his having done so as a special inspiration—he builded better than he knew—or else as an irrepressible outbreaking of the national character. This, however, will not be so palpable a mischance when an improvement still hoped for shall, in less burdensome days, be carried to completion, and, the old facade being done away with, the main front shall be brought forward into the prominence which is its right; by which means the central portion will not seem to be about to be crushed by the dome above; the present wings, instead of seeming separate parts of a block, will secure a normal connection with the building, and there will appear to be some original unity of design about the whole disjointed group of porticoes and pillars. . . .

The old Capitol, from which the new wings are extended, was constructed of a sandstone from Acquia Creek, which is painted white—one of those economical artifices which are ultimately an extravagance, as the rains affect the stone badly, and it is constantly requiring to be repainted. The extensions are of marble, from Massachusetts and Maryland, of shining quality and particularly choice veining. The columns were all brought from their place of debarkation, it is said, after an exceedingly primitive method of rolling them along the ground with ropes; this being complained of at the time, it was found upon experiment that it was altogether the safest way of transporting them, as only those broke in which hidden flaws made it desirable that if they were going to break at all they should do so before being set in their final places under the superincumbent weight of architrave and entablature. The dome, which was originally of wood, is now of cast iron, weighing more than four thousand tons, or eight million pounds; one can scarcely believe the enormous figures when catching the first glimpse of that light and airy case with which it lifts its rich decorations into the sunshine; its foundations, however, are said to be adequate to a much heavier pressure. The ascent is up a winding flight of stairs between the outer and inner shells, and is a morning's journey; but once there the climber hangs over a landscape that lies beneath, broadening away into mellow distances, overswept by sailing cloud-shadows, and threaded by the sliver of the Potomac.

It is within the old Capitol that some of our earlier statesmen rivaled one another in the decorative arts—Jefferson, evincing here a good deal of architectural taste and capacity in pillars carved after the likeness of sheaves of our native maize, the ears and blades and silk forming the capital, the clustered, jointed stems bound together for the shaft; and also in designs where the blossoms and foliation of the tobacco-plant make an effect as exquisite to the full as that of the old acanthus leaf; and John Quincy Adams, emulatory, grouping some figures in an allegorical representation on a frieze. . . .

Passing from wing to wing of the Capitol, since its extension, affords the visitor quite a stroll. The passage being something more than the eighth of a mile in length there is always a fresh wind blowing through it and slamming the great doors, which resound with multitudinous echoes. One finds upon the way a place known as the Temple of the Winds, in which the miniature model of an ancient temple has been set bodily; it has its use in the system of ventilation, but with a truly national largeness of temperament its frequenters, said a witty guide, use it for a cuspidor. Up its hollow depth come cold draughts, suggestive of shivering *oubliettes* and dungeons underneath; but there is nothing of the sort beneath, other than that great gloomy chamber with its low and heavily vaulted roof and gigantic Egyptian columns, in the central crypt of which it was first intended to entomb the remains of Washington, with statues of his generals keeping guard in a charmed circle around him; and farther away the quarter where the burnished engines slide silently to and fro by day and night, sending volumes of air over leagues of hot tubes in the winter-time to diffuse a soft warmth every where; and in the summer fanning up equal volumes over great blocks of ice, distilling coolness and freshness in like manner, and forming all the diablerie to be found in the place. It is in this same substratum of the Capitol that the marble-lined baths, luxurious enough for a Roman, are situated. Certainly our legislative work ought to be done with clean hands, for no appliance, no delicacy, no delight of the bath is wanting; foreign soaps and essences and cosmetics and perfumes, damasks soft as satin, and attendants deferential as slaves, all being supplied to our lawgivers without money and without price. And this facility for purification is by no means an unwise provision at the public expense, for a glance at some of its participants is sufficient to show that they would never have it at their own. . . .

We come now to the grand staircase by which we ascend to the gallery of the new Hall of Representatives. The balustrades of this staircase are of a gray marble from the quarries of Tennessee, so beautiful in tint, and susceptible of so brilliant a polish, that it is amazing it should be so seldom used elsewhere. This staircase has a massive majesty of its own, as has also its companion of the Senate Chamber. The light falls full upon it and shows it solid enough to endure for ages. At one point upon it you turn and look upward where story after story of panel and pilaster rises light and graceful, though emblazoned with florid and unmeaning ornament. It is quite stately and noble, and seems to be the benefiting entrance to these halls of empire. . . .

The Hall of Representatives is a great oblong chamber, which, although very lofty, affords you a contrary impression, owing to the deep caissons of the ceiling, which, being planted between huge pendants of gilding, and the panes of glass being stained with the arms of the several States, give a sense of low-browed heaviness. An untraveled citizen can hardly obtain a better idea of the vastness of his country than when he takes his place in the galleries of this hall—entrance to which, very differently from the arrangements of the English Houses of Parliament, he finds to be unrestricted—and, looking down at the mob of members, recalls to himself all that they represent, and fancies that he sees at one glance the rock-bound sea-coast of New England, the impassable mountains and wild rivers of the West, the savannas of the South. . . .

Very different is the scene presented by the Senate Chamber, where calm dignity sits enthroned, and where business really seems to be done. This room, in the opposite wing, is much smaller than that of the other branch, yet has a gaudier appearance, being tawdrily furnished in jarring colors, the carpet bright scarlet and yellow, the sofas a dull magenta tint, which is, however, a trifling matter, and which, as it may by-and-by so easily be rectified, need not annoy any one who wishes to listen forgetfully to the orotund sentences of deep-mouthed Senators.

The lobby of the Senate is at present much the superior of the Senate Chamber itself, with its lofty groined arches covered by an arabesque of scrolls and floral suggestions in decorative plaster-work; and the committee-rooms opening upon it, and the reception-room for the wives and friends of Senators, rejoice in windows, each of which seems only the setting to a lovely picture. There are, however, other entrances to these sacred floors, reserved to the members of Congress themselves and to their attachés, few of whom, it may be doubted, know half how beautiful are the passages through which they daily hasten. Here, for instance, is a staircase of bronze and brass, which, being erected in a well of darkness, is seen only when some occasion lights the gas, and then only imperfectly, unless the visitor's pocket-match comes to the rescue; yet it is a wonder of art, its balustrade being a lattice-work of exquisitely executed fancies—the forest-creature plunging between the boughs with his horns bent back—naked little boys at play with leaf and spray—mother-birds bringing food to their fledglings—a snake twisting up a tree to protrude his fangs into a nest over which the parent-birds flutter helplessly—the great shield of the eagle sealing it as the republic's property. This staircase, and its companion in the other wing, costing severally eighteen thousand dollars, and not to be valued in gold or silver, are monuments of a nation's liberality of which we may well be proud.

The President's room, a few steps beyond the last place of which mention has been made, and into which the Chief Executive comes to sign those bills hurriedly passed at the close of a session, is a collection of choice fresco-work, splendidly executed portraits of our illustrious ancestry, and a slightly improved version of the fresco in the roof of the rotunda, where the Father of his Country again appears ringed about by bright allegorical damsels; and although the greater part of the work is very finely done, especially the portraits of Franklin, Jefferson, and their compeers, yet the whole effect is a confusion of rich color, and one is wearied with a single glance by the quantity which reverses the old rule of "nothing too much." That, indeed, is the chief defect through the whole vast pile: its designers do not seem to have known how to spend their unlimited resources. Every thing is massive and stupendous throughout the building; the arched carriage-ways under which you drive are as superbly solid as the pyramids: but, not content with that, every thing is gilded and ornamented and painted and finished beyond the last point of endurance. There are but few really good paintings on all the square roods of the wall, and there are some that are atrocious; an equestrian Washington hangs over the landing of one of the staircases, a waking nightmare; and Congress, it is said, has some idea of giving Powell another great place to lay waste; but a portrait in the apartment of one of the dignitaries, and the copy of a Murillo in that of another, are at present almost the only things of merit to be found. How superb the great stretches of the walls might be if Bierstadt and Church should spread their splendid colors there in pictures of our wild vast scenery, with the mountains of the Yo Semite and the rapids of Niagara, does not seem to have occurred to our purveyors of public taste, who throw away our treasure on canvases violating every law of perspective and chromatics. . . .

[W]e do not forget that this same room where now congregate the intellects of the bar is the arena where formerly contended those who have gone into history; and the memories of Webster and Calhoun, Crittenden and Clay, like gigantic Caryatides, are holding up the roof to-day. . . .

FREDERICK JACKSON TURNER,
"ARCHITECTURE THROUGH OPPRESSION," 1884

Frederick Jackson Turner is known to us as perhaps the most influential American historian. That fame stems from a speech he delivered nine years after this one: "The Significance of the Frontier in American History." In that essay, he argues that the experience of frontier conquest and settlement stripped away Europeanness and created a people distinctly American. This lecture, delivered when Turner was still a student at the University of Wisconsin, deals with the history of architecture, yet reaches for some of the same themes: the history of architecture, he argues, is intimately connected with the history of oppression. Democratic societies, like nineteenth-century America, await an architecture of freedom.

To an American standing in some venerable city of the old world, the architecture seems strangely different from that of New York or Boston. About him rise spires, pinnacles and minarets; his step resounds along the naves of vast cathedrals and his heart is thrilled with strange emotion at the sight of:

> High embowed roof
> And antique pillars massy proof,
> And storied windows richly bright,
> Casting a dim religious light.

His eye wanders among the wilderness of beautiful carvings and mouldings until he stands bewildered at these treasures of the mediaeval past. He searches for the secret of these works of architecture, and he learns that Nature furnished the designs. "The groves were God's first temples!" Filled with memories of the forest, man wrought in stone the effect it had on him, and wondrous palaces and Parthenons begemmed the earth. In America we have giant cathedrals, whose spires are moss clad pines, whose frescoes are painted on the sky and mountain wall, and whose music surges through leafy aisles in the deep toned bass of cataracts or winds about in aeolian harmonies breathed from the forest harps. But in America where nature yet displays these grand suggestions, we build our buildings common, angular and plain. The places and cathedrals of the old world belong to a different age from ours. Our times are plebeian; it is visible in our architecture.

The history of humanity has been a romance and a tragedy! In it we read the brilliant annals of the few who seemed born to reap the fruits of the earth. For them were the glories of wealth, for them the glitter and glamour of life, and for them this "blossoming in stone." But the tragedy of humanity! Millions groaning that one might laugh, servile tillers of the soil, sweating that others might dream; drinking the logwood of life, while their masters quaffed its nectar. Many are the historians who have painted the glories of the past; few there are that tell the "lamentation and the ancient tale of wrong." It was from the extortion of the despot that the magnificent mosques of the Orient were built. When the freedom of Rome had departed and her peasantry had been crushed into

Speech originally printed in *University Press* 15, June 21, 1884.

serfdom, then the rich and cultivated nobleman adorned his villa with the gems of art, and Italy was decked with splendid palaces. Many a castle on the Rhine remains to furnish quaint old legends, and to tell a story of the robber baron who, spider-like drew within that strong walled seat of his fruit of the common people's toils.

Art is a glorious gift to man; these works of architecture are a splendid contribution from those who were actors in life's romance, but how ill they suit with the state of the common men in the times in which they rose! When we think of the countless masses who wore the fetters of oppression how dark a shadow their anguish casts about these miracles of stone and marble that their sorrows helped to build. Gloriously rise the spires and minarets of many a mediaeval cathedral, but even by its side was built the hovel of the serf, and as the solemn wail of the *miserere* steals along the stately aisles, seems to bear a burden from the men worn out with toil and slavery! How heavy, gloomy, and how awful stand the pyramids upon the sands of Egypt, telling of—

> The detested task
> Of piling stone on stone, and poisoning
> The choicest days of life
> To sooth a dotard's vanity.

And the deep-wondering, placid face of the Sphynx gazes toward the heavens in a kind of enquiry of how long the children of the earth must be oppressed. So it has looked for centuries, in mute trusting appeal against man's inhumanity to man.

Art is too divine a thing to live by the throes of the people. The civilization of the past, which was the condition of art's existence, left it sadly marred by the incompleteness, the distortion of that civilization. But now the world begins to see that true progress, true enlightenment, means the progress, the enlightenment of all. In this wave of democratic utilitarianism, that is sweeping over the earth, art may seem engulfed, refinement destroyed, and men may shudder as the wave seems about to hide forever all that remains of the ancient idea of the Beautiful. But the fear is groundless! In the very breadth and depth of the inundation lie the possibilities of a grander future. The Greek upreared the Parthenon and sneered at the world as barbaric. The Nineteenth century is striving to build humanity into a glorious temple to its God,—his only fitting temple. When the greatest happiness of the greatest number shall have become something like a reality, when life's tragedy shall cease to clash with life's romance, and the squalor of the hovel shall no longer mar the cathedral's beauty,—then again may "music freeze into marble," and forests blossom into stone.

MONTGOMERY SCHUYLER, "THE POINT OF VIEW," 1891

Montgomery Schuyler, a journalist who wrote importantly about architecture, delivered this speech at a pivotal moment in American architectural history. On one hand, the practice of architecture itself had become professionalized. Trained either in Europe or in the studios of other architects, a new generation of architects had come to maturity. On the other hand, those architects found a fruitful source of commissions in the new, booming industrial cities and from newly wealthy industrialists. It is no accident that Chicago—mentioned here by Schuyler—stood at the forefront of American architectural developments at the end of the nineteenth century. No city grew faster or more spectacularly, and after it was devastated by fire in 1871, the city became an architectural tabula rasa. Notice as well the moral language with which Schuyler discusses architecture—beauty and function are simply not enough, architecture needs to express "truth."

I do not know that I can make a clearer or briefer statement than I made in a speech delivered, in response to the toast of "Architecture," at the fifth annual banquet of the National Association of Builders, given February 12, 1891, at the Lenox Lyceum, in New York. Accordingly I reprint here the report of my remarks:

"Mr. Chairman and Gentlemen of the National Association of Builders,—You will not expect from me, in responding to this toast, any exhibition of that facetious spirit with which some of my predecessors have entertained you. It has, indeed, been said that American humor has never found full expression except in architecture. It has also been said by an honored friend of mine, himself an architect, whom I hoped to see here to-night, that American architecture was the art of covering one thing with another thing to imitate a third thing, which, if genuine, would not be desirable. But I hope you will agree with me that, though the expression is comic, the fact, so far as it is a fact, is serious even to sadness. It is a great pleasure and a great privilege for me to speak to this sentiment, and it is especially a privilege for me to speak upon it to an association of builders, because it seems to me that the real, radical defect of modern architecture in general, if not of American architecture in particular, is the estrangement between architecture and building—between the poetry and the prose, so to speak, of the art of building, which can never be disjoined without injury to both. If you look into any dictionary or into any cyclopedia under 'architecture,' you will find that it is the art of building; but I don't think that you would arrive at that definition from an inspection of the streets of any modern city. I think, on the contrary, that if you were to scrape down to the face of the main wall of the buildings of these streets, you would find that you had simply removed all the architecture, and that you had left the buildings as good as ever; that is to say, the buildings in which the definition I have quoted is illustrated are in the minority, and the buildings of which I have just spoken are in the majority; and the more architectural pretensions the buildings has, the more apt it is to illustrate this defect of which I have spoken.

"It is, I believe, historically true, in the history of the world, with one conspicuous exception, that down to the Italian Renaissance, some four centuries ago, the architect was himself a builder. . . . Why, before the fifteen century, I don't suppose any man who

Originally printed in *Inland Architect and News Record* 17 (February 1891): 5–6.

began to build a building ever thought in what style he should compose it any more than I thought before I got up here in what language I should address you; he simply built in the language to which he was accustomed and which he knew. You will find this perfect truth is the great charm of Grecian architecture, and ten or fifteen centuries later it was the great charm of Gothic architecture; that is to say, that it was founded upon fact, that it was the truth, that it was the thing the man was doing that he was concerned about, even in those pieces of architecture which seem to us the most exuberant, the most fantastic, like the front of Rouen, or like the cathedral of which Longfellow speaks, as you all remember:

> 'How strange the sculptures that adorn these towers!
> This crowd of statues, in whose folded sleeves
> Birds build their nests; while, canopied with leaves,
> Parvis and portal bloom like trellised bowers,
> And the vast minister seems a cross of flowers.'

Even in those things there was that logical, law-abiding, sensible, practical adherence to the facts of construction, to the art of building, which we have so long lost, and which I hope we are getting back again.

"There are examples, in the work of our modern architecture, of architects who design with this same truth, with this same reality, with this same sincerity that animated the old builders before the coming-in of this artificial and irrelevant system of design, and one of them is the building in which I am informed a great many of you spent last evening; I mean the Casino. I don't know any more admirable illustration of real, genuine, modern architecture than that building; and among all its merits I don't know any merit greater than the fidelity with which the design follows the facts of structure in the features, in the material, in everything. It is a building in baked clay; there isn't a feature in it in brick or in terra-cotta which could be translated into any other material without loss. It is a beautiful, adequate, modern performance. I say this without any reservation, because unfortunately the genius who, in great part, designed that building has gone from us; and there are many things by living architects, whom I cannot mention because they are living, which exhibit these same merits. There is one other example that I would like to mention here, because many of you know his work; I mean the late John Wellborn Root, of Chicago. I shouldn't mention him either if he hadn't, unfortunately, gone from us. Mr. Root's buildings exhibit the same true sincerity—the knowledge of the material with which he had to do, the fulfilment of the purpose which he had to perform. I don't know any greater loss that could have happened to the architecture of this country and to the architecture of the future than that man dying before his prime. These are stimulating and fruitful examples to the architects of the present time to bring their art more into alliance, more into union, more into identity, with the art of building; and it is by these means, gentlemen, and by these means only, that we can ever gain a living, a progressive, a real architecture—the architecture of the future."

JOHN DOS PASSOS, EXCERPT FROM *THE BIG MONEY,* 1936

The Big Money is the last volume in Dos Passos's monumental *U.S.A.* trilogy, tracing a broad arc of America's decline from the First World War to the Great Depression. Innovating in their structure, the novels splice together fictional narrative with "newsreels" of actual current events and short biographies of real people of prominence. The excerpt here is Dos Passos's quick biographical sketch of Frank Lloyd Wright. Wright stands unarguably as the most important American architect of the twentieth century, and while we have avoided the focus on specific architects, their particular styles and schools, Dos Passos paints Wright in the most broadly "American" terms and does so with such efficiency and energy that we couldn't resist.

Frank Lloyd Wright was the grandson of a Welsh hatter and preacher who'd settled in a rich Wisconsin valley, Spring Valley, and raised a big family of farmers and preachers and schoolteachers there. Wright's father was a preacher too, a restless illadjusted Newenglander who studied medicine, preached in a Baptist church in Weymouth, Massachusetts, and then as a Unitarian in the middle west, taught music, read Sanskrit and finally walked out on his family. . . .

His training in architecture was the reading of Viollet le Duc, the apostle of the thirteenth century and of the pure structural mathematics of gothic stonemasonry, and the seven years he worked with Louis Sullivan in the office of Adler and Sullivan in Chicago. (It was Louis Sullivan who, after Richardson, invented whatever was invented in nineteenth century architecture in America).

When Frank Lloyd Wright left Sullivan he had already launched a distinctive style, prairie architecture. In Oak Park he built broad suburban dwellings for rich men that were the first buildings to break the hold on American builders' minds of centuries of pastward routine, of the worn out capital and plinth and pediment dragged through the centuries from the Acropolis, and the jaded traditional stencils of Roman masonry, the halfobliterated Palladian copybooks.

Frank Lloyd Wright was cutting out a new avenue that led towards the swift constructions in glassbricks and steel foreshadowed today.

Delightedly he reached out for the new materials, steel in tension, glass, concrete, the million new metals and alloys.

The son and grandson of preachers, he became a preacher in blueprints, projecting constructions in the American future instead of the European past. Inventor of plans, plotter of tomorrow's girderwork phrases, he preaches to the young men coming of age in the time of oppression, cooped up by the plasterboard partitions of finance routine, their lives and plans made poor by feudal levies of parasite money standing astride every process to shake down progress for the cutting of coupons. . . .

To the young men who spend their days and nights drafting the plans for new rented aggregates of rented cells upended on hard pavements, he preaches the horizons of his boyhood, a future that is not the rise of a few points in a hundred selected stocks, or an increase in car loadings, or a multiplication of credit in the bank or a rise in the

Originally printed in *The Big Money* (New York: Harcourt, Brace and Company, 1936), 428–33.

rate on call money, but a new clean construction, from the ground up, based on uses and needs, towards the American future instead of towards the pain smeared past of Europe and Asia. Usonia he calls the broad teeming band of this new nation across the enormous continent between Atlantic and Pacific. He preaches a project for Usonia. . . .

Like the life of many a preacher, prophet, exhorter, Frank Lloyd Wright's life has been stormy. He has raised children, had rows with wives, overstepped boundaries, got into difficulties with the law, divorce courts, bankruptcy, always the yellow press yapping at his heels, his misfortunes yelled out in headlines in the evening papers: affairs with women, the nightmare horror of the burning of his house in Wisconsin. By a curious irony the building that is most completely his is the Imperial Hotel in Tokyo that was one of the few structures to come unharmed through the earthquake of 1923 (the day the cable came telling him that the building had stood saving so many hundreds of lives he writes was one of his happiest days) and it was reading in German that most Americans first learned of his work.

His life has been full of arrogant projects unaccomplished. (How often does the preacher hear his voice echo back hollow from the empty hall, the draftsman watch the dust fuzz over the carefully contrived plans, the architect see the rolled up blueprints curl yellowing and brittle in the filing cabinet.)

Twice he's rebuilt the house where he works in his grandfather's valley in Wisconsin after fires and disasters that would have smashed most men forever.

He works in Wisconsin, an erect spare white haired man, his sons are architects, apprentices from all over with him, drafting the new city (he calls it Broadacre City). . . .

Building a building is building the lives of the workers and dwellers in the building. The buildings determine civilization as the cells in the honeycomb the functions of bees.

Perhaps in spite of himself the arrogant draftsman, the dilettante in concrete, the bohemian artist for wealthy ladies desiring to pay for prominence with the startling elaboration of their homes has been forced by the logic of uses and needs, by the lifelong struggle against the dragging undertow of money in mortmain, to draft plans that demand for their fulfillment a new life; only in freedom can we build the Usonian city. His plans are coming to life. His blueprints, as once Walt Whitman's words, stir the young men:

Frank Lloyd Wright, patriarch of the new building, not without honor except in his own country.

9

MARY HORNADAY, "MELTING POT OF ARCHITECTURE," 1937

The melting pot as a metaphor for American society became popular in the early years of the twentieth century. It expressed both the reality of a population made remarkably diverse by immigration from Southern and Eastern Europe and a hope by some that all that cultural diversity—differences in language, religion, customs, and so on—would be "melted down" to create a more homogenous nation. Mary Hornaday has applied that metaphor to American architecture. Specifically, she reports on the findings of the Works Progress Administration's survey of local American architecture. Vernacular architecture, the architecture of the ordinary and everyday, Hornaday tells us, is also a marvelous melting pot of different traditions.

If you came from the Middle West, your birthplace was probably modeled after a Greek temple. If you belong to one of the F. F. V's (First Families of Virginia), your family may have had a Georgian mansion of the type that flourished in eighteenth-century England. If you are a Californian, the chances are your homestead had a Spanish touch.

Your family home may have been of French, Dutch, German, Swedish or even Chinese architectural descent—anything but American. Until recent years, there was little real American architecture in the United States. In its early days, the nation was a melting pot for architecture from all over the world, just as it was for people.

This fact is being forcefully brought out in an extensive government study of historic American buildings, directed by the National Park Service.

Several hundred draftsmen and photographers, paid with WPA funds, have been engaged during the last three years making records of fast disappearing early American buildings of all kinds and shapes. As fast as these records are completed, they are filed in the Library of Congress in Washington for the use of architects, students, government departments and the general public. Information on more than 3000 buildings, selected by local advisory committees as being worthy of note, is already in hand in Washington.

Now architect-officials of the survey are taking a retrospective look to see what conclusions can be drawn from the pictures and drawings. They find that geography, climate, wars, European ties, slavery, proximity of building materials, limited transportation, and even religious beliefs, played parts in determining the appearance of early American homes, business houses and public buildings.

In New England, dwellings were compactly built with barns, sheds and houses joined together to make the journey between them less arduous in wintry weather. In the South, on the other hand, porticos and balconies were built to create shade and breezy corners for hot weather.

Early Virginian houses, usually of brick made from native clay, reflected the taste of well-to-do home owners in England. It was natural that these colonists, many of whom built on lands granted them by their kings, should remain true to English architecture. New England dwellings, though usually more puritanical, followed the same general Georgian style.

Thomas Jefferson was the first great enthusiast for the classical style. He went to Italy, was captivated by Roman architecture, and designed the University of Virginia buildings according to its rules. A passion for columns was started that spread throughout the South.

Slavery also imprinted its mark on southern architecture—so much so that many of the mansions built in the grand style before the Civil War have proved ill-adapted to modern-day living.

Originally printed in *Christian Science Monitor Monthly Magazine*, June 2, 1937. Copyright by Mary Hornaday, *The Christian Science Monitor* 1937.

Dwellings and public buildings built in the manner of the Greek temple came into favor around 1825, after the Greek war for independence had stirred popular imagination. The fashion spread westward along the newly opened Erie canal. Greek-inspired dwellings began to take the place of humble log cabins. The Treasury in Washington was built in this period.

The fancy for Greek classical architecture lasted until the Civil War. After that, the fast-growing nation adopted the showy Victorian Gothic, commonly known as the "gingerbread" style. No house, built in that period was complete without a cupola. The more trimmings, the handsomer the building, it was thought then.

As a matter of fact, the Government has been skipping over these "gingerbread" buildings, chiefly because they are not real pioneer architecture. Many architects think that this period in American building development is not worth remembering anyway.

The present inventory includes no houses built after 1860, except in a few slowly developing communities such as the Kentucky mountains, where building design is still in its pioneer stage.

While Anglo-Saxons were stamping their tastes on eastern architecture, the Spanish influence was making itself felt on the Pacific coast. It flourished there side by side with the crude frame buildings associated with western mining towns.

In New Orleans, the French left their handiwork. Around Philadelphia, German and Dutch styles and simple square buildings, suited to the Quakers' dislike of ostentation, sprang up from native stone. In isolated Salt Lake City, where dug-out and sod hut might have been expected, government investigators found Brigham Young's "beehive house" erected 1000 miles from civilization in best New England fashion, only seven years after the city was settled.

Indigenous American buildings, the Survey reveals, are about as scarce as hen's teeth. Most people will say that the log cabin is American, but many architectural experts trace even it back to Sweden and Finland, declaring that colonists from these northern European countries imported the plans to Delaware and the north woods.

One of the few 100 per cent American dwellings is the Indian pueblo of the Southwest, which is almost as primitive now as it ever was. The Historic Buildings Survey made extensive studies of the Acoma pueblo, 75 miles southwest of Albuquerque, said to be the oldest continuously occupied village in the United States.

Other early types of architecture for which no foreign prototype has been discovered are the so-called "dog-run" houses, with an open passage in the center, found in Tennessee and other southern states; the "Sunday house," a small community dwelling erected in Texas by German settlers for week-end use; and the garrison house, a combination fort and home built chiefly in New England to combat Indian attacks.

The Survey has not been limited to houses. New England churches, Minneapolis flour mills, covered bridges, opera houses, and taverns have been carefully measured and photographed. The Library's index of record runs: "sod houses, stables, state capitols; theaters, town halls, towers," and so on. Draftsmen have measured shelves and rail fences. Architects have drawn pictures of hinges, millwheels and unusual nail heads. Clerks have answered questions as to owner, date of erection, architect, builder, present condition, number of stories and materials of construction. . . .

From now on, if anybody wants to rebuild any of these historic landmarks, the

Government archives will help them out. The records now being gathered are considered to be a form of insurance against the loss of data, as well as a contribution to the history of American architecture.

Some of these places have been destroyed since Government agents worked on them. A century-old covered bridge near Homer, Illinois, collapsed three weeks after draftsmen had measured it. The Cross Keys Tavern, near Shelbyville, Kentucky, erected in 1800, burned to the ground after its record had been made.

Wreckers were already at what is believed to be the oldest building on Manhattan Island—a Dutch house under the shadow of Brooklyn Bridge—when Survey scouts discovered it. At Newburyport, Massachusetts, draftsmen went out the back doors of a row of old houses as wrecking crew came in the front with orders to make room for a new boulevard.

Directors of the Survey think the attention the Federal Government has been giving to historic buildings has played a part in arousing localities to preserve and restore their landmarks. Preliminary surveys are now under way in preparation for the restoration of the first permanent white settlement in the United States, picturesque St. Augustine, Florida. There is talk of restoring Annapolis, colonial capital of Maryland. Restorations which have already used records made by the Survey include that of Vernon, at Germantown, Pennsylvania, and Gilreath's Hill Tavern at Natchez, Mississippi.

Data from the Survey's files helped the inaugural committee erect a faithful likeness of Jackson's home, "The Hermitage," as a White House reviewing stand and enabled Capitol architects to reproduce certain decorations after installing an air-cooling system recently.

10

TALBOT F. HAMLIN, EXCERPT FROM "THE ARCHITECTURE OF THE FUTURE," 1943

For many Americans, the Second World War was nothing less than a titanic struggle between democracy and tyranny, between individual freedom and totalitarian repression. Writing in the midst of the war, Talbot Hamlin urges Americans that the lessons and meaning of the war be translated in the architecture and design of postwar America. In his plea that this new architecture reflect American democracy, Hamlin, who was both an architect and an architectural historian of some importance, harkens back to writers of the early Republic who believed that American architecture ought to embody American political principles. Here, however, Hamlin writes that the highest value that architecture needs to express is "the conscious life of individuals."

Originally printed in *New Pencil Points* 24 (March 1943): 64–69.

Today, architectural practice is in large measure non-existent; when the war ends it will resume in an unprecedented flood. Is it not time for the architect to think seriously of what forms that flood will take, of how the architect may use his creative power to fulfill the needs society will present, of the materials and structural methods with which his designs will be built, and of how his particular talents can be brought to bear? Even if there is no place in a wartime economy for many architects, surely this is no excuse for their failure to use their best imagination, their most stringent powers of analysis, their creative efforts now, with the aim of being better prepared and more thoughtfully aware, so that their work, when the time comes, will be more realistic, in the sense that it is based on the actual needs of people, and more idealistic, in the sense that it is more consciously devoted to the public welfare. If this is an aim, then we must examine not only revolutions in industrial techniques, but the much more subtle problems of the relation of design to human life.

This attitude will condition the looks of buildings as well as their plans, for, however much present-day social and economic pressures and the necessity of building with a minimum of materials and money have tended to minimize esthetic ideals, it is nevertheless true that architecture is a matter of "looks" as well as of other more obvious utilities. . . .

This is a war for democracy. I can see no more important connotation of democracy than the stimulation of the rich, conscious life of individuals. It is, therefore, on the individual that our architecture after a victorious war must be founded, and all matters of collective controls—economic, cultural, or industrial—must exist solely as means to the enhancement of individual living. From this will be developed the one great criterion of success or failure in architectural design. This will be the controlling idea which must override all preconceived attitudes toward styles, toward novelty *per se*; this will be the great standard by which we may judge such industrial aids as prefabrication and the furnishing of new materials.

This ideal should affect pre-eminently the problem of housing and community form. That community or that housing group will be most successful in which each inhabitant has the greatest opportunity to develop his own individuality, in which each feels himself a "person" and not merely a member of a class. This same attitude should apply to residential developments for all economic levels.

But there is another element in democracy which must also have its effect. Not only is each individual in a democratic society allowed to be himself; each individual, each self, is an integral part of the co-operative working whole which is society. His selfness must not be allowed to interfere with the selfness of others. Just as in law there is a continual search for the limits between anarchy and co-operation, so in architectural communities there must be a continual search for basic community harmony as well as for individual expression.

To understand the architecture which the future should bring, we must therefore understand people—their extraordinary variety, their creative differences—and yet we must also understand their basic desire, when unspoiled by outside pressures, to help one another and live together as fellow beings. We must understand and respect the fact that there are people who like urban conditions, those who like small communities, those who like the solitude of country living. We must understand that even in a single urban community there are people who like the privacy of individual houses, and others who prefer the ease and freedom of the co-operative services of an apartment hotel. There are people gregarious, and people solitary. It is no impossible task for the community planner and the architect, working together, to take care of all these types, to give to each the kind of environment in which it can flower in the most creative and, at the same time, most socially-useful ways.

If this is true, then one of the greater sins against the spirit of postwar architecture would be standardized monotony. Standardization of house unit or of apartment layout may, to a certain degree, become inevitable, owing to the industrial development of pre-fabrication, in whole or more probably in part. But of the monotonous rows of identical buildings, spaced at approximately equal distances, which have been too often the results of much governmental housing in the past, there should be an end. . . . They are barracks essentially, and the idea of the barrack *must* be the submersion of the individual within a class. We must get rid of the "low-cost housing complex" and, whatever the cost of the buildings we are working for, we must build not for an "income level" but for the people.

This will affect, first of all, the question of community scale. . . . I feel we must reconstitute our whole concept of housing communities. Any community, it seems to me, will in the future consist of several different types of shelter. There will be different building heights; there will be many different types of layout. The young married couple without children, or the older couple whose children have gone out on their own, may perhaps prefer to live high above the ground in a tall apartment—perhaps with a co-operative restaurant within the building The family with children will want to find either an apartment of sufficient size, closely related to play space outdoors and with sufficient indoor area so that little John and his electric train are not always underfoot, or perhaps a row house with its own back yard. Every housing group of any size should contain all these elements, and the idea of forcing families of all sizes and kinds into buildings of one type will appear the ridiculous denial of individuality which it is. The kind of implied segregation which has followed the development of certain very large and very monotonous USHA developments in the past is, I believe, a danger to society and one of the reasons why there has been so much hostility on the part of many estimable people toward the whole housing movement. . . .

Perhaps the most expressive example in contemporary architecture of the kind of development we should be able to expect is furnished by the revolution in school design which has been so noticeable in the Middle West and the Far West in the last ten years. The best of the new schools are human, intimate, designed for children for whose use they are built. One feels that the unit of measure which has controlled them is the measure of the child personality. Just so, we may hope for communities in the postwar period which are as definitely to be measured by the wants and needs, the desires and ideals, of adult individuals.

Somewhat the same kind of freedom of form, generated by humanity of ideal, has distinguished large numbers of one-story houses along the West Coast. There, too, graciousness and beauty and a kind of winning naturalness have followed when the real needs of persons have been allowed completely to dominate conventions of lot usage or house shape and the applied clichés of styles. The best of them are buildings designed not to be photographed but to be lived in. May not an architecture of a victorious democracy be expected to proceed much further along this path, as more and more people gain the right and the ability to live the lives they want, and as more architects learn what people really are and feel?

The freedom of form inherent in this conception entails no denial of the industrialization or rationalization of building itself. Industry is a tool; the greater the flexibility and power of this tool, the more easily will human wants be satisfied. It is only an unimaginative use of industrialized building which produces the monotony of repeated units. The reason for the stupid ugliness of many prefabricated war housing groups lies not in the machinery of fabrication but in lack of creative thought. . . . Let us not forget . . . that the personality—the human quality—of a community can be gained by careful, imaginative, and realistic site planning, by curved streets and varied setbacks, by studies of street, playground, or yard views, by architectural planting.

Moreover, these new tools have already increased enormously the alphabet of architectural forms. The increasing presence, for example, of curved lines in industrial buildings—owing to the use of laminated wood frames, lamella roofs, or various types of shell concrete construction—is an outstanding quality of today's most "practical" buildings. This is perhaps one of the most significant form trends in recent architecture. We may look forward confidently to a broadening of the esthetic imagination, so that it will cease to design merely in terms of T-square and triangle. This has been foreshadowed in much of the best recent work of Frank Lloyd Wright, where complete freedom from conventional thinking in plan, exterior, and interior has recaptured something of the three-dimensional poetry of the Pantheon.

The architecture of the future, then, will be a democratic architecture, because its conceptions will be based on individuals rather than on class. It will demand of its architects the greatest human imagination—the ability to pierce through the inarticulateness of the average American and perceive his real ideals and desires. It will have a harmony and human graciousness which bear to the 20th Century the same relationship that the beauty of such towns as Nantucket or Marshall, Michigan, bore to the early 19th Century. It will be regional, because American culture is a complex harmony with many regional strains, and because of the variety of climates and of local materials. It will be an architecture freer from style clichés than any architecture in our lifetime, and as such it will develop inevitably a rich and expressive style of its own—American because built for us.

11

G. E. KIDDER SMITH, EXCERPT FROM "THE TRAGEDY OF AMERICAN ARCHITECTURE," 1945

The Second World War had just ended when G. E. Kidder Smith wrote this long, angry rant about the state of American architecture. There is much here that rings familiar: the complaint that Americans do not like to plan their cities and towns; the condemnation that Americans borrow their architectural styles from the past and from Europe; the conviction that what Americans build is really only façade deep. But Smith also aggressively advocates

Originally printed in *American Magazine of Art* 38 (November 1945): 255–60.

modernism and the application of modernist principles of design to architecture and planning—big, planned "super-blocks," lots of car-carrying highways, the smooth integration of technology into the home. In this sense, Smith reveals that belief among modernists in the wake of the war that modern architecture could fundamentally reshape the world.

I have recently returned from a series of countrywide trips which permitted me to see much of the cream of our modern American architecture. . . .

I had naively imagined before starting out that California would be bursting with all manner of modern work. . . . There is no general acceptance of modern architecture in California, or in the East—much less the South. It was ridiculous for me to have thought so.

Because America does not realize the fundamental approach of modern architecture and the great benefits (which we hope to make clear) accompanying it, it neither knows nor cares about it. It does not seek buildings generated by plan instead of by façade; it does not look for living beauty and restfulness in its houses; it is horrified at anyone proposing that some responsible and capable authority plan its subdivisions and highways in an effort to make its cities and surroundings coherent and beautiful. . . . It is altogether as one to preserve the architectural anarchy that has so far blighted our cities and our land.

Will our postwar houses, highways, schools and stores meet their requirements any more successfully than those we built before the war, when almost everything we designed bulged with fakeries and artificiality, when sham exteriors dominated actual needs of building, when hideous, unplanned cities and ruinous, uncontrolled developments seemed to be demanded and so many were produced?

This 20th century archeology has got to stop. It is imperative for our future that we shake loose our feeble planning efforts and our befuddled designing. Our new architecture must grow from the *needs* of the problem; it cannot continue to be a collection of debased "styles" with rooms (even towns) warped to fit—if that were possible. Our cities, our villages, our very school yards must be planned as they never were before, and planned in relation to themselves, their neighborhoods and their communities. Trees and sunshine must fill the cities of tomorrow, and their buildings must be products of the genius our science and technology have given the world in almost every other field. Does our present disgraceful insistence upon the antique give us hope for such a future?

Our doctor's office is filled with the latest theories of sulfa drugs and penicillin; our industrialists seek only the most efficient production methods; our accountants, our business associates, we ourselves, conduct our affairs according to the most up-to-date and progressive means. Yet when we see our architect—and even this is too rarely done—we *demand* that he revert to the most aged stylistic conception he can conjure up! The more our house looks like the ones the Pilgrims built on Cape Cod, the more closely it follows Williamsburg or some Spanish villa, the more satisfactorily are our desires answered. . . .

Look at our cities: Thoughtless checkerboards superimposed over a prostrate nature without the slightest regard to natural features, site adaptability . . . Is there one in the entire country, with the exception of a few villages in old New England and a sprinkling elsewhere, which altogether has any semblance of charm or beauty? Parts of some are good, and others impress with the power of the skyscrapers; but go down any commercial street of any town in the United States and really look at what surrounds you. There is no order, no unity, no convenience, no plan, no peace nor quiet, merely a collection of excessively unattractive and repugnant buildings flashing modernistic superficiality. . . .

This chaos does not have to be: Such structural brutality is not mandatory, nor does any civic code prescribe ten circuits of the block before a parking space will be granted. There is only one reason why all of our cities are not filled with parks and playgrounds, why parking places are not integrated with city plans, why express boulevards do not whisk us home at night, why our buildings are not inspiring examples of American capability instead of miserable imitations of something Europe discarded decades ago. That reason is because you and I do not demand it, or are not interested, or are too lazy. . . .

Examine the buildings which make up this jumbled urban sordidness; multitudinous parades of cheap, flashy stores, each trying to outdo its neighbor, each spouting arrays of [ ] signs in a veritable forest of unbridled wires, awnings and marquees. And at night such confusion is embellished with multi-colored flashing lights. Nothing is integrated, no one regards his neighbor, no block is planned as a unit, each is an individualistic accretion—everyone suffers. . . .

The apartment houses in our cities, from Park Avenue to Midwest suburbia, are cages of little cells, boxed in with fake Elizabethan "half timber," corseted with Greek pilasters, festooned with idiocies. The idea of large, sunny windows, pleasant flower-lined balconies and open planning never seems to occur—it would involve annoying originality; the banks and the F.H.A. wouldn't like it. The rational notion that some advantage might be gained by coordinating the planning of several such buildings so that parks flow by each and trees brush your balcony, as could be so magnificently done, is ridiculed as "foreign" and "European stuff." Accordingly, we put on sack cloth and ashes and live in architectural sin the rest of our lives.

For houses we have tight little boxes with holes punched in the walls for windows, with interiors cluttered with cornices, mouldings and panels; with chopped up walls, busy-busy surfaces, poorly laid out, poorly oriented, wretchedly conceived. Yet, as we have seen, the houses of which American architects are capable are breathtaking. Houses so altogether livable and gracious that "period" imitations seem intolerable beside them. Houses which relish steep hills that defy the colonial, and from such vantage points throw themselves open to inspiring views. Houses which delight in the imaginative challenge of difficult sites, yet equally well met banal, flat city lots with fenced or walled gardens into which the interior flows, as one indoor-outdoor space, filled with flowers and trees yet ever private. Houses designed for modern carefree living, for your site and climate—not mechanically plucked from some contractor's dream book and slapped up with scant regard for you or your neighbors. And houses with a convenience, ease of upkeep, a color and beauty never known before.

But look at what surrounds us on all sides. Even our kitchens, in spite of all their fancy fixtures, are rarely more than rooms filled with unintegrated mechanical furniture. Each item has been so advertised and ballyhooed as a unit by itself, that in planning the meal workshop, the architect must perforce use stoves, refrigerators, sinks, washing machines, etc., as so many individual pieces instead of being able to tie them all together, as he could if they were flexible, interchangeable units fitting any layout the design called for.

This individual furniture obsession has reached such fatuous proportions that one of the leading producers of electric ice-boxes pays a well-known industrial designer a reported $25,000 *each year* to restyle his product with some foolishness or "streamlining" (in case of floods?), so that it would look out of date in a few years' time, and one would feel ashamed of a 1940 model in a 1945 kitchen. An ice box is a freezing machine, not a fashion fancier. . . .

What then, we may ask, is modern architecture and how is its approach so fundamentally different that it, together with modern planning, can offer us a greater and better life. Before beginning to define it, we had first better clear up the difference between real modern architecture and two spurious imitations, both of which have discredited the modern movement. The first of these is the "moderne," and this is basically nothing more than an old classic form with most of the excess ornaments scraped off. Its face has been lifted, the Greek columns have become rectangular piers and the ponderous cornices have been shaved down. However, the rigidity of plan, the all-prevailing symmetry, the unfunctional conception remain the same. A branch of this style is also called the "Federal." It generally has eagles out in the front.

The second imitation is more confusing (and more harmful), for it consciously apes and elaborates on many of the external features of good modern work without regard for their origin or purpose. It then throws everything together in a fantasy of tasteless materials and a potpourri of surfaces either bent into collapsed curves or overlapped and built-up into such jazz formations that steady study is guaranteed to produce organic twitchings or nervous collapse. This jitterbug approach is the "modernistic." It is common with many theaters and stores, some radios and all jukeboxes. Its houses look like hard little cubes with no eyebrows. We must, therefore, be careful to avoid calling a modern building modernistic, for modernistic defines only the most bizarre and jazzy concoction of shallowest appeal.

True modern (i. e. logical) architecture began as a reaction to the façade school because such a degree of absurdity had been reached and the results were patently so untenable that a fresh attack from the ground up was obviously needed. The modern architect, therefore, begins anew with each problem and considers it not as a preconceived outside shell to be slipped straightway on a steel frame, or a house (in any style) to be drawn in a moment's notice, but as a series of inter-related problems that involve not only the building's immediate functions but its multiple uses, relation to the community (and city itself), orientation, climate, materials available, traffic, client, and those other technical and sociological considerations whose analyses make up the many problems to be answered *before* the building design itself is even begun. The modern architect's every step is based on reason, his entire motivation—uninhabited by limitations of the renaissance, colonial, etc.—is towards solving a problem completely and beautifully—and with imagination, a factor which perforce the "styles" can never admit.

With the modern school—and it includes many of the older men as well as most of the younger—it is axiomatic that all considerations which affect the use of a building shall be weighed in its design. The points we have just mentioned are only a few whose incorporation will naturally give a more beautiful, restful and livable home, a more workable and flexible school, a more efficient library, factory or office building. Why? Because all the ideas generating the design were based on the exact solution of these various problems as we are capable of solving them in the 20th century America, and were not a synthesized assimilation of needs stuffed willy-nilly into an antique box.

However, this new architecture can live and flourish only in planned communities. Our cities stand in desperate need of a new scale, a scale of the superblock, of trees and parkways, a scale of the automobile. We need an intelligent use of the land for the benefit of all, not the uncontrolled speculation of the few. We need zoning in both town and country that protects not only the buyer but the citizen spectator. We also need a far greater integration of nature and city.

It is indeed strange that we must be taught that which can offer us more in livable comfort, beauty, and convenience than any previous architecture and planning ever offered any previous people, yet the new architecture requires an education by ourselves, our schools, our builders, and banks. We must get to know it, our children must know it, for it is only from the people that a great architecture can arise. And the more we know it, the more we will demand it, the greater will be the rewards, the more wonderful our cities.

1 2

JOHN A. KOUWENHOVEN, EXCERPT FROM "WHAT IS 'AMERICAN' IN ARCHITECTURE AND DESIGN? NOTES TOWARD AN AESTHETIC OF PROCESS," 1961

John Kouwenhoven stands as one of the foundational figures in what was the new field of American studies in the generation after the Second World War. In the tradition of early "men of letters," Kouwenhoven had a varied career as a high school teacher, an editor at *Harper's*, and as an instructor at Barnard College. This excerpt comes from his classic collection of essays, *The Beer Can by the Highway*. What Kouwenhoven noticed about Americans was our fascination with speed, with force and with motion. In this piece, he sees an American architecture embodied in, among other things, vernacular designs that express structural tensions and competing forces.

We may ask what is "American" in architecture and design because we want to establish their continuity with buildings and objects of the past. And if this is our motive in asking the question we will, of course, be most interested in those buildings and objects whose structure and aesthetic effect are clearly related to, and thus comparable with, those of their predecessors in the Western tradition. We will concern ourselves, that is, with architecture in its textbook sense, as a fine art which has developed continuously, with local and national variants, throughout the Western world.

If we approach the question in this way, taking "architecture" to mean churches, government buildings, and palaces (for princes or merchants), and taking "design" to include what the nineteenth century lumped as "Industrial Art" (manufactured objects to which one could apply "arts and crafts" decoration, such as pottery, textiles, bijouterie, and the printed page), we will probably conclude that the "American" quality is catholicity. We can

Kouwhenhoven, John A. *The Beer Can by the Highway: Essays on What's American about America*, pp. 139–62. © 1961 John A. Kouwenhoven. Reprinted with permission of The Johns Hopkins University Press.

find in the United States an imitation of almost any architectural style or decorative mannerism which ever existed in any other nation. And when we have done so, all we shall have demonstrated is what we already knew: that Americans came from everywhere, and brought with them the traditions—architectural and decorative as well as social and religious—of which they were the heirs. We shall have learned what is English or Spanish or German about our architecture and our design, and therefore how they relate to the Western tradition; but we shall know as little as ever about their "American" quality, if such there be....

The question can be asked, however, not in hopes of establishing ties to the past but in hopes of discovering those elements of creative energy and vitality which can evolve forms and structures appropriate to a world of flux and change—the "American" world—even at the risk of devaluing or destroying much that we have cherished and loved in the past. If this is our motive, we must look at those structures and objects which were not thought of as "Architecture" or "Industrial Art" by those who designed or paid for them. We must look, in other words, at those structures and objects which have been unself-consciously evolved from the new materials, and for the unprecedented psychological and social uses present in the "American" environment.

If we go at the question in this way, we will discover, I think, that the "American" quality is the product of a vernacular which has flourished in the United States....

I am . . . using the term *vernacular* as a descriptive label for the patterns and forms which people have devised, usually anonymously, in attempting to give satisfying order to the unprecedented elements which democracy and technology have jointly introduced into the human environment during the past hundred and fifty years or so.

Actually there are two ways in which people can order the elements of a new environment. One is to cramp them into patterns or forms which were originally devised to order other and quite different elements of another and quite different environment....

The other way is to shuffle and rearrange the unfamiliar elements until some appropriate design is empirically discovered. The vernacular patterns or forms so devised will often be ungainly, crude, or awkward in contrast with those evolved and refined over the centuries to order the elements of the pre-democratic, pre-industrial world, but they will at least bear a vital relation to the new environment of whose elements they are composed. More importantly, they will contain within themselves the potentiality of refinement and . . . of transfiguration by the hand of genius....

If we turn . . . to building we may perhaps more easily see the way in which vernacular forms and patterns can become expressive elements in creative design. In the past thirty years many structural elements which were developed in vernacular building have become characteristic features of contemporary architecture. One has only to look at the accompanying pictures of a century-old iron loft building, the glass-enclosed verandahs of a seaside hotel of the eighteen eighties, and an abandoned tobacco factory to be aware of the vernacular roots of important elements in the architectural design of such buildings as Albert Kahn's tank arsenal, the Farm Security Administration's utility building for a California migrant camp, and Raymond Hood's magnificent McGraw-Hill building—done after he had learned to dispense with the Gothic trappings of the Tribune Tower.

Thus far we have touched upon examples of the vernacular which were evolved primarily to cope with or exploit those elements of the new environment which were introduced by technology—by developments in the machining of metal, in frame construction, and in the manufacture of glass. But the vernacular as I have tried to define it is by no means the product of technology alone. It is a response to the simultaneous impact of technology and democracy. . . . New techniques and new materials have not been the only constituents of the new environment for which men have had to discover appropriate forms. There have also been new amalgams of thought, of emotion, and of attitude. . . .

By now it is clear that many of the constituents of contemporary design which at first struck us as alien and strange evolved from our vernacular. The molded plywood which seemed so startling when it appeared in chairs exhibited at the Museum of Modern Art in the late thirties and early forties was the conventional material for seats in American ferryboats in the 1870's. The spring-steel cantilever principle, which attracted world-wide attention when Mies van der Rohe use it in a chair he designed at the Bauhaus, had been standard in the seats of American reapers and mowers and other farm machines since the 1850's. Built-in furniture, the "storage wall," and movable partitions to create flexible interior space, all three were employed in an ingenious amateur house plan worked out in the 1860's by Harriet Beecher Stowe's sister, Catherine Beecher, a pioneer in the field now know as home economics. The provision of storage facilities in interchangeable units, which can be rearranged or added to, as changing needs and circumstances require, had a long history in office equipment, kitchen cabinets, and sectional furniture before it was recognized as an appropriate element in creative design.

What is important about such instances, from the point of view of this article, is that so many of them reflect a concern with process, especially as it is manifest in motion and change; for it is this concern, as I have said, which seems to me to be central to that "American" quality which we are trying to define. . . .

In an earlier essay I have tried to show that the quality shared by all those things which are recognized, here and abroad, as distinctively "American"—from skyscrapers to jazz to chewing gum—is an awareness of, if not a delight in, process: that universal "process of development" which, as Lancelot Law Whyte has said, man shares with all organic nature, and which forever debars him from achieving the perfection and eternal harmony of which the great arts of Western Europe have for centuries created the illusion. In the hierarchical civilizations of the past, where systems of status kept people as well as values pretty much in their places, men were insulated against an awareness of process to an extent which is no longer possible. In an environment dominated by technology and democracy, a world of social and physical mobility and rapid change, we cannot escape it. And our awareness of process is inevitably reflected in the vernacular, just as our occasional dread of it is witnessed by our continuing commitment to the cultivated forms inherited from a world in which permanence and perfection seemed, at least, to be realities.

It is the ideas, emotions, and attitudes generated by this conscious or unconscious awareness of process which account, I think, for a basic difference between the aesthetic effects of vernacular forms and those of the cultivated Western tradition. Inevitably, the forms appropriate to our contemporary world lack the balanced symmetry, the stability, and the elaborate formality to which we are accustomed in the architecture and design of the past. They tend, instead, to be resilient, adaptable, simple, and unceremonious. Serenity gives way to tension. Instead of an aesthetic of the arrangement of mass, we have an aesthetic of the transformation of energy. Only in some such terms as these, it seems to me, can we describe the so-called "American" quality which we detect in our architecture and design.

It is not possible in a brief essay to do more than suggest the implications of such an approach to the question asked in our title. Obviously it restricts our attention to a limited field of structures and objects, and diverts it from some of the most charming and interesting things which have been produced in this country. But it has the merit, I think, of converting a question which can easily become a mere excuse for a naïvely nationalist antiquarianism, or an equally naïve internationalism, into one which may help us discover the aesthetic resources of an "open-ended" civilization, of an "American" environment which reaches far beyond the borders of the United States. It also has the modest merit of requiring us to look with fresh eyes at things around us—not just the things in the decorators' shops and museums, but the humbler things which, because the people who made them took them, as we do, for granted, are often spontaneously expressive of those elements in our environment which do not fall naturally into traditional forms and patterns.

One way to emphasize the point I am trying to make is to contrast a product of the vernacular with a masterpiece of the cultivated tradition. Books on the architecture of bridges do not, so far as I know, refer to structures such as the bridge built in 1882 across the Canyon Diablo in Arizona, on what is now the Santa Fe Railroad. Seen in contrast with the majestic Pont du Gard, one of the most perfect examples of Roman masonry construction, which rises 155 feet above the river Gard near the French city of Nîmes, this spider-web truss of iron, carrying heavy locomotives and cars 222 feet above the bottom of the canyon, dramatically illustrates the utterly different aesthetic effects produced in response not only to new techniques and materials but also to new attitudes and values. The two structures, embodying fundamentally different conceptions of time, of space, of motion, and of man's relation to external nature, make essentially different demands upon our attention.

If we can put aside, for the time being, all question of which structure is the more beautiful, there will be no difficulty in recognizing which of the two is embodied in a scheme of forms that is capable of becoming a vehicle for an architecture expressive of the American environment. . . .

[A] Tennessee architect named Harrison Gill . . . argues, the very fact that it does not rely on compression alone, but employs tension as well. By its use of tension it "comes closer to the forces and mechanics of nature than ever before. . . . The ability of a stalk of corn to stand erect lies in the tensile strength of its outer layers. Man and beast can move and work because of the elastic tension and sinew. All living things exist in a state of constant tension. . . . All truly modern building is alive."

Here, then, from vernacular roots a scheme of forms has evolved which is capable of expressing a humanism which takes man's mind as well as his body, his knowledge as well as his feelings, as its standard of reference, a humanism which sees man not as a stranger trying to assert his permanence in the midst of nature's inhuman and incomprehensible flux, but as a sentient part of nature's universal process.

13

DOUGLAS DAVIS, "TOWERS OF MAMMON," 1973

Sitting at the bottom of Manhattan Island, New York's World Trade Center, its twin towers, became among the most instantly recognizable signature buildings in the world. It was precisely this symbol of New York and of America that terrorists attacked on September 11, 2001. After the horrific attacks that caused their destruction, it became easy to forget just how controversial the towers were when they were proposed, and after they were completed. (It is ironic that these towers, designed by the same architect who designed Pruitt-Igoe, were completed at almost exactly the same moment as the hated housing project was torn down.) Far from being universally loved, these buildings generated intense animosity, as in Douglas Davis's piece here. The tallest buildings in the world (at least for a time), they culminated a half century of skyscraper construction, and represented the peak—or nadir—of the International Style. For those seeking a new direction in American architecture, the twin towers became a touchstone of what not to build.

The only way to grasp the enormity and the ugliness of New York's controversial World Trade Center is by air. From up there, flying across the Hudson River from New Jersey, the eye perceives the center's two aluminum, steel and glass towers standing like maidens of innocence against the grimy landscape of lower Manhattan. The 110-story twin towers are taller than the Empire State Building, stretching almost 1,400 feet into the sky, dwarfing the mere 50 and 60-story structures beneath them. The maidens are not fully decked out yet—floors remain to be finished, the roofs completed—but when they emerge, fully clothed, in a year or two, they will accommodate 9 million square feet of office space and house a potential daily population of 130,000 people.

The towers approximate the human body in fact as well as in metaphor: controlled at their center by a computer brain, they regulate themselves every minute of the day, automatically adjusting to external heat, cold, wind and rain. They use more electricity than Stamford, Conn.; their cooling plant is the largest in the world. The maidens sweat and excrete, too, emitting tons of sewage daily. . . .

Certain WTC advocates think this complex is the symbol of a new, automated skyscraper age, eclipsing the previous generation of tall buildings symbolized by WTC's uptown rival, the Empire State Building. And, indeed, skyscrapers are going up across the U.S. now, in Chicago, Houston, New Orleans and beyond. Minoru Yamasaki, the architect of WTC, believes that his towers humanize the art of skyscraping, inspiring their occupants with "pride and a sense of nobility." The Port Authority of New York and New Jersey, the owner of the towers, credits them with stimulating growth throughout the Metropolitan area.

A fraction of these claims is true. Unlike New York's Seagram Building, the World Trade Center is not a work of skyscraper art but it is definitely a marvel of engineering. It is constructed on principles and with materials not available to the Empire State generation. The massive towers support themselves by means of their walls, rather like a hollow box. This frees the floors from the crowding presence of columns and opens them up

1.4. World Trade Center towers, view from Manhattan Bridge, 1970. Photograph by Camillo Vergara. The tallest buildings in the world when they were built (the Sears Tower in Chicago would eclipse them in 1974, barely a year after their opening), the World Trade Center towers represented a remarkable engineering achievement and the peak of the modernist skyscraper era. For many, however, Minoru Yamasaki's towers also represented the lowest point in the development of the skyscraper. Massive, impersonal, antiurban—to many the twin towers represented how far wrong architecture had gone over the past half century. (It is a stunning irony that just as the World Trade Center was going up, another Yamasaki project—the Pruitt-Igoe low-income housing complex in St. Louis—was being demolished as an utter failure.) In the aftermath of the terrorist attack of September 11, 2001, however, it was hard not to remember the twin towers more generously.

horizontally, freeing both the eye and gobs of rentable space (the inside of the towers is easily their most pleasing feature). The walls, which are covered with a tough, whitish aluminum alloy, are so strong that the maximum "sway" of the building is a mere 11 inches, even at the very top.

The next generation of tall buildings will surely go even higher and, hopefully, learn from the mistakes of the present and past generations, as the WTC did not. It is a single-use center, doggedly devoted to business and nothing else, which means both economic risk and a failure of social resourcefulness and imagination, unlike Chicago's new John Hancock Center, which is designed for multiple use—living, playing, recreation, as well as offices. At a time when office space is a drug on the market, the World Trade Center is staying economically alive only because it is a quasi-public creature of the Port Authority, paying taxes at a lower rate than private industry, and pricing its space below its neighbors and competitors. Even so, it has gambled too heavily on one use, in the midst of a skittish, changing economy.

Also, the World Trade Center is an esthetic failure, a classic attempt to compromise too many motives and ideologies at once, soured further by a dose of hubris. Yamasaki has tried to marry capitalism and religion in his attempt to humanize the vastness of his structure; he has also tried to bridge the dry form-to-function ideology of Mies Van der

Rohe with the dainty arabesques of the post-Mies generation, of Philip Johnson and Edward Durrell Stone. The most glaring example of this is in his lobbies, where a combination of stainless steel, marble and 73-foot Gothic columns (curving up to cathedral windows at the top) becomes sheer bombast.

Yamasaki succeeded not in humanizing his building by these pretentious references—or by his open, sterile plaza—but in further alienating man from his environment. Both the art and the function of the contemporary skyscraper remain to be defined. The theories of Paolo Soleri (who argues that we must build up to keep the land around us open and free) and the example of the John Hancock tower may yet accomplish that. The architects of the World Trade Center have succeeded only in their aggressive aim to dominate the skyline of Manhattan, a motive that cannot be disguised by lobbies gilded in Gothic, or columns plated in white.

14

VINCENT SCULLY, "TOMORROW'S RUINS TODAY," 1999

Vincent Scully, Yale University's legendary professor of architectural history and unyielding critic of all that he saw as shallow and antiurban in the world of architecture, offers his none-too-hopeful view of what in America's built environment will endure for the centuries, to the next millennium. He hopes for the grand national lawn—the Mall in Washington—but fears that it will be the underground nuclear waste dump that lasts. Unwilling to be overly pessimistic, Scully finds in the New Urbanism (discussed in the Urbanism chapter) hope for the future of American architecture. Finally, he suggests, we have begun again to build places we love and hope to have last more than fifty years.

Most of what we build today won't be around in 100 years, let alone 1,000. Our steel-frame and curtain-wall skyscrapers are major symbols of our age, but there is every reason to surmise they won't be here for long. Their life expectancy is 50 years or so, and that assumes assiduous maintenance. It's also hard to believe that people in 1,000 years will still be willing to sit in cells up there pushing pieces of paper around. This is a very special, recent, odd way of life, vastly at variance with the grand fantasy of its setting.

Of course, we cannot know what society in the year 3000 will be like. We can only hope that it will be more civilized than our own and will cherish the city more than we have come to do. If so, New York's powerful grid plan, an indelible impress of human order on the earth, will be there for the people of that time to build upon in their own way, perhaps long after the skyscrapers have rusted into dust. Or it may be that generations to come will love the skyscrapers to distraction—let us hope especially the Chrysler Building and the Empire State Building—and thus save them despite everything.

From the beginning, cities have been coupled in the human mind with the idea of

Originally printed in *New York Times Magazine*, December 5, 1999, p. 38.

immortality, as indeed most architecture has been up to our time. In the great Mesopotamian epic that bears his name, Gilgamesh, King of Uruk, searched the world for eternal life and concluded in the end that immortality could be attained only by building. The "well-fired bricks" he used for the temple of Uruk's goddess shaped the future well beyond his own lifetime, and the city, whose buildings were constructed in relation to those built by the generations that had gone before and lasted in turn beyond the lives of those who made them, became the most effective instrument of permanence to which human beings could aspire.

Gilgamesh and his descendants in Mesopotamia piled up ziggurats of brick, mountains where no mountains were, the most enduring kind of building they could imagine. The Egyptians shaped their pyramids of cut stone, more enduring yet, and much later the Maya built theirs of masonry and concrete, echoing the shapes of the mountains around them.

The Greeks also built for endurance, but they changed the sacred type. Instead of mimicking natural forms, their temples, made up of stone columns, suggest a human image. Even after being leveled by earthquakes, the columns lay in disciplined rows, outlasting their gods. Many still stand in their landscapes as permanent images of mankind and could well be standing 1,000 years from now. The Romans, as always, were different. They built of concrete, in great masses, enclosing high volumes of space, as in the Pantheon in Rome. Even though in many cases the vaults fell long ago, the eroded walls remain indestructible still.

Do we build anything so solid today? Unappetizing examples come first to mind: manmade mountains of garbage, like Fresh Kills, on Staten Island. Perhaps some of our new "super max" prisons, which are now enjoying a building boom in the service of one of our fastest growing industries, the incarceration of human beings. The confinement of wasted lives in immortal containers constitutes our most ambitious public work today.

The need to dispose of nuclear waste has also inspired, if that is the word, an architecture that will last. The government's underground nuclear-waste repositories are the only things being built today that are specifically intended to last millenniums. Semioticians have proposed signs for the planned repository at Yucca Mountain meant to be understood by future cultures long after all of earth's present languages have passed away.

Also likely to endure are the roadways we've built to accommodate our automobiles, though nobody in his right mind can believe that the automobile will still be infesting the earth in 1,000 years. Long after the car is extinct, the ruins of our highway system will be here. And how spectacular they are! Though we cannot forget how these highways have torn our cities apart, it is nevertheless inspiring to see them swooping across the flat lands, rushing up the slopes of the Rockies, tunneling like lasers through the rock. Someday quite soon they will be recognized as ghosts of a vast human obsession, enormous terrestrial patterns to be interpreted by nut cases of the future as signaling to Mars.

What is most in and of the earth will outlast everything else. This ancient idea received its most stirring expression at the turn of the last millennium, when many people feared the world was about to end. When that didn't happen, people at once began, in a profound gesture of optimism about the future, to build churches of stone. This in itself was nothing new, but for the first time these churches were given stone vaults, roofed over like caverns in the rock. They were Roman vaults revived, now built not of concrete shoveled in by gangs of slaves but of beautifully cut masonry blocks carved by dedicated craftsmen. Within 50 years the new architecture of stone, which we call the Romanesque, had spread through southern and central France, creating the massive geometries of churches like St. Etienne de Nevers, and sometimes rising, like St. Front at Perigueux, to celebrate the domed landscape around it.

The Romanesque way of building, in barrel vaults, cross vaults and domes, has remained Europe's most enduring. Gothic architecture pushed its lithic permanence to the structural limit. The Renaissance changed the details back to classical and returned to round-headed forms. Vaulted and domed, St. Peter's in Rome and the thousands of Baroque and modern churches after it are all children of the Romanesque, born out of the safe arrival of the year 1000 and the endurance of the Christian faith, and they may easily last out the millennium to come.

It is only a footnote to that majestic sequence to observe that in America, in a new place, Henry Hobson Richardson revived the forms of the Romanesque to endow 19th-century New England with an architectural antiquity far more ancient than any it had really known. Yet durable as Richardson's buildings were, his aesthetic of permanence would not itself survive.

For the first time since cities began to be built, architecture in the 20th century has been dominated by an aesthetic of impermanence. The new industrial materials embraced by modern architects—steel and glass, especially, along with light-frame structures clad with plastics and other things that blow away—made the new approach possible. But there was also something in the air, some need to outdo the Abstract painters in their break with convention, to outface Nature and to encourage perpetual revolution, in which nothing could be decently allowed to last too long. All that resulted in the lightness and transparency of most modern work. Its sense of hazard culminated in Frank Lloyd Wright's transcendent Kaufmann House, Fallingwater, whose concrete slabs, first anchored deep in the rock, are then pushed way out there, too far, perennially cracking, deflecting, threatening to collapse and break our hearts. Like much of Wright's work, Fallingwater is a challenge to natural forces, heedless or heroic as one wishes to see it.

The aesthetic of impermanence—the willingness to say "to hell with history"—is especially strong today among neo-modernist architects and critics reacting against the recent revival of vernacular and classical traditions of architecture. Rightly or wrongly, Frank O. Gehry's Guggenheim Museum, in Bilbao, so beautifully sited in relation to the city's natural setting and its dark grid of streets, clearly gives the impression that it is much less permanent than they are. It is at once protean: a crashed ship, a conical hill, a fish, a cloud—and ephemeral: a light skeleton structure supporting a quaking feuillage of winking titanium leaves. We have come a long way from the Romanesque. But that is probably the point.

Perhaps for things to last one has to love their physicality in old, premodern ways. But can we ever love an individual building again as the people of the 11th century loved their churches? It is true that we mourn Wright's Larkin Building, in Buffalo, and McKim, Mead & White's Pennsylvania Station, in New York, but when we try to tally the architecture that will be around in the year 3000, it is of places, rather than buildings, that we are likely to think today. We think of cities, even as they are going to pieces around us. How we pray, perhaps against all the odds, that Rome and Paris will still be there in 1,000 years, and St. Petersburg and San Francisco and many others as well. Most of them are much better than we once thought. The meanest of them stir our novelists with endless images of intense life: Roth in Newark, Bellow in Chicago, Updike in God knows what benighted burg in Pennsylvania.

One prays, too, for the Mall in Washington. It is at least built to last, all Greek temple and Egyptian obelisk; only the iron dome of the Capitol needs to be preserved from rust. The track record of classical architecture suggests that these structures may still be here in the year 3000, so that schoolchildren of that time may well conflate, and rightly, the murder of the Kennedys with that of the Gracchi. Maya Lin's Vietnam memorial will recall the brave fragility of human life so long as people still have names and cuts in the earth endure. Of course, these reasonable assumptions could be undone by a less admirable human creation: global warming, which threatens to put the Mall—only a few feet above sea level—under water in 1,000 years.

A few years ago, we tended to look at the future through one of two veils. The first made us see the future as utopia, the other as a wild, uncivilized place, stunned by total cataclysm. It is hard to say which was the more depressing projection. In the first, Nature had pretty much disappeared and mankind lived in high-tech megastructural nightmares designed by mad architects. In the other, the world had gone back to jungle, nurturing new Eves and Adams. Now we don't look at things that way. We tend to hope that New York and Chicago will stay pretty much as they are. We now believe, perhaps naively, that they will escape the bombs and the germs and, though their skyscrapers will fall, that their indomitable inhabitants will have cleared away the rubble by the year 3000 and put up something more permanent in their place. It is, finally, the urban grid that counts, the firm plan at human scale.

Here at the end of the century, we are, I think, finally beginning to understand how we would like to live and how architecture can serve us best. Architects like Andres Duany and Elizabeth Plater-Zyberk and their colleagues have already constructed a gentle model upon which our near and far-distant futures might reasonably be built, disciplining the automobile and shaping our towns and cities as pleasant and stable places for people at all economic levels to live. That model, first tried at Seaside, in Florida, is based on the scale of the neighborhood; its major elements are the grids, streets, squares, boulevards and parks of traditional American city planning, which modernists had disastrously cast aside. Its proponents call it the New Urbanism, but it is in fact a renewal of ends and means as old as the city itself, as old as Gilgamesh, who built structures for the goddess of the place, who outlasts time. As the Greeks knew, Eros builds everything that counts and takes care of it. In architecture, love conquers and endures.

CHAPTER 2

"They Do Things Better in Europe": Americans View the World

By 1931 when F. Scott Fitzgerald wrote the essay "Echoes of the Jazz Age," he had, like so many expatriates in the 1920s, gone to Paris searching for a better cultural life. And like so many of that generation, he returned to America. Looking back on the 1920s he defiantly wrote, "Who could tell us anymore what was fashionable and what was fun?" Here was Fitzgerald, participating in the tradition of Ralph Waldo Emerson, Walt Whitman, and others, declaring America's cultural independence yet again from the Old World.

Throughout the nineteenth century, Americans lived, or perceived that they lived, in the long shadow of European culture, and many wanted desperately to get out from under it. Europeans did their part to foster that sense of cultural inferiority. Commenting caustically on the state of American literature, English critic Sydney Smith quipped in the pages of the *Edinburgh Review* in 1818, "why should the Americans write books, when a six weeks' passage brings them in our own tongue, our sense, science and genius, in bales and hogsheads?" "In the four quarters of the globe," Smith went on, "who reads an American book?" One hundred years later, whether self-consciously or not, Fitzgerald was still speaking to Smith.

Portraits of the United States drawn by visiting Europeans became a staple of the travel literature genre, especially in the antebellum period, when the very existence of the United States seemed such a novelty. Alexis de Tocqueville, for example, produced *Democracy in America*, a volume of remarkable perception and enduring importance, after his tour of the country. Others were less charitable.

But the transatlantic traffic went in two directions, and Americans also went abroad looking to see what the world might have to offer a new nation looking to build itself. A trip abroad to compare the United States with places in the "Old World" was not without its psychic risks. As Thomas Jefferson mused in 1787, "Travelling. This makes men wiser, but less happy. When men of sober age travel, they gather knowlege [*sic*] which they may apply usefully for their country, but they are subject ever after to recollections mixed with regret, their affections are weakened by being extended over more objects, & they learn new habits which cannot be gratified when they return home."

Still, risking the acquisition of unfulfillable habits, Americans did venture forth in increasing numbers as the nineteenth century wore on. A growing middle- and upper-middle-class wealth made overseas excursions economically possible for more people, and their trips were facilitated by innovations in steamship travel that cut down considerably on travel time. In 1865, Robert Tomes wrote in *Harpers* as if describing a new species: "The American is a migratory animal. He walks the streets of London, Paris, St. Petersburg, Berlin, Vienna, Naples, Rome, Constantinople, Canton, and even the causeways of Japan with as confident a step as he treads the pavements of Broadway."

Some walking those streets prepared to defend American institutions and ideals against all comers. Others searched for some ineffable something that the United States

2.1. Jasper Francis Cropsey, *Coliseum*, c. 1848. Courtesy of the Newington-Cropsey Foundation. When Americans ventured to Europe they found ruins. For some, those ruins symbolized the decay of an old culture. For others they stood as romantic evocations of a grand and glorious history, just the sort of history that many found lacking in the American landscape.

simply lacked. Still others went with an open mind, looking for adventure and discovery. They took the measure of their difference from other societies, and in that measure found either relief or yearning. Whatever the case, they wrote copiously about their experiences.

Travel writing, as a genre, dates almost coterminously with the European "Age of Exploration"—which is to say that nearly as soon as voyaging out became a central part of European nation-building, writing and reading about it became a central part of the world of letters. Americans too quickly became enthusiastic travelers, travel writers, and readers of travelogues. As the head of Harper & Brothers, then the largest publishing house in the nation, put it in the mid-nineteenth century, "Travels sell about the best of anything we get hold of. . . . They don't always go with a rush, but they sell longer, and in the end pay better." Henry David Thoreau, Walt Whitman, and Emily Dickinson never left this country: beyond these, one is hard pressed to come up with any serious American writer in the nineteenth century who did not try his or her hand at travel writing: Irving, Cooper, Hawthorne, Twain, James, Wharton—the list could go on.

The selections in this chapter are drawn largely from this body of American travel writing, and as a consequence some deal with the built environment explicitly, others only implicitly. We include them because they help us understand the cultural context in which Americans shaped their own built environment. Architecture is rooted in its own history, perhaps more than other fine art, and for Americans that history was largely European. It was a history that could either inspire—as in Jefferson's case—or oppress, but that could not be ignored. Further, what struck Americans who traveled overseas, whether they articulated it or not, was the way the in which the different customs, older histories, and other faiths they encountered were embodied in the architecture and built environment.

In the nineteenth century, the question the more thoughtful among these travelers posed of their journeys and to their readers might be simply put: What does the Old World have to teach us? For those of a certain cast of mind, the answer was quite lengthy indeed—Europe as the source of the culture, learning, and history so lacking in America; Asia as the source of ancient spiritualities and sensualities too subtle to be appreciated in the materialistic and Puritanical United States. For others, the answer was defiantly short: the Old World was old in the worst sense, replete with all the signs of an aged, tired, and feeble society. Ruins, after all, that most emblematic symbol of decay in the landscape, was what Europe had to offer in abundance, and this provided a stark contrast to the muscular, energetic youth of the United States.

At the turn of the twentieth century, Edith Wharton and Henry James best exemplified, at least in America's higher literary echelon, the powerful Europhilia that continued to cast America in an inferior light. Both spent extensive periods of time traveling and writing about Europe—James, in fact, left the United States altogether and took British citizenship at the end of his life—and both believed that America would never be a place where art, culture, or architecture for that matter could develop in any serious way. Only Europe possessed that sense of history out of which sprang great art and architecture, and the traditions and manners so that it could be appreciated.

At the same time, a quite different set of observers found a quite different set of things to admire in late-nineteenth-century Europe. Many of those Americans associated with the movement called Progressivism looked to Europe both for philosophical and theoretical inspiration for their efforts, and for examples of those principles made concrete. Jane Addams, for example, who founded and ran Hull House in Chicago, the most famous of the American settlement houses, did so after visiting London and seeing Toynbee Hall, the very first settlement house. She also took a pilgrimage to see the Russian author/philosopher Leo Tolstoy, whose ideas about poverty, peace, and pacifism would influence not only her but also Mahatma Ghandi and eventually Martin Luther King, Jr. Though James and Addams lived vastly different lives with vastly different concerns, they each found Europe to be the source for their inspiration.

Reformers who hoped to address the problems of the turn-of-the-century city found in Europe examples of everything from working-class housing to street lighting and sewers to municipal finance. What these reformers envied in Europe was not necessarily history and culture, but a more energetic and centralized state that made large-scale reform efforts easier to achieve than they were in the United States where the federal government, and many state governments, remained loath to involve themselves too much in reform. The model American Progressives saw in Europe was new design ideas linked to a more expansive state authority.

James died in 1916, in the middle of the First World War. His death symbolized the passing of a generation of Americans who looked to Europe with a set of nineteenth-century sensibilities about culture. The generation of writers and critics, artists and architects that came of age during the war rejected much of what James stood for in their bitter alienation and disillusionment. The old Europe, after all, despite or perhaps even because of its encrusted history and stultifying culture, had torn itself apart in an orgy of violence unmatched in human history. "A botched civilization," according to poet Ezra Pound, "an old bitch gone in the teeth."

While these intellectuals turned their backs on much of that old Europe, they now looked to Europe—especially Paris—for what was modern or, more properly, Modern. Early in the twentieth century in Paris, Picasso had invented Cubism, the most revolutionary and most profound of the modern art movements. In the 1920s Paris was still the center of the modern art world, and Weimar, home to the Bauhaus, was a mecca of modern ideas about architecture. Americans had received their first, shocking introduction to the Modern in 1913 at the Armory Show—the International Exhibition of Modern Art—in New York. After the war, a vast number of writers, artists, musicians, and others were drawn to Europe eager to participate in the creation of Modern culture. It was in this particular cultural context that Fitzgerald wrote so defensively.

By the first quarter of the twentieth century, Americans built bigger, taller, and more grandiose buildings than anyone else, but many felt that the truly important ideas about new architecture still came from Europe. Looked at this way, the United States seemed hopelessly old-fashioned and bourgeois, its artistic tastes rooted in the sentimental and the mediocre. Worse yet, in the roaring 1920s, the United States seemed so consumed with money-making as to create a society downright toxic to real culture, architectural or otherwise. By the 1920s, the skyscraper was the quintessential American architectural invention, but for many critics this represented not so much the perfection of architectural form and technique as the most efficient accumulation of rentable space.

And thus many left, with their disaffection in tow, hoping in Paris to write one great novel, or paint one important painting. In this sense, these expatriates, called a "Lost Generation" by Gertrude Stein, were not so different from Henry James after all. They weren't fair or generous or even right, many of these expats, in their anger with the United States. Indeed, it was in the 1920s, probably for the first time, that large numbers of Europeans began to take the pure products of America quite seriously. Jazz, the musical form that could have come only from the United States, represented some of the most daring, avant-garde culture, combining musical experiments and the crossing of racial boundaries in bold ways. And while American critics might hold their nose at the crass commercialism of skyscrapers, many Europeans were simply dazzled by them. Bauhaus experiments might have tried to rid architecture of the burdens of history and put it to use for social reform, but the American skyscrapers, cloud-piercing symbols of American engineering and private capital, made people dizzy, inspired them to take photographs and to write poetry.

The expatriate love affair with Europe in the 1920s came to its own unhappy end with the advent of economic depression and the rise of fascism. American intellectuals came home in the 1930s, and many of them felt an obligation to put their services to use creating a better society out of the ash heap of the Great Depression. Many writers, artists, and others embraced left-wing politics, with varying degrees of eagerness, and like the Progressive reformers of a previous generation, saw in totalitarian states the rational planning and state control they thought were necessary to rebuild a society destroyed by reckless capitalism.

Whatever inspiration American builders might have found in the great state building programs of Stalin's Soviet Union, or Mussolini's Italy, in the 1930s was quickly extinguished by the Second World War, and the growing awareness of what really went on behind the iron curtain. Whatever political disappointments that caused for those on the left in the 1930s, for artists and architects perhaps it did not matter that much. After the war, the United States emerged as powerful culturally as it was militarily and economically. Paris was still charming, but New York had replaced it as the cultural capital of the Western world.

For architects in particular the ideal, and increasingly the practice, was international. That was the name given to the style that grew out of theories of the German Bauhaus during the 1920s and 1930s. After the war the rise of the International Modern style resulted from both an ideological position that internationalism, rather than nationalism, was the only thing that could save the world from further war, and the fact that the war made refugees of many of those architects and designers who transplanted the International Modern style to the United States. Frank Lloyd Wright had designed the Imperial Hotel in Tokyo as early as 1916, but it was only after the Second World War that the United States became a net exporter of modern architecture abroad.

By the second half of the twentieth century, architecture had succeeded in some measure in transcending the strictly national boundaries that had defined it in the past. American architects built buildings from London to Dacca, and foreign architects designed and worked widely in the United States. Indeed, by the late twentieth century many Europeans had begun to complain about an overreaching American cultural imperialism. Sydney Smith's question had been entirely inverted, whether in Hong Kong or in Paris: who in the world read anything other than an American book, or listened to anything other than American music, or watched television programs and movies produced anywhere else? By the end of the twentieth century, the view from abroad had grown to resemble the view from home quite considerably.

15

THOMAS JEFFERSON, LETTERS FROM PARIS, 1785–1786

Thomas Jefferson occupies a singular place in the nation's architectural history. No other national leader saw the connection between forms of government and forms of architecture as deeply as he did. Jefferson did not simply speculate about these matters, of course, but took an active part in shaping the new nation politically and in designing real buildings. As president, he actively oversaw plans for the new capital at Washington, D.C., and as a Virginia aristocrat he turned his plantation home at Monticello into a showplace of architectural experiment. In these two letters, he discusses the building of the new Virginia capitol in Richmond, another building over which he had enormous influence. Jefferson had fallen in love with the Maison Quarrée in Nismes, France, and thought it ought to be the model for Virginia's new capitol, quite oblivious to the irony of using a building built by a Caesar and restored by Louis XIV as a model for a state capitol in a new republic.

LETTER TO JAMES MADISON, FROM PARIS, SEPTEMBER 20, 1785

Dear Sir,

   ... I received this summer a letter from Messrs. Buchanan and Hay, as Directors of the public buildings, desiring I would have drawn for them, plans of sundry buildings, and, in the first place, of a capitol. They fixed, for their receiving this plan, a day which was within about six weeks of that on which their letter came to my hand. I engaged an architect of capital abilities in this business. Much time was requisite, after the external form was agreed on, to make the internal distribution convenient for the three branches of government. This time was much lengthened by my avocations to other objects, which I had no right to neglect. The plan, however, was settled. The gentlemen had sent me one which they had thought of. The one agreed on here, is more convenient, more beautiful, gives more room, and will not cost more than two-thirds of what that would. We took for our model what is called the *Maison Quarrée* of Nismes, one of the most beautiful, if not the most beautiful and precious morsel of architecture left us by antiquity. It was built by Caius and Lucius Caesar, and repaired by Louis XIV, and has the suffrage of all the judges of architecture who have seen it, as yielding to no one of the beautiful monuments of Greece, Rome, Palmyra, and Balbec, which late travellers have communicated to us. It is very simple, but it is noble beyond expression, and would have done honor to our country, as presenting to travellers a specimen of taste in our infancy, promising much for our maturer age. I have been much mortified with information, which I received two days ago from Virginia, that the first brick of the capitol would be laid within a few days. But surely, the delay of this piece of summer would have been repaired by the savings in the plan preparing here, were we to value its other superiorities as nothing. But how is a taste in this beautiful art to be formed in our countrymen unless we avail ourselves of every occasion when public buildings are to be erected, of presenting to them models for their study and imitation? Pray try if you can effect the stopping of this work. I have written also to E.R. [Edmund Randolph] on the subject. The loss will be only of the laying the bricks already laid, or a part of them. The bricks themselves will do

Originally printed in Albert Bergh and Andrew Lipscomb, eds., *The Writings of Thomas Jefferson* (Washington, D.C.: Thomas Jefferson Memorial Association, 1905), 5:134–37.

again for the interior walls, and one side wall and one wall may remain, as they will answer equally well for our plan. This loss is not to be weighed against the saving money which will arise, against the comfort of laying out the public money for something honorable, the satisfaction of seeing an object and proof of national good taste, and the regret and mortification of erecting a monument of our barbarism, which will be loaded with execrations as long as it shall endure. The plans are in good forwardness, and I hope will be ready within three or four weeks. They could not be stopped now, but on paying their whole price, which will be considerable. If the undertakers are afraid to undo what they have done, encourage them to it by a recommendation from the Assembly. You see I am an enthusiast on the subject of the arts. But it is an enthusiasm of which I am not ashamed, as its object is to improve the taste of my countrymen, to increase their reputation, to reconcile to them the respect of the world, and procure them its praise.

LETTER TO THE DIRECTORS, FROM PARIS, JANUARY 26, 1786

Gentlemen,

I had the honour of writing to you on the receipt of your orders to procure draughts for the public buildings, and again on the 13th of August. In the execution of those orders two methods of proceeding presented themselves to my mind. The one was to leave to some architect to draw an external according to his fancy, in which way experience shows that about once in a thousand times a pleasing form is hit upon; the other was to take some model already devised and approved by the general suffrage of the world. I had no hesitation in deciding that the latter was best, nor after the decision was there any doubt what model to take. There is at Nismes in the South of France a building, called the *Maison Quarrée*, erected in the time of the Caesars, and which is allowed without contradiction to be the most perfect and precious remain of antiquity in existence. . . . Having not yet had leisure to visit it, I could only judge of it from drawings, and from the relation of numbers who had been to see it. I determined therefore to adopt this model, & to have all its proportions justly drewed. As it was impossible for a foreign artist to know what number & sizes of apartments could suit the different corps of our government, nor how they should be connected with one another, I undertook to form that arrangement, & this being done, I committed them to an Architect (Monsieur Clerisseau) who has studied this art 20 years in Rome, who had particularly studied and measured the *Maison Quarrée* of Nismes, and had published a book containing 4 most excellent plans, descriptions, & observations on it. He was too well acquainted with the merit of that building to find himself restrained by my injunctions not to depart from his model. In one instance only he persuaded me to admit of this. That was to make the Portico two columns deep only, instead of three as the original is. His reason was that this latter depth would too much darken the apartments. Economy might be added as a second reason. I consented to it to satisfy him, and the plans are so drawn. I knew that it would still be easy to execute the building with a depth of three columns, and it is what I would certainly recommend. We know that the *Maison Quarrée* has pleased universally for near 2000 years. By leaving out a column, the proportions will be changed and perhaps the effect may be injured more than is expected. What is good is often spoiled by trying to make it better.

The present is the first opportunity which has occurred of sending the plans. You will accordingly receive herewith the ground plan, the elevation of the front, and the elevation of the side. The architect having been much busied, and knowing that this was all which would be necessary in the beginning, has not yet finished the Sections of the building. They must go by some future occasion as well as the models of the front and side which are making in plaster of Paris. These were absolutely necessary for the guide of workmen not very expert in their art. It will add considerably to the expense, and I would not have incurred it but that I was sensible of its necessity. The price of the model will be 15 guineas. I shall know in a few days the cost of the drawings which probably will be the triple of the model: however this is but my conjecture. I will make it as small as possible, pay it, and render you an account in my next letter. You will find on examination that the body of this building covers an area but two-fifths of that which is proposed and begun; of course it will take but about one half the bricks; and of course this circumstance will enlist all the workmen, and people of the art against the plan. Again the building begun is to have 4 porticos; this but one. It is true that this will be deeper than those were probably proposed, but even if it be made three columns deep, it will not take half the number of columns. The beauty of this is ensured by experience and by the suffrage of the whole world; the beauty of that is problematical, as is every drawing, however well it looks on paper, till it be actually executed: and tho I suppose there is more room in the plan begun, than in that now sent, yet there is enough in this for all the three branches of government and more than enough is not wanted. This contains 16. rooms. To wit 4. on the first floor; for the General court, Delegates, Lobby, & Conference. eight on the 2nd floor for the Executive, the Senate, & 6 rooms for committees and juries: and over 4. of these smaller rooms of the 2nd floor are 4. Mezzaninos or Entresols, serving as offices for the clerks of the Executive, the Senate, the Delegates & the court in actual session. It will be an objection that the work is begun on the other plan. But the whole of this need not be taken to pieces, and of what shall be taken to pieces the bricks will do for inner work, mortar never becomes so hard & adhesive to the bricks in a few months but that it may easily be chipped off, and upon the whole the plan now sent will save a great proportion of the expense. In my letter of Aug. 13, I mentioned that I could send workmen from hence as I am in hopes of receiving your orders precisely in answer to that letter I shall defer actually engaging any till I receive them. In like manner I shall defer having plans drawn for a Governor's house until further orders, only assuring you that the receiving and executing these orders will always give me a very great pleasure, and the more should I find that what I have done meets your approbation. I have the honour to be, etc. etc.

16

ANONYMOUS, EXCERPT FROM "DESCRIPTION OF THE CITY OF MOROCCO," 1795

Morocco was surely among the most exotic places Americans could imagine in the late eighteenth century, sitting as it does at the cultural crossroads of North Africa, the Ottoman Empire, and Europe, all of which contribute to the physical fabric of the place. Yet

Originally printed in *Massachusetts Magazine, or, Monthly Museum of Knowledge and Rational Entertainment*, vol. 7, October 1795.

the author of this piece has not stressed that exotic otherness. Instead, he or she has chosen a carefully descriptive style typical of the travel writing of this period. As a result, the essay is anonymous both because no one has signed the piece and because the author has revealed little of his or her personality. The author is struck by the "devastations of different conquerors" and the destruction brought by revolutions. Implicit is an anxiety common among Americans at the time over what happens when "contending factions" in a great empire fight.

The city of Morocco is situated in a pleasant plain, planted with palm-trees, having Mount Atlas to the east, which has a fine and romantic effect. The numerous streams which meander through this fertile plain render it capable of the highest cultivation. It was formerly divided into a prodigious number of enclosed gardens and beautiful plantations of olive trees, which have, in part, escaped the barbarous devastations of contending factions. More than six thousand springs poured their waters from Mount Atlas to fructify and enrich this plain, which was filled with country houses and pleasure grounds; but these have all been laid in ruins by the revolutions which proceeded and distinguished the reign of Moley Ishmael; and it was with difficulty, that, in 1768, the course of twelve hundred streams which wind through this fertile country was renewed. The city of Morocco itself, exposed to the devastations of different conquerors, has preserved nothing but its form. The extent of the walls which still exist entire, except in some few places, supposes a city, which might contain three hundred thousand souls; at present this capital is little better than a desert. The ruins of houses, heaped one upon another, serve only to harbour thieves, who lurk among them to rob the passengers. The quarters, which have been rebuilt, are considerably distant from each other: and the houses are low, dirty, and extremely inconvenient. It is difficult to conceive how an imperial city can have become so miserable and so deserted. I doubt whether it contains thirty thousand inhabitants, even when the court is there.

Morocco possesses several large mosques, but they have no pretensions to magnificence. One of these has a tower similar to those at Sallee and Sevile, and which may be seen at a very great distance. Within the walls are a number of large enclosed spaces, almost entirely detached, containing gardens of orange trees, and pavilions in which the princes lodge. These pavilions, covered with colored tiles, are the more remarkable, as the gaiety and splendor of their appearance form a striking contrast with the wretchedness and poverty of the surrounding buildings.

Among the number of the public edifices at Morocco, we must not forget to mention the Elcaisseria, a place where stuffs, and other valuable commodities, are exposed to sale. We find similar buildings in all the other cities of the empire; but in Barbary they are by no means equal to those of the same kind in Turkey called Bezestins. . . .

The emperor's palace, at the extremity of the city of Morocco, fronting Mount Atlas, is a very expensive and solid building. The principal gates are gothic arches of cut stone, embellished with ornaments in the Arabian taste. Within the walls are various courts and gardens, elegantly laid out by European gardeners. In each of these gardens is a pavilion, to which the Emperor frequently retires to take his repose, or amuse himself with his courtiers. These pavilions are square pyramidal edifices, about forty feet in length, and somewhat less in height; they are covered with varnished tiles of various colors; the inside is a kind of a spacious hall, that receives light and air from four large doors in the four sides, which are opened, more or less, according to the position of the sun, or the coolness they may produce. These halls within are painted and gilt in the style we call arabesque, and ornamented with cartouches, containing passages of the Koran, or other Arabic sentences. The furniture of these apartments is very simple; it consists only of a couch, some arm chairs, tables and china, or other embellishments; tea equipage, clocks, arms hung round the walls, a water pot, and carpets for prayers.

The pavilion, containing apartments for the Emperor and his women, is in one of these gardens. This is a very spacious building, according to the usual way of living among the Moors; for the taste of different nations, in this respect, always depends on their manners and customs. The furniture of this palace displays no splendid ornaments, but is in a style of the greatest simplicity. These climates are unacquainted with that profusion of fantastic novelties which are every day multiplied by the industry, luxury, and caprice of Europe.

The present Emperor, who has shown an exclusive preference to the city of Morocco, has added to his palace, a large piece of ground, on which he has caused to be built, by Europeans, regular pavilions in the midst of gardens. These are of cut stone, have handsome windows, are finished in an excellent taste, and give an air of grandeur and magnificence to this part of the palace which we do not see any where else. Between these pavilions and the old palace is a large vacant space, enclosed with walls, called Meshooar, where the Emperor gives public audience four times in a week. This place is entered from without the town by a large gate which is only opened an hour before the Meshooar.

17

ANONYMOUS, EXCERPT FROM "SKETCH OF AMSTERDAM," 1804

The traveler to Amsterdam at the turn of the nineteenth century encountered one of the busiest, most bustling commercial centers in Europe, and that energy caused this traveler a certain ambivalance. On one hand, he or she finds the city one of the most beautiful in Europe and sees much to call "charming." On the other, he or she is repulsed by the poverty of the Jewish quarter of the city and finds the public spaces inadequate. Perhaps most interestingly, the writer complains that in this dense urban environment, nature has been squeezed out. Many Americans believed that their cities could preserve some connection to the natural world and worried that as they grew to resemble places like Amsterdam, they too would lose that connection.

Amsterdam is one of the largest, and I believe I may add, one of the most beautiful cities of Europe, and strongly fortified. The streets are all broad, well paved, and, as in the other cities of the Netherlands, kept very clean. The most beautiful of the streets are

Originally printed in *Literary Magazine*, vol. II, September 1804.

incontestibly the four called *gragts,* which derive their names from the four broad canals which flow in a right line through the city for about four miles and a half. These canals have, on each side, broad streets, planted with rows of trees, and connected by beautiful drawbridges. . . . but then this pleasantness is counterbalanced by many disagreeable circumstances. The canals serve to the inhabitants as a receptacle for all kinds of filth, which they cast into the water from their houses; this occasions, especially in summer, a pestilent and intolerable stench. . . . In winter, the canals send forth a nebulous exhalation, which begins to rise at about sun-set, and continues often till nine o'clock in the morning: this fog is frequently so dense, that it is impossible to distinguish the street from the canal, whence many an unwary stranger loses his life by falling into the water. These exhalations likewise force the inhabitants to observe the high degree of cleanliness which prevails here, and which is absolutely necessary for the preservation of their health and of the external beauty of their houses, which would otherwise soon be covered with a thick black incrustation. Next to these *gragts,* the most beautiful street of Amsterdam is the *Kalvers straat,* not so much on account of its breadth and cleanliness (for it is narrow and dirty) but because it extends above a mile and a half in length, and every house presents to the eye of the stranger new objects to occupy his attention and to excite his desires. The whole street is one continued fair, where everything, from the most trifling necessaries of life, to the most costly articles of luxury may be purchased; every house is a warehouse, vying with one another in the rarity and richness of the commodities they contain.

The most disagreeable part of the city is the quarter of the Jews, who, before they were admitted to the rank of citizens, were obliged to dwell, with very few exceptions, in a distinct part of the city, which, indeed, lies within the gates and walls of Amsterdam, but is separated by the Amstel from the habitations of the christians, communicating therewith only by means of a bridge. The filth in the streets inhabited by the Jews, and the excessive nastiness of the houses, surpass all power of description; and are more disgusting, as one is quite unaccustomed here to such a sight. The Jews themselves are, for the most part, clothed in dirty rags, make a disagreeable noise, crowd around the stranger, begging of him, and teazing him to buy some of their wares; and, if an opportunity offers, picking his pocket, so that one cannot be too much on his guard against the tricks of such dexterous and cunning thieves.

The houses in Amsterdam are in general built in an old-fashioned style: only a few in the *Heerengragt* are distinguished by a better taste. As the population of Amsterdam . . . before the last revolution, by which this city, from obvious causes, lost a number of its inhabitants . . . had, by degrees, greatly increased; this naturally occasioned a want of room, the consequence of which was, that most of the private houses are so narrow, and the broadest of them has not above six windows in front. The most beautiful houses are in the *gragts,* which are inhabited by private persons and placemen, and therefore are the dearest. But here too the houses are narrow from want of room; they have, therefore, sunk stories, through which the usual entrance leads: but, besides, every house has steps, which lead directly into the first story, and the way by which strangers and visitors usually enter.

The public edifices in Amsterdam deserve the most honorable testimony: here there has been no sparing of the ground; for they are all large, and some of them beautiful buildings. . . .

On the other hand there is a total want of beautiful and spacious public places or squares. That in which the town-house . . . and now likewise the tree of liberty . . . stand, is very irregular, and too much crowded with buildings. The market-places, as the butter-market, the water-market, &c. scarce deserve to be mentioned. The most pleasant spot in the whole city I found on the bridge know by the name of *Pont des Amowrena,* where there is an excellent prospect. On the one side I glanced over the river down upon the city, and the busy bustle of its laborious inhabitants; . . . I overlooked many of the bridges situated lower; and the houses, which, with the row of trees on the Amstel, form two beautiful side-lines, end in the back-ground in the shape of an amphitheatre, to which the lofty spires that emulously rise at a greater distance in the city, give a picturesque appearance.

This is the most charming spot in Amsterdam, and I am almost tempted to say, the only one which can have any charms for a stranger. Public walks there are none, except what are called *Plantagen* be reckoned such: but these consist of only some rectilinear stiff rows of trees, planted, however, at so great a distance from one another, that they only serve to excite an unsatisfied longing after shade. He who has accustomed himself to seek for delight and refreshment in the charms of nature . . . to awaken his slumbering faculties, and raise his depressed spirits by the sight of the various and grand creations of her unceasing activity; or to animate his heart with fresh courage and hope by her soft and blissful pictures . . . he must not choose Amsterdam for his place of abode.

For men, the coffee-house is the chief place of recreation and centre of amusement. This appears from the extraordinary number of such houses, which are always crowded. Politics form the principal part of the entertainment here. They read as many news-papers as possible, and then discuss their contents, whilst smoking a pipe of tobacco. A few indeed occasionally play at chess or billiards; but rarely, however, and for the most part only young people.

From this short sketch you see that a man of a cultivated taste can find no recre-ation in the public amusements of Amsterdam; and his lot will appear still more worthy of commiseration, when I assure you, that for the polished stranger there is not enter-tainment to be found in private companies. This is not owing to any want of hospitality or obliging disposition on the part of the citizens of Amsterdam, but to their contracted and partial views of things.

18

CATHERINE MARIA SEDGWICK, EXCERPT FROM
LETTERS FROM ABROAD TO KINDRED AT HOME, 1841

Catherine Maria Sedgwick was a prolific antebellum author, writing twelve novels in addition to her travelogues. In this excerpted selection, drawn from her time in London, Sedgwick

Originally printed in Catherine Maria Sedgwick, *Letters from Abroad to Kindred at Home* (New York: Harper, 1841).

does not discuss architecture or the city at all. We include this piece, however, because she does speak directly to that gnawing cultural unease that many Americans felt in the presence of their European acquaintances. Any comparison Americans made between their own cities and those of the Old World was drawn within the context of this inferiority complex. The United States, Sedgwick discovers, still does not rank high in the esteem of the Londoners she encounters, not even as high as the tiny country of Malta.

You will perhaps like to know, my dear C., more definitely than you can get them from these few anecdotes of my month in London, what impressions I have received here; and I will give them fairly to you, promising that I am fully aware how imperfect they are, and how false some of them may be. Travellers should be forgiven their monstrous errors when we find there are so few on whose sound judgments we can rely, of the character of their own people and the institutions of their own country.

In the first place, I have been struck with the *identity* of the English and the New-England character—the strong family likeness. The oak-tree may be our emblem, modified, but never changed by circumstances. Cultivation may give it a more graceful form and polish, and brighten its leaves, or it may shoot up more rapidly and vigorously in a new soil; but it is always the oak, with its strength, inflexibility and "nodosities."

With my strong American feelings, and my love of home so excited that my nerves were all on the outside, I was a good deal shocked to find how very little interest was felt about America in the circles I chanced to be in. The truth is, we are so far off, we have so little *apparent* influence on the political machinery of Europe, such slight relations with the literary world, and none with that of art and fashion, that, except to the philosopher, the man of science, and the manufacturing and labouring classes, America is yet an undiscovered country, as distant and as dim as Heaven. It is not, perhaps, to be wondered at. There are new and exciting events every day at their own doors, and there are accumulations of interests in Europe to occupy a lifetime, and there are few anywhere who can abide Johnson's test when he says that, "whatever withdraws us from the power of our senses; whatever makes the past, the *distant,* or the future predominate over the present, advances us in the dignity of thinking beings." Inquiries are often put to me about my country, and I laugh at my own eagerness to impart knowledge and exalt their ideas of us, when I perceive my hearers listening with the forced interest of a courteous person to a teller of dreams.

One evening, in a circle of eminent people, the question was started, "what country came next in their affections to England?" I listened, in my greenness expecting to hear one and all say "America"; no, not one feeble voice uttered the name. Mrs. ———, with her hot love of art, naturally answered, "Italy is *first* to us all." "Oh, no," replied two or three voices, "England first, and next—Germany." "England first," said Mrs. A., "Germany next, and I think my third country is—Malta!" I thought of my own land, planted from the English stock, where the productions of these very speakers are most widely circulated, and, if destined to live, must have their longest life; the land where the most thorough and hopeful experiment of the capacity of the human race for knowledge, virtue, happiness, and self-government is now making; the land of promise and protection to the poor and disheartened of every country; and it seemed to me it should have superseded in their affections countries comparatively foreign to them.

I have seen instances of ignorance of us in quarters where you would scarcely expect it; for example, a very cultivated man, a bishop, asked K. if there was a theatre in

America! and a person of equal dignity inquired "if the society of Friends was not the prevailing religious sect in Boston!" A literary man of some distinction asked me if the Edinburgh and Quarterly Reviews were read in America; and one of the cultivated women of England said to me, in a soothing tone, on my expressing admiration of English trees, "Oh, you will have such in time, when your forests are cut down, and they have room for their limbs to spread." I smiled and was silent; but I saw in vision our graceful, drooping, elm-embowering roods of ground, and, as I looked at the stiff, upright English elm, had something of the pharisaical "holier than thou" flit over my mind, I may be forgiven.

I was walking one day with some young Englishwomen, when a short, sallow, broad man, to whom Nature had been niggardly, to say the least of it, passed us. "I think," said I, "that is a countryman of mine; I have seen him in New-York." "I took him for an American," said one of my companions, with perfect nonchalance. "Pray tell me why." "He looks so like the pictures in Mrs. Trollope's book!" It is true, this was a secluded young person in a provincial town, but I felt mortified that in one fair young mind Mrs. Trollope's vulgar caricature should stand as the type of my countrymen.

I have heard persons repeatedly expressing a desire to visit America—for what? "To see a prairie"—"to see Niagara"—"to witness the manner of the help to their employers; it must be so very comical!" but, above all, "to eat canvass-back ducks!" The canvass-backs are in the vision of America what St. Peter's is in the view of Rome. But patience, my dear C. In the first place, it matters little what such thinkers think of us; and then things are mending. The steamers have already cancelled half the distance between the two continents. . . .

19

CONSTANCE FENIMORE WOOLSON, EXCERPT FROM
MENTONE, CAIRO, AND CORFU, 1896

Traveling and writing late in the nineteenth century, Woolson wrote descriptions of Cairo that played to her audience's taste for the exoticness and mysteriousness of the "East." This passage focuses on the architecture of Cairo's mosques and begins by telling the reader that Cairo, whatever its long history, belongs to the Arab world. As with fellow nineteenth-century travel writers, Woolson is drawn to scenes of decay and ruin, even as she chides Egyptians for not maintaining their architectural heritage. While clearly fascinated by the architecture and social function of these mosques, she is not above comparing them a bit invidiously to Western religious buildings, reminding readers that real religious beauty, as it is given architectural form, belongs to Christendom.

Originally printed in Constance Fenimore Woolson, *Mentone, Cairo, and Corfu* (New York: Harper & Brothers, 1896), 263–69.

Mosques

It must be remembered that Cairo is Arabian. "The Nile is Egypt," says a proverb. The Nile is mythical, Pharaonic, Ptolemaic; but Cairo owes its existence solely to the Arabian conquerors of the country, who built a fortress and palace here in A.D. 969. . . .

There are over four hundred mosques in Cairo, and many of them are in a dilapidated condition. Some of these were erected by private means to perpetuate the name and good deeds of the founder and his family; then, in the course of time, owing to the extinction or to the poverty of the descendants, the endowment fund has been absorbed or turned into another channel, and the ensuing neglect has ended in ruin. When a pious Muslim of to-day wishes to perform a good work, he builds a new mosque. It would never occur to him to repair the old one near at hand, which commemorates the generosity of another man. It must be remembered that a mosque has no established congregation, whose duty it is to take care of it. A mosque, in fact, to Muslims has not an exclusively religious character. It is a place prepared for prayer, with the fountain which is necessary for the preceding ablutions required by Mohammed, and the niche towards Mecca which indicates the position which the suppliant must take; but it is also a place for meditation and repose. The poorest and most ragged Muslim has the right to enter whenever he pleases; he can say his prayers, or he can simply rest; he can quench his thirst; he can eat the food which he has brought with him; if he is tired, he can sleep. In mosques not often visited by travelers I have seen men engaged in mending their clothes, and others cooking food with a portable furnace. In the church-yard of Charlton Kings, England, there is a tombstone of the last century with an inscription which concludes as follows: "And his dying request to his Sons and Daughters was, Never forsake the Charities until the poor has got their Rites." In the Cairo mosques the poor have their rites. . . . The sacred character of a mosque is, in truth, only made conspicuous when unbelievers wish to enter. Then the big shuffling slippers are brought out to cover the shoes of the Christian infidels, so that they may not touch and defile the mattings reserved for the faithful.

After long neglect, something is being done at last to arrest the ruin of the more ancient of these temples. A commission has been appointed by the present government whose duty is the preservation of the monuments of Arabian art; occasionally, therefore, in a mosque one finds scaffolding in place and a general dismantlement. One can only hope for the best—in much the same spirit in which one hopes when one sees the beautiful old front of St. Mark's, Venice, gradually encroached upon by the new raw timbers. But in Cairo, at least, the work of repairing goes on very slowly; three hundred mosques, probably, out of the four hundred still remain untouched, and many of these are adorned with a delicate beauty which is unrivalled. I know no quest so enchanting as a search through the winding lanes of the old quarters for these gems of Saracenic taste, which no guide-book has as yet chronicled, no dragonman discovered. The street is so narrow that your donkey fills almost all the space; passers-by are obliged to flatten themselves against the walls in response to the Oriental adjurations of your donkey-boy behind: "Take heed, O maid!" "Your foot, O chief!" Presently you see a minaret—there is always a minaret somewhere; but it is not always easy to find the mosque to which it belongs, hidden, perhaps, as it is, behind other buildings in the crowded labyrinth. At length you observe a door with a dab or two of the well-known Saracenic honeycomb-work above it; instantly you dismount, climb the steps, and look in. You are almost sure to find treasures, either fragments of the pearly Cairo mosaic, or a wonderful ceiling, or gilded Kufic (old Arabian text) inscriptions and arabesques, or remains of the ancient colored glass which changes its tint hour by hour. Best of all, sometimes you find a space open to the sky, with a fountain in the centre, the whole surrounded by arcades of marble columns adorned with hanging lamps (or, rather, with the bronze chains which once carried the lamps), and with suspended ostrich eggs—the emblems of good-luck. One day, when my donkey was making his way through a dilapidated region, I came upon a mosque so small that it seemed hardly more than a base for its exquisite minaret, which towered to an unusual height above it. Of course I dismounted. The little mosque was open; but as it was never visited by strangers, it possessed no slippers, and without coverings of some kind it was impossible that unsanctified shoes, such as mine, should touch its matted floor; the bent, ancient guardian glared at me fiercely for the mere suggestion. One sees sometimes (even in 1890) in the eyes of old men sitting in the mosques the original spirit of Islam shining still. Once their religion commanded the sword; they would like to grasp it again, if they could. It was suggested that the matting might, for a baksheesh, be rolled up and put away, as the place was small. . . . the three or four Muslims present withdrew to the door, and the unbeliever was allowed to enter. She found herself in a temple of color which was incredibly rich. The floor was of delicate marble, and every inch of the walls was covered with a mosaic of porphyry and jasper, adorned with gilded inscriptions and bands of Kufic text; the tall pulpit, made of mahogany-colored wood, was carved from top to bottom in intricate designs, and ornamented with odd little plaques of fretted bronze; the sacred niche was lined with alabaster, turquoise, and gleaming mother-of-pearl; the only light came through the thick glass of the small windows far above, in downward-falling rays of crimson, violet, and gold. The old mosaic-work of the Cairo mosques is composed of small plates of marble and of mother-of-pearl arranged in geometrical designs; the delicacy of the minute cubes employed, and the intricacy of the patterns, are marvelous; the color is faint, unless turquoise has been added; but the glitter of the mother-of-pearl gives the whole an appearance like that of jewelry. Upon our departure five blind men were found drawn up in a line at the door. It would not have been difficult to collect fifty. . . .

It may be asked, What is the shape of a mosque—its exterior? What is it like? You are more sure about this shape before you reach the Khedive's city than you are when you have arrived there; and after you have visited three or four mosques each day for a week, the clearness of your original idea, such as it was has vanished forever. The mosques of Cairo are so embedded in other structures, so surrounded and pushed and elbowed by them, that you can see but little of their external form; sometimes a façade painted in stripes is visible, but often a doorway is all. One must except the mosque of Sultan Hassan (which, to some of us, is dangerously like Aristides the Just). This mosque stands by itself, so that you can, if you please, walk round it. The chief interest of the walk (for the exterior, save for the deep porch, which can hardly be called exterior, is not beautiful) lies in the thought that as the walls were constructed of stones brought from the pyramids, perhaps among them, with faces turned inward, there may be blocks of that lost outer coating of the giant tombs—a coating which was covered with hieroglyphics. Now that hieroglyphics can be read, we may some day learn the true history of these monuments by pulling down a dozen of the Cairo mosques. But unless the commission bestirs itself, that task will not be needed for the edifice of Sultan Hassan; it is coming down, piece by piece, unaided. The mosques of Cairo are not beautiful as a

Greek temple or an early English cathedral is beautiful; the charm of Saracenic architecture lies more in decoration than in the management of massive forms. The genius of the Arabian builders manifested itself in ornament, in rich effects of color; they had endless caprices, endless fancies, and expressed them all—as well they might, for all were beautiful. The same free spirit carved the grotesques of the old churches of France and Germany. But the Arabians had no love for grotesques; they displayed their liberty in lovely fantasies. Their one boldness as architects was the minaret.

It is probably the most graceful tower that has ever been devised. . . .

The Cairo mosques are said to allow the purest existing forms of Saracenic architecture. One hopes that this saying is true, for a dogmatic superlative of this sort is a rock of comfort, and one can remember it and repeat it. . . .

2 0

MARK TWAIN, EXCERPTS FROM
THE INNOCENTS ABROAD, 1869

The Innocents Abroad appeared in 1869 and was Twain's first book. It remains the most popular travel book written by an American. Twain always portrayed himself as the comic tourist, rather than as a "traveler," the humor of his travel writing coming in part from his stating nakedly and explicitly what other writers delicately danced around: "We wanted something thoroughly and uncompromisingly foreign," he writes, "foreign from top to bottom." These two selections, the first about his visit to Tangiers, and the second about his stop in Odessa, make a nice counterpoint. In deeply "foreign" Tangier, Twain is overwhelmed by a sense of history that makes even the landscapes of Europe seem young and immature. By the time he reaches Odessa, he is delighted to find himself in a place that feels just like America.

This is royal! . . . Tangier is the spot we have been longing for all the time. Elsewhere we have found foreign-looking things and foreign-looking people, but always with things and people intermixed that we were familiar with before, and so the novelty of the situation lost a deal of its force. We wanted something thoroughly and uncompromisingly foreign—foreign from top to bottom—foreign from centre to circumference—foreign inside and outside and all around—nothing anywhere about it to dilute its foreignness—nothing to remind us of any other people or any other land under the sun. And lo! in Tangier we have found it. Here is not the slightest thing that ever we have seen save in pictures—and we always mistrusted the pictures before. We can not anymore. The pictures used to seem exaggerations—they seemed too weird and fanciful for reality. But behold, they were not wild enough—they were not fanciful enough—they have not told half the story. Tangier is a foreign land if ever there was one; and the true spirit of it can

Originally printed in Mark Twain, *The Innocents Abroad* (New York: Harper's, 1869), 61–65, 306–7.

never be found in any book save the Arabian Nights. Here are no white men visible, yet swarms of humanity are all about us. Here is a packed and jammed city enclosed in a massive stone wall which is more than a thousand years old. All the houses nearly are one and two-story; made of thick walls of stone; plastered outside; squared as a dry-goods box; flat as a floor on top; no cornices; whitewashed all over—a crowded city of snowy tombs! And the doors are arched with the peculiar arch we see in Moorish pictures; the floors are laid in vari-colored diamond-flags; in tesselated many-colored porcelain squares wrought in the furnaces of Fez; in red tiles and broad bricks that time can not wear; there is no furniture in the rooms (of Jewish dwellings) save divans—what there is in Moorish ones no man may know; within their sacred walls no Christian dog can enter. And the streets are oriental—some of them three feet wide, some six, but only two that are over a dozen; a man can blockade the most of them by extending his body across them. Isn't it an oriental picture? . . .

What a funny old town it is! It seems like profanation to laugh, and jest, and bandy the frivolous chat of our day amid its hoary relics. . . . Here is a crumbling wall that was old when Columbus discovered America; was old when Peter the Hermit roused the knightly men of the Middle Ages to arm for the first Crusade; was old when Charlemagne and his paladins beleaguered enchanted castles and battled with giants and genii in the fabled days of the olden time; was old when Christ and his disciples walked the earth; stood where it stands to-day when the lips of Memnon were vocal, and men bought and sold in the streets of ancient Thebes!

The Phoenicians, the Carthagenians, the English, Moors, Romans, all have battled for Tangier—all have won it and lost it. . . .

Five days journey from here—say two hundred miles—are the ruins of an ancient city, of whose history there is neither record nor tradition. And yet its arches, its columns, and its statues, proclaim it to have been built by an enlightened race.

The general size of a store in Tangier is about that of an ordinary shower-bath in a civilized land. The Mohammedan merchant, tinman, shoemaker, or vendor of trifles, sits cross-legged on the floor, and reaches after any article you may want to buy. You can rent a whole block of these pigeonholes for fifty dollars a month. The market people crowd the market-place with their baskets of figs, dates, melons, apricots, etc., and among them file trains of laden asses, not much larger, if any, than a Newfoundland dog. The scene is lively, is picturesque, and smells like a police court. The Jewish money-changers have their dens close at hand; and all day long are counting bronze coins and transferring them from one bushel basket to another. They don't coin much money now-a-days, I think. I saw none but what was dated four or five hundred years back, and was badly worn and battered. These coins are not very valuable. Jack went out to get a Napoleon changed, so as to have money suited to the general cheapness of things, and came back and said he had "swamped the bank; had bought eleven quarts of coin, and the head of the firm had gone on the street to negotiate for the balance of the change." I bought nearly half a pint of their money for a shilling myself. I am not proud on account of having so much money, though. I care nothing for wealth. . . .

We have got so far east, now—a hundred and fifty-five degrees of longitude from San Francisco—that my watch can not "keep the hang" of the time anymore. It has grown discouraged and stopped. I think it did a wise thing. The difference in time between Sebastopol and the Pacific coast is enormous. When it is six o'clock in the morning here, it is somewhere about week before last in California. . . .

* * *

Odessa is about twenty hours' run from Sebastopol, and is the most northerly port in the Black Sea. We came here to get coal, principally. The city has a population of one hundred and thirty-three thousand, and is growing faster than any other small city out of America. It is a free port, and is the great grain mart of this particular part of the world. Its roadstead is full of ships. Engineers are at work, now, turning the open roadstead into a spacious artificial harbor. It is to be almost inclosed by massive stone piers, one of which will extend into the sea over three thousand feet in a straight line.

I have not felt so much at home for a long time as I did when I "raised the hill" and stood in Odessa for the first time. It looked just like an American city; fine, broad streets, and straight as well; low houses, (two or three stories,) wide, neat, and free from any quaintness of architectural ornamentation; locust trees bordering the sidewalks (they call them acacias;) a stirring, business-look about the streets and the stores; fast walkers; a familiar *new* look about the houses and every thing; yea, and a driving and smothering cloud of dust that was so like a message from our own dear native land that we could hardly refrain from shedding a few grateful tears and execrations in the old time-honored American way. Look up the street or down the street, this way or that way, we saw only America! There was not one thing to remind us that we were in Russia. We walked for some little distance, reveling in this home vision, and then we came upon a church and a hack-driver, and presto! the illusion vanished! The church had a slender-spired dome that rounded inward at its base, and looked like a turnip turned upside down, and the hackman seemed to be dressed in a long petticoat without any hoops. These things were essentially foreign, and so were the carriages—but every body knows about these things, and there is no occasion for my describing them.

We were only to stay here a day and a night and take in coal; we consulted the guide-books and rejoiced to know that there were no sights in Odessa to see; and so we had one good, untrammeled holyday on our hands, with nothing to do but idle about the city and enjoy ourselves. We sauntered through the markets and criticised the fearful and wonderful costumes from the back country; examined the populace as far as eyes could do it; and closed the entertainment with an ice-cream debauch. We do not get ice-cream every where and so, when we do, we are apt to dissipate to excess. We never cared anything about ice-cream at home, but we look upon it with a sort of idolatry now that it is so scarce in these red-hot climates of the East. . . .

21

EDITH WHARTON, EXCERPT FROM
ITALIAN VILLAS AND THEIR GARDENS, 1904

In a genre crowded with writers, Edith Wharton's travel writings stand as classics of their kind. Best known for her novels about society and manners, Wharton's first book was, in fact, her study of Italian villas and gardens, from which this selection is excerpted. Like her friend Henry James, Wharton found much to admire in the way European history, culture,

2.2. Edith Wharton's house, The Mount, 1902. Yale Collection of American Literature, Beinecke Rare Book and Manuscript Library. Writer Edith Wharton (1862–1937) was one of those of the American elite who, at the end of the nineteenth century, saw in Europe a deeper cultural sensibility than existed in the United States. She lived with her family for a number of years in Europe and later moved to Paris. When she built her own house in the Berkshire Mountains of Massachusetts in 1902, she took inspiration from places she had seen on her travels. The Mount has a French courtyard and an Italian garden, and the house itself is modeled after the seventeenth-century Belton House in England, albeit with the typical green shutters of a New England homestead. Wharton clearly believed that the best European traditions could be adapted to a uniquely American setting.

and sensibilities were expressed in the European landscape. This passage stands as a gentle rebuke to Americans who have tried to recreate the "magic" of the Italian garden without understanding at all the principles of those places, in much the same way her novels and those of James play on Americans' inability to grasp the rules of European society.

The Italian garden does not exist for its flowers; its flowers exist for it: they are a late and infrequent adjunct to its beauties, a parenthetical grace counting only as one more touch in the general effect of enchantment. This is no doubt partly explained by the difficulty

Originally printed in Edith Wharton, *Italian Villas and Their Gardens* (New York: The Century Co., 1904), 5–13.

of cultivating any but spring flowers in so hot and dry a climate, and the result has been a wonderful development of the more permanent effects to be obtained from the three other factors in garden-composition—marble, water and perennial verdure—and the achievement, by their skilful blending, of a charm independent of the seasons.

It is hard to explain to the modern garden-lover, whose whole conception of the charm of gardens is formed of successive pictures of flower-loveliness, how this effect of enchantment can be produced by anything so dull and monotonous as a mere combination of clipped green and stone-work.

The traveller returning from Italy, with his eyes and imagination full of the ineffable Italian garden-magic, knows vaguely that the enchantment exists; that he has been under its spell, and that it is more potent, more enduring, more intoxicating to every sense than the most elaborate and glowing effects of modern horticulture; but he may not have found the key to the mystery. Is it because the sky is bluer, because the vegetation is more luxuriant? Our midsummer skies are almost as deep, our foliage is as rich, and perhaps more varied; there are, indeed, not a few resemblances between the North American summer climate and that of Italy in spring and autumn.

Some of those who have fallen under the spell are inclined to ascribe the Italian garden-magic to the effect of time; but, wonder-working as this undoubtedly is, it leaves many beauties unaccounted for. To seek the answer one must go deeper: the garden must be studied in relation to the house, and both in relation to the landscape. . . .

The Italian country house, especially in the centre and the south of Italy, was almost always built on a hillside, and one day the architect looked forth from the terrace of his villa, and saw that, in his survey of the garden, the enclosing landscape was naturally included: the two formed a part of the same composition.

The recognition of this fact was the first step in the development of the great garden-art of the Renaissance: the next was the architect's discovery of the means by which nature and art might be fused in his picture. He had now three problems to deal with: his garden must be adapted to the architectural lines of the house it adjoined; it must be adapted to the requirements of the inmates of the house, in the sense of providing shady walks, sunny bowling-greens, parterres and orchards, all conveniently accessible; and lastly it must be adapted to the landscape around it. At no time and in no country has this triple problem been so successfully dealt with as in the treatment of the Italian country house from the beginning of the sixteenth to the end of the eighteenth century; and in the blending of different elements, the subtle transition from the fixed and formal lines of art to the shifting and irregular lines of nature, and lastly in the essential convenience and livableness of the garden, lies the fundamental secret of the old garden-magic. . . .

The inherent beauty of the garden lies in the grouping of its parts—in the converging lines of its long ilex-walks, the alternation of sunny open spaces with cool woodland shade, the proportion between terrace and bowling-green, or between the height of a wall and the width of a path. None of these details was negligible to the landscape-architect of the Renaissance: he considered the distribution of shade and sunlight, of straight lines of masonry and rippled lines of foliage, as carefully as he weighed the relation of his whole composition to the scene about it. . . .

It is because, in the modern revival of gardening, so little attention has been paid to these first principles of the art that the garden-lover should not content himself with a vague enjoyment of old Italian gardens, but should try to extract from them principles which may be applied at home. He should observe, for instance, that the old Italian garden was meant to be lived in—a use to which, at least in America, the modern garden is seldom put. He should note that, to this end, the grounds were as carefully and conveniently planned as the house, with broad paths (in which two or more could go abreast) leading from one division to another; with shade easily accessible from the house, as well as a sunny sheltered walk for winter; and with effective transitions from the dusk of wooded alleys to open flowery spaces or to the level sward of the bowling-green. He should remember that the terraces and formal gardens adjoined the house, that the ilex or laurel walks beyond were clipped into shape to effect a transition between the straight lines of masonry and the untrimmed growth of the woodland to which they led, and that each step away from architecture was a nearer approach to nature.

The cult of the Italian garden has spread from England to America, and there is a general feeling that, by placing a marble bench here and a sun-dial there, Italian "effects" may be achieved. The results produced, even where much money and thought have been expended, are not altogether satisfactory; and some critics have thence inferred that the Italian garden is, so to speak *untranslatable*, that it cannot be adequately rendered in another landscape and another age.

Certain effects, those which depend on architectural grandeur as well as those due to colouring and age, are no doubt unattainable; but there is, none the less, much to be learned from the old Italian gardens, and the first lesson is that, if they are to be a real inspiration, they must be copied, not in the letter but in the spirit. That is, a marble sarcophagus and a dozen twisted columns will not make an Italian garden; but a piece of ground laid out and planted on the principles of the old garden-craft will be, not indeed an Italian garden in the literal sense but what is far better, *a garden as well adapted to its surroundings as were the models which inspired it.*

This is the secret to be learned from the villas of Italy: . . . so the garden-lover, who longs to transfer something of the old garden-magic to his own patch of ground at home, will ask himself, in wandering under the umbrella-pines of the Villa Borghese, or through the box-parterres of the Villa Lante: What can I bring away from here? And the more he studies and compares, the more inevitably will the answer be: "Not this or that amputated statue, or broken bas-relief, or fragmentary effect of any sort, but a sense of the informing spirit—an understanding of the gardener's purpose, and of the uses to which he meant his garden to be put."

22

SYLVESTER BAXTER, EXCERPT FROM
"THE GERMAN WAY OF MAKING BETTER CITIES," 1909

Sylvester Baxter was among the first generation of professional urban planners, and the excerpted selection is a technical report from Germany, where urban planning was regarded

Originally printed in *Atlantic Monthly*, July 1909.

as most advanced. Baxter's report was intended to offer models for Americans looking for enlightened solutions to their own urban crises—especially of housing in booming, rapidly expanding industrial cities. In this sense, Baxter is participating in the larger Progressive movement of reform that was most influential in the years before the First World War. Progressives, on both sides of the Atlantic, believed that professional expertise could be brought to bear on any number of pressing social problems. If Baxter's essay reads a bit stiffly and seems dull, it reflects a technician's sense of carefulness and detail common to many Progressive reformers.

In no other country has the art of city planning been carried to so high a degree as in Germany today. This is due to several important factors. Among them are the extraordinary industrial progress in the past quarter century, the highly organized character of German institutions, the thoroughness with which the Germans attack their problems, and the strongly idealistic quality of the national temperament. The unification of Germany in 1871 made possible the development of large plans and vast enterprises, political, economic, and industrial. The great industrial movement, favored by a generation and more of uninterrupted peace, has vastly enhanced national prosperity and created an enormous volume of new wealth. The growth of urban population—the creation of new centres, the expansion of villages into cities, of small cities into large ones, and of the larger ones into complex metropolitan communities—has not been surpassed by similar movements of population in newer-settled countries like our own.

The German urban movement in a great measure is marked by elements of conscious development, of finish, of well-considered attainment of definite ends deliberately aimed at. The same skill, the same deliberately conscious determination, that has given Germany the industrial primacy of Continental Europe, has been applied to the development of her cities. Here the demand has induced the supply. With the creation of so many new centers of trade and industry, and with the certainty that this meant an indefinite continuance of urban expansion, it was felt that this growth should be intelligently provided for. Thereby what is practically a new art, a new science, came into being. Like architecture, it is both a fine art and a technical science. Like landscape architecture, it may be regarded as a phase of architecture. It is akin both to landscape architecture and to structural architecture, but it has qualities that carry it beyond the limits of either profession. The members of both are drawn to practice it, but to practice it successfully, needs further training and the acquisition of new points of view. It means something more than planning. The planning of cities, both intelligently and unintelligently, is something very old. Were it merely city-planning, it would be worth ranking as a new profession. The German name has the merit of a greater precision than English speech can impart. *Städtebau,* literally translated, would be "citybuilding." But the term is a shade more inclusive than that would imply; "city-development" more nearly expresses the comprehensively formative nature of the task. . . .

The new art, as practiced in Germany, is a gradual development away from formal and geometrical ideas embodied in the checkerboard and gridiron plans that, in fact, derive themselves from a remote antiquity rather than from a Philadelphian modernity, and from the diagonal and radial systems for which the plans of Paris and Washington, as masterworks of the kind, are prototypes. Vienna, with its radical reconstruction in the middle of the nineteenth century, also furnished another master example. Here as in Paris, the razing of fortifications struck the keynote. It created the typical circumferential way: the boulevards of Paris, the Ringstrasse of Vienna. So the word boulevard; a French attempt to speak the German military term *bollwerk* (English *bulwark*) harking back to its ancestral home, give rise to the *Anlagen,* or "layingsout,"—the irregular rings of promenades, drives, and gardens replacing the ancient walls, so charmingly typical of nearly all the old German cities. . . .

The reckless planner cuts and slashes at will in pursuit of his "ideals." All this makes improvements unduly costly, and often prohibits them altogether. The modern German school, however, keeps a constant eye upon the taxpayer; it cherishes a tender regard for the "pocket nerve" and the city treasury. Economy in money, as well as in energy, is a cardinal principle. Hence a careful adjustment of plan to property lines, and a thorough studying of all existing conditions, is precedent to taking any given work in hand. . . .

Another important matter, in which the old-time architects thoroughly understood what they were about, was the placing of their churches and other public buildings. The nineteenth century was marked by a general disposition to "improve" things by opening up to view great cathedrals and other monumental edifices. The cathedrals of Cologne, of Milan, and of Notre Dame in Paris, are famous examples of the procedure. While the buildings are thereby placed in striking relations to the vistas thus developed, the results on the whole are disappointing. In fact, the impressiveness of an oldtime building thus dealt with is diminished rather than enhanced. A modern building, like the Capitol at Washington and other monumental structures there, or like such stately European examples as the Opera House in Paris, carefully planned with particular reference to vistas, axes, etc., may be superbly effective in its deliberate adjustment to its environment. Cities planned in this grandiose fashion have a festal and spectacular splendor. We would not have Washington or Paris otherwise. But when such an all-pervading formality sets a fashion to be followed, the sameness that comes from set rules makes one city too suggestive of another, and becomes tiresome—just as, in a still worse way, the aping of New York and Chicago skyscraping precedents by our minor cities, all the way from Atlanta to Oshkosh, makes for monotony. In city development, as in landscape design, the spontaneous or unpremeditated effects in grouping and in the relations of monumental landmarks to their surroundings are what most charm and delight. . . .

It is pointed out that a long arterial thoroughfare should occasionally change in direction, at least slightly, and likewise in width and in other distinctive characteristics, in order to avoid the tedium proceeding from keeping on and on in a straight line, as if interminably. A trip over a route diversified by changes in direction and in the character of the way seems much shorter and more interesting than a straight route of the same length. Capital illustrations of this principle are to found in the new quarters of Munich, where the main streets, keeping in the same general direction, curve very slightly here and there, according to topographical circumstances; the distance is not appreciably increased and the interest of the street is very considerably enhanced. These streets are instinctive features of Henrici's masterly plan for the extension of Munich, which is considered one of the most successful achievements among modern examples of the kind.

One feature of these new Munich streets is the way in which they break with one of the most venerated dogmas of conventional planning, that the lines of a street must invariably be parallel. These long streets broaden out here and there in gently curves, giving space perhaps for a cabstand, for a group of trees, or to make some notable architectural feature more conspicuous. In this sort of planning advantage is taken of any circumstance that may lend diversity to the work. Old roads or cartpaths suggest ways to be followed; property lines likewise indicate how best to run the new streets in order to effect the most economical distribution of building sites, as well as the desirable individuality in development. . . .

It should not be inferred, however, that the way to better things has been wholly a smooth one. The Germans have found the path beset with a due amount of obstacles. Human nature in Germany is very much the same as human nature elsewhere, and no nearer perfection. Their large measure of success has chiefly been due to the organizing capacity which has been encouraged by the development of their national institutions. This has made them open to regard such problems in a rational, logical manner. Extraordinary progress has been made. The art, considered definitely as such, dates its conscious beginnings from the appearance of the last part of Camillo Sitte's important work, *Der Stadtebau nach kunstlicheren Grundsatzen*, previously referred to. Sitte demanded liberation from the intellectually desolate schematic methods of the day, and urged the artistic procedure that comes with freedom of treatment. Naturally, the greatest impediment has been presented by the obstacles imposed by selfish real estate interests, which, in Germany as elsewhere, look at such matters purely with regard to their own profit. Excellent as municipal government is in Germany, the landed interests tend to be unduly influential in the city councils. The extraordinary expansion of the cities has led to corresponding opportunities for land speculation. Many great fortunes have been made in this way. . . .

German procedure in the encouragement of better housing is remarkably flexible. Methods vary according to circumstance. There is no cut and dried formula. In some instances, the municipality builds the houses directly; again, it encourages in various ways, by loans or otherwise, building societies organized for the purpose; and it even offers extraordinary inducements to regular builders to supply the demand. . . . Mutual building societies (*gemeinnutzige Bauvereine*) have long been a popular institution in Germany. . . . Societies of this sort, whose resources would be slender when unaided, are often powerfully supported by municipalities or other public institutions, in ways that vastly increase their efficiency, and at the same time amply secure the parties advancing the funds against possible loss. Occasionally a municipality will aid such a society with land for building, and perhaps with financial assistance as well.

A striking instance of cooperative activity is that whereby the imperial government recently bought a tract of land in a Dresden suburb for about $60,000 and leased it on a groundrent of about $1340 a year for eight years to a local savings and building society, which has covered it with model dwellings for nearly one thousand people. . . .

In building these homes for working people, Ulm has adopted the democratic policy of not separating socially the various classes of the community. The quarter is therefore planned with particular reference to the erection by the city of numerous new houses designed especially for middleclass occupants. Since the workingmen's houses are tastefully built, there is nothing about the neighborhood to repel the other class. It is notable that in Berlin the proposed establishment of a village colony near the city was objected to, on the part of the workingmen, for the reason that it tended to separate and isolate the classes and correspondingly weaken their sense of mutual interest. This policy of bringing the classes together in the same neighborhood is one of the distinctive features of the garden-city movement in England. In countries with practically homogeneous populations, like Germany and England, such measures are attended with less difficulty than would be the case under our American conditions, where the existence of so many unassimilated foreign elements in the working classes, with habits and standards of living so radically different from that of the native population, tends to make their neighborhood undesirable for a better-circumstanced class. An important result of the policy adopted by Ulm has been the attraction of a higher class of working people, and, consequently, the development of improved industrial advantages, which encourage manufacturing and promote local prosperity, by a body of skilled workingmen, contented, and identified with the community by the possession of homes which, under the economical system adopted, cost less than otherwise would have to be paid out in rent. . . .

The examples cited above are typical of what many German cities are doing, both in the way of broad general improvements and in directly bettering the conditions of life for their people. The movement has manifold aspects, economic, social, and artistic. Its influence, already great outside of Germany, has been particularly strong in Great Britain, where in organizing movements for garden cities and model villages, and in shaping legislation dealing with town planning and the housing question, many leaves have been taken from German experience. . . . Here in America we can at present hardly hope to go beyond the stage of admiration for successful and humane achievement that eventually may make our public opinion receptive as to possibilities of commensurate results under a quite different environment.

23

MALCOLM COWLEY, EXCERPT FROM
EXILE'S RETURN: A LITERARY ODYSSEY OF THE 1920s, 1934

As a young man, Malcolm Cowley made his way from Pittsburgh to Greenwich Village, where he became part of an extraordinary collection of writers, artists, political activists, and other bohemians who made the Village an epicenter of America's cultural avant-garde in the years before the First World War. After the war, however, this new generation of intellectuals, many of whom had, like Cowley, fled to New York from somewhere else, had grown tired even of New York. While this selection was not written from Europe, it captures wonderfully the allure of Paris for a disillusioned generation. And while this younger generation, in their politics, artistic goals, and cultural outlook, differed dramatically from their elders like Henry James and Edith Wharton, they shared a fundamental belief that the crass, materialistic, Puritanical United States would never be a place conducive or receptive to serious art. Even New York in the Jazz Age, the premier city in the United States, could not compare culturally to Paris and other European capitals. Like James before them, Cowley, Ernest Hemingway, and others fled across the Atlantic believing "They do things better in Europe."

Originally printed in Malcolm Cowley, *Exile's Return: A Literary Odyssey of the 1920s* (New York: Norton, 1934), 74–80.

2.3. Ernest Hemingway, Sylvia Beach, and friends in front of the Shakespeare and Co. bookstore in Paris, 1928. Princeton University Library. Sylvia Beach Papers, Manuscripts Division, Department of Rare Books and Special Collections, Princeton University Library. A new generation in the early decades of the twentieth century picked up where the nineteenth-century elite left off—fleeing to Europe for inspiration. For many young artists, writers, and radicals of the 1920s, Paris was the place to be in the aftermath of the First World War. From Gertrude Stein to Hemingway to Edith Wharton, the inspiration of Paris—its architecture and its urban vitality—served as a continuing reminder that Americans would continue to import ideas, and architecture, from Europe.

But there was one idea that was held in common by the older and the younger inhabitants of the Village—the idea of salvation by exile. "They do things better in Europe: let's go there." This was not only the undertone of discussions at Luke O'Connor's saloon; it was also the recurrent melody of an ambitious work, a real symposium, then being prepared for the printer.

Civilization in the United States was written by thirty intellectuals, of whom only a few, say ten at the most, had been living in the Village. There were no Communists or even right-wing Socialists among the thirty. "Desirous of avoiding merely irrelevant criticism," said Harold Stearns in his Preface, "we provided that all contributors to the volume must be American citizens. For the same reason, we likewise provided that in the list there should be no professional propagandists . . . no martyrs, and no one who was merely disgruntled." All Village cranks were strictly excluded. But Harold Stearns, the editor, lived in a remodeled house at 31 Jones Street. The editorial meetings were conducted in his basement while often a Village party squeaked and thundered on the floor above. And the book that resulted from the labors of these thirty intellectuals embodied what might be called the more sober side of Village opinion. . . .

As a matter of fact, their book was more modest than its pretentious title. They were not trying to present or solve the problem of American civilization as a whole. They were trying to answer one question that touched them more closely: why was there, in America, no satisfying career open to talent? Every year hundreds, thousands of gifted young men and women graduated from our colleges; they entered life as these thirty intellectuals had entered it; they brought with them a rich endowment, but they accomplished little. Why did all this promise result in so few notable careers? . . .

Here again the thirty intellectuals have the same story to tell. . . . One after another they come forward to tell us that American civilization itself is responsible for the tragedy of American talent.

Life in this country is joyless and colorless, universally standardized, tawdry, uncreative, given over to the worship of wealth and machinery. "The highest achievements of our material civilization . . . count as so many symbols of its spiritual failure." . . . "The most moving and pathetic fact in the social life of America today is emotional and aesthetic starvation." And what is the remedy? . . .

The intellectuals had explored many paths: they had found no way of escape; one after another they had opened doors that led only into the cupboards and linen closets of the mind. "What should a young man do?" asked Harold Stearns in an article written for the *Freeman*. This time his answer was simple and uncompromising. A young man had no future in this country of hypocrisy and repression. He should take ship for Europe, where people know how to live.

Early in July 1921, just after finishing his Preface and delivering the completed manuscript to the publisher, Mr. Stearns left this country, perhaps forever. His was no ordinary departure: he was Alexander marching into Persia and Byron shaking the dust of England from his feet. Reporters came to the gangplank to jot down his last words. Everywhere young men were preparing to follow his example. Among the contributors to *Civilization in the United States*, not many could go: most of them were moderately successful men who had achieved security without achieving freedom. But the younger and footloose intellectuals went streaming up the longest gangplank in the world; they were preparing a great migration eastward into new prairies of the mind.

"I'm going to Paris," they said at first, and then, "I'm going to the South of France . . . . I'm sailing Wednesday—next month—as soon as I can scrape together money enough to buy a ticket." Money wasn't impossible to scrape together; some of it could be saved from one's salary or borrowed from one's parents or one's friends. Newspapers and magazines were interested in reports from Europe, two or three foundations had fellowships for study abroad, and publishers sometimes made advances against the future royalties of an unwritten book. In those days publishers were looking for future authors, and the authors insisted that their books would have to be finished in France, where one could live for next to nothing. "Good-by, so long," they said, "I'll meet you on the Left Bank. I'll drink your health in good red Burgundy, I'll kiss all the girls for you. I'm sick of this country. I'm going abroad to write one good novel."

And we ourselves, the newcomers to the Village, were leaving it if we could. The long process of deracination had reached its climax. School and college had uprooted us in spirit; the war had physically uprooted us, carried us into strange countries and left us finally in the metropolis of the uprooted. Now even New York seemed too American, too close to home. On its river side, Greenwich Village was bounded by the French Line pier.

In the late spring of 1921 I was awarded an American Field Service fellowship for study at a French university. It was only twelve thousand francs, or about a thousand dollars at that year's rate of exchange, but it also entitled my wife and me to a reduction of fifty per cent in our cabin-class steamship fares. We planned to live as economically as a French couple, and we did. With the help of a few small checks from American magazines, the fellowship kept us in modest comfort, even permitting us to travel, and it was renewed for the following year. When we left New York hardly anyone came to the ship to say good-by. Most of our friends had sailed already; the others were wistful people who promised to follow us in a few months. The Village was almost deserted, except for the pounding feet of young men from Davenport and Pocatello who came to make a name for themselves and live in glamour—who came because there was nowhere else to go.

24

FRANK LLOYD WRIGHT, EXCERPT FROM "ARCHITECTURE AND LIFE IN THE U.S.S.R.," 1937

Frank Lloyd Wright stands as probably the most internationally influential American architect of the twentieth century not simply because of the collection of buildings he designed, but because of the vast body of writing he left. Several of his essays have become well-known classics of architectural writing, though the one we offer here is certainly lesser known. In it, Wright—not known for his generosity of spirit—offers an enthusiastic endorsement not only of contemporary Soviet architecture and architects, but of the new world they purported to build. While it might strike us as odd today that Wright would embrace the Soviet Union so fully, this essay reminds us that many Americans, especially in the 1930s as the United States floundered through the Great Depression, found inspiration in Soviet society. In 1921 journalist Lincoln Steffens returned from a tour of the U.S.S.R. and pronounced: "I have seen the future. And it works." Wright concurs in this essay, saying he has seen the future of how architecture can help build a new society.

Now that I am back at Taliesin again, my Moscow colleagues are far enough away for perspective to assert itself. I enjoyed them so much, was personally so much in sympathy with them while there, that appraisals made on the spot might easily have been overdrawn. They were not.

Reprinted with permission from *Architectural Record* 1992, a McGraw-Hill Construction publication.

As I see across the Pole—my friends in Moscow and their work appear the more extraordinary. I went to them intending to do what little I could to end the confusion I thought I saw among them. I disliked the Soviet Work Palace exceedingly—do so yet—hoped to change the minds entangled with its erection, but the foundations were in.

And I found that in Russia now, as in the United States long ago, the masses who had nothing and to whom the landed aristocracy appeared to have everything had their turn to be pleased. Nothing pleases them so much as the gleam of marble columns under high ceilings, glittering chandeliers, unmistakable luxury as they had to look up to it when it decided their fate, when they ate out of luxury's hand if they ate at all.

But reassurance for me lay in the attitude of the Soviet architects themselves. I may mention Alabyan, Colly, Jofan, the Vesnins, Nikolsky, Chuseff and the editor, Arkin, as personal acquaintances in this connection. All of them took the present situation calmly with Russian humor and a touch of fatalism, characteristically Russian.

Just now is no time to offer the liberated ones the higher simplicity which repudiates the falsity of that sort of luxury. This is not the time to insist upon something they could not yet understand—the higher simplicity that has turned upon that flagrant artifice as the people themselves turned upon its possessors. So in the Soviet Union, I saw the cultural lag again as I have seen it and have fought against it for a lifetime in these United States. With the Russians, as with the Americans, several more generations must pass away before a more natural way of life and building can take the place of the old order. The Russian people see viciousness in that old order where human rights are concerned, but the masses of the people are yet unable to see viciousness in the old order in that higher realm of created things of which architecture is the highest.

The architects, however, at least those I have named, are men who do see and realize it. They are men who say, "Never mind, we will tear it down in ten years."

Who can help loving such liberal great-hearted fellows? What colleague would not do anything he could do under heaven to help them? The result might be help *from* them.

Said they: "We have faith in our people. We Russians are by nature artists. We love the beautiful. Our sense of life is deep and rhythmic. We will create a new Russia. You will see."

I believe I do see even now in their efforts, a new organic Russia slowly entering into their buildings "through closed doors." And I see no necessity for Russia to die that the Soviet Union may live.

If Comrade Stalin, as disconcerted outsiders are saying, is betraying the revolution then, in the light of what I have seen in Moscow, I say he is betraying it into the hands of the Russian people. . . .

Plans for the new Moscow are far ahead of any city planning I have seen elsewhere. There is splendid opportunity to make the city over because no private property, nor sentimentality, can say no when the great plan requires the blowing up of whole sections of old buildings. Even sacred old landmarks are blown into the air to make spacious streets where dirty obscure lanes existed. The scope and liberal character of the proposed changes and extensions is astonishing. When completed, Moscow will inevitably be the first city of the world. But, to me, that can only mean something already dated and outlived by the advanced thought of our today.

All of the new city will be much too high—the same premium put upon congestion seemingly that landlordism places on it here. And I suppose this is partly because the industrialist, still clinging to his habits of congestion, is ahead of the agrarian in the

U.S.S.R. He is still ahead in our own U.S.A. For some reason, there will be regimented areas, too, in the "classic" manner, where inevitable freedom should be. There will be four-story schoolhouses, knowledge factories, where two stories would be too high. And while the entire outer belt is a park area, it should be the other way around. The best of the traditional and official buildings should stand in a big central park, buildings growing higher as they extend outward into the country. But much that is splendid is already done—wide avenues and park spaces. The ancient Moscow River is being walled with cut granite blocks, sweeping in a fine curve from the water to the upper levels. The ancient Kremlin walls and domes stand nobly above these new granite slopes.

The Moscow subway is a succession of well-planned palatial stations. I like the more simple ones, built at first, with columns containing lights, the shafts rising and spreading dendriform into the overhead. Later ones are richer and more spacious. The Moscow subway makes the New York subway look like a sewer when one returns to compare them. . . .

Chuseff and I stood together in his great new Soviet Hotel, a great constructed thing, done in what I told him should be called "the Metropolitan style" because you could see it, with such virtues as it has and all its faults, in Philadelphia or any big city of the world. A comfortable hotel though, and I exaggerated a little because in many respects it was better done, with more comfort provided for an occupant, but still the building was the type of hotel we Americans are learning to hate. Mere size seems to captivate the Russians as it seduced us earlier. Of course, all this is reaction in action. . . .

The building occupied by "Pravda," I saw as the more creditable of the left-wing "modernistic" attempts by the Russians but because of its negative and unconstructive precedents, such is not for the Russians—too laborious stylization of too little spirit and small content. I see the Russians discontented with less than something profound, when culture catches up—say, in ten years. . . .

What a pity that architecture in Soviet Russia is not as free as the man, so that the millennium might be born at once where the road is more open than anywhere else, instead of again wearisomely temporizing with the old time lag and back drag of human ignorance where culture is concerned. It is hard for me to be reconciled to the delays Russia herself is experiencing, no matter how cheerfully, in getting architecture characteristic of her new life and freedom.

I saw the admirable models for Soviet Russia's new towns and cities in various places, all better than good but too many concessions to the time lag in culture. I suppose the marvel is that a country so backward as Russia was should have these fine things at all, at least have them so soon, perhaps too soon. I grant all that and still regret.

But I saw something in the glimpses I had of the Russian people which overcomes the regret and makes me smile in anticipation. The Russian spirit! There is nothing quite like that spirit anywhere in the world today. I felt it in the air, saw it as a kind of aura about the wholesome maleness of her men and femaleness of her women; in this new gospel of work; in the glad open expressions of the faces of workmen and workwomen. Freedom already affects the unconsciously proud way they carry themselves. Especially the women. I could not help feeling "what a mother this new Russia is going to have." . . .

Having seen and sensed the Russian spirit, I should say that enemies interfering with the Soviet Union would not only have to reckon with the whole male population bearing arms, but with the women too, and every child above nine years of age. Nothing less than total extermination could conquer Soviet Russia. . . .

It is true. Russia may yet give to this money-minded, war-minded, quarreling pack of senile races that make up the world, the soul they fail to find within themselves, and I hope, in time to prevent the suicide their nations are so elaborately preparing to commit.

25

DOUGLAS HASKELL, EXCERPT FROM "RECENT ARCHITECTURE ABROAD," 1940

By the mid-twentieth century overseas travel was growing more common and writers could no longer simply play on a sense of the unknown and the exotic. Rather than write impressionistically or emotionally about architecture, as writers in the nineteenth century had, Douglas Haskell writes quite technically about architectural developments in Europe, though he was not writing for a professional architectural journal. Part of what is remarkable about this piece is the even-handed way he treats the fascist architecture of Germany and Italy despite the fact that war had already broken out in Europe. He does conclude by drawing a comparison with the contemporary architecture of Sweden and a rousing call for American architecture to more boldly embody democratic ideals—a call reminiscent of writers from the early nineteenth century.

In reviewing recent architecture abroad it seems important to stress the totalitarian states. Theirs is the building program which in the United States has been most generally misunderstood, when, indeed, our own professional press has not completely ignored it. Our natural habit is to think that a dictatorship over the arts must quickly result in manifest inferiority and decay. That is not the case. On the contrary, the first outcome of a dictatorship is that planning and architecture take on the appearance of conspicuous unanimity and startling success. Many who observe this fact are swept off their feet into the belief that in this field the claims of the dictators to superiority are valid after all. But the immediate success has been gained by sacrificing larger, more difficult aims. . . .

In examining recent architecture in Germany and Italy there is another common habit of thought that we must transcend. In our own architectural press there is a controversy under way about the merit of the "traditional" as against the "modern" approach to architectural style. Now the German trend is traditional and the Italian is modern but both are used in basically the same way. In either country a part of what has been given up is the hope that progress can be achieved by the voluntary association of individuals for purposes of production and free exchange. In both countries the leaders have restricted themselves to uniting their followers, destroying those who refuse to unite, and seeking improvement through conquest. Architecture is a tool of such union. It must declare continuity with a glorious past that led to former conquest. It must secure the individual to

Originally printed in *American Scholar*, July 1940.

the group; and, since hope of change in his own status is indefinitely deferred, he must be supplied with a sense of security and unique pride on occupying the station where he is. The architectural means of expressing all this are found by instinct as well as choice. Thus German fairy-tales would be inconceivable in a setting of flat roofs. In German folk-lore the high pitched roof is quintessentially Germanic, associated with the prehistoric German forest and later with the castles of medieval knights. . . .

The assiduous attention paid to the rural landscape has the aim of keeping the peasant proud of being one. Romantic restudy is bestowed upon the plans of medieval farm courts and their intricate, ritualistic framing. The occurrence in such a plan of a manure pile out-side the peasant's living-room window, or the fact that the whole *menage* is labor-devouring rather than labor-saving, brings no challenge, because our own ideal of a progressive, educated, independent population of farmers is not even raised. . . .

The highest outlet for German pride is supposed to be found in direct worship of the State; the latest available accounts indicate that not even the war has stopped the vast building program designed to "put the stamp of National Socialism forever" on the larger cities. In Berlin the North-South, East-West Crossing, a scheme so vast that the Kaiser's *Siegesallee* is reduced to a mere appendage, is already well under way. Whether in the exterior of the formidable reinforced concrete Air Ministry, in Hitler's own huge Chancellery, or the enormous new *Tempelhof* airport (with arched wings that will carry 80,000 spectators on their grandstand roofs) the architecture is a congeries of eclecticisms that adds up to the unique neo-classic of the "General Architectural Inspector," Dr. Albert Speer. The size compels awe; but those who have felt the incandescence of 20th-century architecture at its best cannot be deeply impressed by the intellectual approach.

Nazi architecture, in summary, serves the myth of the German race and State. It concentrates upon those emotional symbols that can produce union. Within the picture there is one apparent contradiction that really is none. Factories and workplaces have the most nearly international appearance of any part of the scheme. Indeed, new airplane plants such as those for Henschel or Junkers are sharply functional. They, however, are the tools of conquest and they strictly mean business.

On the surface Italian architecture today differs strongly from German. Mussolini took power earlier and thought of fascism as a logical step of rational evolution. So the "modernist" architects were eagerly accepted and told they had nothing to fear from bold innovation. The contemporary Italian architect commands some special resources. . . .

What especially concerns us here is its present evolution as a whole. The functionalist elements appear to be receding; what is advancing is more nearly functionary. Close study reveals, indeed, that the calm and assurance of Italian modern architecture arose largely from the fact that the individual elements of which it was assembled were taken over, all finished and ready to hand, from the democratic countries of the north. "Modern" Italian architecture employs an elegant vocabulary of smooth *clichés*. The process appears to be related to that which built ancient Rome. And contemporary Italian building, which began by recalling Rome, seems gradually to be imitating it. The situation becomes more clear. From their early role of conveying a sense of progress, Mussolini and his architects are turning to glorification of the past. The purpose is to prepare a psychology of chauvinism and conquest. . . .

The most direct antithesis to the architectural approach of the totalitarian countries is to be found in Scandinavia....

This Swedish example is dwelt upon because of its importance to America. There is a temptation to be impressed by Italian monumentality and German organization. Both, however, are less than completely human. Neither terror nor pride in status or hope of conquest produces democracy. Our promise was that every individual should have the chance to realize himself in peace. If groups such as the Okies permanently lose hope the chance is gone for democratic architecture as well as democratic life. With Nazi and Communist agents spying out every discontent it is imperative that the effort to supply secure and decent shelter, once begun under the Farm Security Administration, be resumed on a vastly larger scale.

Democratic architecture must not only give every citizen his chance to have an agreeable home but must declare its aims in emotional terms....

It is contended here that the present reverse trend toward "traditionalism" (really revivalism), although in one way evidence of democratic diversity, represents an emotional retreat into the past and a portentous failure inwardly to affirm the liberal hope of progress.

Most of Washington is under the same dead hand. The rows of columns still being added to other rows are inferior to Hitler's in that they represent not even a bad idea. Our finest single architectural project of the day is perhaps the vast scheme of the TVA, where rugged, honest, clean-cut and beautifully detailed structures proclaim in their forms and arrangement the power of a democratic government, without pomp, to organize conservation for its citizens. TVA is equal or superior to anything Germany or Italy has done, and so too were the buildings for the Government at the San Francisco Fair. If our Government always told its story in terms so charming and fresh and devoted to common welfare, who could help believing in democracy with "heart and head and hand"?

26

GEORGE BIDDLE, EXCERPT FROM "ISRAEL: YOUNG BLOOD AND OLD," 1949

The creation of the state of Israel stands as one of the most extraordinary events to have occurred in the wake of the Second World War. To document this event, the *Atlantic* sent George Biddle for a month-long tour of the new country. Biddle, an artist who had done sketches of figures at the Nuremburg Trials, was by no means an expert on the politics or social issues confronting Israel, and his report back to *Atlantic* readers has the quality of sketchy journal entries. Biddle is struck by the tremendous influx of new Israelis from all parts of the world, by the layers of history—European, Arab, Roman, Biblical—that intermix

Originally printed in *Atlantic Monthly*, October 1949, 19–25.

in the landscape—and by the destruction and rebuilding going on with extraordinary energy, an energy he imagines the American founders might have felt.

Tel Aviv, April 21, 1949.—The modernistic, stuccoed, matchbox, balconied buildings: the tropical shrubs and trees: the crowds thronging the Sir Herbert Samuel Square on the shore of the Mediterranean. A vital, energetic, up-to-date, youthful, and enthusiastic crowd. The faces might come from any city where type, color, and dress are not too rigidly stressed; from Geneva or Lausanne, from the French towns of the Mediterranean, from North Italy or Barcelona. Nothing particular to mark them; youth, a high proportion of physical beauty, healthy vitality, politeness, good nature. Many young soldiers in English uniform: boys and girls, single and in groups. A look of "belonging," which one had not associated with an all-Jewish population. . . .

It is impossible to get rooms anywhere. Much building is going on. All in brick and stucco on steel girders. It continually reminds me of Rio: the heavy-ladened, tropical-odored sea air; the modern balconied architecture and the mingling of the occasionally exotic, dark-skinned, sensuous slant-eyed women and strikingly handsome boys. . . .

April 29.—After lunch I walked to Jaffa, one of the most ancient cities in the world. The former Arab section was completely and systematically destroyed by Hebrew bombing during the war. Yet—by intent—only one mosque was damaged. I have seen no city in Europe more ruthlessly demolished. Entire blocks were heaps of rubble, the height sometimes of a two-story building.

I continued along King George V. Avenue, down King Feisal Avenue around the old fortress overlooking the port, whose arrogantly solid masonry dates from the days of Suleiman and the Crusaders. All this section of old Jaffa encompasses slums as miserable as any I have seen in San Antonio, Mexico, or Algiers. Heaps of swill and rubbish lay piled by the houses. The sewage trickled down the middle of the unpaved streets. Snotty, half-naked babies and slatternly women in filthy rags crawled in and out of the dark stinking alleys and among the wreckage left by the bombing. . . .

April 30.—Lunched at the Tel Aviv Museum, where I met Dr. Haim Gamzu, the Director, and saw a very fine retrospective exhibition of Hanna Orloff. At times her work approximates arts and crafts and is pretty weak in design, and some of her portraits are frank caricatures, and mediocre. Others of her portraits are exceedingly sensitive and sculpturesque.

The galleries were packed with young people, eager, vivacious, alert. It suggested to me what might have been the enthusiasm of the Italian youths during the High Renaissance. Often I think, too, of the same mental eagerness, democratic simplicity, pride, and prophetic sense of fulfilling a world mission that shine through the writings of Americans at the birth of our country—particularly Jefferson and the Adamses. . . .

Jerusalem, May 1.—Where Tel Aviv is all modern—but tawdry and completely lacking in architectural distinction—Jerusalem is a jumble of many styles, brought, however, into some sort of fusion by the warm color, austerity, and fine solidity of the almost universal cut stone. I was immensely impressed by the Jewish Agency Building, wrecked during the war, but already completely restored. John Ratner, a Jerusalem architect, designed it. The Yeshurun Synagogue by Rubin is also very fine. The Anglo-Palestine Bank by Eric Mendelsohn and the Post Office by an English architect, Harrison, who also did the Rockefeller Museum in the old city and the Government House, have great style.

All these buildings have individual distinction and are a sober and intelligent adaptation of the modern. . . .

May 12.—I visited the Al Hamei Tiberia baths a mile below the walled-in town of Tiberius. Here was a melting-pot of the Jews of four continents. Hasidic elders in long yellow and black or rose-colored striped gowns; European Jews, speaking English, German, or Yiddish; Druse women, squatting in the shade, eyes and mouths hid with white burnooses; tattooed Bedouins from the desert; city Arabs in Western dress with thinly veiled faces: Yemenite women in close-fitting embroidered black trousers, tucked into long GI woolen stockings; Yemenite men with flowers embroidered in wool on white vests; Sephardic Jews from Turkey or Persia; soldiers; boys and girls in the universal khaki shorts or slacks and khaki shirts; and the attendants in short white togalike gowns and green aprons above their brown legs and sandaled feet. . . .

The heavy walls of cut stone circling the old Roman city, and the bastions and towers built by Tiberius, are still standing. He, too, unquestionably bathed in the hot sulphur Al Hamei Tiberia baths. To the casual traveler these walls are the only enduring symbol, in these parts, of the splendor of Roman civilization. Like the petrified footprints, or bones of huge mastodons, these skeleton vestiges of the tremendous energy and life drive of former civilizations are to me very dramatic.

What dynamic drive the Arabs must have had! How can one explain their architecture and achievements in mathematics, war, medicine and humanities in terms of the apathy, filth, disease, degradation, and laziness of their descendants? I have felt the same way in attempting to measure the furious thrust of the Spanish conquistadores in some lazy, half-buried Guatemalan town, rotting away in apathy, pellagra, and undernourishment. . . .

May 22.—The PIO got me a plane to fly down to Sodom—the Sodom of Genesis— on the Dead Sea. As we approached the Dead Sea the sullen landscape became more terrifying in appearance. The black crust of the earth was split with broad chasms, canyons, barrancas, arroyos, dried rivulets, wriggled and zigzagged in all directions. One would suppose that not a living thing, a lizard, a bird, a plant, could suck nourishment or moisture from that torrid, salty, sun-baked clay. The earth was totally without color, but ranged from a dead black to every tone of gray and dirty white, by the edges of the sea. . . .

My visit to Israel has been uneventful; certainly much less exciting than the stay in Germany during the Nuremberg trials or the year in North Africa, Sicily, and Italy during the war. . . .

But for me the real excitement has been to watch in its early germination a social and moral experiment in government. Other nations have professed, but Israel is putting into practice, asylum, without prejudice as to origin, to all Jewish victims of religious persecution. They boldly proclaim: We must, we can, and we will integrate them all into our national ideal: the Algerian, the Yemenite, the Oriental, the Russian, Polish, English, German, African, or Chinese.

And they have done this during their first bitter war year, during the throes of the creation of a new state, at the rate of one quarter of the total population of the first year, without any wealth or housing facilities or capital resources; relying of course heavily on the hope of American help; but even more on the spiritual faith that burst into flame in the concentration camps of Europe.

27

PAUL GOLDBERGER, EXCERPT FROM
"THE INTERNATIONAL STYLE AFTER HALF A CENTURY," 1983

This essay, which appeared originally in 1982, marks the fiftieth anniversary of perhaps the most important museum exhibition of architecture ever mounted, the "International Exhibition of Modern Architecture" held at the Museum of Modern Art in 1932. Those who mounted the show did so to proselytize for these new architectural ideas, and they successfully reshaped contemporary architecture in America and how architectural history would be written. The arrival of International Modern in America had two important implications for America's cultural relationship with Europe. First, it suggested that architecture could truly become international, transcending the national boundaries and cultural prejudices that had previously existed; second, while the theories of International Modern originated primarily in Europe, many of its most important monuments were built in the United States, signaling that America was no longer on the architectural periphery, but now at the very center of architectural developments.

If any fact can be said to underscore how quickly revolutions age, it is that half a century has passed since the day the Museum of Modern Art put a few photographs and models into its galleries under the title "International Exhibition of Modern Architecture." Behind that bland and unassuming label was one of the most determined efforts at design proselytizing this or any other museum has ever engaged in. For this exhibition was the celebrated International Style show, in which the museum presented the stark, white buildings of stucco and glass and metal by Le Corbusier, Walter Gropius, Mies van der Rohe, and others who it wanted us to think would pull us out of the stultifying classicism of the nineteenth century and pave the way to a glorious new world.

How old all of this now seems, and how far away from what has happened to architecture since. The freshness, the daring, the triumphant sense of newness that was the International Style's stock in trade is today neither fresh nor daring, and least of all is it new. If anything, the works of architecture that appeared in the exhibition by now seem quaint: the sense of revolution they represented comes across now not as powerful but more as prim, puritanical, and not a little innocent.

Architecture has gone in different directions altogether, since the day, fifty years ago this month, that the International Style exhibition opened. It is not that modernism did not turn out to amount to anything—it amounted to very much indeed, since buildings in some way influenced by the International Style dominated the American downtown for decades. Without the International Style, there would have been no Third Avenue—or at least a very different Third Avenue.

But the stark boxes of modernism are now, clearly, the buildings of the past. We still build in glass, and we still build sleek, crisp forms, but we have almost completely given given up the International Style's cold, rigorous austerity. And what we have wisely given up on altogether is the International Style's firm moral posture—the sense its architects had that they knew what was right for us, the belief that the precise and hard-edged

2.4. American Embassy Chancellery, London, 1960. Courtesy of Yale University Press. By mid-century, America had taken the Bauhaus ideas, which had been born of social demo-cratic ideology in Germany, filtered them through the modern capitalist economy of the United States, and produced the International Style. Soon it was the United States that was exporting modernism, in the form of corporate skyscrapers and political architecture. The American architect Eero Saarinen (who had emigrated from Finland) won the competition to design the new Chancellery building of the American Embassy in Grosvernor Square.

lines of modernism were a positive force liberating us from the harsh stranglehold of history.

This was precisely the stance taken by the museum's International Style exhibition. The show, which was organized by Philip Johnson, who began his career as the museum's first curator of architecture, was seen by 33,000 people at the museum and by thousands more as it traveled around the country. Several times this many people, of course, have read and continue to read the book *The International Style* by Henry-Russell Hitchcock and Mr. Johnson, which appeared at the same time. Together the exhibition and the book are gen-erally thought of as comprising a watershed event in the history of modern architecture. The exhibition was a sort of debutante cotillion at which the style was dressed up and given its formal presentation to a waiting world; the book recorded the happy debut for posterity.

The importance of this event has always been more symbolic than real, fifty years ago as much as today. In February 1932, the International Style was not really brand

new—its great monuments, buildings like the Villa Savoie in Poissy, France, by Le Corbusier; the Bauhaus in Dessau, Germany, by Walter Gropius; or the Tugendhat House in
Brno, Czechoslovakia, by Mies van der Rohe, had all been complete for at least two years
and were fairly well known. And by then the style had already begun to cross the Atlantic,
too. The exhibition contained such American buildings as the Starrett Lehigh Building in
New York of 1931, by Russel G. and Walter M. Cory; Raymond Hood's McGraw-Hill
Building, also in New York, of 1932; and Richard Neutra's Lovell House, in Los Angeles,
of 1929.

What this famous exhibition and the long-lived book that accompanied it did was
to grant a certain legitimacy to a style that was coming, by virtue of forces far more powerful than those controlled by anyone at the Museum of Modern Art, to play a larger and
larger role in shaping the cityscape. The Museum of Modern Art's stamp of approval
made the International Style's growth somewhat smoother and easier, but it did not, of
course, bring all this modern architecture into being in the first place. Popular writers
such as Tom Wolfe have lately made great sport of the myth that the International Style
was some sort of foreign plot foisted upon an unwilling America by a group of European
intellectuals led by the Museum of Modern Art; in fact, Frank Lloyd Wright's American
architecture was an important International Style antecedent. And acceptance of modernism in its various forms had been growing slowly for years; the museum show merely
confirmed that fact. . . .

Modernism continued to spread through this country for at least four decades after
the exhibition, but not quite in the way the museum's proselytizers had hoped it would.
Its acceptance was fueled less by esthetics than by the economics of the postwar years, as
glass curtain walls finally became cheaper than masonry and as the decline in craftsmanship made it seem financially prudent to join the parade against ornament. By 1950 modern architecture had become the American corporate style, its clean, sparse lines ideally
suited to the cool and anonymous world of American Business in the postwar years.

As the style grew, however, it became harder and harder to tell what was the International Style and what was not. By the late 1950's we were seeing not only more and
more weak imitations of International Style masters—the kind of bargain-basement
Mies van der Rohe that fills Third Avenue—but also the flamboyant shapes of Eero
Saarinen, whose picturesque architecture at its best has an appealing stage-set quality;
the decorative modernism of Minoru Yamasaki and Edward Durell Stone, who tried to
break away from the International Style toward a delicate, rather prissy kind of architecture; and the powerful imagery of Kevin Roche, whose buildings back then had a strong,
almost brutal sculptural quality to them.

So there was considerable diversity in modernism—modern buildings were more
than just products of the single-minded, narrow dogma of the International Style itself.
But there was a kind of hubris to all of this architecture, a certainty that it represented
the right way, the one true way to the making of right buildings. And if the International
Style did not encompass all that modern architecture was about, it certainly exemplified
modernism's hubris. Nowhere but here did there seem to be such narrow dictates, nowhere but with the gurus of the International Style was there so much concern with pro-
nouncing buildings acceptable or unacceptable.

And this is where the Museum of Modern Art exhibition played a major role—it
presented what amounted to a set of rules for the making of modern architecture. There
was a right way, which was to create buildings that fit into a particular esthetic, and a

wrong way, which was to do anything else. The International Style was never really about much of anything except esthetics anyway, in the end. There was much talk about social responsibility, and about using new technology and modern materials, but these factors could never hold a candle to the question of how a building looked. . . .

That esthetics alone could do this [improve society] is something almost no one, not even our most zealous architects, believes anymore. We ask of our architecture today something much more particular, something much less moralistic. We expect it to shelter us and, quite frequently, we expect it also to please and even entertain us. At its best—when its aspirations to art are the most serious—we hope that it will uplift us. But we still do not look to it for a cleansing of the soul; neither do we look to it for a sense of absolutes.

And thus there is, at this moment in architectural history, no clear sense of style at all. Our best architects are divided between those who seem to be taking some modernist themes—a sense of sleekness and abstraction—and using them in a far more decorative and playful way than the International Style architects did, and those who are trying to reject all that modernism has been about and bring into their work the very aspects of historical architectural style that the International Style rejected. . . .

It is perhaps no accident that fifty years after the International Style's great exhibition the work of those architects with whom the International Style's practitioners felt in deepest competition, the eclectic architects of the 1920's, is riding a crest of popularity. The picturesque, relaxed, and easy Georgian mansions of Delano & Aldrich, the sumptuous Renaissance buildings of McKim, Mead & White, the lush Gothic of James Gamble Rogers are all very much in fashion now. They are admired by historians and, more significantly, they are imitated by younger, postmodern architects.

The best eclecticism of the 1920's and 1930's was an architecture of a certain ease, a certain self-indulgent but not unsophisticated pleasure. It displays far more knowledge of what makes buildings physically and emotionally comfortable than the International Style was ever able to do. But what makes eclecticism most appealing right now is that it is an architecture without dogma—an architecture without a rigid ideology to foist upon the world. The International Style was a kind of missionary architecture, and it is that, more than anything else, that sets it apart from the sensitivities of our age today.

2 8

SUZANNE STEPHENS, "MANIFEST DISNEY," 1992

One of the most controversial events in Europe late in the twentieth century was the opening of "Euro-Disney" just outside of Paris. Plagued at the outset with financial, labor, and public relations problems, Euro-Disney struck many Europeans as the worst example

Originally printed in *Architectural Record*, vol. 180, June 1992. Reprinted with permission from *Architectural Record* 1992, a McGraw-Hill Construction publication.

of American cultural imperialism, a sense captured wryly in the very title of Suzanne Stephens's piece. As she points out, in the demarcated spaces of amusement parks, "entertainment architecture" strives to achieve the same ersatz effects everywhere. This last essay of this chapter poses the question, What if the view from abroad looks just like the view from home?

Euro Disneyland opened on April 12 with explosive fanfare from the popular media and a barrage of criticism from French intellectuals. In essence it was both praised for being fun, and criticized for being fake. Although only 20 miles east of Paris, the 4,800-acre American implant of make-believe castles and mountains with Main Street, Mickey, Donald Duck, and Goofy could be anywhere. Plopped down in the green pastures of Marne-la-Vallée, this colony appears self-sufficient. The inclusion of 5,200 hotel rooms and a restaurant/nightclub complex next to the amusement park is key to Disney's success: With the hotels easy to see and easy to walk to, there is no need to stay in Paris. After all, as Disney CEO Michael Eisner points out, "Research shows that Paris is an adult attraction."

To help make the Euro Disney Resort more delectable as a tourist destination to adults and children alike, the Disney Company, led by Eisner, hired high-profile American architects Frank Gehry, Michael Graves, Antoine Predock, and Robert Stern, along with respected French architect Antoine Grumbach, to design five hotels and an entertainment complex (RECORD, August 1990, pages 72–79). The concept, already initiated at Disney World in Orlando, Florida, presumably would instill in the buildings an element of sophistication appealing to grown-ups, while still accounting for Disney's reputation for being CG-13—anyone over 13 should be accompanied by a child.

Clearly "entertainment architecture," the epithet for the output of these architects, comes with a different set of requirements and expectations than "regular architecture." The question then is what are those expectations and how well does this group of high-design architects live up to them? More importantly, what implications does this type of architectural effort have for architecture in general? With the architects feeling figuratively pushed to the edges of the built world these days, some could hope that entertainment architecture is a way of finally convincing the public of its need for the real thing. As in Disney's box-office hit *Beauty and the Beast,* a happy ending would be in store when the public, drawn into entertainment architecture, learns to love architecture for its soul and accepts it in all its outward, even ugly, guises.

The hotels by Graves, Grumbach, Predock, and Stern, along with the entertainment complex by Gehry, are clustered in their own compound around a lake and an adjoining creek. While separated from the amusement park itself by the rapid transit and high-speed railroad stations that link Euro Disney to Paris and (eventually) southern Europe, they are only a short stroll from the heart of the action. One hotel, however, is not part of this cluster. The Disneyland Hotel is the gateway entrance to the amusement park, a high-Victorian-style confection with rabbit-eye pink wood siding and lobster-red turreted and mansarded roofs. Its foofa-raws, frills, and furbelows go the whole nine yards of entertainment architecture. . . .

For his part, Gehry simply convinced Disney that his entertainment center didn't need an overt theme. So his Festival Disney looks like a bunch of weird, jaggedly patterned, quilted stainless-steel columns with some giant bloblike hangar spaces dropped in. This is just how Gehry wanted it—although Disney countered with themed-to-the-

2.5. Where are we? A photograph like this one might well have been taken in Southern California or southern Florida. In fact, it shows a street in Thailand. Even here the Golden Arches preside over the built environment, and Colonel Sanders smiles on the scene.

hilt bars and restaurants inside. Festival Disney looks great by night when the open net-like canopy of small lights creates a web of stars directly overhead. In the cold light of day, however, the jazzy columns and dropped-in shapes have the morning-after look of a discothèque at 10 A.M. with all the lights turned on. One thing for sure: Festival Disney is a long way from Hotel Disneyland, although it's just next door.

If the individual buildings by the famous architects have their ups and downs, there is always the urban ensemble to consider. Having the oblong pond of water function as the central organizing device brings to mind the plan of the Chicago World's Fair of 1893. When Montgomery Schuyler analyzed this famous American predecessor of entertainment architecture, he commented that the White City succeeded because of the unity of the ensemble of buildings, their magnitude, and the success of the illusion. At Euro Disney Resort, the unity comes through common theming and general building height, not through one architectural style. Architectural presence is achieved through hotel size and guestroom number, not through awesome proportions, and illusion gives way to allusion. Because of the wide ranging assortment of styles closely arrayed, the illusion of the geographical place, when created, is right away subverted by the immediate juxtaposition of another place and style. No effect is allowed to last in this constant flow of images—a Disney trait that is characteristic of its amusement parks.

This shift, nevertheless, creates the most interesting paradox. Since the architecture fights the creation of a cohesive urban ensemble, paradoxically Euro Disney Resort is almost too much like reality today. It is a condensed version of the surface discontinuities and ruptures typical of the world outside Disneytopia. The architects' efforts haven't gone far enough to help us escape from that reality into the harmonious, cohesive, glamorous, romantic simulation we expect from the movies—and from Disney.

If the entertainment architecture isn't escapist enough, then one might wonder if it could be reclassified as Architecture with a capital A. That depends on one's definition. True, architects have believed for decades that architecture should express our culture and our times. Yet a number of architects also maintain that architecture should not necessarily console and comfort, or spoonfeed the familiar to an already stuffed public. It should provoke and challenge it. Others argue that architecture should heighten the spiritual appreciation of its physical possibilities through the manipulation of space, light, and materials. And, instead of architecture reflecting what we are, it should conjecture what we might be. Finally, alas, Euro Disney has told us devilishly only what we are. And that picture is a static one. It neither provokes us into examination of these facts, nor helps us transcend them.

2.6. Guggenheim Museum, Bilbao. Courtesy of Laura Goldfeld. Without question, the most celebrated building of the end of the twentieth century was Frank Gehry's Guggenheim in Bilbao. Built as an attempt to attract tourists to a depressed city, the museum dazzled the world with its curving, sparkling titanium. Designed by an American architect, built in an obscure corner of Europe, and looking like nothing anyone had ever seen before, Gehry's Guggenheim underscores just how international the ideas and practice of architecture have become.

3.1. *In the Yosemite Valley,* by Albert Bierstadt. Oil on canvas, 1866. Wadsworth Atheneum, Hartford. Bequest of Elizabeth Jarvis Colt. This painting, like so many of the late nineteenth century, celebrated the majesty of the American "wilderness." Bierstadt and fellow travelers found in the West landscapes equal to the cathedrals and ancient cities of Europe. Here would be the youthful country's claim to an ancient history and beauty.

CHAPTER 3

So Glorious a Landscape: Shaping Nature the American Way

The cultural critic Raymond Williams wrote that in the definition of the word "nature" lies much of the cultural history of Western civilization, for it speaks directly to how we conceive of human beings in relation to their surroundings. The mythos of few nations have been bound more closely to the many definitions and contradictions of the word "nature" as that of the United States. This is in large measure because of its close connection to the idea of "wilderness" existing beyond the reach of human influence, which has been so central to American identity.

Perhaps the most important single sentence written by an American historian referred directly to the wilderness of the American West. In 1893, at the annual meeting of the American Historical Association in Chicago, the year of the World's Columbian Exposition, Frederick Jackson Turner delivered his presidential address, "The Significance of the Frontier in American History," with the stunning line "The existence of an area of free land, its continuous recession, and the advance of American settlement westward, explain American development."

But nature, however defined, is not equivalent to landscape. The origins of the term "landscape" derive from the Dutch *landskip,* which had equally to do with looking at the natural world as with the natural world itself. As architectural historian Dell Upton has written, nature may be defined in opposition to landscape. Nature is the "undisciplined landscape." We focus in this chapter not on the whole history of American views and approaches to nature more generally, but on the history of landscape, or "disciplined nature": nature as crafted and constructed and cajoled into particular forms and views by human society.

The goal of American thinking about landscape has been to domesticate nature in the midst of human civilization, to exploit the seemingly limitless resources of the continent without despoiling nature's power of renewal and redemption. Different ideas about disciplining nature confronted each other in the birth of the United States. Native American ecological patterns—living on the land and transforming it with the purpose of maintaining its ongoing productivity—clashed with and rapidly lost out to a European invasion characterized by owning and bounding land, and harvesting single crops for sale on an international agricultural market.

Cultivation of the American landscape was intimately tied to the continuing success of the republican experiment in the United States, and the preservation of republican virtue. In the minds of many of the founding thinkers, especially James Madison, the very openness of the American land would be the guarantor of republicanism, at least for a time. Ultimately, however, the vastness of the United States, Madison feared, would undermine the bonds of community and frustrate the delicate balance of representative democracy. The power of this undisciplined and overwhelming natural environment threatened the cohesion of the new nation even as it offered opportunities for individual freedom.

Although most of the United States remained rural through the nineteenth century, the restless acquisitiveness of a burgeoning market economy and the growing cities and industries of the antebellum period provoked a powerful intellectual response: a romantic pastoralism that sought in communing with nature an antidote to the ills of the modernizing nation.

Thoreau's *Walden* (1854) was the epitome of this intellectual flowering, but the sense of nature's wisdom and man's destructiveness resonated throughout many areas of intellectual and cultural life. The image of tree stumps in the art of the era, for example, echoed a long-standing trope in American culture. Dating from the beginning of the new nation, artists, such as Thomas Cole, and writers, like Thoreau and Cooper, had used tree stumps and, implicitly, the axes that cut them down, as visual and literary symbols of the destructive side of the American character. But the metaphor went further: the stumps of ancient trees, felled in an instant, posed a "temporal crisis," as art historian Barbara Novak has called it. They suggested that humans—and especially Americans—were promoting "extraordinary accelerations" in the pace of change, literally unsettling notions of time itself. In the city the disparities in the movement of time, between humans and nature's representatives, were all the more striking and troubling. The "hurricane of the axe," which Thomas Cole decried in the 1830s, ravaged not only trees but also the invented idea of a cohesive, consensual community.

At the same moment, the continental vision of American political leaders—celebrated or lamented—meant that Native Americans would be moved aside so that the young nation could achieve its Manifest Destiny, a phrase used beginning in the 1840s to justify America's expansion to the Pacific. The "free land" Frederick Jackson Turner spoke about at the end of the century had never been free of people and settlement. Indeed, estimates of the number of Native Americans who occupied the Americas before the arrival of Europeans in the sixteenth century reach the millions. The antebellum march of Manifest Destiny, which only quickened after the Civil War, displaced and destroyed Native American cultures, and replaced landscapes of nomadic hunting and gathering and subsistence agriculture with landscapes of individual landownership, commercial agriculture, and mining over the breadth of the North American continent. In this sense, the great "free land" of the American West whose loss Frederick Jackson Turner lamented was the most powerfully constructed of all landscapes, connected almost umbilically to urban markets and urban capital.

For some in the mid-nineteenth century, however, landscapes of nature need not exist in polar opposition to urban ones. Beginning with Andrew Jackson Downing's writings on the value and design of country houses, a pastoral cemetery movement, and finally the urban parks movement of the latter half of the nineteenth century, Americans experimented with merging nature and an industrializing, urbanizing nation. Frederick Law Olmsted was the most influential force in this movement. He championed a vision of urban parks and park systems that fully accepted and embraced the American urban and industrial future while hoping to ameliorate the social and physical stresses of the modern city. In designing his parks, he created new landscapes on top of an older nature. So successful was this "second nature," that many came to see his designs as "true" nature preserved in the midst of the city. His parks were, in many ways, constructions as artful as the skyscrapers that would come to encircle them. Even more influential than his park designs was Olmsted's development of the idea of the suburban home amid a suburban community. Emphasizing a careful balance of lawns and parks, tree-lined streets and rapid transit connections to the city, Olmsted set the stage for the dominant American landscape of the next century: the suburban home and lawn.

The Progressive Era saw the tension over how best to preserve and exploit America's landscapes manifest itself in a debate between conservationists and preservationists. The former, President Theodore Roosevelt most prominent among them, believed that with rational planning and regulation, nature could be made productive forever. Roosevelt set aside millions of acres, mostly in the West, as National Forests to be managed by the Federal Forest Service so that Americans would have both forests to enjoy and timber with which to build. Preservationists, like John Muir, founder of the Sierra Club, thought large areas of American wilderness ought to be set aside and left permanently alone. It was he who declared, on traveling to the Sierras in 1868, that he had never seen "so glorious a landscape, so boundless an affluence of sublime mountain beauty." In many ways, this Progressive Era debate over how best to treat what remained of American nature lies at the heart of environmental debates today.

The New Deal brought a radical shift in attitude toward the shaping of the American landscape. The experimentation of government control and regulation of American life that characterized the New Deal was also brought to bear on nature. Though the New Deal would fund the development of new towns, which more fully integrated nature with urban planning, it was the enormous infrastructure projects that were of greater lasting impact. The massive dams of the Tennessee Valley Authority transformed the flow of rivers; Works Progress Administration bridges and highways made forbidding natural obstacles navigable; the trails and roads of the Civilian Conservation Corps brought vast numbers of Americans in contact with state and national parks. As the United States entered the Second World War, there was a pervasive new confidence in the government's ability to shape the American landscape.

In the postwar period, tensions over how to treat the American landscape only intensified. On one hand, Americans forced their landscapes into increasing artificiality, exemplified by the carefully crafted and near ubiquitous suburban lawn. Even in the deserts of Arizona, Americans built lush, green golf courses, and in semiarid valleys in California, farmers began to grow rice, all made possible with heavily subsidized and environmentally destructive irrigation. Whatever attempts had been made in the nineteenth century to create an artful merging of nature and civilization were abandoned in large parts of the country.

At the same time that these suburban trends were homogenizing the landscape, a powerful intellectual assault was taking place. Critics assailed the ugliness of the American landscape, its "junkyard" appearance, and its desecration of spectacular natural scenery. Calls for more careful growth planning and design guidelines bore fruit, not immediately, but in the 1970s and 1980s and sought to stem the tide of suburbanization and homogenization of the landscape. "Smart growth" ordinances became the center of political debate in dozens of states and localities in the 1990s.

Finally, under the inspiration of Rachel Carson's manifesto, *Silent Spring* (1962), a remarkably powerful environmental movement was reinvigorated. Although the environmental movement gained notable victories in the Great Society programs of Lyndon Johnson—the Clean Air and Water Acts, the Highway Beautification Act—it was actually in the 1970s that the movement fully matured into a powerful political force. Indeed, it remains one of the most long-lasting and most widely supported of the social movements of the 1960s.

By the close of the twentieth century it is a remarkable irony that while the American landscape has been transformed dramatically over the course of two hundred years, in many ways the terms of debate over that landscape remain the same. The commitment to the idea of wilderness—that there are truly wild and uninhabited places that hold precious moral lessons and spiritual uplift—has distant roots in our history. At the same time, as we write this President Bush, pliant servant of the oil industry, continues to push hard to open the Arctic National Wildlife Refuge to oil drilling. At the start of the new millennium, Americans have created landscapes that are at once more artificial than ever and also more sensitive than ever before to an attempt to live in concert with natural forces. How this balance will be tipped is the question of the next decades.

C. W. SHORT, "ANTIQUITIES OF OHIO," 1817

Reporting from the far frontier of Kentucky in 1817 to East Coast readers, C. W. Short relayed a letter from General Harrison describing one of the hundreds of Native American mounds settlers encountered in the Ohio and Mississippi Valleys. Just who built them and for what reasons constituted one of the great debates among learned Americans in the first half of the nineteenth century. It is both amusing and predictable that the general should describe this particular earthwork as a military installation. Americans who explored these mounds often projected onto them their own fantasies about their use and about the people who built them. These mounds did serve as reminders for Americans settling the "virgin" wilderness west of the Appalachian Mountains that this land had, in fact, already been occupied for a long time.

Dear Sir—As some pages of your interesting miscellany have already been devoted to the aboriginal remains of our country, I am induced to send you the annexed draught of an ancient work, in Hamilton county, Ohio. It is situated immediately at the confluence of the Ohio and Great Miami rivers, on the estate of general Harrison; and in the opinion of the proprietor (who is certainly well qualified to judge), and indeed of all who have examined it, is one of the few works evidently intended for military defence, among the many others more probably consecrated to religious or social purposes, which are dispersed over all the western section of the union. As a more full description of this work may not be uninteresting, I take the liberty of extracting part of a letter, written by general Harrison to a gentleman in Cincinnati, who had requested some information on the subject.

"It is situated," says the general, "on the high ridge which borders the Ohio, and precisely at the point where it is terminated by the coming in of the Miami. The hill is perhaps two hundred feet above the level of the adjacent bottom, and the sides are so steep that there are few places where it can be ascended on horseback. The work contains by estimation fifteen acres, and occupies the whole width of the ridge; the wall, both on the Ohio and Miami sides, being as near as possible to the brink of the hill; from this circumstance, and from the ridge growing constantly narrower as you approach the Miami, the eastern wall or curtain is twice the length of that which forms the western defence of the fort, and the distance from the latter to the very point of the hill opposite to the junction of the rivers, an hundred and fifty feet. Immediately upon the point is a tumulus, of about half the elevation of that in Cincinnati. The two long walls immediately upon the brink are nowhere so high as those of the ends, their situation subjecting the earth of which they are made to be washed down the precipice. Indeed it is probable they never were so high, as, from the same cause, the approach to them was rendered very difficult. In one instance only, where it crosses a considerable ravine, the side-wall on the Ohio mounts to the present height of the end-walls. Of the latter, that on the west is the highest, being at present perhaps fifteen feet—a precaution dictated, no doubt, by the ground over which it passes being more level than at any other place. The ridge is here, however, too narrow, and the hill on each side too steep, to make it the point at which an assault

Originally printed in *Port Folio* IV (1817): 179–81.

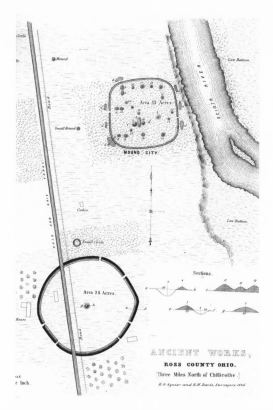

3.2. Mound City, Ohio, 1848, Ephraim Squier and Edwin Davis. Nineteenth-century Americans marveled at the mounds that lay scattered throughout the landscape of the Ohio and Mississippi Valleys. There was wild speculation about who built them and how they functioned. Squier and Davis were the first American archaeologists to attempt a systematic survey of these mounds with anything like scientific precision.

could be made with the greatest prospect of success. It is moreover covered by an out-work; for such I deem the mound or tumulus abovementioned. The weakest point of the position is to be found, on the eastern side, where the ridge, spreading out to a considerable extent, would allow a large army to approach and form near the work. It is here, therefore, that the ingenuity of the persons who constructed it has been most successfully exerted. There is at this place a considerable and irregular sink in the hill, which might afford cover to an offending enemy; but the line has been so run as to command every part of it. It appears also that the engineer was not unacquainted with the great efficacy of flank defences. He has therefore secured this curtain, by a projection from each angle, which answer the purpose of our bastions. These bastions are formed by two parallel lines, twenty-fire or thirty feet in length, and at the distance of ten or twelve feet apart. Had these lines been drawn at different angles with the main work, they would have answered, without any additional labour, for the defence of the side-curtains also, as the modern bastions do: as it is, they defend the eastern face only; for in each of the lines which compose them, the one is drawn at right angles (or nearly so) with the eastern wall—the other a prolongation of the side-wall. The foundation of the whole wall is of stone, without any appearance of cement, and not laid horizontally, but vertically, wedged in with each other as closely as possible. Upon this foundation the eastern parapet is raised."

30

ANONYMOUS, "PINE LANDS OF NEW JERSEY," 1829

While present-day New Jersey is popularly known as the state of interstate highways, it was also once known as the state of forests, with the "pine lands" covering much of the state. The author of this selection is awed not as much by the immensity of these forests, but by the rapidity with which they are being chopped down to feed the unstoppable demand of steamboats. The author laments the passing of the pine lands not so much because of their natural beauty (this would be the heart of the environmental protection movement of the late 20th century) but because of what it signified about the larger culture: an anxiety toward technology, a fear of the speed of change, and a resentment toward the market and its voracious appetite for new forms of profit.

Thirty years ago the immense forests which cover so large a portion of this state, were not worth more than six to ten cents an acre. There was no inducement to make them productive, because there were no visible means. No demand existed for the timber, for oak was preferred for household purposes; neither was it an object to clear the land for agricultural purposes, because, when cleared, it was not worth tilling, and that which was, had been farmed long before. By degrees, however, Furnaces were established among the woods; yet, though they made great havoc, no reduction was apparent in the huge wilderness of pines. Next came the Steamboats. For a few years they traversed our waters, propelled by timber from New Jersey, yet without sensibly diminishing the density of the forests. In a few years more, their number was doubled—trebled—quadrupled. Their huge maws, though supplied with thousands of shallop-loads of pine, were yet unsatisfied. The demand for fuel, became immense, and the almost worthless pine lands of New Jersey rose rapidly in value, until they constituted an essential item in the profits of the farmer. Four dollars was not thought too great a price for an acre, and owners even showed a disposition to hold on, rather than sell, wisely foreseeing that, instead of a decrease in the demand, an immeasurable increase must ensue. In this posture of affairs, the inexhaustible depositories of Coal upon the Lehigh were laid open to the astonishment and gratification of the whole country. The bowels of the earth were penetrated for the hidden treasure—more valuable than all the mines of Carolina and Virginia, because they require labor to transmute them into gold—and coal became the universal favorite.

Originally printed in *Register of Pennsylvania*, reprinted from the *Saturday Bulletin* 82 (July 25, 1829): 63.

But before it could be used, charcoal must be used to ignite it—and here again, a new in-road must be made into the Pine Lands of New Jersey for a supply. This was an entirely new market opened for her formerly useless timber. Nay, there are not less than one thousand furnaces used in this city, for culinary purposes, which, during the summer months, consume nothing else than charcoal. In fact, the mighty march of steam upon her neighboring waters have nearly revolutionized New Jersey. Her pine lands, in place of bringing ten cents an acre, are now worth six dollars—an advance, in thirty years, of nearly six thousand percent! Yet we have no doubt, but that in a few years hence, there will be no such thing as a pine forest within her borders. The steam engine must be satisfied. It will eat up every tree upon her soil; and as the oak springs up where the pine has flourished, and the pine where the oak has grown, a century at least must pass away before a second forest of pine can be worthy of the axe. What then, shall be done, when all this wilderness shall be burnt away, and the ground left bare and barren, like the prairies of the Mississippi? In place of pine, the bowels of the earth must be digged to stop the outcry of the steam engine, since that which grows upon its surface has been unable to satisfy its cravings. Coal must be substituted for wood. It has been done already, and will be done still more extensively, it is used to drive our steam ferry boats and it is shipped to the West India Islands, where it is advantageously employed in boiling sugar. How vast the changes which the discoveries of steam and anthracite have made! How mighty the effects which they are yet destined to produce. They have diminished distances to mere pleasure-trips—they swallow up whole forests, leaving nothing in their place, and make the wilderness itself to blossom like the rose.

31

JOHN MCPHEE, EXCERPT FROM *THE PINE BARRENS*, 1967

John McPhee is one America's great journalists, with the uncanny ability to find and tell the stories of obscure corners of life—from the history and theory of growing oranges to the way basketball star and future senator Bill Bradley had a sense of where he was on the court, to the class relations on a windy Scottish isle. In this piece McPhee shows the 1829 visitor to the "pine lands" of New Jersey to have been right to stand in awe at the immense pine forests, but wrong in his prediction that "in a few years hence, there will be no such thing as a pine forest within her borders." Indeed, in McPhee's portrait the Pine Barrens remain a world apart from the developing suburban landscape of New Jersey, a place of rich folklore and impenetrable beauty, a unique place in a state criticized for creating the ultimate in homogenized landscapes.

From the Fire Tower on Bear Swamp Hill, in Washington Township, Burlington County, New Jersey, the view usually extends about twelve miles. To the north, forest land reaches to the horizon. The trees are mainly oaks and pines, and the pines predominate. Occasionally, there are long, dark, serrated stands of Atlantic white cedars, so tall and so closely set that they seem to be spread against the sky on the ridges of hills, when in fact they grow along streams that flow through the forest. To the east, the view is similar, and few people who are not native to the region can discern essential differences from the high cabin of the fire tower, even though one difference is that huge areas out in this direction are covered with dwarf forests, where a man can stand among the trees and see for miles over their uppermost branches. To the south, the view is twice broken slightly—by a lake and by a cranberry bog—but otherwise it, too, goes to the horizon in forest. To the west, pines, oaks, and cedars continue all the way, and the western horizon includes the summit of another hill—Apple Pie Hill—and the outline of another fire tower, from which the view three hundred and sixty degrees around is virtually the same as the view from Bear Swamp Hill, where, in a moment's sweeping glance, a person can see hundreds of square miles of wilderness. The picture of New Jersey that most people hold in their minds is so different from this one that, considered beside it, the Pine Barrens, as they are called, become as incongruous as they are beautiful. West and north of the Pine Barrens is New Jersey's central transportation corridor, where traffic of freight and people is more concentrated than it is anywhere else in the world. The corridor is one great compression of industrial shapes, industrial sounds, industrial air, and thousands and thousands of houses webbing over the spaces between the factories. Railroads and magnificent highways traverse this crowded scene, and by 1985 New Jersey hopes to have added so many additional high-speed roads that the present New Jersey Turnpike will be quite closely neighbored by the equivalent of at least six other turnpikes, all going in the same direction. In and around the New Jersey corridor, towns indistinguishably abut one another. Of the great unbroken city that will one day reach at least from Boston to Richmond, this section is already built. New Jersey has nearly a thousand people per square mile—the greatest population density of any state in the Union. In parts of northern New Jersey, there are as many as forty thousand people per square mile. In the central area of the Pine Barrens—the forest land that is still so undeveloped that it can be called wilderness—there are only fifteen people per square mile. This area, which includes about six hundred and fifty thousand acres, is nearly as large as Yosemite National Park. It is almost identical in size with Grand Canyon National Park, and it is much larger than Sequoia National Park, Great Smoky Mountains National Park, or, for that matter, most of the national parks in the United States. The people who live in the Pine Barrens are concentrated mainly in small forest towns, so the region's uninhabited sections are quite large—twenty thousand acres here, thirty thousand acres there—and in one section of well over a hundred thousand acres there are only twenty-one people. The Pine Barrens are so close to New York that on a very clear night a bright light in the pines would be visible from the Empire State Building. A line ruled on a map from Boston to Richmond goes straight through the middle of the Pine Barrens. The halfway point between Boston and Richmond—the geographical epicenter of the developing megalopolis—is in the northern part of the woods, about twenty miles from Bear Swamp Hill.

Technically, the Pine Barrens are much larger than the thousand or so square miles of them that remain wild, and their original outline is formed by the boundaries of a thick layer of sand soils that covers much of central and southern New Jersey—down the coast from the outskirts of Asbury Park to the Cape May Peninsula, and inland more than halfway across the state. Settlers in the seventeenth and eighteenth centuries found these soils unpromising for farms, left the land uncleared, and began to refer to the region as the Pine Barrens. People in New Jersey still use the term, with variants such as "the pine belt," "the pinelands," and, most frequently, "the pines." Gradually, development of one kind or another has moved in over the edges of the forest, reducing the circumference of the wild land and creating a man-made boundary in place of the natural one. This transition line is often so abrupt that in many places on the periphery of the pines it is possible to be at one moment in farmland, or even in a residential development or an industrial zone, and in the next moment to be in the silence of a bewildering green country, where a journey of forty or fifty miles is necessary to get to the farms and factories on the other side. I don't know where the exact center of the pines may be, but in recent years I have spent considerable time there and have made outlines of the integral woodland on topographic maps and road maps, and from them I would judge that the heart of the pine country is in or near a place called Hog Wallow. There are twenty-five people in Hog Wallow. Some of them describe it, without any apparent intention to be clever, as a suburb of Jenkins, a town three miles away, which has forty-five people. One resident of Hog Wallow is Frederick Chambers Brown. I met him one summer morning when I stopped at his house to ask for water.

32

WASHINGTON IRVING, EXCERPT FROM
A TOUR ON THE PRAIRIES, 1835

Washington Irving toured the "Indian Territories" in 1832, in the midst of a renewed government effort to push Indian tribes off eastern lands. He produced *A Tour on the Prairies* in 1835, just three years before the "Trail of Tears," the forced removal of the Cherokee from the Southeast to Oklahoma. Inevitably, a tour of the American West had to involve the pursuit of buffalo, with the intent to kill. The killing of the buffalo, who in their great numbers symbolized the abundance of the West as well as the world of the Native American, was a central cultural act on the part of invading European-Americans. There is a sense of awe Irving hopes to communicate—the solitude of the prairie, the immensity, the emptiness. But, in seeming to honor the beauty and power of this unique American landscape, Irving replicates a growing cultural trope: that the West is "without a sign of human existence" and "far beyond the bounds of human habitation." In those simple words, replicated thousands of times in accounts of the West, were justifications for displacing Native Americans, settling the land, and making it "productive" as private property.

Originally published in Washington Irving, *A Tour on the Prairies* (Philadelphia: Carey, Lea & Blanchard, 1835), 171–77.

After proceeding about two hours in a southerly direction, we emerged toward mid-day from the dreary belt of the Cross Timber, and to our infinite delight beheld "the great Prairie" stretching to the right and left before us. We could distinctly trace the meandering course of the main Canadian, and various smaller streams, by the strips of green forest that bordered them. The landscape was vast and beautiful. There is always an expansion of feeling in looking upon these boundless and fertile wastes; but I was doubly conscious of it after emerging from our "close dungeon of innumerous boughs."

From a rising ground Beatte pointed out the place where he and his comrades had killed the buffaloes; and we beheld several black objects moving in the distance, which he said were part of the herd. The Captain determined to shape his course to a woody bottom about a mile distant, and to encamp there for a day or two, by way of having a regular buffalo hunt, and getting a supply of provisions. As the troop defiled along the slope of the hill toward the camping ground, Beatte proposed to my messmates and myself, that we should put ourselves under his guidance, promising to take us where we should have plenty of sport. Leaving the line of march, therefore, we diverged toward the prairie; traversing a small valley and ascending a gentle swell of land. As we reached the summit, we beheld a gang of wild horses about a mile off. Beatte was immediately on the alert, and no longer thought of buffalo hunting. He was mounted on his powerful half-wild horse, with a lariat coiled at the saddle-bow, and set off in pursuit; while we remained on a rising ground watching his maneuvers with great solicitude. Taking advantage of a strip of woodland, he stole quietly along, so as to get close to them before he was perceived. The moment they caught sight of him a grand scamper took place. We watched him skirting along the horizon like a privateer in full chase of a merchantman; at length he passed over the brow of a ridge, and down into a shallow valley; in a few moments he was on the opposite hill, and close upon one of the horses. He was soon head and head, and appeared to be trying to noose his prey; but they both disappeared again below the hill, and we saw no more of them. It turned out afterward the he had noosed a powerful horse, but could not hold him, and had lost his lariat in the attempt.

While we were waiting for his return, we perceived two buffalo bulls descending a slope; toward a stream, which wound through a ravine fringed with trees. The young Count and myself endeavored to get near them under covert of the trees. They discovered us while we were yet three or four hundred yards off, and turning about, retreated up the rising ground. We urged our horses across the ravine, and gave chase. The immense weight of head and shoulders, causes the buffalo to labor heavily up hill; but it accelerates his descent. We had the advantage, therefore, and gained rapidly upon the fugitives, though it was difficult to get our horses to approach them, their very scent inspiring them with terror. The Count, who had a double-barreled gun loaded with ball, fired, but it missed. The bulls now altered their course, and galloped down hill with headlong rapidity. As they ran in different directions, we each singled one and separated. I was provided with a brace of veteran brass-barrelled pistols, which I had borrowed at Fort Gibson, and which had evidently seen some service. Pistols are very effective in buffalo hunting, as the hunter can ride up close to the animal, and fire at it while at full speed; whereas the long heavy rifles used on the frontier, cannot be easily managed, nor discharged with accurate aim from horseback. My object, therefore, was to get within pistol shot of the buffalo. This was no very easy matter. I was well mounted on a horse of excellent speed and bottom, that seemed eager for the chase, and soon overtook the game; but the moment he came nearly parallel, he would keep sheering off, with ears formed and pricked forward, and every symptom of aversion and alarm. It was no wonder. Of all animals, a buffalo, when close pressed by the hunter, has an aspect the most diabolical. His two short black horns, curve out of a huge frontlet of shaggy hair; his eyes glow like coals; his mouth is open, his tongue parched and drawn up into a half crescent; his tail is erect, and tufted and whisking about in the air, he is a perfect picture of mingled rage and terror.

It was with difficulty I urged my horse sufficiently near, when, taking aim, to my chagrin, both pistols missed fire. Unfortunately the locks of these veteran weapons were so much worn, that in the gallop, the priming had been shaken out of the pans. At the snapping of the last pistol I was close upon the buffalo, when, in his despair, he turned round with a sudden snort and rushed upon me. My horse wheeled about as if on a pivot, made a convulsive spring, and, as I had been leaning on one side with pistol extended, I came near being thrown at the feet of the buffalo.

Three or four bounds of the horse carried us out of the reach of the enemy; who, having merely turned in desperate self-defense, quickly resumed his flight. As soon as I could gather in my panic-stricken horse, and prime the pistols afresh, I again spurred in pursuit of the buffalo, who had slackened his speed to take breath. On my approach he again set off full tilt, heaving himself forward with a heavy rolling gallop, dashing with headlong precipitation through brakes and ravines, while several deer and wolves, startled from their coverts by his thundering career, ran helter-skelter to right and left across the waste.

A gallop across the prairies in pursuit of game is by no means so smooth a career as those may imagine, who have only the idea of an open level plain. It is true, the prairies of the hunting ground are not so much entangled with flowering plants and long herbage as the lower prairies, and are principally covered with short buffalo grass; but they are diversified by hill and dale, and where most level, are apt to be cut up by deep rifts and ravines, made by torrents after rain; and which, yawning from an even surface, are almost like pitfalls in the way of the hunter, checking him suddenly, when in full career, or subjecting him to the risk of limb and life. The plains, too, are beset by burrowing holes of small animals, in which the horse is apt to sink to the fetlock, and throw both himself and his rider. The late rain had covered some parts of the prairie, where the ground was hard, with a thin sheet of water, through which the horse had to splash his way. In other parts there were innumerable shallow hollows, eight or ten feet in diameter, made by the buffaloes, who wallow in sand and mud like swine. These being filled with water, shone like mirrors, so that the horse was continually leaping over them or springing on one side. We had reached, too, a rough part of the prairie, very much broken and cut up; the buffalo, who was running for his life, took no heed of his course, plunging down break-neck ravines, where it was necessary to skirt the borders in search of a safer descent. At length we came to where a winter stream had torn a deep chasm across the whole prairie, leaving open jagged rocks, and forming a long glen bordered by steep crumbling cliffs of mingled stone and clay. Down one of these the buffalo flung himself, half tumbling, half leaping, and then scuttled along the bottom; while I, seeing all further pursuit useless, pulled up, and gazed quietly after him from the border of the cliff, until he disappeared amidst the windings of the ravine.

Nothing now remained but to turn my steed and rejoin my companions. Here at first was some little difficulty. The ardor of the chase had betrayed me into a long, heedless gallop. I now found myself in the midst of a lonely waste, in which the prospect was bounded by undulating swells of land, naked and uniform, where, from the deficiency of landmarks and distinct features, an inexperienced man may become bewildered, and lose his way as readily as in the wastes of the ocean. The day, too, was overcast, so that I could not guide myself by the sun; my only mode was to retrace the track my horse had made in coming, though this I would often lose sight of, where the ground was covered with parched herbage.

To one unaccustomed to it, there is something inexpressibly lonely in the solitude of a prairie. The loneliness of a forest seems nothing to it. There the view is shut in by trees, and imagination is left free to picture some livelier scene beyond. But here we have an immense extent of landscape without a sign of human existence. We have the consciousness of being far, far beyond the bounds of human habitation; we feel as if moving in the midst of a desert world. As my horse lagged slowly back over the scenes of our late scamper, and the delirium of the chase had passed away, I was peculiarly sensible to these circumstances. The silence of the waste was now and then broken by the cry of a distant flock of pelicans, stalking like specters about a shallow pool; sometimes by the sinister croaking of a raven in the air, while occasionally a scoundrel wolf would scour off from before me; and, having attained a safe distance, would sit down and howl and whine with tones that gave a dreariness to the surrounding solitude.

After pursuing my way for some time, I descried a horseman on the edge of a distant hill, and soon recognized him to be the Count. He had been equally unsuccessful with myself; we were shortly after rejoined by our worthy comrade, the Virtuoso, who, with spectacles on nose, had made two or three ineffectual shots from horseback.

We determined not to seek the camp until we had made one more effort. Casting our eyes about the surrounding waste, we descried a herd of buffalo about two miles distant, scattered apart, and quietly grazing near a small strip of trees and bushes. It required but little stretch of fancy to picture them so many cattle grazing on the edge of a common, and that the grove might shelter some lowly farm-house.

We now formed our plan to circumvent the herd, and by getting on the other side of them, to hunt them in the direction where we knew our camp to be situated; otherwise, the pursuit might take us to such a distance as to render it impossible to find our way back before nightfall. Taking a wide circuit, therefore, we moved slowly and cautiously, pausing occasionally, when we saw any of the herd desist from grazing. The wind fortunately set from them, otherwise they might have scented us and have taken the alarm. In this way, we succeeded in getting round the herd without disturbing it. It consisted of about forty head, bulls, cows, and calves. Separating to some distance from each other, we now approached slowly in a parallel line, hoping by degrees to steal near without exciting attention. They began, however, to move off quietly, stopping at every step or two to graze, when suddenly a bull that, unobserved by us, had been taking his siesta under a clump of trees to our left, roused himself from his lair, and hastened to join his companions. We were still at a considerable distance, but the game had taken the alarm. We quickened our pace, they broke into a gallop, and now commenced a full chase.

33

ANONYMOUS, REVIEW OF ANDREW JACKSON DOWNING, "LANDSCAPE GARDENING AND RURAL ARCHITECTURE IN AMERICA," 1845

Of those who theorized about the American landscape and how it should be shaped in the antebellum period, none was more influential than Andrew Jackson Downing. In seeking to enhance the moral values of the United States through the beautification of the countryside and through "rural architecture," Downing helped create the American suburb. Downing's writings were closely in line with those of the reformer Catherine Beecher (see Chapter 7): both saw the picturesque landscape as inseparable from, and supportive of, the ideal single-family home where women would hold sway and produce a morally uplifting revitalization. Indeed, Downing envisioned the creation of the picturesque country house and garden as promoting a "genuine patriotism." We include here a review of Downing's book in order to convey a sense of how his ideas were received.

Whoever has sailed up the Hudson, in a clear day, may have observed, among other noble and beautiful sights that greeted him on the banks of that majestic river, the residence of the accomplished author of the volumes bearing the above-named titles. After leaving the wilder and bolder scenery of the highlands, at the opening where the hills begin to recede and stretch away with a somewhat more subdued sweep and even outline, he may have noticed at the left on the northern side of the village of Newburgh, a chaste and finished villa, in the Tudor gothic style, with growing trees surrounding it, marking the taste of an individual who has given a fine practical illustration, as well as an acceptable theory, of both Architecture and Gardening. Our country has not yet dedicated many temples to Beauty. We do not suppose that Mr. Downing would wish his quiet home to be regarded by the public as one of her shrines. But from his books we should believe him to be himself a sincere and enthusiastic lover of more than one of the "beautiful sisterhood" of the elegant arts; a willing and prompt encourager of whatever fosters and enlarges our æsthetic culture; a scholar of comprehensive views and a refined heart, and a hospitable gentleman of course. Such is the sort of person, we presume, that almost every reader of these works places before his mind and associates with the pages; and he is certainly an author of no ordinary good fortune who can convey through his writings so favorable and so true an impression of his qualities.

At any rate, in the department of toil and study which he has chosen and thoroughly given himself to, Mr. Downing stands, as an American, quite alone. It is, indeed, but a few years since he first made himself known in connection with the subject. The first edition of his "Landscape Gardening" was published in 1841. And whatever degree of merit may attach to his efforts, that merit can yet be shared, so far as the community is aware, by no other of our countrymen. He has neither companion nor rival. The ground is all his own. For any appearance of a competitor hither to question his claims or dispute his positions, or supersede his labors, he may be as dictatorial and as despotic as he pleases. We regard this as a circumstance by no means to be rejoiced in, for the country's

Originally printed in *United States Magazine and Democratic Review* 16 (April 1845): 348–63.

sake; we wish a multitude were reaching towards the same distinction when we take the general interest into consideration. And we cannot doubt that this Sir Joshua Reynolds of our rural decorations himself, if he might but advance the people at large to a deeper and more active interest in his favorite cause, would be ready to divide his empire and distribute the prerogatives of his sovereignty. Meantime, we will be grateful for what he has done. We will hope that he has communicated an impulse that shall not be soon spent; that he is kindling up an admiration for sylvan scenes and natural beauties that will not die till it has wrought out some worthy and durable results. And we will rejoice that a generous and liberal science has fallen, for its early advocacy, into the hands of no unscrupulous speculator on the one hand, or narrow-minded bigot on the other.

There are many things to be said, however, explanatory and vindicatory of whatever apparent deficiency exists among our people in regard to matters of taste. In the first place, the indifference is not so remarkable as it has been; it is beginning to be broken up: it is yielding to a more genial influence. There never was a stubborn hostility to artistic pursuits here. They have been neglected rather. But the circumstances of the time did not favor a very thorough or assiduous application to them. Every age has its work; every period its pressing necessity; every era its own glory. We have never heard that a nation in the first half-century of its existence, engaged too in a sharp struggle for its liberties, nay for its life, has devoted itself much to laying out flower-gardens, trimming hedges, or transplanting shrubbery. Our fathers, grave and earnest men, have had solid tasks on their hands. If the founders of the Republic had been inclined to push their horticultural experiments to much extent, they must have turned up the soil with their bayonets, literally made their swords their ploughshares, and without any transformation of the article, used the spear of a pruning-hook. They were not wandering like Arcadian lovers in search of luxurious valleys bathed in a perfume and dreamy air. Even that romantic and magnificent nature which the new world disclosed to their eyes hardly awakened a thought that could compare in majesty with the great thought of Freedom, Justice, Equality and Right which had taken firm possession of their souls. They did battle for the honest cause first; were loyal to the dictates of divine conscience; and is not that enough? Is it magnanimous in our transatlantic neighbors, especially for our brothers in England, to taunt the men they provoked with oppression and drove into hard necessities, with the reproach that they did not busy themselves with founding schools in the fine arts instead of thrusting back the arm of despotism? That they did not expend their energies in adorning Bunker Hill with comely terraces and covering it with parterres of roses, instead of shaping its summit into a rough redoubt and enriching it with heroes' blood?

But, what might have been foolish effeminacy or shameful unfaithfulness in the Puritans and first Republicans, is a very different thing to their posterity. The period of comparative poverty that followed the Revolution, imposing the necessity of rigorous exertion and strict private economy, is giving place to an easy condition. Wealth has begun to heap up its revenues, and it is time to study a wise, rational expenditure of it. Men of leisure, opulence and education are multiplying; and it ought to be a serious inquiry how they shall devote their resources for the common benefit, in methods worthy of the consideration of the age. The interests of even the subordinate departments of national endeavor demand consideration now. No nation can be said to have a harmonious and complete development or a true greatness, unless it has its Art. That element is essential. When it is wanting, something is wanting in the mind and heart of the people. If there is no constant ardor or devotion to the Beautiful; if no hands "build altars to the Sublime;" if there are no

> ——"longings to obey
> The haunting oracles that stir our clay,
> To make the unseen with actual glories rife
> And call the starred ideal into life;"

then the culture of that people has no founded and full perfection, its growth is not symmetrical, but one-sided and partial.

And this has begun to be understood and felt, here as well as elsewhere. There has been, within a few years past, a perceptible awakening of interest in these subjects. The attention of large numbers of persons has been directed to rural improvements, as well, indeed, as to artistic studies in general. In the vicinity of nearly all our cities are to be found mansions and villa residences, surrounded by grounds whose arrangement gives ample evidence that while much has been done, much more is to be expected. If there is any doubt that a new regard for gardening is springing up and growing, a few moments' examination of the establishments of Messrs. Hovey & Co., of Boston, or of Thornburn, of N. Y., or of Sinclair & Co., of Balitmore, or of Landreth, of Philadelphia, or of Prince, of Flushing, or of the Horticultural Magazine, started ten years ago and still conducted by the former firm, will satisfy the most incredulous. Individuals of competence are breaking away from the old rules or no-rules respecting architecture, becoming independent of the wretched customs that have been too prevalent, and asking for cultivated artists to design their buildings instead of ordinary carpenters; excellent and worthy men are carpenters, but justice to them does not require that they should be subjected to the mortification of a failure in attempting to do what they have not been educated to do. And justice to the interests of all requires that the higher processes of this, as of other intellectual vocations, should be assigned to a distinct and learned profession. The sort of structures that have been common—dull, inexpressive and heavy as they often are,—is to be exchanged for a positive and intelligent style. Convenience and elegance are about to be consulted, and not a senseless habit, nor a degenerate imitation of classic models. Kitchens, parlors and sleeping-rooms are not to be always thrown into the form of the Greek temple, nor domestic comfort sacrificed to the proportions of the Parthenon. Modifications of the Gothic and Italian, thanks to Mr. Downing and others such as he, are frequently tried already. To pretend that we love, or can love at present anything like a fixed, regular, original American style, would, of course, be preposterous.

A tendency to imitation—not merely a contemplation and study, for the discipline and expansion of the artist's faculty—but to imitation of the forms of antiquity, we regard, indeed, as the fault of all countries in this century, and not of ours alone. But long perseverance will bring such a style as we just spoke of, a style having reference to our climate, position and habits, and adapted in all respects to our needs. Human beings must have permanent habitations, from the burrowing Troglodyte to the luxurious *millionaire,* as long as their human hearts retain their social affections, and their physical constitution is unequal to the exposure of an unsheltered life, under the cold canopy of heaven. Then, every individual who erects an abode for himself or for another, should be conscious of his responsibility. He engages in a serious act. The consequences of what he does he ought not to regard as trifling or transient. They will remain after he has gone to a more silent mansion. Disease and mortality, inestimable misery may be entailed on a family, and on many families, by a careless builder. And harm no less real and lasting may be inflicted on the taste of the community. Whoever orders and superintends the erection of a human home, places that upon the earth which must, in the ordinary course of things, stand there and speak and exert its share of influence, for good or for evil, in moulding the preferences and guiding the future methods of more than one generation. Whoever builds an ill-proportioned, unsightly house, insults the community, wrongs his neighbors, perhaps lowers the standard of taste and detracts from the common weal. We are indebted, then, deeply, to those who, by their writings or their example, stir up a spirit of investigation, elevate the tone of feeling, and honestly help on a better day.

Besides, our population exhibits every day a quicker apprehension and appreciation of the results of art. Painters, sculptors, architects and musicians, are characters that constantly become more significant among us, and more operative. A disposition for travel is spreading. All classes find a new joy in turning their backs on cities, the artificial usages that exert a tyrannical dominion there, the conventionalities and outside vanities that glitter and mislead and bewilder there. The centralization that goes on at the bidding of commerce and manufactures is felt to carry with it a dangerous trial for purity of heart. It is found a salutary thing that the pulse, heated and swollen in the ambitious strifes and competitions of masses, should be quieted by the cool breath of solitude. The acquaintance between men and nature promises to strengthen into an intimacy. Nature in her holy simplicity is revealing herself, with all her wonderful and enrapturing loveliness, to watchful eyes. She calls the children of the land to witness that she has finer sights to offer than dioramas and panoramas, feeble theatricals and vaulting buffoons. She would turn off their eyes from sunsets of machinery, lamp-light and screens, and lead their feet up her steep mountain-sides till they stand face to face before the august splendors of an autumnal nightfall. She would show them a pomp and pageantry around their daily walks more gorgeous than in all the costliness of St Peter's. She would wean them from "the world's accursed sorcery," and lift up their hearts in loving worship to Him who made

> "the hills
> Rock-ribbed and ancient as the sun; the
> vales
> Stretching in pensive quietness between,
> The venerable woods—rivers that move
> In majesty, and the complaining brooks
> that make the meadows green; and
> poured round all,
> Old ocean's grey and melancholy waste."

. . . For this reason, the present should be regarded as the great opportunity to introduce enlightened views. The face of the country at its first settlement, and in many places that stage has not yet been passed, resembles the out-spread canvas with only outlines drawn, the colors not yet laid on; or rather, it is like the stucco while moist, ready for impressions, waiting to receive and promising to return the fresco-painter's touch. The form into which the virgin soil is now moulded must be retained for a long time to come. The contour of plantations, the curves of groves, roads, walks and river-banks, and the prominent features of architecture, cannot be easily obliterated. Inquiry ought therefore to be aroused and kept alive. Judicious and learned treatises ought to be written and circulated and read. Each citizen should feel that a personal responsibleness is devolved on himself, and contribute his own share to the advancement of the whole.

Should we be fortunate enough to have annals and reach a reverend age, it would be desirable that the masters of taste and the lovers of beauty in that remote epoch, looking back on our achievements and the impulse we shall have given, either in a right or wrong direction, shall find something in us to eulogize and be thankful for. Whatever tendency we encourage, let us remember that verdict of the hereafter. Should not we kindly provide for future antiquarians too? Should not we be gathering some worthy materials for decent ruins and interesting relics? In case such despisers of their present, and such lovers of the mouldering past,—of whatever "comes down covered with the awful hoar of innumerable ages," should, by any possibility, ever live upon these shores, as were Struvius and Camden and Stowe, or the Laird of Monkbarns himself, willing to pass their days tracing faded inscriptions, like old Bosius, in subterranean chambers, would it not be a bitter cruelty to disappoint their wonder-seeking curiosity? To leave them nothing but melancholy proofs that their ancestors had no eye nor hand for the elegant, or the graceful, or the endearing, but were only plodding disciples of the awkward and the temporary? Unlikely as it may seem now, little as the spirit of the times seems to favor such a prophecy, it is not impossible that men may again be born as richly inspired with veneration for what is ancient, and high, and hallowed by the centuries, as Burke and Sir Thomas Browne. We are amenable to posterity for what we do with our noble heritage.

In climate, as well as other fixed natural conditions requisite for success in the different departments of gardening, America enjoys the most various advantages. The United States alone, embracing so vast a latitude, include almost every possible temperature of atmosphere, and so admit nearly every kind of growth except those which belong to tropical and frigid extremes. They offer variety of surface enough to satisfy the most fastidious demand. They contain abundant opportunities in numberless localities, to secure within given limits a perfect harmony of the parts and an entire unity of expression. Art could carve our hills into monuments of combined beauty and grandeur much more easily than Stasierates could carve Mount Athos into a colossal statue of Alexander. There is smoothness and grace of outline in our scenery, sufficient to delight the author of the "Essays on the Sublime and Beautiful," with bold bluffs, and rugged peaks, and broken chasms, and romantic glades, enough to inspire an Ossian. Streams, lakes, rivulets, cascades, either make artificial works in water superfluous, or supply the means for their construction. There are slopes of as accurate a pitch of elevation as those that have made so fine an exposure of the plains of oriental celebrity in Media and Persia. There are forest trees of wonderful and diversified beauty, scattered in waving profusion over our hill sides and plains from the Penobscot to the Columbia. And as to foreign kinds not yet imported, we have a commercial intercourse that might enable us to vie with England, which has introduced into the island, within a century, some thirteen or fourteen hundred species. It will be deeply to be deplored if in ruthless haste we insult the Dryads, strip our land of its noble ornaments, cut trees away and never plant them, lay our homes and fields bare in a shameful nakedness, expose ourselves to the burning rays of summer and the bleak winds of winter,—all, when we might have enjoyed the delicious coolness, or the sheltering protection of shady groves and groups. We inherit English blood, too, and by virtue of that we should be gifted with an ardent love of whatever is picturesque and charming in rural life. . . .

We wish he [Downing] would only popularize his work still more; or that he would write another for a cheaper sale, and in that way made secure of a wider circulation. Not that he should abate one jot from the high standard of a pure taste; not that he should concede anything to false principles in the art. This would be one of the most pernicious of all possible mistakes. We have suffered enough from it already; we have had examples in abundance of a defiance of certain primary, fundamental rules that ought never to be violated. In the attempt to imitate grand classical models with the outlay of a few dollars; to reconcile a vast design with a small fortune; to compress the various beauties of antiquity into dimensions of a few feet—without marble, or anything in fact, but the lighter kind of materials, all fitness and comeliness have been sacrificed. The orders have been grossly insulted, the eye painted, Art burlesqued. Let the principles therefore be preserved and insisted on in their purity, at all hazards. Real artists must guide and sway, or there will be no lofty attainments. The past shows that if it shows anything. But practicability must be consulted. Common builders, all through the land, need instruction, instruction that they will heed, feel to be reasonable, and follow. A spirit of Art must be enkindled among the people. Great models must rise to plead silently with their subduing eloquence; and then the people must be drawn to behold them, to gaze upon them, to appreciate them, in the secret confession of enraptured minds. How was it in Florence and Venice and Rome, in the fifteenth century? The patronage we want is the patronage of the whole community, the riches of the opulent with the toil and the emotions of the poor. If the theory is correct, that the arts can flourish only under monarchs and a nobility, only amidst striking inequalities in all physical advantages, only amidst enormous accumulations, in a few hands, of affluence, luxuries and power, why then we must prepare our minds for a sad deprivation; we must despairingly conclude to dispense with the arts, and on those terms, we, for our part, will resign them cheerfully. But we cherish a different belief. What we are longing to see is a country covered with neat, tasteful, appropriate homes, in keeping with the scenery and simply adorned,—improvements of our natural inheritance. In order to see that, the people at large, we repeat, must be touched, moved or taught.

In conclusion, we have to say of our national prospects in these studies and toils of art: Let us be of good cheer: Let not the slowness of results dishearten us. The future has something in store for us, not only in triumphs of physical science, but in other kinds also. By and by, perhaps mechanism will even stop and wait a little for the beautiful arts to come up. Perhaps both will advance, with even step, together. When love-letters and business epistles are blown from New York to Boston, in an air tube, in half an hour; when the Mexican President and the Esquimaux chief, the one in his chair, the other on his mat of state, hold a pleasant after-dinner chat by the magnetic telegraph; when steam engines, waking the echoes of the Rocky Mountains, leave only some forty-eight hours' journey between Washington and Astoria,—then at least, if not before, we will have "Landscape Gardening and Rural Architecture" on a satisfactory scale. We cannot seriously bring ourselves to believe, as some seem disposed to think, that we are at present to be exiled from the whole Paradise of Beauty, and only permitted to glance back, with trembling and sighs of despair, at the cherubs' flaming swords.

34

H. M. ALDEN, EXCERPT FROM
"THE PENNSYLVANIA COAL REGION," 1863

The rise of a mature industrial economy in the latter half of the nineteenth century transformed the American landscape in countless ways and in countless places. Coal, perhaps
more than any other single thing, made that industrialism possible. H. M. Alden takes us on
a tourist excursion through the coal regions of Pennsylvania. Alden rides on the train, itself powered by coal, and presents this area in the form of a travelogue. While it may
seem strange to make a tourist destination out of an industrial landscape, Alden stresses
the natural beauty of the region and gives his readers a glimpse into a world most will
never see, though one which is already transforming all their lives.

There are few trips so delightful as that through the great Coal Fields of Pennsylvania,
made by means of the NEW JERSEY CENTRAL RAILROAD and its connections. For the time,
one can hardly choose amiss, from May, when the region puts on its robe of greenery, till
November, when it assumes its gorgeous autumnal attire.

The starting-point from New York will be the dépôt of the Central Railroad at Jersey
City. Avoiding the southern portion of New Jersey, which is one unbroken plain of sand,
as also the northern, which is hilly and for the most part but poorly cultivated, our course
lies through the very centre of the State—a region made up of alluvial valleys containing
some of the richest soil that is to be found in the country—and after this transit of New
Jersey, our route takes in quite entirely the eastern half of Pennsylvania. . . .

Now let us take a glance at the mines. . . .

If you wish to descend into the mine itself you will step into the car, which, after
having been emptied above, is again descending into the shaft. You are let down about
two hundred feet into the dark, holding one of the miner's lamps in your hand. But even
with your lamp you can see scarcely a rod ahead of you, and seem to be in perpetual danger of being run over by the coal-cars that rattle along the narrow defile, meeting you or
pursuing you. Soon you accustom your eye and feet to the features of your novel situation, and closely following your guide, you begin to thread the labyrinthian chambers,
narrow and low, that stretch away in all directions. Soon you come to an abrupt termination. Here you must tread carefully, for there may be danger ahead. The rock is mined
here by blasting. . . . You smell gunpowder—your guide hails out ahead—it is all right—
you come up just in time to hear of an accident which, not five minutes ago—indeed in
the last blasting—came near to proving fatal to a miner in the vicinity who mistook the
signal! You tremble for your fate, and are half-angry with your guide, who insists on
showing you how the thing is done—not the accident, but the process of blasting!

You are now quite willing to ascend again into the upper air, and are led back to the
entrance. You came down in a cart—but how are you to get back? The carts which go up
are filled with coal, so that you must go up some other way. You stumble against a slender framework which looks very like a gallows: it is upon this that your ascent is to be effected. The lower piece of the frame is not half a foot wide, and upon this piece your
guide steps, bidding you to follow. You expostulate, meekly expressing your preference

Originally printed in *Harper's New Monthly Magazine* 27 (September 1863): 455–67.

for the full coal-cart or any thing else; but it's of no use—the gallows or nothing!—and up you totter, clinging to the sleeve of your guide....

From Easton we return on the Central Railroad of New Jersey back to New York, having seen probably a greater variety of natural scenery than is usually the lot of railroad travelers, and having witnessed some of the most remarkable specimens of human ingenuity and skill which the country can furnish.... [T]here are few regions in which a summer vacation can be more pleasantly passed.

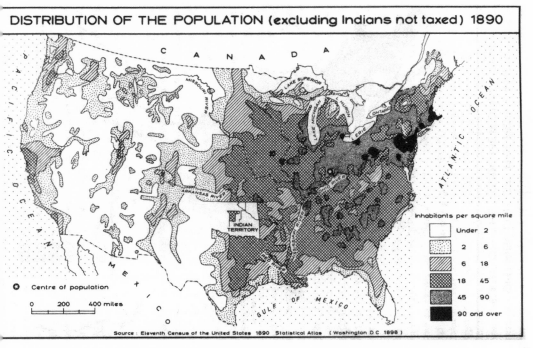

3.3. 1890 census map. At the World's Columbian Exposition, Frederick Jackson Turner declared that the 1890 census had concluded that there was no longer a frontier. We can see here, in the map to which he referred, that, indeed, there was no clear line between settled areas of the East and Midwest and those of the Great West. But, of course, there never was a clear line of settlement, with "Americans" on one side and empty frontier on the other. Native Americans had lived in great numbers and in a variety of settlements for millennia and even the recent European migrants had extended in waves across the southwest and California.

35

FREDERICK LEWIS ALLEN, "OUR NATIONAL SHABBINESS," 1915

"Our cities and towns and countryside are . . . undeniably shabby." So begins an eloquent and increasingly typical jeremiad against the state of the American landscape. It would be a theme Allen, editor of the *Atlantic Monthly, Century,* and *Harper's* magazines and best-selling author of a history of the 1920s, picked up from nineteenth-century cultural critics and would be amplified in the twentieth century. Even as Americans celebrated the unique beauty and possibility of the American landscape, many criticized what the new nation had done to the landscape in its frenetic growth. Allen is prescient in his focus on the auto-mobile as the cause of much of this shabbiness, even though the popular use of the automobile was just beginning. In 1901, there were nine miles of paved roads in the coun-try; by 1915, the number had reached into the hundreds. This attack on the effects of the car, especially in the postwar years, came to dominate critics of the American way of building. Finally, and perhaps inevitably when it came to evaluating the beauty of the archi-tecture and landscape that America had built, a comparison with Europe is made. Allen finds the "typically trim and orderly English town" a welcome sight in stark opposition to the already-sprawling American cities and towns.

Any sensible man, if he wishes to pass critical judgment upon a piece of his own work, puts it away for a while, letting other work and other thoughts occupy his attention. Fi-nally, coming back to his own production, he is able to see its real value—its special mer-its and special faults. For exactly the same reason, the man who wishes to see the peculiar virtues and shortcomings of his own country travels to Europe, or South America, or Canada, and on his return gains the sudden power of looking at familiar objects from a fresh angle. Things that he has always taken for granted—the behavior of his friends, the prevailing methods of business, the lay of the land—he sees projected in bold relief against a foreign background. All at once these things appear to him in their true rela-tions. He finds much to admire and be thankful for, of course; but he also finds much to criticize. And one of his most disappointing discoveries is likely to be that our cities and towns and countryside are in appearance undeniably shabby.

This melancholy fact first strikes the prodigal American when he lands at Hoboken or East Boston, and looking upon the dingy piers and sheds, and the staring brick build-ings of the waterfront, thinks of the trim docks at Plymouth, England, or at Cherbourg. Having survived the welcome of the United States Customs, the Prodigal goes out into the streets of the city. He finds them wide and untidy. The brick houses are expressionless; their windows are just so many square holes in the wall. Battered street-cars clang along under trolley-wires strung between sagging poles; the paving-stones are slippery with mud; stray newspapers flap feebly in the ooze and refuse of the gutters. The Prodigal con-soles himself with the thought that this district is not representative, and that he, perhaps, missed the corresponding portions of foreign cities; he postpones judgment, and goes on.

As he passes through the city, he naturally sees much of compelling beauty. Many of our public buildings and private residences testify to the skill and vision of our archi-tects. Fifth Avenue rivals Piccadilly and the Boulevards. Nothing in Europe has the pecu-

Originally printed in *House Beautiful* 32 (January 1915): 33–36.

liar magnificence of our skyscrapers. Yet on the other hand a vague feeling of disappointment must follow the Prodigal in his survey of New York or Boston or Chicago or any other American city, large or small. The average street has an unfinished appearance, resulting from the disturbing lack of anything like uniformity. A ten-story apartment-house or office building of dazzling brick and stone towers between a one-story shack and a frowzy vacant lot. Here and there loose gravel takes the place of the brick pavement; a passing wind picks up this gravel and carries it down the street in a regular Sahara dust-storm. The Prodigal hails a dingy street-car as with a long-drawn, heart-rending scream it turns the corner, climbs aboard, settles into a wicker-backed seat, and looks out of the window. As he watches, the vacant lots become more frequent, until they finally cover large districts; and the side streets at length degenerate into mere strips of macadam making off ambitiously through acres of tousled grass, piled with ashes, cans, and rubbish, and disfigured by rows of signboard, advertising everything from corsets and "Moxie" to last winter's theatrical attractions. A few ungainly houses rise here and there from the waste. The Prodigal is sickened by the utter and uncompromising dreariness of the picture. He had perhaps forgotten that a more or less continuous belt of this dump-heap desolation surrounds most of our big cities.

Finally the car sets the Prodigal down in an average suburb of the factory or mill type. Here rise the high chimneys of great prison-like factories of blackened brick; and about them huddle wooden shacks of the flimsiest description; unpainted (except, perhaps, for a huge advertisement of "Bull Durham" glaring from the roof), dilapidated, dismal. Rows of freight cars; rows of three-decker tenements lining the roads of cinder and dust; weeds and matted grass eking out a thirsty existence in the little front yards. Small wonder that the foreigner who looks upon such a scene thinks that Americans have no God but the Dollar. If they had any other idea in life, he argues, how could they live in such a scene, or—what comes to almost the same thing—let it surround their fellow men at their very back door?

The Prodigal continues his impartial investigation, and seeks out a typical seashore or lakeside "summer resort," being careful to select not a fashionable or in any way exceptional one, but an average settlement by an average beach, to which the average man can afford access. What does the Prodigal see? Rank on rank of little box-like cottages, which look as though they had been patched together yesterday and would fall to pieces tomorrow. Their only concession to beauty is a little jig-saw work along the eaves. Their screened porches give upon a sizzling tarvia boulevard, with telegraph-poles as a dominant theme in the general decorative effect. Motors passing and repassing without end; a view, of other little collar-box houses; a few trees, their leaves whitened by dust from the motors; and toward the sea, a great waste of sand disfigured by unsightly bath-houses—this is what our shoddy civilization has made of the seashore. Squalor and filth have no foothold here, to be sure; there is much sanitary plumbing and healthy living behind these blistered clapboards; but what an appalling aesthetic poverty! What a miserable cardboard makeshift of a village!

Farther away from the cities—in the mountains or the forests—the same ramshackle habitations have sprung up in the track of the pioneer; man has made a travesty of his appreciation of the beauty of hill and glade and field, by laying a tar road across them, and setting up in the most favored spots his general stores, his ice-cream parlors, his fruit stands, his bowling alleys, his auto repair shops, his gasoline supply tanks. The architecture of the ice-house and the bowling-alley is good enough for this average practical

American; he seems to have no realization of the utter lack of paint and finish and refinement in this mushroom village down whose dusty street the Prodigal sees him lolling in his jersey and khaki trousers and soiled sneakers.

My picture may not seem fair. I shall probably be told that I have dwelt only on the ugly, disregarding the beautiful. In all honesty, I do not believe that this objection holds. Even our "show towns," like Marblehead and Nantucket—to name two which are famous for their quaintness and charm—disappoint the Prodigal in so far as they are shabby. The artist who searches these towns for possible subjects finds everywhere a superfluity of straggling, unpainted wooden fences, of scrawny telegraph-poles, of dingy front yards, which obtrude themselves upon the most favorable compositions. And in the average American town the artist finds practically nothing to delight the eye; for every picture which the place offers, the most unpromising French or English village would offer a dozen. How one misses, in our country, those little refinements which are responsible for so much of the special beauty of even the humblest English villages: the smooth lawns, the well-clipped hedges, and above all, the gardens and window-boxes everywhere gay with flowers!

Again, compare our representative county hotels with those inns which correspond to them on the Continent. I doubt not that our hotels are cleaner "behind the scenes"— that there is better sanitation, that the flies are fewer—but the foreign inn is at least swept and garnished, with a gravel or brick terrace and a brave showing of flowers, whereas our typical hotel smoking-room is all spittoons and blue smoke; the windows more than likely to be unwashed; the unkempt or overdressed servants sling dishes about with a prodigious clatter of crockery. The landlord's generous hospitality is offered with few arts and graces; and one notices that his cultivation of the place is extensive rather than intensive; he had rather build a new wing or print a high-flown and redundant menu than trim his lawn or put a clean coat on the waiter.

What is the reason for this disheartening national shabbiness?

Many reasons suggest themselves. While Europeans construct their houses of brick and stone and stucco, we use wood largely. Wood is unsubstantial, and its decay is unpicturesque. Furthermore, paint wears off speedily; repainting is expensive, and the lack of paint is not becoming to a clapboarded house; it contributes more than almost anything else to give the general impression which I have described. Then again, our country is less fertile than England at any rate. The worst English lawns make some of our prize putting greens look moth-eaten. We are ever handicapped because the vegetation will not spring up to hide the scars on the face of the earth. And vegetation covers a multitude of sins.

Another reason is the enormous industrial growth of our country. We are cumbered more than other nations with the machinery of the railroad, the telephone, the telegraph, the trolley-car—until the air is full of wires and the cities are surrounded by train yards. Look at a Union Pacific locomotive, think of the tiny green toy which drags freight on the English railways, and you will understand our artistic handicap; for the locomotive, wonderful and inspiring as it is, can hardly be called an agent of neatness and cleanliness. And the expansion of advertising, side by side with our commercial expansion, serves to make the countryside hideous.

Let us see, though, if there are not causes which lie deeper still. Wood construction and advertising and commercial expansion are merely superficial allies of the Philistinism; what of us ourselves, the American people?

Ever since the Declaration of Independence, we have been proud of our democratic ideals. It is our boast that we don't care for appearance, that we extend the glad hand to our neighbor whether or not he sits on his piazza in his shirt-sleeves, provided his heart beats warmly beneath his President suspenders. The result follows as inevitably as night follows day. If we welcome a good fellow, shirt-sleeves or no shirt-sleeves, the good fellow will keep his coat off and be proud to show his sleeve-elastics. And he will say of his house, "I don't care how it looks so long as it's comfortable." Intellectual honesty this is, perhaps; beside it European anxiety to keep up appearances may be a whited sepulcher; but the European vice at least appeals more to the eye than the American virtue.

Besides, we Americans lack thoroughness. We build for the moment only. Why do more? we say. Our vaulting ambition tells us that progress is ever onward and upward, and that the American who is worth his salt is continually replacing little old things with big new things. Why make the country store a permanent structure? It will soon be outgrown. Such an argument, consciously or unconsciously formulated, accounts for much that is sordid and down-at-the-heel wherever the spirit of '76 has percolated. We exult fiercely in the growth of our country, our cities, our industries. While the European takes pride in the oldest house or church his town possesses, it is our delight to stand on the edge of a chasm in the street and say, "They're building here the biggest subway in the world. Within thirty years they'll have to rip it all to pieces and build a bigger one." For ourselves we build houses of shingles that will rot soon and lose their paint still sooner. Architecture doesn't much matter; bless us, we'll be in a man-sized house where we can afford architecture as soon as our ship comes in.

The vastness of our country, too, gives us a sense of elbow-room. If our own town is ugly, we are under no compulsion to set it to rights; we can always move out into the country. There is still plenty of land to go round. Instead of burying our rubbish, we pile it in the woods behind the house; nobody will see it there. When we go on a mountain-top picnic, we throw our boxes and egg-shells over the cliff, "out of everybody's way." The results of this amiable delusion are evident to anybody who glances at the waste lands about our cities and towns.

But are these the only reasons for our national shabbiness? I do not believe so. The incontrovertible fact remains that no man of good taste—no matter how ambitious or democratic or conscious of elbow-room—could put up the dreary shacks that line our streets; and no man whose neighbors had good taste could live very long in one of these shacks without realizing that it was offensive to the community. As a nation, we lack taste. It is true that we have made big strides since the days when our barbarism was the laughing-stock of Europe. Nevertheless, beauty is not with most of us a guiding principle of life; it is a luxury, a sort of candy to be enjoyed as an exception to our practical fare of beef and potatoes. To look for beauty in the commonplace things of our normal, worka-day existence simply never occurs to us.

I am told that the owner of the grimy shop can't afford to paint it. I reply that if the community had a developed artistic taste, he couldn't afford not to. Under such conditions, a trim shop would be the best possible advertisement, and the shopkeeper would soon realize the fact. Again I am told that the suburban householder can't afford to set his place in order. Very well; let us make the experiment; let us add a hundred dollars to his income. He will spend the money on a dozen useful objects, no doubt; but the odds are overwhelming that he won't think of wasting the money on window-boxes, or flowers for his front yard, or a can of paint for his blinds. Add five hundred dollars to the man's income, and we find him proposing to buy a Ford. House-painting can wait, he says. No, let us not blame his income. The trouble is with his scale of values.

In these days when the nations of Europe are blowing each other to pieces, and when the phrase "European civilization" is become a mockery, it is only too easy for us three thousand miles from the shock of war to pooh-pooh all things European, with an easy feeling that the "good old U.S.A." needn't worry about lessons to be learned on the Continent. Yet from the very civilization which is being hourly devastated we can learn much; and our task is to try in all humbleness of heart to learn it.

The Village Improvement Societies and the "Clean Up and Paint Up Weeks" have made a beginning. What must supplement these scrappy and insufficient efforts is the slow and painful process of educating people to see the difference between the beautiful and the ugly, and what is more, to realize that everything in this wide land can be made good to look upon—not only dwelling-houses and formal gardens and parks, but office-buildings and market-buildings and the smallest, humblest grass-plot. A hopeless task, it almost seems. All the clearer, then, is the call for us to face it, and little by little to eradicate this national disgrace.

36

DOUGLAS HASKELL, "ARCHITECTURE OF THE TVA," 1941

Douglas Haskell, one of America's important architectural critics, offered soaring praise of the Tennessee Valley Authority's program of dams, which transformed the valley's landscape and offered the prospect of cheap electricity to some of the poorest areas in the United States. The TVA represented potentially the most revolutionary aspects of Franklin Roosevelt's New Deal, far more radical than most of his more moderate reforms. Haskell seems here to recognize the uniqueness of the TVA's architectural undertaking. He is impressed by both the remarkable size of these public projects and the total design they required: merging the work of engineers and architects and transforming not a plot of land but all of the environment. There is a dark underside to this praise, however. For it was the hubris of grand public projects that, at the time, was also being applied to the delicate order of the city, to great destructive effect. The idea of "unbounded power," as Haskell writes, used with alleged "unreserved magnanimity" produced much of the urban renewal devastation of the post–Second World War world.

Quite plainly there is something unusually heartening and bracing about the architecture of the TVA, with its huge program of eleven dams and associated power plants, navigation locks, fertilizer plants and other industries, its fish hatcheries, its highways through recreational parks, its reforestation showing as pattern on the ground, its erosion-control projects, rural electric lines, defense plants, and new communities. Writers try to

Reprinted with permission from the May 17, 1941, issue of *The Nation*.

deal with the Tennessee Valley like Whitman. Younger architects report an experience not unlike getting religion. The director of the Museum of Modern Art in New York, in the course of opening the current show, said bluntly that the architecture of the TVA was "the greatest that America had yet produced."

The show itself is built around the magnificent photographs for which the Authority is noted, and which translate the homogeneity of the endeavor with a fine consistency of their own.

What is there about a building project such as that of the TVA that puts it so entirely apart from other large correlated ventures such as Rockefeller Center? The difference lies in the sense of something big being done for literally everybody, of unbounded power used with unreserved magnanimity.

Even in technical terms, the problem set in the Tennessee Valley had an unprecedented scope, complexity, and grandeur of scale, and the designers knew it. Of architecture as an art it used to be said that it dealt with the enclosure of space. That was when the primary concern was with individual buildings. The projects of a higher class were conceived—involving a consistent character for whole city areas or royal estates, as in the squares of Bloomsbury, the boulevards of Haussmann, the gardens of Versailles. In the Valley, however, architecture has taken hold of an area of 40,000 square miles, inhabited by 2,000,000 people, based on 650 miles of the all-important river.

Really to get hold of the idea, it is necessary to be quite strict in thinking of the whole Valley as the unit that was reshaped. The dams are merely the climaxes. The wooden areas and more level farms are an element that it was not necessary to touch. Nevertheless, they played their assigned parts in a grand theme first announced through the contour plowing of sloping hillsides, and then carried with ever-increasing complexity into the industrial culmination.

Before going into the handsome way in which this larger theme was knit, it may be well to speak of the most obvious part, the dams, locks, and power houses. The grand scale was not frittered away. The usual American dam is a giant with Lilliputian scholars and clowns posturing all over his back in togas or cap and bells. The ruggedness at TVA, the blocky big simplicity that is found even in auxiliary structures such as, for example, the control house at Gunthersville, may seem to casual visitors to be a natural consequence or purely "functional." This is not so. It is carefully evoked, a matter of design having to do with proportion, craftsmanship with materials, placing, scale, and a sense of the drama in the whole thing. Consider, if you will, the tall dam at Norris with the power house at its foot. The stately curved profile of the dam itself results of pure engineering calculation, but the way in which the power house below has been juxtaposed as a compact cube, off-center, and the way its openings have been cut in the geometrically patterned surface, even the way the roof has been covered with concrete slabs chiefly for the appearance from above, all are architecture in its oldest and most basic sense.

Much could be written on the cunning correlations made all up and down the line, and the more serious reader is referred to as *Architectural Forum* for August and *Pencil Points* for November, both 1939. These magazines, along with the exhibit at the Modern Museum, give some notion of what was produced in the way of a new index of current American design, in which the controlling thought was to hold to the larger purposes, to be neither clumsy nor over clever, to do generously the job at hand and then quit.

What remains to be done here is to insist on the larger view of architecture itself that TVA has generated. A glimpse of this larger formative pattern might be found in the cunning that quarried the stone so as to leave behind parking slips for pleasure boats after the water had risen. The same thought could be found in the design of roads as a new kind of "freeway" assuring both more rapid deliveries for farmers and a greater enjoyment of the landscape for the visitor on vacation. It could be found in the multiple-minded fashion in which means were shaped to several sets of ends and the entire area so homogenously treated that there could be no reason for confining the term "architecture" to the one part where the materials used happened to be concrete and steel instead of soil, trees, water surfaces, or rock. Here all elements conveyed the same theme—of nature tended and controlled so as to yield nourishment, power, and enjoyment all together.

It's as if Joshua had fit a new battle of Jericho and the walls had come tumblin' down. In the forward view that is opened at TVA the walls, even the big ones, have dropped to a minor role. The glimpse that is given is of man working upon the *whole* of his environment to put it into habitable, workable, agreeable, and friendly shape. As a concept architecture can today be no less.

The spirit manifest in TVA shows that the designers were aware of such an aim and sought for architectural expression that would make it speak. There is something still further that seems important in the Valley. Here the complexity of the planning put the American people to a severe test, and they came out of it with colors flying, with a *collaborative* venture. Not only did the architects collaborate with the engineers, and both with the farmers, and so on, but nobody had his name put on a commemorative tablet. All the inscriptions give only the date and the motto, "Built for the People of the United States." It could have been added, "—and by Them." In this collaborative effort the people of America showed themselves so much more than the equals of any loudmouth for some superimposed "new" order that their doubts ought to dissolve away.

Mayor LaGuardia told, with great effect, how close we came at the start to thinking it was "too big" for us and "giving it all away." The thought that a people might turn nerveless now that a TVA has been built, and proceed to give over, is enough to make one sick.

37

JOHN D. MACDONALD,
"LAST CHANCE TO SAVE THE EVERGLADES," 1969

Rachel Carson's *Silent Spring* (1962) was for the environment what Jane Jacobs's *Death and Life of Great American Cities* (1961) was for cities: a call to arms against the dominant, and in their minds, destructive approach to growth and development. Long after the social movements of the 1960s withered, the environmental movement remained powerful. Indeed, at the beginning of the twenty-first century, the environmental movement remains one of the few social movements of the 1960s that has been able to galvanize those on the right and the left wings of the political spectrum. Here, John MacDonald argues pas-

Originally printed in *Life*, September 5, 1969. © 1969 Life Inc., reprinted by permission.

sionately against a new "jetport" adjacent to the Everglades. The argument, reminiscent of many writings about the loss of environmental treasures, declares imminent doom in the face of massive development and governmental inaction, but offers the saving grace of citizen action.

In the beginning you do not see very much or hear very much, and you do not understand.

Then one afternoon there was no movement of the air. There was heat, sweat and a silence so vast that when I heard a mosquito near my ear, it was exactly like a night sound of long ago in Mexico, hearing a truck in its lowest gear whining down the mountains miles away. A thunderstorm moved toward me and toward the west. By the time it began to stir the air in hot gusty puffs, it was a startling indigo wall across the world, a constant rumbling, and I stood in strange golden yellow light waiting for it.

Cooler air then, and good wind, with each gust making its own shape, as it came across the saw-grass pastures. Fat pink lightning banging down, and then the oncoming roar from far away of the smashing, drenching rain. When it ended, I could hear the same roar, receding, hurrying west. Incredible smell of a well-washed twilight, and 10 trillion frogs and toads and peepers welling into a deafening rain-chorus. Birds in that straight, no-nonsense flight pattern of heading for the rookery. Fragile insects flying. (How did they escape the smashing rain?) Some blooms closing, and leaves folding, and other blooms, spicier, opening on the hammocks and uplands where the tree frogs are.

Then I began to understand that it is not memorable fragments, but a complex unity, all of it a savage and symmetrical pattern of interwoven, interdependent lives, from gator to gnat, from bald cypress to microdot of green algae, from giant metallic dragonfly to spider-shaped invisibility of the redbug. It is a complexity which took eons to style and plan itself for this special place, climate, condition, through unending trial and error.

Now we are on the brink of destroying that complex unity. Experts in such matters—biologists, hydrologists, geologists—have all come to the same alarming conclusion: if we proceed with the plans to establish a commercial jet port squarely across the last natural watershed in south central Florida, we will kill what is left of the Everglades, kill the Everglades National Park, upset the water tables and the water supply in all south Florida, cripple the shrimp industry, stunt commercial and sports fishing, invite salt intrusion and possibly even alter the very climate of the Florida peninsula.

The jetport tract, all 39 square miles of it, is 45 miles west of Miami, about 55 miles east of Naples on the gulf, roughly a third of it in Dade County, the rest across the line to the west in Collier County. In late September of 1968, less than a week after the first parcels of land were acquired by condemnation proceedings, the Dade County Port Authority at Miami let a contract for a two-mile east-west jet training runway with taxi strips and aprons. The strip is completed. It is the first phase of the plan to build the world's largest jetport—big enough to enclose Los Angeles Airport, Dulles, Kennedy, San Francisco and a cluster of several smaller fields as well. Federal funding for this monster project could exceed half a billion dollars.

The commercial-political-financial establishments of Dade, Collier and Monroe counties are sweaty with the excitement of a new boom, huge profits, explosive growth. Every bit of this silent wilderness land around the jetport site is privately owned, and much of it has already changed hands in heavy-risk commitments. One Miami real estate agent has assembled a package almost as big as the proposed jetport itself for a single corporate buyer. Collier County leaders have stated in Naples that they intend to make the jetport area the largest industrial center in Florida, and boosters are already talking about such projects as cutting a deep-water canal from the gulf to the jetport to barge in the jet fuel and construction materials, and getting the authorized extension of Interstate 75 from Tampa to Miami officially realigned to bisect the jetport, with a thousand-foot right-of-way from the gulf to the Atlantic.

The Everglades National Park is already in such fragile condition that only by the most careful planning could it be nurtured back to health and stability. So why save a sick park when it stands in the way of progress?

If it were merely that it is a unique 1.4 million-acre wonderland, visited by over a million people a year, merely an eerie, silent environment for gator, wood ibis and tree snail, one might be able to make some kind of a feeble case for the proposed jetport location. But over the last 40 years the U.S. Army Crops of Engineers has demonstrated for all of us what the death of the Everglades might mean.

The jumbo jetport will go right in the path of this ancient flow, and even if great care is taken within the jetport areas to keep that flow moving as naturally as possible, the urban growth and industrialization around the jetport would make such concern futile.

It is the entire complex that will finish off the park, mostly by dramatically altering the volume and the characteristics of the essential water flow. That southward flow will be used water, treated and released. It will leave so much nitrogen-compound nutrient from animal and human waste in the water that, according to Frank Nix, long-time hydrologist at the park, the explosive growth of undesirable algae would crowd out the natural algae, fundamental to the life support system of the Glades and the park.

In addition to water pollution, there will be soil pollution—the inevitable fallout from the unburned components of jet fuel, inefficiently consumed at low altitudes, and unburned fuel jettisoned in emergency situations.

Nor is jet noise compatible with that strange and unique flavor of the Everglades, with a silence so brooding and intense that the sudden slap-splash of a feeding fish is as startling as an explosion. What such noise might do to the reproduction rate of the wild birds, already diminished thanks to the ingestion of DDT in the food chain, is not yet known, but one could hardly expect it to be beneficial.

The Everglades and the national park cannot survive this final insult. The ramifications of the death of an entire ecological system have always been more grave, more far-reaching, more deadly to man himself than anyone realized until the long process of decay was too far along to be reversed.

The equation is simple, clear and elegant. Is this the place where, finally, we stop brutalizing our environment in the name of that sort of progress which makes things quite different—but never any better, and usually worse than we could have believed?

38

JOHN A. KOUWENHOVEN, EXCERPT FROM "PRELIMINARY GLANCE AT AN AMERICAN LANDSCAPE," 1961

Over a century after Washington Irving's celebrated visit to the prairie, John Kouwenhoven, along with many others, returned there to find the essence of the American landscape in the mid-twentieth century. Kouwenhoven took the train through this most "characteristic landscape." A train trip like this, however, had become increasingly anachronistic. In the postwar period the word "glance" in Kouwenhoven's title would define the experience of the American landscape, but that glance came from a car window. Never before had so many so completely found their view of the American landscape defined by a view from the road.

From the blister-dome of the Wabash Railway's *Blue Bird*, en route from St. Louis to Chicago, the spring landscape of central Illinois is one of wide, level horizons with now and then a clump of leafed-out willows or a brief row of maples or elms which have budded enough to look hazy. It is a land of pale coffee-colored fields, darkened in irregular blotches where cloud shadows lie and in strips where a tractor-drawn disc harrow has recently passed. A lone man driving a tractor is the only human being you are likely to see for miles, but there are many other living things: cattle—black, or black and white, and still winter-fuzzy—standing or lying in the unplowed fields; pigs and sheep whose young scamper away from the fenced railroad track when the train passes, though their elders are accustomed and remain still; and quite often a pheasant, green neck feathers shining in the sun, standing close to the track, always with his back turned to the passing train, looking over his shoulder at it but not otherwise disturbed.

The only city you go through is Decatur, a momentary collection of factories, warehouses, and handsome grain elevators, and a business district with some stone buildings of modest dimensions. Most of the towns you go through are small and irregularly square, with streets at right angles to the railroad, many of which do not cross the track but stop short at earth mounds partly covered with grass. Each town has a corrugated sheet-metal grain elevator and a Quonset warehouse or two near the wooden station. The houses are wood, with fruit trees blooming in their board-fenced yards. But there are almost no people in sight, just a few cars moving in the streets or parked at the curbs. And in less than a minute you are out on the prairie again.

Occasionally the level fields are studded with shining ponds, and now and then you see small streams whose flashing surfaces are almost flush with the fields they flow through, or shallow gullies banked with tin cans and bottles which glitter in the sun. Running alongside the track all the way, three tiers of shining wires dip from and rise to the crossbars on the telegraph poles—each of the three crossbars with room for ten bright insulators, some missing, leaving gaps like broken rake teeth. Sometimes the ground bordering the track also dips and rises where the right of way has been sliced down to grade through long, flowing swells of land. But the only real break in the general flatness is a huge eroded mesa, man-made

Originally printed as the Introduction to *The Beer Can by the Highway: Essays on What's American about America*, pp. 13–19 © 1961 John A. Kouwenhoven. Reprinted with permission of The John Hopkins University Press.

from the waste of what may be strip-mining operations, which stretches along west of the track for miles, somewhere near Reddick or Essex judging by the timetable.

Most of the time there is just the wide, flat landscape of harrow-smoothed earth, ruled into squares by lines of wire fence strung on thin metal posts (not split wooden posts, as in New England), and along the fences there is a fringe of the dry, blond husks of last year's uncut grass, with now and then a large, unaccountable sheet of wilted brown paper caught on the wire barbs. Once in a huge, immaculate field near Symerton, roughly forty-seven miles out of Chicago, I saw a rock. It was about the size and shape of a dented watermelon, but no one had bothered to move it; the parallel harrow tracks in the smooth dirt diverged to avoid it, then came together again.

Once in a while you see white roads taped across the landscape, and if they cross the track the diesel honks at them. Once in a while you see a lonely schoolhouse, usually of wood, with a flag flying briskly from a pole in front and a yellow bus standing in the grassless yard. Once in a while a field is dotted with round metal grain bins with cone-shaped roofs, looking like a battery of stumpy, unlaunchable rockets. And once in a while, too, near one of the clumps of trees, you see a white farmhouse, with red or white barns—big barns, with ventilators on their roofs looking like little barns straddling the ridgepoles of the big ones. Near the houses tall windmills stand on spindly iron legs, mostly with broken blades in their fans, and almost every farm has a gawky television antenna in the yard as tall as, or taller than, the windmill.

This is a landscape which a century ago looked to a Chicago newspaperman like "the untilled and almost untrodden pastures of God." Standing with a group of excursionists in the middle of the rolling prairies, the reporter, Benjamin F. Taylor, felt as if he were in the center of a tremendous dish.

> Not a tree nor a living thing in sight; not a sign that man had ever been an occupant of the planet . . . The great blue sky was set down exactly upon the edge of the dish, like the cover of a tureen, and there we were, pitifully belittled.

A century later the pastures of God are well-tilled and much trodden. The prairie has become, in fact, a technological landscape: subdivided by wire fences, smoothed by tractors, tied to the urban-industrial world by wires, roads, and rails, and by the invisible pulses felt in the lofty antennas. The height of those antennas measures the strength of the city's pull. As you leave St. Louis they grow taller and taller until, in central Illinois they outtop and almost outnumber the trees. As you approach Chicago they grow shorter until, when you reach the suburban landscape of supermarkets, drive-ins, and rows of little square houses with little square lawns, they need be only small, solicitous bundles of branching wire rods attached to the house chimneys.

The prairie landscape no longer belittles man. It is still vast, and you see very few people as you watch from a train window. But man's technology has modified everything from the texture of the earth itself to the stance of the pheasants.

This landscape, through which I last traveled three years ago, came freshly to my mind as I began to assemble and revise the essays in this book. It did so, I think, because it embodies a number of the forms and patterns which seem to me to be characteristic of a civilization based as ours is upon a distinctive blend of technology and a somewhat untidy but dynamic form of democracy. And it is with some of these characteristic forms and patterns, and the indigenous energies they express, that these essays are primarily concerned.

There are other American landscapes, some of which embody forms and patterns that seem to have little in common with those of the prairies: the landscape of Maryland's trim and cultivated Eastern Shore; the barbaric splendor of the Southwest's mesas and canyons; the grim and powerful landscape of River Rouge; and—more like the prairies than at first appears—the New York skyline.

The most endearing and comfortable landscape, to me, is in Vermont, where I spend the summers on a farm which lies like a large green saddle blanket on the small of the back of a mountainous ridge along the western border of the state. Eastward from the farm you can look down into the domesticated Vermont valleys of Pawlet and Dorset, with pasture clearings running well up the enclosing slopes. Westward you look out over a widening, open-ended valley where the tree-hidden village of Rupert lies, where dogs bark distantly in the evening, and where an occasional light blinks through the trees after dark. At the far, open end of the valley the D & H Railroad comes down from the north and curves westward into New York State toward the Hudson and the Susquehanna. You cannot see the trains but when the rain is right—when rain is coming—you can hear the imitation steam-whistle which the railroad, in tune with the industrial sentimentality, has substituted for barking horns on its diesels. And beyond the valley's open end the continent rolls gently westward through the Mohawk Valley and then invisibly onward past the Great Lakes, lifting easily across the prairies and plains. You can believe that if the atmosphere were glass-clear and the earth did not curve you could see two thirds of the way to the Pacific, for there is nothing high enough to block the view till you come to the Laramie Range and the big horns. Closed and friendly to the east, open and inviting to the west, it is a likable landscape.

It is, I suppose, the landscape of this eastward-and-westward-looking Vermont farm, superimposed upon the landscape of New York's skyline, which controls the point of view from which I have looked at America. But the characteristic landscape of the America I have looked at in these essays seems to me to be the "interminable and stately prairies," as Walt Whitman called them, ruled off by roads and fences into a mathematical grid. They have become, as Whitman thought they would become, the home of "America's distinctive ideas and distinctive realities." They produced Abraham Lincoln and the city of Chicago—both of which are ideas as well as realities and both of which seem to me, at least, to be distinctively American.

39

WILLIAM F. BUCKLEY, EXCERPT FROM "THE POLITICS OF BEAUTY," 1966

William F. Buckley, the founder of the *National Review*, agrees that beautifying and protecting the natural and human environments is important. In this way, he follows the writings

Originally printed in *Esquire* 66 (July 1966): 50–53, 116.

of one of his columnists, Russell Kirk (see his essay in Chapter 8), who lambasted corporations who had little concern for historic sites, except as obstacles to profit. Indeed, the nostalgic longing for an earlier time of small towns and "order"—well in evidence in this piece—was in line with conservative philosophy of the postwar era. But Buckley resists the solution increasingly put forward by liberals: that protecting and beautifying the environment require governmental regulation and intervention. For Buckley, great architecture and a beautiful natural environment can spring only from the "genes of a community" and cannot be legislated from state houses and Congress.

It is a thesis of the literature of protest against the way physical America is shaping up that external harmony is necessary for the repose of the soul. I suppose I am not absolutely certain that this is so, but I do know that it is so for some people (for instance myself), though not necessarily for those people who, according to fashion's book, are the most to be admired in the human race. These last include the inner-directed types of whom the absentminded professor is the most widely caricatured example, who are generally oblivious to external surroundings. And there are the hard intellectuals, whose physical life is mostly spent inside the cavernous libraries, and whose intellectual life is in the mind; who could not care less whether one, two, or a dozen trees grow in Brooklyn.

One's own experience counts greatly. Mine, during my childhood, was a continuing confrontation with beauty. I do not know whether I'd recognized it as such, or even whether I'd have thought back about it as such, except that my father was constantly calling attention to it, wherever we were—and that was, on account of the travels to which his work took him, all over the place. He had lived, after college, in Mexico, and intended to settle there and would have, except that he backed the wrong revolution, which was easy enough for a political activist to do since during the period there was almost always an incumbent revolution. So he left, escorted to the border by armed guard, in 1921, and took with him the plans for a beautiful house and garden he had just begun to build on which he had lavished infinite attention. He bought a large house in Sharon, drawn to the little town in northwest Connecticut for the simple reason of its extraordinary beauty. We went to Paris, and Switzerland, and London, for protracted stays when I was a boy, but kept popping back to Sharon, where we settled more or less permanently during the Thirties, spending winters in Camden, South Carolina, where my father undertook the rehabilitation of a derelict antebellum house which is surrounded now, the fruit of his diligent supervision, with whole terraces of flowers, red and white and lavender. I remember as a boy my older brothers and sisters giving vent to their underworld amusement because, not withstanding my father's vigilance, a red azalea had had the nerve to raise its head smack in the middle of a bed of white azaleas, quite against my father's orders, which no vertebrate had ever been known to defy. . . .

I am, then, myself committed to the notion that attractive external surroundings can mean a great deal, and to the corollary that something ought to be done about it: just how and just what being, of course, the question. Next in order of consideration is the question, *Who knows what is beautiful?* Perhaps it boils down to the easier question, *Who will decide what is beautiful?* That, after all, is merely a matter of political arrangement. The Congress of the United States, for instance, is absolutely in charge of deciding what is beautiful and what isn't in respect to its own quarters. Sam Rayburn was in charge of the Congress of the United States at the time the plans were drawn for a new House Office Building, and so it came about that the sovereign legislature of the United

States, representing all the people, devised and constructed a building not merely lacking in beauty, but positively drunk in its featurelessness, $86,000,000 worth of white neo-classical blah. The thing was, presumably, designed by an architect, which therefore raises the other question, *Is there an expertise in beauty?* To which the answer of course is, yes and no; yes in that some people's eyes are better than other people's; no in the sense that there is continuing disagreement on just whose eyes are operatively better. And this, in turn, makes insufficient the recommendation of Mr. Daniel Patrick Moynihan, a very fashionable intellectual who also happens to be very bright, that the architectural "profession" form a lobby. "There wasn't a special interest in America that didn't have a hunk of [the highway] bill except the architects," he observed at one of our regular conferences of disgust over the deteriorating face of America, enjoining the architects to become "a lobby." Why not? The most beautiful buildings in the world are designed by architects. But so are the ugliest buildings in the world, and it isn't that the beautiful buildings are beautiful because they are free of the pressures of the marketplace, though those pressures do figure, often for the worse, in certain types of buildings. Disagreements about architecture—and indeed about all art—are often written about as though they were being fought between the beautiful spirits and the Philistines, which is all very well until the moment comes when with absolute confidence we are asked to distinguish between the two in such a way as is aesthetically, or politically, acceptable. The monster that rises over the Grand Central Building in New York is despised by Norman Mailer, and adored by August Heckscher. Heckscher is In, culture-wise; indeed he was J.F.K.'s Number One on-duty aesthete, and Mailer is concededly erratic; but he is in very steady company in his dislike of the Pan Am Building, and quite apart from that, greatly respected for the occasional jewel that washes in with the flotsam and jetsam that inundates us from his ongoing collision with the world he lives in. The most galvanizing words recently uttered on the matter of saving America the Beautiful came from the President of the United States, whose superb French cook, inherited from J.F.K., recently resigned in despair after the superordination of a dietitian from Austin, Texas, who ordered him to serve beets with cream on them at affairs of state. Can a man who thus misorders his own kitchen be trusted to design the Acropolis?

It is not safe, in a word, to assume that great and beautiful buildings are automatically what happen when you allocate more money to be spent on great and beautiful buildings—even when you give the money to those among our highest political authorities who bloviate most regularly on the subject of the beautiful life. To say that taste differs is not to concede, to be sure, that all tastes are equally defensible. It is merely to say that the demonstration of the poorer and better taste is not easy to make, that it often depends not merely on a blackboard demonstration whose at-onceness overwhelms the Philistine; but on a lengthening perspective; the kind of thing which over a period of several hundred years came absolutely to establish that Westminister Abbey and Chartres, both built about the same time, were respectively a catastrophe and a thing so sublime as might have been designed by God Himself. There weren't any art critics in the thirteenth century who attended cathedral openings, but it isn't necessary, in order to make the point, that there should have been. The "finest" available designers and craftsmen were called together at about the same time to construct the two elysian cathedrals. They did their best, and there is no reason to believe that a talented designer doing his best doesn't, during the period of his absorption with his fancy, proceed with as much conviction—and as much of a right to his conviction—as the critic. If a well-trained architect can act as a defective impulse, so can a well-trained critic. It is time that gradually erodes the dross, settling the impression, and making possible the universal judgment. When Johann Sebastian Bach died, the obituarists acclaimed him as a choirmaster and organist, and his son Carl Philipp Emanuel as the composer. Obviously this is not an argument against all public buildings. Familiarity breeds contempt, a Cambridge debater argued before the First War, opposing the maximization of contact between His Majesty's and the Kaiser's subjects. "True," his opponent observed, "but a lack of familiarity breeds nothing at all." . . .

As regards the first, I fear greatly that it is only a matter of time before some President will think to declare War against Ugliness. He may very well be a President who couldn't care less about ugliness, but who is desperate for programs by which to confer Democratic benefits on his people. When that happens, theoretical arguments will rage, even as, less conspicuously, they rage at this moment, for instance on the question of what are the rights of the collectivity over the individual. Some hard thought should be given to that problem and the sooner the better, and herewith a modest and, I hope, heuristic contribution.

The role of our various governments, local, state and Federal, ought to remain primarily negative. Governments are as a rule better at reeling off prohibitions than fancying themselves as creative artists. I have mentioned the overarching problem: how is the government going to decide what is beautiful; will the Library of Congress send down a memo on the matter? And secondly, don't we need to understand that the kind of organic beauty we most greatly need to encourage in our towns and cities can issue only from the genes of the community. Infusions of Federal money and Federal bureaucrats tend, as Jane Jacobs has amply demonstrated in her book on the life and death of the great American cities, to upset the glandular balances of individual neighborhoods; and the baby is deformed.

In some areas, the Federal Government has intruded probably forever. One never quite realizes, in retrospect, why the Federal Government had to get into some of the acts, but so it happened. As regards highway building, for instance, the program arose like Venus from the Cyprian seas ordaining that henceforth the government would pay ninety percent of the cost of building interstate highways. That, of course, gave the Federal Government a little leverage, which it sought to exercise, by happy accident, for the common good—by offering a bribe (an extra one-half of one percent) to those states which would agree to ban billboards along the banks of the highways. Only seven states have qualified for that subsidy. . . .

As regards the maintenance of the natural beauty of great parts of the nation, the weight of the argument is, once again, on the side of the public. The present Secretary of the Interior Department, Mr. Stewart Udall, is, I think it is fair to say, as aggressive a champion of the necessity to maintain oases of natural beauty as anyone who ever held high Federal office. Sometimes, to be sure, he does leave the impression that he resents any private dwelling at all, on the grounds that it is liable to get in the way of a meandering buffalo. But his occasional excesses, unlike those of some of his own coadjutors, are tolerable in an age that very much needs to be reminded of the factor of beauty, natural and man-made. Mr. Udall has launched a great land-acquisition program, attempting to husband the natural parks to the use of the public. I must depart from the company of those conservatives who are always resenting the acreage owned by the government, always provided said government does not go hog wild, and that the great reservations continue—as some of the city parks for instance do not—to be dedicated to the enjoyment of the public (42,500,000 people visited one or another of our natural parks during the last year, which suggest Udall must be doing something right). The withholding of land, to be retained in its supernal beauty, is a legitimate function of government, as Adam Smith was among the first to observe. . . .

The community. It is cursed by indifference. That indifference is perhaps exaggerated, but it is most certainly there. "Indifference," sighs Herbert Read, "is endemic. . . . a disease which has spread through our whole civilization, and which is a symptom of a lowered vitality. The sensibilities are dulled and the average human being no longer cares to feel the keen edge of life, to have freshness in vision or zest and savor in the senses." Mr. Read is very largely correct, but it is demoralizing to take his conclusions as an absolute judgment on the current state of mind, because if one does, one faces a dilemma. It is, very simply, that the only way to do anything about the problem of natural beauty and architectural harmony is to do so athwart the people's indifference; indeed, by extension, athwart their will.

At this point a word should be said about the Very Gloomy. The point can be made, as with Mr. Udall, that their exaggerations are galvanizing. But the opposite point can also be made, that their gloom is so total as to invoke not the impulse to reform, but the impulse to despair.

Herewith Miss Marya Mannes on her especial irk:

"*Cans. Beer cans. Glinting on the verges of a million miles of roadways, lying in scrub, grass, dirt, leaves, sand, mud, but never hidden. Piels, Rheingold, Ballantine, Schaefer, Shlitz, shining in the sun or picked by moon or the beams of headlights at night; crashed by rain or flattened by wheels, but never dulled, never buried, never destroyed. Here is the mark of the savages, the testament of wasters, the stain of prosperity.*" And her climax: "*Slowly the wasters and despoilers are impoverishing our land, our nature, and our beauty, so that there will not be one beach, one hill, one lane, one meadow, one forest free from the debris of man and the stigma of his improvidence.*" Now: does that kind of thing make you want to give up beer cans, or does it make you wonder whether Miss Mannes has, as regards beer cans, the same kind of problems that the fellow had who went to the psychiatrist and kept brushing the mosquitoes off his arms and legs?

Or there is the crushed poet, an anonymous employee of the Department of the Interior, who comes up with the grisliest metaphor of the season in, no less, an official publication of DepInt:

"The shift of our Nation from a predominantly rural to an urban population *has made a sinister sandwich of much of our land, buttering our soil with concrete and asphalt, piling people on people, and then hanging a pall of polluted air over all.*" And, not to be outdone by Miss Mannes, he reaches his own immolation: "*If current trends continue unchecked, in another generation a trash pile or piece of junk will be within a stone's throw of any person standing anywhere on the American continent.*" Surely before that happens the hungry cosmos will have gulped down the sinister sandwich and eliminated all of our worries?

40

PETER BLAKE, EXCERPT FROM *GOD'S OWN JUNKYARD*, 1964

Peter Blake's book falls into the jeremiad tradition of Frederick Allen and the earlier "pine lands" commentator. In a relentless portrait of the ways in which Americans were participating in the "planned deterioration" of America's landscape, Blake saw much more than a visually degraded world; he believed he was witnessing the destruction of civilization in America itself. A series of works sprang from Blake's *God's Own Junkyard* in the following decades, highlighting the "uglification" of the American landscape and the decline in the "sense of place." Though it was Gertrude Stein who demeaned Oakland by declaring that "there is no there there" (and not insignificantly shaping the image of that city for generations), it was Blake, and John Brinckerhoff Jackson among others, who launched an intellectual assault against the "placelessness" of the American landscape. In the 1970s and 1980s, that intellectual assault became a policy assault leading to design controls, slow-growth legislation, and the expansion of historic preservation efforts.

For the sad fact is that America's Suburbia is now functionally, esthetically and economically bankrupt.

> The vital statistics of the suburban sprawl are terrifying:
> Some 50,000,000 Americans live in suburban developments.
> Within twenty years, another 50 million are expected to move into them.
> Since World War II, about 6 million acres of our countryside have been covered with little houses on little lots (and the services that go with this).

Consider now these detailed statistics: Nassau County, New York, which is almost entirely suburban, grew from a population of 672,675 in 1950 to 1,300,171, in 1960—interpreted, this means that in this one county alone some 90,000 additional acres were swallowed up—almost half the county's land. Irving, Texas, a suburban community near Dallas grew from 2,621 inhabitants in 1950 to 45,985 in 1960—all of them suburbanites, all spread out over some 13,000 acres of newly developed land (and the town is trying to annex another 60,000 acres for additional suburban development). Orange County, in California, which forms a large chunk of Los Angeles' Suburbia, more than tripled its population between 1950 and 1960. And Phoenix, Arizona, moved up from being the ninety-eighth city in the United States in 1950 to the twenty-ninth in 1960—almost all the growth taking place in vast suburban developments that now cover the once-beautiful desert like some sort of skin cancer.

There is not much that we can do about the population explosion that lies at the base of all this; but there *is* something we should have done long ago about the pattern of housing this exploding population. For the suburban pattern that has developed in the United States not only eats up land at a mammoth rate, but is bankrupting most suburbs and is, further, making life there only slightly less intolerable than on tenement streets.

The mess that is suburban America departs from the sentimental assumption, fos-

Originally published in Peter Blake, *God's Own Junkyard* (New York: Holt, Rinehart and Winston, 1964).

3.4. Strip mall, Cherry Hill, New Jersey, 1992. Courtesy of Iguana Photo, www.iguanaphoto.com. The dominant Amercan landscape in the second half of the twentieth century comprised the highways and strip malls that came with the rise of the automobile as the primary means of moving. The strip mall is designed entirely for the convenience of drivers. Though it might be anywhere, this strip is located in the suburbs of Camden, New Jersey, and was built to serve white suburbanites who fled an increasingly black city.

tered by the early agrarians, that everybody should live in their own house on a small lot. The most common residential "unit" today is a single house of about 1,200 square feet placed on a lot that is 60 feet wide and about 120 feet deep. The house is set back some 25 feet from the sidewalk and about 10 feet from each of the side lines of the property. Because the owners have but limited resources of time and money, they often improve only that part of their lot which represents their "front" to the outside world. These front yards are, of course, unusable for outdoor living because common restrictions against fences rob them of all privacy. The rear yard is frequently neglected, and in any case, it is not really big enough for growing children to play in. The results are palpable: children play in the street; parents spend most of their time maintaining a front garden which they can't use; the community has to maintain long roads and long utility lines to service its strung-out houses; and the suburbs go broke.

There is a better way. It is entirely possible to build 1,200-square-foot, two-story houses on lots that measure only 20 feet wide by 60 feet deep. Such houses would be attached to one another, yet they could be staggered so that each would have a completely private patio space of its own, big enough for large outdoor parties and small enough for any family to maintain without trouble. The "surplus land" thus saved—something like 6,000 square feet per family—could then be pooled to create several large communal parks and playgrounds, each big enough for community offerings or athletic events, each maintained by a small annual contribution from member families. (It is much cheaper to maintain a single large park than hundreds of small gardens; and it is much cheaper for a builder to bypass a hilly and wooded site than to flatten it with bulldozers and to cut down all its trees.) This sort of plan not only preserves much of the natural beauty of the areas that surround our cities but also reduces the cost of roads and utilities and, thus, the suburban tax burden.

The wholesale destruction of our countryside is clearly not the inevitable result of the population explosion. It is the result of incompetence and ignorance on the part of those who determine the shape of our suburbs. And it is also the result of pressures from those who speculate with land and who have a vested interest in making buildable land scarce and, thus, increasingly valuable. Under the present system of suburban development, the land speculator has been able to make phenomenal profits: between 1950 and 1960, while the Consumer Price Index went up just a little more than 10 per cent, the price of suburban land rose anywhere from 100 to 3,760 per cent, and the end is nowhere in sight.

In architectural terms, throughout the history of Western civilization, good communities have been made up of three elements: utilitarian buildings (places where people live and work), which may be entirely plain and unpretentious in character; symbolic buildings (places that form some sort of focal points in a community), which are likely to have a much more distinctive appearance, size, and location, depending, of course, on what they are meant to symbolize; and finally (and most importantly), outdoor spaces of different size and character.

In today's Suburbia, it is virtually impossible to create outdoor spaces of *any* character. Individual little houses plonked down on individual little lots do not form continuous "walls" of the sort we still find along the cobblestone streets of Beacon Hill. Our little houses form, at best, a ragged fence, full of gaps; they face each other across wide streets and deep front yards, so that the distances between them are likely to measure at least 100 feet; and because our little houses are generally low-slung, the "ragged fences," created by them, together with the wide distances between parallel "fences" add up to absolutely nothing in terms of definable, outdoor space. For any "outdoor room," just like any indoor room, depends for its success upon the proportions of height to width to length. Suburbia's streets are "outdoor rooms" 100 feet wide, lined (if you look closely) with ragged walls that may be 12 feet high, and completed at each end by an intersection or, possibly, a fire hydrant. No city builder of the Middle Ages or the Renaissance would have dared to propose anything so ridiculously amorphous; if he had, his fellow citizens would have run him out of town.

As for symbolic buildings, what do we see in Suburbia? It is true that there are probably some churches along the nearest highway. But while the churches of our early New England towns and villages were tall enough (and sufficiently close by) to be visible from almost everywhere, the sprawl of today's Suburbia has pushed the churches so far out that their spires are no longer visible farther than a block away. (The Howard Johnson spire, more often than not is more visible.) This condition may, of course, be an accurate reflection of today's relative values, but it is also a further contribution to the formlessness of modern Suburbia. One of the important functions of a tall building in any community is to serve as a point of reference, to permit people to find their way about without trouble, much as a lighthouse helps a ship's captain to chart his route.

Suburbia's other "symbolic" buildings are those of the shopping center, which is certainly symbolic of *some*thing—though perhaps not of anything we would particularly want to symbolize. (Some new shopping centers have tried to become "community centers" in a broader sense, and perhaps there is some validity in this.) Then there are schools, police stations, fire houses and, indeed, somewhere, there may even be a town hall.

The meaning of all this is twofold: first, we do not seem, at this time, to possess the sort of common faiths that shaped cities like Florence (whose only tall buildings were the symbols of religion and of government) or, at least, we do not seem to be very strongly committed to any common faiths; and, second, one reason we are not so committed is, quite clearly, that nobody living in Suburbia (and very few people living in Urbia) is conscious of the physical symbols of democratic government—the one faith we do claim to hold in common.

This is not merely an esthetic problem, or even primarily an esthetic problem, because Suburbia, in its present form, is incapable of generating significant outdoor spaces and is so spread out that its few, symbolic buildings are lost among the forests of telephone poles; moreover, we find ourselves with 50 million suburbanites most of whom are totally disinterested in local government, refuse to participate in it, and frequently don't even know what community (if that is the appropriate word) they belong to. The only local issue that arouses any degree of passion is taxes—and that one tends to generate more furor than constructive illumination.

It is all so much easier to "buck the trend," especially when the trend, as Anthony West put it, "is up." The only trouble, of course, is that the trend is down: the kind of stratified, anesthesized and standardized society being bred in America's present-day Suburbia is not one to look forward to with pleasure. Nor are the purely practical, economic problems being created in and by Suburbia likely to be solved by inaction and insouciance. There are some pretty terrible things that are happening to our cities, partly as a result of the engulfing suburban sprawl: like the suburbs themselves, our cities are becoming ghettos of one sort or another; and like the suburbs themselves, they are rapidly losing all sense of communal identity.

41

MICHAEL POLLAN, "ABOLISH THE WHITE HOUSE LAWN," 1991

No aspect of the twentieth-century American landscape has come to dominate the American imagination more than the lawn. Hardly "natural" in virtually any sense of the word, the American lawn is an invention of the nineteenth century which grew in direct proportion to the growth of the private home and suburbs. Michael Pollan, executive editor of *Harper's* and one of the most astute critics of contemporary attitudes toward nature, offers here a modest proposal for challenging the ubiquity of the American lawn. While shocking at first glance—How many times have we seen presidents and heads of state stride across the thick green carpet of the White House lawn?—the case is compelling. Pollan writes at an ambiguous moment in the history of American attitudes

Originally printed in *New York Times*, May 5, 1991, sec. 4, p. 17, col. 2.

toward the natural landscape. On one hand, suburbanization continues apace, with houses and lawns growing in size as Americans retreat to their private castles. On the other hand, there is a powerful and growing environmental movement that is having a far-reaching influence on growth policies and even, perhaps, on American attitudes toward what we consider beautiful and necessary.

Three years after candidate George Bush told us he wanted to be remembered as the "environmental President," he has done little to earn that distinction—unless one regards his catch-and-release policy on bonefishing as a major environmental initiative.

We know the excuses by heart: A Treasury that is broke, an economy too fragile to bear the weight of new environmental regulations and a skeptical chief of staff, John Sununu, who remains unperturbed by the threat of acid rain, ozone loss and the greenhouse effect.

Still, I'm inclined to take the President at his word when he voices his concern for the planet. So I want to offer him a suggestion—a simple, constructive step that would save the Treasury money, impose no new burdens on the economy and that even Mr. Sununu might endorse.

True, it is only a symbolic step, but its symbolism is so potent that it could conceivably set off a revolution in consciousness—just the sort of revolution that may be needed if we are ever to strike a healthier relationship between the American people and the American land.

I propose that, tomorrow morning, President Bush issue an executive order to the Park Service to rip out the White House Lawn.

I imagine that, at first blush, most Americans will be as disturbed by this idea as I was. We are great lovers of lawn, and the White House rendition is quite possibly the best there is. I have seen it up close. I have even run my hand through that smooth, emerald crewcut, and can report that at 1600 Pennsylvania Avenue there stands the platonic ideal of Lawn.

There is justice in this: We Americans have traditionally looked on our front lawns as nothing less than an institution of democracy. Beginning in the 19th century, at the urging of such landscape designer-reformers as Frederick Law Olmsted and Andrew Jackson Downing, we took down our old-world walls and hedges (which they had declared to be "selfish" and "undemocratic") and spread an uninterrupted green carpet of turfgrass across our yards, down our streets, along our highways and, by and by, across the entire continent.

Front lawns, we decided, would unite us, and, ever since, their maintenance has been regarded as an important ritual of consensus in America, even a civic obligation. Indeed, the citizen who neglects to vote is sooner tolerated—and far more common—than the citizen who neglects to mow: in hundreds of communities the failure to mow is punishable by fines. That's because our quasi-public unhedged front yards all run together—in a sense, the White House lawn is contiguous with every other lawn in the land—and the laggard who neglects to tend his lawn spoils the effect for everyone.

The democratic symbolism of the lawn may be appealing, but it carries an absurd and, today, unsupportable environmental price tag. In our quest for the perfect lawn, we waste vast quantities of water and energy, human as well as petrochemical. (The total annual amount of time spent mowing lawns in America comes to 30 hours for every man, woman, and child.) Acre for acre, the American lawn receives four times as much chemical pesticide as any U.S. farmland.

The White House has declined to tell me how much, or what kind of chemicals it applies to its lawn. But it doesn't take a Freedom of Information Act request to figure out that this lush, supergreen and weed-free carpet is being maintained with frequent, heavy doses of poison. For that reason alone, it would make ample sense for this Administration to set an example and say no to lawn drugs.

But the deeper problem with the American lawn, and the reason I believe the White House lawn must go, is less chemical than metaphysical. The lawn is a symbol of everything that's wrong with our relationship to the land. Lawns require pampering because we ask them to thrive where they do not belong.

Turfgrasses are not native to America, yet we have insisted on spreading them from the Chesapeake watershed to the deserts of California without the slightest regard for local geography. Imposed upon the land with the help of our technology, lawns encourage us in the dangerous belief that we can always bend nature to our will. They may bespeak democratic sentiments toward our neighbors, but with respect to nature the politics of lawns are totalitarian.

What we need is for the President to take the lead—to stride out onto the South Lawn, drive the sharp edge of his spade into that unnaturally plush sod and toss the first chunk of White House lawn onto the compost pile. To do so would constitute an act of environmental shock therapy.

The President's choice of a replacement for the White House lawn gives him an unprecedented opportunity to reinvent the American front yard—and, in the process, promote a saner approach to the environment.

With that end in view, let me offer the President a few suggestions for the new White House grounds:

Meadow. By letting the lawn go and gradually allowing so-called "weed" species to take hold, the White House lawn could be transformed into a meadow that would require only a single annual mowing or scything. This is the cheapest alternative.

I would recommend mowing a few paths through the tall grasses. One path might lead to the Capitol, symbolizing a new spirit of common purpose; another could form a spur to the Appalachian Trial, recalling us to the great beauty and variety of the American landscape.

Wetland. With the help of the Army Corps of Engineers, we could restore a portion of the White House ground to its original condition, which historians tell us was wetland.

The political symbolism of the White House standing in the middle of what used to be called swamp might be troubling to some, however apt. But we now recognize wetlands as one of the richest and most crucial of habitats; a White House wetland would express a fresh appreciation for the land's history and a respect for the well-being of other species. One small but not insurmountable problem would be figuring out where TV correspondents could safely tape their nightly standups without having to don unstylish waders.

Vegetable garden. Imagine an 18-acre victory garden on the grounds of the White House, managed according to the highest organic principles. This garden, which need not contain any broccoli, would stand as a paradigm of environmental responsibility.

3.5. *NYC Skyline from the Fresh Kills Landfill,* 1998. Photo by Michael Falco. The largest "natural" feature of New York City's landscape—reaching 225 feet above sea level and covering 2,200 acres—is an utterly man-made one: the Fresh Kills landfill on Staten Island. But a remarkable transformation has taken place in anticipation of its closing (which was delayed because of the attacks of September 11, 2001, on the World Trade Center, visible in the distance): Fresh Kills has begun to be converted into natural landscape, a form of second nature.

The White House has enough land to become self-sufficient in food—a model of Jeffersonian independence and thrift. Alternatively, a White House garden could help supply food for Washington's poor. Depending which party is in power, a few elephants or donkeys should be maintained for the purpose of fertilization.

Orchard. This is my preferred solution. An orchard of apple trees, underplanted with meadow grasses, would not only make the grounds productive but also beautiful at every season. And like the lawn it would replace, an orchard of apple trees would celebrate our democratic spirit—but without offending nature.

"The apple is, beyond all question, *the* American fruit," the minister Henry Ward Beecher declared in 1874. "It is a genuine democrat. It can be poor [in soil], while it loves to be rich; it can be plain, although it prefers to be ornate . . . But, whether neglected, abused, or abandoned, it is able to take care of itself, and to be fruitful of excellences. That is what I call being democratic."

42

WILLIAM CRONON, "THE TROUBLE WITH WILDERNESS," 1995

William Cronon has revolutionized the study of American history by helping to invent the new field of environmental history, which sought to tell the history of humans and nature and not simply as humans versus nature. His works and those of his colleagues have sought to tell the stories of how humans shaped and were shaped by the natural world. Where we have traditionally seen "nature"—unchanged and uninhabited—Cronon and his colleagues have found extensive human manipulation and resultant environmental changes.

Here he makes a less than modest proposal: that we abandon the term "wilderness." He argues that the term has helped perpetuate the notion that there are places beyond human impact, untouched and unchanged, in order to push scholars and policy makers alike to see the constant and age-old interactions of humans and their environments. Not surprisingly, Cronon has received much criticism for these views, in part because the dedication to the idea of wilderness has been a powerful organizing principle for environmental activists. In the face of assaults on the environment by Republican administrations and corporations, many activists have resisted undermining such a basic concept in the struggle.

Preserving wilderness has for decades been a fundamental tenet—indeed, a passion—of the environmental movement, especially in the United States. For many Americans, wilderness stands as the last place where civilization, that all-too-human disease, has not fully infected the earth. It is an island in the polluted sea of urban-industrial modernity, a refuge we must somehow recover to save the planet. As Henry David Thoreau fatuously declared, "In Wildness is the preservation of the World."

But is it? The more one knows of its peculiar history, the more one realizes that wilderness is not quite what it seems. Far from being the one place on earth that stands apart from humanity, it is quite profoundly a human creation—indeed, the creation of very particular human cultures at very particular moments in human history. It is not a pristine sanctuary where the last remnant of an endangered but still transcendent nature can be encountered without the contaminating taint of civilization. Instead, it is a product of that civilization. As we gaze into the mirror it holds up for us, we too easily imagine that what we behold is nature when in fact we see the reflection of our own longings and desires. Wilderness can hardly be the solution to our culture's problematic relationship with the nonhuman world, for wilderness is itself a part of the problem.

To assert the unnaturalness of so natural a place may seem perverse: we can all conjure up images and sensations that seem all the more hauntingly real for having engraved themselves so indelibly on our memories. Remember this? The torrents of mist shooting out from the base of a great waterfall in the depths of a Sierra-Nevada canyon, the droplets cooling your face as you listen to the roar of the water and gaze toward the sky through a rainbow that hovers just out of reach. Or this: Looking out across a desert canyon in the evening air, the only sound a lone raven calling in the distance, the rock walls dropping away into a chasm so deep that its bottom all but vanishes as you squint into the amber light of the setting sun. Remember the feelings of such moments, and you

Originally printed in *New York Times Magazine*, August 13, 1995, pp. 46–47.

will know as well as I do that you were in the presence of something irreducibly non-human, something profoundly Other than yourself. Wilderness is made of that too.

And yet what brought each of us to the places where such memories became possible is entirely a cultural invention.

For the Americans who first celebrated it, wilderness was tied to the myth of the frontier. The historian Frederick Jackson Turner wrote the classic academic statement of this myth in 1893, but it had been part of American thought for well over a century. As Turner described the process, Easterners and European immigrants, in moving to the wild lands of the frontier, shed the trappings of civilization and thereby gained an energy, an independence and a creativity that were the sources of American democracy and national character. Seen this way, wilderness became a place of religious redemption and national renewal, the quintessential location for experiencing what it meant to be an American.

Those who celebrate the frontier almost always look backward, mourning an older, simpler world that has disappeared forever. That world and all its attractions, Turner said, depended on free land—on wilderness. It is no accident that the movement to set aside national parks and wilderness areas gained real momentum just as laments about the vanishing frontier reached their peak. To protect wilderness was to protect the nation's most sacred myth of origin.

The decades following the Civil War saw more and more of the nation's wealthiest citizens seeking out wilderness for themselves. The passion for wild land took many forms: enormous estates in the Adirondacks and elsewhere (disingenuously called "camps" despite their many servants and amenities); cattle ranches for would-be rough-riders on the Great Plains; guided game hunting trips in the Rockies. Wilderness suddenly emerged as the landscape of choice for elite tourists. For them, it was a place of recreation.

In just this way, wilderness came to embody the frontier myth, standing for the wild freedom of America's past and seeming to represent a highly attractive natural alternative to the ugly artificiality of modern civilization. The irony, of course, was that in the process wilderness came to reflect the very civilization its devotees sought to escape. Ever since the 19th century, celebrating wilderness has been an activity mainly for well-to-do city folks. Country people generally know far too much about working the land to regard unworked land as their ideal.

There were other ironies as well. The movement to set aside national parks and wilderness areas followed hard on the heels of the final Indian wars, in which the prior human inhabitants of these regions were rounded up and moved onto reservations so that tourists could safely enjoy the illusion that they were seeing their nation in its pristine, original state—in the new morning of God's own creation. Meanwhile, its original inhabitants were kept out by dint of force, their earlier uses of the land redefined as inappropriate or even illegal. To this day, for instance, the Blackfeet continue to be accused of "poaching" on the lands of Glacier National Park, in Montana, that originally belonged to them and that were ceded by treaty only with the proviso that they be permitted to hunt there.

The removal of Indians to create an "uninhabited wilderness" reminds us just how invented and how constructed the American wilderness really is. One of the most striking proofs of the cultural invention of wilderness is its thoroughgoing erasure of the history from which it sprang. In virtually all its manifestations, wilderness represents a flight from history. Seen as the original garden, it is a place outside time, from which human beings had to be ejected before the fallen world of history could properly begin. Seen as the frontier, it is a savage world at the dawn of civilization, whose transformation represents the very beginning of the national historical epic. Seen as sacred nature, it is the home of a God who transcends history, untouched by time's arrow. No matter what the angle from which we regard it, wilderness offers us the illusion that we can escape the cares and troubles of the world in which our past has ensnared us. It is the natural, unfallen antithesis of an unnatural civilization that has lost its soul, the place where we can see the world as it really is, and so know ourselves as we really are—or ought to be.

The trouble with wilderness is that it reproduces the very values its devotees seek to reject. It offers the illusion that we can somehow wipe clean the slate of our past and return to the tabula rasa that supposedly existed before we began to leave our marks on the world. The dream of an unworked natural landscape is very much the fantasy of people who have never themselves had to work the land to make a living—urban folk for whom food comes from a supermarket or a restaurant instead of a field and for whom the wooden houses in which they live and work apparently have no meaningful connection to the forests in which trees grow and die. Only people whose relation to the land was already alienated could hold up wilderness as a model for human life in nature, for the romantic ideology of wilderness leaves no place in which human beings can actually make their living from the land.

We live in an urban-industrial civilization, but too often pretend to ourselves that our real home is in the wilderness. We work our nine-to-five jobs, we drive our cars (not least to reach the wilderness), we benefit from the intricate and all too invisible networks with which society shelters us, all the while pretending that the things are not an essential part of who we are. By imagining that our true home is in the wilderness, we forgive ourselves for the homes we actually inhabit. In its flight from history, in its siren song of escape, in its reproduction of the dangerous dualism that sets human beings somehow outside nature—in all these ways wilderness poses a threat to responsible environmentalism at the end of the 20th century.

Do not misunderstand me. What I criticize here is not wild nature, but the alienated way we often think of ourselves in relation to it. Wilderness can still teach lessons that are hard to learn anywhere else. When we visit wild places, we find ourselves surrounded by plants and animals and landscapes whose otherness compels our attention. In forcing us to acknowledge that they are not of our making, that they have little or no need of humanity, they recall for us a creation far greater than our own. In wilderness, we need no reminder that a tree has its own reasons for being, quite apart from us—proof that ours is not the only presence in the universe.

We get into trouble only if we see the tree in the garden as wholly artificial and the tree in the wilderness as wholly natural. Both trees in some ultimate sense are wild; both in a practical sense now require our care. We need to reconcile them, to see a natural landscape that is also cultural, in which city, suburb, countryside and wilderness each has its own place. We need to discover a middle ground in which all these things from city to wilderness can somehow be encompassed in the word "home." Home, after all, is the place where we live. It is the place for which we take responsibility, the place we try to sustain so we pass on what is best in it (and in ourselves) to our children.

Learning to honor the wild—learning to acknowledge the autonomy of the other—means striving for critical self-consciousness in all our actions. It means that reflection and respect must accompany each act of use, and means we must always consider the possibility of nonuse. It means looking at the part of nature we intend to turn toward our own ends and asking whether we can use it again and again and again—sustainably— without diminishing it in process. Most of all, it means practicing remembrance and gratitude for the nature, culture and history that have come together to make the world as we know it. If wildness can stop being (just) out there and start being (also) in here, if it can start being as humane as it is natural, then perhaps we can get on with the unending task of struggling to live rightly in the world—not just in the garden, not just in the wilderness, but in the home that encompasses them both.

CHAPTER 4

One Nation, of Many Parts: Regionalism and the Built Environment

Nations spring first from the imagination before they exist as accomplished political or social facts. The Constitution, ratified in 1787, imagined a framework for national government well in advance of there being a nation to govern in any real or meaningful sense. Indeed, the thirteen disparate colonies that joined together long enough to achieve independence from Britain could first only agree to a confederation before they moved to become United States.

At the outset of the new republic, with the bulk of the country's Euro-American population still hugging the eastern seaboard, the "nation" might better be thought of as a collection of three regions stitched loosely together: New England, the mid-Atlantic, and the South.

The expansive, aggressive, imperial growth of the United States during the nineteenth century came not only by adding states to the union but also by annexing sections that became defined as regions. The Atlantic south evolved into the upper or old South and the lower or new South during the first half of the nineteenth century. The northwest territories quickly aged into the "old northwest" as the Mid-west itself divided into upper and lower. And, of course, the frontier West emerged in the American consciousness in the middle of the nineteenth century, disappeared as a demographic fact by 1890, and remains permanently fixed in the American imagination.

Locale, rather than nation, remained the way most Americans saw their own identity and their connection to place well into the nineteenth century. In his classic study *The Search for Order*, Robert Wiebe demonstrated just how powerful local and regional identities remained into the last quarter of the nineteenth century, and similarly in his study of the 1893 World's Columbian Exposition in Chicago, James Gilbert notes how most visitors saw themselves first as residents of a particular state, or even of a smaller unit, rather than as citizens of the nation.

Regions can be defined in a number of ways. Geography is perhaps the first and most obvious—we speak of the "East Coast," though generally we don't mean the entire stretch of coast by that term; the "Rocky Mountain West"; the piedmont areas of Virginia and North and South Carolina. Some regions can be defined economically, like the "industrial Mid-west," or the "cotton South."

There is another factor complicating our understanding of American regionalism: Because the business of writing and publishing centered around Boston, New York, and Philadelphia primarily, especially in the nineteenth century, the nation was viewed, at least in the world of letters, largely from that vantage point. The economics, social relations, and physical shapes of the industrializing, urbanizing Northeast were taken as the benchmark, and the rest of the country measured against it. Thus, as some of the selections in this chapter demonstrate, the South was often seen as "backward" and the West as "wild."

Most intriguing and most elusive, regions stand as cultural markers, differentiating

4.1. *Across the Continent:* "*Westward the Course of Empire Takes Its Way.*" Publisher:
Currier & Ives, 1868. Museum of the City of New York, The Harry T. Peters Collection.
This popular image, produced just after the Civil War, when thousands of settlers streamed
across the trans-Mississippi West, captures the sense that the West was an empty space, waiting for Americans to manifest their destiny. It was not, as the few Native American figures
left literally in the dust remind us.

one group of people from others. "Appalachia," to which Americans began to refer after
the Civil War, denotes a physical geography, but more important, a social geography as
well—a region of poverty and "backwardness." The extent to which America is a map of
cultural regions has been much debated. Whether there was a distinctive "New England
mind," for example, or an indigenous linguistic pattern in Appalachia are questions that
folklorists, historians, sociologists, and others have studied.

Without weighing in on these debates, we can say that Americans did develop different regional styles in their built environment, especially in the eighteenth and nineteenth centuries. These vernacular approaches to building developed as the ethnic
traditions Euro-Americans brought with them encountered the new landscapes, climate,
and functional necessities in a new world.

Seventeenth-century New England Puritans brought the patterns of English domestic architecture with them, but quickly sheathed them in wood clapboards because
wood was so much more available than it had been back in England. Spanish settlers to

the Southwest brought with them the red tile of Spain and were influence by the adobe construction of the indigenous Native American architecture. Perhaps most dramatically, the German and Scandanavian farmers who turned the Great Plains into the grain belt often lived first in houses built from sod bricks, cut out of the very land they farmed.

Indeed, the images we have of different regions are more often than not embodied by vernacular architecture. When we think of Charleston, we think of the double-gallery houses, short end facing the street. When we think of New Orleans, we think of the ornamented balconies of town houses facing onto Bourbon Street, or shotgun shacks in poorer neighborhoods. And when we conjure an image of New England, we think of the town green with a steepled church at one end. The agricultural Mid-west is synonymous in the mind's eye with the farmsteads that German, Irish, and English farmers built. In this sense, architecture is central to our notion of regional identity and distinctiveness.

Counterpoised against the rich diversity of regional vernacular architecture in the nineteenth century, however, was often a commonality of architectural vocabulary for larger, more public buildings. State capitols, whether in Harrisburg, Pennsylvania, or Olympia, Washington, drew from the Roman classical. Courthouses, city halls, and public schools too participated in nineteenth-century neoclassicism. Gothic, in its nineteenth-century revival form, was preferred for churches and college campuses whether in New England or in Wisconsin.

In response to the rapid and chaotic urbanization of the late nineteenth and early twentieth centuries, several cities developed local solutions to the housing shortage each now faced. The Lower East Side of New York became equated with the dumbbell tenement. Boston and cities in the region housed people in "triple deckers"; Philadelphia and Baltimore built squat brick row houses—in Philadelphia called a "trinity"—by the tens of thousands.

The erosion of regional architectural distinctiveness paralleled the rise of the United States as a more coherent, unified political and economic entity in the years after the Civil War. Railroads made possible an integrated national market, tying the farmers of Nebraska with consumers in New York, and they imposed a single standard time on the nation in the 1880s. The federal government grew in scope, significance, and influence and continued to do so throughout the twentieth century, helping to reshape the way people thought about their relationship to the nation.

The decline of regional distinctiveness did not proceed in a straight line, following exactly the rise of industrial capitalism. The first major colonial revival, for example, launched at the 1876 Centennial Exhibition in Philadelphia, gave New England vernacular forms new currency and, in a way, made them a national style. The interest in all things colonial (that is, New England colonial) simmered throughout the coming twentieth century, and has never truly disappeared.

Still, by the first quarter of the twentieth century, what had been vernacular variety became increasingly standardized. Families anywhere in the country could now buy a home design or kit from the Sears and Roebuck catalogue, whose reach was tentacular.

The slow disappearance of regional distinctiveness may explain why some American critics, writers, and intellectuals in the 1920s and 1930s rushed to "discover" local cultures and extoll their virtues. For some, these "folk" traditions, representing what appeared to be a simpler way of life, provided an antidote to the corrosive acids of modernity. For others, "regionalism" served as a battle cry in the war to define what was distinctly American about American culture.

The fascination with American regionalism in the interwar period had a more profound impact on American writing and painting than it did on American architecture. The writings of the southern Agrarians, of John Steinbeck and Sherwood Anderson, the folkloric research of Zora Neale Hurston and Alan Lomax, and the paintings of Thomas Hart Benton and John Stuart Curry have no equivalent architectural parallel.

The economic and social forces that undermined regional variations in the country's architectural landscape only accelerated after the Second World War. Local idiosyncrasy and vernacular tradition has been replaced with corporate homogenization.

The Levitt brothers did not invent the standardized home design, but in the late 1940s they did perfect the process of mass producing housing units on a scale hitherto unimaginable. In so doing, their Levittowns became the model for nearly every postwar housing development across the country. While Levitt adapted the New England "cape" as his prototype house, his new towns hardly inspired a resurgent regionalism. Indeed, American housing built in the last half of the twentieth century is virtually indistinguishable in any architecturally significant way, whether in suburban Bucks County, Pennsylvania; Rolling Meadows, Illinois; Cobb County, Georgia; or Irvine, California. By the end of the twentieth century, the houses that a vast number of Americans lived in were no longer the product of particular landscapes and climates acting upon specific ethnic traditions, but rather they became the prepackaged plans of large real estate development companies.

The increasing integration of a national marketplace, and the increasing reach of companies who could operate nationally, has also meant that the architecture of commercial spaces no longer retains much regional variation either. Indeed, certain corporations, like McDonald's, depend for their success precisely on the promise that every single franchise will be identical—the golden arches is, along with Mickey Mouse, the most universally recognized corporate symbol in the world. (McDonald's did, to a greater extent than other fast-food chains, change their cookie-cutter design to fit into community on a few occasions.)

Large-scale shopping malls in the last thirty years of the twentieth century were built by the same small number of firms and all included the same set of elements: waterfalls, glass atriums, food courts, and the like. Strip malls in southern California might have some ersatz "Spanish"-style decoration slapped on them, but their design layout and function doesn't really differ from those of strip malls in the Mid-west or in New England; and in any event, to call any of them "architecture" probably overstates the case.

In reaction to these developments, citizens in big cities and small towns grouped together to save historically significant buildings and in some cases whole neighborhoods. Aided by the historic landmarks and historic district legislation passed by Congress in 1966, historic preservation efforts responded to the loss of distinctive places as urban renewal projects tore them down and suburban sprawl buried them. Whether in German Village in Columbus, Ohio, or the Vieux Carre district in New Orleans, these preservation efforts attempt to save what is unique about a particular city or town.

Regionalism of various kinds continued to matter in the late twentieth century. The "Sun Belt," a broad area across the South and Southwest, boomed as a major center of population and economic growth. Conversely, the "Rust Belt," the swath of the Northeast and Great Lakes most heavily industrialized, became synonymous with economic collapse and urban decline. The two often stared at each other antagonistically. At the same time, suburbia emerged as the most powerful "region" in the country, pitted against both urban and rural areas whether in Orange County, California, or in Chester County, Pennsylvania.

There was also, in the late twentieth century, a small resurgence of regional consciousness. Some cities, most notably San Francisco, passed design guidelines that were intended to preserve the particular vernacular traditions of the Bay Area. In the South, since the Civil War the region most immersed in its own history, a new wave of scholars have pursued the unique cultures that flourished in the region. This new interest in southern regional distinctiveness was encapsulated with the enormous popular publication *The Encyclopedia of Southern Culture*. As in the earlier fascination with regional cultures, however, architecture has perhaps been the least influenced of the arts.

At the end of the century, a movement of architects and planners, calling themselves the "New Urbanists," worked to incorporate and update regional building and town planning forms in their projects. In their best moments, the New Urbanist towns— Seaside in Florida, Kentlands in Maryland—stand as examples of how we might build modern new communities based on sound local traditions. At their worst, they are merely new Levittowns, with regional forms appropriated as a "selling point" in the heated suburban real estate market.

In the end, all this renewed interest in regional culture and regionalism has had little impact on the vast majority of new developments. By the end of the twentieth century much of what constituted the country's regional architectural traditions was gone.

For those who hope to turn the tide, however, the one reason for hope is that there remain underlying structures laid down over the past several centuries—street patterns and lot lines, parks and rivers and grand public buildings—to set apart one community from the next and one region from another. A renewed regionalism will have to be built upon those persistent forms.

43

ANONYMOUS, EXCERPT FROM "TOPOGRAPHICAL SKETCHES OF THE COUNTY OF ESSEX," 1792

This excerpt comes from a lengthy piece that describes the towns situated in Essex County, Massachusetts. While it may be hard to imagine what readers would have found captivating here, the piece does illustrate several important points. First, it is written in the detached dispassionate voice of a natural scientist and, in this sense, is much like the writings penned by Americans about foreign countries in the same period. Facts are laid out with a minimum of editorial content, though there is a small bit of boosterism in the writer's discussion of Ipswich. Second, by taking Essex County as the geographical boundaries of this essay, the writer reminds us that in the early Republic, the county was probably the most significant political and social unit for most Americans. Finally, in devoting so much space to the towns of a single county not too far from Boston, the writer underscores that most Americans simply did not travel very far in the course of their lives and probably would not have been familiar with places even relatively close at hand.

Ipswich, by the aboriginal inhabitants called *Agawam,* is divided into five parishes. Through the centre of the town passeth Ipswich river, which has its rise in Wilmington in Middlesex county, and passing through Reading, Middletown, Topsfield and Ipswich, falls into Ipswich bay, at the southwest end of Plumb Island. It is navigable for vessels of considerable burthen three miles from its mouth. Here it is obstructed by a fall, and at a quarter of a mile higher is another fall, both carrying grist and saw mills. Between these two falls on the post road from Boston to Newbury-port, is an excellent stone bridge, composed of two arches, built in the year 1764 at the joint expense of the county and town, and executed under the direction of the late Hon. Judge Choate, in a style of strength and neatness hitherto unequalled in this county. The inhabitants are chiefly employed in agricultural pursuits, except those living in the compact settlement near the river. Here something is done in the fishery and a few vessels trade to the Westindia Islands. Silk and thread lace of an elegant and lasting texture are manufactured in large quantities by women and children, and sold for use and exportation in Boston and the other mercantile towns. This was heretofore a place of much more consideration than at present, wearing evident appearances of decay. Its natural situation is pleasant, being agreeably variegated with hills and vales. The river, the falls, the plentiful surrounding country, the number of inhabitants almost without employment, point this out as a place well calculated for manufacturers of consequence. Travellers have been sensibly impressed with this idea in passing through the town, and it is hoped that ere long the attention of the inhabitants will be drawn to the subject, and their great natural advantages no more remain so ill improved. . . .

Gloucester, more commonly known by the name of *Cape Anne,* is divided into five parishes, besides a society of universalists under the instruction of the Rev. John Murray, who may well be stiled the father of the sect in this country. This is one of the most considerable fishing towns in the commonwealth.

Originally printed in *Massachusetts Magazine, or, Monthly Museum of Knowledge and Rational Entertainment,* vol. 4, February 1792.

At the *harbour*, properly so called, are fitted annually from 60 to 70 bankers, and from *Squam* and *Sandy-bay*, two small out ports, the bay fishery is carried on with great spirit and to a large amount.

The principal compact settlement is at the harbour; and here, besides fishing vessels, a number are employed in European and Westindia voyages. A distilling house and spermaceti works have been built here since the revolution by Mr. David Pearce, an enterprizing and industrious merchant, and are conducted by him with much spirit. The soil of this town being in general very rocky and stubborn, very little is obtained from its cultivation, the inhabitants depending for their supplies on other towns. On Thatchers island, off the head of the cape, are two stone light houses bearing of each other S. S. W. ¹/₄ S. and N. N. E. ¹/₄ N.

Manchester is a small fishing town situated on the sea coast between Capeanne and Beverly, and consists of one parish. The fishery is carried on from this port chiefly in the vessels, and for the account of merchants in Boston and other places. . . .

Essex Bridge was erected in the year 1788, over the river between Beverly and Salem. A well contrived draw, with a pier on each side, renders the passage of vessels very speedy and convenient. The expense of this bridge is said not to have exceeded one third part of that of Charles River bridge, yet it is esteemed quite equal in strength, and is thought by travellers to be superior in point of beauty.

Salem, the largest town in the county, and the oldest, except Plymouth, in the Commonwealth, was settled in 1628, by Governor Edincott before mentioned and was known to the aboriginals by the name of *Naumkeag*. Here are a meeting of quakers, an episcopal church, and five congregational societies. The town is situated on a peninsula, formed by two small inlets of the sea, called north and south rivers. The former of these passes into Beverly harbour, and has a draw bridge across it, built many years ago at private expense. At this place some part of the shipping of the town is fitted out; but the principal harbour and place of business is on the other side of the town, at south river, if that may properly be called a river, which depends on the flowing of the sea for the water it contains. So shoal is this harbour that vessels which draw more than ten or twelve feet of water must be laden and unladen at a distance from the wharves by the assistance of lighters. This inconvenience notwithstanding, more navigation is owned and more trade carried on in Salem than in any port in the Commonwealth, Boston excepted. The fishery, the trade to the West Indies, to Europe, to the coast of Africa, to the East Indies, and the freighting business from the Southern States, are here all pursued with energy and spirit. The enterprise of the merchants of this place is equalled by nothing but their indefatigable industry and severe economy. This latter virtue forms a distinguishing feature in the character of the people of this town. . . . A general plainess and neatness in dress, buildings and equipage, and a certain stillness and gravity of manner, perhaps in some degree peculiar to commercial people, distinguish them from the citizens of our metropolis. It is indeed to be wished that the sober industry here so universally practiced may become more extensive through the union, and form the national character of federal Americans. . . .

The melancholy delusion of 1692 originated in this town, in the family of the Rev. Mr. *Paris*, the then minister, and here was the principal theatre of the bloody business. At the upper end of the town, at a place called, from the number of executions which took place there, *gallows hill*, the graves of the unhappy sufferers may yet be traced. Though this unfortunate and disgraceful business was chiefly transacted here, it is well known that the leading people both of church and state in the colony took an active part in it. Unjust therefore and highly absurd it is to fix a peculiar odium on the town of Salem for what was the general weakness or crime of the country. While the sarcastick smile is excited among the vain and unthinking, or the insulting abuse of illiberal prejudice is unjustly thrown upon this shocking tragedy, the serious cannot but lament to find the human mind, subject to so gross deceptions, and the man of candour will hasten to drop the curtain on the dismal scene.

44

ANONYMOUS, EXCERPT FROM "AN ACCOUNT OF MORAVIAN SETTLEMENTS," 1796

This essay begins with an editorial note that the "the following is the result of actual observation." In a magazine originating in Boston, this note serves to give authority to the subsequent discussion. The tone of the piece, while still descriptive and empirical, gives the reader the sense that Bethlehem, Pennsylvania, might as well be an even more distant exotic land. In fact, of course, it was to a certain extent. In the eighteenth century, Pennsylvania in particular, because of its tradition of religious tolerance, attracted a whole range of different religious sects, many like the Moravians from Germany and surrounding regions. These groups came not so much to join in the mainstream of American life—if there could even be said to have been a single mainstream—but to establish religious utopias quite separate and apart from the rest of American society. This is what the writer has stumbled upon, like an intrepid explorer, in Bethlehem.

Bethlehem is situated in a pleasant, fertile country, 52 miles Northwest from the metropolis of Pennsylvania. It was settled about 50 years since, by a company of Moravians, who left their former residence in Georgia, from opposition to certain military demands of that colony. The territory, they at present possess, was purchased of the Rev. George Whitefield.

The village, we have mentioned, stands on the river Leheigh, a considerable stream, which rises in the great pine swamp, on the border of Luzerne county, and falls into the Delaware at Eanon.

As the place is approached from the South, it presents a prospect, beautiful and enchanting, in the highest degree. The rolling thro' a rich country; a variegated scene of hills and vales, of groves and meadows; with the village itself, covering the side of a high, conical hill; are among the objects, which, on a sudden, meet the eye, and captivate the fancy.

A strong and convenient bridge has lately been erected over the Leheigh, supported by abutments; and well calculated to resist the impetuosity of the winter and vernal current. Stability, not elegance, was the object of the proprietors.—This very useful piece of

Originally printed in *Massachusetts Magazine, or, Monthly Museum of Knowledge and Rational Entertainment*, September 1796.

4.2. Ephrata Cloister. In the eighteenth and nineteenth centuries, Pennsylvania was a magnet for a variety of different religious groups from Europe and especially from German-speaking areas. Landing in Philadelphia, where religious tolerance was a cornerstone of William Penn's "holy experiment," many often journeyed into the hinterland to set up their own religious communities. Founded by Conrad Beissel in 1732, the Ephrata Cloister was a communal society where men and women lived and prayed and developed music in their own musical notation system, all in half-timbered buildings reminiscent of their Rhenish origins.

architecture, is the only one of a similar construction in the state of Pennsylvania; it was effected with difficulty after long deliberation; and now produces ten per cent, free of deduction. . . .

Bethlehem, though almost the largest place in Northampton county; is a small, yet very compact settlement. The houses are built of stone; which, at a favourable situation, have a pleasing effect on the eye. A great proportion of them are appropriated to public uses. The largest in the place, denominated the Brother's House, is a college, in which young men of the Moravian society are educated in the mechanic arts. It has formerly been occupied by a numerous brotherhood; though, at present, its inhabitants are few. The Sister's House is now the residence of a large society of females; who retire, in a great measure from the world, and devote themselves to curious and useful arts, and to the exercises of piety. Carding, spinning, embroidery, &c. are among their occupations; in the pursuit of which, is observed every appearance of innocent, unmingled pleasure. Their apartments are numerous; each seems an abode of industry, contentment, and peace.— Many members of this *sororum societas* appear far advanced in life; and have probably, been long contented with the virgin institution; and, as probably will long continue so. There are, in the edifice, two large apartments for lodging; containing eighty small beds, arranged in perfect order; which exhibit a very grotesque appearance. A large lantern hangs in the middle of each apartment; which, in the night is kept constantly burning. Besides which, for greater security, several persons, every night, in rotation, abstain from sleep; who frequently visit the lodging-room, to see if all is safe. There is likewise a large chapel, in which devotional exercises are performed every morning and evening; which consists of prayers, by the principal of the society, and of music, by a select band, all females.

A widow's house, and one for the accommodation of ministers, add to the number of public buildings in Bethlehem.

But the capital institution, in the place, is the academy for the education of young females. This has existed not more than five or six years. It is under the direction of a learned gentleman, who is principal; and a number of preceptresses, to whom belongs the immediate care of government and instruction. The members of this seminary are collected from various parts of the continent; their number, at present, is more than a hundred. They are taught the English and German languages, music, embroidery, arithmetic, &c. and in all, so far as is observed, they seem to be good proficients. Their embroidery is truly admirable. In a body, they constantly attend public worship, conducted by their preceptresses. They appear to have lively impressions of religion, created by the peculiarities of the Moravian forms of worship; which, however, may exist independent of too strong an attachment to the forms themselves. Rigour of confinement or government, is, by no means, a defect in this institution. Observation will suggest a wish, that more restraint than we actually find, might be laid on the volatility of youth. Their amusements are various, and such as are calculated to attach them to the society, to make them healthy and happy. . . .

The chapel of the Moravians is simple and unadorned. A chair and a table, somewhat elevated, answers for a pulpit. On the right hand of the minister, are long seats for the men; on the left, for the women. Their music is excellent. Their public concerts are frequent.

The Moravians are exceeding plain in their manners, and in their dress. The men wear their hair short in their neck; and women and girls wear caps, fitting close to their heads. Gravity sits in every countenance, generally tinctured with melancholy. They are honest, industrious, and innocent. The laws of their society are such, that no one continues a member of it, but on condition of good behavior. Hence there is every where the appearance of sobriety and virtue; which, tho it may seem to depend too much on external constraints, to evince reality; yet, has an admirable effect in perpetuating the order and existence of the society.—Attached to their own manners and customs, the Moravians neither borrow from foreign nations, nor copy those of their nearest neighbours. Among themselves, they use the German language; yet most of them speak the English with ease.

There was, formerly, a community of goods in the Moravian society; tho now we find a separate interest, with respect to many occupations; particularly those of tradesmen and merchants. Land is still common property. Tenants are procured and paid by the society. The direction, emolument, and expenses of all public institutions, appertain to the whole society.

45

Z, EXCERPT FROM "DOMESTIC ARCHITECTURE," 1832

At one level, this essay is part of the long tradition of lament over the state of American architecture. In this case, however, the author has couched his discussion in regional terms. Acknowledging that New England constituted a region quite different from the mid-Atlantic states of New York and Pennsylvania, Z points to the domestic architecture of that region to draw a complaining comparison with his own. The cultural geography of American regionalism could, like the comparisons made with Europe, be a goad to improve architecture closer to home. There is also a strong moralistic strain in this essay, as the author suggests, in an architectural version of the transitive property, that love of luxury leads to bad domestic architecture, which in turns leads to the ruination of families.

GENTLE READER! Wert thou ever so far forsaken by thy good Genius, as to be left to build a house? If thou has not been, thank thy stars most devoutly that thou has been spared, and pray that the "*mania a domu*" may never seize thee. If, however, thou hast, like us, been engaged in racking thy brains, fretting thy patience, and exhausting thy purse, to bring into being a pile of timber, and brick and mortar, bearing the cognomen of a House, thou needest not be told, that Architecture furnishes a vast theme for solemn reflection. . . .

We speak now of the dwelling houses of our citizens, the homes of our men of business, as well as of the few men of fortune, who are scattered through the country, and in these we include all who are able to own the estates which they occupy. On this subject, sober judgement and our daily observation are utterly opposed to each other. Neatness, comfort, and economy are sacrificed to fashion and false pride; and go where we may in New-England, and, especially in Massachusetts, the traveler finds few things, so much to be lamented, as the sacrifice which is thus made to false taste, false judgement, and a falser estimate of what is valuable.

In the first place, our houses are too large for comfort, convenience, or beauty. The consequence of erecting them of such dimensions is, often, that they remain unfinished and incomplete; and, instead of the neat rural villa, which almost every farmer might own and enjoy, we see huge houses, the original cost of erecting which, too often, has entailed upon its tenant a load of debt, which he can never remove during his life, and he lives on, toiling to keep down the accumulating interest of the money, thus expended for what he cannot enjoy, with a consciousness, every year, that his chance of redemption is becoming less, and that his children must, ere long, yield their paternal acres to some stranger, who will enter to enjoy, if he can, the mansion, for which the tenant has sacrificed the best years of his life, and the best hopes of his family.

This weakness is, if we mistake not, a peculiarity of New-England, and New-England men. We should look in vain, for such an idle expenditure of money among the thrifty descendants of the Dutch and Germans, in New-York or Pennsylvania. They understand these things better. Whatever they expend, in the way of buildings, is put to actual use. They have large barns, and large granaries, because they can fill them, and if

Originally printed in *New England Magazine*, vol. 2, January 1832.

they know not the luxury of a fine house, they know the comfort of a full and warm one; and never think, while thus enjoying ease and competence, of voluntarily becoming the tenants of a griping landlord, and paying rent in the form of interest, for money expended in enlarging their dwelling houses, and contracting their means of enjoyment.

It has so often been our misfortune to trace the progress of a farmer or mechanic, who has, indiscreetly, run into debt to build, or purchase a larger house than he has had occasion to put to actual use, that we can almost infallibly tell, at the first sight, the precise stage of his career of ruin. Here might very easily be formed a pretty accurate scale, by which we could determine the condition of a stranger by the external marks, that meet the eye of a traveler while passing by his dwelling house. If we see a large house, with here and there a tattered garment supplying the places of broken panes of glass, we expect soon to see the shingles or clapboards loose, the doors with broken hinges, the fences broken down or carried away for fuel; and we soon look for the last step in this downward scale, a sheriff's flag hanging from the premises, to tell the passers-by that the tenant's equity of redemption in those premises is about to be sold to pay a store debt, or settle a tavern score. We might point out, too, the marks of this progress of poverty, within the doors of such an estate; but the dwelling soon becomes too desolate, and the wife and children too strongly marked with the seal which ruin has set upon them, to make such a spectacle any thing but painful and melancholy.

Let no man imagine that this is a fancied picture. It may be seen in almost every town in New-England. Go with us to the registry of deeds for any county in Massachusetts, and, we doubt not, we can point to instances, in every volume of its records, of mortgages of estates made to secure the payment of money borrowed to renew or enlarge the buildings upon those estates, and where the whole has been forfeited by the borrower, who, otherwise, might have been the independent tenant of the acres he had purchased, or inherited. Of the propensity to which we have referred, though it is the besetting weakness of our men of moderate fortunes, it is difficult to trace the origin or the cause of its general prevalence. We are willing to ascribe it to honorable and praiseworthy considerations, but we think them unfortunate and indiscreet.

There is a feeling of independence, and of republican equality among our citizens, which, if properly directed, makes them the best citizens in the world; but which, if misapplied, makes them the veriest slaves. And this feeling may be traced in the style of our farm houses, as well as in other objects of luxury or convenience. No man is willing to be out done, if he can avoid it, by his neighbor. In the consciousness of acknowledged equality, he cannot bear with patience to be surpassed in the *externals* of style or independence. Instead of converting this feeling into an incentive to greater exertions gradually to attain to an actual equality with his more fortunate neighbors in wealth, and the means of display, too many begin with assuming the appearance of this equality, which they cannot sustain, and thereby take a load upon themselves that sinks them to the dust. Fashion in this thing is a tyrant, to whom they blindly submit, even with all their high notions of independence, which spurn every appearance of control. They are dazzled by the hugeness of the idol they worship, and lie down to be crushed by the wheels of his car, the willing victims of their own idolatry. We have, again and again, seen families of limited means, forego the very necessaries of life, in order to keep up the appearance of being able to enjoy its luxuries, and this, because they were unwilling to seem inferior to those with whom they have been accustomed to associate in life. . . .

And there it is, towering up into its two stories in height, with its large and numerous windows, its white glaring walls, and, if you please, (for we will take one of the best we can find) its white fence in front, enclosing a green plat of untrodden grass, but without a tree near it to shade or shelter it from the sun and storm, or a shrub, or a vine, to relieve the eye as it gazes upon it. What can, in fact, be more ill-suited than that pile for the purposes for which it was designed? It is an independent farmer's dwelling house, and one half of it is scarcely ever, if ever, brought into use. The wind moans along its wide entries, and through its unoccupied rooms, when the weather is cold, with a sound that is truly appalling; and anon, when the summer heat drives us to seek a shelter from the scorching rays of the sun, we may see them pouring into those open windows, which seem intended to expose the inmates to the gaze and the pity of the spectator, while they are suffering from the oppressive heat of the climate, rather than let in the pure light of heaven, and the cooling breeze, as they may be wanted for the convenience or comfort of its occupants. Where shall we look in such an object for either the beauties of nature, or of art, or of these combined? Nature is, indeed, shut out entirely. She is not permitted to lend the cooling shade of her forest trees, nor the bright and beautiful flowers of her exhaustless store of shrubs, to deck what man, not art, has tortured into the adobe of a rational being, in whom nature originally implanted a fondness of her simple beauties. If we lay out of view the future destiny of such an estate, and regard only the uses to which it is applied by its present possessors, is there a man in his sober senses, who can call the construction of it a wise or a judicious expenditure of money, or one which indicates a man of native refinement, or of cultivated taste?

To test this style farther, let us turn our eyes for a moment towards that little cottage, (for we have a few such) which we see yonder among the trees. Go there, and we shall see neatness, and comfort, and taste combined. Its white walls peep out from among the trees that surround it, like a rose amidst its own green leaves, and the eye is delighted and relieved by the order and symmetry that prevails through every part of the little grounds that surround it. You may enter the humble door of that cottage, over which a woodbine has been trained, or look into its windows through the honey-suckles that are climbing over them, and you will find every thing convenient, though every spot is occupied for some useful purpose. And yet that is the dwelling house of a mechanic of humble means, who has made his own estate by industry, and knows how to enjoy it to the utmost. The first cost of that cottage was but trifling, compared to the large mansion of his neighbor, and it has been by his own hand, and without interfering with his accustomed employments, that he has planted these trees, and shrubs, and vines, and made that little spot so charming and inviting.

No traveler can pass these two dwellings, without almost envying the scene of comfort and good taste which the one presents, and almost pitying the tenant of the other, whenever a comparison is made between them. . . .

We ask no finer scenery, or brighter suns, or milder skies, than nature offers in our own New-England. But where we look for the objects of art, for the ornaments which nature borrows from the taste and skill of man, we look, too often, in vain. We have the most cheering and animating scenes of business and enterprise on every side. At one point, the towering walls of a Factory, surrounded with its clusters of dwelling houses and shops; at another, the huge proportions of the village Tavern, and its neighboring stores, and shops of artisans; and on every side are objects indicating the busy, bustling habits of our people, and the eagerness with which they pursue the acquisition of wealth. But how few are the marks of that cultivated taste, which we might look for in a country enjoying so many means of knowledge and cultivation? Where do we look for the neat cottages, with their enclosures of hedges and their beautiful draperies of flowers and foliage? or, in short, where shall we look for many of those simple and unpretending beauties, which give so much interest to an English landscape in description or representation? The answer and the reason is, not that nature has been sparing on her part, but man, the lord of this part of the creation, will not follow her hints nor improve the advantages which she places within his reach.

46

W. E. B. DU BOIS, EXCERPT FROM *THE SOULS OF BLACK FOLK,* 1903

W. E. B. Du Bois stands unquestionably as the leading black intellectual of the first half of the twentieth century. His purpose in writing the essay "Of the Black Belt," Chapter 7 in his masterpiece *The Souls of Black Folk,* was decidedly not to give his primarily Northern readers a description of the landscape of southern Georgia. His goal here, and in the rest of his book, was to elucidate the problems facing American blacks in the era after the sad failure of Reconstruction. In this chapter, however, Du Bois has taken his readers on a tour of rural Georgia and inscribed racial issues and their history onto the landscape he describes. A Northerner himself, Du Bois has come to the epicenter of black America and found a place filled with strange and terrible traditions, a landscape of simultaneous abundance and decay. In this sense, he participates in the tradition of Northern writers who viewed the South as virtually another country, and certainly as a failed, backward society.

Out of the North the train thundered, and we woke to see the crimson soil of Georgia stretching away bare and monotonous right and left. Here and there lay straggling, unlovely villages, and lean men loafed leisurely at the depots; then again came the stretch of pines and clay. Yet we did not nod, nor weary of the scene; for this is historic ground. Right across our track, three hundred and sixty years ago, wandered the cavalcade of Hernando de Soto, looking for gold and the Great Sea; and he and his foot-sore captives disappeared yonder in the grim forests to the west. Here sits Atlanta, the city of a hundred hills, with something Western, something Southern, and something quite its own, in its busy life. And a little past Atlanta, to the southwest, is the land of the Cherokees, and there, not far from where San Hose was crucified, you may stand on a spot which is to-day the centre of the Negro problem,—the centre of those nine million men who are America's dark heritage from slavery and the slave-trade. . . .

But we must hasten on our journey. This that we pass as we leave Atlanta is the ancient land of the Cherokees,—that brave Indian nation which strove so long for its

Originally printed in W. E. B. Du Bois *The Souls of Black Folk* (Chicago: A.C. McClurgh & Co., 1903), 83–97.

fatherland, until Fate and the United States Government drove them beyond the Missis-sippi. If you wish to ride with me you must come into the "Jim Crow Car." There will be no objection,—already four other white men, and a little white girl with her nurse, are in there. Usually the races are mixed in there; but the white coach is all white. Of course this car is not so good as the other, but it is fairly clean and comfortable. The discomfort lies chiefly in the hearts of those four black men yonder—and in mine.

We rumble south in quite a business-like way. The bare red clay and pines of North-ern Georgia begin to disappear, and in their place appears a rich rolling land, luxuriant, and here and there well tilled. This is the land of the Creek Indians; and a hard time the Georgians had to seize it. The towns grow more frequent and more interesting, and brand-new cotton mills rise on every side. Below Macon the world grows darker; for now we approach the Black Belt,—that strange land of shadows, at which even slaves paled in the past, and whence come now only faint and half-intelligible murmurs to the world beyond. The "Jim Crow Car" grows larger and a shade better; three rough field-hands and two or three white loafers accompany us, and the newsboy still spreads his wares at one end. The sun is setting, but we can see the great cotton country as we enter it,—the soil now dark and fertile, now thin and gray, with fruit-trees and dilapidated build-ings,—all the way to Albany....

For a radius of a hundred miles about Albany, stretched a great fertile land, luxuri-ant with forests of pine, oak, ash, hickory, and poplar; hot with the sun and damp with the rich black swamp-land; and here the corner-stone of the Cotton Kingdom was laid.

Albany is today a wide-streeted, placid, Southern town, with a broad sweep of stores and saloons, and flanking rows of homes,—whites usually to the north, and blacks to the south. Six days in the week the town looks decidedly too small for itself, and takes fre-quent and prolonged naps. But on Saturday suddenly the whole county disgorges itself upon the place, and a perfect flood of black peasantry pours through the streets, fills the stores, blocks the sidewalks, chokes the thoroughfares, and takes full possession of the town. They are black, sturdy, uncouth country folk, good-natured and simple, talkative to a degree, and yet far more silent and brooding than the crowds of the Rhine-pfalz, or Naples, or Cracow. They drink considerable quantities of whiskey, but do not get very drunk; they talk and laugh loudly at times, but seldom quarrel or fight. They walk up and down the streets, meet and gossip with friends, stare at the shop windows, buy cof-fee, cheap candy, and clothes, and at dusk drive home—happy? Well no, not exactly happy, but much happier than as though they had not come.

Thus Albany is a real capital,—a typical Southern country town, the centre of the life of ten thousand souls; their point of contact with the outer world, their centre of news and gossip, their market for buying and selling, borrowing and lending, their foun-tain of justice and law. Once upon a time we knew country life so well and city life so lit-tle, that we illustrated city life as that of a closely crowded country district. Now the world has well-nigh forgotten what the country is, and we must imagine a little city of black people scattered far and wide over three hundred lonesome square miles of land, without train or trolley, in the midst of cotton and corn, and wide patches of sand and gloomy soil.

It gets pretty hot in Southern Georgia in July,—a sort of dull, determined heat that seems quite independent of the sun; so it took us some days to muster courage enough to leave the porch and venture out on the long country roads that we might see this un-known world. Finally we started. It was about ten in the morning, bright with a faint breeze, and we jogged leisurely southward in the valley of the Flint. We passed the scattered box-like cabins of the brick-yard hands, and the long tenement-row facetiously called "The Ark," and were soon in the open country, and on the confines of the great plantations of other days. There is the "Joe Fields place"; a rough old fellow was he, and had killed many a "nigger" in his day. Twelve miles his plantation used to run,—a regular barony. It is nearly all gone now; only straggling bits belong to the family, and the rest has passed to Jews and Negroes. Even the bits which are left are heavily mortgaged, and, like the rest of the land, tilled by tenants. Here is one of them now,—a tall brown man, a hard worker and a hard drinker, illiterate, but versed in farm-lore, as his nodding crops declare. This distressingly new board house is his, and he has just moved out of yonder moss-grown cabin with its one square room. . . .

The whole land seems forlorn and forsaken. Here are the remnants of the vast plantations of the Sheldons, the Pellots, and the Rensons; but the souls of them are passed. The houses lie in half ruin, or have wholly disappeared; the fences have flown, and the families are wandering in the world. Strange vicissitudes have met these whilom masters. Yonder stretch the wide acres of Bildad Reasor; he died in war-time, but the upstart overseer hastened to wed the widow. Then he went, and his neighbors too, and now only the black tenant remains; but the shadow-hand of the master's grand-nephew or cousin or creditor stretches out of the gray distance to collect the rack-rent remorselessly, and so the land is uncared-for and poor. Only black tenants can stand such a system, and they only because they must. Ten miles we have ridden to-day and have seen no white face. . . .

Now and again we come to churches. Here is one now,—Shepherd's they call it,—a great whitewashed barn of a thing, perched on stilts of stone, and looking for all the world as though it were just resting here a moment and might be expected to waddle off down the road at almost any time. And yet it is the centre of a hundred cabin homes; and sometimes, of a Sunday, five hundred persons from far and near gather here and talk and eat and sing. There is a school-house near,—a very airy, empty shed; but even this is an improvement, for usually the school is held in the church. The churches vary from log-huts to those like Shepherd's and the schools from nothing to this little house that sits demurely on the county line. It is a tiny plank-house, perhaps ten by twenty, and has within a double row of rough unplaned benches, resting mostly on legs, sometimes on boxes. Opposite the door is a square home-made desk. In one corner are the ruins of a stove, and in the other a dim blackboard. It is the cheerfulest schoolhouse I have seen in Dougherty, save in town. Back of the schoolhouse is a lodge-house two stories high and not quite finished. Societies meet there,—societies "to care for the sick and bury the dead"; and these societies grow and flourish. . . .

How curious a land is this,—how full of untold story, of tragedy and laughter, and the rich legacy of human life; shadowed with a tragic past, and big with future promise! This is the Black Belt of Georgia. Dougherty County is the west end of the Black Belt, and men once called it the Egypt of the Confederacy. . . .

Then came the black slaves. Day after day the clank of chained feet marching from Virginia and Carolina to Georgia was heard in these rich swamp lands. Day after day the songs of the callous, the wail of the motherless, and the muttered curses of the wretched echoed from the Flint to the Chickasawhatchee, until by 1860 there had risen in West Dougherty perhaps the richest slave kingdom the modern world ever knew. A hundred and fifty barons commanded the labor of nearly six thousand negroes, held sway over farms with ninety thousand acres of tilled land, valued even in times of cheap soil at three millions of dollars. Twenty thousand bales of ginned cotton went yearly to England, New and Old; and men that came there bankrupt made money and grew rich. In a single decade the cotton output increased four-fold and the value of lands was tripled. It was the heyday of the *nouveau riche*, and a life of careless extravagance reigned among the masters. Four and six bob-tailed thoroughbreds rolled their coaches to town; open hospitality and gay entertainment were the rule. Parks and groves were laid out, rich with flower and vine, and in the midst stood the low wide-halled "big house," with its porch and columns and great fire-places.

And yet with all this there was something sordid, something forced,—a certain feverish unrest and recklessness; for was not all this show and tinsel built upon a groan? "This land was a little Hell," said a ragged, brown, and grave-faced man to me. We were seated near a roadside blacksmith-shop, and behind was the bare ruin of some master's home. "I've seen niggers drop dead in the furrow, but they were kicked aside, and the plough never stopped. And down in the guardhouse, there's where the blood ran."

With such foundations a kingdom must in time sway and fall. The masters moved to Macon and Augusta, and left only the irresponsible overseers on the land. And the result is such ruin as this, the Lloyd "home-place":—great waving oaks, a spread of lawn, myrtles and chestnuts, all ragged and wild; a solitary gate-post standing where once was a castle entrance; an old rusty anvil lying amid rotting bellows and wood in the ruins of a blacksmith shop; a wide rambling old mansion, brown and dingy, filled now with the grandchildren of the slaves who once waited on its tables; while the family of the master has dwindled to two lone women, who live in Macon and feed hungrily off the remnants of an earldom....

This was indeed the Egypt of the Confederacy,—the rich granary whence potatoes and corn and cotton poured out to the famished and ragged Confederate troops as they battled for a cause lost long before 1861. Sheltered and secure, it became the place of refuge for families, wealth, and slaves. Yet even then the hard ruthless rape of the land began to tell. The red-clay sub-soil already had begun to peer above the loam. The harder the slaves were driven the more careless and fatal was their farming. Then came the revolution of war and Emancipation, the bewilderment of Reconstruction,—and now, what is the Egypt of the Confederacy, and what meaning has it for the nation's weal or woe?

It is a land of rapid contrasts and of curiously mingled hope and pain.... [A] pall of debt hangs over the beautiful land; the merchants are in debt to the wholesalers, the planters are in debt to the merchants, the tenants owe the planters, and laborers bow and bend beneath the burden of it all. Here and there a man has raised his head above these murky waters. We passed one fenced stock-farm, with grass and grazing cattle, that looked very homelike after endless corn and cotton. Here and there are black freeholders: there is the gaunt dull-black Jackson, with his hundred acres; "I says, 'Look up! If you don't look up you can't get up,' " remarks Jackson, philosophically. And he's gotten up. Dark Carter's neat barns would do credit to New England. His master helped him to get a start, but when the black man died last fall the master's sons immediately laid claim to the estate. "And them white folks will get it, too," said my yellow gossip.

I turn from these well-tended acres with a comfortable feeling that the Negro is rising. Even then, however, the fields, as we proceed, begin to redden and the trees disappear. Rows of old cabins appear filled with renters and laborers,—cheerless, bare, and dirty, for the most part, although here and there the very age and decay makes the scene picturesque. A young black fellow greets us. He is twenty-two, and just married. Until last year he had good luck renting; then cotton fell, and the sheriff seized and sold all he had. So he moved here, where the rent is higher, the land poorer, and the owner inflexible; he rents a forty-dollar mule for twenty dollars a year. Poor lad!—a slave at twenty-two. . . .

The Bolton convict farm formerly included the neighboring plantation. Here it was that the convicts were lodged in the great log prison still standing. A dismal place it still remains, with rows of ugly huts filled with surly ignorant tenants. "What rent do you pay here?" I inquired; "I don't know,—what is it, Sam?" "All we make," answered Sam. It is a depressing place,—bare, unshaded, with no charm of past association, only a memory of forced human toil,—now, then, and before the war. They are not happy, these black men whom we meet throughout this region. There is little of the joyous abandon and playfulness which we are wont to associate with the plantation Negro. At best, the natural good-nature is edged with complaint or has changed into sullenness and gloom. And now and then it blazes forth in veiled but hot anger. I remember one big red-eyed black whom we met by the roadside. Forty-five years he had labored on this farm, beginning with nothing, and still having nothing. To be sure, he had given four children a common-school training, and perhaps if the new fence-law had not allowed unfenced crops in West Dougherty he might have raised a little stock and kept ahead. As it is, he is hopelessly in debt, disappointed, and embittered. He stopped us to inquire after the black boy in Albany, whom it was said a policeman had shot and killed for loud talking on the sidewalk. And then he said slowly: "let a white man touch me, and he dies; I don't boast this,—I don't say it around loud, or before the children,—but I mean it. I've seen them whip my father and my old mother in them cotton-rows till the blood ran; by—" and we passed on. . . .

I remember wheeling around a bend in the road beside a graceful bit of forest and a singing brook. A long low house faced us, with porch and flying pillars, great oaken door, and a broad lawn shining in the evening sun. But the window-panes were gone, the pillars were worm-eaten, and the moss-grown roof was falling in. Half curiously I peered through the unhinged door, and saw where, on the wall across the hall, was written in once gay letters a faded "Welcome."

47

CLIFTON JOHNSON, EXCERPT FROM
HIGHWAYS AND BYWAYS OF THE SOUTH, 1904

At virtually the same time that W. E. B. Du Bois took his trip to the South, this now for-gotten writer from Hadley, Massachusetts, also journeyed through the region and pub-lished a book about his experiences. Johnson stopped in Tuskegee, Alabama, home to the

Originally printed in Clifton Johnson, *Highways and Byways of the South* (New York: Macmillan, 1904), 75–77, 78, 88–91, 94–95.

4.3. Shotgun shack, New Orleans, John Michael Vlach. Houses like this one became a distinctive architectural form throughout the south in the nineteenth century. Long and narrow, they take their name from the folk saying that one could fire a shotgun clear from one end of the house to the other. These houses represented a clear case of the migration of building traditions from Africa through the Carribbean and into the United States, as well as adaptations made to fit local tastes and climates.

Tuskegee Institute, the most famous black institution in the South at the turn of the twentieth century. What Johnson describes, in a gently condescending tone, is a sleepy, Southern town, which has neither recovered from the effects of the Civil War nor participated in the much vaunted revival of the "New South." People lounge and nap and spit tobacco on unpaved streets and outside rickety buildings. That this conforms almost precisely to the image that most Northerners probably already had of the South goes almost without saying, as does Johnson's praise for the energy and purpose of the Tuskegee Institute. Given the condition of black people in the South, Johnson concludes, the work of the institute and its powerful leader Booker T. Washington is deeply important.

Tuskegee is best known as the home of Booker T. Washington's famous negro school, but the school is on the village outskirts, and the place has a well-defined character of its own. It is a typical Southern country town, and is a centre for the country population from miles around. Thither the people flock every market day for news and gossip, for buying and selling, borrowing and paying, and for justice and law. The town is wide-streeted and placid, with a broad public square at its heart, bounded about by brick and wooden stores, livery stables, law offices, etc. These structures are one and two stories high, and are pretty sure to have projecting from their fronts, across the sidewalk, an ample board roof to furnish shade; and between the supports of the roof, on the outside of the walk, is usually a plank seat. The walk is a good deal encumbered with displays of various goods, and here and there are careless huddles of empty whiskey-barrels and other receptacles. The barrels and boxes, in common with the plank seats and sundry doorsteps and benches, are utilized very generally by loungers. The populace like to sit and consider, and they like to take their ease when talking with their friends; while it occasionally happens that a darky will be so overcome by weariness or *ennui* that he will stretch out on one of the larger boxes to enjoy a nap. A more aristocratic loitering-place than any provided by chance or intention as adjuncts of the stores, is a group of chairs at the rear door of the court-house. Every pleasant day these chairs are brought out into the shadow of the building and the near trees, where they are occupied by some of the village worthies for purposes of mild contemplation and discussion.

The court-house stands in the centre of the square, on a generous grassy oval that is separated from the rutted sandy earth of the rest of the square by a low fence. The building is a solid, but rather battered structure of brick, with quite a pleasing air of sedate age. On the lower floor are the county offices, and among the other rooms is one reserved for the grand jury—a most rudely furnished apartment with a small fireplace and a deeply sanded floor. This sand is, I believe, intended to ameliorate the unevenness of the original floor of brick, which is badly worn, but it makes the room look as if it had been prepared for the caging of wild beasts.

Upstairs is the court-room—a plain, old-fashioned apartment, heated by two small stoves. Its most noticeable characteristic is its odor of nicotine. The Southern men are famous smokers and chewers, and they spit copiously and emphatically all day long. If they are where a fireplace or stove is handy, they make that their target, but in public buildings or conveyances they drench the floors, and the court-room had been thus soaked for two generations. I remember with what serious thoughtfulness and regularity the judge expectorated on the occasion when I was present. . . .

The principal streets radiating from the Tuskegee town square are broad and tree-lined, and are flanked by fine old mansions, some in serene retirement beyond a formal garden, some approached by an avenue of great trees. Tuskegee was one of the richest towns in the state "befo' the war"; but, while the vicinity was never fighting-ground, the conflict left it devastated and ruined, in common with the rest of the Confederacy, so that, although you still find the old-time mansions and the ample grounds, they are not, as a rule, well kept up, and some are far gone in decay and dilapidation. The dwellings are of two types—the low and spreading with wide piazzas, and a higher and more imposing style with pillared fronts like Greek temples. On warm days the doors are thrown wide open and you can see straight through the central hall which penetrates and ventilates these homes of the sunny South front to rear.

Just outside of the village is the white folks' cemetery, of which they are very proud, for it is full of monuments, and receives constant care; but to me it looked like a desert—as if the spot was blasted. It is a wholly grassless waste of sand, relieved only by clumps of flowering shrubs and scattered trees. Roads and paths are marked by bordering lines of bricks set up on edge so as to overlap each other in saw-toothed fashion, and family plots are ordinarily enclosed either by a brick wall or, more likely, by a forlorn-looking wooden fence. An old negro is kept busy hoeing up such stray spears of grass and sproutings of weeds as chance to start, and owners of plots often supplement his labors in keeping the earth befittingly barren by bringing rakes and brooms and giving the sand above their family graves a thorough scratching and brushing. Then it appears beautiful in their eyes. Grass seems to them unkempt.

A great deal of money has been spent on the monuments, and the desire to emulate others in funeral display has plainly resulted in expenses far beyond the means of many who have put up these fine stones. Very few of them date back more than thirty or forty years. They have nearly all been bought in the period of the town's poverty.

The negroes have a separate cemetery. If a colored person was to be buried among the whites, the latter would all rise from their graves in indignation. How they tolerate the "niggers" in heaven is a mystery, unless the mansions there are provided with kitchens and stables. But, whatever the state of affairs in heaven, no mixing is allowed in this Tuskegee burial-place, and the negro dead are interred a half-mile farther on, where cultivated fields give way to scrubby woodland. In a humble way their cemetery is a copy of that of the whites. Fences have been built around quite a number of family plots, and the ground in some cases is kept free from greenery by occasional hoeings and sweepings. Several of the graves were marked with diminutive slabs of marble; others had neatly painted white boards set up; but most, if marked at all, had only bits of wood, though not infrequently the graves were outlined by a border of bricks or bottles. The cemetery was not enclosed, and many of the rude fences about the family plots were falling to wreck. Its pleasantest features, as I saw it, were the tufts of wild violets that grew plentifully and two black-gum trees all ahum with honey-gathering bees. . . .

I left the hollow not far from Mr. Washington's school, and, on climbing a high zigzag fence, startled a young negro student who had secretly constructed here an amateur hothouse. He had taken some discarded windows and other odds and ends and tinkered up a structure three of four feet square and six or seven high, that was quite ingenious. He had contrived to keep it heated with a cast-off lamp that he set inside an old tin pail to form a kind of furnace. To a certain extent this hothouse was a plaything, yet he was by its means doing some genuine investigation into the principles of plant growth and nurture. He was perhaps making more of his school opportunities than most; but the students, as a whole, are remarkably earnest, and are intent on getting all the good they can out of their course. I doubt if there is a white school in our entire country where the mental and moral atmosphere is so good. The students are not merely working to help themselves, but to be uplifters of their race. They are obliged to subsist on the plainest fare, to learn order, cleanliness, industry, and promptness. Small vices are not tolerated, nor any tendency to foppish display.

The school is an inspiration, and the master spirit is Booker T. Washington—a man who, in spite of his fame, continues unspoiled; a man of rare simplicity and ability and hard sense, giving his life to stem the tide of ignorance and poverty and the attendant evils that weigh down his people. One does not have to be long in the South to appreciate the immense need and importance of his work.

48

CORRA HARRIS, EXCERPT FROM
"THE ABOMINATION OF CITIES," 1914

Traveling from her home in an unnamed Georgia valley, Corra Harris came to New York and found it horrifying. Her critique—mixing equal parts pastoral idealism, Protestant Christianity and Southern hostility toward the North—is familiar: the city enervates men, robbing them of their vitality, distancing them from the honest and real work of farming and forcing them to be parasites on the labor of others. In this sense, Harris contributes to two traditions. The first is the antiurban bias in American thought, articulated most famously by Thomas Jefferson. This tradition enjoyed something of a revival in the years before the First World War as American cities grew to enormous size and seemed to generate unsolvable social problems. The second is a more distinctively Southern pastoralism, which insisted that the South and its way of life represented the real virtues of America more fully than the urbanized North. This strain of thought traces back to the proslavery apologists of the antebellum period who defended slavery as more human than the "wage slavery" of the North, and forward to the collection of writers known as the "Agrarians" who took their stand in defense of the South in the 1920s.

I reached New York one week ago tonight. The whole city swung like an iridescent bubble in the luminous darkness—so different from the Valley where the earth lay wrapt in sweet repose like a virgin beneath a pale star-shining coverlid. The streets were canals of streaming splendor. The darkness was far above where the stars should have been dark. The light was far below where it should have been dark. The throngs seemed to be treading light, pilgrims walking in a strange illusion. There were no signs of poverty anywhere. The shops blazed with magnificent displays of every imaginable luxury. The people were better clothed than we ever could be in the Valley. Yet somehow I knew that they were all poverty stricken. The petulant faces of handsomely gowned women floating past in noiselessly moving motor cars, the arid gaiety of others, the look of desperate expectancy upon all faces, the hurried eyes of the men, the awful alertness everywhere—all declared "want." I knew, of course, that what they really wanted was to come home, say their prayers beneath the roof of homestead trees, be forgiven their childish trespasses and find repose. But no man, nor any woman could prove that to these people. They are by reason mad. They live by what they see, what they have got, or have not got, and by what they know here. It is a false standard. The only way to live is by faith. These people live by fear, by anxiety, by indulgence, according to frightful needs for which they can not substitute that faith which is the substance of things hoped for, the evidence of things not seen. . . .

[L]ife in a city destroys the nerve of a man to take his chances with just nature. He would rather risk pauperism to get a "job" than to endure with fortitude the chances of the seasons in the country. He has lost his plowhandle muscles, and his capacity to hope for a harvest just from the earth. He wants wages "by the day" or the month. He lacks the courage to believe in the soil, to endure the hardships of cold in the winter and of heat in the summer. He has been taught by a false system to look to a fresh air fund vacation. He cannot stand more than two weeks in the country. The space, the silence, the peace of it

Originally printed in *Independent* 77 (January 26, 1914): 129–31.

4.4. "The David Hilton Family, near Sargent, Nebraska," 1887. Nebraska State Historical Society. The Homestead Act made millions of acres of grassland in the Great Plains available for settlers in the decades after the Civil War. Finding themselves in a treeless landscape, often hundreds of miles from stone quarries, these settlers, like the Hilton family, simply cut bricks of sod out of the ground to build homes and barns. There is probably no more dramatic example of a vernacular building style than the sod houses that these settlers built across the Great Plains. In the foreground, however, stands a sign that the Hilton family was not so rustic and set off from the urban commercial culture as so many were willing to assume. Increasingly, all of America became interconnected, with everything—even pianos—available through mail-order catalogues. This would mark the erosion of some regional distinctiveness.

depresses his spirit. You need not doubt this, it requires natural manhood, natural strength, natural courage and tremendous faith to live upon a hill and to earn bread and the mere necessities of life from tilling the soil. And we are losing that more and more. The weaker men even who are born there always leave it and come to the city. One young man told me since I have been here, that after spending a month in a "sleepy Southern community" he felt like an octogenarian. He blamed the community, the conditions there. The fact is, New York made him the octogenarian. It came out on him there like a disease or reaction, once he lacked the awful intoxication of life here to keep him stimulated. He had sobered up and did not know what was the matter with him. Every drunkard has this downcast octogenarian depression after a prolonged spree.

But the other more important reason why you cannot drive these wretched souls back to nature and healthy employment is because the men who cultivate the soil must get enough out of it to support themselves and enough more out of it to afford luxuries to the rich in New York and other markets where men gamble upon everything the earth brings forth. The Southern farmer must sell his cotton at a price so much lower than it is really worth in order that the Northern capitalist who owns a factory for making cotton goods can have the means to own a yacht and four touring cars, can give his wife a splendid establishment and his mistress splendid diamonds, so that he can make his idle son an allowance of from three to twenty thousand dollars a year while the son pretends to study the economics and mathematics of civilization at Yale or Harvard, and lastly, so that he can pose as a great philanthropist and an uplifter of mankind. Such men are always natives of New York or some other city like it. They are produced by conditions there, by its enterprises, its opportunities and its hypocrisies. Show me the greatest, richest city in this country and I will show you the greatest, most ruthless criminal in it, no matter how many schools and universities it contains, no matter how many good people. They cannot be really good. They are only as good as they can be under wicked conditions which work untold hardships upon those who live in the mountains and in the fields where they belong.

This is the only curse I have found upon life in our Valley at home, the shamefully low prices received for produce, the outrageously high prices paid for what is bought. . . .

It is all wrong. We shall not see it, nor our children, but our children's children may see sheep pastures on Manhattan Island, because things have got to be made right. That is the Law which outlasts all of our mere laws.

49

J. W. HOOVER, EXCERPT FROM "HOUSE AND VILLAGE TYPES OF THE SOUTHWEST AS CONDITIONED BY ARIDITY," 1935; AND TALBOT HAMLIN, EXCERPT FROM "WHAT MAKES IT AMERICAN? ARCHITECTURE IN THE SOUTHWEST AND WEST," 1939

Americans rediscovered regional variety with a new enthusiasm in the 1930s. The cosmopolitan, urban world celebrated in the 1920s by writers and intellectuals seemed to have come crashing down spectacularly with the stock market in 1929, and part of the response to the Depression was to search for some kind of stability represented by different regional traditions. As Talbot Hamlin, representative of the East Coast intelligentsia, writes in this piece: "I have been discovering parts of the United States new to me, and it has been thrilling." For Hamlin, J. W. Hoover, and countless others, the American Southwest

Reprinted with permission from *Scientific Monthly,* March 1935. Copyright 1935. American Association for the Advancement of Science.

stood as the most interesting, alluring, and distinctive region in the nation. Home to a mixture of three cultures, indigenous, Spanish/Mexican, and Anglo, the Southwest's distinctive culture was seen to have developed out of its long history and particular conditions. Hoover's dry essay—forgive the pun—roots the particular building tradition of the Southwest in its harsh climate. Elsewhere in the essay, he underscores the long history of the region by linking the climatologically driven methods and practices of building here with those in similar climates around the world and across time—Assyria, Chaldea, Egypt, and the like. The lesson to be drawn from this, Hoover implies, is that the architectural solutions developed in the past to deal with the climate could and should be adapted for present buildings. Hamlin is more interested in the current state of building in the Southwest and California, but he also concludes that climate, ultimately, dictated the architecture of Spanish colonial past, and that it should the present as well. Hamlin writes with the breathlessness of new discovery, though we might chuckle that that wide-eyed wonder merely reflects his own provincialism. Ultimately Hamlin thinks he has discovered the true "American" architecture.

J. W. Hoover, excerpt from "House and Village Types of the Southwest as Conditioned by Aridity"

The sub-tropical hot desert type of climate of the lower Colorado River drainage basin and the upper valley of the Rio Grande with their bordering steppes constitute a region of distinct character as contrasted with other parts of the United States. Here, then, we may look for distinctive human adjustments to climatic conditions resulting in peculiar or indigenous forms. Most universal and conspicuous of cultural forms are house and village or community building types. Yet often in the more highly developed districts of the arid Southwest one fails to be impressed with anything distinctive architecturally except a few scattered old houses or neglected old buildings in less frequented locales which have failed to share in the general quickening prior to 1930. Outside of New Mexico, where a conservative Spanish-speaking population of low living standard is considerably in the majority, there has been considerable leveling of structural types due to mobility of population and fluidity of ideas shared with other parts of the country. So local indigenous forms have often been submerged among the exotic styles introduced through a rapid influx of population, steeped in the culture of a different clime and uninured to the modes of the desert. Will the desert eventually impress its stamp upon this heterogeneity to produce a fusion in harmonious adjustment?

For that which is more typically desertic, we may look to the simpler indigenous cultures and even to the adjustments of the American pioneer settlers. Indian cultures were supplemented by Spanish or Mexican culture and house types. The first American settlers, isolated from their kind, adopted the forms of those who had preceded them in the land. Later settlers, coming in larger numbers and less completely cut off from old cultural ties, employed their accustomed building methods and materials, but modified their style of building to suit the climate.

Conditioning Factors

The character of the desert house is determined largely by two sets of natural facts: (1) Conditions imposed by climate; (2) materials available for construction.

The climate factors which taken together set apart the areas designated as a climatic province in the United States are the same as characterized all the arid regions of the world bordering on the tropics. They are: (1) *Low rainfall,* generally less than 10 inches, although the limit will vary with temperature and other conditions; as affecting cultural forms, no definite limit can be set. (2) With low rainfall invariably goes *low atmospheric humidity,* which more directly affects human comfort. (3) Also continuous sunshine. (4) Very high summer temperatures. (5) Mild winters with little freezing weather. (6) High diurnal range, commonly over 25 degrees.

The matter of building materials is of paramount importance where the desert community is isolated or the standard of living is low, and diminishes in importance with ease of communication and greater wealth. The materials of the desert are earth (adobe) or stone, with perhaps sufficient woody growth to supply beams or even upright supports.

Clayey soil makes up for the scarcity of wood in the arid zone. It can be easily molded and will absorb substances which solidify and harden it when dried in the sun or baked in the fire. The clay is also used for cooking utensils and for vessels to contain and to cool liquids, as the well-known *olla* of the Southwest. In Northern Africa and Southwest Asia even clay furniture and earthenware chests are used. If one is looking for beginnings, he will learn that architecture using bricks did not originate in the places where it is developed farthest to-day, but in the arid regions of the world. In districts arid enough for the use of sun-dried brick, clay has always maintained its supremacy. The great Chaldean and Assyrian palaces, even those which succeeded them in western Asia up to the time of Alexander, were built almost exclusively of clay. "The native of such regions is earthy in the most literal sense of the word;—earth in his domicile, whether he builds upon the ground or conceals himself within."

The need of protection from nomadic tribes is a social factor which often has played a large part in structural arrangements.

The Typical Desert House Type

In its simple form the mud or adobe block house, characteristic of the Mexican villages, may be taken as the general and well-nigh universal type of arid and semi-arid fixed habitations. Toward it the more primitive house types tend in their evolution. From it as the basic form emerge more elaborate forms of more highly bred cultures of the dry regions.

The adobe house is usually simply rectangular in form, flat-walled and flat-roofed, with little window space. If larger it takes the form of an L, T or U, or it may enclose a court. A space partly enclosed by the house may be completely enclosed by an added adobe wall forming a "patio." Built of the earth on which it stands, the drab buff of walls and roof blend with the same color of the soil. The universality of this as a desert form is evidence of fitness to the environment. The thick adobe walls, roof and floor are effective insulation from the glaring heat of the desert. Deep-set windows in thick walls emit little or no direct sunlight, and from the heat of the desert the cool dim light is inviting. During the heated part of the day doors and windows are closed and house remains very comfortably cool until lengthening shadows break the glare of the sun and the heat begins to moderate. During the night the temperatures drop from 25 to 35 degrees or even more, and the house is again effectively cooled for the coming day.

It seldom rains; so the pitched roof of rainy or snowy climes is not needed. The roof is commonly built by laying beams or rafters on top of the walls. Across these, poles are laid close together. These, covered with grass or weeds, support in turn a few inches thickness of earth. Such a roof may suffer severe erosion during occasional sporadic downpours characteristic of the desert. Or if there is an unusual rainy period, the roof and even the walls may become soaked, and the house with contents seriously damaged.

In parts of the world where the supply of wood for beams is scant or has been depleted, an inverted basin-like dome or cupola must be resorted to cover the space between walls. With the disappearance of the supporting wooden framework for the roof goes also that of the runway for dripping rain. Cupola construction, mothered by necessity, is also widely distributed, and represents the highest structural achievement of some groups. It is an especially common form through southwestern Asia and may be witnessed even in the Sahara. In Kurd villages of Turkestan and the villages of the Alepp Plain of Syria, the earthen or brick dome becomes the entire house, a beehive form with the flat walls eliminated.

Instead of being domed, the rectangular rooms are sometimes barrel-vaulted, a form especially common in Egyptian villages and in Mesopotamia. Neither the barrel-vault nor the cupola have entered into the primitive house construction of the Southwest, most likely because of the availability of material for beams large enough for the roofing of small structures. However, the rudiments of such construction are found in the sizeable ovens of the Papago Indians, the Hopis and the Rio Grande pueblos.

The simplicity of the adobe house is also due in large part to the fact that the climate makes so few demands upon shelter. Most of the life is out of doors. Even the outdoor patio and the roof of the house become important outdoor adjuncts of the house and accommodate a large share of the household activities and diversions. In this respect the native of the Southwest is somewhat like the Egyptian, who does not build for his own use and comfort, but who lives out of doors in the open sunlight the year around, using his house only as a shelter for the night. Nor does he need shelter like the peasant of northern countries for the long gloomy evenings of the winter.

The clay of the desert is rich calcareous material which in nature forms calcareous concretions or the hard stratum of "caliche" beneath the surface. This, dried in the abobe blocks, hardens and binds them. Its natural consistency is reinforced with weeds or stubble mixed with the mud, and it is then put into molds and allowed to harden into blocks of varying sizes; but blocks about 14 inches by 12 inches by 4 inches are the most conveniently handled. . . .

"Like house, like village." In Arizona the Mexican villages are seldom more than adjuncts of the American towns; but in New Mexico, they are as distinctively Mexican and as frequent as south of the International Boundary. Low and dull-colored, they squat upon the land, blending with the color of the dry earth, or massed on slight eminences they appear as flat prominences. Except for the arrangement of houses in rows or around courts, they have little plan. Seldom is a house more than one story high. Rising above the general flatness of the village is one conspicuous structure, the church, surmounted by a wooden cross. Yet how common is the type with a few variations in many parts of the world. . . .

American Construction in the Arid Southwest

The early American settlers in the Southwest were effectively isolated from their fellows and adapted themselves to the country. In this period, the latter half of the nineteenth century, American and Mexican villages were hardly distinguishable architecturally. Sometimes even the early white settler had to start his new home with a crude wattle shelter like those of the Indians. Even as late as 1877 the first Mormons, coming into southern Arizona and settling on the Salt River, had at first to imitate their Indian neighbors along the river, using the material close at hand. Some of these first shelters had one room with low dirt floor and walls of arrow-weed and poles plastered with mud. . . . Prescott, the early capital and metropolis of Arizona, was different in its highland environment of cool climate and pine trees. Early writers described it as like a New England village. But not so the desert settlements, Tucson, Phoenix, Florence or Yuma. Even today the old adobe houses predominate in the older quarters, which have now become the Mexican quarters. These early settlements and settlers were effectively isolated from the culture and its materials whence they sprung. Of necessity they adopted the indigenous desert house and adapted themselves to the conditions found in the desert, much as the Indians and Mexicans had done before them.

Throughout the state of New Mexico, with its predominant Spanish and Mexican population, the villages are nearly all made up of the low one-storied rectangular mud houses. The church, with its earth or frame tower mounted by a cross, is always the dominant and only conspicuous structure of the village. . . .

Following the building of the Southern Pacific Railway, which entered the state in 1878, there was an influx of settlers into the valley who came too rapidly to be assimilated by the indigenous culture. Swifter and cheaper transportation brought also building materials to which the new settlers had been accustomed, and a new period of lumber and brick construction was ushered in during the eighties.

However, this was before the day of general refrigerators and electric fans or of easy escape from the summer heat to the neighboring highlands by auto over smooth highways, and building construction had to be adapted to making the best of the long season of excessive heat. Winters were short and mild and made few demands and made possible lighter construction. Adequate facilities for heating even in this sub-tropical climate were commonly neglected, the cheerful but inefficient open fireplace playing the principal rôle.

Most of the farm houses of the valley were built in this period. The inside arrangement of rooms on both sides of the wide hall was according to the conventions of the period, but the arrangements for outdoor sleeping with unscreened porches on one, two, three or all sides of the house was a conspicuous adaptation. High ceilings and attics protected the lower story or stories. The larger and better houses were built with two stories, but the typical house had one story with an attic, under a long square diamond roof sloping down over the screened porches on three or all sides.

In the town, roofs or porches commonly extended over the sidewalks, providing the best possible comfort to pedestrians and loafers. Hotels, like houses, provided outdoor sleeping quarters, and openly exposed sides and fronts were faced with verandas for each story. Each room had its door opening upon the sleeping porch, shared by all. Lack of privacy in sleeping quarters has never been immodest in Arizona, as considered in other parts of the country, and night dress was modest there long before the day of motion picture display and street pajamas. The street porch is for many of the older humbler village houses still the family sleeping room. The adaptations of this period were utilitarian but inartistic, with rusty screens and weather-beaten canvas shades on the porches, and the sidewalks covered with narrow roofs heterogeneous in height and angle, supported by slender posts or props. Yet there was an inviting hospitality about the old style house with its cool verandas and in the covered sidewalks, inviting to loiter and to loaf.

The modern metropoli of the desert, such as Phoenix, Tuscon and El Paso, have developed rapidly in late years, along the most modern lines, chic, fresh and new, in imitation of the Southern California towns. The easy hospitality of the clime, expressed in their older styles, has given way to brisk commercialism. The sheltered sidewalks have almost disappeared. These cities would by their dress belie the summer heat, but what an opportunity is lost for individual expression of fitness to environment, both comfortable and artistic. There are local suggestions for pleasing, harmonious and utilitarian planning in the arcades and towers of San Zavier Mission near Tucson, in the terraced pueblos of the Indians and in the "Governor's House" of the Spanish period in Santa Fé. In the latter city there is much construction in imitation of the Spanish and the Indian pueblos but no concerted plan.

In these desert oasis cities of recent rapid growth there are rows of attractive appearing small homes built without regard to summer comfort in imitation of styles developed in other climes. However, the better-built homes now incorporate insulation wall materials, and the larger and better public and commercial buildings and hostelries have installed systems of air-cooling, permitting greater independence of form. So while in the future the desert climate will continue to impinge upon the evolving culture of the arid Southwest, the resultant distinctive qualities of the architecture may be more in the internal structure and in the use of special appliances rather than in the external expression of form.

TALBOT HAMLIN, EXCERPT FROM "WHAT MAKES IT AMERICAN? ARCHITECTURE IN THE SOUTHWEST AND WEST"

I have been discovering parts of the United States new to me, and it has been a thrilling and an encouraging discovery. I have seen the rich rolling Texas country, with old German-settled towns of white frame houses and picket fences. In San Antonio I saw a city born of two cultures, Spanish-Mexican and American. I have seen the desert flash by, with marching cactus plants like soldiers, and prickly pears like Dali visions, and great urn-shaped cactuses with rows of pale spikes and pinkish flowers climbing up the curved edges. I've watched lean cattle prowling over dry country, and I've seen the windmills of distant ranches rising above the sage. I've been delighted by bare cliffs pink and purple in the sunset, and at night seen the airplane beacons flashing red and white on mountain tops.

And I've seen fertile villages, and farms; the sudden rich lushness of the irrigated valley near El Paso, rows of orange trees in California, and in the Salinas valley 25 miles of lettuce waiting for the pickers and conjuring up visions of migratory labor and *The Grapes of Wrath.* I've seen little Arizona towns announcing themselves from afar by dumps of tin cans and rusting automobile corpses, and by the forest of telegraph and wireless aerial poles which proclaim human residence today. In the middle of the desert, miles from anywhere, I've seen the red-and-blue neon signs, "Joe's Café, Air Conditioned Dine Dance."

Out of this confusion of buildings, new and old, of town and country, of the Spanish past and the 20th Century, of automobiles and radio, of mission buildings and mod-

Originally published in *Pencil Points* vol. 20, December 1939.

ern houses, little by little there has grown, for me at least, a clearer idea of what American architecture is and might become. . . .

But San Antonio was a new adventure. It is a city of enormous charm, and the preservation of the winding river banks as parks, with lush semi-tropical foliage, makes any walk through the town a delight. San Antonio has the great advantage of a double parentage, and the Spanish-Mexican culture which built its magnificent missions is still vividly alive; the Mexican market on Saturday evening gives remarkable evidence of the variety of living which America can compass. San Antonio is not less American because of this, but more.

Under all the country to which my trip took me lay the old Spanish tradition, inherited through Mexico and the missions. That is a brilliant tradition, and it is not strange that in the days of rampant eclecticism it was eagerly seized upon by architects and welcomed by their clients. It was exploited in every possible and impossible way. It is amazing, however, to discover that in this exploitation the architects saw only an opportunity for baroque detail on the one hand, and a flurry of sentiment on the other. In San Antonio, in Los Angeles or any of its older suburbs, in many parts of San Francisco, one can see, all too plain, the evidences of this unthinking attempt to out-Spanish the Spanish. Candy-stick twisted columns, broken pediments, and iron grilles burgeon over and around doors and windows, and vie with over-rustic tile roofs and windows and panels and niches to give these buildings their strange and repellent appearance of a particularly new and artificial unreality. Often what was planned to look antique now looks only shabby; what was supposed to be rich now seems merely vulgar.

Hardly anywhere, until recent years, was there a real attempt to learn the true lesson which is to be read in the Spanish Colonial missions and houses. And it is a lesson as true now as it ever was: the lesson that good building—building that is an enduring enrichment of life—arises naturally from a frank acceptance of the climate and the available materials, used in the best way at one's command and with all the sense of proportion and simplicity with which one is endowed. The Spanish colonial builder, in the mission churches, gave of his best. He might decorate the façade with all the richness and skill of which he was capable. In the front of the mission of San Jose de Aguayo in San Antonio, he produced, in 1731, a piece of Churrigueresque as exquisite in conception, as perfect in execution, as anything in Spain; and the San Antonio churches likewise are nobly proportioned and beautifully vaulted. But usually, in the monastery buildings and the houses, simplicity and the most direct fulfillment of the needs is the rule, whether in the plain, rough stonework of the Purisma Concepción and the Governor's Palace in San Antonio, or in the cruder wide arches of the California missions.

It is interesting, too, to note that as the years passed, as "Americans" joined the Spanish and the Mexicans in Texas and California, the buildings of both cultures came more and more to be alike. Could this combination, this as it were joint result, be a kind of first distillation of a true architecture of the United States? Could its qualities give an indication of the secret of American architectural development? The old Greek Revival houses of San Antonio of the forties and fifties are as much at home there as the missions, for they have felt and accepted climate and materials. It is impossible to say of such a group as the Ursuline Convent there that it is either Classic Revival or Spanish Mission. It is neither, and it is both. It is San Antonio American.

And this is even more true of the Monterey buildings. There one sees "Spanish" structures with delicate woodwork of almost Adam type, and houses built after the Mexican war which are indistinguishable from those built before. For the character of both was determined by the damp Pacific winds, the warm days, the habit of outdoor living, and the materials at hand.

The chief qualities of all of this are easy to see. First of all, there is a definite trend towards simplicity—that basic simplicity that is at the heart of the classic concept. Second, there is great skill and inventiveness in using materials well—rough stone, adobe, or wood; roofs flat or pitched, of timber covered with clay or metal, tiles or shingles. Roofs, for some reason, tend towards a slope of between 30 and 40 degrees, very similar to the slope of many New England roofs. Third, there is a special facility in handling wood, both in slim structural elements and in trim. Fourth, there is an unusual readiness to let differences in climate or local taste create local variations. And, last, there is in almost all the work, even the most unassuming, a natural sense of good proportion and harmony. These, then, seem the basic qualities of the tradition of the Southwest, as they are of early New England. Might they not be, somehow, deep unconscious expressions of American democracy in building? . . .

This movement towards freedom has even permeated far into the speculative house field. Not always, however; around Los Angeles the speculative architecture is chaotic, varying from some of the freest and most creative to the worst and most banal. The latest fashion there in some areas is the Williamsburg fashion, with false chimneys, one at each end. The only hope is that this fashion, too, will die out as rapidly as those which preceded it, and that the native excellence of the simple direct design of the best work will continue. By and large, the whole picture one gets of speculative housing in both San Francisco and Los Angeles is sunny and cheerful, and there is a surprising amount which will wear well because it is restrained, styleless, and well planned. . . .

It is this feeling—that the house is the thing, and not its style—which is recreating the domestic architecture of California and, at least in part, of Texas. These houses I saw are definitely American, unlike those to be found anywhere else in the world, not because of any vaunting nationalism, any attempt to impose on refractory form an intellectually chosen style, but because their architects, working simply, have created houses above all else. O'Neil Ford's Texas buildings like many of those designed by Howard Meyer of Dallas, are as direct and as simple in their approach as the California work. It would seem, therefore, that here we are dealing, not with a mere local and accidental development, but rather with a growing trend, originating perhaps in California and gradually spreading eastward—a trend toward a kind of house design which is modern in its results because it is modern in its purposes, and not because its architect had some fixed prejudice as to what was modern in style. . . .

Such are the ideas behind a large amount of present-day domestic work in California and parts of Texas, expressed with varying degrees of completeness and success. Such are the ideas, it seems to me, at the bottom of the essential American tradition; and that is why this recent domestic work of the West and the Southwest is one of the greatest hopes for the future of American architecture.

50

PHYLLIS FENNER, EXCERPT FROM
"GRANDFATHER'S STORE," 1942

Dripping with a saccharine nostalgia, this essay evokes one of the most important institutions in any small town or city neighborhood: the local store. For small towns, especially in remote places, the general store or mercantile functioned as among the most important connections local residents had to the wider world, providing them with the latest consumer goods, news, and mail. More than that, as Phyllis Fenner remembers of her grandfather's country store, these places served as community centers, helping to cement social ties among people who often lived quite isolated lives.

The little general store that my grandfather ran in the New York State village of my childhood was the mainspring of our lives. Everything we ate, wore, owned came from it. Our playhouse was an old yellow delivery wagon taken off its wheels. Large cardboard discs from cracker barrels made wonderful shields to carry in our squirt-gun battles. All our family stories came from there, too, going back to my great-grandfather's time when goods were brought by canal.

My delight was to be sent to the store's fragrant cellar with an empty lard pail for a quart of molasses. What a delicious, heady smell! A whiff of molasses from the big barrels lying on their sides; the tang of vinegar; the pungent reek of tar paper; a strong undercurrent of rubber from boots that hung in pairs along the wall. And over all other smells was the odor of damp, earthy floor.

On one side of the store as you entered were the dress goods and notions. Men's clothing was in the back.

And down the other side were the groceries—not many canned things then, mostly good, honest staples. You smelled the spices and flavoring extracts right away. Vanilla was in a beautiful glass jar, usually with a drop hanging on its edge that I made for first thing. There was Jamaica ginger, which fat Bill Boyd used to buy by the quarter's worth, tip up the bottle and drink 'er down. They were strong men in those days.

The men congregated around the big stove in back, sitting on barrels or leaning against the coffee grinder. Even now I can smell the steam from their damp clothing and felt boots. The grinder was red and had an enormous wheel with a wooden handle. I could give myself a good push off and ride around on it—if no one was looking. Coffee was ground by hand, and getting 20 or 30 pounds ready for the wagon deliveries was a job. One night when the usual gang of boys was hanging around, my grandfather offered a cent to the boy who could grind a pound the fastest—and got all his orders put up for one penny....

Near the stove stood the high desk, with wire grating around the top, where my grandfather sat on a spindly stool and figured up his accounts. Leaves from his ledger are like ages of social history, chronicling changes in customs over the years....

One of Grandfather's sayings was that "an honest man with no job is a better risk than a crooked one with money." He presented his bills once a year, when the farmers had sold their crops. He had his own method of collecting when that was necessary....

Some people Grandfather carried on the books for years without ever expecting

Reprinted with permission from the June 1942 *Reader's Digest*, pp. 57–60.

payment. Lib Little was a queer soul, still wearing the curls of an earlier day. A small sum of money for her support had been turned over to Grandfather years before. When it was gone he kept right on sending whatever groceries she wanted, including snuff—"to kill the bugs," she said.

Because of Grandfather's reputation for square dealing, old maids and widows brought him their savings to keep for them and he paid them interest. He handled mortgages for the farmers, too; he was Justice of the Peace, and postmaster for years.

The only amusement place in town was the large hall above the store. Square dances were held there. Jingling sleigh loads of men and women would pile in from the farms bringing box suppers with them. We children got great fun out of watching bearded old men and farm wives in their funny clothes "cutting her down" on the corners to the tune of Tommy Regan's fiddle. . . .

Nearly everyone used kerosene for light and heat in those days, and every Saturday night the floor of the store would be covered with five gallon cans waiting to be filled. But the men didn't mind waiting. They'd cut a plug from the long, brown, fruity smelling strip of chewing tobacco back of the counter (we became quite expert at imitating them; working up a nice brown spit with licorice root), and gather round the stove. An enormous spittoon stood beside it, but Jake Hogan would always walk way to the front door to spit, and then come back to finish his yarn. Night after night they'd drop in before going to bed, for a bit of gossip or to settle the world's and their neighbors' affairs—young and old, lawyer, doctor, town bum, politician, swapping yarns and ideas: Many a local social problem was settled around that stove; and sometimes the law was taken into private hands. . . .

If a new doctor wished to locate in town, he wrote my grandfather first. If someone wanted information about a man's credit, or reputation, he wrote to my grandfather. That round stove was in many ways the real hub of the community.

Grandfather must have built well, for though chain stores have come and gone on each side of it, Fenner's Store is still doing business. The molasses comes in tins now; and customers are more likely to ask for gasoline than kerosene. Instead of the sociable round stove, there's a furnace in the cellar. No one stands around that of an evening. And no longer do folks know it's time to go to bed by the store's lights blinking out, for it closes at six. Most folks are off to the nearest movie, anyway. I wonder if they find it as much fun?

51

CAREY MCWILLIAMS, EXCERPT FROM "LOOK WHAT'S HAPPENED TO CALIFORNIA," 1949

Strictly speaking, California is a state, not a region. But as the cliché goes, it isn't really so much a state as a state of mind. It certainly dazzled the American imagination after the

Originally printed in *Harper's Magazine*, October 1949, pp. 21–29.

Second World War when California exploded with new residents, building new towns and creating a unique culture. More than any other place, California exemplified the growth of the West as an economic, social, and political force in the second half of the twentieth century. Indeed, it has driven that growth with, as this essay captures nicely, a bewildering and chaotic energy.

During the war and the ensuing years, Californians were vaguely aware of a phenomenal increase in population. But the full shock of recognition did not come until August 1947, when the Bureau of the Census released a report on population shifts for the period from April 1, 1940 to July 1, 1947. Then came amazing news. California had gained *three million new residents in seven years*—had absorbed, in less than a decade, about as many people as live in the whole state of Virginia, or the whole state of Iowa, or as lived in California itself at the time of the first world war. Thus the state had reached a total population of ten million—more people than there are in all of New England. California had passed Illinois and Ohio in population and had edged close to Pennsylvania, the second most populous state in the Union.

No other state has ever shown a volume of increase through migration even remotely approaching this; it is so large as to represent a substantial redistribution of the population of the United States. Historically we have learned to think of the westward movement of population, but what we do not realize is that for the past forty years the westward movement of population has been primarily a movement of people to California.

Nor has this movement stopped. California is still a very young state whose area is virtually limitless in comparison with its present population. California's present population density, per square mile of arable land (not counting mountains, desert, and forest), is still only one-eighth that of Massachusetts, the first state to be settled. If California continues to follow what population experts call the law of growth, it will expand at an almost constant, but gradually declining rate for the next two or three decades. The experts now forecast that California will show an additional gain of 2,650,000 in the 1950's, that it has not yet reached the mid-point in its growth, and that 20,000,000 people will eventually reside within its boundaries.

Such population shifts have a dual significance: one region's gain must necessarily represent another region's loss. In the past eight years, nine states actually lost population: Arkansas, Kentucky, Mississippi, Oklahoma, West Virginia, Nebraska, North and South Dakota, Idaho, and Montana. . . .

Just what does it mean, in human terms, to dump 3,000,000 people into a state—even a state as large as California—in the brief period of seven years? Although the absorptive capacity of the state is still very great, the latest rush of people to California has produced an impact not unlike that of the gold rush a hundred years ago. (Actually thirty times as many people have come to California in the past eight years as came during the gold-rush decade.) The effect of this latest migration has been all the greater by reason of the fact that the war migrants surged into a limited number of already crowded cities, mainly San Francisco, Oakland, San Diego, and Los Angeles. Since most of the migrants came to Los Angeles, it is to this city that one must turn for illustrations of the new type of community that has come into being. . . .

Although the wartime migrants to California have been a mixed lot, coming from different places and backgrounds, this general heterogeneity is sometimes deceptive. For in many cases groups of migrants have come from the same place, from the same background, and have settled in the same areas. In this event, the similarity in background and origin have served as a temporary cement to hold the migrants together as a social group, and to assist in their adjustment. Hence the new California phenomenon of "group migration," of community transplantation. . . .

With all these inhibitions of the planning function, how then does it happen that the influx of 3,000,000 people did not produce a state of sheer chaos? There are many answers to this question. For one thing, California has space to burn. The city of Los Angeles has a larger land area than any other city in America: 44 miles by 25 miles, enough land to support a population of between eight and ten million people. The county of Los Angeles, with 4,038 square miles, is about the size of the state of Connecticut. If Los Angeles had been a compact, centralized city, the migration of the past eight years would have had a devastating impact; as things are, the newcomers simply fill up the vacant spaces.

The spread-out character of Los Angeles, plus the volume and velocity of migration, has resulted in a natural, and from many points of view a highly desirable, dispersion of population. Industries are widely scattered in Los Angeles. For the most part the wartime growth has taken place round the edges of the community, rather than at the center. By an accident, therefore, Los Angeles has become the first modern, widely decentralized industrial city in America. For, with the growth taking place in the peripheral areas, the city has found it more convenient to decentralize services and facilities than to attempt a new integration from the center. As fast as new areas have developed, the chain stores, the department stores, and the drive-in markets have chased after the people, setting up new shopping districts and establishing new neighborhood centers. With more automobiles per capita than any other city in America, and with the worst rapid-transit system, Los Angeles was almost ideally prepared for a decentralization which it did not plan but from which it will profit in the future.

One of the great problems in Los Angeles is that many of the city's institutions have not adjusted to the decentralized pattern of the city. The metropolitan daily newspapers have simply resigned from the task of multiple community reporting and have increasingly fallen back on county-wide, national, and international news. On the other hand, some 250 separate newspapers have sprung up all over Greater Los Angeles, to reflect the interest and news of particular neighborhoods and communities. . . .

This, then, is California in 1949, a century after the gold rush: still growing rapidly, still the pace-setter, falling all over itself, stumbling pell-mell to greatness without knowing the way, bursting at its every seam. Today it has 10,000,000 residents; tomorrow it may have 20,000,000. California is not another American state: it is a revolution within the states. It is tipping the scales of the nation's interest and wealth and population to the West, toward the Pacific.

52

CHARLOTTE CONWAY,
"WHY IS THIS AN AMERICAN STYLE HOUSE?" 1951

Of all building types on the American landscape—church, courthouse, school, factory—
none has been more significant than the single-family house. In the United States, homeownership is a more important goal, both financially and culturally, than perhaps in any
other Western nation. At some basic level, homeownership is at the heart of the very
definition of what makes Americans different from Europeans and others in the first
place. While Americans had written about, sketched, and theorized what the ideal home
should be since the antebellum period, the post-Second World war boom in new suburban housing construction allowed ideas about home design to be realized on an unprecedented scale. In this piece author Charlotte Conway dissects the new suburban house,
looking for what makes it distinctly "American." What she finds primarily is convenience.
By calling this an "American" house, Conway has underscored that regional differences in
housing disappeared with the great tide of suburban development.

This is a house-and-garden that demonstrates the core of the American Style idea from
one property line to the other. Each room has its "garden" and they all interlock so that
you can scarcely tell where one stops and the other begins. Outdoors, there's always a
choice of sun and shade, cool spots or warm ones—and for a great deal more of the year
than you would think possible. And even in bad weather, each room has its visual link
with the out-of-doors. This house is designed so you can't tell where indoors ends and
outdoors begins. As a result the house seems "as big as all outdoors," even though it's a
relatively small one.

A house should give you freedom of choice in living space, for any time of day or
year. It is too much to expect of any one room or any one garden that it be equally pleasant, day-round and year-round. That's one of the main reasons we build houses—to win
the luxury of choosing sun or shade, warmth or coolness, privacy or outlook, as we desire. That's why this house, with its interlocking indoor and outdoor living spaces, is
American Style.

A place for everything and everything in its place is not hard to achieve if you know
what you're after before you start. This house, designed for people who go to the country
because they like the outdoors, has pre-planned space for every kind of outdoor activity.
It is ringed with spaces for sun-bathing, lounging, dining, and plain gardening. At the
same time, all these areas are designed to give maximum visual enjoyment when seen
from indoors. Thus, in any weather, the landscape is a source of pleasure.

The house itself is so planned that normal family activities can be carried on easily,
without conflict or confusion. The study, for instance, is placed off beyond the living
room with its own bath, so that occasional guests can sleep as late as they like. Kitchen,
garage, and service yard are similarly isolated. A large, covered parking court lies between
the house and street. It is neatly landscaped for looks and separated from the bedroom
wing by a tall wood fence for privacy.

A wide, sheltering roof protects walls from weathering, windows from reflected heat

Originally printed in *House Beautiful*, 93 (February 1951): 80–83.

and glare. Along the southeast, it extends to form a great airy porch whose brick-paved floor continues out to form a sunny terrace. Fences give privacy.

"Borrowed" space makes the living room larger. Designed as a unit with living porch, it is divided from it only by a glass wall. Thus, in good weather, living space is actually doubled, in bad weather visually so. See how simple use of unpainted wood serves as background for fine furniture.

A private retreat for the masters of the house, the main bedroom is quiet and handsome. Also, because bath and dressing room are isolated, it is easily tidied, can serve as a secondary living room for the parents when necessary. Sunny bay window faces lawn.

LET YOUR KITCHEN DO THE WORK

If your kitchen work is so easy you hardly know you're doing it, your kitchen measures up to the standards of the American Style, as this one does. Many factors are involved: good light, cross ventilation, a pleasant outdoor view, accessibility from the rest of the house (and from the garden, too), convenient entrance for tradesmen, spaciousness without waste of space, uncomplicated traffic lanes, placement of cabinets and equipment in logical work sequence to save steps and time, selection of materials so durable and easy to clean that they need no special pampering.

Everything you need for kitchen and laundry is assembled in a space approximately 22'6" long x 13' wide. One end of this space, separated from the rest with only a semi-partition, is the laundry. The rest holds all the equipment demanded by 1951 standards to store, prepare, and serve food, to clean up afterward, and to do it easily.

LAUNDRY

No trekking up and down stairs, in and out of doors in all kinds of weather, to get the laundry done! No heavy loads to haul! Laundry is part of the kitchen, yet separated from it. You can keep one eye on the stew, toss a load of soiled clothes into the washer, transfer them to the dryer, and sit down at the ironer to ready them for the linen closet. This way you cut your time and energy expenditure to the bone, and have clothes that are really clean.

SNACK BAR

Because Americans like informal living and also like to make housework as easy as is consistent with gracious living, we have adopted wholeheartedly the idea of eating in the kitchen. Here a built-in snack bar saves space in a comparatively small kitchen. One end of it doubles as a planning desk. An extension of it, outside the window like a wide window sill, is a convenient shelf to simplify serving meals in the garden, designed as it is for outdoor dining.

FREEZER CENTER

With a freezer in the kitchen, you have a home "shopping center" always at hand. It saves you time, work, and money by letting you buy in quantity, take advantage of food bargains, cook ahead, and solve the problem of leftovers. Moreover, it lets you eat better quality and greater variety than you have ever known before. This freezer has 8.8 cubic feet of storage space, holds 308 pounds of food and maintains a temperature of about zero throughout.

FOOD PREPARATION

No servant problem here! There are six to do the work for you automatically and without human failure. There is the big refrigerator, a double-oven, double broiler range, a front-opening dishwasher . . . , leaving unbroken work surface above, a food-waste disposer, a freezer, and storage cabinets. Black Vitalast counters are heat-, grease-, and acid-resistant, wipe clean with damp cloth, just as easily as the white enamel cabinets do.

53

THOMAS GRIFFITH, "SHOW ME THE WAY TO GO HOME," 1974

This essay is largely a personal mediation by writer Thomas Griffith on the connection people have to the place where they grew up—in his case, the Pacific Northwest. He believes that while Americans are constantly in motion, relocating all the time, they seldom identify themselves with the places to which they have moved. And yet, at the same time, what it means to come from specific parts of the country has largely evaporated, under "powerful" forces that nationalize us. Regionalism, he writes, "today exists mostly as a fact of nature and climate." He also comments on the proliferation of tourist attractions that further diminish the sense that one region is, culturally, any different than another. There is something of a lament here, as Griffith sees Madison Avenue advertisers, national retail chains, and Disneyfication—though he does not use that term—as homogenizing us all.

Can it be that regionalism in America is declining in the same way that patriotism has—that it is more noisily insisted upon, but by fewer and fewer people? It used to be a peculiarly American trait to brag on where you lived. The most aggressive of these geographical chauvinists would extol their climate and belittle everyone else's, would rhapsodize over the outdoor beauty to be found close at hand, and would solemnly assert that their region molded people of superior character.

I know that attitude well, since I myself come from God's country. Those wide open spaces out West were thought to broaden your horizons even if they only left you with an unfocused, far-off stare. Being spread out was supposed to make you more self-reliant. We pitied the herded eastern cities with their squalid political machines, and persuaded ourselves that we were the true, think-for-yourself democrats.

And when critics came along and said that all our Main Streets looked alike, with a Woolworth's here and an A&P there, we thought they were judging merely by externals, and had missed what was stubbornly individual in us. We could have our cake mixes and eat them too, without jeopardizing our Garden of Eden. I don't believe that anymore.

I would argue that regionalism in America today exists mostly as a fact of nature and climate. Among man-made things, it survives mainly in parody. And in people it

Originally printed in *The Atlantic*, December 1974.

persists more as sentimental illusion, a pride of memory, than as distinctiveness of character. America has lost the battle to the common ooze spread by giantism.

The forces that mold us as a nation are now more powerful than those that differentiate us by regions. Big businesses—big super-markets to handle their wares, big television budgets to clear their shelves—depend at every stage on efficient uniformity. Let any enterprising local owner of a highway fast-food franchise try to vary his menu by adding a regional specialty, and he'll get a quick rocket from headquarters to stop that nonsense—everything must be similar from Bellingham to Key West, or the customer would feel disoriented.

Of course, if a wanderer through America feels the need to savor local atmosphere, he can, for a price, subject himself to roadside inns which flaunt a halfhearted and usually spurious regionalism—from fake beams to cutesy menus full of ship-ahoy gabble about Gloucester fish or chuck-wagon metaphors to sanction the toughness of the beef. (Often the only discernible linkage between a roadside Colonial tavern and its Revolutionary past is the conviction that the dollar isn't worth a continental.)

Just as much a parody of the past, though more endearing, are those one-day festivals in Midwestern small towns where local high school girls put on wide smiles and Swiss dirndls or Dutch wooden shoes to celebrate their ethnic origins. Actually, true ethnic survival in America depends on the much tougher proposition that "I'm not inferior; I count too; you must reckon with me." This attitude is more deeply felt and more insistent than any regionalism is. Challenging a man's regionalism just does not touch him to the quick anymore. You don't have to smile, ponder, when you confront a Virginian; his suburbs are much like yours. Nor is he any longer instructed that, for politeness' sake, he must "never throw up to a Yankee the fact of his birthplace."

Even the touristy landmarks of any region seem diminished now, and not just by being surrounded and overwhelmed by souvenir stands and litter. They are diminished by accessibility, as Samarkand and Xanadu are. Those brave parents who—scorning the convenient plane—crisscross the American West with their children, journeying from camper site to Indian battleground, may travel in monotonous ease across expanses of tableland ringed by mountains, but at least they get some transitional sense of the agonizing distance and receding horizons of those who, in creaky Conestoga wagons, journeyed into the unknown a century earlier.

Soon it won't be necessary to travel such distances to see dispersed artifacts. Those convenient cultural conglomerates, our proliferating Disneylands, tidily bring together in one place Wild West towns, antebellum mansions, Mississippi riverboats, or roadside jungles stocked from elsewhere. After moving comfortably from one such dollop of recreated history to another, it's but a short ride back to the motel swimming pool.

But the real distinctions between regions grow fewer as people no longer live in isolated and narrow cultures on which the outside world only rarely impinges. Even the Old South that once made a literary eloquence out of the bonds of defeat now resounds with the affirmative business aggressiveness of the New South, the kind that used to be deplored as northern materialism.

All of us, in our million, who began there and ended here, have our passports heavily stamped by else-wheres. We have not only become victims of the ooze but are carriers of the virus. We bunch together in cities and expanding suburbs where the market strategists—those students of similarity and harbingers of uniformity—can have at us easily. In their corporate boardrooms, and on Madison Avenue, they don't look at the familiar map of the fifty states as we do, as a variegated, history-sanctioned collection of contraries.

They focus instead on densely populated clots—the kind that the government calls Standard Metropolitan Statistical Areas—and have so studied the "A and B Counties" of city and suburb that they are experts in how most cheaply to reach the masses who buy cornflakes, or to single out those families, known as "upscale in income and education," who can be sold brand-name Scotch and elaborate sound systems. Everyone's level of sophistication, earnings, and schooling has been efficiently calibrated, and if you get your regional charts right, the same dollar-rated entertainers will be admired to the same degree, and the same products will sell best.

We have all been made more similar than we like to admit. At best, we hold dual citizenship: in the place of our origins, and in a nationalized culture which is in part political but mostly a shared community of experiences, references, entertainments, celebrities, and the commercial inundation not only of products but of their sell, made familiar to us in insistent melodies—all of this giving us not so much a national outlook as a common subjection to a homogenous palaver.

54

JOHN BRINCKERHOFF JACKSON, EXCERPT FROM "A VISION OF NEW FIELDS," 1984

The American West remains the most persistently fascinating American region, one that represents the sharpest contrasts in American life. Defined by landscapes of supreme grandeur and, it would appear, pure wilderness, the West is also the environment most fundamentally shaped by human beings, with whole ecologies transformed by settlement, corporate agriculture, dams, and mining. And this most "wild" of regions has also become the setting for the most rapidly growing cities and suburbs in the country, with Las Vegas, Houston, and Phoenix leading the wave that threatens to undermine regional distinctiveness. Few writers have been as influential in shaping how we look at the natural and built environments in the United States as J. B. Jackson. Because of J. B. Jackson, we now see architecture and cultural meaning in mobile homes, courthouse squares, and as in this piece, crop circles. Jackson reminds us of the persistence of regional differences underlying a growing homogenization and suggests that from high above, in an airplane, we might gain a new appreciation of those differences.

The best place to find new landscapes is in the West. Pictures painted on canvas is not what I mean, nor glimpses of pleasant rural scenery, but landscapes as we are now learning to see them: large-scale organizations of man-made spaces, usually in the open country.

Originally printed in *Discovering the Vernacular Landscape* (New Haven, Conn.: Yale University Press, 1984).

4.5. "Across the American Landscape," Alex MacLean. In this photograph, Alex MacLean has captured a sense of both the enormity of the Western landscape that has always awed Americans and the immensity of the large-scale agricultural enterprises that have come to fill it up. These crop circles are created by huge irrigation systems revolving around a central point. The systems pump water up from underground aquifers, which are being depleted far faster than they are replenished in this arid area.

Spaces of this sort are common everywhere, but it is in the West that they have been given unusual forms and dimensions: compositions of fields hard to interpret when seen at eye-level as we pass through them, but clear and sharply defined when seen from the air; and it is when we fly over it that we begin to understand the American landscape from a new perspective.

I am thinking in particular of the mosaics of irrigated land we so often fly over when traveling from East to West. They are of two kinds: those we see in Nevada and Utah and Arizona stand out in vivid contrast to their pale and empty background of desert, whereas those we see when we are above parts of eastern Washington or west Texas or Colorado or Nebraska have a far less dramatic setting; they seem gradually to emerge out of the rolling prairie. To me these latter irrigated landscapes are the ones especially worth our attention. . . .

We traveled too fast, and still travel too fast for fresh thinking about what we see below. But flying over that other kind of High Plains irrigated landscape proves to be a different experience. It is so huge and yet so simple in composition that we can study it as we look down, perceive it in other than painterly terms. We no longer see the surface as concealing what is beneath it, but as explaining it.

Only about three decades ago did this new kind of irrigated landscape begin to evolve, and not in the desert but in the rangeland of the High Plains—a region somewhat removed from the main routes of transcontinental air travel, which is perhaps why it has long remained unnoticed. Its most conspicuous feature is the great number of perfectly circular green fields. Almost completely devoid of familiar human installations—houses and roads and towns and groves of trees—this landscape is hard for the eye to measure, but each of these round fields contains 130 acres and is enclosed in a square each of whose sides is a quarter mile long. In parts of the High Plains these round fields seem to stretch without interruption in uniform rows almost to the horizon. Interspersed among them are many large fields which are severely rectangular, some of them long and narrow, others square. No details, natural or man-made, interrupt the expanse of simple geometrical forms. The few roads and highways conform to the overall grid pattern. There is a predominance of shades of green. The landscape is one of extraordinary simplicity and enormous size, but because of its monotony it is best experienced briefly and from the air.

The High Plains is an open, undulating region east of the Rockies, extending from the Canadian border down into west Texas. . . . Rainfall is barely sufficient for farming, and there are few streams for irrigation. But beneath the surface there is a large supply of water, and thanks to new engineering and agricultural techniques and the former availability of cheap energy, this supply has been tapped and brought to the surface for irrigation, and these round fields are the result. There are more than 10,000 of them in western Nebraska, and in west Texas and parts of Colorado and Kansas, even more.

What distinguishes this new irrigated landscape from the older ones, as well as what gives it its circular form, is the fact that the fields are watered not by a ditch or system of dams and ditches leading from some lake or reservoir. Each field has its own central well. A motor, located at the wellhead, drives a perforated aluminum pipe on wheels, a pipe a quarter of a mile long, around the field. Water is dispensed in a uniform spray as the pipe moves at any speed between one revolution a week or one revolution an hour. . . . Once the schedule or irrigation is programmed, a single experienced central pivot operator can take care of at least ten fields. . . .

Still, as air travelers, as amateur viewers of the landscape, our role is simply to look at the visible results of these projects and problems and to postpone the passing of ecological or social judgment until all the evidence is in. . . . A sustained interest in this landscape should eventually lead us to look for signs of change in the panorama below us. Already by looking closely, we can observe that the perfectly circular field of 130 acres of greenery has in many places begun to reach out and occupy some of the hitherto neglected corners which the rotating pipe could not reach. Eventually we will see square fields, and that, I think, from the spectator's point of view will be a loss.

In the meantime we would do well to recall that newer definition of a landscape—an organization of man-made spaces—and with an artist's eye interpret what we see. Obviously we are looking down on what must be the most artificial, the most minutely planned and controlled agricultural landscape in America. But artificiality to a greater or lesser extent is part of every landscape, and what we should also note is that this kind of irrigation requires little or no modification of the topography. . . . So these definitely artificial fields—artificial in form, artificial in content—merely lie on the surface and represent no permanent topographical change. Unlike the irrigated fields in the older landscape—bulldozed, leveled, sliced and scarred by ditches—these round fields can be abandoned without leaving a trace, just as traditional fields eventually revert to second growth and wilderness. In time we will see this happen again.

Perhaps the most significant feature of this High Plains landscape is the extraordinary self-sufficiency, the autonomy and functional isolation of each of these innumerable green circles; like billiard balls, they barely touch their neighbors, and nothing except propinquity seems to relate them one to another. Each grows its own crop according to its own individual schedule, each depends for its survival not on a common (or communal) supply of water or on a common tradition of farming or even on a common weather pattern, but solely on its own individual supply coming from its own well. We are confronted with the realization that these are not fields in the accepted sense of the word; these are areas or spaces rigidly defined by an influence or power emanating from a central source. Such is the scientific use of the world field, but we must now use it in discussing a farm landscape: the central agent of course is the pump, or the flow of water it produces, and these are fields of energy, for once given visible form.

It is surely a development of some significance when an ancient and familiar word begins to shift in definition, for it suggests that many other commonly accepted features of the landscape are likewise undergoing transformation. It would be foolish to attach too much importance to the development of a new and perhaps short-lived type of irrigation landscape. At the same time, it would be more than foolish to discount the many changes which have taken place over the last generations. And these changes are not merely a matter of shape and scale in the landscape, evident in the mile after mile of identical discs of green, slipping by beneath us like items on an assembly line, nor even a matter of the invisible power of computers to change the microclimate and the growth of plants. The real change is in ourselves and how we see the world. Flight has given us new eyes, and we are using them to discover a new order of spaces, new landscapes wherever we look.

55

STEVEN CONN, "BULLDOZING OUR SENSE OF PLACE," 1999

The loss of regional distinctiveness in America's built environment happened through countless small projects and local zoning decisions, as well as through the expansion of interstate highways and the proliferation of McDonalds. This essay begins with one of those small, local fights to muse on the connection between culture, identity, and a genuine sense of place. Bucks County was home to a distinctive regional architecture, born out of waves of Welsh, English, and German farmers, who arrived in the seventeenth and eighteenth centuries, and later, in small railroad towns that grew up along lines that radiated out from Philadelphia. It has now largely disappeared.

Originally printed in *Philadelphia Inquirer*, July 22, 1999.

The folks in Newtown Township, Bucks County, are hopping mad.

It seems that township officials had granted permission to a developer to build some tract mansions on a piece of old farmland only after the developer promised to preserve an 18th-century barn on the site.

Then, last week, one of the bulldozers on the job—oops—tore the barn down anyway.

Township officials had hoped that the barn would serve, like some ghostly museum piece, as a reminder of what the land had once been. Of what Bucks County had once been. Township officials temporarily suspended construction while they steamed about what to do next.

I wasn't surprised to hear about this rogue bulldozer and the flattening of another historic structure. I went out to Bucks County recently to visit family and discovered that Bucks County is gone. Vanished. Disappeared under a smothering tide of subdevelopments, strip malls, shopping centers, McMansions and road projects.

Given what's happened to Bucks County over the past generation, I was only surprised that this time people got so mad about a single barn. Even if Newtown Township wins the fight to get its barn reconstructed, the war over what the future of Bucks County will look like was lost long ago, and without much of a resistance.

Barns once dotted the gently rolling agriculture land in Bucks, land once extraordinarily productive. Those barns defined, as much as anything else, a distinctive American landscape. Once upon a time, and not that long ago, Bucks County looked and felt as different from the farming villages of New England as it did from the vast agricultural spaces of the Midwest and the farm country of the South.

The barns of Bucks were also remarkable pieces of design. Functionally efficient—these farmers would have had it no other way—the barns also managed to be starkly beautiful. No wonder this combination of form and function inspired the work of Charles Sheeler, perhaps America's greatest modernist painter, in the 1920s.

Sheeler went to Bucks County early in his career, searching for a way to wed a sensitivity to the past with his modernist aesthetic. What he found were Bucks County barns. In a series of stunning paintings, he immortalized them.

Sheeler was not alone in finding inspiration in Bucks County. His mentor, the eccentric Henry Mercer, filled his extraordinary museum in Doylestown with objects he collected largely from Bucks County. Pearl S. Buck, Nobel Prize-winning writer and humanitarian, lived there, as did composer Oscar Hammerstein. James Michener, too, grew up there. Twentieth-century American culture owes an outsized debt to Bucks County and the artists it nurtured.

All found a source for artistic production in Bucks County's combination of tidy compact towns, surrounded by peaceful countryside, with remarkable proximity to two great urban centers. Bucks County inspired people because once upon a time, and not that long ago, Bucks County had a singular sense of place.

In only 50 years, that sense of place has been destroyed, town by town, field by field. Barn by barn. It disappeared as hordes of new settlers, following fleets of bulldozers, came looking for it. The greatest of all the ironies about suburbanization is that it has ruined precisely those things that made leaving the city attractive in the first place.

Suburbanites came flooding into Bucks County like seekers after a holy lifestyle grail. Open spaces, quiet living, no traffic hassles. Now many of them realize that suburbia's promise has in large measure proved illusory. Plenty of traffic—more every day—and vanishing open spaces. After a series of tragedies like Littleton, Colo., comedian

Chris Rock began cracking that suburban parents now want to send their kids to city schools. Much safer.

The latest barn razing in Newtown Township reminds us, however, that at stake in the debates over suburban sprawl is the question of whether America will continue to have landscapes that give us a sense of place, as Bucks County once did.

Or are we inevitably and inexorably going to create homogenous, culturally flat and utterly banal landscapes? Strip malls and subdevelopments from sea to shining sea?

That question isn't about the trivialities of "lifestyle," but rather about our connection to place, and what grows out of that: a connection to our past. If Pearl Buck or Oscar Hammerstein or James Michener came to Bucks County today, I doubt very much whether any would find their muse there. There are no more barns left for Charles Sheeler to paint.

CHAPTER 5

Urbanism, Real and Imagined

In a letter to Dr. Benjamin Rush in 1800, Thomas Jefferson wrote, "I view great cities as pestilential to the morals, the health and the liberties of man. True, they nourish some of the elegant arts, but the useful ones can thrive elsewhere, and less perfection in the others, with more health, virtue and freedom, would be my choice." Almost a century and a half later, E. B. White, the greatest defender of cities, imagined the nightmare of an atom bomb dropping on New York: "If it were to go, all would go—this city, this mischievous and marvelous monument which not to look upon would be like death." This deep, long-standing ambivalence toward cities is at the heart of American culture, as it has come to pit nature versus culture, independence versus dependence, immigrants versus "Americans," farmers versus laborers, community versus individualism, good versus evil. In this chapter, we trace the contours of this ambivalence. The selections included here do not simply document the rise of cities, and the reaction to it, but comment on the development of urbanism, that is, the ideas and cultures around the building and imagining of cities.

Thinking about the building of cities preoccupied not only reformers in those large and growing centers, but also utopians who built communities in rural New York and Kentucky, western miners who built "instant cities" in the West, and architects who built temporary fantasies of ideal cities, such as the White City of Chicago's Columbian Exposition in 1893 and the Futurama display at the 1939 World's Fair in New York. The drama of America's urban growth comes not only from overwhelming statistics of the growth of urban population, economic output, and physical expansion. It also derives from the aggressive and passionate attempts to develop cities, to promote them, to fight against them, and to interpret them. It is the attempt to cope with the new cities—to develop them, control them, enhance them, interpret them, celebrate them, and denigrate them—that is the most fascinating story of all.

It is natural to begin, as we do, with the founding of the new nation, and with the design of Washington, D.C. But it merits noting that a long history of American urbanism existed well before the new republic. In 1630, John Winthrop envisioned the Puritan settlement of Massachusetts Bay as "a city upon a hill," but in fact, the oldest Euro-American city in the country is Santa Fe, New Mexico, founded by Spanish explorers and missionaries in the sixteenth century. Well before that, however, Native Americans, especially in the Southwest, lived in some of the most carefully designed and planned cities, dating back at least as far as 900 of the common era (C.E.). These pueblos were followed by other important urban centers, such as Mesa Verde in Colorado. There were urban Americans long before there was a United States with a central capital.

When the decision to build Washington, D.C., as the nation's capital was made in 1789, the new American government relied on a Frenchman, Charles L'Enfant, to design a grand capital city of boulevards punctuated by public buildings and monuments. It was to be unlike any of the other major cities of the time—Philadelphia with its grid and

Boston with its network of streets and wharves. But the new Congress also chose a location geographically "out of sight and out of mind," a symbol of the relative weakness of this government in the new Constitution. Furthermore, in the very design of the city was a map of the new Constitution: long axes connected the three branches of the new federal government. While there remains a debate whether the metaphorical swamp Washington has come to represent was actually built upon a swamp, it is clear that the city design made for an inhospitable stay for its inhabitants, who usually did all they could to leave as soon as the Congress was adjourned.

Although the United States would remain demographically rural until 1920 (when the census noted that more people lived in cities than in small towns or in the country), American cities expanded with a remarkable rapidity through the nineteenth century. Most cities, however, remained largely unplanned, and grew with a haphazard energy. While the plan for Washington, D.C., suggested that Americans were amenable to the planning of their cities by governmental fiat, this was hardly the case in the years that followed Washington's founding. Public planning on the scale represented by Washington stands as the exception to the rule of private development in American urban history, especially in the antebellum period. A somewhat disheveled proximity remained the hallmark of urbanism in the nineteenth century.

Counterpoised against the chaotic life of early nineteenth-century cities, handmaidens of America's growing commerce, were the remarkable number of "utopias" that sprouted up at the same moment: Shaker villages in Massachusetts and New York, New Harmony, Indiana, as well as the gridded towns that began to be settled across the Ohio Valley and into the Great West. Each in their own way, these communities tried to create a new, more perfect society, and to give those ideals physical shape in these places.

It would seem as if American cities grew naturally and inevitably, if not always pleasingly, through the nineteenth century, sprouting up full-blown where nothing had been before. But for every St. Louis, Denver, and Chicago, there was also a Superior, Wisconsin; Galena, Illinois; and Galveston, Texas—places that were promoted by their founders to become the next New York or Philadelphia but that floundered when a railroad bypassed them or an industry moved to a more convenient destination. Los Angeles was stagnant as a city until two railway lines to the area launched a massive advertising campaign to lure tourists and residents there. Across the country, and especially in the American West, the landscape is littered with ghost towns haunted by their own delusions of grandeur. The history of American cities is of both its glorious successes and its disappointing failures.

The aftermath of the Civil War brought the urbanization of the United States to a new level. By 1900 there were six cities with more than half a million people. Although New York had become the largest city and dominated the economic and cultural life of the nation, it was Chicago that seemed the most extraordinary, especially in its rate of growth. Founded in 1830 and virtually destroyed in the Great Fire of 1871, it more than tripled in size between 1880 and 1900 to 1.5 million people. With the creation of vast corporations, as well as a network of railroad lines, it was to cities that industry moved, and cities became the engines of the nation's economy. By 1890, according the federal census, the value of manufactured products exceeded the value of agricultural products for the first time. Jefferson must have rolled over in his grave.

Such spectacular urban growth was impossible, of course, without a constant influx of immigrants. In the century after 1830 some 40 million people emigrated to the United States, 23 million of those after 1880. A high proportion of this century-long wave of immigration was drawn to America's cities. In those places, away from the watchful eye but under the foot of speculative developers and landlords, these immigrants built dense, vibrant, but usually impoverished communities.

Just as immigrants flowed into American cities to serve as laborers in the burgeoning American industrial economy, so too did the wealth of the United States flow into America's great cities, remaking them into cities of "sunshine and shadow," as the cliché of the day portrayed it. Slowly and steadily, the "walking city" of the early nineteenth century, where rich and poor lived adjacent to one another, began to give way to segregation by wealth and poverty. A new wave of urban planning began, to address the social, economic, and aesthetic problems of the modern city.

The post–Civil War period also brought the first substantial attempt to positively shape American cities. Frederick Law Olmsted, who drew intellectual sustenance from landscape architect and writer Andrew Jackson Downing, brought Downing's ideas to the city. His plan for Central Park introduced into the most dynamic American city a place of repose, designed to be the antithesis of the dirty, harried, tense city. Olmsted had strong ideas about how visitors to his park should act. Indeed, he saw the park as a place where behavior would be the opposite of that engaged in in the rest of the city. Olmsted's vision went far beyond parks, however. He envisioned a park system, with large parks linked to smaller ones by wide, tree-lined parkways bearing public institutions alongside. While he designed and inspired dozens of remarkable urban spaces across the country, only in Boston and its "emerald necklace" of parks was he able to achieve, at least for a time, something of this ideal.

The problems of the new industrial city generated the era of reform activity we call Progressivism. Progressives who sought to reform city government corruption, to replan and redesign the city; architects who offered new forms for industry and commerce; social reformers who fought for better tenements for the poor, expanded public schooling, and built welfare organizations all recognized the power and inevitability of urbanization but also remained shocked by the horrible effects in terms of poverty, crime, and disease.

Jacob Riis pioneered the concept of investigative journalism in his now classic *How the Other Half Lives* (1890). Not content simply to document the crowded, disease-ridden tenements (New York's Lower East Side held upward of one thousand people per acre, higher than present-day Calcutta), Riis used his journalism to demand both the demolition of slums and the building of new forms of low-income housing and creation of neighborhood parks. On another side were aesthetic reformers, purveyors of what culminated in a City Beautiful Movement, propounding an ideal that called for making American cities equal in beauty and grandeur to their European counterparts.

In the midst of this era of Progressive urban reforms came the World's Columbian Exposition in Chicago in 1893. City planners drew enormous inspiration from this temporary "White City." Well planned, orderly, and clean—the White City seemed to represent everything the real city wasn't, even if the fantasy lasted only the six months before the fair closed. The inspiration planners drew, however, focused less on the ways of making the American city healthier or more just. Rather, these citybuilders followed Olmsted in their call for comprehensive planning (although they put far less emphasis on ecological planning of the city). Where the practical Progressive reformers hoped to soothe the tensions of the industrial city through better housing, schools, and parks, aesthetic reformers hoped to Americanize immigrants through the uplift provided by beautiful surroundings.

Neither set of reformers was able to fully implement their plans, due largely to the long-standing resistance to government intervention in the marketplace of space. Public housing was largely rejected, and plans for wholly replanning street arrangements to create the "city beautiful" were rejected by property owners. Thus, the dominant building image of the age was not the boulevard or grand public buildings, but the private skyscraper, designed for speculation and for advertising the great invention of the age, the modern corporation. The horizontal city of public affairs was vastly overshadowed by the vertical city of business.

Only with the New Deal in the 1930s did city government gain the legal and financial backing of the federal government to take large swaths of land for public housing and other public projects. New Deal efforts to remake American cities were politically palatable because some of the worst effects of the Depression were felt in American cities. Detroit teetered on the verge of bankruptcy, and in Toledo, unemployment reached a staggering 80 percent. Faced with these drastic times, Americans embraced the experiments in public housing and slum clearance conducted by the New Dealers. These projects, along with the soaring bridges and early highways also built in the 1930s, foreshadowed of the massive remaking of cities undertaken by the federal and state governments after the Second World War.

America's industrial cities boomed during the Second World War and seemed to emerge from it bigger, stronger, and more culturally central than ever before. But beneath this surface lay the seeds of an urban crisis that by the 1970s and 1980s would take the older American cities to their lowest state. In fact, those seeds had been planted during the Second World War. The war created a housing crunch for returning veterans; the explosion of defense industries in the South and West called for massive new housing developments. Traditional industries followed quickly in the aftermath of the war, and people followed in their wake, all taking a new system of interstate highways (built throughout the 1950s, especially after the 1956 Highway Act) to cheaper land and labor. By the 1970s, America's urban geography had divided into the Rust Belt, stretching from Boston and New York, across Pennsylvania to the cities of the Great Lakes, and the Sun Belt, boom cities like Atlanta, Phoenix, Dallas, and especially Los Angeles.

The response to the urban crisis of the nation's older cities in the postwar era was a series of programs called urban renewal. Within America's large and small cities alike, planners remade the urban fabric to accommodate the automobile as well as modernist ideas of aesthetics and efficiency. Dense, old neighborhoods—now often called "slums"—were demolished to make room for wide-open plazas and high-rise office blocks. Under the leadership of a cadre of urban renewal planners and mayors—such as Robert Moses of New York and Richard Lee of New Haven—American cities were torn down with a violent abandon and rebuilt with highways, parking garages, and public housing high rises. The era of urban renewal marked the achievement of a long-standing goal of urban reformers: the power and finances to redesign cities in the manner of European cities. The scale of these efforts, funded in large part with federal money, was unprecedented; the damage to the urban fabric was incalculable.

By the early 1960s, these urban renewal programs had already generated an opposition on the part of people who saw the cities they loved destroyed to make room for highways, parking lots, and corporate office towers. That opposition galvanized around the 1961 publication of Jane Jacobs's book *The Death and Life of American Cities*. Jacobs, herself a New Yorker when she wrote the book, extolled the virtues of city life lived at pedestrian speed. Rather than decry the crowded messiness that so many urban renewers saw, Jacobs, and others like William Whyte, celebrated the heterogeneity, the bustle, the "organized complexity" that took place in city neighborhoods. *The Death and Life of American Cities* joined that small collection of books written for a broad public—*Uncle Tom's Cabin*, *The Jungle*, and *Silent Spring* among them—that profoundly influenced the course of politics and policy.

Such influence would take two decades to bear fruit, however. Throughout the 1960s and 1970s, the decline of urban fortunes continued. Indeed, the flight of capital and of people out of the older cities accelerated, even amid the general prosperity of the country. American cities, which had experienced a rapid influx of African-Americans from the South from the 1920s onward, now saw whites flee, along with industry and tax dollars. Roughly two million white residents left America's ten largest cities in the 1960s alone. As a result, American cities became increasingly Black and Latino and increasingly poor. These older cities hit their low-water mark between the mid-1970s and mid-1980s: New York City verged on bankruptcy in 1975 and the federal government refused to intervene to help; the steel industry in and around Pittsburgh collapsed virtually all at once; crack cocaine in the early 1980s swept through urban neighborhoods, bringing violence and destroying lives in the process; the automobile industry in and around Detroit moved much of its manufacturing out of state.

To see cities in this period only as warehouses of social and economic problems misses too much. Around the corner from where Jane Jacobs was celebrating small blocks and the corner grocer were some of the most vibrant settings for theater, music, and art, as well as more informal settings of cultural and social innovation. Although a city like Detroit, once the "arsenal of democracy" during the Second World War, became the poster child of urban decay just two decades later, it also served as home to Motown and its revolutionary influence on American popular music. Indeed, the flowering of American popular culture—in music and art and dance—still happened in cities. The death of the old cities had been exaggerated.

More recently, there is some tentative evidence that the pendulum has begun to swing back. Older cities became "hot" during the 1990s, fueled in part by a booming economy and federal tax policies that fostered reinvestment in cities and in part by a renewed appreciation for the value of urban life. In addition, life in the suburbs and in the boom cities of the Sun Belt began to look less attractive. Choking traffic in these auto-addicted places made the air unbreathable; rampant, largely unplanned growth gobbled up open space and made the suburbs just as crowded as the cities. Taking inspiration from Jane Jacobs, the postmodern movement in architecture, and the gentrification of older parts of cities, a growing group of architects and planners have urged a dramatic shift away from the approaches to city building that have been dominant in the United States for at least a half century. While these "New Urbanists" have built some attractive communities—such as Seaside, Florida, and Kentlands, Maryland—they have also inspired a spate of developments that have marketed nostalgia by creating instantaneous towns that mimic in stilted ways the principles of community development laid out by Jane Jacobs. (Post's Riverside, discussed in a document in Chapter 8, is one such development.)

And perhaps most important, American cities remained, as they always have been, the first destination of new immigrants, who arrived in record numbers during the 1990s. As a result, the census of 2000 revealed that the populations of some cities, after declining steadily for half a century, had stabilized, or even increased. In the second half of the twentieth century, America's older cities suffered the worst body blows of bad policy, bad planning, racial tensions, and economic decline, and yet still managed to demonstrate a tremendous resilience, to be places where culture flourished, where new ideas blossomed, and where new Americans pursued their own American dreams.

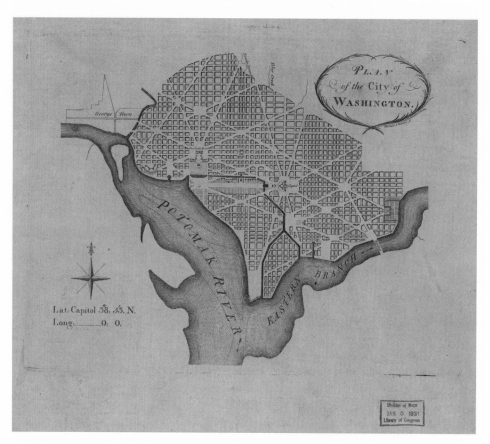

5.1. Plan of Washington, D.C., 1791. When Congress decided to move the nation's capital to the newly created District of Columbia, the plan for this new city served as a chance to give physical form to the political principles of the new nation. Not a few commentators noted the irony that the plan was drawn by a Frenchman and took the gardens of Versailles as its model.

56

THE REVEREND DR. DUCHE, "DESCRIPTION OF PHILADELPHIA," 1789

Although American cities bore no resemblance to the vast metropolises of Europe at the end of the eighteenth century, they were nonetheless far more central to American economic and cultural life than one would expect from the image of America as a rural nation. Indeed, as Gary Nash has written, it was the port cities of colonial America that were the "crucibles" of the Revolution, and none more so than Philadelphia. William Penn's city was, by the late eighteenth century, the largest, busiest, most dynamic city in the New World. Reverend Duche describes it for us, sitting at his window.

I am now sitting at a window that overlooks the majestic Delaware, compared with which our Isis and Cherwell, though immortalized in song, would appear but little babbling brooks. The woods along the opposite shore of New Jersey are clothed in their brightest verdure, and afford a pleasing rest and refreshment to the eye, after it has glanced across the watry mirror. Whilst I am writing this, three topsail vessels, wafted along by a gentle southern breeze, are passing by my window. The voice of industry perpetually resounds along the shore; and every wharf within my view is surrounded with groves of masts, and heaped with commodities of every kind, from almost every quarter of the globe.

I cannot behold this lively active scene, without lamenting, that the streams of commerce should ever be checked in their course, or directed to wander in other channels, than those which they not possess.

Dean Prideaux, in his connexion of the old and new testament, speaks of William Penn's having laid out his new city after the plan of Babylon. Perhaps it might be difficult at this time to ascertain, what this plan was. Be this as it may, I am not so well versed in antiquity to be able to pronounce, whether there is the least resemblance or not betwixt Babylon and Philadelphia. Of this, however, you may be certain that no city could be laid out with more beauty and regularity than Philadelphia. Its streets cross each other at right angles: those which run from north to south being parallel to each other, as well as those from east to west. Notwithstanding the vast progress that has been already made, a considerable time must elapse before the whole plan is executed. The buildings from north to south, along the bank of the Delaware, including the suburbs, now extend near two miles, and those from east to west, about half a mile from the river. But, according to the original plan, they are to extend as far, nay farther, I believe than the beautiful river Schuylkill, which runs about two miles west of Delaware.

The principal street, which is an hundred feet wide, would have a noble appearance, were it not for an ill-contrived court-house, and a long range of shambles, which they erected in the very middle of it. This may, indeed, be very convenient for the inhabitants, and, on their market-days, exhibits such a scene of plenty, as is scarcely to be equalled by any single market in Europe. But I am apt to think, that moveable stalls, contrived so as to afford shelter from the weather, would have answered the purpose full as well, and then the avenue might have been left entirely open. The streets are all well

Originally printed in *American Museum*, March 1789, 234–38.

paved in the middle for carriages, and there is a foot-path of hard bricks on each side next to the houses. The houses in general are plain, but not elegant, for the most part built upon the same plan, a few excepted, which are finished with some taste, and neatly decorated within. The streets are well lighted by lamps, placed at proper distances; and watchmen and scavengers are constantly employed for security and cleanliness.

Almost every sect in Christendom have here found an happy asylum; and such is the catholic spirit that prevails, that I am told, they have frequently and chearfully assisted each other in erecting their several places of worship. These places too generally partake of the plainness and neatness of their dwelling houses, being seldom enriched by costly ornaments. Here are three churches that use the liturgy and ceremonies of our church of England; but only two of them are under any episcopal jurisdiction. Christ church has by far the most venerable appearance of any building in this city; and the whole architecture, including an elegant steeple (which is furnished with a complete ring of bells) would not disgrace one of the finest streets in Westminster. The eastern front is particularly well designed and executed; but its beauty is in a great measure lost, by its being set too near the street, instead of being placed, as it ought to have been, forty or fifty feet back.

The state-house, as it is called, is a large plain building, two stories high—the lower story is divided into two large rooms, in one of which the provincial assembly meet, and in the other the supreme court of judicature is held—the upper story consists of a long gallery which is generally used for public entertainments, and two rooms adjoining it, one of which is appropriated for the governor and his council; the other, I believe, is yet unoccupied. In one of the wings, which join the main building, by means of a brick arcade, is deposited a valuable collection of books, belonging to a number of the citizens, who are incorporated by the name of the library company of Philadelphia. You would be astonished, at the general taste for books, which prevails among all orders and ranks of people in this city. The library assured me, that for one person of distinction and fortune, there were twenty tradesmen that frequented this library.

Behind and adjoining to the statehouse, was some time since erected a tower, of such miserable architecture, that the legislature have widely determined to let it go to decay (the upper part being entirely of wood) that it may hereafter be built upon a new and more elegant construction. Mr. Franklin, the late speaker of the assembly, with whom I have several times conversed, informed me, that the plot of ground, on which the statehouse stands, and which is one of the squares of the city, is to be planted with trees, and divided into walks, for the recreation of the citizens. I could not help observing to him, that it would be a considerable improvement of their plan, if the legislature could purchase another square, which lies to the south of this, and apply it to the same salutary purpose; as otherwise, their walks must be very contracted, unless they make them of a circular or serpentine form.

57

ANONYMOUS,
"DESCRIPTION OF THE CITY OF WASHINGTON," 1791

The founding of Washington, D.C., became a remarkable opportunity to give the princi-ples of American constitutional government a physical form. Writing in 1791, this author does not yet have much of a city to describe, and indeed well into the nineteenth century many Americans viewed Washington as "out of sight" and thus "out of mind." So instead, this author plays the booster, and discusses the natural advantages the new city possesses much in the way older cities were described. In fact, Washington never developed the port or commercial life this author predicts. It remains largely a one company town.

The *City of Washington*, stands at the junction of the rivers Potowmack and the Eastern branch, extending nearly four miles up each, including a tract of territory, exceeded in point of convenience, salubrity, and beauty, by none in America, if any in the world.—For, although the land is apparently level, yet, by gentle and gradual swellings, a variety of ele-gant prospects are produced; while there is a sufficient descent to convey off the water oc-casioned by rain. Within the limits of the city, are a great many excellent springs, and by digging wells, water of the best quality may readily be had; besides, the never failing streams, that now run through that territory, are also to be collected for the use of the city.

The Eastern branch is one of the safest and most commodious harbours in America, being sufficiently deep for the largest ships, for about four miles above its mouth, while the channel lies close along the edge of the city, and is abundantly capacious.—The Potowmack, although only navigable for small craft, for a considerable distance from its banks adjoining the city (excepting about half a mile above the junction of the rivers) will nevertheless afford a capacious summer harbour; as an immense number of ships may ride in the great channel, opposite to, and below, the city.

This metropolis, being situated upon the great post road, exactly equidistant from the northern and southern extremities of the Union, and nearly so from the Atlantick to Fort Pitt, upon the best navigation and in the midst of the richest commercial territory in America, commanding the most extensive internal resources, is by far the most eligi-ble situation for the residence of Congress; and as there is no doubt of its being pressed forward, by the publick spirited enterprise of the people of the United States, and by for-eigners, it will grow up with a degree of rapidity hitherto unparalleled in the annals of cities, and will soon become the admiration and delight of the world.

The plan of this city, agreeable to the directions of the President of the United States, was designed and drawn, by the celebrated *Major l'Enfant*; and is an inconceivable im-provement upon all other cities in the world, combining not only convenience, regularity, elegance of prospect and a free circulation of air, but every thing grand and beautiful, that can possibly be introduced into a city.

The streets, in general, run due north and south, and east and west, forming rectan-gular squares.—The area for the *Congress house*, is situated upon the most beautiful em-inence, little more than a mile from the Eastern branch, and not much more from the

Originally printed in *Massachusetts Magazine, or, Monthly Museum of Knowledge and Rational En-tertainment*, vol. 3, December 1791.

Potowmack; commanding a full and complete view of every part of the city, as well as a considerable extent of the country around.—The *President's house* will stand upon a rising ground, not far from the banks of the Potowmack, possessing a delightful water prospect, together with a commanding view of the Congress house and most of the material parts of the city. The houses for the great departments of State, the supreme court house and judiciary offices, the national bank, the general exchange, and the several market houses, with a variety of other publick buildings, are all arranged with equal propriety, judgment and taste, and such situations as, in practice, will be found the most convenient and proper.—Due south from the President's house, and due west from the Congress house, run two great pleasure parks, or malls, which intersect and terminate upon the banks of the Potowmack, and are ornamented at the sides with a variety of publick gardens and elegant buildings, &c.—Regularly interspersed through the city, where the most material streets cross, in the most important situations, are a variety of open areas, formed in various regular figures, which in great cities are extremely useful and ornamental.—Fifteen of the best of these areas may be appropriated to the different States composing the union, not only to bear their respective names, but as proper places for them to erect statues, obelisks or columns, to the memory of their favourite heroes or statesmen; providing they contribute towards the improvement of the lots around these areas, in such a manner as may be agreed upon.—From the Congress house, the President's house, and some of the other important areas in the city, run transverse avenues, or diagonal streets from one material object to another, which not only produce a variety of charming prospects, and facilitate the communication through the city, but remove that insipid sameness that renders Philadelphia and Charleston unpleasing.—These great leading streets are all 160 feet wide, including a brick pavement of 10 feet, and a gravel walk of 30 feet, planted with trees, on each side; which will leave 30 feet of paved street for carriages.—The rest of the streets, are in general, 130 and 110 feet wide, and are now mostly run out upon true principles, from celestial observations, by the Geographer general of the United States, whose astronomical knowledge and scientifick talents, are so universally known and admired.

58

M. G. UPTON, EXCERPT FROM
"THE PLAN OF SAN FRANCISCO," 1869

The dream of building the next great metropolis—especially the next New York City—
preoccupied city builders of the nineteenth century. The rapid development of the West
along the lines of railroad led to the creation of "instant cities," places where a city of ten
thousand appeared in the course of a year or even in months. It is not surprising that observers would repeatedly predict unending growth. Upton's discussion of the laying out of
San Francisco's street grid also reveals the homogeneity of American town planning ideals
in the nineteenth century amid a landscape of remarkable diversity. The gridded town
plan, following Philadelphia's model and the plan of the Northwest Ordinance of 1789,
was replicated across the United States. Often, as in San Francisco, cities were built with
complete disregard to the topography of their site, creating bizarre living conditions that
persist to this day.

It was to Monsieur Vioget that the astonishing idea of laying out a city upon the peninsula of San Francisco was first presented in a serious and business-like manner. We know
but little of the personal history of that child of sunny France. It is certain, however, that
he was not called upon to found the future metropolis of the Pacific because of any experience which he had previously enjoyed in the matter of surveying places for the future
residence of large populations. . . . The cause of his selection for the performance of a
duty with which immortality is usually associated, was that he was an engineer, and was
in possession of the only instruments which could then be discovered in all Yerba Buena.
It would perhaps be unjust to enter upon a criticism of his work till at least the circumstances by which he was surrounded were recalled. Even in those early days there were
men of faith in the scattered hamlet by the Golden Gate. They looked down upon the
broad expanse of a noble bay, and they said to themselves: "As sites for cities are getting
scarce, a great emporium must, some time in the far-off future, spring up here." In
imagination they beheld streets, and squares, and promenades, take the place of the
chapparal and the sand dunes by which the face of nature was covered; but without any
very clear idea of the causes which were to promote their construction, or the manner in
which the details were to be carried out. Some, in their hilarious moments, at least saw a
new New York rise, as if by magic, in dazzling splendor out of the scrub-oak bushes
through which they were in the habit of forcing a toilsome passage; others, a modernized
Philadelphia, with its streets at right angles, its rows of severely identical buildings with
solid wooden shutters. . . .

The basis for all these dreams was a few houses scattered about the peninsula, built

Originally printed in *Overland Monthly* 2 (February 1869): 131–36.

of adobe. The engrossing subject of conversation was hides and tallow. The bells of the old Mission tolled, every Sabbath, away in the distance, and the good missionaries celebrated their masses, it is to be feared almost exclusively for the poor Indians who found, to their great contentment and satisfaction, that Christianity was only another name for regular ration duly and fairly distributed. The waters of the bay then washed the eastern line of Montgomery Street, and where stately structures now rise, boats were once beached. The peninsula, as you looked westward, presented the appearance of a lump of baker's dough, which had been kneaded into fantastic hills and vales—a lump of baker's dough, too, which, after having been worked, had been forgotten so long that the green mould had begun to creep over it. For, upon this windy tongue of land, the forces of nature had been operating through long geological ages. The westerly wind blowing upon it with ceaseless moan for the greater part of every recurring year, had rolled up the sand from the bottom of the quiet Pacific, and then, when it had been accumulated on the firm land, had fashioned it into the most grotesque shapes. . . .

Whatever be the true geological history, Telegraph, Rincon and Townsend Street Hills rose up on the point of the peninsula, like weird shapes beckoning the adventurers to this rich and wonderful land, while Russian Hill stretched itself in all its wealth of nondescript topography, parallel to them, but further to the west. It was upon a site so unpromising that Monsieur Vioget was called upon by the united acclaim of his fellow-citizens to lay out a city. Looking back at what was then done with such solemnity and pretence of deliberation in the interests of civilization, it is a matter for regret that these early settlers did not leave the tracery of their streets to that bovine instinct of which we have such a brilliant and altogether admirable illustration in the city of Boston. These intelligent animals always furnish evidence that they believe in the maxim, that the longest way around is often the shortest way home. It is altogether possible that if the outlines of the streets were conformed to the paths which the cows of the early villagers made for themselves, on their way to and from their respective corrals, we would have easier and more rational grades, and a more picturesque and interesting city than Monsieur Vioget has given us, with all his wealth of theodolites, and the ceremony of running lines and erecting monuments. . . .

Who, therefore, can with justice censure Monsieur Vioget for going heartily with those who employed him? He made an observation so as to fix one point, and then drew off the future metropolis of the Pacific, with the greatest ease and the most remarkable celerity. For the topography with which he had to deal he manifested a contempt entirely proper in a person engaged in an engineering romance. The paper upon which he sketched his plan was level, and presented no impediment to the easy transit of the pencil. He gave us, with that disregard for details which is always characteristic of great minds, the *Quartier Latin*, improved and modified by Philadelphia, for a site as rugged and irregular as that to which Romulus and Remus applied themselves on the banks of the Tiber. Over hill and dale he remorselessly projected his right lines. To the serene Gallic mind it made but very little difference that some of the streets which he had laid out followed the lines of a dromedary's back, or that others described semi-circles—some up, some down—up Telegraph Hill from the eastern front of the city—up a grade, which a goat could not travel—then down on the other side—then up Russian Hill, and then down sloping toward the Presidio. . . .

His work was fair to look upon on paper—very difficult if not bewildering to follow out on foot. These streets pushed ahead with stern scientific rigor. Never did rising city start upon more impracticable courses. . . .

It did not take [Mr. O'Farrell] long to discover that the plan upon which Vioget had laid out the city was entirely unadapted to the site. A large amount of engineering knowledge was not necessary to enable him to reach that conclusion. A superficial acquaintance with the modes and appliances by which locomotion is achieved among men was all that was required to reveal to him the errors of his predecessor. He proposed to change the lines of the streets so as to conform as much as possible to the topography, but his suggestions were not received with the favor which he expected. There was not an incipient millionaire then in all San Francisco who did not have safely locked up in his trunk the title-deeds to the lot or lots that were going to be the most valuable. It is possible that nobody had made up his mind as to the particular use for which his property would be required. It might be needed for a Custom House, or the Capitol of the new State, the germ of which Marshall had found in the mill-stream, near Sutter's Fort, or some grand and inexplicable structure necessary to the new order of things. Whatever it might be, each settler's lot was *the* lot above all lots—sure to prove the focus of the new city, gradually unfolding its outlines, if not the hub of creation. . . .

It can hardly be expected that a plan conceived under the circumstances above set forth, and carried out in the way we have briefly sketched, could have resulted in anything very complete in itself, or very pleasant to look upon. The stranger, as he paces the deck of the incoming steamer, at night—for a stranger among us always takes the shape of a passenger by sea, and never of a solitary horseman slowly ascending a rugged pathway—is enraptured with the sight which San Francisco presents. As the steamer passes Black Point, the dull red haze upon which he had been gazing with such intensity begins to assume shape and form; when he rounds Clark's Point, a spectacle is revealed which more than repays him for all the dangers and hardships of the voyage. On either side of him rise Telegraph and Rincon Hills like luminous cones, while, in the background, towers above all Russian Hill in stories of light. Nor is the illusion at all dissipated as he is whirled from the wharf, through the well-lighted streets, to his hotel. Unfortunately his enthusiasm is not destined to last long. When he comes to walk abroad in the full light of day, he sees fine structures, it is true—stores, brilliant enough for Broadway, or the *Boulevards* and a style of architecture more elegant and graceful than is generally to be found in American cities, particularly in the case of private dwellings, and well-built though somewhat dirty streets. But as soon as he begins to trace out the lines of the great thoroughfares, he finds that Nature, wherever he turns, has been cut and slashed, dug down and filled up, out of existence; unsightly defiles confront him wherever he goes. . . . From the first error there is, of course, no escape. San Francisco will have to grow in accordance with the lines originally marked out for her. The gage of battle, which Monsieur Vioget in such a light and careless manner flung down to Nature on this peninsula, has provoked a struggle which cannot be ended probably in the life-time of the present generation. The work of grading, cutting down, and filling up, will have to be continued till the logical result of the contest has been reached. In the end we shall probably have a metropolis in every way adapted for trade and commerce; but by no means as handsome and picturesque a city as might have been built, if some attention had in the beginning been paid to the suggestions of Nature.

59

THE REVEREND JOSIAH STRONG, EXCERPT FROM
"THE PROBLEM OF THE TWENTIETH CENTURY CITY," 1888

Few among the intellectual critics of the city rose to the rhetorical levels of Josiah Strong, who called cities the "serious menace to our civilization." In this piece, Strong is more reasoned and less impassioned. Indeed, he is quite prescient that the United States will become an urban nation, leaving its rural roots behind. He argues that the problem of the city in the twentieth century will be how to create a "higher type of citizenship" out of the increasingly diverse immigrant masses who made up American metropolises. He is decidedly pessimistic about the city's ability to create efficient, uncorruptible governments. But he holds out hope that educating the young might create, in a generation, a new type of citizen.

Legislative enactment creates a "Greater New York." It has also been decreed by the laws of our social life that there are to be a greater Boston and Philadelphia, a greater Chicago and San Francisco. The city is to contain an ever-increasing proportion of the population and to constitute a factor of ever-increasing importance in the national life.

The accelerated rate of growth of the city in modern times is illustrated by New York. Settled in 1614, it took the city 175 years to gain the first 33,000 inhabitants. During the next 50 years it gained 280,000. During the next 30 years it gained 630,000; and during the next 21 years, which ended in 1890, it gained 859,000. In the last short period the gain was twenty-six times as great as during the first long period, and the rate of gain was 208 times greater. The census of 1890 showed that this metropolitan city contained a larger population than any one of twenty-eight great states of the Union. . . . .

This sudden concentration of population is often spoken of as a congestion, and is believed by many to be abnormal and temporary. It has brought perplexing problems, as yet unsolved, which some have imagined would find their solution in a reaction of population toward the country. But no warrant for such an expectation is to be found in the causes of the city's recent growth. This movement of population from country to city, which is one of the most significant phenomena of modern times, is due primarily to three causes: (1) The application of machinery to agriculture, which enables four men to do the work formerly done by fourteen; (2) the rise of manufactures in the cities,

Originally printed in *North American Review* 165 (1888): 343–49.

5.2. *Baxter Street Alley,* circa 1898. Museum of the City of New York, The Jacob A. Riis Collection. No one better documented the human misery of the "foul core of New York" than did Jacob Riis, a Danish immigrant and photojournalist working at the turn of the century. His *How the Other Half Lives* (1890) was intended to awaken the consciences of government and philanthropists, to work toward solving the problem of the slum. Riis insisted that it was the physical conditions of the slums that caused disease, crime, and immorality of all types. His photographs may have also fanned the reactionary fervor of such writers as Josiah Strong and Madison Grant, who would, by the 1920s, successfully push for immigration restriction laws.

which attracts the men released from the farms; and (3) the railway, which not only makes the transfer of population easy, but, which is more important, makes it possible to feed a massed population, no matter how vast.

There is a gregarious instinct in men, which has always made the city as large as it could well be; and these three causes have liberated and emphasized this instinct during this century. As this instinct and these causes are all permanent, it is obvious that this tendency will prove permanent.

Some have imagined that the pressure upon the city might be relieved and the miseries of the slum modified by removing families to unoccupied lands and teaching them to engage in agriculture, and steps have been taken in this direction. But those who expect to solve or even to simplify the problem by this method fail to appreciate the profound change which has come over the world's industry during this century, by which it has ceased to be individual and has become organized; a change which is destined to exert more influence on material conditions and on the social, intellectual, moral, and spiritual life of man than did the discovery of America, the invention of gunpowder or the art of printing. Doubtless this transition is the most important material change which has ever taken place in the history of the race. It has separated as by an impassable gulf the simple, homespun, individualistic life of the world's past from the complex, closely associated life of the present and of the world's future. . . .

Poets have sung the independence of the farmer, but that independence forever ceased with the transition from the age of homespun to that of the division and organization of labor; and this fact has a most significant bearing on the future growth of cities. . . . There are already more persons engaged in farming than are needed, with the improved agricultural implements of recent years, to supply the world's demands for food, and that accounts for the general depression of agriculture in Europe and America during recent years.

If we could transfer 100,000 families from our crowded cities to unoccupied land, and so train them as to make them successful farmers, the world would not consume any more food to accommodate them. They could succeed only by getting the market, and they could get the market only by driving 100,000 other farmers out of it, which would mean driving them off the farm and into the city. . . .

Of course population will increase; but increased production by reason of improved methods is likely to keep pace with it for many years to come. Good judges tell us that our present agricultural product could be doubled without any increase of acreage under cultivation, simply by reasonably good methods.

It has been pointed out that the world's demand for food is necessarily limited. This fact places a natural limit to the number of men who can successfully devote themselves to producing the food supply; but there is no such natural and necessary limit to the world's consumption in other directions. In palaces and gardens, in furniture and equipages, in dress and ornaments, in paintings and statuary, the purse sets the only limit of expenditure. If the world were a thousand times as rich as it is, it could spend a thousand times as much as it does on such objects; it could consume but little more food.

This harmonizes perfectly with what is known as Engel's economic law. Dr. Engel, formerly head of the Prussian Statistical Bureau, tells us that the percentage of outlay for subsistence grows smaller as the income grows larger; that the percentage of outlay for rent, fuel, light, and clothing remains the same, or approximately the same, whatever the income; and that the percentage of outlay for sundries becomes greater as income increases.

From all this it follows that, as population and wealth increase, an ever-enlarging proportion of men must get their living by means of the mechanical and the fine arts; or, in other words, an ever-increasing proportion of population must live in cities.

Our free institutions are based on two fundamental principles, viz.: local self-government and federation. . . .

But while patriotism was at the front defending the Union, the other fundamental principle was being quietly subverted at home. Selfish men gained control of municipal governments for personal ends. Conditions made it easy for the political boss to compact his power and to perfect his machine. The inevitable result was the development of bottomless corruption and unblushing outrage upon the rights and liberties of the people; and, as a rule, the larger the city the more completely did it become boss-ridden.

Professor Bryce declares that the one conspicuous failure of American institutions is the government of our great cities, which every intelligent man knows to be true. The State limits the liberties of its cities. It does not dare to trust them with full autonomy. Thus one of our two fundamental principles, that of local self-government, is in question; and in our great cities it has failed. This makes painfully significant and ominous the rapid and inevitable growth of our cities.

We have for years relied upon the country vote to hold the cities in check, but the time is soon coming when the cities will take matters into their own hands. If the rate of growth from 1880 to 1890 continues, in 1920 the cities of the United States will contain 10,000,000 more than one-half of the population. The city will then control State and nation. What if the city is then incapable of self-government?

The greater part of our population must live in cities—cities much greater than the world has yet seen—cities which by their preponderance of numbers and of wealth must inevitably control civilization and destiny; and we must learn—though we have not yet learned—to live in cities with safety to our health, our morals, and our liberties. . . .

The problem of the twentieth century city, therefore, demands for its solution a higher type of citizenship, for which we must look chiefly to those who direct the education of the young. Evidently our public schools must give to the children and youth of today such instruction in the duties and principles of good citizenship as earlier generations did not have. Literature dealing with American citizenship, adapted to all ages, from the high school down to the kindergarten, should be absorbed by the scholars until an intelligent civic patriotism becomes a matter of course.

60

JULIAN RALPH, EXCERPT FROM "COLORADO AND ITS CAPITAL," 1893

The expansion of a railroad network across the continent meant that towns and cities no longer had to be located at places of obvious "natural advantage" like harbors or the

Originally printed in *Harper's New Monthly Magazine* 86 (1893): 935–48.

confluence of rivers. In the post–Civil War period small urban centers popped up repeatedly, each hoping that with a good railroad connection it would grow to be the next important city. Prominent among these railroad cities in the trans-Mississippi West in the late nineteenth century was Denver. Here Julian Ralph has described this boomtown, and found it to be quite charming. It is even beginning to develop its own culture. For every urban success like Denver, however, were urban busts—places that existed briefly, or only in the dreams of real estate speculators, before the railroads passed them by.

Denver's peculiarity and strength lie in its being all alone in the heart of a vast region between the Canadian border and the Gulf of Mexico; but it has been brought suddenly near to us. Not all the fast railway riding is done in the East in these days. The far Western steeds of steel are picking up their heels in grand fashion for those who enjoy fast riding. On a palace-car train of the Union Pacific Railroad between Omaha and Denver the regular time is nearly fifty miles an hour, and the long run is made in one night, between supper and breakfast. Denver is only fifty-three hours of riding-time from New York as I write—twenty-five hours from New York to Chicago, and twenty-eight hours from Chicago to Denver.

I am going to ask the reader to spend Saturday and Sunday in Denver with me. Instead of dryly cataloguing what is there, we will see it for ourselves. I had supposed it to be a mountain city, so much does an Eastern man hear of its elevation, its mountain resorts, and its mountain air. It surprised me to discover that it was a city of the plains. There is nothing in the appearance of the plains to lead one to suppose that they tilt up like a toboggan slide, as they do, or that Denver is a mile above sea-level, as it is. But a part of its enormous good fortune is that although it is a plains city, it has the mountains for near neighbors—a long peaked and scalloped line of purple or pink or blue or snow-clad green, according to when they are viewed. There are 200 miles or more of the Rockies in sight in clear weather. . . .

We have looked on Denver's patent map, and know where we are. Every Western city has its own patent map, usually designed to show that it is in the centre of creation, but Denver's map is more truthful, and merely locates it in the middle of the country west of the Mississippi. It shows the States east of that river without a single railroad, while a perfect labyrinth of railroads crisscross the West in frantic efforts to get to Denver, . . . with Denver in its centre, you would discover no real competitor; but the people have adopted what they call their "thousand-mile theory," which is that Chicago is 1000 miles from New York, and Denver is 1000 miles from Chicago, and San Francisco is 1000 miles from Denver, so that, as any one can see, if great cities are put at that distance apart, as it seems, then these are to be the four great ones of America.

Denver is a beautiful city—a parlor city with cabinet finish—and it is so new that it looks as if it had been made to order, and was just ready for delivery. How the people lived five years ago, or what they have done with the houses of that period, does not appear, but at present everything—business blocks, churches, clubs, dwellings, street cars, the park—all look brand-new, like the young trees. The first citizen you talk to says: "You notice there are no old people on the streets here. There aren't any in the city. We have no use for old folks here." So, then, the people also are new. It is very wonderful and peculiar. Only a year ago Mr. Richard Harding Davis was there, and commented on the lack of pavements in the streets, and I hear that at that time pedestrians wore rubber boots, and the mud was frightful. But now every street in the thick of town is paved with concrete or Belgian blocks as well as if it were New York or Paris. The first things that impress you in the city are the neatness and width of the streets, and the number of young trees that ornament them most invitingly. The next thing is the remarkable character of the big business buildings. It is not that they are bigger and better than those of New York and Chicago— comparisons of that sort are nonsensical—but they are massive and beautiful, and they possess an elegance without and a roominess and lightness within that distinguish them as superior to the show buildings of most of the cities of the country. . . .

The residence districts are of a piece with the rest. Along the tree-lined streets are some of the very prettiest villas it is any man's lot to see at this time. They are not palaces, but they are very tasteful, stylish, cozy, and pretty homes, all built of brick or stone, in a great variety of pleasing colors and materials, and with a proud showing of towers, turrets, conservatories, bay-windows, gables, and all else that goes to mark this period, when men build after widely differing plans to compliment their own taste and the skill of originating draughtsmen. The town spreads over an enormous territory, as compared with the space a city of its size should take up, but we must learn that modern methods of quick transit are so cheap that they are being adopted everywhere, and wher- ever they are used the cities are spreading out. Denver has cable and electric cars, but it is the electric roads that are the city-spreaders. They whiz along so fast that men do not hesitate to build their homes five or six miles from their stores and offices, where they can get garden and elbow room. We are going to see all our cities shoot out in this way. It promotes beauty in residence districts, and pride in the hearts of those who own the pretty homes. . . . But it entails a great new expense upon modern city government, for the streets and the mains and sewers and police and fire systems all have to be extended to keep pace with the electric flight of the people, who, in turn, must stand the taxes. Not that they are high in Denver, or in those other electric-car-peppered capitals, Minneapo- lis and St. Paul, but they are higher than they would be if the people were crowded into smaller spaces. . . .

We shall see that on its worst side the city is Western, and that its moral side is East- ern. It will be interesting to see how one side dominates the other, and both keep along together. But in the mean time what is most peculiar is the indifference with which the populace regards murder among those gamblers and desperadoes who are a feature of every new country, and who are found in Denver, though, I suspect, the ladies and chil- dren never see them, so well separated are the decent and the vicious quarters. It is said that not very long ago it was the tacit agreement of the people that it was not worth while to put the county to the cost or bother of seriously pursuing, prosecuting, and hanging or imprisoning a thug who murdered another thug. It was argued that there was one bad man less, and that if the murderer was at large another one would kill him. The axiom that "only bad men are the victims of bad men " obtained there, as it did in Cheyenne and Deadwood, and does in Butte. To-day a murder in a dive or gambling-hell excites lit- tle comment and no sensation in Denver, and I could distinctly see a trace of the old spirit in the speech of the reputable men when I talked to them of the one crime of the sort that took place while I was there.

The night side of the town is principally corralled, as they say; that is, its disorderly houses are all on one street. There is another mining-town characteristic—wide-open gambling. The "hells" are mainly above stairs, over saloons. The vice is not flaunted as it is in certain other cities; but once in the gaming-places, the visitor sees them to be like those my readers became acquainted with in Butte, Montana—great open places, like the board-rooms in our stock exchanges, lined with gambling lay-outs. They are crowded on this Saturday night with rough men in careless dress or in the apparel of laborers. These are railroad employés, workers from the nearest mines, laborers, clerks—every sort of men who earn their money hard, and think to make more out of it by letting it go easily.

61

JOHN COLEMAN ADAMS, EXCERPT FROM "WHAT A GREAT CITY MIGHT BE—A LESSON FROM THE WHITE CITY," 1896

Like many before him and so many commentators after him, the Reverend John Coleman Adams lamented how Americans had failed to create beautiful and dignified cities. The "great blemish upon our cities," he writes, "is the fact that their natural advantages have been squandered." But at the White City of the World's Columbian Exposition of 1893, Coleman found "a dream." He was not alone. The 1893 White City became a huge influence on the future of architecture and city planning. What Adams admired was how the White City created order, safety, and cleanliness—quite the opposite of the real Chicago just beyond the fair gates. Of course, fair organizers did acknowledge that the White City might prove a bit dull, and they also organized the Midway Plaisance, complete with the world's first Ferris wheel, to entertain the millions who came to Chicago.

While many observers during the great Chicago Exposition, made public their impressions of the artistic and industrial phases of the White City. . . there is one whole aspect of the Exposition which received altogether too little attention. Yet it is a side which contained much food for thought certainly as any other for the American citizen. Nothing in any of the exhibits within the walls of those great buildings, illustrating the achievements of human skill and power, was half so interesting, so suggestive, so full of hopeful intimations, as the Fair in its aspect as a city by itself. In the midst of a very real and very earthly city, full of the faults which Chicago so preeminently displays, we saw a great many features of what an ideal city might be, a great many visions which perhaps will one day become solid facts, and so remove the blot and failure of modern civilization, the great city of the end of the century. The White City has become almost a dream; but it is well to go back to it, after this interval, and study anew some of its lessons.

In the first place, when one entered the gates of the White City, he felt that he was in the presence of a system of arrangements which had been carefully and studiously planned. The city was orderly and convenient. The plotting of the grounds, the manner of their development, the placing of the buildings, the communicating avenues and canals and bridges, all exhibited a prevision, a plan, an arrangement of things with reference to each other. The problems of the architect, the landscape gardener and the engineer had been thoroughly thought out before the gates were opened. The result was

Originally printed in *New England Magazine*, new ser. 14 (March 1896): 3–13.

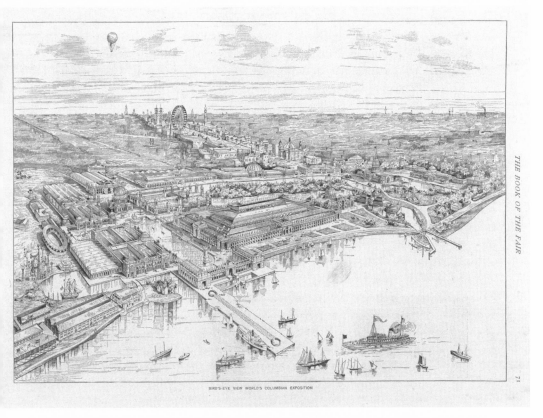

BIRD'S-EYE VIEW WORLD'S COLUMBIAN EXPOSITION

5.3. World's Columbian Exposition, bird's-eye view, 1893. Paul V. Galvin Library, Illinois Institute of Technology. Twenty-five million Americans came to Chicago in the summer of 1893 to see the world's fair. It was surely the biggest event of the era and had a profound impact on the way American cities were shaped subsequently. The order and rationality of the White City, in the foreground, inspired the City Beautiful movement, while the Midway, featuring the first Ferris wheel, became a model for the twentieth-century amusement park. Though park organizers and social reformers focused their efforts on building the White City, most visitors flocked to the Midway, its beer gardens, rides, and risqué entertainment.

preeminently satisfying. The features of the Fair could be studied as a whole, or the details could be taken up without loss of time or distraction of attention. The mind was helped and not hindered by the planning of the various parts. They seemed to be the details of an organism, not the mere units of an aggregation. The buildings were not a heap and huddle of walls and roofs; they were a noble sketch in architecture. The streets were not a tangle of thoroughfares representing individual preference or caprice; they were a system of avenues devised for the public convenience.

Of course every dweller in a great city will recognize the fact that these particulars represent just what most of our larger cities are not. If we except some of the newer cities of the West, we have extremely few in which there are any evidences of deliberate and intelligent plan, the perception of the end to be attained, and the effort to gain that end. Life in our cities would be vastly easier if only they had been planned with some reasonable foresight as to results and some commonsense prevision in behalf of the people who were coming to live in them. The great blemish upon our cities is the fact that their natural advantages have been squandered by uses which had no forethought of future needs. The blunders and stupidity of those who have developed them have laid heavy expense upon those who shall come after and try to remodel the territory they have spoiled. That work has hardly begun. When it is undertaken there will be anathemas profound and unsparing upon the shortsightedness which permitted narrow streets and omitted frequent parks and open squares; which reared monumental buildings, and failed to dig tunnels for local transportation; which carried sewage away in drain pipes, only to bring it back by the water tap.

Of course the answer and defence made to this complaint is a general denial of the possibility of doing otherwise, and a claim that the conditions in the two cases were all so different that it is unfair to expect like results. The claim may be partly conceded. The American city is, in general, a surprise to its own inhabitants. It grows beyond all prophecy; it develops in unexpected directions; it increases in territory and population at a pace which is scarcely less than appalling. All these conditions make foresight difficult and possibly debar hindsight from criticism. But the trouble has been that the builders of our cities have been blind because they would not see. . . . For many years it has been possible to forecast the growth of our cities as certainly as it was possible to predict that the daily population of the White City would be anywhere from 100,000 to 800,000 people. Our mistakes are therefore gratuitous and wilful.

But there were other hints of the order which might exist in our great cities, conveyed in the general cleanliness and neatness of the Exposition grounds. The management had grave difficulties in its way. It had to contend with a great untaught multitude which had never learned in real cities how to be neat in this mimic one. They were as careless and untidy here as they were in their own cities and towns. They littered the ground; they covered the floors; they filled the waters with the rubbish of lunch baskets and the debris of unconsumed luncheons; they tore up their letters and tossed the tatters into the air, they threw away in one building the cards and circulars they had collected in others. But every night when they were gone the patient attendants did their best to clean up after them and to present the grounds fresh and bright for the new crowd next day. When shall we carry the same methods into our municipal affairs? Why may we not at once take a hint in our every-day towns from this city of a few weeks? There is no reason (save such as are discreditable alike to our minds and our morals) why New York and Philadelphia, Boston and Chicago, should not be swept and scrubbed every night in preparation for the uses of every new day. Sometime they will be. Perhaps that day will come all the sooner for the lesson of the White City.

It may be cited as an evidence of what the American populace might be trained to do in the care of its own city premises, that no great multitude of people ever took better care of itself nor showed more love of order in behavior than the throng which came and went every day through the gates of Jackson Park. That fact has been too often cited with praise to demand any emphasis here. It is only called up to show that the American people possesses that self control which can be made the basis of municipal neatness and order. The American citizen understands that he can have a good time without boisterousness or disorder. He knows that the good order of a crowd is only the good order of every individual in it. Once teach him that neatness in the streets can only be secured by the care of every man, woman and child who walks those streets, and we shall be as distinguished for our clean cities as we are for our well-behaved and good natured crowds. . . .

But the White City presented yet another hint of a possibility of every great city, in the remarkable safety which it afforded its temporary citizens. Every provision was made to take care of the people and to guard their lives and limbs. The sense of absolute safety within those avenues was delicious. The visitor could give his whole mind to the business in hand without one thought of peril—of falling into any hole, of being hit by any missile. Coming to these grounds from the crowded thoroughfares of Chicago, where the sharp gong of the street cars and the rumble of vehicles was an interminable reminder of the constant threat to personal safety in the crowded streets, it was an unspeakable and indescribable relief to move freely in the midst of the great throngs and not feel in imminent danger. The visitor did not have to think of his personal safety at all. The slow watering-carts and the occasional ambulance on its errand of relief were all that interfered with pedestrians. The railway overhead and the lagoon at one side furnished all the rapid transit without interference of any sort with the sightseers. Suppose that the same sort of care were taken of our lives and persons in a modern great city. It would be worth one's while if he could be as safe in Brooklyn or New York as he was in the streets of the Exposition. But he never will be as long as selfish and mercenary corporations are allowed to capture our thoroughfares and disregard the rights of the people in their use of them. . . .

Much the same things might be said of the facilities for cleanliness and comfort which in the White City were so amply provided. It was a decided novelty, anywhere in America, to be in a miniature great city, where for a nickel one could get at frequent intervals clean hands and face and a smooth head of hair. But the novelty was of a sort which commanded universal approval. Everybody liked the arrangements at the Fair; and everybody would doubtless like to see similar arrangements in his own city. Who will be first to furnish them? A good profit awaits his investment. . . .

The unanimous opinion [of critics] was that it would give a great impulse to architecture, to the construction of civic buildings, to the study of artistic effects in public and private constructions. Not that anybody expects to see those great buildings reproduced anywhere else. That would be to repeat the old stupidities of our architectural bungling and botches, which have given us Greek temples for dwelling houses and an enlargement of the settler's log cabin for a church. But there will be a new spirit growing out of the discovery of what is possible in the way of beautiful public buildings. We have had very little so far in our national life; and we have had, certainly until this latest time, extremely little good private architecture. After the awful monotony of ugliness in the domestic and public architecture, of cities like Brooklyn and New York and Philadelphia, the White City was not only a revelation but a benediction. But it forecast a duty, too. It is time we awoke from our nightmare of ugliness and builded better. We are on the eve of a great revival in architecture. . . .

The American visitor to the Fair was permitted another sensation as unusual as it was agreeable, and as strange as it was unexpected. He was treated to the extraordinary experience of feeling that all this beauty, order, protection and display were for his sake, to minister to his enjoyment and to his ease. He knew that the White City was built and furnished on his account, and that everything had been done with a view to making him feel at home in the enjoyment of his inheritance. There was not another place in America where the American citizen could feel so much of the pride of popular sovereignty as he could after he had paid his half dollar and become a naturalized resident of this municipality. Once within those grounds he was monarch of all he surveyed. He could go anywhere.

He could see everything. He was welcome to all that he found inside those gates. He could feel for once in his life that he was not liable to be snubbed by the police, nor bullied by car-conductors, nor brow-beaten by salesmen. His temporary citizenship entitled him to the same large privileges which are his by right in any permanent city—with this difference, that for once his title was recognized and his rights respected. It was a great experience for the patient, submissive, long-suffering American. It gave him a hint of his own deserts. It taught him what he had a right to expect by virtue of his citizenship. . . .

Such an era of real liberty in which the city is devoted to the good of the citizen, is perfectly possible, but only under the same conditions as those which made the White City so conspicuous. The splendid administration of that six-months' city was secured by enlisting in its service the best brains and the best dispositions available. The talent and the character of at least one city government in America were level with the task which was set for them. The source and secret of the order, the safety, the beauty, the devotion to the good of the people, which were found in that one small municipality, lay in the fact that the best were called upon to produce the best. Those beautiful grounds were planned by the best minds that could be brought to the undertaking. The beautiful buildings were decorated by the best artists who could be secured. The president of the Directory was one of the foremost business men of Chicago. The executive talent in that wonderful city (which abounds in that particular commodity) was laid under contribution to administer the enterprise. It was a clear case of cause adequate to effect. When our great cities can and will observe the same law; when they realize that it takes the best to make the best; when they feel that personal comfort, safety, and enjoyment are worth having and worth working for; then indeed we may expect to see the ideals suggested in the White City realized in Boston, New York, Brooklyn and Chicago, in every great city in the land.

The great White City has disappeared. Its walls have fallen, its attractions have vanished, its glories have faded like the summer which marked its life. But in its place, heirs of its uses, its beauties, its order, we shall yet see springing into being throughout the land cities which shall embody in permanent form the splendors, the noble suggestions, the dignified municipal ideals of this dream city. In the day in which the better, the best, American city shall become a common spectacle, we shall perceive how much sooner it came by reason of the vision of the White City which we all beheld upon the shores of the great lake.

62

ANONYMOUS, EXCERPT FROM
"ART AND RAILWAY STATIONS," 1909

It is almost a cliché to say that the railroad was the great symbol of industrial America in the late nineteenth and early twentieth centuries. Nothing symbolized the significance of the railway in all facets of American life more than the grand, imposing, sometimes gargantuan railroad stations built in America's major cities. After the 1893 World's Fair in Chicago, where neoclassical architecture made a triumphant revival, many of these stations were built as great Roman monuments, including the one mentioned here, Pennsylvania Station in New York, which took as its model the Baths of Caracalla. The author of this short piece argues that the railroad station is to modern times as the cathedral was to the Middle Ages, the best embodiment "of the vast energy and insistent utilitarianism of this twentieth century."

A few years ago it was the fashion to indulge in artistic sneers at the sky-scraper. Our Pharisaical painters passed it by on the other side of the street. They turned, instead, to the barren reaches and rocks of Brittany or to the ruined castles of the Rhineland, as fitter subjects for their art. Today it is a different tale. The office buildings of Manhattan, clothed in their wreaths of smoke and steam, our avenues, glistening in rain-wetness, reflective of lights from arc lamps and shop windows, have become an almost banal feature of current magazines and contemporary exhibitions. They are, at last, recognized themes for the painter and the etcher, as for the artist in words. Nowadays, Ruskin to the contrary notwithstanding, there is also a moving beauty in our railways. . . .

Even Henry James has felt something of the unexploited poetry of the railway. His confession of the kindness that he feels for stations is just what one had a right to expect: half whimsical, half serious; He likes them aesthetically, he tells us; he views them with complacency, even when he would neither come nor go. "They remind me," he says, in one of his essays, "of all our reciprocities and activities, our energies and curiosities." And the spectacle of Paddington or Euston offers an exhibition of variety in type which compensates him for having to live a part of his year in London.

Time was when the railway station was called a "deepo" and was an architectural horror. In those days there was indeed much need to philosophize and transcendentalize if one was in the least to enjoy its "spectacle." As we have watched the construction of the newest of the New York stations, we have, however, felt that the building of the past and that of the present are two very different matters. Just as the mystical imagination and aspiration of the Middle Ages found their ultimate expression in cathedrals which remain to-day, centuries after, the noblest monuments of Christian faith and of European civilization, so is the modern railway station a kind of memorial and evidence of the vast energy and insistent utilitarianism of this twentieth century. We live in the age of the machine; what more proper than that we should express ourselves in brick and stone dedicated, not to a Saint, but to the heroes of our Dusk of the Gods, the twin daemons Steam and Electricity. And the greatest temple to these demigods thus far erected is the building that fills four blocks in this city, and that will soon be sending its trains out to east and to west, to north and to south, through tunnels that burrow under great rivers. We are proud, in our way, of our demigods, and of their celebrants.

Sometimes, in viewing the pictures of our office-buildings, with their noses pricking the clouds, we have thought the artist's work too cleverly managed for anything except effectiveness. The veils of smoke and of steam have been adjusted almost too coquettishly. There is at least no need to idealize these new railway stations, for which we hope some Monet will in time emerge. Monet has found Charing Cross and Montparnasse subjects worthy of the brush that renders the flower-gardens and the mists of his

Originally printed in *Nation*, September 16, 1909.

exquisite Giverny. Who will prove to be the Monet of Eighth Avenue? "I would give any-thing," Lafcadio Hearn once wrote, with London roaring in his ears, and his heart full of the bitterness of things, "to be a literary Columbus, to discover a romantic America." As to the matter of an America romantic for the man of letters, we dare not answer very positively. If, however, Laurence Sterne could discover the poetry of a *desobligéante,* why should not his literary heirs find it in a Pullman coach? And certain it is that for the painter a romantic America stands very close at hand.

63

CHARLES MULFORD ROBINSON, EXCERPT FROM "IMPROVEMENT IN CITY LIFE: AESTHETIC PROGRESS," 1899

One of the main proponents of the City Beautiful movement at the start of the twentieth century, Charles Mulford Robinson was the author of *The Improvement of Cities and Towns* (1901), a key text of that movement. In this article from 1899, Robinson unwittingly re-veals the biases of the movement: a focus on "aesthetic progress" rather than addressing the causes of the poverty, crowding, and disease which made cities unappealing. While his later writings and those of other reformers focused more on the total planning of the city, it was the appearance of cities—creating boulevards and plazas, fashioning noble pub-lic buildings, planting street trees, and beautifying parks—that evoked the greatest passion of its proponents. Robinson's agenda is starkly different from that of another classic work written in 1899: W. E. B. Du Bois's *The Philadelphia Negro*, which is excerpted in the next document.

One who would chronicle the development of American cities on strictly aesthetic lines faces a difficult undertaking, not because there is so much to record, but because the de-velopment is diversified, widely scattered, and lacking in harmony. But such a chronicle has value in showing a general realization of the shortcomings of our cities, from the aes-thetic point of view, and a surprisingly common awakening of a wish to improve them. There is beginning to appear, also, an endeavor to harmonize these efforts, to treat con-ditions scientifically and systematically.

During the summer and autumn of the world's fair at Chicago, when the country was carried away by the exposition's unexpected beauty, it was common to hear it spo-ken of as "the white city" and "the dream city." In these terms was revealed a yearning toward a condition which we had not reached. To say that the world's fair created the subsequent aesthetic effort in municipal life were therefore false; to say that it immensely strengthened, quickened, and encouraged it would be true. The fair gave tangible shape to a desire that was arising out of the larger wealth, the commoner travel, and the provi-sion of the essentials of life; but the movement has had a special impetus since 1893.

Originally printed in *Atlantic Monthly* 83 (June 1899): 771–85.

When one speaks of the aesthetic side of American cities, one thinks at once of their public buildings; of their parks, statues, and boulevards. But in any right conception of urban loveliness these would be only the special objects of a general and harmonious beauty. A great work in the creation of fairer cities is to be done in directions less striking. A boulevard may do less to improve the general appearance of a city than the putting of its wires underground; a beautiful park may give to it less natural charm than would be restored by the abatement of the smoke nuisance; and a statue may fail to impart the artistic character that an orderly skyline and harmony in the facades of its business blocks would give. It was appreciation of this fact which the world's fair especially extended. . . .

We shall not attain to cities really beautiful, then, until we learn artistically to plan them. Transformations may help us greatly, as London and Paris show; but the pity is that we displayed so little wisdom in the rare opportunity granted when our cities were yet on paper. After actual city building is begun, effort toward beauty is delayed by the strength of the demand for necessities. As long as each new year makes imperative many miles of paving, the laying of miles of sewers, extension of water, and protection from crime and fire over larger areas, it is explicable that weary taxpayers should suffer their ideal of a fairer city to grow dull. Rapid transit aided civic adornment in many ways, but in largely extending city lines an immediate effect was also to increase the burden of necessary expenditures. As a rule, however, the newer parts of our cities, with their broader streets, circles, and spaces set aside for adornment by turf and flowers, are better than older portions. This is hopeful and educating; and there is a widespread effort to mend existing conditions in the older parts, though a mended article can never be as good as one well made at first. Many of the new bridges are worthy of cities of high ideal. In Washington, the Civic Centre has done much in converting blind alleys into open thoroughfares. In San Francisco, a public-spirited woman, who has provided a worldwide competition of architects for artistic designs for the University of California, has recently offered to provide plans for beautifying the entire city by a similar international competition, and the city is well situated financially to avail itself of the chance. Cleveland also is fortunate in an opportunity for contemplating the simultaneous erection of a new court house, post office, library, city hall, and chamber of commerce. The wish has arisen to group these buildings, if possible, and to construct them on one harmonious architectural plan that shall create a magnificent centre of public business. . . .

Better street cleaning, since the success which attended the efforts of Colonel Waring in New York, has been the most popular direction for the municipal aesthetic effort to take. It has lately absorbed a good deal of the movement's enthusiasm, but one is not inclined to quarrel with its prominence. Good pavements are a demand which clean pavements involve, and together they may be said to be the essentials of municipal dignity. As a man is judged by his linen, a city is judged by its streets. . . .

Of more distinctly aesthetic purpose is effort for the beautifying of the streets. It rests mainly with the people, and properly, since in any case they must be depended upon to protect and cultivate grass, flowers, and shrubbery. Examples of the effort are seen in the greater care of lawns and trees, the removal of front fences, the planting of vines, and the "parking" which gives to city sidewalks vistas almost like country paths. . . .

City parks at once suggest themselves. Two years and a half ago, a writer in The Atlantic Monthly, on The Art of Public Improvement, said that "parks have become a necessity of our cities and towns," and a very interesting sketch was published of their origin with us, and their rapid development. Historically, the thought of large parks for American cities hardly goes back of the early fifties; and "only persistent and unremitting effort on the part of a few determined souls" was able then to get consideration for the project. An official who has made a study of the park statistics of twenty-five principal cities is my authority for saying that, except in a few of the largest, it is only within the last decade that a general interest in park development has appeared. He adds that in every case the park acreage has more than doubled in that time. . . .

The park acreage of Greater New York, authorized by public liberality exceeds that of Greater London or of Paris, and is four times that of Berlin. There is little need here to speak of the park systems of Boston,—the Boston within the city, and the Metropolitan without. For the land alone which is comprised in the first the city has paid something more than $6,000,000, without considering the old Common or the Public Garden; and it has added something more than $7,500,000 for improvement and adornment. The Metropolitan Park Commission, which enables the towns and cities about Boston to co-operate with the big city in the selection of contiguous park lands and their harmonious treatment, was created by legislation only as late as 1893. The commission now controls more numerous large pleasure grounds than are held by any public authority on the continent except the national government. The great systems of boulevards and park-ways, which are characteristic of the development of this land, are distinctly an aesthetic feature. They have become a distinguishing part, also, of the fine park system of Chicago, which, through their means, encircles the city on the land side. With proverbial large-mindedness, Chicago is now extending one of them, the famous parkway, Sheridan Drive, with the aid of the towns and villages to the north, along the lake shore clear to Milwaukee, a distance of some eighty miles. . . .

A large amount of endeavor, however, is informal. Sometimes an individual, whose motive may or may not be public spirited; sometimes a society, or a collection of individuals united only for a moment by common impulse, and often with the wish for the aesthetic adornment of the city completely secondary to that for perpetuating a memory, offers to give an art object. In this way a degree of adornment has been gained for which our cities might have waited vainly many years, had they depended upon the societies regularly organized for municipal improvement. Recent notable examples are the great Washington Monument, which was presented to Philadelphia by the Society of the Cincinnati of Pennsylvania, and which is said to be the finest of its kind in the country; the Stephen Girard statue, in the same city; the beautiful Shaw Memorial, at Boston; the Grant tomb and the Washington Arch, in New York. . . .

Municipal advance on aesthetic lines has been supported by an interesting economic argument. This was not needed, but of late it has been so much referred to that it cannot be properly passed over. It expresses the value of civic attractiveness in dollars. When the Municipal Improvement Association of New Orleans wished to close one of its printed addresses with a strong appeal, it said: "New Orleans could be one of the most attractive cities in the world, and visitors should come in large numbers; and if this condition of affairs should be reached, then the income derived from this source would be, perhaps, as important as that derived from the trade of the city." . . .

But there is other value in municipal beauty than that indicated by money value. There is a sociological value in the larger happiness of great masses of people, whose only fields are park meadows, whose only walks are city streets, whose statues stand in public places, whose paintings hang where all may see, whose books and curios, whose drives and music, are first the city's where they live. The happier people of the rising City Beautiful will grow in love for it, in pride in it. They will be better citizens, because better instructed, more artistic, and filled with civic pride.

64

W. E. B. DU BOIS, EXCERPT FROM
THE PHILADELPHIA NEGRO: A SOCIAL STUDY, 1899

W. E. B. Du Bois's study of African-Americans in Philadelphia stands as one of the foundations of modern sociology. In it, Du Bois offered dramatically new ways of analyzing city life. In the place of soaring rhetoric celebrating or decrying cities, or providing sweeping visions for improving the beauty and functioning of cities, Du Bois offered detailed statistics of housing conditions, producing in the process a damning indictment of white society that helped create these conditions. Du Bois hoped to demonstrate two things: first, that the African-American ghetto was the result of structural discrimination; and second, that the African-American community experienced the same class stratification as the white community. While working at the University of Pennsylvania and writing *The Philadelphia Negro*, Du Bois lived in the long and narrow Black district of Center City Philadelphia. Following the tradition of settlement house workers, Du Bois launched a century-long genre of urban studies: the scholar-writer immersed in the life of a (usually poor and minority) community.

The Seventh Ward, 1896.—We shall now make a more intensive study of the Negro population, confining ourselves to one typical ward for the year 1896. Of the nearly forty thousand Negroes in Philadelphia in 1890, a little less than a fourth lived in the Seventh Ward, and over half in this and the adjoining Fourth, Fifth and Eighth Wards:

Ward.	Negroes.	Whites.
Seventh	8,861	21,177
Eighth	3,011	13,940
Fourth	2,573	17,792
Fifth	2,335	14,619

The Seventh Ward starts from historic centre of Negro settlement in the city, South Seventh street and Lombard, and includes the long narrow strip, beginning at South Seventh and extending west, with South and Spruce streets as boundaries, as far as the Schuylkill River. The colored population of this ward numbered 3621 in 1860, 4616 in 1870, and 8861 in 1890. It is a thickly populated district of varying character; north of it is the

Originally printed in W. E. B. Du Bois, *The Philadelphia Negro: A Social Study* (Philadelphia: University of Pennsylvania Press, 1899), 58–65, xxx–297.

residence and business section of the city; south of it a middle class and workingmen's residence section; at the east end it joins Negro, Italian and Jewish slums; at the west end, the wharves of the river and an industrial section separating it from the grounds of the University of Pennsylvania and the residence section of West Philadelphia.

Starting at Seventh street and walking along Lombard, let us glance at the general character of the ward. Pausing a moment at the corner of Seventh and Lombard, we can at a glance view the worst Negro slums of the city. The houses are mostly brick, some wood, not very old, and in general uncared for rather than dilapidated. The blocks between Eighth, Pine, Sixth and South have for many decades been the centre of Negro population. Here the riots of the thirties took place, and here once was a depth of poverty and degradation almost unbelievable. Even to-day there are many evidences of degradation, although the signs of idleness, shiftlessness, dissoluteness and crime are more conspicuous than those of poverty.

The alleys near, as Ratcliffe Street, Middle alley, Brown's court, Barclay street, etc., are haunts of noted criminals, male and female, of gamblers and prostitutes, and at the same time of many poverty-stricken people, decent but not energetic. There is an abundance of political clubs, and nearly all the houses are practically lodging houses, with a miscellaneous and shifting population. The corners, night and day, are filled with Negro loafers—able-bodied young men and women, all cheerful, some with good-natured, open faces, some with traces of crime and excess, a few pinched with poverty. They are mostly gamblers, thieves and prostitutes, and few have fixed and steady occupation of any kind. Some are stevedores, porters, laborers and laundresses. On its face this slum is noisy and dissipated, but not brutal, although now and then highway robberies and murderous assaults in other parts of the city are traced to its denizens. Nevertheless the stranger can usually walk about here day and night with little fear of being molested, if he be not too inquisitive.

Passing up Lombard, beyond Eighth, the atmosphere suddenly changes, because these next two blocks have few alleys and the residences are good-sized and pleasant. Here some of the best Negro families of the ward live. Some are wealthy in a small way, nearly all are Philadelphia born, and they represent an early wave of emigration from the old slum section. To the south, on Rodman street, are families of the same character. North of Pine and below Eleventh there are practically no Negro residences. Beyond Tenth street, and as far as Broad street, the Negro population is large and varied in character. On small streets like Barclay and its extension below Tenth—Souder, on Ivy, Rodman, Salem, Heins, Iseminger, Ralston, etc., is a curious mingling of respectable working people and some of a better class, with recent immigrations of the semi-criminal class from the slums. On the larger streets, like Lombard and Juniper, there live many respectable colored families—native Philadelphians, Virginians and other Southerners, with a fringe of more questionable families. Beyond Broad, as far as Sixteenth, the good character of the Negro population is maintained except in one or two back streets. From Sixteenth to Eighteenth, intermingled with some estimable families, is a dangerous criminal class. They are not the low, open idlers of Seventh and Lombard, but rather the graduates of that school: shrewd and sleek politicians, gamblers and confidence men, with a class of well-dressed and partially undetected prostitutes. This class is not easily differentiated and located, but it seems to centre at Seventeenth and Lombard. Several large gambling houses are near here, although more recently one has moved below Broad, indicating a reshifting of the criminal centre. The whole community was an earlier immigration from Seventh and Lombard. North of Lombard, above Seventeenth, including Lombard street itself, above Eighteenth, is one of the best Negro residence sections of the city, centering about Addison street. Some undesirable elements have crept in even here, especially since the Christian League attempted to clear out the Fifth Ward slums, but still it remains a centre of quiet, respectable families, who own their own homes and live well. The Negro population practically stops at Twenty-second street, although a few Negroes live beyond.

We can thus see that the Seventh Ward presents an epitome of nearly all the Negro problems; that every class is represented, and varying conditions of life. Nevertheless one must naturally be careful not to draw too broad conclusions from a single ward in one city. There is no proof that the proportion between the good and the bad here is normal, even for the race in Philadelphia; that the social problems affecting Negroes in large Northern cities are presented here in most of their aspects seems credible, but that certain of those aspects are distorted and exaggerated by local peculiarities is also not to be doubted.

In the fall of 1896 a house-to-house visitation was made to all the Negro families of this ward. The visitor went in person to each residence and called for the head of the family. The housewife usually responded, the husband now and then, and sometimes an older daughter or other member of the family. The fact that the University was making an investigation of this character was known and discussed in the ward, but its exact scope and character was not known. The mere announcement of the purpose secured, in all but about twelve cases, immediate admission. Seated then in the parlor, kitchen, or living room, the visitor began the questioning, using his discretion as to the order in which they were put, and omitting or adding questions as the circumstances suggested. Now and then the purpose of a particular query was explained, and usually the object of the whole inquiry indicated. General discussions often arose as to the condition of the Negroes, which were instructive. From ten minutes to an hour was spent in each home, the average time being fifteen to twenty-five minutes. . . .

On December 1, 1896, there were in the Seventh Ward of Philadelphia 9675 Negroes; 4501 males and 5174 females. . . .

Age.	Male.	Female.
Under 10	570	641
10 to 19	483	675
20 to 29	1,276	1,444
30 to 39	1,046	1,084
40 to 49	553	632
50 to 59	298	331
60 to 69	114	155
70 and over	41	96
Age unknown	120	116
Total	4,501	5,174

Grand Total   9,675

. . . There were a considerable number of omissions among the loafers and criminals without homes, the class of lodgers and the club-house habitués. These were mostly males, and their inclusion would somewhat affect the division by sexes, although probably not to a great extent. The increase of the Negro population in this ward for six and a half years is 814, or at the rate of 14.13 per cent per decade. This is perhaps somewhat smaller than that for the population of the city at large, for the Seventh Ward is crowded and overflowing into other wards. Possibly the present Negro population of the city is between 43,000 and 45,000. At all events it is probable that the crest of the tide of immigration is passed, and that the increase for the decade 1890–1900 will not be nearly as large as the 24 per cent of the decade 1880–1890.

The division by sex indicates still a very large and, it would seem, growing excess of women. The return shows 1150 females to every 1000 males. Possibly through the omission of men and the unavoidable duplication of some servants lodging away from their place of service, the disproportion of the sexes is exaggerated. At any rate it is great, and if growing, may be an indication of increased restriction in the employments open to Negro men since 1880 or even since 1890.

The age structure also presents abnormal features. Comparing the age structure with that of the large cities of Germany, we have:

Age.	Negroes of Philadelphia.	Large Cities of Germany
Under 20	25.1	39.3
20 to 40	51.3	37.2
Over 40	23.6	23.5

Comparing it with the Whites and Negroes in the city in 1890, we have:

Age.	Negroes of Philadelphia, 1896 Seventh Ward.	Negroes* of Philadelphia, 1890.	Native Whites of Philadelphia, 1890.
Under 10	12.8%	15.31%	24.6%
10 to 20	12.3	16.37	19.5
20 to 30	28.7	27.08	18.5
30 and over	46.2	41.24	37.4

*Includes 1003 Chinese, Japanese and Indians.

As was noticed in the whole city in 1890, so here is even more striking evidence of the preponderance of young people at an age when sudden introduction to city life is apt to be dangerous, and of an abnormal excess of females.

For the last ten or fifteen years young Negroes have been pouring into this city at the rate of a thousand a year; the question is then what homes they find or make, what neighbors they have, how they amuse themselves, and what work they engage in? Again, into what sort of homes are the hundreds of Negro babies of each year born? Under what social influences do they come, what is the tendency of their training, and what places in life can they fill? To answer all these questions is to go far toward finding the real causes of crime and pauperism among this race. . . .

THE ENVIRONMENT OF THE NEGRO

Houses and Rent.—We see that in 1848 the average Negro family rented by the month or quarter, and paid between four and five dollars per month rent. The highest average rent for any section was less than fifteen dollars a month. For such rents the poorest accommodations were afforded, and we know from descriptions that the mass of Negroes has small and unhealthful homes, usually on the back streets and alleys.

The accommodations furnished for the rent paid must now be considered. The number of rooms occupied is the simplest measurement, but is not very satisfactory in this case owing to the lodging system which makes it difficult to say how many rooms a family really occupies. A very large number of families of two and three rent a single bedroom and these must be regarded as one-room tenants, and yet this renting of a room often includes a limited use of a common kitchen; on the other hand this sub-renting family cannot in justice be counted as belonging to the renting family. The figures are:

```
829   families live in 1 room, including families lodging, or 35.2 per cent
104      "      "    "  2 rooms . . . . . . . . . . . . . . . . . . . . . or  4.4    "
371      "      "    "  3    " . . . . . . . . . . . . . . . . . . . . . or 15.7    "
170      "      "    "  4    " ⎱
127      "      "    "  5    " ⎰ . . . . . . . . . . . . . . . . . . or 12.7    "
754      "      "    "  6    " or more . . . . . . . . . . . . . . or 32.0    "
```

The number of families occupying one room is here exaggerated as before shown by the lodging system; on the other hand the number occupying six rooms and more is also somewhat exaggerated by the fact that not all sub-rented rooms have been subtracted, although this has been done as far as possible.

Of the 2441 families only 334 had access to bathrooms and water-closets, or 13.7 percent. Even these 334 families have poor accommodations in most instances. Many share the use of one bathroom with one or more other families. The bath-tubs usually are not supplied with hot water and very often have no water-connection at all. This condition is largely owing to the fact that the Seventh Ward belongs to the older part of Philadelphia, built when vaults in the yards were used exclusively and bathrooms could not be given space in the small houses. This was not so unhealthful before the houses were thick and when there were large back yards. To-day, however, the back yards have been filled by tenement houses and the bad sanitary results are shown in the death rate of the ward.

Even the remaining yards are disappearing. Of the 1751 families making returns, 932 had a private yard 12 x 12 feet, or larger; 312 had a private yard smaller than 12 x 12 feet; 507 had either no yard at all or a yard and outhouse in common with the other denizens of the tenement or alley.

Of the latter, only sixteen families had water-closets. So that over 20 per cent and possible 30 per cent of the Negro families of this ward lack some of the very elementary accommodations necessary to health and decency. And this too in spite of the fact that they are paying comparatively high rents. Here too there comes another consideration, and that is the lack of public urinals and water-closets in this ward and, in fact, throughout Philadelphia. The result is that the closets of tenements are used by the public. . . .

This is the origin of numbers of the blind alleys and dark holes which make some parts of the Fifth, Seventh and Eighth Wards notorious. The closets in such cases are sometimes divided into compartments for different tenants, but in many cases not even this is done; and in all cases the alley closet becomes a public resort for pedestrians and loafers. The back tenements thus formed rent usually for from $7 to $9 a month, and sometimes for more. They consist of three rooms one above the other, small, poorly lighted and poorly ventilated. The inhabitants of the alley are at the mercy of its worst tenants; here policy shops abound, prostitutes ply their trade, and criminals hide. Most of these houses have to get their water at a hydrant in the alley, and must store their fuel in the house. These tenement abominations of Philadelphia are perhaps better than the vast tenement houses of New York, but they are bad enough, and cry for reform in housing. . . .

The rents paid by the Negroes are without doubt far above their means and often from one-fourth to three-fourths of the total income of a family goes in rent. This leads to much non-payment of rent both intentional and unintentional, to frequent shifting of homes, and above all to stinting the families in many necessities of life in order to live in respectable dwellings. Many a Negro family eats less than it ought for the sake of living in a decent house.

Some of this waste of money in rent is sheer ignorance and carelessness. The Negroes have an inherited distrust of banks and companies, and have long neglected to take part in Building and Loan Associations. Others are simply careless in the spending of their money and lack the shrewdness and business sense of differently trained peoples. Ignorance and carelessness however will not explain all or even the greater part of the problem of rent among Negroes. There are three causes of even greater importance: these are the limited localities where Negroes may rent, the peculiar connection of dwelling and occupation among Negroes and the social organization of the Negro. The undeniable fact that most Philadelphia white people prefer not to live near Negroes limits the Negro very seriously in his choice of a home and especially in the choice of a cheap home. Moreover, real estate agents knowing the limited supply usually raise the rent a dollar or two for Negro tenants, if they do not refuse them altogether. Again, the occupations which the Negro follows, and which at present he is compelled to follow, are of a sort that makes it necessary for him to live near the best portions of the city; the mass of Negroes are in the economic world purveyors to the rich—working in private houses, in hotels, large stores, etc. In order to keep this work they must live near by; the laundress cannot bring her Spruce street family's clothes from the Thirtieth Ward, nor can the waiter at the Continental Hotel lodge in Germantown. With the mass of white workmen this same necessity of living near work, does not hinder them from getting cheap dwellings; the factory is surrounded by cheap cottages, the foundry by long rows of houses, and even the white clerk and shop girl can, on account of their hours of labor, afford to live further out in the suburbs than the black porter who opens the store. Thus it is clear that the nature of the Negro's work compels him to crowd into the centre of the city much more than is the case with the mass of white working people. At the same time this necessity is apt in some cases to be overestimated, and a few hours of sleep or convenience serve to persuade a good many families to endure poverty in the Seventh

Ward when they might be comfortable in the Twenty-fourth Ward. Nevertheless much of the Negro problem in this city finds adequate explanation when we reflect that here is a people receiving a little lower wages than usual for less desirable work, and compelled, in order to do that work, to live in a little less pleasant quarters than most people, and pay for them somewhat higher rents.

The final reason of the concentration of Negroes in certain localities is a social one and one peculiarly strong: the life of the negroes of the city has for years centered in the Seventh Ward; here are the old churches, St. Thomas', Bethel, Central, Shiloh and Wesley; here are the halls of the secret societies; here are the homesteads of old families. To a race socially ostracized it means far more to move to remote parts of a city, than to those who will in any part of the city easily form congenial acquaintances and new ties. . . . At the same time color prejudice makes it difficult for groups to find suitable places to move to—one Negro family would be tolerated where six would be objected to; thus we have here a very decisive hindrance to emigration to the suburbs.

65

LOUIS SULLIVAN, EXCERPT FROM "THE TALL OFFICE BUILDING ARTISTICALLY CONSIDERED," 1896; AND HENRY JAMES, EXCERPT FROM *THE AMERICAN SCENE*, 1907

After training briefly in Philadelphia with architect Frank Furness, Louis Sullivan moved to Chicago where he became one of the most influential American architects of the late nineteenth and early twentieth centuries, training, among others, Frank Lloyd Wright. Sullivan came to Chicago when it was arguably the most architecturally dynamic city in the nation, and where the modern skyscraper was invented. In trying to develop a skyscraper aesthetic in this essay, Sullivan proceeds from the assumption that the skyscraper represents something altogether new in architecture, and he classes it with the Greek temple and the Gothic cathedral. Such a revolutionary building form demands, according to Sullivan, a new set of design rules, governed by the principle that function will dictate form.

Just a few years after Sullivan celebrated the possibilities of the "tall building," novelist Henry James returned to the United States after a nearly quarter century absence and recorded his disappointed observations in the book *The American Scene*. James hated these new skyscrapers, as he saw them in New York, "extravagant pins in a cushion already overplanted." Through the characteristic opacity of his prose is an insightful critique of these new buildings: more than anything they are profitable, piling rentable space on top of rentable space in an effort James calls "the last word of economic ingenuity."

Originally printed in *Lippincott's*, 57 (March 1896): 403–9.

5.4. Tribune Tower, exterior from the south. Raymond Hood & John Mead Howells, architects. From the Architecture Photography Collection. Photograph courtesy of The Art Institute of Chicago. In 1922, the Chicago *Tribune* newspaper company held a competition for the design of its new headquarters. The competition attracted a stunning array of designs that served as models for skyscraper design during the next fifty years. The winning design looked both forward and backward: it recognized that the skyscraper had become the preeminent architectural symbol of the United States, but it refused to abandon traditional historical styles. The Gothic-inspired skyscraper, which had found its most glorious rendition in the Woolworth Building in New York (1912) proved to be short-lived and would be supplanted by modernist designs, like those which had been rejected in the *Tribune* competition.

Louis Sullivan, "The Tall Office Building Artistically Considered"

The architects of this land and generation are now brought face to face with something new under the sun—namely, that evolution and integration of social conditions, that special grouping of them, that results in a demand for the erection of tall office buildings.

It is not my purpose to discuss the social conditions; I accept them as the fact, and say at once that the design of the tall office building must be recognized and confronted at the outset as a problem to be solved—a vital problem, pressing for a true solution.

Let us state the conditions in the plainest manner. Briefly, they are these: offices are necessary for the transaction of business; the invention and perfection of the high-speed elevators make vertical travel, that was once tedious and painful, now easy and comfortable; development of steel manufacture has shown the way to safe, rigid, economical constructions rising to a great height; continued growth of population in the great cities, consequent congestion of centers and rise in value of ground, stimulate an increase in number of stories; these successfully piled one upon another, react on ground values—and so on, by action and reaction, interaction and inter-reaction. Thus has come about that form of lofty construction called the "modern office building." It has come in answer to a call, for in it a new grouping of social conditions has found a habitation and a name.

Problem: How shall we impart to this sterile pile, this crude, harsh, brutal agglomeration, this stark staring exclamation of eternal strife, the graciousness of those higher forms of sensibility and culture that rest on the lower and fiercer passions? How shall we proclaim from the dizzy height of this strange, weird, modern housetop the peaceful evangel of sentiment, of beauty, the cult of a higher life? . . .

It is my belief that it is of the very essence of every problem that it contains and suggests its own solution. This I believe to be natural law. Let us examine, then, carefully the elements, let us search out this contained suggestion, this essence of the problem.

The practical conditions are, broadly speaking, these:

Wanted—lst, a story below-ground, containing boilers, engines of various sorts, etc.—in short, the plant for power, heating, lighting, etc. 2nd, a ground floor, so called, devoted to stores, banks, or other establishments requiring large area, ample spacing, ample light, and great freedom of access. 3rd, a second story readily accessible by stairways—this space usually in large subdivisions, with corresponding liberality in structural spacing and expanse of glass and breadth of external openings. 4th, above this an indefinite number of stories of offices piled tier upon tier, one tier just like another tier, one office just like all the other offices—an office being similar to a cell in a honey-comb, merely a compartment, nothing more. 5th, and last, at the top of this pile is placed a space or story that, as related to the life and usefulness of the structure, is purely physiological in its nature—namely, the attic. In this the circulatory system completes itself and makes its grand turn, ascending and descending. The space is filled with tanks, pipes, valves, sheaves, and mechanical etcetera that supplement and complement the force-originating plant hidden below-ground in the cellar. Finally, or at the beginning rather, there must be on the ground floor a main aperture or entrance common to all the occupants or patrons of the building. . . .

Hence it follows inevitably, and in the simplest possible way, that if we follow our natural instincts without thought of books, rules, precedents, or any such educational impediments to a spontaneous and "sensible" result, we will in the following manner design the exterior of our tall office building—to wit:

Beginning with the first story, we give this a main entrance that attracts the eye to its location, and the remainder of the story we treat in a more or less liberal, expansive, sumptuous way—a way based exactly on the practical necessities, but expressed with a sentiment of largeness and freedom. The second story we treat in a similar way, but usually with milder pretension. Above this, throughout the indefinite number of typical office tiers, we take our cue from the individual cell, which requires a window with its separating pier, its sill and lintel, and we, without more ado, make them look all alike because they are all alike. This brings us to the attic, which, having no division into office-cells, and no special requirement for lighting, gives us the power to show by means of its broad expanse of wall, and its dominating weight and character, that which is the fact—namely, that the series of office tiers has come definitely to an end. . . .

It demands of us, what is the chief characteristic of the tall office building? And at once we answer, it is lofty. This loftiness is to the artist-nature its thrilling aspect. It is the very open organ-tone in its appeal. It must be in turn the dominant chord in his expression of it, the true excitant of his imagination. It must be tall, every inch of it tall. The force and power of altitude must be in it, the glory and pride of exaltation must be in it. It must be every inch a proud and soaring thing, rising in sheer exultation that from bottom to top it is a unit without a single dissenting line—that it is the new, the unexpected, the eloquent peroration of most bald, most sinister, most forbidding conditions.

The man who designs in this spirit and with the sense of responsibility to the generation he lives in must be no coward, no denier, no bookworm, no dilettante. He must live of his life and for his life in the fullest, most consummate sense. He must realize at once and with the grasp of inspiration that the problem of the tall office building is one of the most stupendous, one of the most magnificent opportunities that the Lord of Nature in His beneficence has ever offered to the proud spirit of man.

That this has not been perceived—indeed, has been flatly denied—is an exhibition of human perversity that must give us pause. . . .

Certain critics, and very thoughtful ones, have advanced the theory that the true prototype of the tall office building is the classical column, consisting of base, shaft and capital—the moulded base of the column typical of the lower stories of our building, the plain or fluted shaft suggesting the monotonous, uninterrupted series of office-tiers, and the capital the completing power and luxuriance of the attic.

Other theorizers, assuming a mystical symbolism as a guide, quote the many trinities in nature and art, and the beauty and conclusiveness of such trinity in unity. They aver the beauty of prime numbers, the mysticism of the number three, the beauty of all things that are in three parts—to wit, the day, subdividing into morning, noon, and night; the limbs, the thorax, and the head, constituting the body. So they say, should the building be in three parts vertically, substantially as before, but for different motives. . . .

Others, seeking their examples and justification in the vegetable kingdom, urge that such a design shall above all things be organic. They quote the suitable flower with its bunch of leaves at the earth, its long graceful stem, carrying the gorgeous single flower. They point to the pine-tree, its massy roots, its lithe, uninterrupted trunk, its tuft of green high in the air. Thus, they say, should be the design of the tall office building; again in three parts vertically. . . .

All of these critics and theorists agree, however, positively, unequivocally, in this, that the tall office building should not, must not, be made a field for the display of architectural knowledge in the encyclopædic sense; that too much learning in this instance is fully as dangerous, as obnoxious, as too little learning; that miscellany is abhorrent to their sense; that the sixteen-story building must not consist of sixteen separate, distinct and unrelated buildings piled one upon the other until the top of the pile is reached. . . .

This view let me now state, for it brings to the solution of the problem a final, comprehensive formula.

All things in nature have a shape, that is to say, a form, an outward semblance, that tells us what they are, that distinguishes them from our styles and from each other. . . .

It is the pervading law of all things organic and inorganic, of all things physical and metaphysical, of all things human and all things superhuman, of all true manifestations of the head, of the heart, of the soul, that the life is recognizable in its expression, that form ever follows function. This is the law.

Shall we, then, daily violate this law in our art? Are we so decadent, so imbecile, so utterly weak of eyesight, that we cannot perceive this truth so simple, so very simple? Is it indeed a truth so transparent that we see through it but do not see it? Is it really then, a very marvelous thing, or is it rather so commonplace, so everyday, so near a thing to us, that we cannot perceive that the shape, form, outward expression, design of whatever we may choose, of the tall office building should in the very nature of things follow the functions of the building, and that where the function does not change, the form is not to change?

Does this not readily, clearly, and conclusively show that the lower one or two stories will take on a special character suited to the special needs, that the tiers of typical offices, having the same unchanging function, shall continue in the same unchanging form, and that as to the attic, specific and conclusive as it is in its very nature, its function shall equally be so in force, in significance, in continuity, in conclusiveness of outward expression? From this results, naturally, spontaneously, unwittingly, a three-part division, not from any theory, symbol, or fancied logic.

And thus the design of the tall office building takes its place with all other architectural types made when architecture, as has happened once in many years, was a living art. Witness the Greek temple, the Gothic cathedral, the medieval fortress.

And thus, when native instinct and sensibility shall govern the exercise of our beloved art; when the known law, the respected law, shall be that form ever follows function; when our architects shall cease struggling and prattling handcuffed and vainglorious in the asylum of a foreign school; when it is truly felt, cheerfully accepted, that this law opens up the airy sunshine of green fields, and gives to us a freedom that the very beauty and sumptuousness of the outworking of the law itself as exhibited in nature will deter any sane, any sensitive man from changing into license, when it becomes evident that we are merely speaking a foreign language with a noticeable American accent, whereas each and every architect in the land might, under the benign influence of this law, express in the simplest, most modest, most natural way that which it is in him to say; that he might really and would surely develop his own characteristic individuality, and that the architectural art with him would certainly become a living form of speech, a natural form of utterance, giving surcease to him and adding treasures small and great to the growing art of his land; when we know and feel that Nature is our friend, not our implacable enemy—that an afternoon in the country, an hour by the sea, a full open view of one single day, through dawn, high noon, and twilight, will suggest to us so much that is rhythmical, deep, and eternal in the vast art of architecture, something so deep, so true, that all the narrow formalities, hard-and-fast rules, and strangling bonds of the schools cannot stifle in it us—then it may be proclaimed that we are on the high-road to a natural and satisfying art, an architecture that will soon become a fine art in the true, the best sense of the word, an art that will live because it will be of the people, for the people, and by the people.

Henry James, excerpt from *The American Scene*

The "tall buildings," which have so promptly usurped a glory that affects you as rather surprised, as yet, at itself, the multitudinous sky-scrapers standing up to the view, from the water, like extravagant pins in a cushion already overplanted, and stuck in as in the dark, anywhere and anyhow, have at least the felicity of carrying out the fairness of tone, of taking the sun and the shade in the manner of towers of marble. They are not all of marble, I believe, by any means, even if some may be, but they are impudently new and still more impudently "novel"—this is common with so many other terrible things in America—and they are triumphant payers of dividends; all of which uncontested and unabashed pride, with flash of innumerable windows and flicker of subordinate gilt attributions, is like the flare, up and down their long, narrow faces, of the lamps of some general permanent "celebration."

You see the pin-cushion in profile, so to speak, on passing between Jersey City and Twenty-third Street, but you get it broadside on, this loose nosegay of architectural flowers, if you skirt the Battery, well out, and embrace the whole plantation. Then the "American beauty," the rose of intermingled stem, becomes the token of the cluster at large—to that degree that, positively, this is all that is wanted for emphasis of your final impression. Such growths, you feel, have confessedly arisen but to be "picked," in time, with a shears; nipped short off, by waiting fate, as soon as "science," applied to gain, has put upon the table, from far up its sleeve, some more winning card. Crowned not only with no history, but with no credible possibility of time for history, and consecrated by no uses save the commercial at any cost, they are simply the most piercing notes in that concert of the expensively provisional into which your supreme sense of New York resolves itself. They never begin to speak to you, in the manner of the builded majestics of the world as we have heretofore known such—towers or temples or fortresses or palaces—with the authority of things of permanence or even of things of long duration. One story is good only till another is told, and sky-scrapers are the last word of economic ingenuity only till another word be written. This shall be possibly a word of still uglier meaning, but the vocabulary of thrift at any price shows boundless resources, and the consciousness of that truth, the consciousness of the finite, the menaced, the essentially *invented* state, twinkles ever, to my perception, in the thousand glassy eyes of these giants of the mere market. Such a structure as the comparatively windowless bell-tower of Giotto, in Florence, looks supremely serene in its beauty. You don't feel it to have risen by the breath of an interested passion that, restless beyond all passions, is for ever seeking more pliable forms. Beauty has been the object of its creator's idea, and, having found beauty, it has found the form in which it splendidly rests.

Originally printed in Henry James, *The American Scene* (New York: Harper & Brothers, 1907), 60–61.

66

The 1920s was a decade of bigness—of corporations, of popular heroes, and also of cities. While many reveled in the size of what America made, not far beneath the surface was a fear of America's growth, and particularly the growth of American cities. The editors of *Commonweal* scoff at those who imagine the problem of the "super-city" as simply one of logistics, solved mechanically in the same way Henry Ford solved the problem of Model T production quotas. In fact, the threat of the city is something much more abstract, and much more "terrible": "Is it possible to stem the creation of monster communities with no soul, and work back to groups who know each other?" At stake is nothing less than the loss of connection citizens have to each other and to society in this "super-city."

A topic of the most serious importance and complex nature was brought to the surface once more by President Coolidge, in his speech on what is pleasantly spoken of as the national highway crisis. . . .

But President Coolidge's thought leaped out beyond the mere matter of getting about. The size of cities, as a huge complex of the near future, worried him. He was right; it is one of the biggest subjects calling for the consideration of practical politicians. The President's broaching it is an instance of a certain quality of the super-commonplace in his imagination. . . .

The fact is, that when the growth of cities is spoken of—say the growth of New York to 20,000,000 inhabitants by the year 1950, or 50,000,000 inhabitants by the year 2000—the common popular reaction is a sort of fatuous pride—as if mere numbers made greatness. Even enlightened leaders of thought, instead of asking what the life of such a community would be, materially or spiritually, indulge in dreams of marts and markets, air lanes and subterranean passages, electrical homes, and art peddled by radio from municipal stations to the convertible bed-dining-sitting-working-room, of which the ultimate home of the too, too many millions would have to consist. We have all seen the diagrams and pictorial layouts in the Sunday newspapers—map of New York in nineteen-something, taking in all Long Island and New Jersey as far as Trenton, with the Hudson Valley as far as Newburgh thrown in. . . .

President Coolidge was evidently impressed with this feature of the whole conception—the difficulty of making it work, perhaps; of making it fool-proof.

But in fact its worst evil, its direct tragedy, does not lie in its inevitable malfunctioning upon occasions. Its success would be the real disaster. It is impossible to conceive of these teeming millions in their physical multiplication, and in their spiritual loneliness, without repulsion. It needs but a little thought to show that in these regimented crowds, all the essential qualities and enjoyment of citizenship and civilization must be lost. It is a question today whether the limit of numbers permitting the community sense has not already been surpassed. In the dream city of the future, one feels that the intimacy of feeling and interest which makes the spiritual bond, would be attenuated to the danger point. Multiply the appeal by three, or four, or twenty—and we arrive at a stage where a

Originally printed in *Commonweal* 2, no. 1 (May 13, 1925): 1. © 1925 Commonweal Foundation, reprinted with permission. For subscriptions <www.commonwealmagazine.org>.

public-spirited man may perhaps have an affection for his borough or his ward with an understanding of its advantages and needs, but is repelled even to anger by the exigencies of a rival quarter, which he has never visited, and whose people he regards with suspicion and dislike.

Social intercourse has greatly diminished in American cities, at least as regards the home. The multiplication of obligations leads to even the best and finest being ignored; and the mechanical difficulties of getting together, the enormous rivalry of other duties and attractions, have completely changed the lives of the people in the last twenty-five years. The end of New-Year-calling, is an illustration. New York is too big and too hard to circulate in for mere casual observances. A result already felt is the loneliness of the young people and the isolation of the old. How much more hopeless the mechanism of community living, how vain the hope of any genuine social intercourse among 20,000,000 people without common idea or purpose, and living often fifty miles apart!

President Coolidge has raised a very large question—and it may be a tragic one of the future—in turning the public eyes upon the problems of the super-city of the future. He had the mechanical ones in mind mainly, it would seem; but they are simple as compared with the cultural and moral ones. So devious are these that the true question for civic leaders is—whether it is not time to call a halt? Can it be done? Is it possible to stem the creation of monster communities with no soul, and work back to groups who know each other—who have ideals as well as subways, and inspirations as well as airless entertainment? At bottom, the question is one of soul—but the practical problem is one of better distribution of population.

67

NORMAN BEL GEDDES, EXCERPT FROM *MAGIC MOTORWAYS*, 1940

Just as the 1893 World's Columbian Exposition in Chicago provided a powerful set of examples and ideas for those who would remake cities in the early twentieth century, so too the Futurama display at the New York World's Fair in 1939 fired the imaginations of the planners, politicians, and corporations who presided over the era of urban renewal after the Second World War. For Bel Geddes, who had made a name for himself designing theater sets, all urban problems could be traced to one cause: traffic. And thus there was one answer for redesigning cities: highways. We can hear in Bel Geddes's book, published in response to the tremendous popularity of Futurama, the echo of Progressives and New Dealers who called for greater, more thorough, more centralized planning. We can also see in Futurama, an exhibit sponsored by General Motors, all the elements of postwar urban policy—the clearance of vast areas in the central city, the creation of high-rise complexes

Originally printed in Norman Bel Geddes, *Magic Motorways* (New York: Random House, 1940), 3–13, 223–45.

surrounded by open plazas, the construction of multilane expressways through cities. Bel Geddes put his future city at the distant date of 1960. By 1960, many American cities had begun to resemble Futurama to a remarkable extent.

Five million people saw the Futurama of the General Motors Highways and Horizons Exhibit at the New York World's Fair during the summer of 1939. In long queues that often stretched more than a mile, from 5,000 to 15,000 men, women and children at a time, stood, all day long every day, under the hot sun and in the rain, waiting more than an hour for their turn to get a sixteen-minute glimpse at the motorways of the world of tomorrow. There have been hit shows and sporting events in the past which had waiting lines for a few days, but never before had there been a line as long as this, renewing itself continuously, month after month, as there was every day at the Fair.

The people who conduct polls to find out why other people do things, and the editorial writers, newspaper men and columnists who report daily on the doings of the human race, all had their theory as to why the Futurama was the most popular show of any Fair in history. And most of them agreed that the explanation was really very simple: All of these thousands of people who stood in line ride in motor cars and therefore are harassed by the daily task of getting from one place to another, by the nuisances of intersectional jams, narrow, congested bottlenecks, dangerous night driving, annoying policemen's whistles, honking horns, blinking traffic lights, confusing highway signs, and irritating traffic regulations; they are appalled by the daily toll of highway accidents and deaths; and they are eager to find a sensible way out of this planless, suicidal mess. The Futurama gave them a dramatic and graphic solution to a problem which they all faced.

Masses of people can never find a solution to a problem until they are shown the way. Each unit of the mass may have a knowledge of the problem, and each may have his own solution, but until mass opinion is crystallized, brought into focus and made articulate, it amounts to nothing but vague grumbling. One of the best ways to make a solution understandable to everybody is to make it visual, to dramatize it. The Futurama did just this: it was a visual dramatization of a solution to the complex tangle of American roadways.

As all those who saw it know, the Futurama is a large-scale model representing almost every type of terrain in America and illustrating how a motorway system may be laid down over the entire country—across mountains, over rivers and lakes, through cities and past towns—never deviating from a direct course and always adhering to the four basic principles of highway design: safety, comfort, speed and economy. The motorways which stretch across the model are exact replicas, in small scale, of motorways which may be built in America in the near future. They are designed to make automobile collisions impossible and to eliminate completely traffic congestion. Particular features of the motorways may perhaps be improved on, details of future road construction and engineering may differ, but the design of these motorways has been carefully and thoughtfully worked out and is suggestive of probable future developments.

Much of the initial appeal of the Futurama was due to its imaginative quality. But the reason that its popularity never diminished was that its boldness was based on soundness. The plan it presented appealed to the practical engineer as much as to the idle daydreamer. The motorways which it featured were not only desirable, but practical.

As each spectator rode around the model in his comfortable, upholstered armchair, he listened to a description of it in a voice which came from a small speaker built into the back of the chair. This recorded description synchronized with the movement of the chairs and explained the main features of what was passing before the spectator's eyes. It directed his attention to the great arterial highways which were segregated into different speed lanes and which looked so different from the roads of today. It pointed out the overpasses, high-speed intersections and wide bridges over which tear-drop motor cars whisked by at a hundred miles an hour. It commented in passing on the surrounding scenery, the planned cities, decentralized communities and experimental farms. . . .

The Motorway System as visualized in the Futurama and described in this book has been arbitrarily dated ahead to 1960—twenty years from now. But it could be built today. It is not too large a job for a generation which has replaced the plodding horse and buggy with the swift-moving automobile, which has grown wings and spanned the world with them, which has built skyscrapers a thousand feet high. Modern engineering is capable of magnificent accomplishments. . . .

New York is a prize exhibit of almost everything, including sluggishness. But there are other cities with the same characteristics. Detroit, a city dedicated to automotive progress, already confessed itself stymied by the time its main industry got into full swing. In 1805 a master plan was designed to take care of the city's future growth, but in 1924 an official report said that "Detroit is being strangled for lack of sufficient circulating facilities for its people." Unfortunately, this statement is as true today as it was then.

Pittsburgh, with its famous triangle—formed by the meeting of two rivers plus the skyrocketing of a half dozen industries—also is a trouble point. The first street plan was drawn up in 1795—when the rivers were there, but not the industries. That street plan still operates. In attempts to offset the increasing pressure of traffic flow over such inadequate thoroughfares, Pittsburgh has tried and is still trying many methods of traffic control. One-way streets, coordinated traffic signals, the limited and the restricted varieties of curb parking, street carloading platforms with and without curb cut-back for a traffic by-pass, prohibited turning movements within intersections, no stopping during the rush hours, enlarged curb radii for easier turning, and so on—in other words, splints, bandages and liniments applied to a battered traffic body.

Nor are St. Louis, Los Angeles and Chicago immune. They all suffer from the same thing: street layouts too inflexible to adjust themselves to changing conditions and growth. All three are great department-store cities. The stores settled down where the traffic was heaviest, so as to be available to the most people. And then their presence increased traffic congestion in these same areas. An exceptionally heavy burden was thrown upon the streets in the vicinity of the stores. Office buildings multiplied. In St. Louis and Detroit office buildings, the daily passenger traffic was estimated to be about four visitors for each worker. That meant still more stores and accommodations—but no change in the street plan. One suggested solution is to stagger the working hours and so ease the agonies of the rush hour. In Los Angeles, a number of large concerns and government buildings have done this. This measure acts as a palliative at the peak of the crisis, but it is not a basic enough remedy to solve the fundamental problems: concentration and congestion. It is not only that the public is sadly inconvenienced by the immobile automobile, but the existence of stores and businesses is actually threatened by it. Often, after businesses feel themselves threatened by the very congestion they have helped to create, they find they have to move on. Industry is tending to move toward the limits of large cities not only to escape taxes, but perhaps even more directly to escape the cost of traffic congestion. . . .

We face an inescapable choice between planning and chaos. Our sprawling, tangled cities must be transformed. Our city streets must be redesigned. Just as it is time for us to start replacing the forests which we have over-cut, it is time for us to let light and air into the cities which we have over-built. The cost will be great, although engineering studies made for the city of Chicago have proved that elevated highways can be designed at a cost much lower than that of street-widening projects. It is impossible to speed up city traffic by one hundred per cent, at this stage of the game, on a pittance. Twenty years ago the cost would have been much less; twenty years from now the cost will be much greater. But the cost of failure to do so will be greater still. No city can afford the stagnation toward which many are heading.

Hope for the future lies in our determination to rebuild and redesign our cities to prevent the evils which have accumulated as a consequence of lack of planning. The success of the design, physical structure and economy of our future cities will depend on the enterprise and vision which we show today.

68

E. B. WHITE, EXCERPT FROM "HERE IS NEW YORK," 1949

E.B. White's writings for the *New Yorker* constitute perhaps the finest defense of American cities offered by any writer. In this piece—observations of his New York really—he captures the complex and contradictory things that define the city. Every kind of human experience is to be found here, including a deep connection with the past. The joyous chaos that White loves, and that he so lovingly describes, is muted at the end of the piece as White admits to an anxiety of living in a city at the dawn of the nuclear age, a fear that he shared with many Americans. In the wake of the attacks of September 11, 2001, this part of White's essay was widely distributed, as an almost uncanny prediction of that day.

On any person who desires such queer prizes, New York will bestow the gift of loneliness and the gift of privacy. It is this largess that accounts for the presence within the city's walls of a considerable section of the population; for the residents of Manhattan are to a large extent strangers who have pulled up stakes somewhere and come to town, seeking sanctuary or fulfillment or some greater or lesser grail. The capacity to make such dubious gifts is a mysterious quality of New York. It can destroy an individual, or it can fulfill him, depending a good deal on luck. No one should come to New York to live unless he is willing to be lucky.

New York is the concentrate of art and commerce and sport and religion and entertainment and finance, bringing to a single compact arena the gladiator, the evangelist, the promoter, the actor, the trader and the merchant. It carries on its lapel the inexpungable odor of the long past, so that no matter where you sit in New York you feel the vibrations of great times and tall deeds, of queer people and events and undertakings. I am sitting at the moment in a stifling hotel room in 90-degree heat, halfway down an air shaft, in midtown. No air moves in or out of the room, yet I am curiously affected by emanations from the immediate surroundings. I am twenty-two blocks from where Rudolph Valentino lay in state, eight blocks from where Nathan Hale was executed, five blocks from the publisher's office where Ernest Hemingway hit Max Eastman on the nose, four miles from where Walt Whitman sat sweating out editorials for the Brooklyn *Eagle,* thirty-four blocks from the street Willa Cather lived in when she came to New York to write books about Nebraska, one block from where Marceline used to clown on the boards of the Hippodrome, thirty-six blocks from the spot where the historian Joe Gould kicked a radio to pieces in full view of the public, thirteen blocks from where Harry Thaw shot Stanford White, five blocks from where I used to usher at the Metropolitan Opera and only 112 blocks from the spot where Clarence Day the Elder was washed of his sins in the Church of the Epiphany (I could continue this list indefinitely); and for that matter I am probably occupying the very room that any number of exalted and somewise memorable characters sat in, some of them on hot, breathless afternoons, lonely and private and full of their own sense of emanations from without. . . .

There are roughly three New Yorks. There is, first, the New York of the man or woman who was born here, who takes the city for granted and accepts its size and its turbulence as natural and inevitable. Second, there is the New York of the commuter—the city that is devoured by locusts each day and spat out each night. Third, there is the New York of the person who was born somewhere else and came to New York in quest of something. Of these three trembling cities the greatest is the last—the city of final destination, the city that is a goal. It is this third city that accounts for New York's high-strung disposition, its poetical deportment, its dedication to the arts, and its incomparable achievements. Commuters give the city its tidal restlessness, natives give it solidity and continuity, but the settlers give it passion. And whether it is a farmer arriving from Italy to set up a small grocery store in a slum, or a young girl arriving from a small town in Mississippi to escape the indignity of being observed by her neighbors, or a boy arriving from the Corn Belt with a manuscript in his suitcase and a pain in his heart, it makes no difference: each embraces New York with the intense excitement of first love, each absorbs New York with the fresh eyes of an adventurer, each generates heat and light to dwarf the Consolidated Edison Company.

The *commuter* is the queerest bird of all. The suburb he inhabits has no essential vitality of its own and is a mere roost where he comes at day's end to go to sleep. Except in rare cases, the man who lives in Mamaroneck or Little Neck or Teaneck and works in New York, discovers nothing much about the city except the time of arrival and departure of trains and buses, and the path to a quick lunch. He is desk-bound, and has never, idly roaming in the gloaming, stumbled suddenly on Belvedere Tower in the Park, seen the ramparts rise sheer from the water of the pond, and the boys along the shore fishing for minnows, girls stretched out negligently on the shelves of the rocks; he has never come suddenly on anything at all in New York as a loiterer, because he has had no time between trains. He has fished in Manhattan's wallet and dug out coins but has never listened to Manhattan's breathing, never awakened to its morning, never dropped off to sleep in its night. About 400,000 men and women come charging onto the island each weekday morning, out of the mouths of tubes and tunnels. Not many among them have ever spent a drowsy afternoon in the great rustling oaken silence of the reading room of the Public Library, with the book elevator (like an old water wheel) spewing out books onto the trays. They tend their furnaces in Westchester and in Jersey but have never seen the furnaces of the Bowery, the fires that burn in oil drums on zero winter nights. They may work in the financial district downtown and never see the extravagant plantings of Rockefeller Center—the daffodils and grape hyacinths and birches and the flags trimmed to the wind on a fine morning in spring. Or they may work in a midtown office and may let a whole year swing round without sighting Governors Island from the sea wall. The commuter dies with tremendous mileage to his credit, but he is no rover. His entrances and exits are more devious than those in a prairie-dog village, and he calmly plays bridge while buried in the mud at the bottom of the East River. The Long Island Rail Road alone carried forty million commuters last year, but many of them were the same fellow retracing his steps. . . .

A poem compresses much in a small space and adds music, thus heightening its meaning. The city is like poetry: it compresses all life, all races and breeds, into a small island and adds music and the accompaniment of internal engines. The island of Manhattan is without any doubt the greatest human concentrate on earth, the poem whose magic is comprehensible to millions of permanent residents but whose full meaning will always remain elusive. . . .

It is a miracle that New York works at all. The whole thing is implausible. Every time the residents brush their teeth, millions of gallons of water must be drawn from the Catskills and the hills of Westchester. When a young man in Manhattan writes a letter to his girl in Brooklyn, the love message gets blown to her through a pneumatic tube—*pfft*—just like that. The subterranean system of telephone cables, power lines, steam pipes, gas mains, and sewer pipes is reason enough to abandon the island to the gods and the weevils. Every time an incision is made in the pavement, the noisy surgeons expose ganglia that are tangled beyond belief. By rights New York should have destroyed itself long ago, from panic or fire or rioting or failure of some vital supply line in its circulatory system or from some deep labyrinthine short circuit. Long ago the city should have experienced an insoluble traffic snarl at some impossible bottleneck. It should have perished of hunger when food lines failed for a few days. It should have been wiped out by a plague starting in its slums or carried in by ships' rats. It should have been overwhelmed by the sea that licks at it on every side. The workers in its myriad cells should have succumbed to nerves, from the fearful pall of smoke-fog that drifts over every few days from Jersey, blotting out all light at noon and leaving the high offices suspended, men groping and depressed, and the sense of world's end. It should have been touched in the head by the August heat and gone off its rocker. . . . But the city makes up for its hazards and its deficiencies by supplying its citizens with massive doses of a supplementary vitamin: the sense of belonging to something unique, cosmopolitan, mighty, and unparalleled. . . .

The oft-quoted thumbnail sketch of New York is, of course: "It's a wonderful place, but I'd hate to live there." I have an idea that people from villages and small towns, people accustomed to the convenience and the friendliness of neighborhood over-the-fence living, are unaware that life in New York follows the neighborhood pattern. The city is literally a composite of tens of thousands of tiny neighborhood units. There are, of course, the big districts and big units: Chelsea and Murray Hill and Gramercy (which are residential units), Harlem (a racial unit), Greenwich Village (a unit dedicated to the arts and other matters), and there is Radio City (a commercial development), Peter Cooper Village (a housing unit), the Medical Center (a sickness unit) and many other sections each of which has some distinguishing characteristic. But the curious thing about New York is that each large geographical unit is composed of countless small neighborhoods. Each neighborhood is virtually self-sufficient. Usually it is no more than two or three blocks long and a couple of blocks wide. Each area is a city within a city within a city. Thus, no matter where you live in New York, you will find within a block or two a grocery store, a barbershop, a newsstand and shoeshine shack, an ice-coal-and-wood cellar (where you write your order on a pad outside as you walk by), a dry cleaner, a laundry, a delicatessen (beer and sandwiches delivered at any hour to your door), a flower shop, an undertaker's parlor, a movie house, a radio-repair shop, a stationer, a haberdasher, a tailor, a drugstore, a garage, a tearoom, a saloon, a hardware store, a liquor store, a shoe-repair shop. Every block or two, in most residential sections of New York, is a little main street. A man starts for work in the morning and before he has gone two hundred yards he has completed half a dozen missions: bought a paper, left a pair of shoes to be soled, picked up a pack of cigarettes, ordered a bottle of whiskey to be dispatched in the opposite direction against his home-coming, written a message to the unseen forces of the wood cellar, and notified the dry cleaner that a pair of trousers awaits call. Homeward-bound eight hours later, he buys a bunch of pussy willows, a Mazda bulb, a drink, a shine—all between the corner where he steps off the bus and his apartment. So complete is each neighborhood, and so strong the sense of neighborhood, that many a New Yorker spends a lifetime within the confines of an area smaller than a country village. Let him walk two blocks from his corner and he is in a strange land and will feel uneasy till he gets back. . . .

The Consolidated Edison Company says there are eight million people in the five boroughs of New York, and the company is in a position to know. As in every dense community, virtually all races, all religions, all nationalities are represented. Population figures are shifty—they change almost as fast as one can break them down. It is safe to say that about two million of New York's eight million are Jews—roughly one in four. Among this two million who are Jewish are, of course, a great many nationalities: Russian, German, Polish, Rumanian, Austrian, a long list. The Urban League of Greater New York estimates that the number of Negroes in New York is about 700,000. Of these, about 500,000 live in Harlem, a district that extends northward from 110th Street. The Negro population has increased rapidly in the last few years. There are half again as many Negroes in New York today as there were in 1940. There are about 230,000 Puerto Ricans living in New York. There are half a million Irish, half a million Germans. There are 900,000 Russians, 150,000 English, 400,000 Poles, and there are quantities of Finns and Czechs and Swedes and Danes and Norwegians and Latvians and Belgians and Welsh and Greeks, and even Dutch, who have been here from way back. It is very hard to say how many Chinese there are. Officially there are twelve thousand, but there are many Chinese who are in New York illegally and who don't like census takers.

The collision and the intermingling of these millions of foreign-born people representing so many races, creeds, and nationalities make New York a permanent exhibit of the phenomenon of one world. The citizens of New York are tolerant not only from disposition but from necessity. The city has to be tolerant, otherwise it would explode in a radioactive cloud of hate and rancor and bigotry. If the people were to depart even briefly from the peace of cosmopolitan intercourse, the town would blow up higher than a kite. In New York smolders every race problem there is, but the noticeable thing is not the problem but the inviolate truce. Harlem is a city in itself, and being a city Harlem symbolizes segregation; yet Negro life in New York lacks the more conspicuous elements of Jim Crowism. Negroes ride subways and buses on terms of equality with whites, but they have not yet found that same equality in hotels and restaurants. Professionally, Negroes get on well in the theater, in music, in art, and in literature; but in many fields of employment the going is tough. The Jim Crow principle lives chiefly in the housing rules and customs. Private owners of dwellings legally can, and do, exclude Negroes. Under a recent city ordinance, however, apartment buildings that are financed with public moneys or that receive any tax exemption must accept tenants without regard to race, color, or religion. . . .

The slums are gradually giving way to the lofty housing projects—high in stature, high in purpose, low in rent. There are a couple of dozens of these new developments scattered around; each is a city in itself (one of them in the Bronx accommodates twelve thousand families), sky acreage hitherto untilled, lifting people far above the street, standardizing their sanitary life, giving them some place to sit other than an orange crate. Federal money, state money, city money, and private money have flowed into these projects. Banks and insurance companies are in back of some of them. Architects have turned the buildings slightly on their bases, to catch more light. In some of them, rents are as low as $8 a room. Thousands of new units are still needed and will eventually be built, but New York never quite catches up with itself, is never in equilibrium. In flush times the population mushrooms and the new dwellings sprout from the rock. Come bad times and the population scatters and the lofts are abandoned and the landlord withers and dies. . . .

The subtlest change in New York is something people don't speak much about but that is in everyone's mind. The city, for the first time in its long history, is destructible. A single flight of planes no bigger than a wedge of geese can quickly end this island fantasy, burn the towers, crumble the bridges, turn the underground passages into lethal combers, cremate the millions. The intimation of mortality is part of New York now: in the sound of jets overhead, in the black headlines of the latest edition.

All dwellers in cities must live with the stubborn fact of annihilation; in New York the fact is somewhat more concentrated because of the concentration of the city itself, and because, of all targets, New York has a certain clear priority. In the mind of whatever perverted dreamer who might loose the lighting, New York must hold a steady, irresistible charm. . . .

Along the East River, from the razed slaughterhouses of Turtle Bay, as though in a race with the spectral flight of planes, men are carving out the permanent headquarters of the United Nations—the greatest housing project of them all. In its stride, New York takes on one more interior city, to shelter, this time, all governments, and to clear the slum called war. New York is not a capital city—it is not a national capital or a state capital. But it is by way of becoming the capital of the world.

69

SIMONE DE BEAUVOIR,
AMERICA DAY BY DAY (L'AMÉRIQUE AU JOUR LE JOUR), 1954

On her tour of the United States, the celebrated author Simone de Beauvoir took an afternoon stroll through the Maxwell Street market on the west side of Chicago. In the 1940s and 1950s, Maxwell Street and its bustling market became, with the arrival of waves of African-American migrants from the South, the birthplace of the urban electric blues, a place where Muddy Waters, Robert Nighthawk, Little Walter, Hound Dog Taylor, and many other musicians transformed an African-American musical form into the foundation of modern popular music. Europeans had long been fascinated by the diversity of American life, especially its African-American communities and their peculiar—and unequal—place in American life. But here de Beauvoir also highlights the unique characteristics of American immigrant neighborhoods in cities: their ability to serve as crucibles of cultures and their commercialism of the street.

This afternoon C. L. has left her bookshop to join me on a walk through the streets of Chicago. On the edge of the black, Greek, and Italian neighborhoods, we discover, by chance, one of the biggest markets I've seen since the Djelma el Fna Square in Marrakech. It stretches for more than a mile along the pavement and sidewalks of a broad street. The sun is punishing, a midsummer sun, and dark Chicago has suddenly become an exotic village, hot and colorful, the way I'd imagined San Francisco would be. The men are wearing shirts of pale blue, delicate green, shrimp pink, salmon, mauve, sulfur yellow, and indigo, and they let their shirts hang outside their trousers. Many women have knotted the ends of their white blouses above their navels, revealing a broad strip of midriff between skirt and bodice. There are many black faces, others olive, tan, and white, often shaded by large straw hats. To the right, to the left, people in wooden stalls sell silk dressing gowns, shoes, cotton dresses, jewelry, blankets, little tables, lemons, hot dogs, scrap iron, furs—an astonishing mixture of junk and solid merchandise, a yard sale mixed with low-priced luxury. On the pavement small cars drive around selling ice cream, Coca-Cola, and popcorn; in a glass cage the flickering flame of a little lamp heats the kernels and makes them pop. There's a tiny man in rags with the face of an Indian, wearing a big straw hat and with a hearing device fixed behind his dirty ear; he's telling fortunes with the help of a machine. The apparatus is very complicated, truly magical: on a moving cart there's a glass column full of liquid in which little dolls jump up and down. A customer approaches—a black woman with a naked midriff, who seems at once provocative, skeptical, and intimidated. She puts her hand against the glass; the bottle-imps jump up and sink into the invisible depths of the instrument, which spits out a strip of pink paper on which the customer's fate is written. This mechanical apparatus in the service of magic, the hearing aid beneath the exotic hat, these juxtapositions give this market its unexpected character. It's an eighteenth-century fair in which drugstore products are sold amid the clamor of four or five radios. There's another charlatan worthy of the old Pont Neuf: he has twined a snake around his neck and is selling a black elixir that's supposed to

Originally printed in Simone de Beauvoir, *America Day by Day* (*L'Amérique au jour le jour*) (Paris: Gallimard, 1954).

be a cure-all, and he describes the fabulous properties of this universal panacea through a microphone. Another man specializes in headaches, curing them through a simple laying on of hands. He, too, pitches his sales talk through a microphone, and behind him there's a highly scientific anatomical drawing representing the human brain. There are shops on the sidewalks, often below street level, as in the Jewish neighborhood in New York, and their merchandise spills out onto the pavement. Through an open door, I see a gypsy covered with scarves and veils in a darkened room; she's kneeling beside a basin, washing her linen. The radios blare, and each is playing a different tune.

On the street corner, some blacks are holding a religious meeting. The men are in ordinary clothes, but the women wear long black robes and veils edged in white, just like the nuns of certain orders. They are singing in chorus, and above their heads, a black family is sitting on a balcony lazily listening to them sing stirring spirituals. A little farther on, a black preacher is speaking passionately, and guitarists are playing jazz tunes on the edge of the sidewalk. Another black speaker with a red skullcap is gesticulating vehemently: he angrily singles out other preachers for preaching the God of the white man; in contrast, he is invoking the God of Black people, and he exhorts his brothers to come to him and no one else. Sects that are openly against white people have arisen recently, but only a few. For the most part they are Islamic, worhsiping the god of Muhammad, not the Christian god, and they look to the brown people of Asia Minor and Africa for the salvation of the black race. This preacher probably belongs to the "Moors," which is not only a religious sect but also a small economic community with a harem. It includes two hundred blacks, mostly women, who live in one of the nearby slums. We listen, we look.

Superstitions, science, religion, food, physical and spiritual remedies, rags, silks, popcorn, guitars, radios—what an extraordinary mix of all the civilizations and races that have existed throughout time and space. In the hands of merchants, preachers, and charlatans, the snares sparkle and the street is full of the chatter of thousands of brightly feathered birds. Yet under the blue sky, the grayness of Chicago persists. At the end of the avenue that crosses the glowing bazaar, the pavement and light are the color of water and dust.

70

JANE JACOBS, "DOWNTOWN IS FOR PEOPLE," 1958

Jane Jacobs was born in 1916 in Scranton, Pennsylvania, but, as she would later write, found her fortune in New York City. As the urban renewal era was in full swing, with wrecking balls across the country demolishing thousands of acres of supposed "slums," Jacobs was already penning sharp critiques of this movement for urban redevelopment. While planners were increasingly designing cities and regions from high above the street, with both eyes focused on the needs of the automobile, Jacobs was going in the opposite

Originally printed in *Fortune*, v. 57 April 1958, 133–40, 236, 238, 240–42. Reprinted by permission of *Fortune* magazine.

5.5. Hudson Street at Perry Street, Greenwich Village, New York. Courtesy of Iguana Photo, www.iguanaphoto.com This view, from a window adjacent to the home where Jane Jacobs resided as she wrote her seminal work *The Death and Life of Great American Cities*, reveals a beauty we can appreciate only after reading her observations. Looking out her window at 505 Hudson Street, Jacobs saw a messy vitality in the short blocks, the old and new buildings, the stores and homes atop one another that created a unique urban culture. Where others saw a slum, Jacobs saw a neighborhood that worked, socially and economically. Her way of seeing transformed American architecture, planning, and urban life.

direction: she told the stories of how cities worked at the street level. And she sounded the warning of what big highways, huge public housing complexes, and empty plazas would do to urban life. This essay for *Fortune* magazine, which urged that those who plan cities go out and actually see how cities work in reality, led directly to her masterwork, *The Death and Life of Great American Cities* (1961). That book shifted the momentum away from urban renewal, away from the suburbs, and toward "great American cities" once again.

This year is going to be a critical one for the future of the city. All over the country civic leaders and planners are preparing a series of redevelopment projects that will set the character of the center of our cities for generations to come. Great tracts, many blocks wide, are being razed; only a few cities have their new downtown projects already under construction; but almost every big city is getting ready to build, and the plans will soon be set.

What will the projects look like? They will be spacious, parklike, and uncrowded. They will feature long green vistas. They will be stable and symmetrical and orderly. They will be clean, impressive, and monumental. They will have all the attributes of a well-kept, dignified cemetery.

And each project will look very much like the next one: the Golden Gateway office and apartment center planned for San Francisco; the Civic Center for New Orleans; the Lower Hill auditorium and apartment project for Pittsburgh; the Convention Center for Cleveland; the Quality Hill offices and apartments for Kansas City; the downtown scheme for Little Rock; the Capitol Hill project for Nashville. From city to city the architects' sketches conjure up the same dreary scene; here is no hint of individuality or whim or surprise, no hint that here is a city with a tradition and flavor all its own.

These projects will not revitalize downtown; they will deaden it. For they work at cross-purposes to the city. They banish the street. They banish its function. They banish its variety.

Almost without exception the projects have one standard solution for every need: commerce, medicine, culture, government—whatever the activity, they take a part of the city's life, abstract it from the hustle and bustle of downtown, and set it, like a self-sufficient island, in majestic isolation.

There are, certainly, ample reasons for redoing downtown—falling retail sales, tax bases in jeopardy, stagnant real-estate values, impossible traffic and parking conditions, failing mass transit, encirclement by slums. But with no intent to minimize these serious matters, it is more to the point to consider what makes a city center magnetic, what can inject the gaiety, the wonder, the cheerful hurly-burly that make people want to come into the city and to linger there. For magnetism is the crux of the problem. All downtown's values are its byproducts. To create in it an atmosphere of urbanity and exuberance is not a frivolous aim.

We are becoming too solemn about downtown. The architects, planners—and businessmen—are seized with dreams of order, and they have become fascinated with scale models and bird's-eye views. This is a vicarious way to deal with reality, and it is, unhappily, symptomatic of a design philosophy now dominant: buildings come first, for the goal is to remake the city to fit an abstract concept of what, logically, it should be. But whose logic? The logic of the projects is the logic of egocentric children, playing with pretty blocks and shouting, "See what I made!"—a viewpoint much cultivated in our schools of architecture and design. And citizens who should know better are so fascinated by the sheer process of rebuilding that the end results are secondary to them.

With such an approach, the end results will be about as helpful to the city as the dated relics of the City Beautiful movement, which in the early years of this century was going to rejuvenate the city by making it parklike, spacious, and monumental. For the underlying intricacy, and the life that makes downtown worth fixing at all, can never be fostered synthetically. No one can find what will work for our cities by looking at the boulevards of Paris, as the City Beautiful people did; and they can't find it by looking at suburban garden cities, manipulating scale models, or inventing dream cities.

You've got to get out and walk. Walk, and you will see that many of the assumptions on which the projects depend are visibly wrong. You will see, for example, that a worthy and well-kept institutional center does not necessarily upgrade its surroundings. (Look at the blight-engulfed urban universities, or the petered-out environs of such ambitious landmarks as the civic auditorium in St. Louis and the downtown mall in Cleveland.) You will see that suburban amenity is not what people seek downtown. (Look at Pittsburghers by the thousands climbing forty-two steps to enter the very urban Mellon Square, but balking at crossing the street into the ersatz suburb of Gateway Center.)

You will see that it is not the nature of downtown to decentralize. Notice how astonishingly small a place it is; how abruptly it gives way, outside the small, high-powered core, to underused areas. Its tendency is not to fly apart but to become denser, more compact. Nor is this tendency some leftover from the past; the number of people working within the cores has been on the increase, and given the long-term growth in white-collar work it will continue so. The tendency to become denser is a fundamental quality of downtown and it persists for good and sensible reasons.

If you get out and walk, you see all sorts of other clues. Why is the hub of downtown such a mixture of things? Why do office workers on New York's handsome Park Avenue turn off to Lexington or Madison Avenue at the first corner they reach? Why is a good steak house usually in an old building? Why are short blocks apt to be busier than long ones?

It is the premise of this article that the best way to plan for downtown is to see how people use it today; to look for its strengths and to exploit and reinforce them. There is no logic that can be superimposed on the city; people make it, and it is to them, not buildings, that we must fit our plans. This does not mean accepting the present; downtown does need an overhaul, it is dirty, it is congested. But there are things that are right about it too, and by simple old-fashioned observation we can see what they are.

71

ALFRED KAZIN, "FEAR OF THE CITY, 1783 TO 1983," 1983

Alfred Kazin, one of America's greatest literary critics, is equally well known for his writings about cities. His *Walker in the City* is a classic essay on New York. Kazin, who loves his New York, wrote this article at perhaps the low-water mark of American cities in the twentieth century, when crime, drugs, and economic collapse made many wonder if cities could survive. As he says, "What has finally happened is that fear of the city on the part of those who live in it has caught up with the fear on the part of those who did not have to live in it." But in the end, Kazin seems unwilling to give in to this despair.

The trouble with the city, said Henry James, Henry Adams, and Edith Wharton, *is* democracy, the influx of ignorant masses, their lack of manners, their lack of standards. The trouble with the city, said the angry Populist farmers and their free-silver standard-

Originally printed in *American Heritage*, February–March, 1983, 14–23. Reprinted by permission of *American Heritage*.

bearer Bryan in 1896, is Wall Street, the "moneyed East," the concentration of capital, the banking system that keeps honest, simple farmers in debt. Before modern Los Angeles, before Dallas, Phoenix, and Houston, it was understood that "the terrible town," as Henry James called New York, could exist only in the crowded East. The West, "wild" or not, was land of heart's ease, nature itself. The East was the marketplace that corrupted Westerners who came East. There was corruption at the ballet box, behind the bank counter, in the "purlieus of vice." The city was ugly by definition because it lacked the elemental harmony of nature. It lacked stability and relentlessly wrecked every monument of the past. It was dirt, slums, gangsters, violence.

Above all it was "dark." The reporter and pioneer photographer Jacob Riis invaded the East Side for his book *How the Other Half Lives* (1890) because he was "bent on letting in the light where it was much needed."

Look at Riis's photograph "Bandit's Roost," 59½ Mulberry Street, taken February 12, 1888. "Bandit's Roost" did not get its name for nothing, and you can still feel threatened as your eye travels down the narrow alley paved with grimy, irregularly paved stone blocks that glisten with wet and dirt. Tough-looking characters in derbies and slouch hats are lining both sides of the alley, staring straight at you; one of them presses a stick at the ground, and his left knee is bent as if he were ready, with that stick, to go into action at a moment's notice. The women at the open windows are staring just as unhelpfully as the derbied young fellow in the right foreground, whose chin looks as aggressive as the long, stiff lines of his derby. . . .

ARE CITIES all that important as an index of American health and hope? The French sociologist Raymond Aaron thinks that American intellectuals are too much preoccupied with cities. He neglects to say that most Americans now have no other life but the life in these cities. Paris has been the absolute center of France—intellectually, administratively, educationally—for many centuries. America has no center that so fuses government and intellect. Although Americans are more than ever an urban people, many Americans still think of the city as something it is necessary to escape from.

In the nineteenth century slums were savage places Jacob Riis documented in his photographs, but on the whole the savagery was confined to the slums. The political scientist Andrew Hacker has shown that "there was actually little crime of the kind we know today and in hardly any cases were the victims middle class. The groups that had been violent—most notably the Irish—had by 1900 turned respectable. The next wave of immigrants, largely from Eastern Europe and Southern Italy, were more passive to begin with and accepted the conditions they found on their arrival. . . . they did not inflict their resentments on the rest of society . . ."

What has finally happened is that fear of the city on the part of those who live in it has caught up with the fear on the part of those who did not have to live in it.

American fear of the city may seem ungrateful, since so much of our social intelligence depends on it. But the tradition of fear persists, and added to it nowadays—since all concern with the city is concern with class—has been fear of the "underclass," of blacks, of the youth gangs that first emerged in the mid-fifties. Vast housing projects have become worse than the slums they replaced and regularly produce situations of extreme peril for the inhabitants themselves. To the hosts of the uprooted and disordered in the city, hypnotized by the images of violence increasingly favored by the media, the city is nothing but a state of war. There is mounting vandalism, blood lust, and indiscriminate aggressiveness.

The mind reels, is soon exhausted and turns indifferent to the hourly report of still another killing. In Brooklyn's 77th precinct a minister is arrested for keeping a sawed-off shotgun under his pulpit. On Easter Sunday uniformed police officers are assigned to protect churchgoers from muggers and purse snatchers. In parts of Crown Heights and Bedford-Stuyvesant, the *Times* reports that "there, among the boarded-up tenements, the gaudy little stores and the residential neighborhoods of old brownstones and small row houses, 88 people were killed in one year—16 in one three-block area." A hundred thousand people live and work in this precinct, but a local minister intones that "Life has become a mean and frightening struggle." Gunshots are heard all the time.

I was born and brought up alongside that neighborhood; the tenement in which my parents lived for half a century does not exist and nothing has replaced it. The whole block is a mass of rubble; the neighborhood has seen so much arson that the tops of the remaining structures are streaked with black. Alongside them whole buildings are boarded up but have been broken into; they look worse than London did after the blitz.

Democracy has been wonderful to me and for me, and in the teeth of the police state creeping up elsewhere in the world, I welcome every kind of freedom that leaves others free in the city. The endless conflict of races, classes, sexes, is raucous but educational. No other society on earth tolerates so many interest groups, all on the stage at once and all clamoring for attention.

Still, the subway car I take every day to the city university definitely contains a threat. Is it the young black outstretched across the aisle? The misplaced hilarity proceeding from the drinking group beating time to the ya-ya-ya that thumps out of their ghetto blaster? The sweetish marijuana fumes when the train halts too long in this inky tunnel and that makes me laugh when I think that once there was no more absolute commandment in the subway than NO SMOKING? Definitely, there is a threat. Does it proceed from the unhelpful, unsmiling, unseeing strangers around me? The graffiti and aggressive smears of paint on which I have to sit, and which so thickly cover every partition, wall, and window that I cannot make out the stations? Can it be the New York *Post*— "Post Mortem" as a friend calls it—every edition of which carried the news MOM KILLS SELF AND FIVE KIDS? The battle police of the transit force rushing through one car after another as the motorman in his booth sounds the wailing alarm that signifies trouble?

What a way to live! It is apartness that rules us here, and the apartness makes the threat. Still, there is no other place for me to work and live. Because sitting in the subway, holding the book on which I have to conduct a university seminar this afternoon, I have to laugh again. It is *Uncle Tom's Cabin, or Life Among the Lowly.*

72

CAMILLO JOSE VERGARA, EXCERPT FROM "THE NEW AMERICAN GHETTO," 1994

The photographer and writer Camillo Jose Vergara has spent two decades documenting the changing face of America's older cities, illustrating in pictures and words the steady physical and social collapse of the "new American ghetto." These are not the ghettos of the early part of the century, which housed, in different areas, immigrant groups and African-Americans. Instead there are the devastated neighborhoods created by urban renewal, deindustrialization, and suburbanization after the Second World War. Vergara's images—some of the most powerful recording the physical decline of a single block over the course of a decade or more—are devastating in their impact. They describe a new type of ruin: the urban ruin of once great urban civilizations. As a tragic half-joke, Vergara has proposed that all of downtown Detroit, the city of the automobile, be turned into a memorial to the era of industry in the United States.

A tour of ruined neighborhoods and downtowns in America's once-mighty industrial heartland offers some startling sights: former banks with Classical porticos boarded up; Art Deco automobile showrooms, their wrap-around windows cinderblocked; splendid hotels with silent ballrooms; neo-Gothic churches abandoned in the march of time.

With so many of the surrounding buildings leveled, these substantial "leftover" structures—too costly to tear down—dominate the streetscape in isolated grandeur. Common wisdom tells us to relocate the people, demolish the remains, and rebuild. Structures that attracted immigrants from the entire world, that survived riots and decades of disinvestment now have no future. Although their immediate meaning is of neglect and failure, is it possible for these ghetto cityscapes also to stir our imagination?

This essay looks at two Midwestern cities—Chicago and Gary, Indiana—where the new American ghetto, with its contradictions, inequality, and tragic allure reveals itself to us. Though still a vibrant city, Chicago exhibits erratic patterns of development, where large sections of the urban landscape have been neglected or abandoned. Meanwhile, much of moribund Gary has been leveled by urban renewal and the work of scavengers.

REINVENTING THE CITY

Chicago has lost about 900,000 people since 1950, over 23 percent of its population. Among those fleeing in 1992, more than twice as many were residents of wealthy neighborhoods than of poor ones. But whites weren't the only ones leaving the city. During the 1980s alone, the city lost 100,000 African Americans. "The strongest force behind that migration today," states a December 1993 *Chicago Tribune* study, "is fear of crime." Asked to comment, Mayor Richard M. Daley replied: "You're going to have a smaller city, better quality of life. . . . The city will get smaller and then reinvent itself. You'll start planning it differently in a way." Indeed, Daley keeps the demolition crews busy, clearing space for Chicago to "reinvent itself."

Reprinted with permission from *Architectural Record*, vol. 182, no. 11, November 1994, a McGraw-Hill Construction publication.

5.6. Camillo Jose Vergara, from *The New American Ghetto.* Photograph of downtown Detroit, as seen from Park and Sibley Streets. Like the government photographers of the 1930s, who catalogued the plight of various groups struggling in the Great Depression, Camillo Jose Vergara has documented the changing, and usually declining, inner city of late-twentieth-century America. Especially tragic are his images of Detroit, such as this one, which show how utterly devoid of people and even buildings much of the city is.

On thoroughfares like West Madison Street in Chicago, we can see what is happening to large parts of urban America. Once one of the nation's most important commercial streets, West Madison has been through two riots and four decades of disinvestment and is today mostly gone. Moving west from the Loop (Chicago's still thriving downtown), a buffer zone of institutions and housing leads to five miles of large-scale abandonment, and then to affluent Oak Park.

The process of abandonment, fire, and demolition is repeated throughout Chicago's ghettos, as it was in the South Bronx a dozen years ago. This is happening at a time of particular economic hardship: 21 percent of the population falls below the poverty level—four times the number of poor than in the ring of suburbs surrounding the city. A shortage of affordable housing combined with a scarcity of rent subsidies is forcing destitute residents to double up or live in substandard dwellings.

In many areas of Chicago, according to an official of the Buildings Department, "a building that is not occupied has a very short life because scavengers will come in, strip the plumbing, and cause fires." Yet the city is very slow in transferring the rights to abandoned buildings to non-profit community groups willing to rehabilitate them. Why this is so is a matter of speculation. But many people suspect an undeclared "clearance" policy. In any case, the consensus is that if a structure is not going to be rehabilitated soon, it should be demolished. Last year, the city approved a five-fold increase in its demolition budget, raising it to $10 million.

"Abandonment is old. It may be picking up speed now, but this has been going on since the 1950s," says Professor Charles Hoch of the University of Illinois. This time, however, nobody seems to be surprised that so much of the city is disappearing. "To the banks, to the people who own those buildings, their value in money terms is insignificant even though their value as shelter is still great. Capital is into new edge cities, not into restoration, protection, or preservation."

As privately owned apartment buildings disappear, the only large investment in low-income housing is the rehabilitation of projects belonging to the Chicago Housing Authority (CHA), an institution that has long been associated with mismanagement, semi-abandoned high-rises, concentrated poverty, and high crime rates. Because it provides housing of last resort, the CHA has often been called "Chicago's unofficial shelter system." For nearly three decades, CHA developments, widely resented as "places to load down poor people" and as "hellholes," have defined the city's worse ghettos. . . .

THE CAPITAL OF BLACK AMERICA

Gary ranks first in the nation among cities in population loss during the 1980s. At the National Black Political Convention in 1972, an event held at a time of hope, the 3,500 delegates and alternates were enjoined to "Come Home to Gary." In 1994, the city still wants people to return. Banners strung along Broadway, read "Come Home . . . to Gary."

In his five terms as mayor, from 1968 to 1988, Richard Hatcher linked the city's downtown to the interstate highway system, cleared dozens of acres for reconstruction, and built the Genesis Convention Center. But his goal of building a Civil Rights Hall of Fame at the city's most prominent intersection remains unfulfilled. This is the city that Hatcher wanted to make the capital and economic center of black America. During the first 15 years of his administration, Gary received $300 million from Washington. In 1976, federal funds accounted for 36 percent of the city's entire budget. But during Hatcher's tenure in office, U.S. Steel Gary Works, the company that created the city, eliminated 20,000 jobs.

Steel City looks desolate. Viewed northward from Washington Street, the ruined downtown rises like a mirage above large empty fields. A few prostitutes with harsh faces, working out of semi-abandoned buildings, are what remains of a once legendary red-light district. Street dogs trot along the empty lots. Plywood nailed across openings of vacant buildings has gone from brown to gray, and the boards are falling off, leaving the vacant structures accessible to squatters and scavengers.

Malfunctioning street lights are sometimes cut down as if they were trees stricken by a deadly disease, their jagged aluminum stumps left imbedded in the cement. Overgrown sidewalks line streets that have lost their names and sometimes even their traffic signs. Trees grow from the roofs of abandoned buildings, and in parking lots wild shrubs break out of the concrete. Broadway, the city's main commercial street, has only one building undergoing rehabilitation, a former Sears store. "Fifty years ago, during the war, this was one of the busiest places on the planet," says James B. Lane, professor of history at Indiana University Northwest. . . .

Nationally, we seem unable to achieve the consensus needed to rebuild our cities.

But as we see in Chicago and Gary today, we certainly seem able to blow up and bulldoze structures that we consider useless. Our extraordinary ruins represent a short transitional period when stately structures built for the affluent become the homes, churches, and businesses of the poor, and after decades of neglect and disinvestment are discarded.

America does not share Europe's respect for ruins. From a distance, they are perceived as messengers of bad news. We either ignore them or react to them with anger, resentment, guilt, or despair. Ruins stand as witnesses to their own past, not doing what they were built to do, yet possessing an awesome power to stir the soul.

Historical precedent teaches that it will be a long time before these ruins can be looked upon with anything resembling appreciation. In England, for example, a century elapsed after the abrupt termination of the monasteries in the sixteenth century before observers could view them with interest and esthetic delight.

There is something inspiring about ruins. As witnesses of the urban condition, they urge us to ask: "Is there no choice but to stand by and watch the destruction of our cities?" Stripped to their essences, left-over buildings and discarded spaces form cityscapes of great power.

We need to hear the elemental chant that comes from our skeletal neighborhoods. Their once-familiar song beckons us to come home and perhaps to try again.

73

KURT ANDERSEN, EXCERPT FROM "A CITY ON A HILL," 1997

Flush with industrial fortunes, philanthropists of the late nineteenth century built museums and filled them with treasures. The museum became a way both to legitimate robber baron wealth and to create cultural legitimacy for the cities in which these museums were built. In the last quarter of the twentieth century, museums still functioned as markers of cultural legitimacy, and cities like Seattle, Dallas, and Phoenix built new ones as a way of announcing their arrival into the first rank of urban centers. And just as no other city has been made to feel as bad about its cultural shallowness as Los Angeles, none tried to erase those perceptions as swiftly and as dramatically as Los Angeles when the Getty Museum opened in 1997. The Getty was created by oil baron J. Paul Getty with a bequest of more than a billion dollars, which instantly made the Getty the best endowed museum in the country. With that money, the museum trustees commissioned New York architect Richard Meier to design a campus of buildings atop an undeveloped hill. The results are described enthusiastically by critic Kurt Andersen in this review of the new museum. Though the pieces were not yet installed when Andersen took his tour, he applauds the place and believes it will force the nation's cultural establishment to take Los Angeles more seriously.

Originally published in the *New Yorker*, September 29, 1997, 66–73.

One bright weekend afternoon earlier this year, on a mountaintop in Brentwood, the architect Richard Meier—tall, commanding, magnificently white-haired—was giving a pre-opening tour of his new Getty Center to a few billionaires he knows. (During the past six months, the private pre-opening Getty tour has become an in-the-know V.I.P. perk, the backstage pass of the beau monde.) Aside from Meier, who has spent a week or two every month for the last ten years in a funky, rat-infested house on the construction site, only one member of the group was a local—David Geffen, the entertainment mogul. The group had wandered over acres of gorgeous Italian stone, through impeccably thirty-five-foot-high galleries, and past dozens of glass-walled scholars' offices with dumb-founding Pacific Ocean views, when, as Meier tells it, Geffen suddenly blurted, "this is too good for Los Angeles." He went on to explain, "I love it, but people here won't appreciate it. There's nothing else here that can stand up to this. Look around— everything's transitory. And this is solid. This is permanent."

John Walsh, the vigorous, Waspy director of the Getty Museum, tries to be indulgent of reactions like that. "There are people around here who are nostalgic about the feckless, charming, hedonist Los Angeles of the twenties and thirties," he says. "But Los Angeles is putting a kind of support underneath the cultural structure that was built hastily out of recycled and sometimes cheap parts over its first hundred or so years. We're part of that. This is a process of growing up."

New York passed through its own boomtown phase more than a century ago. The Metropolitan Museum opened at its current site in 1880, surrounded protectively by Central Park, across Fifth Avenue from what was shaping up to be the city's gentry neighborhood. The Met's expansion was underwritten by the Gettys of that era. Los Angeles has just come through half a century of fantastic growth, and now the Getty Center is opening across the San Diego Freeway from that city's gentry neighborhood, atop a hill near the intersection of two of L.A's busiest highways, the 10 and the 405, surrounded protectively by its own square mile of nature. . . .

Since the nineteen-sixties, undertakings of such scale, let alone grandeur, have been unfashionable and unaffordable in this country. It has been left to parvenus in the Middle East and in Southeast Asia—oligarchs enriched by companies like Getty Oil—to create giant cultural institutions out of nothing. Indeed, with dead-rich-white-male values besieged in America, the particular philanthropic hubris of the Getty seems impossibly, thrillingly nineteenth century: a new first-rate museum of old European art and antiquities, plus an expansive scholarly facility, both of them built in fifteen years by a major architect living among a thousand construction workers, and both lavishly underwritten without a single fund-raising gala. . . .

This is just how the future was supposed to be. From the parking garage at the bottom of the hill, it's a winding five-minute ascent on robot tram cars, past groves of California live oak and rusticated stone ramparts, to the Getty Center itself. The combination of microprocessed Epcot efficiency, permanently sunny panoramas, and Meier's highly classicized modernism is like a dream, or a "Star Trek" episode about Periclean Athens in a parallel universe.

The serenity is intense. A grand utopian peacefulness was the intent, and the process of the designing and the building was accordingly slow and steady. When Williams phoned Meier, in 1984, to tell him he had the job, Williams asked, according to the architect, "Can you finish it in three years?" In fact, it was seven years before the final design was unveiled. During his first year on the project, he, Walsh, Williams, and others from the Getty went on several world tours in which they visited libraries and research centers and, in southern Europe, wandered together through gardens and citadels, village squares and hill towns, seeking inspiration.

And so the dense, complicated cluster of Getty structures—there are eleven, occupying a hundred and twenty-four acres—is reminiscent, in its spick-and-span abstract way, of some Old World settlement. Given the traditionalism of the Getty's collection, the hilltop site, and the Southern California climate, the Mediterranean model was irresistible. There are six non-museum buildings, which are clad mainly in Meier's familiar white enamel-covered aluminum panels (*off*-white was his concession to the client and the neighbors), but the five-building museum complex is covered mainly by travertine from a quarry near Tivoli, north of Rome. Over the past two decades, it has become standard to paste thin stone veneers on high-rise office towers, as a kind of attenuated allusion to prewar architecture—class on the cheap. At the Getty there are three hundred thousand substantial chunks of travertine, most of them two-and-a-half-feet square and almost three inches thick. No wonder the original three-hundred-million-dollar construction budget doubled, and finally tripled. . . .

In emphatically multicultural Los Angeles, where the freeways have signs directing motorists to a Museum of Tolerance, the Getty Center is routinely derided as élitist. The critics seem to mean that it is physically very grand, that you can't park right at the front door, and that the collection consists overwhelmingly of works from the European premodern canon. The fact that Meier is a New Yorker and Despont is French probably adds to the sense of élitism. Although a city bus stops at the museum, there is parking space for only twelve hundred automobiles, and each parking space requires a reservation. About this crime against the car-loving people of Los Angeles, Walsh says, "We want to make a place that has a kind of unforgettable intimacy that's peaceful. And it can't be peaceful if it's overcrowded." The élitism charge, Meier says, "is a straw man, a false polemic." . . .

The Getty Center should make Angelenos in general feel a little better, in part by making Los Angeles seem more like a real city. To begin with, there's the view: from the old downtown to Century City and over to the Hollywood Hills and on to the ocean, this is one of the rare local spots from which a person can survey the whole megalopolis. . . .

"I think the Getty Center is going to change what actually happens and what appears to happen in Los Angeles," John Walsh says. "I think it will make it easier for serious people to persuade themselves they might come and live in Los Angeles. It will bring tourists here, and that will change the caricatured view of Los Angeles."

5.7. New York–New York Casino, Las Vegas. Courtesy of Iguana Photo, iguanaphoto.com. Las Vegas's main road is called "The Strip" and is defined by the casino signs that light up the desert landscape—Stardust, Caesar's, Circus Circus. But in the last decade "sin city" has been remade again, this time as a family entertainment center, with vast new inward-turning complexes, designed to ape cities of the world. The new Las Vegas strip begins with Luxor, a hotel and casino disguised as the largest pyramid outside of Egypt; Paris Las Vegas, complete with an Arc de Triomphe, Eiffel Tower, and Opera House; the Venetian, with its own canals and gondoliers; and now, New York–New York, where the Brooklyn Bridge and the Statue of Liberty stand, conveniently, within a few steps of one another.

74

RICHARD TODD, EXCERPT FROM
"LAS VEGAS, TIS OF THEE," 2001

In the same way Washington, D.C., exists only because it is a government center, and
Orlando exists only because of Walt Disney, gambling is Las Vegas's raison d'etre. It over-
simplifies history only a little to say that Las Vegas was founded by gangsters with the sole
intent of providing a haven for legalized gambling in a nation where it was otherwise prohibited. Long regarded as a tawdry town where nothing but sin and vice flourished, Las Vegas attempted to transform itself into a family-friendly entertainment destination. And in
the process, Las Vegas was the nation's fastest-growing city in the 1990s. That transformation has meant removing the physical reminders of the seedier Las Vegas, the famous hotels of the 1950s and 1960s where mobsters hung out, and replacing them with a
collection of new hotels and casinos, extraordinary in their scale and in the variety of
their ersatz architecture. In a sense, Richard Todd finds not so much a city as a theme
park devoted to gambling, and the results are reminiscent of Disney's theme park in Paris.
Todd is more sympathetic than other writers to the "new" Las Vegas, finding that in the
midst of all the architectural fakery he could be no where else but in America.

I hadn't been there for a while. Returning to a place is one of the little pleasures of travel:
you perceive it differently over the years, and it reminds you of who you once were, and
often enough the whole experience spills over into a thoroughly pleasant melancholy. No
danger of this emotional sloppiness in Las Vegas. My last trip happened ten years ago,
and the city I visited then no longer exists. Not that a decade is the relevant interval: the
past four years have seen the arrival of those hotels, Bellagio, Paris, New York–New York,
The Venetian, without which Las Vegas would not be. . . . well, whatever it is. Here is one
virtue of Las Vegas: it changes so fast that it makes you feel more or less eternal.

I was staying at Luxor, built in 1993—the world's third largest hotel. This is not
quite the distinction it might seem, inasmuch as nine of the hotels on the world's top-ten
list can be found along the Strip. Luxor is hard to miss: it's the black-glass pyramid with
the 120-foot obelisk and the ten-story sphinx in front. At night a bright beam shines
forth from the hotel's peak, in imitation, I guess, of the eye in the pyramid on a dollar
bill. Within is the world's largest atrium, providing views from the upper stories that are
not for the vertiginous. At eight years old Luxor shows signs of wear—and why not, since
at any given moment 6,000 or 7,000 people may be staying there? The casino occupies
most of the pyramid's base. When I arrived, its middle-of-the-night cacophony was at
full tilt, and I was disheartened to learn that I had a room on the first floor.

In the morning I set out on foot to tour the Strip, though Las Vegas doesn't exactly
beckon to the pedestrian. (Later, when I had turned to taxis, one driver remarked that
thirty-seven "jaywalkers" had been killed in the city the previous year.) But the walking
tour had its rewards, letting me meet the succession of new spectacles slowly, face to face,
in all their majesty. Walking north from Luxor, I passed up Excalibur, built on a Knights
of the Round Table theme, to get directly to New York–New York, its half-scale Statue of
Liberty rising from a rendition of New York Harbor that includes a tugboat and a fire-

Originally printed in *Atlantic Monthly* 287 (February 2001): 100–102, 104.

boat and a skyline: the Chrysler Building, the Empire State Building, and CBS's Black Rock. Around the corner a bit of the Brooklyn Bridge ornaments the streetside façade.

Architectural collage has emerged as the characteristic gesture of the new wave of Las Vegas building. Bellagio has created an eight-acre lake for its entrance, meant to suggest Lake Como. Paris, across the street, features a louver-like façade merged with that of the Palais Garnier, the whole thing surmounted by an Eiffel Tower whose hind legs actually rest indoors, in the middle of the casino. An Arc de Triomphe (at two thirds the size of the original) dominates the hotel's courtyard. The Eiffel Tower stands only half as tall as the real thing, but like the half-scale Statue of Liberty, it is no small structure. The whole of the Paris casino, with bistros and kiosks, lies beneath a false sky intended to simulate a Parisian twilight. . . .

This exuberance of fakery has its detractors, who tend to take a moral stance toward it. The criticism one hears most frequently is that it substitutes a "sanitized" experience for the real thing, offering the romance of Venice without the crowds and the stench and the language barrier. I harbor suspicions about those who advance this theory—mostly because it seems to give them so much pleasure. True, there have been days in New York when my appetite for that city could have been satisfied exactly by New York–New York, but it's hard to imagine that people think they're having a New York or a Venetian or a Parisian experience in Las Vegas. We like this architecture, if we do, for its ingenuity, not its realism. We're gratified that someone has gone to such lengths to entertain us: it's performance architecture. . . .

The new wisdom in Las Vegas is that people don't come here for the gambling, they come for "entertainment." Logically this has to be true in some sense, since gambling is now so widely available elsewhere. Yet people gamble here who wouldn't gamble elsewhere. They feel free, historically licensed, to do so—that's what the place is for. And gambling still pays the bills: it accounts for about 60 percent of the revenues at an average large hotel. Purists—those who like their corruption uncorrupted—object to the new tourist-paradise Las Vegas, but it may be that the fantasy architecture, like the absence of daylight and clocks inside the casinos, only enhances that sense of suspended reality that can make a hundred-dollar bill look so insubstantial. In any case, whatever the architecture does for the gambling, there is little doubt that the gambling enhances the architecture—it provides the charge in the air, the sense of living dangerously, that keeps the place from being the Disney World it sometimes seems to want to become.

Las Vegas meets one fundamental criterion for a great city: it imposes its own reality on you. The cityscape effectively cuts you off from the outside world, but from time to time you may look down a long side street, get a glimpse of the red mountains beyond, and feel curious about the desert in which the city has grown. One day I rented a car to look around. The desert used to begin right outside the Strip's back door, but Las Vegas has sprawled. Its metropolitan area is the fastest-growing in the country, with a population now of about 1.4 million. (Forty years ago the entire state of Nevada had fewer than 300,000 residents.) To the east and the south development stretches for some twenty miles, all the way to Henderson, and so the drive down toward Hoover Dam (thirty miles from Las Vegas) has become rather dispiriting, in a landscape whose long, treeless views forgive nothing. . . .

It's easy to hate Las Vegas, and it's just about as easy to love it, with a . . . campy embrace of all that glitters. But as I settled in, I came to wonder if the city doesn't deserve the respect we pay other places, the honor of ambivalence. It was the luxury hotel Bellagio, where I started spending most of my time, that got me thinking this way. . . .

Everything is a little bit better at Bellagio. Natural light, in violation of Las Vegas tradition, finds its way into the hotel's common areas through sky-lighted arcades, a conservatory, and even restaurant windows with a view. Italian craftsmen were brought in to lay the beautiful mosaic tile in the lobby. Cut flowers abound, thanks to a garden and a greenhouse staff numbering 150. The casino's machines have been dimmed and muted, and its low ceiling hung with striped silk fabric. The women who serve drinks, instead of looking like Playboy bunnies, dress in little black suits that would be appropriate at Goldman Sachs, if only their hemlines were a foot or two closer to the ground.

Here is a problem of Bellagio: the hotel is not just amusing—it's kind of nice. . . . The rates, of course, reflect the quality: in late fall "deluxe," meaning standard, rooms were around $300 a night. . . .

Each night Bellagio puts on a water show on the lake, geysers erupting from the surface with loud reports, the water exploding into the air like liquid fire-works. The whole show is choreographed to music heard by means of speakers discreetly placed on the perimeter of the lake. The scene we were watching was accompanied by a section of *Appalachian Spring.*

The jets rose and fell in perfect consonance with the swelling music, and in a little interlude just before the Shaker theme is repeated, the sprays dissolved into a cloud of mist. Then, as the stately finale began, the water erupted again, with more force. My companion had of course seen this many times before, but he was smiling with what seemed to be unaffected pleasure, and so was I. "Simple gifts indeed," he said. *Boom!* and a new fountain arose before us. Hearing this music, I can never keep the words out of my head, and there they were again. *'Tis a gift to be simple*—the water shot up on every beat—*'Tis a gift to be free* . . . By the close a wall of water stood before us, obscuring all else. Then, as the last chord resolved itself, the water dropped back into the lake. The mist cleared, and the Eiffel Tower was visible once again, its lights glowing in the dusk. At that moment I could not recall having felt before such an emphatic sense of being where I belonged: in America.

75

MAX PAGE, "ON EDGE, AGAIN," 2001

The terrorist attack on the World Trade Center on September 11, 2001, was a horrific event, claiming nearly three thousand lives when two of the tallest buildings in the world came crashing to the ground, all 110 stories. Along with a billowing cloud of debris and death, it brought long-lasting grief and fear to New Yorkers and Americans. In the aftermath, New York's pain and its resilience earned it a broad glow of affection from around the country and the world, even as the city headed into an economic recession. More ominously, many wondered if the attacks of 9/11 would undermine the resurgence of

Originally printed in *New York Times,* October 21, 2001, sec. 14, pp. 1, 17.

New York City, which had, like other American cities, come out of physical and economic malaise of the 1970s and early 1980s to new energy in the 1990s. In the short run, 9/11 provoked an outpouring of love letters for "The City" which, as this essay argues, seemed again frighteningly mortal.

New York is still the city that never sleeps. Fear will do that.

Fear of death borne in the air: a jet, a microbe. In Lower Manhattan, the dust has been scrubbed away. Night and day trucks rumble off with more rubble. But the fear persists: there are letters to open, cross-country trips to take. The fear is a psychic anthrax, an almost invisible powder creeping under the windowsills of thought, sifting into the corners of each mind.

Fear and this city are no strangers. History reminds us that New York has burned and been occupied by soldiers. It has been besieged by epidemics and riots. Our popular culture has been in dress rehearsal for the city's destruction for decades: in books, at the movies, in computer games, although no amount of history, no number of rehearsals, could prepare New Yorkers for Sept. 11 and the days of grief and worry that followed.

It was the most perfect and horrific demolition job. Two quarter-mile-tall towers exploding, then imploding, one-acre floors falling through the next one, 200 times over.

The survivors, blanketed in the gray mist of urban disaster, headed north and east. The attacks' human spores bearing their stories, their fear, throughout the city.

That unleashed energy was finally absorbed by each resident here, metastasizing into a malaise that has lingered as the country has gone to war and the specter of bioterrorism has grown.

Virginia Woolf wrote in "A Room of One's Own" that after World War I, it was not possible to hum poetry. On the surface, lively lunches at Oxbridge proceeded as before the war. But the "humming noise, not articulate, but musical, exciting" was gone. The war had "destroyed illusion and put truth in its place."

Many suggest that such is the case with Sept. 11: our world has changed. A controlled fear—a constant hum of worry, rather than poetry—seems part of this new world, this new New York. But, after the initial silence, then the muted tones, the city is still somehow humming. Perhaps, Sept. 11 has not created a new city, but in many respects ferried us back to an older, more visceral New York, where it was understood that the city was at risk. And while today the rest of the country is on edge, New York is even more so. New Yorkers understand again that their city is a target.

To 19th-century New Yorkers, who may have been told stories of the city's burning during the seven-year British occupation in the Revolutionary War, or who lost family members to the cholera epidemics of the 1830's, who perhaps watched the burning of much of Lower Manhattan in 1835, or who later saw rioting mobs rage through the city in 1863, the notion that the city was forever was absurd.

Even the city of the 1940's and 1950's was not immune to fears of sudden catastrophe, the distinct possibility of nuclear attack. Sept. 11 bombed us back to the atomic age, when a roar in the sky could instantly evict daydreams from New Yorkers' minds and substitute apocalyptic visions.

Fear and New York are words that have often gone together. Usually, it has been the rest of the country fearing New York, rather than New Yorkers fearing their city. New York, ascending to dominance by the early 19th century, became the most feared city of all. In New York, Americans saw the poor, the immigrants, people of all races. In New

York, crowding, crime, disease and radicalism were not only found but nurtured and propagated.

American movies and television, books and newspapers have projected images of urban fear for more than a century. Urban catastrophe movies and novels, paintings and comic books—many created by New Yorkers themselves—have used New York to try to reveal the dangers of the American city.

American popular culture has returned to the theme of New York's destruction time and again, almost as a leitmotif that resonates with some of the most longstanding themes in American history: the ambivalence toward cities, the troubled reaction to immigrants and racial diversity, fear of technology's impact, and the tensions between natural and humanmade disasters.

In a nation as religious as the United States, with a strong apocalyptic strain in its popular culture, it is not surprising to find so many examples of catastrophe. But more regularly than any other, New York—not only our largest city but "the city" of platonic ideal—has repeatedly met its death by art.

In moments of social upheaval, visions of how New York would be demolished, blown up, swallowed by the sea, or toppled by monsters have proliferated in films and in science fiction novels, as well as in photography, painting and the graphic arts.

In Joaquin Miller's 1886 novel, "Destruction of Gotham," a great fire engulfs the city as lower-class mobs attack the homes and stores of the wealthy. Only when Manhattan had "burned and burned and burned to the very bed-rock" was the apocalypse complete.

Jacob Riis, the photographic chronicler of the slums of the Lower East Side, encapsulated the fears of many Americans in 1890 with his metaphors of the waves of radical immigrants flooding onto the beaches of Brooklyn in his landmark book, "How the Other Half Lives."

At the nearby immigrants' paradise, Coney Island, tenements were routinely set on fire at Dreamland, giving those same immigrants a chance to witness from afar the tenuous world they inhabited on the Lower East Side.

In paintings by the futuristic artist Chesley Bonestell from the cold war 1950's, in popular magazines like Fortune and Collier's, Manhattan is repeatedly devastated by atomic bombs.

In the SimCity software of the 1990's, users could pick what disaster would strike New York, or just watch past disasters play out before their eyes.

And in movie after movie, as has been noted in the past weeks, Hollywood has found inspiration in destroying New York: through earthquake ("Deluge"), tsunami ("Deep Impact"), asteroid ("When Worlds Collide" and "Armageddon"), and monster ("Godzilla" and "King Kong").

Just this summer, in what had become an almost annual rite, New York was destroyed repeatedly on movie screens. The Japanese animated movie "Final Fantasy" showed a devastated Lower Manhattan beneath a dome, to protect it from the assaults of viruslike aliens. In "A.I.," the child robot finds himself drawn to a forbidden zone, called "Man-Hattan," overflowing with water. The World Trade Center towers stand above the water line, one tipped, leaning against the other.

In the millions, we have read these books, watched these movies, played these games, thrilled to the skyscrapers of Manhattan toppling as if it were somehow culturally cleansing. In other words, despite the repeated statement that the events of Sept. 11 were unimaginable, our culture has been imagining, rehearsing, these events for years.

Of course, New Yorkers themselves have been less concerned with catastrophic visions of the city's end, and more preoccupied with the very real catastrophes they have had to confront. José Martí, the Cuban revolutionary who lived in New York in the late 19th century, admired the city's resilience after the crippling Blizzard of 1888.

New York, "like the victim of an outrage, goes about freeing itself of its shroud," he wrote. The democracy of snowfall, covering aristocratic Fifth Avenue as heavily as Mulberry Bend on the Lower East Side, had brought out a "sense of great humility and a sudden rush of kindness, as though the dread hand had touched the shoulders of all men."

The city's early history is studded with events in which distinctions of wealth and race were swept aside by disaster. In a city where rich and poor coexisted, with pigs and prostitutes living alongside Astors and Lenoxes, natural and human disasters were more likely to include everyone.

In the 20th century, disasters have tended not to directly affect the whole city, like the Triangle Shirtwaist Fire of 1911. Even the anthrax attacks, on the news media and at Gov. George E. Pataki's New York office, have been localized. Right now, strangely enough, it is an office problem, a disease that has been spread through the mail, in the windowless mailrooms of the new economy, and eventually landing on cubicle desks. Yes, some workplaces have been threatened, but so far the city as whole has not been at risk, though it feels as if it is.

It's important to remember that New York has always been better at celebration than fear. New York has always prided itself on humming: ticker tape parades down Broadway, the tall ships at the Bicentennial, that memorable V-J Day kiss (caught by Eisenstaedt) in Times Square: these are New York's emotional landmarks.

If the "unexpungeable odor of the long past," as E. B. White wrote in 1948 in "Here Is New York," persists in the city, in the endless sediment of New York's people and their histories, it has been overcome by the daily odors of city life. New Yorkers' notoriously short memories have, even so, kept room for celebration.

All this is why we continue to destroy New York in books, on canvas, on movie screens and on computer monitors: because it is so unimaginable for us, in reality, not to have this city. We have played out our worst fears on the screen and in our pulp fiction because, as the city's oracle, Mr. White, wrote in the shadow of the atomic bomb: "If it were to go, all would go—this city, this mischievous and marvelous monument which not to look upon would be like death."

Maybe fear is the wrong word for what New Yorkers feel now. There is anxiety, there is uncertainty. New York is no longer an invulnerable porcupine of skyscrapers that can never be attacked. Instead, the city has been rediscovered as a fragile community.

A community built on a delicate mix of people and buildings, the solace of anonymity and the thrill of cosmopolitanism, what Jane Jacobs famously called "organized complexity" in her classic study, "The Death and Life of Great American Cities." Only beyond the five boroughs, in the hinterlands, does the city appear to embody raw chaos.

This new uncertainty has brought New Yorkers together in repeated moments of empathy and concern over the recent weeks. But uncertainty could also lead to a pulling away from public life, New York's enduring justification for being, and a mimicking of the fortress mentality that has rolled across the country.

6.1. Mall of America, 1992. Like a ship from outerspace, the Mall of America—all 4.2 million square feet of it—squats on the Minnesota landscape, serving as both one of the largest settings for consumption and as an apt symbol of the dominance of the suburban way of life. The town center of the new suburban America is this: an enclosed, temperature-controlled, police-regulated environment owned by a corporation.

It might, finally, also remind New Yorkers again of the precariousness of this place, its indispensability to a personal and national identity. It might make New Yorkers want to defend the city even more, by starting an era of unprecedented creativity.

The city that never sleeps because of fear of airplanes, fear of powder, might again become a city that never sleeps because it is too busy creating and telling, building and imagining, eating and singing. Jonathan Larson's words in the musical "Rent" could only have been written in and for New York: "The opposite of war is not peace, it's creation!"

E. B. White wrote: "New York is to the nation what the white church spire is to the village—the visible symbol of aspiration and faith, the white plume saying the way is up!"

The white plume we saw on Sept. 11 was the cloudy debris of two massive towers collapsing, shrewdly demolished to turn gleaming symbols of the city into burning signs of terror. Our fantasies and nightmares made real, we now wait, almost expectantly, for the next plume, a puff of powder from a No. 10 envelope.

Still, in this time of New York's haunting, I think White was right. New York will remain the way up for us all, the home of our ideals, and the place to which the world looks, for ideas, for success, for art and for a new start.

CHAPTER 6

Taming the Crabgrass Frontier: The Triumph of the Suburbs

In 1980, the federal census announced what many Americans had suspected for some years: a majority of us now lived in areas defined as "suburbs." Whether or not this demographic finding took people by surprise, it represented an extraordinary shift in the social geography of the nation. In 1920, the very same federal census had concluded that for the first time in the nation's history, a majority of Americans were urbanites. While it had taken well over one hundred years for the United States to become an urban nation, America's urban majority lasted a scant sixty.

While many Americans at the birth of the new nation were suspicious of cities— Thomas Jefferson, most notably, feared that they were the source of corruption that would poison American virtue—in fact, during the course of the nineteenth century the country continued to urbanize. Jefferson might have envisioned a nation of independent rural farmers, but economic and cultural opportunities were increasingly to be found in cities, and Americans flocked there searching for both. This flow helped stoke one of the most significant cultural tensions in nineteenth-century America, that between the city and the country. City dwellers enjoyed countless jokes about country bumpkins and farmers' daughters, while farmers and residents of isolated small towns complained about big city bankers and other "monied interests" who seemed to exercise conspiratorial control over their simple lives. Indeed, the Populist revolt of the 1880s and 1890s—a political uprising of Southern and Midwestern farmers rooted in their economic desperation—can be seen as the most spectacular manifestation of this urban-rural tension in American political life.

By the 1920s, Jefferson's equation had been almost entirely reversed. Cities embodied a certain kind of cosmopolitan ideal, the places where philosopher Randolph Bourne's "Trans-National America" would be fully realized, while the nation's small towns were seen as the reactionary strongholds of bigots and provincials, home to the "boob-ocracy" lampooned by Baltimore newspaper editor H. L. Mencken and satirized bitterly in the novels of Sinclair Lewis.

In the midst of these cultural tensions emerged the suburb. The suburb has occupied a place, both literally and imaginatively, in between, and as such the definition of what constitutes a suburb has not been straightforward and has changed over time. Likewise, its function, its constituency, and its significance in American society have been fiercely debated. Thus, considerations of the suburbs as a phenomenon of American life are necessarily intertwined with discussions of American cities.

In the eighteenth and early nineteenth centuries, American suburbs developed like their European counterparts as loose settlements on the outskirts of larger cities, often serving as the sites for things that city residents did not want, but could not do without— poor people, industrial production, stables, brothels, and the like. Philadelphia's South-wark is typical of the eighteenth-century suburbs that grew up on the fringes of Boston,

New York, and other East Coast cities. Located just south of the city's formal boundary, it housed blue-collar workers, free blacks, slaughterhouses, leather dressers, and a few houses of ill repute. While Philadelphia's wealthy and respectable clustered in the center of town, its "suburban" edges housed the marginal and undesirable. In 1799, the newspaper *Aurora* described a visit to Philadelphia's suburbs this way: "Persons who are disposed to visit the environs of this city, and more particularly on a warm day after a rain, are saluted with a great variety of fetid and disgusting smells, which are exhaled from the dead carcasses of animals, from stagnant waters, and from every species of filth that can be collected from the city, thrown in heaps as if designedly to promote the purposes of death."

In the antebellum period, however, suburbs were reconceived as places that might be deliberately and carefully developed to capture the best of both the city and the country—close enough so that residents could still make their living in the new, booming urban economies; far enough away so that houses could be bigger, surrounded by yards, trees, and other landscaped amenities. The suburbs that grew up in the mid and late nineteenth century beyond city limits, or in undeveloped space within them, often did so along train or trolley lines, linking them umbilically to the city center. Home largely to the middle and upper middle classes, these "street car" or "railroad" suburbs represented the first attempt to create separate residential districts apart from, yet still connected to, the crowded, dense central city.

These new suburbs were theorized by several architects and landscape designers including Andrew Jackson Downing, who published *The Architecture of Country Houses* in 1850; Calvert Vaux, who published *Villas and Cottages* in 1857; and Alexander Jackson Davis, who had the chance to make real his ideas about the "romantic" suburb when he was hired to design Llewellyn Park, New Jersey, just before the Civil War.

Llewellyn Park stands as perhaps the first attempt to create a "picturesque" suburb along the lines described in books by Vaux, Downing, Davis, and others. Designed to highlight the natural features of the place, the development put a "ramble" at the center and houses along curvilinear roads. Though it was only thirteen railroad miles from Manhattan, the builders of Llewellyn Park wanted to create a romantic, rather than agricultural, pastoral ideal. To ensure their vision they stipulated in the original charter that no industrial operation could ever open in their idyll.

Llewellyn Park, and the developments it inspired, drew not only from new ideas about the relationship between the city and the country, the house and the landscape, but on a revolution in notions of domesticity. For the emerging middle class at least, the single-family home became the ideal place to raise children and to foster proper values. The middle-class ideal of the single-family home was given its most encyclopedic formulation in *The American Woman's Home* written by Catherine and Harriet Beecher and published in 1869. The sisters acknowledged that their book would be of value primarily to those "living either in the country or in suburban vicinities as give space or ground for healthful outdoor occupation in the family service." The transformation of the suburb in the nineteenth century meant both a reconception of how people shaped residential spaces and how they lived their family lives.

Of the legacies bequeathed to subsequent generations of suburbs by the landscape ideas of Davis and the domestic ideas of the Beechers, it has probably been the latter that have proved more influential. While the sensitive balance between open space, natural features, and domestic architecture attempted at Llewellyn Park was largely lost in the

suburban developments of the late nineteenth and early twentieth centuries, new building technologies made single-family homeownership more accessible to a growing middle class. By the 1920s, suburbanization largely meant creating affordable, middle-class
enclaves, and homeownership became perhaps the single most important marker of
middle-class respectability. Less important, however, was the desire to balance the best of
town and country.

The Great Depression and the Second World War brought the home construction
industry to a virtual standstill, and with it suburban development. During the worst of
the Depression upward of 80 percent of those who had been employed in the construction industry were idle. As a consequence, fifteen years of pent-up demand exploded after 1945 in an unprecedented spree of suburban building.

Levittown, outside of New York City and built by brothers William and Alfred
Levitt, opened in 1947. Eventually the site would contain 17,400 single-family houses. The
development, on an old farm field, used the techniques of mass production already perfected in the other industries to build houses quickly, inexpensively, and identically. The
Levitts broke up the job of building a house into twenty-seven distinct tasks; everything
that could be preassembled in a central warehouse was, and then was dropped off at precise sixty-foot intervals by fleets of trucks moving from concrete pad to concrete pad in
highly choreographed succession. The results were hugely popular with new families. On
one day in March 1949 alone, fourteen hundred contracts were drawn up. By the time
they retired, the Levitts had built more than 140,000 houses in three separate developments outside New York and Philadelphia, and in the process they invented modern suburbia. Levittown was ridiculed by critics for its banality, sameness, and sterility. Little
boxes, so a popular song went, all made out of ticky-tacky. Little boxes, all the same. Despite what critics like Lewis Mumford might have thought, however, Levittown became
the archetypical suburban model.

If the nineteenth-century suburbs clustered along rail and trolley lines, then the
postwar suburb was shaped almost entirely by the automobile. Americans fell in love
with their cars in the 1920s, but for increasing numbers of suburbanites by the 1950s cars
had become an absolute necessity. New suburban developments were often reachable
only by car; schools, parks, libraries, and shopping too were at such distances from
homes and from each other that one had to drive to reach any of them. Nintey percent of
the residents of new suburbs in the 1950s owned cars—20 percent of those owned more
than one.

These auto-centric suburbs reshaped the design of the American home to include
an indoor garage—often two or three cars wide—accessible directly from the street and
therefore often the most prominent feature of the house. So, too, they also were built
around and helped to drive the huge expansion of highways and other road projects. Authorized and paid for by the federal government in 1947 and again in 1956, the Interstate
Highway system made life in the new suburbs possible. Simply put, without the highway,
the postwar suburb would never have come into being.

Just as the notion of the single-family home in the nineteenth century was predicated on changes in ideas about domesticity and family life, so, too, the postwar suburb
was a highly gendered space constructed on the assumption that families would have one
income earner (dad) and one person to stay home, raise children, and tend to matters of
the home (mom). Less than ten years after Levittown opened for business, sociologists,
critics, and others were noticing the isolating and repressive effects of the new suburbs

on a generation of women. Many feminists of the 1960s and 1970s, like Betty Friedan, had lived in new suburbs in the 1950s, and found the life of the lonely housewife suffocating.

In the same way, the new suburbs were racially exclusive spaces by design. Because of migrations of black Americans from the South to the North, Northern cities found themselves with significant black populations by the end of the Second World War. The new suburbs became the places where white urbanites fled to escape their new black neighbors. In the decade of the 1960s alone, 2 million white residents moved out of America's ten largest cities in the exodus known as "white flight." The racial exclusivity of the new suburbs were ensured by so-called "restrictive covenants," written into the sales contracts of new houses, in which the buyer promised never to sell to a nonwhite person. The racist nature of the new suburbs was exacerbated further by discriminatory lending policies practiced both by private banks and agencies like the Federal Housing Authority. The FHA's "red-lining" rules denied black Americans access to mortgage lending within cities, even as it encouraged "white flight" to the suburbs. While the courts ruled many of these practices to be unconstitutional, they were remarkably effective, even long after court rulings. Even in 1960 not a single one of the 82,000 residents of Levittown, New York, was black.

By the end of the century, some suburban areas, notably around Washington, D.C., and Atlanta, Georgia, had grown somewhat more heterogeneous. Yet while the cultural vitality of urban areas generates, in part, from the mixing and negotiating of different cultures in the public spaces of the city, it remains to be seen whether this new racial diversity in some suburbs makes any real social, cultural, or political difference, since, by their very nature, there are few public spaces in which these different groups can come together.

The racial dimension of American suburbia also had profound political and economic impacts. By their very nature, suburbs have some close relationship to an urban center, but in the postwar period that relationship became increasingly antagonistic and parasitic. White suburbanites took their tax and consumer dollars out of cities, affecting everything from downtown department stores to urban school districts; yet they continued to enjoy the cultural and economic advantages of the metropolis. The political tensions between cities, now increasingly seen as poor and black, and their neighboring suburbs, white and affluent, play out from Boston to San Diego.

By the time the census announced the United States as a suburban nation in 1980, trends in suburban building had begun to shift again. The first generation of postwar suburban houses had been quite modest, designed to appeal to a working and middle class. In the last quarter of the twentieth century, however, real estate developers applied the same tract building techniques to "luxury homes," well beyond the reach of the middle class. While the average size of the American family dropped slightly between 1970 and 2000, the size of the American house doubled as "McMansions" sprung up across the frontier of suburban America, prefabricated markers of status and prosperity, often sitting on multiacre lots.

As the nation's population moved to the suburbs, taking with it its money and political clout by the 1980s and 1990s, so too the suburb became a political topic in the debates over "sprawl." An ugly word to describe an ugly phenomenon, sprawl came to stand both as the description of the unregulated, unplanned proliferation of suburban development, and as a code word for all the social and environmental ill-effects of that development. States, counties, and local municipalities across the country recognized that farmland and open space were disappearing at an astonishing rate, and that over-development threatened the suburban way of life. Some initiated programs to preserve open space, granted development easements to farms, and experimented with new zoning to slow the sprawl. Whatever success these efforts produced, they swam largely against the tide of the much more powerful forces pushing for more development.

In the face of all this, one question looms: why has suburbia triumphed? Simply to make the observation that more and more Americans choose to live suburban lives is, for some, the most eloquent defense of them. And for many, the suburbs provide the convenience, space, and sense of safety they desire. This "triumph of the marketplace" explanation for the huge popularity of the suburbs obscures as much as it reveals, however. Suburban homeownership makes economic sense for many families only because of the hidden ways in which suburban living is subsidized by government at all levels—from school funding formulas, which favor suburban districts, to mortgage deductions on federal income taxes.

In the course of two hundred years, the American suburb has almost completely reversed its social function. Once a home to the proverbial hoi polloi, they have evolved to become segregated by both race and class. They have become increasingly restrictive as well. So-called "gated communities," often fenced off entirely from public access and patrolled by armed security, grew in popularity at the end of the twentieth century and by 2000 housed an estimated 10 million Americans. Gone, however, is the sense of wedding the city and the country that inspired nineteenth-century suburban designers. Indeed, perhaps the final irony of American suburbia at the end of the twentieth century was that, as more and more Americans lived there, the suburbs simply recapitulated all the problems of urban living—traffic jams, overcrowded schools, and the like—while virtually erasing anything natural from the landscape altogether, and without offering the cultural life of real cities as a substitute.

DESIGN XX

VILLA FARM HOUSE

Fig. 76

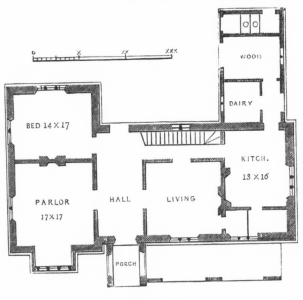

PRINCIPAL FLOOR
Fig. 77

6.2. "Design XX, Villa Farm House," from Andrew Jackson Downing, *The Architecture of Country Houses.* The suburban ideal, as theorized by Andrew Jackson Downing and his colleague Alexander Jackson Davis in the antebellum period, attempted to create a perfect balance between town and country. A product of American romanticism, this ideal included careful design of the landscape and a "picturesque" country house.

76

ANONYMOUS, "LANDSCAPE-GARDENING: LLEWELLEN PARK,"
1857; AND ANONYMOUS, "LLEWELLYN PARK," 1871

The *Crayon* was perhaps the most important magazine devoted to the arts in the United States during the middle years of the nineteenth century. That the journal highlighted Llewellyn Park, New Jersey, underscores that this town was viewed as more than simply a real estate development. Indeed, the writer here believes it "may mark a new era" in suburban development. While areas of settlement just beyond city borders had already existed, developing accidentally, haphazardly, and almost inevitably, Llewellyn Park marks the first attempt to plan a suburban development with any kind of deliberation around what might be called a philosophy. The second essay, written nearly fifteen years later, captures the same sense of enthusiasm for the picturesque, romantic suburb that Llewellyn Park represented. The author describes the same set of design elements, but ends the essay on an unintentionally sinister note by telling readers that, unlike Central Park in New York City, this suburban idyll is strictly private. In so doing, this author has identified a major appeal of suburban living: the retreat away from unruly public spaces into tightly controlled private ones.

ANONYMOUS, "LANDSCAPE-GARDENING: LLEWELLYN PARK"

LLEWELLYN PARK.—This name is given to a recently laid out estate, situated upon the eastern slope of Orange Mountain, N. J., which is the first development, so far as we know, of an idea which may mark a new era in Country Life and Landscape Gardening in this country. So important an enterprise deserves more than a passing notice. The whole estate, of which the Park is a portion, contains about three hundred acres. The situation is elevated, commanding fine views of a wide extent of country, including the city and harbor of New York and its surroundings, and the coast from the Highlands to the south of Sandy Hook. The tract is well wooded, and beautifully broken and diversified. A rocky ravine, through which flows a never-failing brook, divides the estate, and makes one of its finest features. Altogether the location is a happy one.

Mr. L. S. Haskell, the owner of this property, conceived the project, which is now being successfully carried out, of making a beautiful home of this estate not for himself alone, but for many families. Over fifty acres are appropriated to the Park, which is laid out irregularly, including the most beautiful and picturesque portions of the land, surrounded by a delightful drive of nearly three miles. This irregularity of form gives great variety of surface and feeling of size, and it furnishes secluded and quiet nooks and most pleasant surprises. Carefully preserving its natural attractions, the Landscape Gardener's Art develops others: what is artificial is made not only to harmonize with the rustic character of the design, but made with regard to permanence, impressing us as if here, at least, was one work to remain for our children. There are no shams to gratify mistaken economy and offend good taste; but, on the contrary, though simple and rustic, all is honest and pure.

The remainder of the estate is divided into sites of from one to ten acres each. And the same good taste and regard to unity and harmony have directed this division. The

Originally printed in *Crayon*, vol. 4, August, 1857.

lines are run with reference to the nature of the ground, and each lot being complete in itself, contains some special attraction. We are glad to learn that a number of the holders of lots, entering into the spirit of the place and design, intend to improve their lots with reference to each other and the whole enclosure, so that the appearance of one large estate may be suggested.

The whole plot is to be inclosed, and a characteristic gateway and lodge erected. The owners of lots are entitled to all the privileges of the Park, and they are joint proprietors. A person who owns a lot upon this estate has for his use and that of his family over fifty acres of pleasure ground, laid out and ornamented in the highest style of Landscape Gardening, the cost of which only a man of great wealth could afford, but which, divided among so many, becomes a mere trifle, compared to the great advantages obtained. This Park will become not only a source of health and recreation, but of culture and refinement. We trust and believe that this is but the beginning of many such undertakings. There are in the vicinity of our cities many locations now comparatively valueless, which could thus be turned to noblest use, and we know of no way in which combined capital and associated effort could be more worthily employed.

For the benefit of those who may be inspired by this example, we will state the manner in which the money for this Park has been and is to be realized. In addition to the sum paid for his ground, one hundred dollars per acre is required of each purchaser, as a contribution to a fund devoted to improving the Park, which fund will amount to over twenty thousand dollars. We understand the holder of sites have consented to a slight annual assessment for keeping the park in repair. This, it seems to us, is a simple and equitable arrangement, and one that might be readily adopted in similar projects.

The community owe much to Mr. Haskell for the public spirit which suggested the idea, and the enthusiasm and good taste with which (assisted by Mr. Bowman and Mr. Daniels as landscape gardeners,) he has so far executed it.

Anonymous, "Llewellyn Park"

Everybody who visits New York goes to Central Park as a matter of course; but very few people think of going to Llewellyn Park, a place of quite unique loveliness, about an hour's ride from the city. Several years ago Mr. L. S. Haskell purchased a tract of land on nearly 800 acres at Orange, New Jersey, which he laid out in the natural style of landscape-gardening, with picturesque walks and drives, reserving in the centre of the tract about 50 acres as a pleasure ground. The remainder he divided into villa sites of from one to twenty acres, designed for family residence. With its pretty cottages and villas, its shady roads, rustic bridges, and serpentine brooks, Llewellyn Park presents every charm of country life with all the advantages of being within sixty minutes of New York, a special charm for merchants doing business in the city. Llewellyn Park is a private park, and this is perhaps its most important feature. While in extent it nearly equals Central Park, unlike that, it is strictly private, to be used only by the owners and their friends. It is under the control of a board of managers elected annually by the proprietors, and its privacy is secured by lodges and gatekeepers at the entrances. Strangers who wish to visit it, can gain admittance by simply entering their names in a book kept at the main entrance for that purpose.

Originally printed in *Every Saturday* 11 (September 2, 1871): 227.

77

OLMSTED, VAUX AND CO., EXCERPT FROM "LETTER TO THE RIVERSIDE IMPROVEMENT COMPANY," 1868

In this letter to a group of Chicago real estate investors, the firm of Olmsted & Vaux, the preeminent landscape designers in the country, give advice on how to best build a suburb. Frederick Law Olmsted and Calvert Vaux had each established reputations as park planners and writers about matters of architecture and landscape. Here, the Riverside Improvement Company has turned to them for help in planning a new suburban development outside Chicago. Olmsted and Vaux's response demonstrates how theories of beauty, the picturesque, and harmony between town and country shaped ideas about suburban development in the mid-nineteenth century. At the same time, the letter also foreshadows the umbilical dependence of new suburbs on new, bigger, and better roads, which reached its apotheosis with the construction of the interstate highway system one hundred years later. And the letter's addressee reminds us that, whatever the theories behind their appearance, suburbs all originate as speculative real estate developments.

To the Riverside Improvement Company

Gentlemen:

You have requested a report from us, upon an enterprise which you desire to bring before the public, and which appears to rest on the following grounds:

First—Owing partly to the low, flat, miry, and forlorn character of the greater part of the country immediately about Chicago, and the bleak surface, arid soil, and exposure of the remainder to occasional harsh and frigid gusts of wind off the lake, and partly to the fact that the rapidity with which the town is being enlarged, causes all the available environs to be laid out with a view to a future demand solely for town purposes, and with no regard to the satisfaction of rural tastes, the city, as yet, has no true suburbs or quarters in which urban and rural advantages are agreeably combined with any prospect of long continuance.

Second—If, under these circumstances, sites offering any very decided and permanent advantages for suburban residences could be put in the market, there would be at once a demand for them, which would continue and increase with the enlargement and progress in wealth and taste of the population of the city.

Third—You have secured a large body of land, which, must beyond any other, has natural advantages for this purpose.

Fourth—If, by a large outlay, these advantages could be developed to the utmost, and could be supplemented by abundant artificial conveniences of a high order, and the locality could thus be rendered not only very greatly superior to any other near Chicago, but could be made to compare satisfactorily, on the whole, with the most favored suburbs to be found anywhere else, a good return for such outlay might reasonably be expected.

We propose to review these grounds so far as they are not matters of fact easily put to the test of observation by those interested.

To understand the character of the probable demand for semi-rural residences near

Dated September 1, 1868, this letter was originally printed in S. B. Sutton, ed., *Civilizing American Cities* (Cambridge, Mass.: MIT Press, 1971).

Chicago, it must be considered that the most prominent characteristic of the present period of civilization has been the strong tendency of people to flock together in great towns. This tendency unquestionably is concurrent, and probably identical, with an equally unprecedented movement of invention, energy, and skill, toward the production of certain classes of conveniences and luxuries, which, even yet, can generally be fully enjoyed by great numbers of people only in large towns. Arrangements for the easy gratification of certain tastes, which, until recently, were possessed by but a very few, even of the most wealthy class of any country, have consequently, of late, become common to thousands in every civilized land, while numerous luxuries, that the largest fortunes in the old world could not have commanded even half a century since, are enjoyed by families of comparatively moderate means, in towns which have sprung up from the wilderness, within the memory of some still living in them.

Progress in this way was never more rapid than at the present moment, yet in respect to the corresponding movement of populations there are symptoms of a change; a counter-tide of migration, especially affecting the more intelligent and more fortunate classes, although as yet of but moderate strength, is clearly perceptible, and almost equally so, in Paris, London, Vienna, Berlin, New York, Boston and Philadelphia. The most substantial manifestation of it perhaps, is to be found in the vast increase in value of eligible sites for dwellings near public parks, and in all localities of much natural beauty within several hours' journey of every great town. Another evidence of the same tendency, not less conclusive because it indicates an impulse as yet undecided and incomplete, in found in the constant modification which has occurred in the manner of laying out all growing towns, and which is invariably in the direction of a separation of business and dwelling streets, and toward rural spaciousness in the latter. The broader the streets are made, provided they are well prepared in respect to what are significantly designated "the modern conveniences," and especially if some slight rural element is connected with them, as by rows of trees or little enclosures of turf and foliage, the greater is the demand for dwelling-places upon them. . . .

It thus becomes evident that the present outward tendency of town populations is not so much an ebb as a higher rise of the same flood, the end of which must be, not a sacrifice of urban conveniences, but their combination with the special charms and substantial advantages of rural conditions of life. Hence a series of neighborhoods of a peculiar character is already growing up in close relation with all large towns, and though many of these are as yet little better than rude over-dressed villages, or fragmentary half-made towns, it can hardly be questioned that, already, there are to be found among them the most attractive, the most refined and the most soundly wholesome forms of domestic life, and the best application of the arts of civilization to which mankind has yet attained.

It would appear then, that the demands of suburban life, with reference to civilized refinement, are not to be a retrogression from, but an advance upon, those which are characteristic of town life, and that no great town can long exist without great suburbs. It would also appear that whatever element of convenient residence is demanded in a town will soon be demanded in a suburb, so far as is possible for it to be associated with the conditions which are the peculiar advantage of the country, such as purity of air, umbrageousness, facilities for quiet out-of-door recreation and distance from the jar, noise, confusion, and bustle of commercial thoroughfares.

There need then be no fear that a happy combination of these conditions would ever fail to be exceedingly attractive to the people of Chicago, or that a demand for residences where it is found, would be liable to decline; on the contrary, it would be as sure to increase, as the city is sure to increase in population and in wealth, and for the same reason.

We proceed to consider the intrinsic value of your property for the purpose in view.. . .

The chief advantages which a suburb can possess over a town on the one hand, and over a wilderness on the other, will consist in those which favor open-air recreation beyond the limits which economy and convenience prescribe for private grounds and gardens. The main artificial requirements of a suburb then, are good roads and walks, pleasant to the eye within themselves, and having at intervals pleasant openings and outlooks, with suggestions of refined domestic life, secluded, but not far removed from the life of the community.

The misfortune of most existing suburbs is, that in such parts of them as have been built up little by little, without any general plan, the highways are usually adapted only to serve the bare irresistible requirements of agriculture, and that in such other parts as have been laid out more methodically, no intelligent design has been pursued to secure any distinctly rural attractiveness, the only aim apparently being to have a plan, which, seen on paper, shall suggest the possibility of an extension of the town-streets over the suburb, and of thus giving a town value to the lots upon them.

Exactly the opposite of this should be aimed at in your case, and, in regard to those special features whereby the town is distinguished from the country, there should be the greatest possible contrast which is compatible with the convenient communication and pleasant abode of a community; economy of room, and facilities for business, being minor considerations.. . .

We cannot judiciously attempt to control the form of the houses which men shall build, we can only, at most, take care that if they build very ugly and inappropriate houses, they shall not be allowed to force them disagreeably upon our attention when we desire to pass along the road upon which they stand. We can require that no house shall be built within a certain number of feet of the highway, and we can insist that each house-holder shall maintain one or two living trees between his house and his highway-line.

A few simple precautions of this kind, added to a tasteful and convenient disposition of shade trees, and other planting along the roadsides and public places, will, in a few years, cause the whole locality, no matter how far the plan may be extended, to possess, not only the attraction of neatness and convenience, and the charm of refined sylvan beauty and grateful umbrageousness, but an aspect of secluded peacefulness and tranquility more general and pervading than can possibly be found in suburbs which have grown up in a desultory, haphazard way. If the general plan of such a suburb is properly designed on the principles which have been suggested, its character will inevitably also, notwithstanding its tidiness, be not only informal, but, in a moderate way, positively picturesque, and when contrasted with the constantly repeated right angles, straight lines, and flat surfaces which characterize our large modern towns, thoroughly refreshing.. . .

The suggestion that your property might be formed into a "park," most of the land within which might be divided by lines, mainly imaginary, into building lots, and sold as demand should require, has been publicly made with apparent confidence in its feasibility and advantage, and as it seems to have attractions, we shall endeavor to show why we cannot advise you to adopt it.. . .

The essential qualification of a suburb is domesticity, and to the emphasizing of the idea of habitation, all that favors movement should be subordinated. Thus the two ideals are not likely to be successfully followed on the same ground. One or the other should be abandoned wholly. The greater part of your Riverside property has hardly any specially good conditions for a park, while it has many for a suburb.

There are two aspects of suburban habitation that need to be considered to ensure success; first, that of the domiciliation of men by families, each family being well provided for in regard to its domestic indoor and outdoor private life; second, that of the harmonious association and co-operation of men in a community, and the intimate relationship and constant intercourse, and inter-dependence between families. Each has its charm, and the charm of both should be aided and acknowledged by all means in the general plan of every suburb. . . .

We should recommend the appropriation of some of the best of your property for public grounds, and that most of these should have the character of informal village-greens, commons and play-grounds, rather than of enclosed and defended parks or gardens. We would have, indeed, at frequent intervals in every road, an opening large enough for a natural group of trees, and often provide at such points croquet or ball grounds, sheltered seats and drinking fountains or some other objects which would be of general interest or convenience to passers-by. . . .

All desirable improvements of this character, more and better than can be found in any existing suburb in the United States, can be easily supplied at comparatively small cost. That which it is of far more consequence to secure at the outset, and which cannot be obtained at small cost, unfortunately, is a system of public ways of thoroughly good construction.

As we have already shown, in speaking upon the question of approach, your property is not without special advantages for this purpose, and, on the whole, we feel warranted in expressing the opinion that your scheme, though it will necessarily require a large outlay of capital, is a perfectly practicable one, and if carried out would give Chicago a suburb of highly attractive and substantially excellent character. . . .

Respectfully,
Olmsted, Vaux & Co.,
Landscape Architects.
110 Broadway, New York, Sept. 1, 1868.

78

ANONYMOUS, EXCERPT FROM
SUBURBAN HOMES ON THE WEST JERSEY RAILROAD, 1881

All suburban development has depended on reliable transportation connections to the central city. In the post–Civil War period, the growing network of railroads radiating out from central cities provided the fastest and most attractive transportation for suburban-

Originally printed in *Suburban Homes on the West Jersey Railroad* (Philadelphia: Allen, Lane & Scott Printers, 1881).

ites. Railroads did not merely serve as the conveyance of choice for suburban residents, but actively fostered development through publications like the one excerpted here. Presented as a catalogue of stops along the various branches of the West Jersey Railroad, the pamphlet promoted the virtues of the each location, listed the amenities to be found and provided information on the distance from Philadelphia and prices for lots and houses. These descriptions stressed both pastoral nature and urban proximity and highlighted some of the middle-class values that would have appealed to prospective buyers. The boosterism of this 1881 publication worked all too well, as this area of New Jersey has indeed become heavily suburbanized, though largely in a later era, facilitated by big roads rather than trains. And with the railroads, so too has disappeared most of the quaint charm of the area described here.

"To meet the constant and increasing demand for a comprehensive and reliable medium of information, as to the whereabouts of desirable places for out-of-town residence, this pamphlet is presented to the public. Herein will be found a carefully prepared register of the Hotels and Boarding-Houses along the Main Line and the several Branches, with the location and rates of board; and a directory of dwelling-houses for sale and to let, together with notes descriptive of the stations. . . .

To those who desire to dwell amid the beauties of nature and yet be within convenient distance of the city, the locations on the West Jersey Railroad present special attractions, as the line traverses the most delightful portions of New Jersey, and its trains arrive at and depart from the station at the foot of Market Street, within a short walk of the business centre of the city.

WESTVILLE

Distance, 6.4 miles. Single Trip, 18 cents; Two-days' Excursion, 30 cents; 50-trip, $6.40; 54-Trip, $4.50; 46-Trip, $3.60

Westville is situated on Great Timber creek, a stream of considerable size, with a sufficient depth of water to float large boats. Summer visitors are attracted to the place by its excellent facilities for boating and fishing, the latter being good most of the year. The locality is considered healthful, and good water is found at a depth of fifteen feet. There is one church and one school-house in the village, and three stores, where goods can be purchased at Philadelphia prices. . . .

For Sale.—By Samuel S. Kendrick, two houses of four rooms each, one and a half squares from the station, lot 40 x 150, and two houses of six rooms each, lots forty feet front, one square from the station.

S.W. Brooks has the following:-

Cottage of five rooms, with a garden, fruit and shade trees, three squares from station. Price, $300, or will rent for $7 per month.

Fifty building lots, different prices and size, five minutes' walk from station. . . .

In addition to the above, building lots, near station, are on sale, sizes 35 to 40 by 100 to 150. Price, about one hundred dollars each. Apply to station agent, Joseph T. Batten. . . .

WOODBURY

Distance, 9.3 miles. Single Trip, 28 cents; Two Days' Excursion, 45 cents; 50-trip, $9.30; 54-trip, $6.00; 46-Trip, $4.80; Annual Rate, $50

Woodbury is a flourishing and enterprising town of twenty-five hundred inhabitants, situated at the junction of the main line with the Swedesboro Branch and the Delaware River Railroad. . . .

Woodbury also possesses excellent religious, education, and social advantages. Among its public buildings and institutions are nine churches, in which regular services are held; a graded public school and two private schools, which compare favorably with the best in the State; a public circulating library and reading-room, accessible to all; a large public hall for entertainments of various kinds, and an elegant new opera house.

There are also numerous shops, stores, mills, lumber and coal yards. The markets are supplied with the fresh products of the adjacent country, which is one of the finest farming and fruit districts in the State.

There are many inducements offered to those wishing to secure country homes. About a hundred acres of high and beautiful building sites adjacent to the railroad station have been opened and put into market on very advantageous terms. A beautiful public Park, with a miniature lake, is in process of construction. Wide, attractive avenues are being graded on either side of the railroad through the town, and a handsome stone station is to be erected by the Company.

As the tax rate is only one dollar per hundred, the climate salubrious, and the population rapidly increasing, the purchase of real estate is almost certain to be a profitable investment. . . .

For Rent and Sale—Information regarding building lots and a large number of houses for rent and sale, at prices ranging for rent, from $7 to $50 per month, and for sale, from $1000 to $10,000 may be obtained upon application to Geo. H. Barker, real estate agent, Woodbury. . . .

CLAYTON

Distance, 22.5 miles. Single Trip, 63 cents; Two days' Excursion, $1.00; 50-Trip, $22.50; 54-Trip, $9.50; 46-Trip, $7.60

This is a small village in a healthful location, and is conspicuous for its neatness and cleanliness, and the sobriety and industry of its people. It has a town hall, two churches—Presbyterian and Methodist, good schools, a weekly newspaper, four general merchandise stores, drug store, glass and marble works, cast-iron foundry, &c., and is an exceedingly desirable place of residence. . . .

For Sale.—A large number of desirable lots have just been placed in the market, at prices ranging from $75 up. . . .

79

R. CLIPSTON STURGIS, EXCERPT FROM "SUBURBAN HOMES: A PLEA FOR PRIVACY IN HOME LIFE," 1896

The growth of the railroad suburb in the latter part of the nineteenth century generated new writings about how best to design suburban homes. R. Clipston Sturgis begins this essay with a familiar refrain in American architectural writing. Comparing the English country house with the American suburban one, he finds the latter lacking and disappointing. He also echoes the domestic themes that become current in the mid-nineteenth century—the home as refuge from life's stresses and as incubator of better children—that Catherine Ward Beecher among others made popular. Sturgis devotes much of this essay to offering specific design suggestions for making the suburban house into a place more geniunely a home. Yet while he insists that his ideas really are within the reach of everyone, the essay, especially with its focus on the importance of privacy, betrays the exclusivity underneath much suburban development of the era.

In the course of many years spent in England, I was constantly struck with the restful beauty, not only of the more noted country seats for which England is so justly preëminent, but also of the humbler houses which cling to the outskirts of the great cities, or form part of the smaller towns and villages. They have an air of comfort and quiet dignity; they look substantial, respectable, self-contained, inviting. In a word, they are homelike. . . .

I think I am not overstating in saying that with very rare exceptions one sees no such thing here. Our suburbs for the most part are composed of frame houses, looking unsubstantial and temporary. They convey no suggestion of dignity and retirement. They do indeed look hospitable and open, and have an air of saying "All mine is yours; pray, enjoy it." They even invite you to look in on their grounds and through their open windows, where the English house says, "Don't come in unless you know us;" but notwithstanding all this, I think on account of this, they are not so pleasant to look upon nor so sweet to live in. . . .

But there are some homes where love and truth are found, homes which mean to the father a real haven, looked forward to through the day's hard work with eagerness,— to the mother the home of her husband and children where all she loves best are about her, and to the children that safe shelter where loving arms are ever about them. These are indeed places of rest for those who live in them.

To make these homes all that they might and should be there ought to be some real privacy. A flat is better than hotel life, one's own home is better than a flat, and a house with a bit of land, and that land quiet and private, is best of all. Privacy is an essential in the growth of home life,—privacy for the in-door family life and privacy, if possible, for some sort of out-of-door life. Without privacy the tender home affections and associations cannot grow. It is as necessary for the family as a whole to have some time when they are alone, as it is for each individual to have some time to commune with his own soul and be still. We all need breathing places where we can stop and consider our way, and for a family there is the same need to see each other occasionally with no outside

Originally printed in *Cosmopolitan* 21 (June 1896): 180–90.

interests to distract and divert. So only can the mother know her children as they gather at her knee, so only can the father come into true companionship and comradeship with them as they come around him in that "children's hour" for stories or pictures or games.

Many of our city-living people have their houses on the outskirts, where land is cheaper and where one may have a little more air to breathe than can be had in a flat, or even a town house. It is to the dwellers of these suburban houses that I wish especially to appeal. In the title, I use the word homes rather than houses, as it is of homes in the real old English sense that I want to write, not of the houses in which we merely eat and sleep, but of the place that is filled, either with associations, the charm of the past, or with delightful possibilities,—the charm of the future. . . .

The first great essential then of a home is privacy,—the opportunity to consider and treat the family life as something sacred and apart from the outside world with its cares and troubles. A circle to which you will not admit any one lightly and without consideration.

The second important consideration is that it should be beautiful. Whether it be a simple cottage or a great mansion, it may still be beautiful, and fit for its purpose, either, on the one hand, simple, unpretentious, and quiet, in good proportions and of good color; or, on the other, adorned with more stately and magnificent qualities. Each type may have the beauty belonging to it and also be a true home.

The influence and importance of privacy I have already pointed out, and this element of beauty I consider as essential on account of the daily influence (imperceptible perhaps, yet certain) which it exerts on ourselves and those yet more impressionable ones, the little children whom we have received as a precious gift, and on whom the daily associations of childhood will make lasting impression. We appreciate (not perhaps as much as we should) the influence of our own lives past and present on our children. We see reflected in them our childhood's faults, now happily outgrown and perhaps half forgotten, and we note their readiness to pick up from us our bad habits, our hasty speech, our lack of gentleness and forbearance; but we do not so generally appreciate the influence which the material surroundings must exert both on us and on them. It cannot be other than harmful to grow up in daily association with what is ugly, coarse, vulgar, and gross. It cannot but help us to be constantly in surroundings that are refined, quiet, and in good taste. . . .

In these notes I propose to deal only with suburban homes, as being the class of houses most generally built in defiance of the above considerations, and yet most adaptable to the requirements of home life. I will take as examples two classes of houses, first those which are on a small lot sufficient only for the house and a yard or garden, second, places of sufficient size to admit driveways and stables.

First then, for the small lots. . . . The lot is one hundred feet by two hundred feet. If we run the length of the house across the lot, it will cut off from the street the space behind the house. This space, if we allow forty feet for our house and set it back twenty feet from the street, will be one hundred and forty feet by one hundred feet, just the place for a garden. Let us keep this free from intrusion and make it a place where in pleasant weather we can sit and read, while the mother can bring her work and the children their toys, or where, if we are energetic and like exercise after our business hours, we can play a game of tennis. In long summer evenings we may perhaps have our tea on the lawn, with all the privacy of the inside of the house, or we may have a little garden party without feeling that we are entertaining our friends in the street. Surely these are things which are worth some little thought to obtain. There are, however, other necessaries besides gardens which require room outside the house. We do not want the drying of clothes, or the carts of the butcher to mar our bit of garden, so we make on the street or close to it a kitchen-yard, and to avoid having our linen dried in public we can screen it with shrubs and small trees, and these with a few neatly cared for flower beds will make our house and its surroundings sufficiently attractive to the passer-by without giving him any glimpse of our real sanctum beyond. . . .

Contrast such houses and such gardens with the average suburban affair of stained shingle and many hipped roof, planted in the middle of its plot of ground and perhaps approached by an asphalt walk, or guarded by a pair of cast-iron lions. Before it, all is open to the street and its neighbors, and to sit on its apology for a lawn is equivalent to sitting in the street. You cannot even play tennis without having a curious crowd stare at you, and as a matter of fact you generally see none of these things done because most of us happily shrink from such publicity. . . .

If your neighbors follow the same plan, you may consider that you have your money's worth in a pleasanter journey on foot or in the car as you go to and from your home. Your living rooms removed from the noisy street are quiet and free from dust. As you look out on your little garden plot hedged in by trees and shrubs, you can perhaps forget the cares of the office and feel that you have left the city far behind. An hour's play at tennis or at work in your garden will give new strength for the coming day's work, and is a good deal better than sitting on a piazza with a cigar and novel and occasionally noticing a familiar face among the passers-by. All this you have obtained, because by a right arrangement of the house and grounds you have made privacy possible.

And if this is a pleasure and benefit to the head of the house, who sees it but morning and evening, how much more will it mean to his wife and children who live all day in it? Even while the children are quite little they will be safe in the garden without a nurse. A glance from the window keeps them in view, and a good sand-pile will give them endless amusement, and as they grow older, even if the boys generally prefer to play ball outside, the girls will like to sit there and sew, and will welcome the boys to a game of tennis when they come back. The pleasures of such a life will make your house a home, you will love it, and the children though separated from it will never forget it or outgrow its homely influences.

80

CHRISTINE FREDERICK, EXCERPT FROM "IS SUBURBAN LIVING A DELUSION?" 1928; AND ETHEL LONGWORTH SWIFT, EXCERPT FROM "IN DEFENSE OF SUBURBIA," 1928

The 1920s saw the rise and expansion of automobile suburbs. Widespread car ownership permitted real estate development on a much grander scale and across a broader land-

Originally printed in *Outlook* 148 (February 22, 1928): 290–91.

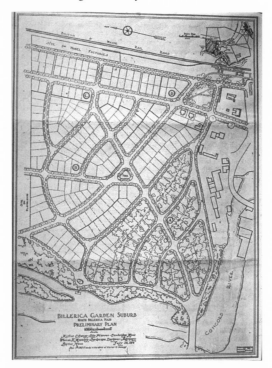

6.3. Plan of a garden suburb, North Billerica, Massachusetts, 1914. The ideal of the garden suburb pioneered by Olmsted survived into the twentieth century, though it was already changing to be more affordable and thus more accessible than its antebellum predecessors. This plan was drawn just before the advent of widespread automobile use. After the 1920s, the automobile would prove to be the single most important factor shaping suburban spaces.

scape because people looking for suburban homes were no longer tied to railroad or trolley lines. The relationship between automobility and suburban development in the 1920s foreshadowed what would happen on a massive scale in the post–Second World War period. These two essays also hint at what would be the major terms of debate between those who reviled the suburbs and those who defended them just as passionately. Christine Frederick, a self-described "sophisticate," finds in the twentieth-century suburbs none of their nineteenth-century promise. It is a place in-between—neither urban nor rural. That in-between space breeds a kind of bourgeois banality, and worse, all the small-minded, conforming pressure of the American small town, which in the 1920s was a target of particular abuse. Not so, replies Ethel Swift several weeks later. In her suburb, north of New York City, she has indeed interacted more regularly with nature and it has given her children a space to play and explore to an extent impossible in the city. Besides, as Swift points out, the "ideal" of having both a genuine country house and an apartment in town is not economically feasible for most people, and thus the suburbs represent the best compromise.

CHRISTINE FREDERICK, EXCERPT FROM "IS SUBURBAN LIVING A DELUSION?"

I have definitely come to the conclusion that suburban living—meaning the neat little colonies of houses in suburban villages—is a snare and a delusion from almost any angle you wish to approach it. Doubtless this will be to many a somewhat startling and sweeping assertion, but I assure you that it is no mere ill-considered whim. My opinion rests upon more than personal preference; I believe that large numbers of people are making this decision on the basis of valuation of the facts—chief of which are the great advance in apartment convenience, on the one hand; and, on the other, the automobile, the bus, and other improved transportation, better roads, the growth of the outdoor idea, and general increase of wealth.

Of course, the suburb has been, and is, an interesting half-way house; in fact, for large numbers of our population it is the best thing available. For many others it is a good temperamental fit. But I am speaking now, not of the general run of people, but of the more sophisticated and individual types. For these the suburb is sometimes utterly intolerable, and nearly always a disappointment. It is the very apotheosis of standardization at its bitter worst.

Now, I believe in standardization *of the mechanism of life.* That is why an up-to-date city apartment is the last word in comfort and preferable to the suburb. The sad truth is that the suburb standardizes those things which a true individual doesn't want standardized, and leaves unstandardized those things he most desires standardized.

The suburban house, for instance. I suppose architects get pleasure out of the neat little toy houses on their neat little patches of lawn and their neat colonial lives, to say nothing of the neat little housewives and their neat little children—all set in neat rows for all the world like children's blocks. . . . The very aspect of it offends me deeply. It is so sugary and commonplace; so pathetic in its pretense of an individualism which doesn't exist. The little gingerbread attempts to achieve difference are so palpably hollow and unsuccessful. The apartment-house is a much more frank standardization of life, and a far more efficient one. It doesn't pretend that it is a country villa when it isn't. It doesn't boast a garden when there is only a patch of grass. It doesn't pretend that it is a Home (with a capital H) when it is only a flat. It doesn't make believe that it gives me elbow room when the breakfast quarrel or the cries of the new baby of the newly-weds in the next suburban home are perfectly audible to two or three neighboring "private homes." . . .

Standardization in the suburbs is not applied, as it should be, to the comfort of living, but to the flattening out of personal individuality. A suburban house at once raises living cost; at once increases the burden of living, and at once makes slaves out of its occupants. It creates a separate menage, with separate furnace, service, repair, cleaning, and supply problems, all of which the apartment leaps over with an agile stride. For what purpose is such an "individual" house? Certainly not to attain separateness, for, as I have just pointed out, there is greater separateness and privacy in an apartment. Certainly not to secure more comfort, for the work burden is doubled and trebled, with often distinctly less comfort. Certainly not to attain beauty and "spacious living," for only the *bourgeois* can see beauty and spacious living in these serried rows of homes. Certainly not to be more independent, for the suburban servant problem is heartrending.

For a long time I was puzzled over the reasons why many people liked the suburbs. I saw them make little use of the boasted open air. I saw them suffer with furnace and servant problems. I saw them assume heavy financial burdens to pay for homes. I saw them inconvenienced, and often ill-tempered about it. I saw them forbear having children, when they had said that they moved to the suburb "for the children's sake." But still they clung to the suburb.

The reason, I finally fathomed, was *social*. There was a magnificent delusion working in their veins. For the truth must be told: the suburb is the social climber's imagined paradise. I say "imagined" advisedly, for those who are sophisticated know very well the silly fallacy in this. . . .

This social delusion has two aspects. One is the honest and praiseworthy desire of parents to have their children "meet nice young folks" and enjoy what they believe will be "a more wholesome social life"—which is believed to come more naturally and easily in a suburb of "charming little homes." The second social delusion is the hope of parents or young married people that they will "get in with" nice groups of people, who are also believed to be present and accessible, more easily and naturally in the suburbs.

In my opinion, these are absolute snares and delusions. What most people fail to realize is that in a suburb you simply recreate the psychology of the small town all over again. Many of the folk who fled from the small town to the large city, thankful to escape from the "narrowness" of small-town social life, now naïvely go to the suburbs expecting a social miracle or utopia. What they get is the same old Main Street!

They encounter the same snobbery, cliques, division of groups on the basis of wealth, the same gossipy, prying standard of the village. . . .

The parents, then, who desire "nice young folks" for their children to meet are soon told by their offspring—if they have not themselves noticed it—that the "charming suburb" is a social desert for any one who won't cut himself to the rigid pattern of a particular group. This pattern is so fixed that the young folks either become just like the rest of the "set," sinking to the level of the common denominator of that "set" and acquiring all the exact habits, slang, tastes, and philosophy of life of that "set," or else they rebel and "high hat" the whole suburb, and go to the city for their social life.

I believe it is splendidly to the credit of a great many young people that they choose the latter course. I hear many pathetic complaints of parents who long ago deliberately moved to the suburb "for the children's sake, socially," and then find that their young folk sneer at the suburb's social life and prefer the city. . . .

As for adult society, the same general principle operates. If you are the kind of person who selects his or her friends on a "neighbor" basis, or a wealth basis, and if you have the rubber soul and cast-iron nerve necessary for social climbing, the suburb may be a good place for you. Doubtless you will get all the bridge parties, country club life, teas, telephone gossip, and invitations your soul craves, if you "play the game," suburban fashion, and aren't overly particular. . . .

The suburb is a makeshift, and as such has its place, especially in slum eradication; but for the art of living by individuals it is, to my way of thinking, a double-dyed falsity.

ETHEL LONGWORTH SWIFT, EXCERPT FROM "IN DEFENSE OF SUBURBIA"

DEFENSIVELY, apprehensively, I have been reviewing my suburban position. . . .

Are we daily deceiving ourselves, I asked myself, in believing that the environment offered by our suburb is to be preferred immeasurably to that offered by a city apart-

Originally printed in *Outlook* 148 (April 4, 1928): 543–44.

ment? Or have we, by accident, got into an unusual suburb? Are we, in measuring the manifest advantages of our home in Suburbia, losing sight of its disadvantages? Indeed, are our minds so dulled by the sugar-coated *bourgeois* existence of life in our little town that we have lost, not only the ability to plumb the depths of cosmopolitan life, but even the insight to recognize our own narrowness? Is our preference a dishonest one?

My answer to all those questions is, *No.* I stand for the suburb. . . . [W]e, like others, have moved to a suburb. We moved because (dare I say it in the presence of those who turn up their sophisticated noses at the suburb and all that therein is?) we liked the country, because we believed that our small children would find there a more normal, healthy environment than the city was providing, and because we ourselves wanted a certain material spaciousness that we hoped could be found even in the atmosphere of "those neat toy houses all set in neat rows."

We have lived in Suburbia for a year, and even an individualist's contempt of our environment fails to make us believe that we have made a mistake.

Two European capitals and the two largest cities of America are included in our experience of apartment life. In the pursuit of "news," which is the commodity which has brought us a living, we have dallied at times in other cities and have tried other forms of metropolitan living, yet we are convinced that at present, in our suburban home, taking into consideration our children and the necessary enriching of their backgrounds, we are living more fully and more graciously than we could do in any city apartment operated on the same annual income.

Our suburb must surely be a typical one. It is neither especially fashionable nor yet notably unfashionable, using those words with their usual connotations. Its people, so far as we can see, are very much the same people who lived about us in New York and Chicago. They have not overwhelmed us with "neighborliness" nor do we have difficulty in avoiding the social life that has been kindly offered to us, but which does not happen to attract us. We have not, to my knowledge, made any enemies; we have made no friends on a purely "neighbor" basis. I do not know the name of a neighbor two hundred feet away, nor was I even conscious of my ignorance until The Outlook's article set me thinking of what I might expect to suffer from my neighbors!

We moved to the suburbs so that we and our children might be near to the grass and the trees. Big elm trees shade our front door. A crooked ledge of gray rock juts out of the hill that rises to the terraced lawn of a suburban house across our street. Ferns grow wild on that ledge in the summer-time. I rake the leaves myself from our seventy-five by one hundred and twenty-five foot garden. My small son builds a hut from packing-boxes in the sumach bushes of the vacant lot next door; my daughter wrestles with a cigar-box which will presently appear as a bird-house meant to lure a bluebird to our garden. The children range about the neighborhood unsupervised. In the city small children cannot be permitted to go far from home alone, a state of affairs which hinders the development of the spirit of independence, so essential to the complete development of the child.

With this suburb as a base, we have rediscovered the out-of-doors. We have tramped the country side for miles about. We have grilled steaks on wooded hills and have built our camp-fires in the snow, and we have thanked Heaven that the suburb gave us a chance to do so. We look back on those days in town when a day in the country (and the average man, be it remembered, has only Saturday and Sunday for such relaxation) was preceded by a long train ride or by hours of driving by car along roads even then overcrowded, and we thank our stars that our lot is now cast in pleasanter places.

For a ridiculously small sum we are able to keep our canoe at the local yacht club. Remember, we are not a fashionable suburb and the "club" is but a shed by the water's edge. We have known the delight of sleeping under blankets in the open air in the shadow of the Hudson's Palisades with a smudge to keep the mosquitoes away, and of waking to see the sun rising over the Westchester hills. . . .

The individualist will find his suburban neighbors as willing, and even as anxious, to let him alone as were his former neighbors of the apartment-house in the city. The custom of calling indiscriminately upon newcomers is dying a logical and natural death in the suburbs. Good riddance to it! The few people who called upon us when we first arrived in Suburbia did so because there was in each case some definite connection either of previous family friendship or similar interests. So conscious were our callers of the desuetude of the old custom that each one, to our amusement, qualified his or her visit with a series of remarks that implied: "Do as you like about making friends with us. We think we could get on with you very well; we have this or that in common, but you are under no obligation, you know."

The very word suburb implies a certain nearness to the city which militates against the close community life that is characteristic of the small town. There is a certain amount of community life, and it is indulged in by those who desire it, particularly those who have regretted its inapplicability to life in the city itself; but those who do not care for it are sufficiently near the city to find there an outlet for their social instincts. Friendships on a basis of common interests are just as possible to suburbanites as to city folk or owners of country houses. . . .

In the morning at this season we awaken to see tiny green buds pricked on the black twigs outside our windows, to be aware of the silent streets, to see last year's dead brown leaves stirring on the ground to the breeze that blows down from the Tappan Zee. At night the sound of the neighbor's gramophone, floating across shrubbery and through the high lilac hedge, is infinitely less noisy than was the combined sound from the radio above us and the piano below us when our rooftree was an apartment-house. No one dances to jazz music over our heads when we want to dream by our log fire. We can talk as loudly as we wish, and even indulge in noisy gayety, without waking the children, who used to sleep within sound of our apartment living-room, and who now are far removed by floors and doors.

The mechanism of life is less standardized, to be sure. The pipes do not always gush hot water at will, and we shovel the snow from our own dooryard. No dumb-waiter buzzes hungrily for a garbage-pail at seven in the morning, nor is there an efficient garbage chute. We must climb a flight of stairs to our bedrooms. There is not even an elevator to speed us to the attic, from which we, unaided, drag down our own fly-screens in the spring, and where, with our own hands, we pack the porch furniture in the autumn. A furnace-man, rather than a janitor, looks after our furnace along with those of several of our neighbors, and he is not at the other end of a telephone wire to be scolded when the house grows unnecessarily cold. We may even have to descend by the stairs to the basement to open the draughts of our own furnace! Help is not so easy to get as in the city, to be sure, nor yet so difficult as the owners of small country houses find it. . . .

Yes, most of us suburbanites, in spite of statements to the contrary, have children. Many of us, in our suburb, are sending them to a private school which was organized co-operatively by a group of parents, and which continues to be operated co-operatively by the parents of the pupils. These suburban parents, believing that the local public school was not sufficiently progressive in method for their children, had with the best educational advise organized a school where every stress was laid upon the capability of the teachers as teachers and where equipment was considered a secondary matter. Many parents send their children to this school at a sacrifice to themselves. The money they pay in school fees might permit them to join one of the country clubs which are popularly believed to be the suburbanite's social mecca; instead, they play their golf on the neighboring community courses, leaving the problem of their social standing for more interested heads to solve.

As to the young folk who are said to sneer so cynically at the social life of the suburb, were not young folks always thus? Their post-adolescent friends of the city sneer at the confinement within four walls of an apartment. Helen of Suburbia, who hates the people "in this dump of a suburb," is matched by the city-bred Dan, who begs his parents to move to a suburb so that "the country club won't be two hours away and there will be some girls in the neighborhood with ideas in their heads beyond drinks, night clubs, and theatres." The younger generation's whines need not be listened to with great seriousness. The suburb is no more a social desert for the young individualist than it is for his seniors.

There is no reason to deny that the suburb is to many a "social climber's paradise." Social ambitions are so universal that they bob their heads up in metropolis, suburb, village, and hamlet. The suburb, fortunately, is able to give some satisfaction to those thwarted souls who found in the city no way to climb the social ladder. My point is that the suburb, though supplying the facilities for this game of ladder-climbing to those who wish to play it, makes no effort to include in the game the thousands of suburbanites who care not a whit for what the world calls "social position," but who are thankful to find that they can live their own lives, without interference, in sight of their own grass and trees and hedges.

Those whose eyes light to see a swirl of dry leaves in the street in the autumn, whose hearts lift at the crunch of hard snow under their feet in the winter, who watch for the first furry signals of the pussy-willow in the springtime, and who, on hot lazy summer afternoons, hear contentedly the locusts and the crickets singing their interminable chorus, thank that enterprising realtor, Babbitt, for the suburb.

81

THOMAS H. AND DORIS REED, WITH MURRAY TEIGH BLOOM, EXCERPT FROM "DOES YOUR CITY SUFFER FROM SUBURBANITIS?" 1952

As the postwar suburban boom was beginning, many observers were quick to recognize the disastrous impact it would have on cities. Suburbanites fled, taking their tax revenues

Originally printed in *Collier's*, Oct. 11, 1952.

6.4. Aerial view of Levittown, Pennsylvania, 1950s. The carefully crafted garden suburb largely disappeared by the 1950s, replaced by the relentless repetition of post–Second World War suburban tract houses. Pioneered by Alfred Levitt, these developments answered the pent-up demand for new housing created by the war and represented exponential growth in suburban living. Not forty years after the war, more Americans lived in suburbs like this than in cities. While suburbs like Levittown gave an increasing proportion of Americans the opportunity to own their own homes, they also increased dependence on the automobile, created sharply segregated communities, and accelerated the decline of America's great cities.

with them and leaving cities "scraping the bottom of the revenue barrel." Unable to reduce expenditures on streets and subways, schools and sewers, cities continued to raise taxes on whoever was left, thereby driving even more people into the suburbs. But the Reeds, urban policy experts, also see economic problems on the horizon for the new suburbs as they face the costs of recreating services already available in cities. The cure for suburbanites, the Reeds argue, is simple: Cities should grow larger by annexing new suburbs. While this solution might have made rational economic and policy sense, and was once the main way cities expanded, by the 1950s it had become far less common, especially in the older cities of the East and Midwest, as suburbs resisted being incorporated into poverty-stricken and racially diverse neighboring cities.

The toughest and most widespread city disease we've encountered is one that two people couldn't begin to cope with. It has already infected hundreds of cities and thousands of suburbs and involves some 85,000,000 Americans. If something isn't done about it soon, it could destroy billions of dollars in city realty, bankrupt entire suburban communities and greatly reduce the value of millions of small homes.

The disease is suburbanitis. It kills cities by choking them off from further growth; by selectively thinning out the city's population—its lifeblood; and by bringing on a host of parasitical communities to feed on the already weakened city.

You know the disease has struck at your community when the suburbs outside the city line suddenly double or triple in population; when your city adopts a wage tax or starts considering one; when you hear city officials talk about "suburban leeches, free-loaders and parasites."

Between 1940 and 1950, the nation's population increased by nearly 19,000,000. About half that growth was in the suburbs of our 168 largest cities; today 35,000,000 Americans live in those suburbs. That is, they live there evenings and week ends. During the day, many of them work in the city.

Nearly 500,000 suburban commuters pour into Manhattan every weekday. They spend comparatively little there, but they use expensive city facilities, such as the streets and the subsidized transit system, and they depend on the city's police and fire protection. At night, the commuters flood back to the suburbs—and that's where the bulk of their money is spent.

Cities can't reduce the cost of government proportionately for every family that moves to the suburbs; it's just about as expensive to provide services for a 20-family block as it was for the same block when it had 30 families. In fact, it's often more expensive. In the older sections of the city, landlords trying to maintain income from vacated apartments often lease single flats to several low income families. When that happens in whole areas, the overcrowding is incredible and health conditions are appalling, and the cost of police, health and fire services balloons to many times that of the normal residential or business area.

With fewer profitable properties to tax and more revenue needed for a multitude of services, the city has to raise real-estate taxes, causing landlords to grumble even louder. Sales taxes are increased, too. That drives a lot of city people out to the suburbs to do their shopping, and soon the merchants follow them there to get the business. Nor does the hapless city stop with the sales and real estate taxes. Why not a tax on cars? On restaurant meals? On cigarettes?

Many of our cities are scraping the bottom of the revenue barrel. Yet cities are the greatest sources of tax revenue for any state. Almost every city gives far more to its state treasury in taxes than it receives back in the form of state aid. States are practically always controlled by rural legislators and they tend, naturally, to vote less money for urban areas.

Made poor by their suburbs and kept poor by their states, the cities have to raise money somehow. They tax their citizens as hard as they can—and then they look to the suburbanites.

Today, there's a payroll tax on everyone who lives or *works* in Philadelphia, Toledo, Columbus, Youngstown, Dayton, Scranton, Louisville and St. Louis. How successful is it? In 1949, Philadelphia got $30,000,000 from this source, more than a fourth of the city's entire income.

But for every city taxing its suburbanites this way, there are many actually helping to *pay* the taxes of parasite suburbs.

In Los Angeles County, for example, there is a huge suburban unincorporated area—that is, one not doing business as a city—called Belvedere. About 90,000 people live in Belvedere, more than in such going cities as Amarillo, Texas, or Manchester, New Hampshire. It costs a lot of money to provide essential services for a community that size. But Belvedere gets along fine; it gets such city services as fire and police protection from the county. Where does the county get the money? From *city* taxpayers, who pay from 80 to 90 per cent of the county general tax fund. . . .

Cities are also faced with another frustrating dilemma; perimeter "bedroom towns" are frequently indifferent to health and crime-prevention programs which cannot succeed without suburban cooperation.

St. Louis, for example, recently had a big smoke-control campaign. It was pretty successful—in St. Louis. But smoke still drifted across the Mississippi River from suburban East St. Louis, Illinois. New York City has a similar problem with suburbs in New Jersey. . . .

But the worst havoc wrought on the cities by their suburbs may yet prove to be the draining off of young, alert citizens who might otherwise become the civic leaders of tomorrow.

One day while lunching at the Hartford Club, the Connecticut capital's leading civic center, we made an informal count and found that 80 per cent of the members eating there lived in the suburbs and thus couldn't take part in Hartford's own political life.

Cities are going to be faced with these problems for a long time. After all, there's a lot to be said for life in the suburbs—even for those of us who don't have atomic jitters. The grass seems greener, the air is often cleaner, sometimes the schools are better. As a matter of fact, we live in Wethersfield, a quiet, green suburb of Hartford. We can appreciate the advantages of suburban living.

For some people, one of the big advantages is that the suburb is a wonderful place to forget city troubles and taxes.

"We're happy by the river and see no reason to assume St. Paul's troubles," the mayor of Newport, Minnesota, a St. Paul suburb, announced not long ago. That pretty well summed up the reactions of thousands of suburban officials to city troubles. It's a form of self-deception that could easily be fatal, for suburbanitis cuts two ways, and the younger, smaller, less resistant communities could succumb long before the tough old cities do.

Is suburban living all it's cracked up to be? Let's see.

Everybody knows that suburban taxes are supposed to be much lower than city taxes. After all, suburbs have no slums, graft, huge relief budgets or armies of politicians on the payroll. Yet some suburbs have *higher* taxes than the nearby cities. For example, comparison between two groups of identical one-family homes, built by the same contractor within Milwaukee's city limits and in the suburb of Granville, revealed that the suburbanites were paying more taxes than their city neighbors—and getting far fewer services. True, that's not common; the high costs of suburban living aren't always so obvious. But they exist. In most cases, you have only to look for them.

Septic tanks, for instance, are all right as a substitute for a sanitary sewer system when houses are far apart. But in the average small-lot suburban development, the septic tank is a makeshift; before long, city-type sanitary sewers will be needed and the cost, perhaps millions, will have to be borne by the homeowners.

The brand-new suburbanite loves to visit the volunteer firehouse, which costs him practically nothing. At least that's what he believes. He forgets that his fire insurance rate is higher than if he were still living in the city. And he doesn't stop to think that most "free" volunteer companies have built-in costs: they often go hog-wild on too much of the very latest and best equipment and there are generally too many volunteer companies in a community. . . .

There are some minor virtues of big-city life that are almost invariably denied the suburbs. A department of weights and measures, for one. Can the suburban housewife always tell if she's being cheated by her butcher or grocer? Even if only one merchant in the village is getting away with short weights, there's a big, invisible tax right there. . . .

From the aches and pains afflicting our suburbs it's clear that they, too, are suffering from suburbanitis, even if there symptoms aren't as marked as those of the city patients.

There is a cure for both city and suburb. The word for it is "annexation," and it works.

Until 1900, annexation was a fairly common method of adding breathing space to a growing city. Then the rurally dominated legislatures got a little worried. Maybe they were letting the cities become too big, politically. Soon onerous restrictions were written into the annexation laws. Later, the suburbs grew to enjoy their independence and the subject became controversial. Today, "annexation" is a shoot-on-sight word in many embattled communities.

"We'll have to pay higher city taxes," protest its opponents. "We'll inherit a corrupt municipal government. Our charming suburban identity will disappear. We'll be lost in the huge city."

Besides these often legitimate objections, county politicians who age perceptibly at the merest whisper of annexation have frequently carried on their campaigns against it with rumors, whispers and downright lies. . . .

There have been a number of other successful annexations in the past few years. Three of the biggest have, naturally, been in Texas: Dallas, Fort Worth and Houston. Memphis, Annapolis and Albuquerque have also had large annexations.

But the most significant of all has been the recent annexation of 83 square miles and nearly 100,000 people to the city of Atlanta. This was accompanied by a redistribution of functions which removes all duplications between Atlanta and Fulton County. The county is now forbidden to provide any of the usual city services, such as police and fire protection, except through contract with the city of Atlanta, thus discouraging the growth of fringe communities around the enlarged city.

Admittedly, making big cities even bigger poses special problems. Cities do become vast and impersonal and their citizens become too removed from their elected local representatives. "Go fight City Hall" becomes the ultimate in hopelessness. Perhaps a stronger form of the New York borough plan, with certain activities allotted to city subdivisions instead of the central city government, might be the answer.

Los Angeles is working out a solution of its own; it has branch civic centers in different parts of the huge metropolis, and is now considering a borough system of government as well, so that community councils could consider minor matters such as local improvements and rubbish collection.

Obviously, every city confronts special problems as its boundaries become uncomfortably tight; annexation certainly isn't the answer in every case. Buffalo cannot annex nearby parts of Canada, even though they are in its metropolitan area, nor can New York City easily annex part of adjacent New Jersey and Connecticut.

But while the problems may vary, all of our cities have this in common: they must be permitted to grow. If they don't, they will die. And that could be catastrophic for the nation.

We're going to have to learn a wholly new concept of a city—a great sprawling community covering hundreds of square miles, in which farms and pastures mingle with intense residential developments, factories and shopping centers, with the entire area run purposefully for the common good, instead of consisting of hundreds of tiny, wasteful, duplicating governmental units working jealously in opposition to one another.

Those wonderful new cities aren't as far in the future as they may sound. We forecast that within the next 10 or 15 years several cities will have successfully taken this drastic cure for suburbantitis. And it's our prediction that they'll live happily ever after.

82

FREDERICK LEWIS ALLEN, EXCERPT FROM "THE BIG CHANGE IN SUBURBIA," 1954

Frederick Lewis Allen was one of the most astute journalists of the middle part of the twentieth century, and his book on the 1920s, *Only Yesterday* (written in 1931), remains a minor classic. In this two-part essay for *Harper's* Allen brings his critical powers to bear on the phenomenon of the postwar suburb, a place he already sees in crisis. In a remarkably penetrating and prescient analysis, Lewis sees that the suburbs as they are currently growing can not escape a fundamental paradox: the open spaces and relaxed lifestyle that draw people to them will inevitably disappear as more and more people move there. The primary reason for this, as he shrewdly points out, is that the new suburbs are autocentric and therefore "open spaces get gobbled up at a rate which has no precedent in history." Lewis's solution to this crisis is large-scale planning and cooperation among governments and agencies so that suburban growth can be managed and directed. Almost nowhere was this advice followed, and the resulting suburban landscape, over-built, choked, and crowded, looks almost exactly like Allen predicted it would.

PART I

A few months ago the editors of *Fortune* went into a huddle and, after elaborate and careful calculations, produced the statement that as many as nine million people have moved to the suburbs of American cities since 1947, and that as a result there are now thirty million suburbanites in the United States: a record number, and by a large margin. The growth of suburbia, said the editors, "is portentous even in a country accustomed to talking of growth in superlatives."

The accuracy of their count may be open to challenge, but there can be little doubt that they put their finger on one of the major changes of our time, which seems destined to alter the face of the land and affect our national way of life for generations to come.

The editors of *Fortune* did not classify as suburbanites everybody who lives on the outskirts of our big cities, or their figures would have been much larger. They included only those who work in the city but "prefer to live where there is more open space": those who are attempting to enjoy, if not the best of two worlds, at least something of the respective blessings of two worlds, the world of the city and the world of the country.

Originally printed in *Harper's Magazine* 208 (June 1954): 21–28.

6.5. Sidney Goodman, *Figures in a Landscape*, 1972–73. Philadelphia Museum of Art. Purchased with the Philadelphia Foundation Fund (by exchange) and the Adele Haas Turner and Beatrice Pastorius Turner Memorial Fund. Postwar suburban development has been critiqued as both environmentally destructive and socially alienating. This painting powerfully captures both of those critiques.

In our modern civilization, the metropolis is an almost irresistible magnet. . . .

But likewise—and especially since the beginning of the automobile age—the metropolis has repelled a considerable number of those whom it drew to it: repelled them with its noise, soot, fumes, barren pavements, traffic tie-ups, nervous pressures, and inhuman dimensions, and especially with the apparent unsuitability of the life it imposes upon small children. It has not repelled many of these people all the way back to the countryside, for its magnetic power is too strong for that; what it has done has been to hold them within its sphere of influence like so many planets—or, more literally, to drive them part way out of town, to attempt to live *by* the city and yet *in* the country. . . .

Such a combination of contrasting values seems temptingly easy. Rapid transit systems, good commuter service on the railroads, and above all the automobile make it, for the time being, at least physically possible. But for his effort the commuter pays a high price—in fact, many prices.

The most obvious one is the sheer cost, in time and energy, of commuting, of repetitive, self-canceling travel. Suppose a man lives 25 miles from his office (not an excessive distance for a commuter): that means some 50 miles of travel a day, 250 miles a week, 12,000 miles a year—perhaps nearly a half a million miles in a lifetime of commuting, without getting anywhere he has not been before. Or to put the cost in terms of time, a man who puts in three hours a day in transit, over a period of forty years, will have devoted considerably over three of those forty years to the mere business of getting there and back. He may have utilized much of this time in reading the paper, or looking over reports, or enjoying bridge games; but these are mitigations of an interminable slavery to the 7:59 and the 5:25.

And there is a curious spiritual cost, too, in that his life is strangely divided. He belongs to the city, but not quite: only as a non-resident, non-dues-paying, and therefore only a partly responsible member. He belongs to his suburb, but only as a part-time person who spends the best of his daylight hours, and of his energies, in exile from it. As my wife once put it, his heart and his treasure are twenty miles apart. He becomes something like a split personality, playing one role by day and another by night and over the weekends. . . .

And in at least one other respect Suburbia tends to be out of balance: it tends to bring together in large communities people of similar economic status, if not of similar occupation. Many things conspire together to bring about this result: the mass-production principle in housing, which invites real-estate developers to make money by building a lot of similar houses which appeal to people in the same income bracket: and also zoning regulations: and also, of course, the natural preference of most commuters, who feel more comfortable when surrounded by people of more or less similar status. We all enjoy, naturally, having the bulk of our intimate, day-to-day contacts with those who look at things with eyes like our own; but the tendency, today, to group together large numbers of people of the same economic status in housing projects, housing developments, and suburban areas may tend to insulate them from the problems and preferences of those in other sections of the population, and thus hinder that approach to the classless civilization which is such a source of American strength.

ANOTHER special characteristic of Suburbia is that the suburban region inevitably is always changing. . . . The more families flee the city for the deep tangled wildwood, the less deep, tangled, and wild does the wood become.

No wonder the suburbanite embraces zoning regulations with all his heart. They represent, it is true, a kind of governmental interference with private enterprise which in another context he might regard with black disfavor; but in fact they appeal to the most conservative instincts in his nature, as protectors of the status quo. And it is fortunate that they do appeal to him: for zoning is one of the few effective instruments available to impose some sort of orderly restraint upon the otherwise disorderly growth of Suburbia.

Yet even zoning regulations cannot stop the influx of newcomers, though they can divert and channel it; and in one way or another the process of change continues, placing new and unexpected difficulties in the way of the family which moved out in the hope of being able to combine the opportunities of the city with the peace of the country. . . .

THE postwar boom in GI housing has been a nation-wide phenomenon, comprising developments both large and small; but to see it on the grand scale you should visit one of the new mass-produced suburbs such as Park Forest outside Chicago, or Lakewood outside Los Angeles, or Levittown, Long Island. . . . Finding a large, almost unoccupied piece of land within striking distance of a city, the developer has built on it a whole town of very similar houses, applying the economies of mass production to the fierce demand for housing which was caused by the halt in building during the war and by the rising marriage rate and birthrate of the nineteen-forties. . . .

These new towns have been laid out with a more thoughtful eye to the realities of the automobile age than most of their predecessors. Levittown, for instance, has wide boulevards for through traffic, well separated from the houses, which stand along narrower, curving roads; the houses themselves are not severely crowded, having ample front grass-plots and room in the rear for gardens; and there is a commendable variety in exterior design and especially in texture and color, so as to mitigate the endless monotony of thousands upon thousands of basically similar houses on flat land.

THE standard form of architecture in such developments is ranch-type, of which the latest variant is "split-level"; they tend to be one-story or story-and-a-half houses, with agreeably long roof lines. One that I went through in an outlying part of New Rochelle, New York, was selling for $25,750, a rather high price for such communities: it had, typically, a picture window for the living-room, a dining area off the living-room, a kitchen waiting for the latest mechanical equipment, and, up a few steps (above the garage), three bedrooms and two baths. The garage was built for two cars, not one. The walls were shingled, and prospective purchasers were informed that they might have "optional brick front on living-room panel."

To a visitor from another area, or from an earlier decade, such houses would seem very small but pleasantly simple and unpretentious, and extraordinarily mechanized: I noted that by paying some $1,250 extra one could get the house I looked at fully air conditioned. Physically, they represent a characteristically American response to an era of high building costs and abundant machinery; spiritually, they represent an abandonment of the dream of old-world charm that flourished in the twenties, and of the dream of old-fashioned American cottage living that accompanied it and then tended to supersede it in the thirties.

Today's dream looks westward to California, and—even on Long Island—envisions a happy family in Technicolor slacks and Hawaiian shirts having a barbecue feast on the terrace, all smiling as in the latest ads....

PART II

One conclusion seems inescapable. The days are passing (if indeed they are not already past) when one could think of a suburban town outside one of our great cities as a village in the country. It would be much wiser, today, to think of it as a more or less comfortably spaced residential area—or residential and business area—within the greater metropolis.

Not only is the countryside which used to surround many of our suburbs getting built up, as the edges of the various suburban developments meet; but the nature of the present changes almost inevitably accelerates the metropolitan process. For it is worth noting that the builders of mass-produced suburbs, and the builders of regional shopping centers, and at least some of the transplanters of business headquarters, have one striking thing in common. *They are all looking for large tracts of open country in which to do their stuff.* And so they are likely to occupy, and metropolitanize, many if not most of the remaining groves and fields which have given the outskirts of our cities the aspect of a countryside.

Nor is this all. For today almost everything that is built outside the central cores of our cities requires much more space than it used to. The reason can be very simply stated. These things are built for the automobile age, and the private passenger car is an inordinate consumer of space—horizontal space.

Think of its various requirements. It needs a place to sit at night. It needs a place to park by the railroad station if its owner is a commuter who takes the train to town. It needs a place to park near his office if he drives all the way to work. It needs further places to park while its occupant is shopping, or visiting, or playing; and, of course, enough room on the roads to get from one place to the next. And although naturally no single car is occupying more than one of these positions at a time, it may need to occupy several of them during a single day, very likely at the same time when other cars will be on similar errands. And since the builders of parking lots want to be able to take care of a peak load, the amount of space required adds up to a big total. I have been told that in an untended parking lot each car needs 330 square feet—which includes, of course, not only the space on which it will sit, but its share of the necessary aisles and entrance and exit areas. Perhaps we could make a wild guess that for every private car, several times that space is required to provide for its several employments.

THE results are visible all about us. The modern factory is no longer, typically, a high building on a city street, which its employees reach by trolley or bus or on foot. Instead, it is a wide-spreading one-story building—preferably outside the city—which must have big parking lots for employees to reach it by car. (One-story factories are preferred because automotive machines, like fork-lift trucks, are in increasing use and operate best on one level: here again the motor age spreads things out.)

The regional shopping center likewise needs immense room—at least two or three square feet of parking space for every square foot of shopping space, it is said, and preferably as much as five to one. The new Northland center outside Detroit, built to accommodate a department store run by the J. I. Hudson Company and some seventy other shops, is providing parking room for 7,000 cars, and as a result is planned to occupy no less than 450 acres—over two-thirds of a square mile! And even these computations do not take into account the probable need for broadening the roads along which people will want to drive to a popular shopping center. Imagine some two or three thousand cars all trying to leave the place at closing time and you will get some idea of the volume of traffic which those neighboring roads will have to handle. . . .

IN ADDITION, as the countryside gets built up, new parkways, turnpikes, or thruways must be constructed to provide for the through traffic, and these, again, eat up land. The next time you drive along such a super-highway, note the width of the belt of land it occupies, and the prodigious dimensions of a clover-leaf intersection for high-speed traffic. And reflect, too, on the fact that the airplane also wants much room: airports are getting to be bigger and bigger, and although heliports will be of much more modest dimensions, the helicopter, too, must have a good many places to sit down if it is to live up to its promise as an aircraft for short hauls.

All this means that when we design things for the automobile age, our open spaces get gobbled up at a rate which has no precedent in history. . . .

Here in the suburbs, at any rate, they think, there will be room enough to indulge the national passion for going everywhere and doing everything by car. But before long they confront once again, and in its pure form, the logic of the automobile age: that the automobile consumes open space at a record rate, and thus robs the suburbs, piece by piece, of their fast-departing rural quality.

AT PRESENT the gobbling up of the open countryside of America is most acutely evident along the Eastern seaboard, and especially in those parts of it where new manufacturing plants like to locate. . . .

BUT it would be a grave mistake to think of the metropolitanizing of Suburbia as a phenomenon confined to the outskirts of a few big cities, mostly on the Atlantic seaboard. What is happening outside New York and Philadelphia offers a preview of what is likely to happen, in one way or another, outside Cincinnati and St. Louis and Kansas City, and has its lessons likewise for Des Moines and Denver. The people who live in and about these smaller cities have a little more time to decide how to control the metropolitanizing process than have the people of Westchester County, New York, or Fairfield County, Connecticut, or Chester County, Pennsylvania: but none too much time.

To the suburbanites of today, the changes taking place may well offer an alarming prospect. For the great majority of them choose their places of residence in the hope of being able to work in the city—with its contracts and opportunities and excitements—and yet live a village life in the country, under stable circumstances. From almost the moment when they moved into their suburban houses they must have realized that they had involved themselves in a process of change that would continue almost uncontrollably. . . .

So frustrating is this process to dreams of rural peace that most suburbanites hate to look ahead and envision the future; they can hardly help wishing that time would stand still. (Is it possible that the political conservatism of most suburban communities is related to this fear of what the future may bring?) But if the commuter can bear to project ahead for as short a period as ten years the present curves of population growth and business expansion in our metropolitan regions, he will realize the trap he is caught in. And if he projects these curves ahead for twenty years, or fifty, or a hundred, he will see the suburban crisis in an even more disturbing guise. . . .

I suggest as a first order of business, for every suburban governmental body and for every suburban citizens' association, a consideration of ways and means for preserving open land for the benefit of succeeding generations. For the change to the greater metropolitan region is upon us. We cannot stop it. We can only channel and direct it. And we cannot even do that, unless we act in good season. For it's later than you think.

83

WILLIAM H. WHYTE, JR., EXCERPT FROM "ARE CITIES UN-AMERICAN?" 1957

Author of *The Organization Man* (1956), a devastating account of the routine of the modern American corporation and its workers, William Whyte is also remembered for his studies of cities, most importantly *The Social Life of Small Urban Spaces* (1980). In this essay, written for *Fortune* magazine during the suburban explosion, Whyte answers the question in his title with a resounding "no." Cities, he argues, remain the rightful centers of industry and commerce and can once again become attractive places to live, despite years of neglect. While he is hopeful for a return from the suburbs and a revitalizing of urban life, he is wary of the urban renewal projects under way, which would be, he fears, a "gigantic bore."

Originally printed in *Fortune* 56 (September 1957): 122–27, 213–14, 218, 220, 223–24, 226. Reprinted by permission of *Fortune* magazine.

Oddly, in this time of "urbanization," when more people are living in metropolitan areas than ever before, the central city itself seems to be getting further alienated from what most people conceive as the American Way of Life. More and more, it would seem, the city is becoming a place of extremes—a place for the very poor, or the very rich, or the slightly odd. Here and there, in pleasant tree-shaded neighborhoods, there are still islands of middle-class stability, but for the young couple on the way up, they are neighborhoods of the past. They are often the last stand of an ethnic group, and the people in them are getting old. The once dominant white Protestant majority has long since dispersed, and among the Catholics and the Jews who have been the heart of the city's middle class, the younger people are leaving as fast as they are able. . . .

Clearly the norm of American aspiration is now in suburbia. The happy family of TV commercials, of magazine covers and ads lives in suburbia; wherever there is an identifiable background it is the land of blue jeans and shopping centers, of bright new schools, of barbecue-pit participation, garden clubs, P.T.A., do-it-yourself, and green lawns. Here is the place to enjoy the new leisure, and as more people make more money and spend less time making it, the middle-class identification with suburbia will be made more compelling yet. The momentum would seem irresistible. It is not merely that hundreds of thousands have been moving to suburbia, here they are breeding a whole generation that will never have known the city at all.

Heterogeneity, concentration, specialization, tension, drive—the characteristics of the city have always been damned in popular American morality, at any rate, but rarely have they been damned with such intensity. "I'm getting out of your skyscraper jungle," says the hero of the typical anti-success novel, and as he tells off the boss, inevitably he tells off the city as well. "To hell with your fur-lined trap, your chrome-plated merry-go-round," he says, with pious indignation, and heads for the country and peace of mind.

Planners, a surprising number of whom don't like cities, have been similarly beguiled. To many, the challenge of the city is meat and drink, but others, appalled at the chronic disorder of it, have turned their eyes outward, and in a burst of glorified provincialism have dreamed of starting afresh with new regional towns. The federal government has no such clear vision in mind, but it shows much the same bias; like the state legislatures, which have always had little use for cities, the federal government has been favoring country over city. The FHA has consistently shown partiality to the suburban homeowner, and in its rules it has created a "legislative architecture" ill adapted to city housing. Lately, it is true, the U.S. has allocated $1.25 billion in capital funds for urban renewal, but for highways it has allocated $33.5 billion, and the effect, if not the deliberate design, will be the enlargement of suburbia. . . .

The City Livable

But the center of the problem is in the center. And it is the center of the biggest, most industrialized, most slum-ridden, noisiest, dirtiest, most congested cities. For these are the engines, after all, of American life. Most of the nation's industry is directed from twenty-four U.S. cities with a population of half a million or more, and within their limits lives almost a fifth of the nation's population.

Their problems are appallingly difficult, not because the cities are "decayed" or "obsolete," but because they have vitality. Their streets are packed because there is business to be done, their slums are jammed because there are jobs to be had. Nor are the cities old and tired. Many are old, but from one of the most venerable of all, Philadelphia, have come more new ideas and experiments in city renewal than in all the younger cities put together.

The big city has already reasserted its function as an industrial center. In all the talk of "decentralization" after the war, there seemed for a while the possibility that the expansion of industry would take place away from the traditional centers. It has not; for all the new plants in small towns, most industrial expansion has been in the big cities.

The city has also reasserted its function as a business center. Not so many years ago, a large-scale exodus of business offices to the countryside seemed imminent; today, the business idyll has proved a contradiction in terms, and the overwhelming proportion of new office buildings has been going up in the big cities. Along several blocks in Manhattan, for example, a prodigious amount of new office space has been constructed; in a great burst of civic energy, Pittsburgh leaders have built virtually a new inner city of office buildings.

But will the city reassert itself as a good place to *live?* To ask this question is to ask whether the city will continue as a dominant cultural force in the U.S. As Pittsburgh's business leaders have found out, the rebuilding of downtown is not enough; a city deserted at night by its leading citizens is only half a city. What the city needs is a core of upper-middle-class people to support its theaters and museums, its shops and its restaurants—even a Bohemia of sorts can be of help. For it is the people who like living in the city who make it an attraction to the visitors who don't. It is the city dwellers who support its style; without them there is nothing to come downtown *to.* . . .

One thing is clear. The cities have a magnificent opportunity. There are definite signs of a small but significant move back from suburbia. There is also evidence that many people who will be moving to suburbia would prefer to stay in the city—and it would not take too much more in amenities and space to make them stay.

But the cities seem on the verge of muffing their opportunities—and muffing it for generations to come. Under the Title I provision of the 1949 Housing Act, cities have been clearing slum areas, marking down the cost, and selling them to private developers. So far, because of financing difficulties, the program is only just beginning to get under way, but already the cities have built, or are in the process of building, some $914 million worth of redevelopment projects (the federal government's contribution: $183 million); in the planning stage are approximately $3 billion worth more.

And what are the projects like? In a striking failure to apply marketing principles and an even more striking failure of aesthetics, the cities are freezing on a design for living ideally calculated to keep everybody in suburbia. . . . These vast, barracks-like superblocks are not designed for people who *like* cities, but for people who have no other choice. A few imaginative architects and planners have shown that redeveloped blocks don't have to be repellent to make money, but so far their ideas have had little effect. The institutional approach is dominant, and unless the assumptions embalmed in it are reexamined the city is going to be turned into a gigantic bore.

84

BETTY FRIEDAN, EXCERPT FROM
THE FEMININE MYSTIQUE, 1963

The Feminine Mystique ranks as one of the most influential books of the second half of the twentieth century, articulating for countless women the frustrations they felt in their lives, and helping to spark a revival of feminism in the 1960s and 1970s. While Betty Friedan is known primarily as a pioneering feminist and a cofounder of the National Organization for Women (NOW), this selection reveals her to be an astute architectural critic as well. She was among the very first to analyze the new suburbia, and especially the new suburban house, in gendered terms. Friedan not only traces the dimensions of the "feminine mystique" but she roots it primarily in the spaces of the postwar suburbs. It is in suburbia that women saw themselves only as wives and mothers, where they experienced increasing social, cultural, and political isolation, and where housework expanded to fill all available time. Though her book is based on dozens of interviews, Friedan knew whereof she spoke. As she wrote later, she had to flee her own suburb after the book was published and move back to the city.

In one upper-income development where I interviewed, there were twenty-eight wives. Some were college graduates in their thirties or early forties; the younger wives had usually quit college to marry. Their husbands were, to a rather high degree, engrossed in challenging professional work. Only one of these wives worked professionally; most had made a career of motherhood with a dash of community activity. Nineteen out of the twenty-eight had had natural childbirth (at dinner parties there, a few years ago, wives and husbands often got down on the floor to practice the proper relaxing exercises together). Twenty of the twenty-eight breastfed their babies. At or near forty, many of these women were pregnant. The mystique of feminine fulfillment was so literally followed in this community that if a little girl said: "When I grow up, I'm going to be a doctor," her mother would correct her: "No, dear, you're a girl. You're going to be a wife and mother, like mummy."

But what was mummy really like? Sixteen out of the twenty-eight were in analysis or analytical psychotherapy. Eighteen were taking tranquilizers; several had tried suicide; and some had been hospitalized for varying periods, for depression or vaguely diagnosed psychotic states. ("You'd be surprised at the number of these happy suburban wives who simply go berserk one night, and run shrieking through the street without any clothes on," said the local doctor, not a psychiatrist, who had been called in, in such emergencies.) Of the women who breastfed their babies, one had continued, desperately, until the child was so undernourished that her doctor intervened by force. Twelve were engaged in extramarital affairs in fact or in fantasy.

These were fine, intelligent American women, to be envied for their homes, husbands, children, and for their personal gifts of mind and spirit. Why were so many of them driven women? Later, when I saw this same pattern repeated over and over again in similar suburbs, I knew it could hardly be coincidence. These women were alike mainly in one regard: they had uncommon gifts of intelligence and ability nourished by at least

Originally printed in Betty Friedan, *The Feminine Mystique* (New York: Norton, 1963), 234–47.

the beginnings of higher education—and the life they were leading as suburban house-wives denied them the full use of their gifts. . . .

On one suburban road there were two colonial houses, each with a big, comfortable living room, a small library, a formal dining room, a big cheerful kitchen, four bed-rooms, an acre of garden and lawn, and, in each family, one commuting husband and three school-age children. Both houses were well-kept, with a cleaning woman two days a week; but the cooking and the other housework was done by the wife, who in each case was in her late thirties, intelligent, healthy, attractive, and well-educated.

In the first house, Mrs. W., a full-time housewife, was busy most of every day with cooking, cleaning, shopping, chauffeuring, taking care of the children. Next door Mrs. D., a microbiologist, got most of these chores done before she left for her laboratory at nine, or after she got home at five-thirty. In neither family were the children neglected, though Mrs. D.'s were slightly more self-reliant. Both women entertained a fair amount. Mrs. W., the housewife, did a lot of routine community work, but she did not "have time" to take a policy-making office—which she was often offered as an intelligent capable woman. At most, she headed a committee to run a dance, or a PTA fair. Mrs. D., the scientist, did no routine community work, but, in addition to her job and home, played in a dedicated string quintet (music was her main interest outside of science), and held a policy-making post in the world-affairs organization which had been an interest since college.

How could the same size house and the same size family, under almost identical conditions of income, outside help, style of life, take so much more of Mrs. W.'s time than of Mrs. D's? And Mrs. W. was never idle, really. She never had time in the evening to "just read," as Mrs. D. often did. . . .

The simple principle that "Work Expands to Fill the Time Available" was first for-mulated by the Englishman C. Northcote Parkinson on the basis of his experience with administrative bureaucracy in World War II. Parkinson's Law can easily be reformulated for the American housewife: Housewifery Expands to Fill the Time Available, or Mother-hood Expands to Fill the Time Available. . . .

One of the great changes in America, since World War II, has been the explosive movement to the suburbs, those ugly and endless sprawls which are becoming a national problem. Sociologists point out that a distinguishing feature of these suburbs is the fact that women who live there are better educated than city women, and that the great ma-jority are full-time housewives.

At first glance, one might suspect that the very growth and existence of the suburbs causes educated modern American women to become and remain full-time housewives. Or did the postwar suburban explosion come, at least in part, as a result of the coinci-dental choice of millions of American women to "seek fulfillment in the home?" Among the women I interviewed, the decision to move to the suburbs "for the children's sake" followed the decision to give up job or profession and become a full-time housewife, usually after the birth of the first baby, or the second, depending on the age of the woman when the mystique hit. With the youngest wives, of course, the mystique hit so early that the choice of marriage and motherhood as a full-time career ruled out educa-tion for any profession, and the move to the suburbs came with marriage or as soon as the wife no longer had to work to support her husband through college or law school.

Families where the wife intends to pursue a definite professional goal are less likely to move to the suburbs. In the city, of course, there are more and better jobs for educated women; more universities, sometimes free, with evening courses, geared to men who work during the day, and often more convenient than the conventional daytime program for a young mother who wants to finish college or work toward a graduate degree. There is also a better supply of full or part-time nurses and cleaning help, nursery schools, day-care centers, after-school play programs. But these considerations are only important to the woman who has commitments outside the home.

There is also less room for housewifery to expand to fill the time available, in the city. That sense of restless "marking time" comes early to the educated, able city housewife, even though, when her babies are little, the time is more than filled with busyness—wheeling the carriage back and forth in the park, sitting on the playground bench because the children can't play outside alone. . . .

It is not surprising, then, that many young wives vote for a move to the suburbs as soon as possible. Like the empty plains of Kansas that tempted the restless immigrant, the suburbs in their very newness and lack of structured service, offered, at least at first, a limitless challenge to the energy of educated American women. The women who were strong enough, independent enough, seized the opportunity and were leaders and innovators in these new communities. But, in most cases, these were women educated before the era of feminine fulfillment. The ability of suburban life to fulfill, or truly use the potential of the able, educated American woman seems to depend on her own previous autonomy or self-realization—that is, on her strength to resist the pressures to conform, resist the time-filling busywork of suburban house and community, and find, or make, the same kind of serious commitment outside the home that she would have made in the city. Such a commitment in the suburbs, in the beginning at least, was likely to be on a volunteer basis, but it was challenging, and necessary.

When the mystique took over, however, a new breed of women came to the suburbs. They were looking for sanctuary; they were perfectly willing to accept the suburban community as they found it (their only problem was "how to fit in"); they were perfectly willing to fill their days with the trivia of housewifery. Women of this kind, and most of those that I interviewed were of the post-1950 college generation, refuse to take policy-making positions in community organizations; they will only collect for Red Cross or March of Dimes or Scouts or be den mothers or take the lesser PTA jobs. Their resistance to serious community responsibility is usually explained by "I can't take the time from my family." But much of their time is spent in meaningless busywork. The kind of community work they choose does not challenge their intelligence—or even, sometimes, fill a real function. Nor do they derive much personal satisfaction from it—but it does fill time.

So, increasingly, in the new bedroom suburbs, the really interesting volunteer jobs—the leadership of the cooperative nurseries, the free libraries, the school board posts, the selectmen-ships and, in some suburbs, even the PTA presidencies—are filled by men. The housewife who doesn't "have time" to take serious responsibility in the community, like the woman who doesn't "have time" to pursue a professional career, evades a serious commitment through which she might finally realize herself; she evades it by stepping up her domestic routine until she is truly trapped.

The dimensions of the trap seem physically unalterable, as the busyness that fills the housewife's day seems inescapably necessary. But is that domestic trap an illusion, despite its all-too-solid reality, an illusion created by the feminine mystique? Take, for instance, the open plan of the contemporary "ranch" or split-level house, $14,990 to $54,990, which has been built in the millions from Roslyn Heights to the Pacific Palisades. They give the illusion of more space for less money. But the women to whom they are sold almost *have* to live the feminine mystique. There are no true walls or doors; the woman in the beautiful electronic kitchen is never separated from her children. She need never feel alone for a minute, need never be by herself. She can forget her own identity in those noisy open-plan houses. The open plan also helps expand the housework to fill the time available. In what is basically one free-flowing room, instead of many rooms separated by walls and stairs, continual messes continually need picking up. A man, of course, leaves the house for most of the day. But the feminine mystique forbids the woman this.

A friend of mine, an able writer turned full-time housewife, had her suburban dream house designed by an architect to her own specifications, during the period when she defined herself as housewife and no longer wrote. The house, which cost approximately $50,000, was almost literally one big kitchen. There was a separate studio for her husband, who was a photographer, and cubbyholes for sleeping, but there wasn't any place where she could get out of the kitchen, away from her children, during the working hours. The gorgeous mahogany and stainless steel of her custom-built kitchen cabinets and electric appliances were indeed a dream, but when I saw that house, I wondered where, if she ever wanted to write again, she would put her typewriter.

It's strange how few places there are in those spacious houses and those sprawling suburbs where you can go to be alone. A sociologist's study of upper-income suburban wives who married young and woke, after fifteen years of child-living, PTA, do-it-yourself, garden-and-barbecue, to the realization that they wanted to do some real work themselves, found that the ones who did something about this often moved back to the city. But among the women I talked to, this moment of personal truth was more likely to be marked by adding a room with a door to their open-plan house, or simply by putting a door on one room in the house, "so I can have someplace to myself, just a door to shut between me and the children when I want to think"—or work, study, be alone.

85

DAVID GUTERSON, EXCERPT FROM
"NO PLACE LIKE HOME," 1992

Like a pith-helmeted anthropologist, writer David Guterson has taken a journey to the latest—one hesitates to say final—suburban frontier: the "master-planned community." In Green Valley, Nevada, which is neither green nor a valley, Guterson reports on life in these new suburbs, dictated to a remarkable degree by the corporations that develop and run them. Responding to a belief that older suburbs have failed to protect their residents from the "problems" they sought to escape—read: crime, race, drugs, and the like—these new communities have left nothing to chance in their effort to maintain property values and guarantee safety. Indeed, for the residents Guterson interviews, "community" has become synonymous with "safety," and paranoia seems to have driven them to this place. While Guterson's observations are sharp and his writing caustic, he also points out that in a society increasingly driven by fear and a desire for security, these places are hugely popular; millions of Americans now live in such planned places behind security walls and more move there every day.

To the casual eye, Green Valley, Nevada, a corporate master-planned community just south of Las Vegas, would appear to be a pleasant place to live. On a Sunday last April—a week before the riots in Los Angeles and related disturbances in Las Vegas—the golf carts were lined up three abreast at the upscale "Legacy" course; people in golf outfits on the clubhouse veranda were eating three-cheese omelets and strawberry waffles and looking out over the palm trees and fairways, talking business and reading Sunday newspapers. . . .

Green Valley is as much a verb as a noun, a place in the process of becoming what it purports to be. Everywhere on the fringes of its 8,400 acres one finds homes going up, developments going in (another twenty-one developments are under way), the desert in the throes of being transformed in accordance with the master plan of Green Valley's designer and builder, the American Nevada Corporation. The colors of its homes are muted in the Southwest manner: beiges, tans, dun browns, burnt reds, olive grays, rusts, and cinnamons. Its graceful, palm-lined boulevards and parkways are conspicuously devoid of gas stations, convenience stores, and fast-food restaurants, presenting instead a seamless facade of interminable, well-manicured developments punctuated only by golf courses and an occasional shopping plaza done in stucco. Within the high walls lining Green Valley's expansive parkways lie homes so similar they appear as uncanny mirror reflections of one another—and, as it turns out, they are. In most neighborhoods a prospective home owner must choose from among a limited set of models with names like "Greenbriar," "Innisbrook," and "Tammaron" (or, absurdly, in a development called Heartland, "Beginnings," " Memories," and "Reflections"), each of which is merely a variation on a theme: Spanish, Moorish, Mexican, Territorial, Mediterranean, Italian Country, Mission. Each development inhabits a planned socio-economic niche— $99,000, $113,900, $260,000 homes, and on into the stratosphere for custom models if a wealthy buyer desires. Neighborhoods are labyrinthine, confusing in their sameness; each block looks eerily like the next. On a spring evening after eight o'clock it is possible to drive through miles of them without seeing a single human being. Corners are marked with signs a visitor finds more than a little disconcerting: WARNING, they read, NEIGHBORHOOD WATCH PROGRAM IN FORCE. WE IMMEDIATELY REPORT ALL SUSPICIOUS PERSONS AND ACTIVITIES TO OUR POLICE DEPARTMENT. The signs on garages don't make me feel any better. WARNING, they read, YOUR NEIGHBORS ARE WATCHING.

I'd come to Green Valley because I was curious to meet the citizens of a community in which everything is designed, orchestrated, and executed by a corporation. More and more Americans, millions of them—singles, families, retirees—are living in such places.

That Sunday afternoon I made my way along peaceful boulevards to Green Valley's civic center, presumably a place where people congregate. A promotional brochure describes its plaza as "the perfect size for public gatherings and all types of social events," but on that balmy day, the desert in bloom just a few miles off, no one had, in fact, gathered here. The plaza had the desultory ambience of an architectural mistake—deserted, useless, and irrelevant to Green Valley's citizens, who had, however, gathered in large numbers at stucco shopping centers not far off—at Spotlight Video, Wallpaper World, Record City, and Bicycle Depot, Rapunzel's Den Hair Salon, Enzo's Pizza and Ristorante, A Basket of Joy, and K-Mart. . . .

Inside the civic center were plenty of potted palms, walls of black glass, and red marble floors, but again, no congregating citizens. Instead, I found the offices of the Americana Group Realtors; Lawyer's Title of Nevada, Inc.; RANPAC Engineering Corporation; and Coleman Homes, a developer. A few real estate agents were gearing up for Sunday home tours, dressed to kill and shuffling manila folders, their BMWs parked outside. Kirk Warren, a marketing specialist with the Americana Group, listened patiently to my explanation: I came to the civic center to talk to people; I wanted to know what brought them to a corporate-planned community and why they decided to stay.

"It's safe here," Warren explained, handing me a business card with his photograph on it. "And clean. And nice. The schools are good and the crime rate low. It's what buyers are looking for."

Outside the building, in the forlorn-looking plaza, six concrete benches had been fixed astride lawns, offering citizens twenty-four seats. Teenagers had scrawled their graffiti on the pavement (DARREN WAS HERE, JASON IS AWESOME), and a footlight beneath a miniature obelisk had been smashed by someone devoted to its destruction. Someone had recently driven past on a motorcycle, leaving tell-tale skid marks.

The history of suburbia is a history of gradual dysfunction, says Brian Greenspun, whose family owns the American Nevada Corporation (ANC), the entity that created Green Valley. Americans, he explains, moved to the suburbs in search of escape from the more undesirable aspects of the city and from undesirable people in particular. Time passed and undesirables showed up anyway; suburbia had no means to prevent this. But in the end, that was all right, Greenspun points out, because master planners recognized the problem as an enormously lucrative market opportunity and began building places like Green Valley. . . . Thirty-four thousand people have filled Green Valley's homes in a mere fourteen years—the place is literally a boomtown.

They have come from Los Angeles, Milwaukee, and New Haven, riding Las Vegas's boom economy—100,000 new jobs in the past four years—but fearful of Vegas's storied sins. . . . Las Vegas is the fourth-fastest-growing metropolitan area in the country and the fastest–growing outside of Florida, and housing starts far outpace the national average. Yet while the city has worked hard to shed its tawdry image, successfully attracting respectable businesses, it still has gangs, a ghetto, and gambling, not to mention cocaine and legal prostitution: it's no place for an accountant to wash the car or raise kids. Real estate agents peddle Green Valley as a place for families, a community where people have returned to basic values—flagrant code phrases offering escape from the fear and threat not only of high rolling Vegas but of modern life in general. . . . [By] 2005, . . . Green Valley's population is expected to double to more than 60,000 residents—larger than the current population of Nevada's 134-year-old capital, Carson City.

Such growth may seem rather odd in a locale whose central fact of existence is barren desert. Green Valley is neither green nor a valley—it's brown and flat. Its stark dry washes lie strewn with sun-faded Budweiser cans, bits of tattered black construction tarp, and leftover concrete hardened into lumps in the desert sand. Green Valley's water flows from the Hoover Dam, twenty miles to the southeast, through ditches, canals, and aqueducts. Like most of the rest of the American West, Green Valley is a desert remade in the image of a garden, a temporary Eden, a mirage. . . .

The characteristic Green Valley family—a married couple with two children under twelve—has an average annual income of $55,000; about one in five are members of the Green Valley Athletic Club, described by master planners as "the focal point of the community" (family initiation fee: $1,000). . . .

In the weight room, I met a man I'll call Phil Anderson, an accountant, who introduced me to his wife, Marie, and to his children, Jason and Sarah. Phil was ruddy, overweight, and sweat-soaked, and had a towel draped over his shoulders. Marie was trim, dressed for tennis; the kids looked bored. Phil had been playing racquetball that evening while Marie took lessons to improve her serve and the children watched television in the kids' lounge. Like most of the people I met in Green Valley, the Andersons were reluctant to have their real names used ("We don't want the reaction," was how some residents explained it, including Marie and Phil). I coaxed them by promising to protect their true identities, and the Andersons began to chat.

"We moved here because Jase was getting on toward junior high age," Marie explained between sets on a machine designed to strengthen her triceps. "And in San Diego, where we lived before, there were these . . . *forces,* if you know what I mean. There were too many things we couldn't control. Drugs and stuff. It wasn't healthy for our kids."

"I had a job offer," Phil said. "We looked for a house. Green Valley was . . . the obvious place—just sort of obvious, really. Our real estate agent sized us up and brought us out here right away."

"We found a house in Silver Springs," Marie said. "You can go ahead and put that in your notes. It's a big development. No one will figure it out."

"But just don't use our names, okay?" Phil pleaded. "I would really appreciate that."

"We don't need problems." Marie added. . . .

Walls are everywhere in Green Valley too; they're the first thing a visitor notices. Their message is subliminal and at the same time explicit; controlled access is as much metaphor as reality. Controlled access is also a two-way affair—both "ingress" and "egress" are influenced by it; both coming and going are made difficult. The gates at the thresholds of Green Valley's posher neighborhoods open with a macabre, mechanical slowness; their guards speak firmly and authoritatively to strangers and never smile in the manner of official greeters. One of them told me to take no pictures and to go directly to my destination "without stopping to look at anything." Another said that in an eight-hour shift he felt constantly nervous about going to the bathroom and feared that in abandoning his post to relieve himself he risked losing his job. A girl at the Taco Bell on nearby Sunset Road complained about Clark County's ten o'clock teen curfew—and about the guard at her neighborhood's gate who felt it was his duty to remind her of it. A ten-year-old pointed out that his friends beyond the wall couldn't join him inside without a telephone call to "security," which meant "the policeman in the guardhouse." Security, of course, can be achieved in many ways, but one implication of it, every time, is that security has insidious psychological consequences for those who contrive to feel secure. . . .

All of Green Valley is defined in this manner, by CC&Rs, as the planners call them—covenants, conditions, and restrictions embedded in deeds. Every community has some restrictions on matters such as the proper placement of septic tanks and the minimum distance allowed between homes, but in Green Valley the restrictions are detailed and pervasive, insuring the absence of individuality and suppressing the natural mess of humanity. Clotheslines and Winnebagos are not permitted, for example; no fowl, reptile, fish, or insect may be raised; there are to be no exterior speakers, horns, whistles, or bells. No debris of any kind, no open fires, no noise. Entries, signs, lights, mailboxes, sidewalks, driveways, rear yards, side yards, carports, sheds—the planners have had their say about each. All CC&Rs are inscribed into books of law that vary only slightly from development to development: the number of dogs and cats you can own (until recently, one master-planned community in Newport Beach, California, even limited the *weight* of dogs) as well as the placement of garbage cans, barbecue pits, satellite dishes, and utility boxes. The color of your home, the number of stories, the materials used, its accents and trim. The interior of your garage, the way to park your truck, the plants in your yard, the angle of your flagpole, the size of your address numbers, the placement of mirrored glass balls and birdbaths, the grade of your lawn's slope, and the size of your FOR SALE sign should you decide you want to leave.

"These things," explained Brad Nelson, an ANC vice president, "are set up to protect property values." ANC owner Greenspun put it another way: "The public interest and ANC's interest are one." . . .

Green Valley is as intricate and hierarchical as feudal England, an 8400-acre kingdom governed by investiture and vassalage and marked by class distinctions. It is composed on paper of five contiguous "villages," with names like "Silver Springs" and "Valley Verde," each designed to have a "village center"—a park, a school, a recreation center. (ANC often advertises its generosity in deeding tracts of desert for these public facilities. Less well advertised is its legal obligation to do so as part of its 1971 agreement with Henderson.) Each "village" contains six to ten developments. The position of each in the pecking order of wealth is best symbolized by the relative ostentation of its entryway—the flamboyance of the sign announcing its name, the demeanor of its guard, the height of its gates, the splendor of the lawns or fountains visible through the portal between its walls.

Development names either strive for the ambience of European luxury—Renaissance, Steeplechase, La Mancha II, Champions Green—or seek to deny the desert's reality—The Fountains, Creekside, Crystal Creek, Bay Breeze. . . .

ANC is not only your neighbor but also a munificent builder of public places—library, recreation center, tennis courts, trails ("the cost of doing business," a master planner explained)—and a medieval-style government that makes vassals out of developers and ministers out of zealous homeowners. Mostly it is blunt about its august powers: in numerous developments and in the only villages that have them, ANC *is* the homeowners' association; the corporation's owners—the Greenspun family—also own Green Valley's only bookstore, cable-television company, and newspaper (the last jointly with Mike O'Callaghan, a former governor of Nevada). Like other master planners elsewhere in the country, ANC shrewdly established a nonprofit community association designed on paper to represent residents' interests but without any political or decision-making power; instead, it offers recommendations and suggestions to city and county officials. ANC patronizes the community association and assists its board members in formulating positions on such matters as the placement of a proposed beltway—about which, incidentally, the corporation and the association concur. They also concur on the need for political redistricting so that at least half the members of the Henderson City Council (Green Valley falls within the boundaries of Henderson) can be drawn from Green Valley neighborhoods.

The irony is that few residents give a damn about corporations or politics. Of the 34,000 people living in Green Valley only some 370 are paid members of the community association that is pitched to them as representing their interest to officialdom; 125 voted in the last board election. The numbers don't represent a boycott, either, of a corporately concocted grass-roots group of well-intended pawns. As I wandered I took an ongoing straw poll that revealed this truth: 99 percent of Green Valley's citizens are glad to live in a planned community. . . .

Most had only a vague awareness of the existence of a corporate master plan for every detail of their community. The covenants, conditions, and restrictions of their lives were background matters of which they were cognizant but about which they were yawningly unconcerned. It did not seem strange to anyone I spoke with that a corporation should have final say about their mailboxes. When I explained that there were CC&Rs for nearly everything, most people merely shrugged and pointed out in return that it seemed a great way to protect property values. A woman in a grocery store checkout line explained that she'd come here from southern California because "even the good neighborhoods there aren't good anymore. You don't feel safe in L.A."

What the people of Green Valley want, explained a planner, is safety from threats both real and imagined and control over who moves in beside them. In this they are no different from the generation that preceded them in search of the suburban dream. The difference this time is that nothing has been left to chance and that everything has been left to the American Nevada Corporation, which gives Green Valley its contemporary twist: to achieve at least the illusion of safety, residents must buy in to an enormous measure of corporate domination. Suburbia in the Nineties has a logo.

But even Eden—planned by God—had serpents, and so, apparently, does Green Valley. Last year a rapist ran loose in its neighborhoods; police suspected the man was a resident and responsible for three rapes and five robberies. George Hennard, killer of twenty-three people in a Killeen, Texas, cafeteria in October 1991, was a resident of Green Valley only months before his rampage and bought two of his murder weapons here in a private transaction. Joseph Weldon Smith, featured on the television series *Unsolved Mysteries,* strangled to death his wife and two stepdaughters in a posh Green Valley development called The Fountains.

The list of utopia's outrages also includes a November 1991 heist in which two armed robbers took a hand-cuffed hostage and more than $100,000 from a Green Valley bank, then fled and fired military-assault-rifle rounds at officers in hot pursuit. The same week police arrested a suspected child molester who had been playing football with Green Valley children and allegedly touching their genitals.

"You can run but you can't hide," one Green Valley resident told me when I mentioned a few of these incidents. "People are coming here from all over the place and bringing their problems with them." Perhaps she was referring to the gangs frequenting a Sunset Road fast-food restaurant—Sunset Road forms one fringe of Green Valley—where in the summer of 1991, according to the restaurant's manager, "the dining room was set on fire and there were fights every weekend." Perhaps she had talked to the teenagers who told me that LSD and crystal meth are the narcotics of choice at Green Valley High School, or to the doctor who simply rolled his eyes when I asked if he thought AIDS had arrived here.

Walls might separate paradise from heavy industry, but the protection they provide is an illusion. In May 1991 a leak at the nearby Pioneer Chlor Al-kali plant spread a blanket of chlorine gas over Green Valley; nearly a hundred area residents were treated at hospitals for respiratory problems. The leak came three years after another nearby plant—this one producing rocket-fuel oxidizer for the space shuttle and nuclear missiles— exploded powerfully enough to register on earthquake seismographs 200 miles away. Two people were killed, 210 injured. Schools were closed and extra police officers called in to discourage the looting of area homes with doors and windows blown out.

And, finally, there is black comedy in utopia: a few days after Christmas last year, police arrested the Green Valley Community Association president for allegedly burglarizing a model home. Stolen items included pictures, cushions, bedspreads, and a gaudy brass figurine—a collection with no internal logic. A local newspaper described the civic leader running from the scene, dropping his loot piece by piece in his wake as he was chased by police to his residence. At home he hid temporarily in his attic but ultimately to no avail. The plaster cracked and he fell through a panel into the midst of the arresting officers. . . .

Some might call Green Valley a simulacrum of a real place, Disneyland's Main Street done in Mediterranean hues, a city of haciendas with cardboard souls, a valley of the polished, packaged, and perfected, an empyrean of emptiness, a sanitized wasteland. They will note the Southwest's pastel palette coloring a community devoid of improvisation, of caprice, spontaneity, effusiveness, or the charm of error—a place where the process of commodification has at last leached life of the accidental and ecstatic, the divine, reckless, and enraged.

Still, many now reside in this corporate domain, driven here by insatiable fears. No class warfare here, no burning city. Green Valley beckons the American middle class like a fabulous and eternal dream. In the wake of our contemporary trembling and discontent, its pilgrims have sought out a corporate castle where in exchange for false security they pay with personal freedoms; where the corporation that does the job of walling others out also walls residents in. The principle, once political, is now economic. Just call your real estate agent.

86

JAMES HOWARD KUNSTLER, EXCERPT FROM "HOME FROM NOWHERE," 1996

James Howard Kunstler has become the standard bearer of the New Urbanism movement that has flourished in the past two decades. Dedicated to developing a new approach to city design based on older models of town planning, the New Urbanists have built a series of new communities, from Seaside in Florida to Kentlands outside of Washington, D.C. Kunstler's first book on the subject—*The Geography of Nowhere* (1994)— detailed the landscape of the late-twentieth-century American city, a place of identical

Originally printed in *Atlantic Monthly*, September 1996. By permission of the author.

6.6. Seaside, Florida, constructed view from the Leon Krier house. Courtesy of Iguana Photo, www.iguanaphoto.com. The vacation community of Seaside, in Florida's panhandle, became the testing ground for the New Urbanism, a set of ideas for rebuilding cities proposed by architects Elizabeth Plater-Zyberk and Andres Duany in the early 1980s. Against both the suburban developments of Levittown and the massive towers and plazas of 1950s urbanism, New Urbanists called for small homes built in local vernacular styles, less dependence on the automobile, greater density, and a mixture of uses woven into the fabric of the community. While some, like James Howard Kunstler, suggest that the New Urbanists have created a revolution in the way we build cities, others argue that the movement has created nothing more than the latest fashion in suburban speculation.

shopping malls and suburban tract housing, created by planners and developers who prostrated themselves before the automobile while ignoring the qualities that made for lively and liveable neighborhoods. In this essay (the basis for a book with the same title), Kunstler lays out the central ideas of the New Urbanist movement: new approaches to zoning that encourages mixed uses and density; an emphasis on walking and other (nonautomobile) forms of transportation, and a dedication to making civic buildings and public places truly public and truly used.

AMERICANS sense that something is wrong with the places where we live and work and go about our daily business. We hear this unhappiness expressed in phrases like "no sense of place" and "the loss of community." We drive up and down the gruesome, tragic suburban boulevards of commerce, and we're overwhelmed at the fantastic, awesome, stupefying ugliness of absolutely everything in sight—the fry pits, the big-box stores, the office units, the lube joints, the carpet warehouses, the parking lagoons, the jive plastic townhouse clusters, the uproar of signs, the highway itself clogged with cars—as though the whole thing had been designed by some diabolical force bent on making human beings miserable. And naturally, this experience can make us feel glum about the nature and future of our civilization.

When we drive around and look at all this cartoon architecture and other junk that we've smeared all over the landscape, we register it as ugliness. This ugliness is the surface expression of deeper problems—problems that relate to the issue of our national character. The highway strip is not just a sequence of eyesores. The pattern it represents is also economically catastrophic, an environmental calamity, socially devastating, and spiritually degrading. . . .

THE NEW URBANISM

The principles apply equally to villages, towns, and cities. Most of them apply even to places of extraordinarily high density, like Manhattan, with added provisions that I will not go into here, in part because special cases like Manhattan are so rare, and in part because I believe that the scale of even our greatest cities will necessarily have to become smaller in the future, at no loss to their dynamism (London and Paris are plenty dynamic, with few buildings over ten stories high).

The pattern under discussion here has been called variously neo-traditional planning, traditional neighborhood development, low-density urbanism, transit-oriented development, the new urbanism, and just plain civic art. Its principles produce settings that resemble American towns from prior to the Second World War.

1. The basic unit of planning is the neighborhood. A neighborhood standing alone is a hamlet or village. A cluster of neighborhoods become a town. Clusters of a great many neighborhoods become a city. The population of a neighborhood can vary depending on local conditions.
2. The neighborhood is limited in physical size, with well-defined edges and a focused center. The size of a neighborhood is defined as a five-minute walking distance (or a quarter mile) from the edge to the center and a ten-minute walk edge to edge. Human scale is the standard for proportions in buildings and their accessories. Automobiles and other wheeled vehicles are permitted, but they do not take precedence over human needs, including aesthetic needs. The neighborhood contains a public-transit stop.
3. The secondary units of planning are corridors and districts. Corridors form the boundaries between neighborhoods, both connecting and defining them. Corridors can incorporate natural features like streams and canyons. They can take the form of parks, nature preserves, travel corridors, railroad lines, or some combination of these. In towns and cities a neighborhood or parts of neighborhoods can compose a district. Districts are made up of streets or ensembles of streets where special activities get preferential treatment. The French Quarter of New Orleans is an example of a district. It is a whole neighborhood dedicated to entertainment, in which housing, shops, and offices are also integral. A corridor can also be a district—for instance, a major shopping avenue between adjoining neighborhoods.
4. The neighborhood is emphatically mixed-use and provides housing for people with different incomes. Buildings may be various in function but must be

compatible with one another in size and in their relation to the street. The needs of daily life are accessible within the five-minute walk. Commerce is integrated with residential, business, and even manufacturing use, though not necessarily on the same street in a given neighborhood. Apartments are permitted over stores. Forms of housing are mixed, including apartments, duplex in single-family houses, accessory apartments, and outbuildings. (Over time streets will inevitably evolve to become less or more desirable. But attempts to preserve property values by mandating minimum-square footage requirements, outlawing rental apartments, or formulating other strategies to exclude lower-income residents must be avoided. Even the best streets in the world's best towns can accommodate people of various incomes.)

5. Buildings are disciplined on their lots in order to define public space successfully. The street is understood to be the pre-eminent form of public space, and the buildings that define it are expected to honor and embellish it.

6. The street pattern is conceived as a network in order to create the greatest number of alternative routes from one part of the neighborhood to another. This has the beneficial effect of relieving traffic congestion. The network may be a grid. Networks based on a grid must be modified by parks, squares, diagonals, T intersections, rotaries, and other devices that relieve the grid's tendency to monotonous regularity. The streets exist in a hierarchy from broad boulevards to narrow lanes and alleys. In a town or a city limited-access highways may exist only within a corridor, preferably in the form of parkways. Cul-de-sacs are strongly discouraged except under extraordinary circumstances—for example, where rugged topography requires them.

7. Civic buildings, such as town halls, churches, schools, libraries, and museums, are placed on preferential building sites, such as the frontage of squares, in neighborhood centers, and where street vistas terminate, in order to serve as landmarks and reinforce their symbolic importance. Buildings define parks and squares, which are distributed throughout the neighborhood and appropriately designed for recreation, repose, periodic commercial uses, and special events such as political meetings, concerts, theatricals, exhibitions, and fairs. Because streets will differ in importance, scale, and quality, what is appropriate for a part of town with small houses may not be appropriate as the town's main shopping street. These distinctions are properly expressed by physical design.

8. In the absence of a consensus about the appropriate decoration of buildings, an architectural code may be devised to establish some fundamental unities of massing, fenestration, materials, and roof pitch, within which many variations may function harmoniously.

Under the regime of zoning and the professional overspecialization that it fostered, all streets were made as wide as possible because the specialist in charge—the traffic engineer—was concerned solely with the movement of cars and trucks. In the process much of the traditional decor that made streets pleasant for people was gotten rid of. For instance, street trees were eliminated. Orderly rows of mature trees can improve even the most dismal street by softening hard edges and sunblasted bleakness. Under postwar engineering standards street trees were deemed a hazard to motorists and chopped down in many American towns. . . .

Human settlements are like living organisms. They must grow, and they will change. But we can decide on the nature of that growth—on the quality and the character of it—and where it ought to go. We don't have to scatter the building blocks of our civic life all over the countryside, destroying our towns and ruining farmland. We can put the shopping and the offices and the movie theaters and the library all within walking distance of one another. And we can live within walking distance of all these things. We can build our schools close to where the children live, and the school buildings don't have to look like fertilizer plants. We can insist that commercial buildings be more than one story high, and allow people to live in decent apartments over the stores. We can build Main Street and Elm Street and still park our cars. It is within our power to create places that are worthy of our affection.

7.1a. Eastern State Penitentiary, Philadelphia, Pennsylvania. "General View, from Southeast, Corner of Corinthian and Fairmont Avenues, HABS, PA, 51-PHILA, 354-1," Historical American Buildings Survey, Prints and Photograph Division, Library of Congress.

CHAPTER 7

Better Buildings, Better People: Architecture and Social Reform

Perhaps more than in any other Western nation, Americans have tried to solve their social problems through architecture. The pervasiveness of the reforming instinct—the belief that the design of homes, institutions, and entire cities should be consciously directed toward influencing behavior—makes the American case special. Long after the ideals that animated the waves of reform efforts that sweep the country every few decades have fallen from favor, the nation's built environment remains littered with the physical remains of efforts to literally build reforming ideals in brick, stone, and steel.

This chapter surveys Americans approaches and responses to the problem of reforming people and societies through architecture. In the nineteenth century, environmental factors replaced essentialist and theological ones as explanations for human behavior, both good and bad. People were born neither intrinsically good nor bad, but wound up that way as a consequence of their surroundings. As a result, many Americans became what we might call "architectural determinists," believing that the shapes, layouts, and designs of buildings could have a profound impact on the moral character of the people who lived and worked in them. Schools properly designed would produce better students; properly built homes would lead to proper family life and better citizens; prisons built according to the right principles would reform criminals.

Underlying these reform movements were conflicted notions about the developing industrial, capitalist society. On one hand, reformers hoped to give poor people the necessary physical surroundings and tools that would enable them to reach middle-class ideals of home and education. On the other hand, the values of a growing market economy rejected government intervention in the economy and looked askance at rewarding those who, in their view, had failed to succeed through hard work. Thus the tenement-dwellers who came to be the symbol of the needy in the late nineteenth century were to be given help, but never enough to raise them out of poverty. For too much aid would encourage dependency and undermine the efforts of the "deserving" poor. The notion of the deserving and the "undeserving" poor powerfully shaped how these reform movements pursued their aims. While reformers sought to transform homes and replan entire cities in order to uplift the poor, they always tempered their efforts, lest they encourage dependence and interfere with the market.

In the nineteenth century, most of these efforts were undertaken by private, often religious, organizations. The Second Great Awakening, an evangelical revival among Protestant denominations of the 1820s and 1830s, spawned a series of movements to redesign the American home, create public schools and libraries, and beautify cities. Toward the end of the nineteenth century, amid the growing distance between wealth and poverty and amid growing strife between capital and labor, it was the Social Gospel movement—a theological argument for Protestant ministers to become actively involved in improving the material reality of all Americans—which spawned the settlement house movement of Jane

Addams and others, the YMCA, and the Women's Temperance Union. That so many of these movements were led and staffed by women was no accident: as Catherine Beecher and others argued, it was women's role to uplift the nation's morals.

The example of prisons illuminates the complexity of the reforming problem during the nineteenth century. The Charles Street Jail in Boston and the Eastern State Penitentiary in Philadelphia were two of the most influential and controversial prison structures in the United States in the nineteenth century. Today both stand empty, closed in the last two decades, and waiting for uncertain futures. At Eastern State Penitentiary (1829), which pioneered what became known as the "Pennsylvania Plan," the building's form—a revolutionary design utilizing a central panopticon rotunda with radiating spokes of individual prison cells—was a physical embodiment of an attitude toward the nature of crime and human behavior. The designers of Eastern State believed that if the prisoners were placed in solitary confinement and forced to confront their crime alone, seek Christian forgiveness, and learn more productive ways of conducting themselves, they might successfully be reintroduced into society. Maximum sentences, therefore, were no more than ten years. John Haviland, whose numerous public buildings in Philadelphia and beyond (especially the "Tombs" Prison in New York City) had brought him great reknown, created an imposing, gothic structure with thirty-foot walls and a massive guard tower. Even as the tower at the center of the radial plan symbolized the watchful eye of the state, the dark entrance building to the prison spoke to citizens on the outside. At Eastern State Penitentiary, reform became almost completely an architectural problem.

Many, however, were suspicious of Eastern State's solution: They saw complete solitary confinement and constant observation as dehumanizing. Even as the first prisoners moved into prison in 1836, there were calls for abandoning the solitary system, which appeared to inspire fury and insanity, and not peace and "penitence." Charles Dickens, on his travels through the United States in 1842, visited Eastern State, which had become one of the country's most popular tourist destinations. He called the system utilized at Eastern State "cruel and wrong." The "Auburn Plan," named after the Auburn, New York, prison structure built in 1820, rejected the notion of strict solitary confinement. Instead, it emphasized silence during days spent working with other inmates, and solitary confinement at night. But, if the agony of Eastern State was to be in the utter lack of human interaction (never fully adhered to as historic photographs show), the Auburn Plan prisons' agony lay in the rigid discipline and corporal punishment employed to break the spirit of hardened criminals.

While Eastern State Penitentiary remains a powerful symbol of nineteenth-century prison design, it is the Charles Street Jail that proved to be the most influential model for prisons in the later nineteenth century and into the twentieth century. Prisons throughout the United States—including H. H. Richardson's Allegheny County Courthouse, a prison complex in Pittsburgh—have followed the outline established in the Charles Street Jail—two or three rows of prison cells fronting onto common space for meals and other activities. Indeed, the breadth of Charles Street's influence is so great that it is rarely remembered as the inspiration for much of our prison architecture.

The religiously inspired moralism of nineteenth-century architects and city builders was evident in a host of other building projects that were, in part, intended to transform, uplift, and improve. Frederick Law Olmsted's parks were in large measure about improving poor people and reforming the interaction between the classes. Nineteenth-century suburbs were predicated on powerful ideas of how the confluence of nature and "country living" would uplift former city-dwellers.

In the twentieth century, the religious roots of this reforming instinct became less overt, but the belief that physical design would promote better citizens and communities persisted. Indeed, one of the greatest outpourings of social reform, the "Progressive Era" of the last decade of the nineteenth century and the first two decades of the twentieth century, was anchored in an environmentalism that assumed a range of forms, including regulating and demolishing slums, building parks and planting trees, devising Beaux Arts city plans, and protecting historic buildings. All were efforts to build one aspect of the Progressive vision, what historian Daniel Rodgers has called the "language of social bonds"—the rhetoric that all parts of society were bound together—into the landscape of the city, and thereby into the minds of its inhabitants, especially those with new and tenuous ties to the United States.

At the cusp of the century reformers like Jacob Riis and Jane Addams began by pursuing private solutions to the problems of the tenements but quickly began to realize that ultimately the government was the only institution powerful enough to achieve the transformations for which they worked. On the national level, Theodore Roosevelt quickly recognized that only the federal government could reign in the massive corporations, regulate working conditions, and protect America's natural landscape. Progressive era reforms have left everything from schools to settlement houses to national parks and forest on the American landscapes.

The culmination of this "age of reform" came with the New Deal of the 1930s, when the federal government became the dominant force in physically transforming the American landscape to uplift and transform citizens. The New Deal also represented a sharp move away from the moralistic tone of reform movements. Reform through architecture became much more of a technocratic enterprise, undertaken by engineers and bureaucrats and dedicated to square footage requirements and tax incentives rather than saving American souls. The legacy on the land of the New Deal's reform efforts was profound: the creation of public housing complexes, new schools, and thousands of public buildings in the signature stripped-down classical style meant to convey permanence and the power of the federal government. While the New Deal produced only a partial welfare state, it also only minimally challenged the private sphere in the physical reforming of the built environment. Over the next several decades public housing, for example, became the housing of last resort for the poor while the private, single-family home because the model for the majority of the country.

Similarly, the urban renewal efforts of the 1950s and 1960s were designed to eliminate "blight" (a keyword of the era) from the midst of older cities. One result of this was the construction of huge public housing projects, designed as improvements over the "slums" that were being demolished at a remarkable rate. At the same time, these efforts to reform the physical fabric of the city also supported the development of suburbs and were crucial in making the automobile the dominant method of transportation and the centerpiece of the postwar economy. All this happened because of the pressure of the private real estate industry and the acquiescence of Congress. Thus, while it was federal government that would dominate the effort to build reform into the environment in the twentieth century, its goals were limited to supporting private capital and supporting services that were deemed unprofitable by the real estate industry.

The result was the creation of what one historian has called "the edifice complex": an obsession with massive highways, public housing, public buildings, replanning of cities at the expense of challenging racial segregation and economic inequality. In translating the welfare state and modern architecture from European countries to the American scene, government officials, under constant pressure from private capital, kept the building forms and eliminated their larger social purposes.

The legacy of the architecture dedicated to reform at the end of the twentieth century is largely one of failure. The United States stopped building public housing; it no longer pursued massive school construction projects or fueled the physical expansion of colleges and universities as it had done with the GI Bill. The only exception was the massive expansion in the number of prisons: they threatened to become the monuments of the age. Indeed, at the dawn of the new millennium, perhaps the greatest reform effort through architecture has taken the form of the wrecking ball. Public housing complexes in Chicago and Newark and Philadelphia have fallen, replaced in some cases by small-scale, single-family houses that have the virtue of not looking like "projects." In many cases, however, the goal was not to replace these failed buildings with new experiments but to leave the land vacant, ready for the investment of private capital. The market, it was argued, would be the greatest reformer of all.

87

CHARLES DICKENS, EXCERPT FROM *AMERICAN NOTES*, 1842

Eastern State Penitentiary, then on the outskirts of Philadelphia, was hardly an obvious stop on a visit to Philadelphia in the 1830s and 1840s. But it became one of the country's most popular destinations, because it was the first solitary confinement prison in the United States. Using a design based on the ideas of English philosopher Jeremy Bentham— in which a central guard station anchored radiating spokes of solitary cells, making each prisoner easily watched—Eastern State served as a model of what reformers hoped would change the course of crime and punishment. Criminals, watched over by reformers and forced to confront their crimes in silence and with nothing but their own prayers for solace, were expected to make a rapid transformation in their ways. But even as the first prisoners moved into Eastern State in 1836, there were calls for abandoning the solitary system which appeared to inspire fury and insanity, and not peace and "penitence." Charles Dickens, the British author, on his travels through the United States in 1842, called the system utilized at Eastern State "cruel and wrong."

In the outskirts, stands a great prison, called the Eastern Penitentiary: conducted on a plan peculiar to the state of Pennsylvania. The system here, is rigid, strict, and hopeless solitary confinement. I believe it, in its effects, to be cruel and wrong.

In its intention, I am well convinced that it is kind, humane, and meant for reformation; but I am persuaded that those who devised this system of Prison Discipline, and those benevolent gentlemen who carry it into execution, do not know what it is that they are doing. I believe that very few men are capable of estimating the immense amount of torture and agony which this dreadful punishment, prolonged for years, inflicts upon the sufferers; and in guessing at it myself, and in reasoning from what I have seen written upon their faces, and what to my certain knowledge they feel within, I am only the more convinced that there is a depth of terrible endurance in it which none but the sufferers themselves can fathom, and which no man has a right to inflict upon his fellow-creature. I hold this slow and daily tampering with the mysteries of the brain, to be immeasurably worse than any torture of the body: and because its ghastly signs and tokens are not so palpable to the eye and sense of touch as scars upon the flesh; because its wounds are not upon the surface, and it extorts few cries that human ears can hear; therefore I the more denounce it, as a secret punishment which slumbering humanity is not roused up to stay. I hesitated once, debating with myself, whether, if I had the power of saying 'Yes' or 'No,' I would allow it to be tried in certain cases, where the terms of imprisonment were short; but now, I solemnly declare, that with no rewards or honours could I walk a happy man beneath the open sky by day, or lie me down upon my bed at night, with the consciousness that one human creature, for any length of time, no matter what, lay suffering this unknown punishment in his silent cell, and I the cause, or I consenting to it in the least degree.

I was accompanied to this prison by two gentlemen officially connected with its management, and passed the day in going from cell to cell, and talking with the inmates. Every facility was afforded me, that the utmost courtesy could suggest. Nothing was concealed or hidden from my view, and every piece of information that I sought, was openly

Originally printed in Charles Dickens, *American Notes* (London: Chapman and Hall, 1842).

7.1b. Eastern State Penitentiary, Philadelphia, Pennsylvania, solitary cell, 1993. Courtesy of Iguana www.iguanaphoto.com. Prisons were built to punish. Penitentiaries were intended to reform the criminals they held so that they could return to be productive members of society. That was the Quaker theory behind the design of Eastern State Penitentiary in Philadelphia. On the outside, the building was meant to be imposing, to frighten potential criminals. Those forced to live inside were subject to a system of solitary confinement in the expectation that they could reflect on their crimes and on the state of their souls. Many, as it turned out, went insane instead. Criticism of the inhumanity of this system—such as that leveled by Charles Dickens—led quickly to the loosening of the rules of solitary confinement.

and frankly given. The perfect order of the building cannot be praised too highly, and of the excellent motives of all who are immediately concerned in the administration of the system, there can be no kind of question.

Between the body of the prison and the outer wall, there is a spacious garden. Entering it, by a wicket in the massive gate, we pursued the path before us to its other termination, and passed into a large chamber, from which seven long passages radiate. On either side of each, is a long, long row of low cell doors, with a certain number over every one. Above, a gallery of cells like those below, except that they have no narrow yard attached (as those in the ground tier have), and are somewhat smaller. The possession of two of these, is supposed to compensate for the absence of so much air and exercise as can be had in the dull strip attached to each of the others, in an hour's time every day; and therefore every prisoner in this upper story has two cells, adjoining and communicating with, each other.

Standing at the central point, and looking down these dreary passages, the dull repose and quiet that prevails, is awful. Occasionally, there is a drowsy sound from some lone weaver's shuttle, or shoemaker's last, but it is stifled by the thick walls and heavy dungeon-door, and only serves to make the general stillness more profound. Over the head and face of every prisoner who comes into this melancholy house, a black hood is drawn; and in this dark shroud, an emblem of the curtain dropped between him and the living world, he is led to the cell from which he never again comes forth, until his whole term of imprisonment has expired. He never hears of wife and children; home or friends; the life or death of any single creature. He sees the prison-officers, but with that exception he never looks upon a human countenance, or hears a human voice. He is a man buried alive; to be dug out in the slow round of years; and in the mean time dead to everything but torturing anxieties and horrible despair.

His name, and crime, and term of suffering, are unknown, even to the officer who delivers him his daily food. There is a number over his cell-door, and in a book of which the governor of the prison has one copy, and the moral instructor another: this is the index of his history. Beyond these pages the prison has no record of his existence: and though he live to be in the same cell ten weary years, he has no means of knowing, down to the very last hour, in which part of the building it is situated; what kind of men there are about him; whether in the long winter nights there are living people near, or he is in some lonely corner of the great jail, with walls, and passages, and iron doors between him and the nearest sharer in its solitary horrors.

Every cell has double doors: the outer one of sturdy oak, the other of grated iron, wherein there is a trap through which his food is handed. He has a Bible, and a slate and pencil, and, under certain restrictions, has sometimes other books, provided for the purpose, and pen and ink and paper. His razor, plate, and can, and basin, hang upon the wall, or shine upon the little shelf. Fresh water is laid on in every cell, and he can draw it at his pleasure. During the day, his bedstead turns up against the wall, and leaves more space for him to work in. His loom, or bench, or wheel, is there; and there he labours, sleeps and wakes, and counts the seasons as they change, and grows old.

The first man I saw, was seated at his loom, at work. He had been there six years, and was to remain, I think, three more. He had been convicted as a receiver of stolen goods, but even after his long imprisonment, denied his guilt, and said he had been hardly dealt by. It was his second offence.

He stopped his work when we went in, took off his spectacles, and answered freely to everything that was said to him, but always with a strange kind of pause first, and in a low, thoughtful voice. He wore a paper hat of his own making, and was pleased to have it noticed and commended. He had very ingeniously manufactured a sort of Dutch clock from some disregarded odds and ends; and his vinegar-bottle served for the pendulum. Seeing me interested in this contrivance, he looked up at it with a great deal of pride, and said that he had been thinking of improving it, and that he hoped the hammer and a little piece of broken glass beside it 'would play music before long.' He had extracted some colours from the yarn with which he worked, and painted a few poor figures on the wall. One, of a female, over the door, he called 'The Lady of the Lake.'

He smiled as I looked at these contrivances to while away the time; but when I looked from them to him, I saw that his lip trembled, and could have counted the beating of his heart. I forget how it came about, but some allusion was made to his having a wife. He shook his head at the word, turned aside, and covered his face with his hands.

'But you are resigned now!' said one of the gentlemen after a short pause, during which he had resumed his former manner. He answered with a sigh that seemed quite reckless in its hopelessness, 'Oh yes, oh yes! I am resigned to it.' 'And are a better man, you think?' 'Well, I hope so: I'm sure I hope I may be.' 'And time goes pretty quickly?' 'Time is very long gentlemen, within these four walls!'

He gazed about him—Heaven only knows how wearily!—as he said these words; and in the act of doing so, fell into a strange stare as if he had forgotten something. A moment afterwards he sighed heavily, put on his spectacles, and went about his work again. . . .

My firm conviction is that, independent of the mental anguish it occasions—an anguish so acute and so tremendous, that all imagination of it must fall far short of the reality—it wears the mind into a morbid state, which renders it unfit for the rough contact and busy action of the world. It is my fixed opinion that those who have undergone this punishment, MUST pass into society again morally unhealthy and diseased. There are many instances on record, of men who have chosen, or have been condemned, to lives of perfect solitude, but I scarcely remember one, even among sages of strong and vigorous intellect, where its effect has not become apparent, in some disordered train of thought, or some gloomy hallucination. What monstrous phantoms, bred of despondency and doubt, and born and reared in solitude, have stalked upon the earth, making creation ugly, and darkening the face of Heaven!

Suicides are rare among these prisoners: are almost, indeed, unknown. But no argument in favour of the system, can reasonably be deduced from this circumstance, although it is very often urged. All men who have made diseases of the mind their study, know perfectly well that such extreme depression and despair as will change the whole character, and beat down all its powers of elasticity and self-resistance, may be at work within a man, and yet stop short of self-destruction. This is a common case.

That it makes the senses dull, and by degrees impairs the bodily faculties, I am quite sure. I remarked to those who were with me in this very establishment at Philadelphia, that the criminals who had been there long, were deaf. They, who were in the habit of seeing these men constantly, were perfectly amazed at the idea, which they regarded as groundless and fanciful. And yet the very first prisoner to whom they appealed—one of their own selection confirmed my impression (which was unknown to him) instantly, and said, with a genuine air it was impossible to doubt, that he couldn't think how it happened, but he was growing very dull of hearing.

That it is a singularly unequal punishment, and affects the worst man least, there is no doubt. In its superior efficiency as a means of reformation, compared with that other code of regulations which allows the prisoners to work in company without communicating together, I have not the smallest faith. All the instances of reformation that were mentioned to me, were of a kind that might have been—and I have no doubt whatever, in my own mind, would have been—equally well brought about by the Silent System. With regard to such men as the negro burglar and the English thief, even the most enthusiastic have scarcely any hope of their conversion.

It seems to me that the objection that nothing wholesome or good has ever had its growth in such unnatural solitude, and that even a dog or any of the more intelligent among beasts, would pine, and mope, and rust away, beneath its influence, would be in itself a sufficient argument against this system. But when we recollect, in addition, how very cruel and severe it is, and that a solitary life is always liable to peculiar and distinct objections of a most deplorable nature, which have arisen here, and call to mind, moreover, that the choice is not between this system, and a bad or ill-considered one, but between it and another which has worked well, and is, in its whole design and practice, excellent; there is surely more than sufficient reason for abandoning a mode of punishment attended by so little hope or promise, and fraught, beyond dispute, with such a host of evils.

88

ANONYMOUS, EXCERPT FROM "THE SHAKERS AT LEBANON," 1851

This essay about the small and, to many, mysterious religious community of the Shakers illustrates a fundamental point about American architecture and reform: from its earliest years, the American republic was populated by a multitude of competing built ideas of how best to uplift and reform American citizens through architecture. The notion of receding from the mainstream to create separate utopian communities, architecturally defined (whether under the aegis of Shakerdom, Fourierism, or communitarianism), is a major element of the American way of building. For the Shakers, as this unsympathetic 1851 account reveals, architecture and religious action were inextricably intertwined. Visitors found the Shaker religion at minimum confusing; usually, they found it disturbing if not downright appalling. But they were impressed by the simplicity and efficiency of their architecture and how thoroughly consistent with their religious ideals was the material culture of the communities, from the round barn down to the now legendary simplicity of their furniture.

The first impression made by the Shakers as you enter their great hall at Lebanon, is that of a ghastly dance of death. The pallid, worn ghosts, in their bleached grave clothes, have taken up their grim orgies on earth, and with rigid muscles and cold lack-lustre eye are

Originally printed in *Literary World* 90, no. 241, (September 13, 1851): 201–2.

7.2. Hancock Shaker Village, Massachusetts. The Historic American Buildings Survey, 1968, Elmer Pearson. Founded in the eighteenth century, the religious sect known as the Shakers flourished in the nineteenth century in a set of settlements ranging from Maine and New Hampshire to Kentucky. They developed an architecture to embody their religious beliefs, including separate living spaces for men and women. Through their architecture—marked by spare, simple furniture, homes, and agricultural buildings—the Shakers hoped to live their religious ideals. They represent one of the earliest of a long string of separatist communities in the United States, for whom design was central to their mission.

performing their cramped revolutions. This certain feeling of terror is succeeded afterwards by disgust as the machinery is a little looked into. But to give our experiences as they occurred. It was a cool bright Sunday morning among the hills of the Taconic, as we rode across the Hancock mountain, from Pittsfield to the Shaker settlement of that name. Heavy summer rains on the previous day had refreshed the vegetation and hardened the usually excellent roads of the region. The cleanly shaved edges of the upland meadows, as they touched the woodland, gave token of the approach to the Hancock Village, for the Shakers are excellent farmers and their fields are nicely groomed. By neat fences and through avenues of shady road-side trees, you approach the variegated houses, red and yellow, rising many stories in height and not unpicturesquely gathered together at regular angles. There is the great circular stone barn, with the huge haymow in the centre, and the numerous stalls where the cattle, each with head toward the great king post, are fed through the cold months of winter. A stone pathway on which you pass a simple dial plate, leads between two groups of houses. Near by, on the opposite side of the road, is the religious house where the services are held of the several families. We found it closed, the brethren, it was said, being off to a meeting on the mountain. This out of door worship is sometimes accompanied by strange fits of enthusiasm. One winter lately the devil was hunted by the Shakers on one of their mountains in solemn procession over the snow drifts. It was satisfactory to learn at that time that he was fairly cornered in the shape of a varmint and was buried with appropriate zeal behind the barn. When you get hold of the devil pin him down. It was a circumstance which created great doubt in the mind of old Dr. Thomas Fuller of the piety of Saint Dunstan, that when, as is well known to all lovers of legend, he had hold of his majesty's nose with a pincers he should let go again.

Three miles farther on is the scattered settlement of the Shakers at Lebanon. Descending upon it from a hill side, groups of carriages were drawn up at the great meeting house, stages, coaches, light wagons, rockaways and others of more city pretence from the fashionable haunts of the neighboring watering place. With the light airy building before them shining with its rounded tin roof in the pure atmosphere, the whole had the gay appearance, with the bustle of the grooms and horses, of a fair or race course. A left hand entrance, past a narrow yard of grass is briefly labeled "Males;" the corresponding doorway being as economically marked "Females." Entering by the former we found ourselves among groups of city-faces and fashionable costume ranged, standing or on benches, the whole length of the edifice. In the middle of the hall, under a vast rounded sounding board, suspended from the ceiling, stood a preacher, a grim, spectral, cold-eyed piece of human timber, boarded up to the oars in a long unwrinkled drab coat. He was in the midst of an exposition addressed to his fashionable audience, which for bathos and cool ignorant impudence, exceeded any address it had ever been our fortune to listen to. It was a polite recommendation to the fat, comfortable, happy looking people in front of him to break up their families, leave their wives or husbands, parents or children, and join the saints of the Millennium which had already begun on earth, the miserable looking, squeaking, jumping beings behind him on the benches, marked with every grade of feebleness and imbecility (with here and there a good face) being its angelic first fruits. Marriage he denounced as belonging to the "natural" man, forgetting that in this division he left himself and his brother celibates to the ranks of the "unnatural." His textual logic seemed a farcical quiz on some of the old Puritan verse-splitting theology. After an enumeration of the various meals which might be eaten in the course of the day, laid down with a confident and dignified assertion, he reminded the company of the persons invited to the supper in the New Testament parable. Several of them had made excuse, one of them had bought a piece of land, another a yoke of oxen, till it came to the man who had married a wife, who asked for no excuse at all, but said simply, he couldn't come. "And why? because there was no excuse to be made. It was out of the question. Had there been any he would have asked for it—thus showing, conclusively, that this condition was utterly incompatible with those heavenly relations?" The millennium, in the Shaker view of it, appears a device to put an end to the world by depopulating it of the good and virtuous. The "calm goblin" then had a shy at the Scarlet lady of Babylon, and by a natural force of logic of his own (slightly at war with physiological experience) went on to condemnation of her daughters—whom he pronounced to be the church of England and the Protestant sects. After some other vulgarities the performance shifted suddenly to a song and a dance. The vocal music had a strong infusion of saw-filing, and the dancing looked hugely like a procession of rheumatic kangaroos. It was a promenade all around in two circles, the adults of both sexes following one another in the outer, and the children (for children they get possession of, like the supernatural hags of old) in the inner, about the vocal group which may be spoken of as the quire for the occasion. The tunes were, some of them, lively and Yankee-doodleish. It was a good business-like trot, with a singular motion of the hands, much like a groceryman "hefting" imaginary pounds of butter. As one tune was finished another began, and on went the dance of death. . . .

The exhibition ended, at last, and the company hurried to their carriages, the Shakers falling into column on their way to the "houses."

It is to be regretted that Mr. Dickens, on his visit to Lebanon, was unable to witness this ceremony. What he did see at the "office" he has left on record, but the world's people at that time were doing penance by a year's exclusion from the interior for some past misdemeanors, and he could not enter. He sums up a pretty fair account of them from hearsay, but bears his testimony to the spirit of the institution in deservedly condemnatory language: "I do abhor," says he, "and from my soul detest that bad spirit, no matter by what class or sect it may be entertained, which would strip life of its healthful graces, rob youth of its innocent pleasures, pluck from maturity and age their pleasant ornaments, and make existence but a narrow path towards the grave; that odious spirit which, if it could have had full scope and sway upon the earth, must have blasted and made barren the imaginations of the greatest men, and left them, in their power of raising up enduring images before their fellow creatures yet unborn no better than the beasts: that in these very broad-brimmed hats and very somber coats—in stiff-necked solemn-visaged piety, in short, no matter what its garb, whether it have cropped hair as in a Shaker village, or long nails as in a Hindu temple—I recognise the worst among the enemies of Heaven and Earth, who turn the water at the marriage feast of this poor world, not into wine, but gall."

The spiritual condition of the Shakers appears to be a junction of extremes—utter negations with old fashioned monkery. It arises with that ancient notion of a portion of the church that the body is wholly corrupt, and that good men should live a life of pure spirit. Hence, ascetic monasticism and intemperance in the name of temperance. It is hardly to be supposed, though, that the sect, notwithstanding an occasional "vision" of the old women, and its grim mountebankery, is sustained by its religious creed. It is probably held together as a low type of associated industry. Labor alone makes it endurable for the individual or the body. It supplies to man what he most seeks, a routine of healthy work, and when the work is done there is the passion of hoarding the profits, which will shine in a miser half an hour before the death he is consciously awaiting, and find its satisfaction in swelling the coffers or adding to the acres of soulless Shakerdom.

The Shakers form a community of associated industry where, at least, the first rude wants of life—pure air, cleanliness, and a sufficiency of food are provided for. Their homes are, to this extent, a refuge for the harassed and destitute. Many disappointed broken down men turn in thither from the buffets of the world and the irresolution of their uncontrolled passions—a safe hand and anchorage for the wreck of a troubled life. The more obvious moralities of life seem to be observed by them with faithfulness. They are honest, sober and industrious. There is a thoroughness of labor in many of their works which commands respect. Slovenly workmanship is a gross practical lie running through the world. The Shakers, limited in the extent of their manufacturers, offer the best of the kind. The covers of their boxes fit, their brooms sweep, their packets of herbs are approved by the physicians, the products of their farms and dairies are sound and wholesome. This, with the fair and exact culture of their land is a virtue before the world. Dealing simply with nature in their relations as agriculturists, in spite of constraint and their barren culture, beauty waits upon them. Their brimming water fountains by the roadside, for man and beast, the cleanliness and order of their farm-yards and meadows, a certain grandeur (of a limited character) in their huge dwellings, the mountain simplicity of their retirement, are tributes to the spirit of Art. Enter their dwellings, and the floors and doors mouldings of the native pine, showing every vein on its unpainted surface, would be an elegance in the cedared palaces of princes. Other features of the interior are curious. The devices for cleanliness remind the traveller of the expedients of the Dutch housewives at Broek. The glazed hard finish of the plaster walls of the large house at Hancock are as pure and fresh at the end of twenty years, as if they had been put up in the city six months since. They have been saved from the impurity of smoke by a small tunnel and pipe, set above each lamp, and leading into the chimney. A broom hangs outside of each house at the doorway. All vanity is eschewed. A tall old family clock stands in the corridor, but some gay flowers on its face had been covered with white paint. You see no flowers in the sister's rooms but a volume of unreadable theology (?) on the Second Advent, with perhaps a pair of crossed spectacles by its side on a small table.

It is a singular proof of the disrelish man has for liberty that the Shakers, renouncing the church governments and magistracies of the world, should at once submit themselves to a burdensome system of routine, restraint and espionage, by which they are converted into machines, with the rigor of a military despotism. Desiring to be free to worship in their own way and advance their spiritual culture, they become slaves of fanaticism and bind new burdens on themselves. No sect is more cramped, maimed, or lamed. Their education goes little beyond enough reading and writing not to be cheated in their dealings with the world; they have no libraries nor literature, unless the title is allowed to a few volumes of spiritual gibberish. Their dialect is uncouth. Their speech has every country provincial vulgarity; but their vanity is blind to the imperfection, and they harangue the brilliant "world's people," the lawyers and others of New York and Boston, assembled from Columbia Hall, as if they were so many Clays and Websters.

Their system has the secret of immobility in the midst of a world which is advancing all around them. There is no relaxation, no improvement. It was brute vulgar toil when they were poor; now that they are rich, it is brute vulgar toil still. They might, one would think, be bachelors and old maids, without sacrificing all the graces of life. Such however may be the necessary tendency of separation of the sexes—in which they demonstrate the fallacy of their own creed, and prove, conclusively, that it is not good for man to be alone.

Strange that the founder and patron saint of these misogynists should be a woman—that there should be a species of Marian worship in their Monkery.

8 9

ANONYMOUS, EXCERPT FROM "COLLEGE EDIFICES AND THEIR RELATION TO EDUCATION," 1847

Of the many efforts in the early nineteenth century to create an "American civilization" equal to the vision of the founders, the design of colleges uniquely suited to the American political system and people ranks high. As the author of this piece notes, the central demands are to "give the public a pledge of the permanency of the institution" and focus on the "moulding [of] the individuals and of the nation." Just as utopian communities dotted the landscape, so too would the American landscape be cluttered with Gothic follies, grandiose Greek Revivals, and Georgian adaptations. Nonetheless, amid this cacophony was a fundamental issue that each college confronted: what architectural attitude to take toward the surrounding towns and cities. Many colleges (such as Amherst and Wesleyan) initially followed Yale College's plan of a row of buildings facing the town, rejecting the cloistered approach of Oxford and Cambridge. But those same colleges later chose to turn away from the city around them and focus inward. In the late nineteenth century, for example, Yale built an imposing line of buildings around its old row, creating a quadrangle. In the 1930s, it would embrace the Oxbridge enclosed college system completely. This dilemma—of the physical relationship between American colleges and the communities in which they stood—continued to define the American way of building colleges through the twentieth century.

Believing that our readers will take no less interest in an object which indicates the progress of learning and art in the country, than in the features of illustrious men, we present them this month with a view of the building which contains the several libraries connected with Yale College. The engraving represents the east front of the edifice, as it will appear when completed. The pinnacles upon the buttresses and a few other particulars are yet unfinished. In its external appearance, it is a Gothic pile of red freestone, one hundred and fifty-two feet in length, including the buttresses, and consisting of a central building with two wings and two connecting wings. The dimensions of the several parts are as follows:

Front of main building, including buttresses,	51 feet
Extreme height of towers,	91 "
Depth of main building,	95 "
Front of each extreme wing,	30 "
Depth of each extreme wing,	67 "
Front of each connecting wing,	26 "
Depth of each connecting wing,	40 "

Each of the five parts of the structure is separated from the rest by solid masonry, constituting a fire proof building by itself. The north and south wings, and the south connecting wing, are fitted up with alcoves, and occupied respectively by the libraries of the Brothers in Unity and the Linonian and Calliopean Societies. The north connecting

Originally printed in *American Literary Magazine* 1, no. 5 (November 1847): 269–74.

7.3. Aerial view of the University of Massachusetts from the northeast, 1958, Everett A. Kosarick, University of Massachusetts News Services. Special Collections and Archives, W. E. B. Du Bois Library, University of Massachusetts Amherst. It has been a central faith of American life that education creates equality of opportunity for everyone. That faith was given a dramatic embodiment with the passage of the Morrill Land Grant Act in 1862. The act helped create state-supported universities around the country, making higher education more democratically available. While many of America's early colleges and universities were modeled after the cloisters of Europe, the modern research university followed modernist planning principles.

wing is occupied by the librarian, and as a reading room for the convenience of those who may wish to consult the books in the library. It communicates by a side door with the main building in which the college library is kept. This is a single room eighty-three feet by forty-one, with a nave fifty-one feet in height and seventeen in width. Between the massive pillars are fourteen alcoves in which the books are arranged according to the subjects upon which they treat. The galleries, which are intended to contain the same number of alcoves, are as yet mainly unoccupied. It is computed that the whole apartment may be so fitted up as to contain sixty or seventy thousand books. A single bust of President Day, just procured by the Alumni of the College, now adorns the interior. It is intended, however, immediately to add several busts and statues which now stand in the Trumbull gallery, and from time to time such other pieces of statuary as may be entrusted to the care of the college.

It will be seen that the edifice is intended to meet the future as well as the present demands of the library, and if we would get a fair impression of the interior we must imagine the time, which we may reasonably place in the youth of the massive structure, when not only the main apartment but the entire range shall be filled with one great and rich library, and embellished throughout with works of art. It contains besides the twenty thousand volumes belonging to the college library, twenty-six or twenty-seven thousand in the several society libraries, making a total of more than forty-six thousand volumes in the building. If we add other libraries belonging to the college, but kept elsewhere for the convenience of the professional schools, we shall have an aggregate of something over fifty thousand. The college library is principally composed of works illustrating the several branches of literature and science pursued in the institution, together with such works of permanent value as are not ordinarily found in private libraries. It is open several hours each day. The society libraries, which are intended to supply the students with general reading and to afford the means of investigating such subjects as are discussed in the societies, are also opened daily.

The expense of the building thus far has been about thirty-four thousand dollars, and six thousand dollars more are wanted to complete it.

This edifice is interesting as an indication of the present aspect and the tendency of American liberal education. The organization of a university system adapted to the genius and circumstances of our people is a task which well may, as it does, engage the minds of our best and wisest men. The circumstances under which universities must here operate, and the nature of the work they have to do, are so new, that we cannot form them after those of any other country. They are not to be, as the English universities have been, mere guardians of an ancient learning and pillars of an old structure of society, nor are they, as in Germany, seminaries for the training of an order or caste of literary men. They must be in sympathy with the popular mind and must act directly upon that mind. They must be distinctly American in their character; with regard to them as with regard to our political institutions, no other land is our model—every other is our example. And we shall be in condition to form our own institutions, just in proportion as we can divest ourselves of that dependence upon the old world which is continually manifesting itself in the various forms of reverence or jealousy or morbid sensitiveness to what European scribblers may say of us.

There is one idea which has some prevalence among scholars which we think an error of serious importance. We allude to the opinion that colleges ought to be conservative in their character. Conservatism—mere resistance—never did any positive good. It never more than delayed an evil. It is often an important work, but unless we assume the postulate that man is incapable of becoming better than he is, we must believe that progress, and not resistance, ought to be the prominent idea of the institutions which are to act upon a free community.

The problem then is, so to form our university system that it shall do its proper work in moulding the mind of individuals and of the nation. This is the object to be kept in view in the whole arrangement of an institution. We introduce it now as the proper point of view from which to consider the subject of college buildings.

A college must have buildings of some kind, because there must be something to give the public a pledge of the permanency of the institution—and something that will be a centre of attachment for its members. How then shall we so adapt the material organization of the institution to the complete education of its students and the advancement of the surrounding community? The founders of Yale College, as well as those of our other institutions, were men of high and comprehensive views. They felt that it was assuming no light responsibility to undertake the education of a youth during the years when he is laying aside the boy and putting on the man. Education in their view meant something more than drilling in the elements of knowledge. It was forming the man as a social and moral, as well as an intellectual being. Hence they felt themselves bound to extend their care to the whole deportment of the student, and, like Christian scholars as they were, they thought it their first duty to surround the members of the institution with influences which should form their characters as well as their minds. It was natural that they should model their system upon that of the English universities in which they had received their own education, and as these in their turn had derived many of their features from the old monasteries, our colleges have had as much of a monastic air as was possible, considering the character of the individuals of whom the community was to be composed. They erected buildings where the student could be under the constant supervision of his instructor; they provided a common table that he might take his meals under the same supervision; and as a further safeguard they made it the specified duty of the older classes to exercise a care over the manners and morals of their younger brethren, who were on their part to render honor and obedience to their seniors. This last part of the system, though a very pleasant application of the theory upon which the whole was constructed, operated in practice as might have been expected, and though long since disused, it is still the subject of a multitude of the most amusing college traditions. Rooms for the officers and students, the commons hall and the chapel, were the frame work of the machinery for social, moral and religious education, and these, with recitation and lecture rooms, completed their catalogue of the indispensable furniture of a collegiate institution. Still they regarded these things rather as the necessary conditions of the existence of a college, than as the proper material organizations of a literary institution. The ten ministers who brought their forty folio volumes to Branford and gave them "for the founding of a college in this colony," understood the true wealth of a college as well as any of their successors. One-third of the number of donations to the college during the first century of its existence were for the increase of its library or apparatus or its other means of exerting and satisfying a taste for learning. But they considered it their duty to provide first the indispensable foundation of good moral influences, and then to furnish the *material* of literature, to the extent of their ability. And in these times, when the privations of poverty were varied only by the calamities of war, they were able to do but little toward rearing their superstructure, so that at the time of the Revolution the colleges which were in existence presented the appearance of mere boarding establishments for men who were preparing for professional life. From that period we are to date the beginning of our intellectual independence. The devotion of the Puritans to learning was of foreign origin, and it was long in taking root in the soil so as to bring forth native fruit. . . .

This new spirit of munificence accompanies a new commercial independence. We are just becoming able to construct our own works with our own capital. The State of Massachusetts, which ten years ago went to Europe for the means of constructing rail roads within her own borders, has now available capital seeking investment in similar works in every corner of the Union, while her manufacturers are searching the windings of all our mountain streams and surveying the rapids of our great rivers to find opportunity to extend their operations. Throughout our business world, we are beginning to feel that confidence in ourselves which leads us to hope that we can pass securely through a crisis which involves the whole trade of England in disaster. In this stage of our progress it is cheering beyond measure to find our Astors, and Lawrences, and Appletons, and Willistons giving abundantly from their abundance to erect upon our own soil temples to learning which shall revive here the glory of the old republics. We feel rebuked when we see a stranger's name united with this central light—the Smithsonian Institute—but when we see this spirit springing up among our own citizens, we feel assured again that we shall yet realize those almost visionary anticipations which could inspire a stranger to make such a gift; and so far as his example has been the means of calling such a spirit into being, he is to be held in lasting honor among those few men of other lands whose noble enthusiasm has made their names familiar to every child in America.

9 0

CATHERINE E. BEECHER AND HARRIET BEECHER STOWE,
EXCERPT FROM *THE AMERICAN WOMAN'S HOME*, 1869

The Beecher sisters came from one of the most remarkable families of the nineteenth century. Among other things, they were at the forefront of the abolition movement in the antebellum period; when President Abraham Lincoln met Harriet Beecher Stowe, he blamed her novel *Uncle Tom's Cabin* for having started the Civil War. In *The American Woman's Home*, the sisters have linked their concern for women's equality with a treatise on "domestic economy." The book is filled with very practical, functional, "scientific" advice about how best to organize and run a household. Behind all these helpful tips lies a deep conviction that the morals of the nation are in the care of women and that they are shaped powerfully by the home.

The authors of this volume, while they sympathize with every honest effort to relieve the disabilities and sufferings of their sex, are confident that the chief cause of these evils is the fact that the honor and duties of the family state are not duly appreciated, that women are not trained for these duties as men are trained for their trades and professions, and that, as the consequence, family labor is poorly done, poorly paid, and regarded as menial and disgraceful.

To be the nurse of young children, a cook, or a housemaid, is regarded as the lowest and last resort of poverty, and one which no woman of culture and position can assume without loss of caste and respectability.

It is the aim of this volume to elevate both the honor and the remuneration of all

Originally printed in Catherine E. Beecher and Harriet Beecher Stowe, *The American Woman's Home* (New York: J.B. Ford and Co., 1869), 13–14, 23–25, 84–87.

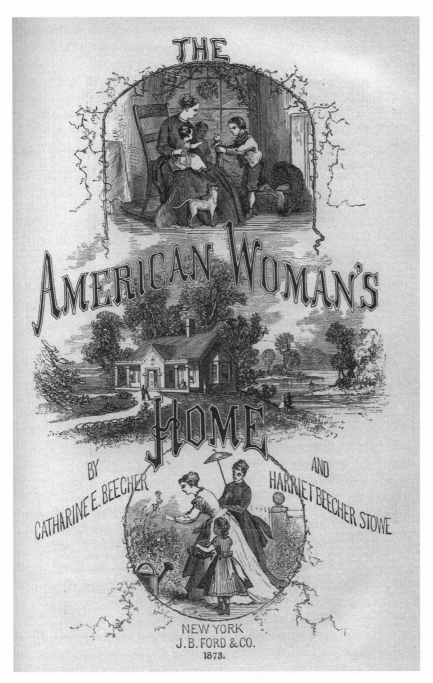

7.4. Cover of Catherine E. Beecher and Harriet Beecher Stowe's *The American Woman's Home*, 1873 edition. These two sisters were among the most dynamic reformers of the mid-nineteenth century, active in the abolition movement and in the movement for women's rights. Their book, a manual of "domestic economy," was intended both to provide women with useful information and to demonstrate that the work of running a home was as important as any other job. Its cover reveals the authors' ideal, one that would become the ideal for a vast number of Americans: a single-family home offering the benefits of nature, watched over by a caring and concerned woman.

the employments that sustain the many difficult and sacred duties of the family state, and thus to render each department of woman's true profession as much desired and respected as are the most honored professions of men.

When the other sex are to be instructed in law, medicine, or divinity, they are favored with numerous institutions richly endowed, with teachers of the highest talents and acquirements, with extensive libraries, and abundant and costly apparatus. With such advantages they devote nearly ten of the best years of life to preparing themselves for their profession; and to secure the public from unqualified members of these professions, none can enter them until examined by a competent body, who certify to their due preparation for their duties.

Woman's profession embraces the care and nursing of the body in the critical periods of infancy and sickness, the training of the human mind in the most impressible period of childhood, the instruction and control of servants, and most of the government and economies of the family state. These duties of woman are as sacred and important as any ordained to man; and yet no such advantages, for preparation have been accorded to her, nor is there any qualified body to certify the public that a woman is duly prepared to give proper instruction in her profession.

This unfortunate want, and also the questions frequently asked concerning the domestic qualifications of both the authors of this work, who have formerly written upon such topics, make it needful to give some account of the advantages they have enjoyed in preparation for the important office assumed as teachers of woman's domestic duties. . . .

In the Divine Word it is written, "The wise woman buildeth her house." To be "wise," is "to choose the best means for accomplishing the best end." It has been shown that the best end for a woman to seek is the training of God's children for their eternal home, by guiding them to intelligence, virtue, and true happiness. When, therefore, the wise woman seeks a home in which to exercise this ministry, she will aim to secure a house so planned that it will provide in the best manner for health, industry, and economy, those cardinal requisites of domestic enjoyment and success. To aid in this, is the object of the following drawings and descriptions, which will illustrate a style of living more conformed to the great design for which the family is instituted than that which ordinarily prevails among those classes which take the lead in forming the customs of society. The aim will be to exhibit modes of economizing labor, time, and expenses, so as to secure health, thrift, and domestic happiness to persons of limited means, in a measure rarely attained even by those who possess wealth.

At the head of this chapter is a sketch of what may be properly called a Christian house; that is, a house contrived for the express purpose of enabling every member of a family to labor with the hands for the common good, and by modes at once healthful, economical, and tasteful.

Of course, much of the instruction conveyed in the following pages is chiefly applicable to the wants and habits of those living either in the country or in such suburban vicinities as give space of ground for healthful outdoor occupation in the family service, although the general principles of house-building and house-keeping are of necessity universal in their application—as true in the busy confines of the city as in the freer and purer quietude of the country. So far as circumstances can be made to yield the opportunity, it will be assumed that the family state demands some outdoor labor for all. The cultivation of flowers to ornament the table and house, of fruits and vegetables for food, of silk and cotton for clothing, and the care of horse, cow, and dairy, can be so divided that each and all of the family, some part of the day, can take exercise in the pure air, under the magnetic and healthful rays of the sun. Every head of a family should seek a soil and climate which will afford such opportunities. Railroads, enabling men toiling in cities to rear families in the country, are on this account a special blessing. So, also, is the opening of the South to free labor, where, in the pure and mild climate of the uplands, open air labor can proceed most of the year, and women and children labor out of doors as well as within. . . .

Having duly arranged for the physical necessities of a healthful and comfortable home, we next approach the important subject of *beauty* in reference to the decoration of houses. For while the aesthetic element must be subordinate to the requirements of physical existence, and, as a matter of expense, should be held of inferior consequence to means of higher moral growth; it yet holds a place of great significance among the influences which make home happy and attractive, which give it a constant and wholesome power over the young, and contributes much to the education of the entire household in refinement, intellectual development, and moral sensibility.

Here we are met by those who tell us that of course they want their houses handsome, and that, when they get money enough, they intend to have them so, but at present they are too poor, and because they are poor they dismiss the subject altogether, and live without any regard to it.

We have often seen people who said that they could not afford to make their houses beautiful, who had spent upon them, outside or in, an amount of money which did not produce either beauty or comfort, and which, if judiciously applied, might have made the house quite charming. . . .

[W]e have seen a dwelling looking very bald and bare, when a sufficient sum of money had been expended on one article to have made the whole very pretty: and it has come about in this way.

We will suppose the couple who own the house to be in the condition in which people generally are after they have built a house—having spent more than they could afford on the building itself, and yet feeling themselves under the necessity of getting some furniture.

"Now," says the housewife, "I must at least have a parlor-carpet. We must get that to begin with, and other things as we go on." She goes to a store to look at carpets. The clerks are smiling and obliging, and sweetly complacent. The storekeeper, perhaps, is a neighbor or a friend, and after exhibiting various patterns, he tells her of a Brussels carpet he is selling wonderfully cheap—actually a dollar and a quarter less a yard than the usual price of Brussels, and the reason is that it is an unfashionable pattern, and he has a good deal of it, and wishes to close it off.

She looks at it and thinks it is not at all the kind of carpet she meant to buy, but then it is Brussels, and so cheap! And as she hesitates, her friend tells her that she will find it "cheapest in the end—that one Brussels carpet will outlast three or four ingrains," etc., etc.

The result of all this is, that she buys the Brussels carpet, which, with all its reduction in price, is one third dearer than the ingrain would have been, and not half so pretty. When she comes home, she will find that she has spent, we will say eighty dollars, for a very homely carpet whose greatest merit it is an affliction to remember—namely, that it will outlast three ordinary carpets. And because she has bought this carpet she can not afford to paper the walls or put up any window-curtains, and can not even begin to think of buying any pictures.

Now let us see what eighty dollars could have done for that room. We will suppose, in the first place, she invests in thirteen rolls of wall-paper of a lovely shade of buff, which will make the room look sunshiny in the day-time, and light up brilliantly in the evening. Thirteen rolls of good satin paper, at thirty-seven cents a roll, expends four dollars and eighty-one cents. A maroon bordering, made in imitation of the choicest French style, which can not at a distance be told from it, can be bought for six cents a yard. This will bring the paper to about five dollars and a half; and our friends will give a day of their time to putting it on. The room already begins to look furnished.

Then, let us cover the floor with, say, thirty yards of good matting, at fifty cents a yard. This gives us a carpet for fifteen dollars. We are here stopped by the prejudice that matting is not good economy, because it wears out so soon. We humbly submit that it is precisely the thing for a parlor, which is reserved for the reception-room of friends, and for our own dressed leisure hours. Matting is not good economy in a dining-room or a hard-worn sitting-room; but such a parlor as we are describing is precisely the place where it answers to the very best advantage.

We have in mind one very attractive parlor which has been, both for summer and winter, the daily sitting-room for the leisure hours of a husband and wife, and family of children, where a plain straw matting has done service for seven years. That parlor is in a city, and these friends are in the habit of receiving visits from people who live upon velvet and Brussels; but they prefer to spend the money which such carpets would cost on other modes of embellishment; and this parlor has often been cited to us as a very attractive room.

91

RICHARD T. ELY, EXCERPT FROM "PULLMAN: A SOCIAL STUDY," 1885

Richard T. Ely, an economist who taught at Johns Hopkins University and the University of Wisconsin, saw in the development of the model company town of Pullman both optimistic and dangerous portents for the future. While calling the idea behind Pullman—of ordering and directing the living conditions of an entire town—"un-American" because of its break from the ideals of personal independence, Ely also praised it, suggesting that it had gone a long way toward solving "one of the great problems of the immediate present, which is a diffusion of the benefits of concentrated wealth among wealth-creators." The irony here is great: in 1894, nine years after the publication of Ely's generally sympathetic view of Pullman, the town and Pullman Palace Car Company factories erupted in one of the great strikes of the nineteenth century.

Sympathy must always be shown to writers who fail to see the future. But the irony of Pullman reveals the weakness of the arguments for architectural determinism, which were so pervasive in nineteenth-century reform movements. The beauty of the town of Pullman could not hide or overcome the structural inequities that animated labor struggles of the late nineteenth and early twentieth centuries.

Originally printed in *Harper's Magazine* 70 (February 1885): 452–66.

7.5. Row houses, including a former corner store, Pullman, Illinois, 1997. Courtesy of Iguana Photo, www.iguanaphoto.com. The line separating social reform from social control blurred almost entirely at Pullman, Illinois. Built by industrialist George Pullman to provide a model community for his workers—and, by extension, to provide a model to his fellow robber barons—Pullman's company town offered much better living conditions than would otherwise have been available to his workers, but at a price: higher rental costs and strict regulation of behavior (including a ban on alcohol).

COMMUNISM, socialism, nihilism, are international words. Understood by people of both hemispheres and of many tongues, and printed daily in ten thousand journals, they are evidence of a momentous social movement. They mean far more than the creeds which under these names find a comparatively limited acceptance. They bear witness to a widespread discontent with things as they are in modern society—a discontent which but rarely goes to the extreme length of what is ordinarily designated by the generic term socialism. The pretty dream of a perfect, natural order of things brought about by the free play of unrestrained social forces has vanished. It has given place on the one hand to pessimism; on the other, and more generally, to a determination not to let things go on of themselves, but to make them go in such manner as may be desired. The conviction has become general that the divine order never contemplated a social and economic world left to itself. Material is furnished out of which man must construct a social fabric according to his lights. This is what modern socialism means, and for this reason it is practical, not romantic, and leaving the dim, artificial light of the study, goes forth into the broad sunlight, seeking immediate realization among the people. . . . [F]or brevity's sake, passing over numerous manifestations of this spirit in our times, this is what is meant by the many attempts of "captains of industry" to step in between those they lead and the unrestrained action of existing economic forces. . . . [T]he most extensive experiment of this character is that now in progress at Pullman, Illinois. It is social experimentation on a vast scale, and this is its significance.

For this reason it challenges attention and discussion at a time when dynamite bombs and revolutionary murmurings terrify monarchs, when an enlarged human sympathy encircles the earth with beneficent institutions, and when an eager interest in social and economic facts more than atones for general indifference to the dogmatic assumptions of classic political economy.

Pullman, a town of eight thousand inhabitants, some ten miles from Chicago, on the Illinois Central Railroad, was founded less than four years ago by the Pullman Palace Car Company, whose president and leading spirit is Mr. George M. Pullman. Its purpose was to provide both a centre of industry and homes for the employés of the company and such additional laborers as might be attracted to the place by other opportunities to labor. Simply as a town, Pullman has not sufficient interest to justify a description of it in a great magazine. Its natural beauties are not remarkable, situated as it is on the low prairie land surrounding Chicago, and its newness makes such romances impossible as one can associate with villages like Lenox, and Stockbridge, and other ancient towns in New England. Like many other Western cities, its growth has been rapid, its population having increased from four souls in January, 1881, to 2084 in February, 1882, and to 8203 in September, 1884. A manufacturing town, it embraces the principal works of the Pullman Palace Car Company, in addition to the Allen Paper Car-wheel Company, the Union Foundry and Pullman Car-wheel Company, the Chicago Steel-works, the Steel-forging Company, and numerous less important enterprises.

Many of the last-mentioned are connected with building operations in the town of Pullman, or furnish commodities to its residents, and in many cases they also supply customers elsewhere, such as the gas works, the ice-houses, the brick-yards, the carpenter shops, and the large farm which receives the sewage of Pullman. The number of men employed in the place is at present about four thousand, of whom over three thousand are employed by the Palace Car Company. The products of the various establishments are valued at many millions of dollars. . . . [T]he purpose of this article is to treat it as an attempt to furnish laborers with the best homes under the most healthful conditions and with the most favorable surroundings in every respect, for Pullman aims to be a forerunner of better things for the laboring classes.

The questions to be answered are these: Is Pullman a success from a social standpoint? Is it worthy of imitation? Is it likely to inaugurate a new era in society? If only a partial success, what are its bright features and what its dark features?

Pullman as an attempt to realize an ideal must be judged by an ideal standard. The measure to be applied is the reasonable ideal of the social reformer. What is this ideal? Is it not that each individual be so situated as to participate, as fully as his nature will allow, in the advantages of the existing civilization? . . . Now what the student of society wants to know is the nearness with which Pullman approaches the social ideal.

Very gratifying is the impression of the visitor who passes hurriedly through Pullman and observes only the splendid provision for the present material comforts of its residents. What is seen in a walk or drive through the streets is so pleasing to the eye that a woman's first exclamation is certain to be, "Perfectly lovely!" It is indeed a sight as rare as it is delightful. What might have been taken for a wealthy suburban town is given up to busy workers, who literally earn their bread in the sweat of their brow. . . .

One of the most striking peculiarities of this place is the all-pervading air of thrift and providence. The most pleasing impression of general well-being is at once produced. Contrary to what is seen ordinarily in laborers' quarters, not a dilapidated door-step nor a broken window, stuffed perhaps with old clothing, is to be found in the city. The streets of Pullman, always kept in perfect condition, are wide and finely macadamized, and young shade trees on each side now ornament the town, and will in a few years afford refreshing protection from the rays of the summer sun.

Unity of design and an unexpected variety charm us as we saunter through the town. Lawns always of the same width separate the houses from the street, but they are so green and neatly trimmed that one can overlook this regularity of form. Although the houses are built in groups of two or more, and even in blocks, with the exception of a few large buildings of cheap flats, they bear no resemblance to barracks. . . . Simple but ingenious designs secure variety, of which the most skillful is probably the treatment of the sky line. Naturally, without an appearance of effort, it assumes an immense diversity. French roofs, square roofs, dormer-windows, turrets, sharp points, blunt points, triangles, irregular quadrangles, are devices resorted to in the upper stories to avoid the appearance of unbroken uniformity. A slight knowledge of mathematics shows how infinite the variety of possible combinations of a few elements, and a better appreciation of this fact than that exhibited by the architecture of Pullman it would be difficult to find. The streets cross each other at right angles, yet here again skill has avoided the frightful monotony of New York, which must sometimes tempt a nervous person to scream for relief. A public square, arcade, hotel, market, or some large building is often set across a street so ingeniously as to break the regular line, yet without inconvenience to traffic. Then at the termination of long streets a pleasing view greets and relieves the eye—a bit of water, a stretch of meadow, a clump of trees, or even one of the large but neat workshops. . . . No other feature of Pullman can receive praise needing so little qualification as its architecture. Desirable houses have been provided for a large laboring population at so small a cost that they can be rented at rates within their means and yet yield a handsome return on the capital invested. Rents are probably about three-fifths what they are in Chicago, and, all things considered, this seems not to be an unfair standard of comparison. It is a mere matter of course that there are architectural defects even in Pullman. The diversity is not quite all that could be desired. What may be called the public buildings, that is to say, the hotel, school-house, arcade, etc., are detached, but no private house stands by itself, though there are quite a number of detached double houses. Spaces have, however, been reserved for a few detached private residences, which will improve the appearance of the town. With the exception of the church and parsonage, built of green serpentine stone from Philadelphia, all the buildings are of brick. This is monotonous, and rather wearying to the eye, but the slate roofs, and a large use of light stone trimmings, and stripes of black across the houses, help matters somewhat. The general character of the architecture is what has been called advanced secular Gothic. This is skillfully varied, and in the hotel particularly there is a feeling of the Queen Anne style. But there ought to be some bold break in the general design. The newness of things, which time will remedy, is a little distressing, as is also the mechanical regularity of the town, and it is this, perhaps, which suggests the epithet "machine-made." The growth of shade trees will break into the sameness, and the magnificent boulevard which divides the shops on the north from the residences on the south, stretching from east to west across the town, and bordered with double rows of elms, will, twenty years from now, be a vast improvement. Great overarching trees will hide one part of the town from another, and give opportunity for pleasant surprises in nature and art.

The interior of the houses affords scarcely less gratification than their exterior. Even the humblest suite of rooms in the flats is provided with water, gas, and closets, and no requisite of cleanliness is omitted. Most of the cottages are two stories in height, and contain five rooms, besides a cellar, closets, and pantry, as seen in the accompanying plan and illustrations. Quite a large number of houses contain seven rooms, and in these larger dwellings there is also a bath-room. . . .

The entire town was built under the direction of a single architect, Mr. S. S. Beman, an ambitious young man whose frequently expressed desire for an opportunity to do a "big thing" was here gratified. This is probably the first time a single architect has ever constructed a whole town systematically upon scientific principles, and the success of the work entitles him to personal mention. . . .

There are over fifteen hundred buildings at Pullman, and the entire cost of the town, including all the manufacturing establishments, is estimated at eight millions of dollars. The rents of the dwellings vary from $4.50 per month for the cheapest flats of two rooms to $100 a month for the largest private house in the place. . . .

The Pullman companies retain everything. No private individual owns to-day a square rod of ground or a single structure in the entire town. No organization, not even a church, can occupy any other than rented quarters. With the exception of the management of the public school, every municipal act is here the act of a private corporation. . . . All this applies only to what is generally known as Pullman, which is in reality no political organization, and is called a town or city simply in a popular sense for the sake of convenience. Pullman is only a part of the large village and town of Hyde Park, but the latter appears to have relinquished the government of this portion of its territory bearing the name of Pullman to private corporations, and the writer was not able to find that a single resident of Pullman, not an officer of the Pullman companies, was either in the board of trustees of Hyde Park or in the staff of officers. The town clerk and treasurer are both officers of the Pullman Palace Car Company, and the directory of Hyde Park reveals the fact that with one exception every member of the board of education of the Pullman school district is an officer of the Palace Car Company or some concern which bears the name of Pullman. . . .

It should be constantly borne in mind that all investments and outlays in Pullman are intended to yield financial returns satisfactory from a purely business point of view. The minimum return expected is six per centum on expenditure, and the town appears to have yielded a far higher percentage on cost up to the present time. . . .

It pays also in another way. The wholesome, cheerful surroundings enable the men to work more constantly and more efficiently. The healthy condition of the residents is a matter of general comment. The number of deaths has been about seven in a thousand per annum, whereas it has been about fifteen in a thousand in the rest of Hyde Park.

It is maintained that Pullman is truly a philanthropic undertaking, although it is intended that it should be a profitable investment, and this is the argument used: If it can be shown that it does pay to provide beautiful homes for laborers, accompanied with all the conditions requisite for wholesome living both for the body and the mind, the example set by Mr. Pullman will find wide imitation. If what is done for the residents of the town were simply a generous gift, another might argue, "If Mr. Pullman chooses to spend his money this way, very well!, I have no objection, but I prefer to keep a stable of blooded horses.

Each one according to his taste!" We may feel inclined to shrug our shoulders at the philanthropy which demands a good round sum for everything it offers, but certainly it is a great thing to have demonstrated the commercial value of beauty in a city of laborers. . . .

But admirable as are the peculiarities of Pullman which have been described, certain unpleasant features of social life in that place are soon noticed by the careful observer, which moderate the enthusiasm one is at first inclined to feel upon an inspection of the external, plainly visible facts, and the picture must be completed before judgment can be pronounced on it.

One just cause of complaint is what in government affairs would be called a bad civil service, that is, a bad administration in respect to the employment, retention, and promotion of employés. Change is constant in men and officers, and each new superior appears to have his own friends, whom he appoints to desirable positions. Favoritism and nepotism, out of place as they are in an ideal society, are oft-repeated and apparently well-substantiated charges.

The resulting evil is very naturally dissatisfaction, a painful prevalence of petty jealousies, a discouragement of superior excellence, frequent change in the residents, and an all-pervading feeling of insecurity. Nobody regards Pullman as a real home, and, in fact, it can scarcely be said that there are more than temporary residents at Pullman. One woman told the writer she had been in Pullman two years, and that there were only three families among her acquaintances who were there when she came. Her reply to the question, "It is like living, in a great hotel, is it not?" was, "We call it camping out." The nature of the leases aggravates this evil. As already stated, all the property in Pullman is owned by the Pullman associations, and every tenant holds his house on a lease which may be terminated on ten days' notice. A lease which lies on the table before the writer reads: "From ___ to ___, unless sooner cancelled in accordance—with the conditions of the lease." It is not necessary that any reason be assigned for the notice; "and it is expressly agreed that the fact that rent may have been paid at any time in advance shall not be a waiver of the right to put an end to the term and tenancy under this lease by such notice." Furthermore, three-fourths of the laborers in Pullman are employed by the Palace Car Company, and many of those who do not work for it are employed in establishments in which the company as such or a prominent member of it is interested. The power of Bismarck in Germany is utterly insignificant when compared with the power of the ruling authority of the Pullman Palace Car Company in Pullman. . . . It is impossible within the realm of Pullman to escape from the overshadowing influence of the company, and every resident feels this, and "monopoly" is a word which constantly falls on the ear of the visitor. . . . A Baptist clergyman, who had built up quite a congregation once ventured to espouse the cause of a poor family ejected from their house, and gave rather public expression to his feelings. Shortly after his support began to fall away, one member after another leaving, and it has since never been possible to sustain a Baptist organization in Pullman. It is indeed a sad spectacle. Here is a population of eight thousand souls where not one single resident dare speak out openly his opinion about the town in which he lives. One feels that one is mingling with a dependent, servile people. There is an abundance of grievances, but if there lives in Pullman one man who would give expression to them in print over his own name, diligent inquiry continued for ten days was not sufficient to find him. . . .

The desire of the American to acquire a home is justly considered most commendable and hopeful. It promotes thrift and economy, and the habits acquired in the effort to pay for it are often the foundation of a future prosperous career. It is a beginning in the right direction. Again, a large number of house owners is a safeguard against violent movements of social discontent. Heretofore laborers at Pullman have not been allowed to acquire any real property in the place. There is a repression here as elsewhere of any marked individuality. Everything tends to stamp upon residents, as upon the town, the character expressed in "machine made." Not only are strikes regarded as the chief of social sins . . . but individual initiative, even in affairs which concern the residents alone, is repressed. Once several of the men wanted to form a kind of mutual insurance association to insure themselves against loss of time in case of accident, but it was frowned down by the authorities, and nothing further has been heard of the matter. . . .

In looking over all the facts of the case the conclusion is unavoidable that the idea of Pullman is un-American. It is a nearer approach than anything the writer has seen to what appears to be the ideal of the great German Chancellor. It is not the American ideal. It is benevolent, well wishing feudalism, which desires the happiness of the people, but in such way as shall please the authorities. One can not avoid thinking of the late Czar of Russia, Alexander II., to whom the welfare of his subjects was truly a matter of concern. He wanted them to be happy, but desired their happiness to proceed from him, in whom everything should centre. Serfs were freed, the knout abolished, and no insuperable objection raised to reforms, until his people showed a decided determination to take matters in their own hands, to govern themselves, and to seek their own happiness in their own way. Then he stopped the work of reform, and considered himself deeply aggrieved. The loss of authority and distrust of the people is the fatal weakness of many systems of reform and well-intentioned projects of benevolence.

Pullman ought to be appreciated, and high honor is due Mr. George M. Pullman. He has at least attempted to do something lasting and far-reaching, and the benefits he has actually conferred upon a laboring population of eight thousand souls testify that his heart must be warm toward his poorer brother. Mr. Pullman has partially solved one of the great problems of the immediate present, which is a diffusion of the benefits of concentrated wealth among wealth-creators.

Pullman is still in its infancy, and great things are promised in the future. . . . It is quite practicable to develop a democracy, or at least what might be called a constitutional monarchy, out of the despotism of Pullman. . . . Some co-operative features might be added, which would be a move in the right direction, and every great philanthropic enterprise ought as soon as possible to be placed on such a footing as not to be dependent upon the life of any one individual. Not a few have ventured to express the hope that Pullman might be widely imitated, and thus inaugurate a new era in the history of labor. But if this signifies approval of a scheme which would immesh our laborers in a net-work of communities owned and managed by industrial superiors, then let every patriotic American cry, God forbid! What would this mean? The establishment of the most absolute power of capital, and the repression of all freedom. It matters not that they are well-meaning capitalists; all capitalists are not devoted heart and soul to the interests of their employés, and the history of the world has long ago demonstrated that no class of men are fit to be intrusted with unlimited power. . . .

If free American institutions are to be preserved, we want no race of men reared as underlings and with the spirit of menials. . . . So when we see such splendid provision for the body as at Pullman, we clap our hands and stop not to ask how all this is to effect the formation of character. And the impassioned pleas for liberty which moved Americans mightily one hundred years ago fall to-day on the ear as something strange and ridiculous. Such thing are straws floating on the stream of social life. Have we reason to be pleased with the direction in which the current is setting?

92

C. JOHN HEXAMER, EXCERPT FROM "MILL ARCHITECTURE" 1885

The industrial economy that expanded in America's urban centers in the years after the Civil War left a variety of marks on the landscape—from great railroad depots and yards to the pits of huge mines to the smokestacks of thousands of factories. The latter sprung up haphazardly in American cities, wherever an industrialist or entrepreneur thought he could manufacture something better and more profitably. In this piece, delivered as a lecture before Philadelphia's Franklin Institute, C. John Hexamer argues in specific and often quite dull detail, that factories need to be planned and designed with great care, especially to prevent fires. Powerful and dangerous industrial machinery and processes required that American architecture be transformed to be safer in all its aspects. A later generation of architects and critics found in the spare, utilitarian factory buildings of the late nineteenth century, the precursors of Modernist design. In these buildings, form always followed function.

The first principle in architecture, and foremost in buildings intended for manufacturing purposes, is utility; and all other considerations are subservient to it. The elements of Vitruvius . . . utility, beauty—still hold good. That mill building is the best which is best suited for its purpose, and that architect is most expert, who exactly knows what changes in his plans are required for every department of manufacture. I, of course, do not mean to say that a mill should be erected in bad proportions . . . on the contrary, an architect shows his superior skill if, notwithstanding the small amounts usually allotted to decorative purposes, and the fetters which that tyrant utility places on him, he is still able to erect an evenly proportioned, well-looking buildings. The higher a building is, the better should be its construction. The simplest of all rules of building, to construct a building safely and solidly, is frequently neglected. . . .

It becomes our problem then to construct each story so that a fire starting in one may be restricted to that story; so that smoke, fire and water used to extinguish the flames, may not harm other stories and their contents. . . .

Brick is the best material for fire construction. It stands long after granite has disintegrated and marble has been burnt into lime. . . .

There are few parts in fire construction which are of so much importance, and

Originally printed in *Journal of the Franklin Institute* 120 (July 1885): 1–17.

generally so little understood, as fire doors. Instances of the faulty construction of these, even by good builders and architects, may be daily seen. . . .

Numerous fires have been caused by lamps in mills. These should be constructed of metal, and not of glass, as the latter readily breaks. High-test oils only, with a flash point of 150 degrees or over should be used.

93

MARY BRONSON HARTT, EXCERPT FROM "BEAUTIFYING THE UGLY THINGS," 1905

Much of what turn-of-the-century social reformers focused on were grand public buildings and the designing of entire communities. But amid the City Beautiful Movement—the nationwide effort to comprehensively replan American cities to make them more efficient and beautiful—was a push to enhance the aesthetics of everyday places. These reformers looked to raise the level of design of stables and bathhouses, water tanks, and back doors, or in Mary Hartt's words, "the devising of comely forms for such uncomely things." Hartt's writing is part of a turn-of-the-century celebration of the "everyday" inspired in part by the ascension of the fields of anthropology and sociology at American universities, which sought to understand how people really lived. It also was a precursor of a later round of this attention to the vernacular, which grew in the 1950s and after under the leadership of J. B. Jackson and Peter Blake. The document also points to a broader idea: that places of beauty, or of historical importance, scattered around American cities and towns would uplift an increasingly diverse and economically divided population.

When apostles of civic improvement paint a vision of that ideal city which is to be—with its parks, its common, its lovely vistas, its business districts uniform of skyline and innocent of advertising atrocities, and its streets of exemplary homes—they commonly leave something out of the picture. What about the ugly things—the factories, the warehouses, the public laundries, the mills? When we gather together the good things of the city, must we quarantine these ugly ones in a place apart?

We might, indeed, establish a manufacturing gehenna, where mills and "works" might set up a crude picturesqueness of their own. The plan has more than once been seriously advocated. But not all ugliness is even crudely picturesque, nor can all unbeautiful utilities be segregated. What about the honest ugly things which we want handy? How about the corner drug-store, the livery stable, the little grocery round the corner? How about "the cheap wee shop" so indispensable, so uncomely? All these we must have. Moreover, we cannot banish our engine-houses, police stations, and car-barns. They must be scattered throughout the fairest of our cities. Shall we then accept them as blots upon the civic beauty we fight for, as things necessary, yet inherently ugly?

Originally printed in *World's Work* 9, no. 4 (February 1905): 5859–68.

No. Reform is outrunning the reformers, and is already doing more and better than they had dared to hope. The movement for civic beauty has grown too big for its instigators. It no longer works putteringly from without, but upheavingly from within. It has got down to the people. The industrialism which produced American bad taste has produced American wealth: American wealth has given Americans education and has sent them to the Old World; and now in good season it is giving them insight and a feeling for good things, as well as the means to secure them. . . . The uplift was bound to show in our building. . . .

Perhaps the most brilliant example is a public laundry just completed in Cambridgeport near Harvard Bridge. The laundry is built in the style of the English Renaissance—did any one ever hear before of a laundry built in any style whatsoever?—of water-struck brick and limestone; it boasts a little copper-topped tower, mullioned windows, decorative cartouches, and carved grotesques along the stone cornice. It is finished with as much attention to detail as if it were devoted to something more dignified than the cleansing of linen.

About the success of the general affect there may be some difference of opinion; but as to the praiseworthiness of the enterprise there can be but one voice. It should have far-reaching consequences; for every car crossing Harvard Bridge runs by the handsome building, and every business man who sees it, and hears the astonished comment of passengers, must be set to thinking about the advertising value of architecture. The laundry bears no sign beyond the familiar monogram of the firm carved in stone. It needs no sign. The unique building speaks louder than printed words, however big.

Just across the way from it stands a storage warehouse which deserves attention. It is scarcely beautiful, and yet its battlemented towers and ornamental cornice raise it above the level of storage-warehouse architecture. It is something more than a huge rectangle of brick. Its semimilitary style makes it a not altogether objectionable neighbor for a fine arsenal next door. Here is food for thought. Can we not make ugly things inconspicuous by harmonizing them with their surroundings? . . .

Do we not all remember when the delivery wagons even of prosperous firms were things of ingenious ugliness? There came one day into a certain city a brand-new, shiny black wagon bearing a sign in Old English lettering in gold. It was scarcely a week before other tradesmen took the hint. Black enamel and tasteful gold lettering supplanted the old-time gaudy paint as fast as new wagons could be ordered or old ones reformed. So it will be with a score of other unbeautiful utilities—when once the way is shown, the commercial world will make haste to supersede them.

Moreover, the American people are quick to learn better ways. Let them once see that industry need not be associated with ugliness, and they will demand that the industries they patronize be housed in sightly quarters. The American people do not always know what is ugly; they will put up with monstrous things in architecture; but—I have it on the authority of an architect of national reputation—give them a really good thing, and they may be trusted to like it. A few generations of good building will open their eyes. They will demand what is good. And what the people want, they will get.

So, then, the city of the future is not to be a thing of patches. Like the Greek cities which antedated the machine age, and those exposition cities of our own day which have risen above the disfiguring influence of the machine, it will be good through and through. Its factories will be sightly, and so will its gas-tanks, its voting-booths, its grain-elevators. The devising of comely forms for such uncomely things will tax the ingenuity of our architects. But success will mean the greater triumph.

94

ISAAC F. MARCOSSON, EXCERPT FROM "GIVING CARNEGIE LIBRARIES," 1905

Carnegie Libraries, which as this essay points out can be found around the country in towns big and small, represent one of the most remarkable philanthropic programs ever undertaken in the United States. Steel magnate Andrew Carnegie had very systematic ideas about why he funded the building of libraries, and, as this piece makes clear, how his program would work. Carnegie was perhaps the most complicated of the robber barons, ruthless as a businessman, almost philosophical as a philanthropist. Whatever one's opinions of him, however, the libraries he left constitute an extraordinary contribution to the cultural infrastructure of the nation and the physical fabric of the communities in which they were built. And they had the power, as Marcosson relates, to change the lives of ordinary people.

In nearly every English-speaking country to-day there is a Carnegie free public library. Altogether there are 1,352. During every hour of every day some of these libraries are open and in use. In New Zealand they enlighten the Maori; in the crowded East Side of New York City they uplift a congested foreign population; in Ireland they influence a struggling race. Without regard to creed or color, they have everywhere taught the value of high intellectual ideals. They have placed (or will place, when the buildings planned are erected) free reading within the reach of 25,000,000 people, and they represent a total benefaction of more than $40,000,000. No individual has ever contributed so much to a single cause or touched so many people. It is the most remarkable public service in the history of philanthropy, and its conduct is as unusual as the personality behind it. . . .

Any English-speaking community in the world may secure a Carnegie Library by making a formal request and fulfilling the business conditions imposed by Mr. Carnegie. Suppose in Nebraska a city of 10,000 people is without a public library building, and a public-spirited citizen, hearing of Mr. Carnegie's library gifts, writes to him asking for a sum of money to build a building. It is a part of the free library system that every letter bearing on a library matter shall be considered and answered. The moment the letter is opened by Mr. Carnegie's secretary, it becomes part of the system which has made it possible successfully to handle the work of more than a thousand libraries, often with the negotiations for several hundred going on at the same time. Immediately upon receipt of the request, Mr. Carnegie's secretary sends a blank form to the applicant, whether it be individual or society, provided they give evidence that the community or their officials are with the project, asking that certain questions be answered. These replies aid Mr. Carnegie in the consideration of the gift. There is a whole series of documents carefully prepared and adapted for every local condition, which is furnished to applicants. It shows how perfect is the method which Mr. Carnegie has adopted. . . .

When these forms have been filled out and returned to Mr. Carnegie, they form a basis for systematic consideration. If the applicant can be favorably considered and allowance be made for a building, Mr. Carnegie requires the council or local governing

Originally printed in *World's Work* 9 (April 1905): 6092–97.

7.6. Carnegie Library, Lexington, Kentucky, 1907. The Historic American Buildings Survey, 1968. Andrew Carnegie lived up to his promise to distribute most of his wealth before he died. Much of it went to building public libraries across the country—he offered one to any community willing to maintain it. Many of the Carnegie libraries, even those in large cities, are quite small, with a neo-Georgian design (as seen here), although there was a great diversity in design types.

body of the community to devote a specific sum yearly (usually 10 per cent of the cost of the building) for the maintenance of the library.

Mr. Carnegie does not provide plans, but he likes to have them submitted for approval. He does not interfere with the local authorities in choosing a site. Believing in home rule, as he does, a site which is satisfactory to the people and their representatives is satisfactory to him.

When all the requirements imposed by Mr. Carnegie have been met, and when the building plans have been sent on and approved, the Library Commissioners receive intimation that Mr. Carnegie's cashier at the Home Trust Company, Hoboken, N. J., will honor their calls to the full amount of the gift. All requisitions for library money must be made by the officers appointed by law to take charge of the library in the community, and must be certified by the architect in charge of the work.

A Carnegie Library building must be used exclusively for library purposes. It must be built on a site furnished by the community or by gift from some benevolent citizen. Although his name, by the common and spontaneous consent of a grateful people, adorns a thousand buildings all over the world, he has never made a request that this be done.

How does Mr. Carnegie know the amount of money to give to a community? The information that he receives on the blank forms largely determines this. It has been his custom to give about $2 for every inhabitant, according to the latest Federal census. A town of 10,000 people usually gets $20,000. It is astonishing how towns grow according to applicants for libraries. Mr. Carnegie's secretary says that if applicants for libraries are to be believed, the next census of the United States will show 150,000,000 people, at least. A claim of a 25 per cent increase since the Federal census of 1900 in considered comparatively modest. . . .

Branch libraries, which bring books close to the people, appeal more to Mr. Carnegie than large central buildings, in which something ornate and monumental is more likely to be the object than a storehouse for books and facilities for their being read. . . .

Only two states—Rhode Island and Arkansas—are without Carnegie Library buildings. Rhode Island is amply provided with libraries, and Arkansas has no library legislation which will permit communities to tax the people. Illinois has sixty cities and towns with sixty libraries, yet New York, with only forty towns with libraries, has 120 such institutions. This is due to the establishment of many branch libraries in New York City with Mr. Carnegie's gift of $5,200,000. The Carnegie Libraries in Illinois are more evenly distributed than in any other State in the Union, because there is only one library in a town. A table of Carnegie Libraries of the United States shows a significant growth in the newer States and particularly in the West. For example, Iowa has fifty-four towns with Carnegie Libraries. California has thirty-six towns with forty-six libraries. Texas has twenty. There are two in Indian Territory, three in Arizona and two in New Mexico. Kansas has sixteen and Nebraska has nine. Illinois leads the Central States, while Indiana is second with forty-nine towns with forty-nine libraries, again showing one library to a town and a wide distribution of the buildings. Massachusetts has only twenty-one Carnegie Libraries, because nearly every town had a library when Mr. Carnegie began his work of establishing them.

Pennsylvania has thirty-four towns with seventy library buildings. This State was first in which a Carnegie Library building was erected, for it was at Allegheny that Mr. Carnegie reared the magnificent building commemorating the kindness of Colonel Anderson. This place and Pittsburg witnessed his great business achievements. At Braddock, Homestead, and Duquesne, where his great steel works employed thousands of people, Mr. Carnegie built libraries for the workmen. He supplemented the library buildings with gymnasiums and meeting places, but it was the library work that began this welfare work for the people who served. . . .

Architecturally the Carnegie Libraries have had an aesthetic and uplifting influence throughout the whole country. Last summer I was driving through a little town in North Dakota. Ten years before it was a group of houses on a river bank and a stopping place for lumbermen on the way from Canada. That day I drove through well-made streets. The driver stopped the carriage before a low, square, classic-looking building surrounded by trees.

"That's our Carnegie Library," he said. "We are mighty proud of it."

"Why?" I asked, curious to find out what he would say.

"Well," he said, "that building has made everybody else here want a nice building." I had a similar experience in Kansas.

In the crowded foreign districts of New York City the Carnegie Free Libraries are making American citizens out of the young boys and girls. I spent an afternoon recently at the free library on Tompkins Square, in the very heart of the Hungarian section. It stands out among the dark, low tenements, giving an aesthetic distinction to the whole community. But it gives more than this. It is not only a place where books are given out and where men, women and children may come to read where it is bright and light and clean. It has entered into the very life and character of the whole district. Here come the mothers with their stories of suffering and distress to find comfort and sympathy and help from the librarians; here assemble the young men who work all day and study half the night, educating themselves and eager to rise out of the sordid conditions in which they live. The children come from dirty homes with clean hands. Standing in line to get books, and respecting the rights of the children who have come before them, is giving them a moral discipline. The little ones carry the methods of the school-room to the library, for they raise their hands and say "Teacher" before asking for a book.

Many incidents enliven the daily round of these East Side libraries. One day a child came in. "Teacher," she said holding up her hand, "I want to get Lamb's Feet."

"Lamb's Feet," said the librarian, "you must be mistaken. There is no such book."

But the child insisted that her school teacher had told her to get it. It turned out that she wanted Lamb's Tales.

Another child said she wanted a book on woman's sufferings. The librarian gave her a medical book.

"That ain't what I want," replied the child. "My mother said it was about votes." She wanted a book on woman's suffrage.

The children are required to give references when they get a card. The meaning of the word "reference" is a stumbling block to many. One day a librarian overheard one boy explaining the meaning of the word to another, as follows:

"A reference is the fellow what sticks up for you."

Tragedies, too, lurk in these places. A short time ago a thumb-marked postal card reached the Tompkins Square Library. Written in pencil in a child's hand was this inscription:

"My sister does not want any more books. She is dead."

What is happening at the Tompkins Square Library is happening at the East Broadway Library in the heart of the Ghetto, and at a half dozen other Carnegie Libraries in New York City. Everywhere they are entering intimately into the life of the people, broadening them and making them better men and women and children. . . .

Thus a man is applying an immense fortune systematically to the constructive work of enlightening English-speaking people. Its significance is world wide; its benefit is not for one generation but for many. That Mr. Carnegie has set about the performance of this task in its largest way is best gathered from his own conception of the spirit and meaning of libraries:

"Free libraries," he says, "maintained by the people are cradles of democracy; and their spread can never fail to extend and strengthen the democratic idea, the equality of the citizen, the royalty of man. They are emphatically fruits of the true American ideal."

95

BENJAMIN MARSH, EXCERPT FROM "CITY PLANNING IN JUSTICE TO THE WORKING POPULATION," 1908

Benjamin Marsh challenged some of the dominant ideas of the City Beautiful movement. He urged a series of concrete, somewhat technical changes so that urban reform would focus not simply on constructing public buildings and parkways but would confer its benefits "upon those most needing such benefits." He urged not just aesthetic change but also such far-reaching reforms as the creation of decent transportation systems and the regulation of house construction. Marsh's look to Britain and the efforts of civic leaders in London, Birmingham, and Liverpool was also typical of the era when crossing the Atlantic occurred as much for social policy as for tourism. Many American city planners looked jealously to Europe, where governments were given much greater powers to condemn property, build public housing, and regulate construction.

All public improvements should be scrutinized with a view to the benefits they will confer upon those most needing such benefits. The grouping of public buildings, and the installation of speedways, parks and drives, which affect only moderately the daily lives of the city's toilers, are important; but vastly more so is the securing of decent home conditions for the countless thousands who otherwise can but occasionally escape from their squalid, confining surroundings to view the architectural perfection and to experience the æsthetic delights of the remote improvements.

The right of the citizen to leisure, to health, to care in sickness, to work under normal conditions, and to live under conditions which will not impair his health or his efficiency, is coming to be recognized as fully as the right of the state to restrain the wrongdoer or its duty to protect property. The recognition of these rights of the citizen carries with it a recognition that the scope of governmental activity needs to be extended, its initiative untrammelled by constitutional limitations and its services given when they will be of the greatest value....

Regulation is the orderly ascertainment of what is a reasonable rate, with its enforcement—confiscation is the seizing of all property or earning power without any allowance as to its compensation.

The spirit of this definition of a well known and astute corporation lawyer we can accept as the basis for the action of a city involved in the term town planning. Recognizing the tendency of industry and commerce to centralization and the consequent growth of cities large or small, the city decides that the rights of those who are here, or who are to come, are paramount, and that no one citizen and no small groups of citizens may mortgage the welfare of others by failing to respect and make provision for such welfare.

England is paying much attention to the proper planning of her cities, and John S. Nettlefold of Birmingham has prepared a bill for the coming session of Parliament providing that a local authority may from time to time by resolution determine that plans shall be prepared indicating the manner in which the making, providing, laying out, widening or improving of any streets or open spaces in their districts or in any part or

Originally printed in *Charities and Commons* 29 (February 1, 1908): 1514–18.

parts thereof shall be carried out, and indicating the method in which the authority may enforce these requirements. . . .

The creation of new congested districts without the necessaries of healthy life now going on in large cities can only be prevented by obtaining power to forbid the erection of any new buildings except in accordance with a general plan for developing all uncovered land within the city boundaries. For the preparation of this plan a special committee should be appointed consisting of representatives from the public works, health, baths and parks, tramways, and housing committees, together with an architect, builder, medical man, lawyer, surveyor, and estate agent to be coopted by the council for their special knowledge of housing requirements and land development.

The need for excess condemnation and larger initiative for the city they appreciate, and assert that "the healthy development of the city would undoubtedly be much assisted if the council could obtain power to purchase land without, as at present, being obliged to specify the exact purpose for which the land is to be used."

Much of our social effort in American cities to better living conditions is aftersight instead of foresight, and we are engaged in the tremendous and impossible task of trying to end the evils we have helped to cause or to perpetuate. The German town plan contemplates a very different attitude. . . .

It is the special purpose of this paper to indicate that such rational planning is essential in order to protect those who without it must sacrifice for mere shelter so much of their income and savings as to compel them to lower their standard of living or to appeal to charity.

To this end five distinct functions should be involved in the system of town planning:

1. The limitation of the area within which factories may be located (like fire lines) and the securing by the municipality of proper facilities for transportation of freight by canal, railroad, subway, etc.
2. The determination by the municipality of the districts or zones within which houses of a given height may be erected, the number of houses which may be erected per acre, the site to be covered and consequently the density of population per acre.
3. The securing by the municipality of the proper means of transportation of the people.
4. The provision of adequate streets, open spaces, parks and playgrounds in anticipation of the needs of a growing community.
5. The right of excess condemnation, i. e., the authority to condemn more than the area to be used for the immediate purposes contemplated by the condemnation, so that ultimately the city makes no net expenditure for land to be used for public purposes.

A few illustrations can be given from actual conditions in various sections of New York. . . .

Manifestly any regulation of land speculation must be put into effect speedily in New York if it is to benefit the working people, thousands of whom are, even with our present standards, on the verge of dependence, and tens of thousands of whom are far below the normal standards of living which we should adopt. It is generally admitted that rents in Manhattan have risen twenty-five per cent to thirty per cent within a very few years, and although exhaustive statistics are lacking, it is also generally admitted that from twenty-five to thirty-five per cent of the earnings of ordinary laborers goes for rent if they have even the minimum accommodations compatible with decency and health.

The standard of living of wage earners may be raised in at least two ways: by increasing their wages or by reducing their expenses. Is it easier to say exclusively and arbitrarily to the employer: "You must increase the wages of your employee irrespective of their earning capacity and the price of your goods," or to say to the speculators in land: "You must limit your profits to a degree consonant with the welfare and earnings of those whose presence alone gives value to the limited commodity they must purchase from you."

Who should be first in Brooklyn, with a density of less than thirty five to the acre, in the Bronx with a density of less than twenty to the acre, in Queens with its 82,000 acres and a density of about three, and in Richmond with a density of two to the acre—the land speculator or the grafting politician, concerned solely for his income, or the municipality with due regard to the interests of all concerned?

To consider the necessity of securing adequate transit facilities for the proper distribution of the population of a city: It is a matter of course that in order to get people to and from their work, proper transit facilities must be provided, and special emphasis has been laid upon the need for proper restrictions regarding land brought into the housing market by increased transit facilities, because of the tendency to speculate in that land as soon as the time element is removed. Is it too much to say that the municipality should insure such transit facilities as will afford every worker a seat and bring him to his place of work in three quarters of an hour, from a home with the conditions above enumerated, and within Greater New York, for a five cent fare? Two hours on a car, in addition to a ten hour day of work mean a twelve hour day with the consequent exhaustion.

The authority which determines the location and nature of residences, and the location of factories, should control, or at least cooperate closely with those controlling the projection of transit facilities for passengers and freight....

The right to condemn a larger area than is needed for the immediate purpose contemplated, follows naturally. This is not a plea for municipal trading; it is merely a plea for the application to the business of a city of the business principles by which the working classes may be saved needless expense in the purchase by the city of those opportunities for which they must help pay, and the acquirement of which is often postponed on the plea that the city can't afford it,—a futile method of stating that the city cannot come into its own.

It is useless to deny that, in such procedure, there is the possibility of graft;—that exists whenever money is paid. To the cities which have now reached the debt limit, it furnishes, however, an important method of extending the protection and relief which the city owes, and of permitting the acquisition at a reasonable price of the land the city must ultimately own to secure the normal development of its citizenship. It is much easier to condemn land, and there is less danger of the cry of confiscation, when the prices demanded have not been inflated by the hopes of a large and unwarranted profit.

Reference has been made chiefly to conditions in New York because the writer is more familiar with conditions in the metropolis. All the boroughs, besides Manhattan, present in substance the problems of town planning—as against town replanning,— which exist in every city of any size; in fact several wards in some of these boroughs are as large and populous as many large cities.

So serious are the problems presented in this cursory review, that they reveal the wisdom of the bill constituting the commission to investigate the subject of public improvements for the Metropolitan District of Boston, which provides that the persons appointed by the governor of Massachusetts and mayor of Boston "shall be persons of recognized qualification and large experience in one or more of the following subjects or professions, namely, finance, commerce, industry, transportation, real estate, architecture, engineering, civic administration and law."

Some similar commission is needed for every large city in the country properly to plan the symmetrical development of our centers of population with due regard to the rights of all constituent members.

96

EDITH ELMER WOOD, EXCERPT FROM "THAT 'ONE THIRD OF A NATION,' " 1940

The title of Edith Elmer Wood's essay refers to a phrase President Franklin Roosevelt used in his second inaugural address in 1937, when despite four years of the New Deal he still saw "one third of a nation ill-clad, ill-fed, ill-housed." In the language of both social science and social activism, Wood makes the case here that publicly subsidized housing of the sort being built in the 1930s was an absolute necessity. Reformers had been for years advocating some sort of housing program to deal with tenements, slums, and the housing shortage in some urban areas. Public housing was counted by some among the New Deal's great successes. Wood suggests that these New Deal programs should not be seen as a short-term solution to the problems brought on by the Depression, but rather as a new role for government in creating a better life for marginalized people.

Equal opportunity which lies at the heart of democracy implies for every man, woman and child at least a sporting chance to attain health, decency and a normal family life. It was because the cards were stacked against a third of the nation that there had to be a new deal in housing. . . .

At present our public housing is also subsidized. The combination offers the only way to arrive at what we are trying to do—provide fit housing for families of the ill-housed and get rid of worn out housing. . . .

At least a third of our housing is bad enough to be a health hazard, but not all in the same way or to the same degree. The coverage of moral hazard is less than that of physical hazard, which is fortunate, as its effects are worse.

About two fifths of our housing is rural, divided more or less evenly between farm and non-farm. The Farm Housing Survey made in 1934 shows an appalling lack of modern

Originally printed in *Survey Graphic: Magazine of Social Interpretation* 29, no. 2 (February 1, 1940): 83–88.

sanitation and conveniences, except in a few favored regions. To call 80 percent of our farmhouses substandard is an understatement. . . . The abundance of blue sky, green grass, sunlight, fresh air and wholesome influences which usually (not always) accompany rural housing atone for some (by no means all) of its shortcomings. . . .

We know beyond a peradventure that areas with high deathrates and high sickness rates, especially for diseases dependent on contact infection, approximately coincide with areas of bad housing. General deathrates and infant mortality in slums are likely to be twice the city average, tuberculosis and pneumonia rates perhaps four times as high. Of course there are other causes, such as lack of medical care, poverty, ignorance, hereditary defect. But physical environment, which is predominantly housing, remains a major factor in the complex.

Not all bad housing areas have a high rate of delinquency or crime, but all areas with high rates of delinquency and crime appear to be areas of bad housing. It is often said that the neighborhood is more important than the house as a factor in producing delinquency. This is probably true, but the statement needs clarifying. To the city planner, "neighborhood" means buildings and open spaces. To the social worker, it means human associates. Both play their part in influencing the growing child, but we need to keep our thinking and our language clear.

The lack of play space for young children inside the crowded home and of yard space immediately outside it force them onto the street at an age when they ought to be still under close maternal care.

The typical near-in slum is a jumble of factories, warehouses, junkyards and tenements, interspersed with saloons, dives and hangouts. Neighborhood children must rub elbows daily with vice and crime. Moral contact infection appears to be more perilous than physical, for there is a wider spread between the juvenile delinquency rates in such a slum area and that in a neighborhood of pleasant homes with house yards than between the corresponding infant mortality rates. Parents, schools, churches, settlements carry on a gallant fight against unwholesome influences. Most slum children do not become criminals. But the casualty rate is much too high.

Still another set of studies in recent years has shown for a number of cities how much the taxpayers are now spending to maintain their slums as slums. In dollars and cents for hospitals and clinics, police, courts, reformatories and jails, made necessary by the excess illness and death, and the excess delinquency and crime, as well as extra costs in fire protection and garbage collection, the taxpayers are now paying out just about as much as it would take to do away with the slums and rehouse their inhabitants.

What have we to show for public housing so far in the United States?

It began in the summer of 1933. The National Industrial Recovery Act opened a crack of the door by naming the clearing of slums and the building of low rent houses among the purposes for which the new Public Works Administration could make loans and grants to public agencies. But there were no public housing authorities in those days, and no local ones could be created without state legislation. The only way to produce results quickly was for the housing division of the Public Works Administration to clear slums and build houses itself, which it proceeded to do. . . .

Fifty-one projects were built in thirty-six communities, containing 21,700 family dwelling units. More than half are on cleared slum sites. Nearly half are occupied by Negro tenants. Whether four-story apartments in New York or one-story bungalows in Miami, all have an abundance of sunlight, air, blue sky and green trees. All have safe play spaces for large and small children. All have the essentials for health and for normal family living.

The first PWA project opened its doors to tenants in Atlanta, in 1936. The last ones were completed after they had been taken over by USHA. Tenants everywhere seem well and happy. Community spirit is high. Maintenance is excellent. Projects are sources of real local pride, pointed out to strangers.

Meanwhile, however, the states had been passing enabling acts under which local housing authorities were being appointed, and the demand grew for permanent housing legislation and for decentralization. Slums and housing are local problems, which ought to be dealt with locally. National financial aid was, however, still obviously necessary if anything important was to be accomplished.

The United States Housing Act of 1937 was the result. Under it, the local housing authority initiates, makes plans, acquires sites, builds, owns and operates projects. It may borrow up to 90 percent of the cost of a project from the United States Housing Authority, which administers the act, and it may receive annual grants from the same source to make possible rents low enough for the groups rehoused. Ten percent of capital costs, and subsidy at least equal to one fifth of the national contribution, must be contributed locally. This last generally takes the form of partial exemption from local real estate taxes.

The USHA was set up on November 1, 1937, and took over the work, records and staff of the PWA housing division. Congress allowed it to make loans to a total of $500 million (increased in 1938 to $800 million) and to make annual grants to $20 million (increased to $28 million). It has the duty of establishing procedure, setting standards and exercising some degree of supervision, as well as being a fiscal agent. Presumably as time passes, local autonomy will increase and central control diminish. . . .

How much public housing must we plan for? That at once suggests "How long must we plan for?" Obviously a long range program is required. To be efficient and effective, it must be continuous.

We do not know what solutions private enterprise may evolve over a term of years. We do not know how much social security, minimum wage, collective bargaining, and the economic situation may change and (one may hope) improve the distribution of income at the lower levels. We are not yet sure what form the undoubtedly needed help to farm and rural housing ought to take. But we may quite safely adopt the recent estimate of Nathan Straus for the subsidized public housing program of 300,000 family units a year for fifteen years, or a total of 4,500,000. That is a large order, but not an impossible one. It leaves plenty of room, not only for private business enterprise but for possible developments in unsubsidized limited-dividend or cooperative housing for the middle third. Its fulfillment depends on Congress, but even more on all of us. Which is just another way of saying that, in a democracy, public housing will go as far and be as sound as the public opinion behind it.

97

JAMES BAILEY, "THE CASE HISTORY OF A FAILURE," 1965

David Harvey, an important urban geographer, has written that the end of modernism can be dated rather precisely to the particular hour in 1973 when the massive Pruitt-Igoe housing development in St. Louis was demolished. The demise of Pruitt-Igoe, by the high modernist architect Minoru Yamasaki (who went on to design the World Trade Center in New York City), after only twenty-four years was a potent symbol of the end of the vision of massive "towers in the park" ideal of some modernists and the slow replacement of that vision with "postmodernism" which was to be, among other things, more respectful of the street, the neighborhood, and historical styles of design. This article, written eight years before the demolition of the complex, highlights the social background of the physical decline of the complex, but primarily focuses on the design failures, especially the overwhelming scale. The larger tragedy is, however, that the fundamental notion underlying the creation of Pruitt-Igoe and modernist design more generally—that a new style of architecture more attuned to modern life could readily transform people's lives, including those of people living in poverty—remained.

In its April, 1951 issue the FORUM featured a St. Louis public housing project which, it claimed, had "already begun to change the public housing pattern in other cities." Called Pruitt-Igoe, its 33 11-story buildings designed by Hellmuth Yamasaki & Leinweber would "save not only people, but money," the FORUM predicted. Two months ago, only ten years after Pruitt-Igoe's completion, the Public Housing Administration announced that it will spend an unprecedented $7 million in an attempt to save it.

What impressed the FORUM were the project's efficient slab buildings incorporating skip-stop elevators opening only on every third floor, which permitted generous galleries, 11 ft. deep by 85 ft. long, at each of the stop floors. Also singled out were the "refreshing" site plan and landscaping design, which called for a minimum of 200 ft. between buildings and a "river" of open space winding among them.

The galleries, the feature which most impressed the FORUM, were conceived by the architects to be "vertical neighborhoods" serving a variety of uses:

- "As a close, safe playground for small children while mothers are doing housework or laundry.
- "As an open air hallway.
- "As a porch in spring, autumn and summer.
- "As a laundry.
- "As storage for such items as bicycles, washing machines, and tools."

Despite its "creative economies," Pruitt-Igoe proved too costly for PHA, which ordered several cutbacks before construction began. The landscaping was reduced to virtually nothing, and such "luxuries" as paint on the concrete block walls of the galleries and stairwells, insulation on exposed steam pipes, screening over the gallery windows, and

Originally printed in *Architectural Forum* 23, no. 5 (December 1965): 22–25.

7.7. Robert Taylor Homes, Chicago, from the Dan Ryan Expressway, 1997. Courtesy of Iguana Photo, www.iguanaphoto.com. Perhaps the most notorious of public housing developments in Chicago, the Robert Taylor Homes stretched for miles south from Chicago's center when it was completed in 1962. The largest public housing project in the country, the twenty-eight identical sixteen-story buildings housed over twenty-eight thousand people and helped solidify residential segregation in Chicago. Some visionary modern architects, such as Le Corbusier, had argued that tall towers set within green space would provide ideal living conditions. The economic and social isolation of the Robert Taylor Homes and the attendant crime and degradation was the most poignant condemnation of the modernist vision. Like the Pruitt-Igoe housing complex in St. Louis—the first of this type of public housing to be torn down—the Robert Taylor Homes have slowly been demolished. Many have cheered, but the question of where low-income residents will live has gone unanswered.

public toilets on the ground floors, were eliminated. But the basic scheme was built essentially as designed by the architects.

Today, ten years after its completion, Pruitt-Igoe bears little resemblance to the architects' early sketches. . . . In a city that suffers from a shortage of low-income housing, it is nearly a third vacant—PHA's major reason for putting up the $7 million. Its buildings loom formidably over broad expanses of scrubby grass, broken glass and litter, and they contain hundreds of shattered windows.

The undersized elevators are brutally battered, and they reek of urine from children who misjudge the time it takes to reach their apartments. By stopping only on every third floor, elevators offer convenient settings for crime. Every so often assailants will jam the elevators while they rob, mug or rape victims, then stop at one of the floors and send the elevator on with the victims inside.

The stairwells, the only means of access to almost [all] the apartments, are scrawled with obscenities; their meager lighting fixtures and fire hoses are ripped out; and they too provide handy sites for predators. The breezeways at the entrances are hangouts for teenagers who often taunt the women and children and disturb those in close-by apartments with their noise.

The galleries are anything but cheerful social enclaves. The tenants call them "gaunt-lets" through which they must pass to reach their doors. Children play there, but they are unsupervised and their games are rough and noisy outdoor pastimes transferred inside. Heavy metal grilles now shield the windows, but they were installed too late to prevent three children from falling out. The steam pipes remain exposed, both in the galleries and the apartments, frequently inflicting severe burns.

The adjoining laundry rooms are unsafe and little used. They never served enough tenants to keep them continuously bustling with activity, and thus invited molesters. Now their doors are kept locked, and keys are distributed to the few tenants who use them. The storage rooms also are locked and empty. They have been robbed of their contents so often that tenants refuse to use them.

SIMPLY TOO BIG

The St. Louis Housing Authority operates seven other public housing developments, and it claims that none of them comes close to Pruitt-Igoe in the proportion of crimes and acts of vandalism committed. Why? Charles L. Farris, the Authority's executive director, says Pruitt-Igoe is simply too big. With nearly 2,800 units and almost 11,000 inhabitants (12,000 if it were full), it is four times the size of the second largest project. Its sheer size and scale, Farris says, thwart all attempts at effective management.

Architect Minoru Yamasaki, who designed Pruitt-Igoe, agrees that its size is objectionable. His original design called for a combination of garden apartments and high-rise buildings accommodating,—a density of 30 per acre. "PHA forced us to almost double the density [to 55]," Yamasaki said. "The best we could do then was to eliminate the low-rise and add more slabs."

As for the misuse of Pruitt-Igoe's communal spaces, Yamasaki said "I never thought people were that destructive. As an architect, I doubt if I would think about it now. I suppose we should have quit the job. It's a job I wish I hadn't done."

Architect Gyo Obata, who joined the firm while Pruitt-Igo was in design, recalled that Yamasaki "tried and fought at every turn" with PHA to get more amenities. "Now," he said, "PHA has gone clear around. They are rehabilitating Pruitt-Igoe because they realize that the human values we fought for are important."

The Rev. John A. Shocklee, pastor of St. Bridget's Catholic Church adjacent to Pruitt-Igoe, criticized the project's lack of public and commercial facilities. "To build a place and offer no services to 2,800 units is ridiculous," he said. "There are no gymnasiums, no barbecue pits, no soda fountains, no decent places for people to gather. The kids have nothing to do; they might as well pull pipes out of the walls and break windows." A community center, built on the site about five years ago, has not worked well because the Housing Authority places too many restrictions on its use, Father Shocklee contended. Also, the community center is the place where tenants pay their rent—a function which underscores their suspicion that it belongs to the Authority, not to them.

Dr. Lee Rainwater, professor of sociology and anthropology at Washington University St. Louis, is heading an exhaustive five-year social study of Pruitt-Igoe through a grant from the National Institute of Mental Health. Though he is reluctant to publicly discuss the study until it is completed, a paper that he delivered to an American Psychological Association conference last fall, based partly on his research at Pruitt-Igoe, reveals some of his conclusions about what he calls "the non-human threats" posed by the physical design of public housing.

These threats, he said, "can be pretty well done away with where the resources are available to design decent housing for lower class people." For example, "In buildings where there are half a dozen or more families whose doors open onto a common hallway, there is a greater sense of the availability of help should trouble come than there is in buildings where only two or three apartments open onto a small hallway in a stairwell."

But, Dr. Rainwater observed, "it would be asking too much to insist that design per se can solve or even seriously mitigate" the human problems of the occupants. At Pruitt-Igoe, these problems are overwhelming.

ABSENTEE FATHERS

The median annual income of the project's 2,100 families is only $2,300, and more than half are receiving welfare payments. Of the 10,736 individuals living there, 98 per cent of whom are Negro, there are only 990 adult males. Missouri law prohibits mothers from receiving public assistance for their children if the father lives at home, and since the aid check is often a family's only stable source of income, many fathers live elsewhere. Father Shocklee considers the absence of so many male heads of households a major cause of its disciplinary and crime problems: "This is the natural result when you drive out any of the strong men. When you remove so much strength from a community, it takes more than the police department to restore the basic structure."

Pruitt-Igoe also is a state of mind. Its notoriety, even among those who live there, has long since outstripped the facts. Its crime rate, though high, is well below that of the surrounding slum neighborhood, and declining. Yet, until recently, the St. Louis Globe Democrat referred to every offense committed anywhere in the general neighborhood as a "Pruitt-Igoe" crime—its way of saying "Negro."

Planner-Architect Albert Mayer, who is advising the Housing Authority and Hellmuth, Obata & Kassabaum in planning the renovation, calls Pruitt-Igoe "a product of the atmosphere of the time. Housing was considered mainly as shelter. Agencies were opposed to anything enlivening, any commercial facilities. There was the crass hostility of real estate interests and the puritanical belief that people could, if they wanted to, earn their own way."

"The success or failure of any housing project," Mayer said, "depends on a combination of social help and alert, understanding management." Pruitt-Igoe, he feels, was deficient in some degree in all three. "Its great size and density," he said, "are accentuated by its relentless over scale. It doesn't stop and it doesn't start. It is a question of endlessness versus definition. Design can provide the definition. But much of this could have been alleviated had the management approached it administratively and socially as a group of smaller entities."

Pruitt-Igoe also is an example of the "not altogether rational craze for open space," Mayer said. "The important thing with open space is what you do with it. At Pruitt-Igoe its relationship to the surrounding slum areas was not sufficiently considered. The adjoining strip of park, bleak and treeless, rather than acting as a link between the project and its neighborhood, serves as a barrier. The open spaces among the buildings are, per se, neutral. They provide too many uncontrolled situations which invite trouble."

The $7 million renovation can do nothing about the building masses, but Mayer has proposed a number of changes designed to relieve the project's sterility and correct its almost total lack of social and recreational facilities. They include many small playgrounds of differing character and designed for different age groups, sitting places, barbecue pits, and wooded picnic areas.

New lighting will be installed, not only for security but, in Mayer's words, "to highlight the arteries of this 'small town's' anatomy."

Circulation will be made to converge on a new central pedestrian "main street," and entrances to the project will be designed to give it greater self-identity. Two cul-de-sac streets will be joined to form a continuous loop. A small private shopping center will be built on a portion of the site to be sold as surplus property. Small buildings of special character which Mayer calls "Everybody's Clubs" will provide informal drop-in and gathering places for all age groups, manned and supervised by tenants.

Within the buildings, the galleries will be narrowed and additional apartment units placed where the laundry and storage rooms are. Laundry facilities will be moved to the ground floor. One of the two breezeways in each building will be partially enclosed for a sheltered play area. Exposed pipes will be covered, raw cement blocks painted, and elevators reconditioned. Public toilets will be installed in the ground floors, and each building group will have a first floor sub-community center. The skip-stop system, too expensive to correct, will remain in all but two buildings to be converted for the exclusive use of the elderly. All elevators will be reconditioned.

Tenant Participation

The Housing Authority, aware that physical rehabilitation may only provide "something else to break," has a series of programs underway to involve the tenants in the process, invite their suggestions, and give them a voice—and hope—in the future. The Authority has also begun a program to coordinate the activities of the scores of Federal, state and local welfare and social agencies, private charitable organizations and sympathetic individuals who are stumbling over each other, and the tenants, in efforts to do something about the human problems of Pruitt-Igoe.

Three years ago, Pruitt-Igoe was selected by the Department of Health, Education and Welfare for its first "concerted services" project, an intense program of health, education, vocational rehabilitation and welfare services. In a report issued last year, HEW admitted that the results have been disappointing, though the same method is working well other places. "Because of the complexity of the problems," said the report, "one can only hope for slow but steady progress in the future."

The same philosophy is being applied to the physical rehabilitation. It will proceed cautiously in four stages over the next five years. After each stage is completed, it will receive a six-month scrutiny so that mistakes can be avoided and new solutions tried in succeeding stages. This time there are no glowing predictions—just hope, and a determination to alter the grim realities of Pruitt-Igoe's first ten years.

98

VINCENT SCULLY, "THE THREAT AND PROMISE OF URBAN REDEVELOPMENT IN NEW HAVEN," 1967

Vincent Scully, professor of art history at Yale University for the entire second half of the twentieth century, did more than almost any critic to highlight the failures of the reform movement called "urban renewal." And it was a reform movement: an organized effort to solve many of the mid-century city's ills through "cataclysmic" physical change, oriented to the automobile and to eliminating the "blight" of poor areas and messy street life. Urban renewal of the 1950s and 1960s was born of new tools—the Federal Housing Act of 1949 and the Interstate Highway Act of 1956—but was derived from a previous half century of urban thought and experimentation led by such reformers as Jacob Riis. At the heart of Scully's eloquent critique of urban renewal in New Haven is a focus on its three-pronged approach: "the cataclysmic, the automotive, and the suburban." In its place, he offers a celebration of the vibrancy of urban street life and the social value of diverse city life.

Urban renewal is in an obvious state of crisis throughout the United States. The architectural and planning concepts of a generation ago, upon which the first phases of urban redevelopment were generally based, have now clearly shown themselves to be obsolete. Hence the threat of redevelopment in New Haven, as elsewhere, derives from the possibility that it might continue to act upon those discredited principles and, by so doing, destroy the town. The promise of urban renewal, on the other hand, rests in the hope that those responsible for it will use their power to restudy the whole problem in a professional manner, so formulating better architectural and sociological principles, through which the city may be saved for all its people and for the generations to come. That hope can be especially strong in New Haven, where a large body of professional assistance lies ready at hand, anxious to be used, and where the mayor and his various agencies of redevelopment were so early on the ground that they need hardly fear to damage their reputations by embracing fresh principles now. It is indeed mandatory that they do so. Everything in life must change, or pass away.

The point is clear: it is certainly not a personal or, in the larger sense, even a political one. It is profoundly professional, having to do with the basic concepts through which all forms are made. And most planning of the past fifteen years has been based upon three destructive fallacies: the cataclysmic, the automotive, and the suburban. These fallacies may be characterized in a few words: the cataclysmic insists upon tearing everything down in order to design from an absolutely clean slate; the automotive would plan for the free passage of the automobile at the expense of all other values; the suburban dislikes the city anyway and would just as soon destroy its density and strew it across the countryside.

Indeed, all the fallacies derive from principles which are fundamentally anti-urban and destructive of the city: the cataclysmic hates the complication of human life which is what a town is all about, just as it is unable to adjust itself to those pre-existing buildings through which the culture of cities—which means human civilization—is handed on from generation to generation. The cataclysmic is therefore also puristic and genteel; it cannot bear the complexity and the splendid mess of towns. The automotive fallacy feeds

Originally printed in *Zodiac* 17 (1967): 171–75.

those same aversions and supports them by substituting vast over-designed highways and connectors for pre-existing neighborhoods, the replanning of which to house a non-affluent population would otherwise pose difficult problems which the redeveloper would rather not face. The cult of the suburb plays its part here as well; the connector becomes a greenbelt through the city, and in that bucolic atmosphere it transports affluent suburbanites directly into the heart of a city which has now been turned into another suburban shopping center for their convenience, while at the same time it has been emptied of the offensive presence of the poor with their messy problems and complicated demands.

Most of the early phases of redevelopment in New Haven—with the proud and honorable exceptions of Wooster Square and Long Wharf—were not untouched by those fallacies and, in my opinion, did the fabric of the city some harm with them. Long Wharf applied similar principles where they made sense—outside the city; and Wooster Square, with the sad exception of the hole cut in it for Russo Park, ignored them all, and so rehabilitated rather than destroyed. Around the square itself, that is, the rest of the area was suburbanized. But a number of the redevelopment projects which lie ahead promise to be of the destructive variety. Among them are the construction of four to six lanes of connector around the center of the city from the Trumbull Street entrance of I-91, and the extension, at present temporarily blocked by citizens action, of the connector which would destroy East Rock Park and might one day blast its way up Armory Street. These two would form the Inner and Outer Circumferential Ring Roads. How the designers involved in these schemes love the roll of such sonorous phrases; they offer the kind of symbolic incantation which serves as a substitute for thought. Soon the city would be chopped up into squirming segments by those vast and sterile barriers. The Oak Street Connector can show us right now what they would look like. But the matter would not end there, because the automobile, given just too much, will take all. Eventually there would be little left but roads, with a neo-suburban shopping center in the middle and a few huddles of captive population, Stalags I, II, etc., scattered about in the toils of the throughway.

The proposed redesign of the Hill neighborhood would not be out of place in that blasted landscape, while the present project for the government complex east of the Green would be an appropriate image for the government of such a province. Its dominant building would be a speculative office tower, owned by a bank and acquired through the public subsidy of the redevelopment program. The historic Green, center of New Haven's civic life and liberties, would, appropriately enough, be ground to nothing by that tower, for which it would serve only as a doormat. At the same time, the definition of the Green would be destroyed by the demolition of the Post Office. The removal of that fine building would serve two cataclysmic purposes, since it would both cut the side out of the Green and, in the manner made famous by Orwell in his 1984, cut a central piece out of our civic memory, through which our dignities as men are developed and sustained.

Again, the three fallacies are present. Cataclysmic: almost all pre-existing buildings gone. Automotive: the Post Office has to go, said the architect, in order to provide uninterrupted basement parking for the bank. Suburban: the cars themselves, and the vast, meaningless open space of the plaza, testify to that arcadian call. So gross is the effect that one cannot really believe that it has been presented without irony. In any event it is an ideal expression of why the cataclysmic, automotive, and suburban fallacies, with their concomitant purism and sick gentility, must all be cast aside.

Instead, all of us who live in cities and care for them must formulate new principles, more broadly and humanly based. We must restudy all the problems of the city in this light: from those posed by the automobile to those raised by the need for decent low-cost housing. We must value the special urban character of low-income neighborhoods more than has been done in the recent past, and we must rescue the traditional street from the impatient calumnies alike of Ville Radieuse and Garden City planners. Here Jane Jacobs, *Death and Life of Great American Cities,* New York, 1961, seems better and better at every rereading. Urban density must be seen as a positive good, in which the buildings of past generations play an important part, since through them the generations communicate with each other and the living complexity of civilization is transmitted across the centuries. Differences are precious; they are what make a city, wherein the complex interaction of individual human lives produce the special hardness, intelligence, and generosity which mark communal form—shaping a family in time, almost immortally.

99

JOHN EDGAR WIDEMAN, "DOING TIME, MARKING RACE," 1995; AND PETER ANNIN, "INSIDE THE NEW ALCATRAZ," 1998

The relationship between architecture and social reform at the end of the twentieth century brings us full circle back to the early nineteenth century and the building of prisons. Both the federal government and the states built prisons at an astonishing rate in the last quarter of the twentieth century, a physical manifestation of the public's desire to "get tough" on crime and criminals. Yet while these buildings proliferated across the landscape—indeed, financially strapped cities and towns often competed for them because they represented the only public works projects available—gone was the social theory of rehabilitation and reform that lay behind the Quaker experiments at Eastern State. John Edgar Wideman writes with great personal anguish about a nation so consumed with building prisons. In so doing, he follows the admonition of the great Russian writer Fyodor Dostoevsky, who said that to truly take the measure of a society, one must look in its prisons. In his essay, Peter Annin takes us on a brief tour of the new federal "supermax" prison, designed to house the worst criminal offenders.

JOHN EDGAR WIDEMAN, "DOING TIME, MARKING RACE"

I know far too much about prisons. More than I ever wished to know. From every category of male relative I can name—grandfather, father, son, brother, uncle, nephew, cousin, in-laws—at least one member of my family has been incarcerated. I've researched the genesis of prisons, visited prisons, taught in prisons, written about them, spent a night here and there as a prisoner. Finally, I am a descendant of a special class of immigrants—Africans—for whom arrival in America was a life sentence in the prison of slavery. None of the above is cited because it makes me proud or happy, but I feel I

Reprinted with permission from the October 30, 1995, issue of *The Nation*.

7.8. The Arizona State Prison complex-Lewis, Buckeye, Arizona. If the Mall of America represents one side of the state of the American built environment at the end of the millennium, the prisons that sprang up at ever more rapid a pace in the 1980s and 1990s represent another. Indeed, the prison construction effort, embodied by the Arizona State Prison complex spread over 284 acres, is the largest public building project since the interstate highway system of the 1950s and 1960s.

should identify some of the baggage, whether bias or insight, I bring to a discussion of prisons.

The facile notion of incarceration . . . as a cure for social, economic and political problems has usurped the current national discussion. Which candidate is tougher on crime was the dominant issue dramatized in TV ads during the last election campaign. And the beat goes on.

"Tougher" seems to mean which candidate behaves more like the bullies I encountered in junior high school, the guys whose fierce looks, macho words and posturing lorded it over the weakest kids, stealing their lunch money, terrorizing and tormenting them to gain a tough-dude image. Cowards at the core, bad actors mimicking the imagined thugs who keep them awake at night.

What bothered me most about the hysterical, bloodthirsty TV ads during the last election was the absolute certainty of the candidates that the prison cells they promised to construct, the draconian prison terms and prison conditions they would impose if elected, would never confine them or those who voted for them. Ignorance, racism, naivete couldn't account for this arrogant, finger-pointing certainty. The only way they could be so sure was to know the deck was stacked, know that they enjoyed an immunity. The ones they were promising to lock up and punish, by design, would never be their people. Always somebody else. Somebody other. Not their kind. The fix was in. Without referring explicitly to race or class, the candidates and their audiences understood precisely who the bad guys were and who the bad guys would continue to be, once the candidates assumed power. I recall a sentencing hearing in a courtroom, the angry father (white) of a victim urging a judge (white) to impose upon a young man (black), who'd pleaded guilty, the most severe punishment because "they're not like us, Your Honor."

Honest fear, thoughtful perplexity, a leavening of doubt or hesitancy, the slightest hint, then or now, that what the candidates insinuated about the "other," about criminals and misfits, also implicated them, would be a welcome relief. Instead, the rhetoric continues, Manichean, divisive and absolute, the forces of light doing battle with the forces of darkness.

As an African-American, as a human being, I haven't yet shaken the sense of being personally assaulted by the campaign appeals to the electorate's meanest instincts. Nor have I been able to forgive the success of the tactic.

Sure enough, our country's in deep trouble. Drastic measures are required. But who says we must always begin at the bottom, taking from those who have least? Why heap more punishment on the losers, the tiny majority of lawbreakers who are dumb enough or unlucky enough to get caught and convicted? Building more prisons doesn't decrease crime. Removing federal money from some citizens' hands (the poor) and placing it in others' (the rich) doesn't save the nation billions. Why are patently false cures proclaimed and believed with such passionate conviction?

Why not start at the top? Limit maximum income. Reduce military spending. Wouldn't it be better to be swept from the earth while trying to construct a just society, rather than holding on, holding on, in a fortress erected to preserve unfair privilege? What indefensible attitudes are we assuming toward the least fortunate in our society? Isn't shame the reason we are desperately intent on concealing from ourselves the simple injustice of our actions?

We're compiling a hit list. Retrogressing. Deciding once more it's in the nation's interest to treat some as more equal than others. Belief that America is burdened by incorrigibles—criminals, the poor and untrained, immigrants too different to ever fit in—is an invitation to political leaders who can assure us they have the stomach and clean hands to dispose of surplus people pulling the rest of us down. We're looking to cold-eyed, white-coated technocrats and bottom-line bureaucrats for efficient final solutions. If this sounds paranoid or cartoonish, you must be unaware of facilities such as Pelican Bay in California, already in operation: chilling, high-tech, supermax prisons driving their inmates to madness and worse.

The sad, defeatist work of building prisons, the notion that prison walls will protect us from crime and chaos, are symptomatic of our shortsightedness, our fear of engaging at the root, at the level that demands personal risk and transformation, of confronting the real problems caging us all.

In the guise of outrage at crime and criminals, hard-core racism (though it never left us) is making a strong, loud comeback. It's respectable to tar and feather criminals, to advocate locking them up and throwing away the key. It's not racist to be against crime, even though the archetypal criminal in the media and the public imagination almost always wears "Willie" Horton's face. Gradually, "urban" and "ghetto" have become code words for terrible places where only blacks reside. Prison is rapidly being relexified in the same segregated fashion.

For many, the disproportionate number of blacks in prison is not a worrisome issue; the statistics simply fulfill racist prophecy and embody a rational solution to the problem of crime. Powerful evidence, however, suggests racism may condition and thereby determine where the war on drugs is waged most vigorously. A recent study, summarized in The New York Times on October 5, indicates that although African-Americans represent about 13 percent of the total population and 13 percent of those who are monthly drug users, they are 35 percent of those arrested for drug possession, 55 percent convicted for possession and 74 percent of the total serving sentences for possession.

We seem doomed to repeat our history. During the nineteenth century institutions such as prisons, orphanages, asylums and poorhouses developed as instruments of public policy to repair the gaping rents in America's social fabric caused by rapid industrialization and urbanization. Politicians driven by self-interest, hoping to woo businessmen and voters with a quick fix, avoided confrontation with the underlying causes of social instability and blamed the poor. Inborn idleness, irresponsibility, uncontrollable brutish instincts, inferior intelligence, childlike dependence, were attributed to the lower classes. Public policies, focusing on this incorrigible otherness, defined the state's role as custodial, separating and controlling suspect populations. State intervention into the lives of the poor neither diminished crime nor alleviated misery but did promote fear and loathing of the victims of chaotic social upheaval.

Today young black men are perceived as the primary agents of social pathology and instability. The cure of more prisons and longer prison terms will be applied to them. They will be the ones confined, stigmatized, scapegoated. Already squeezed out of jobs, education, stable families and communities, they are increasingly at risk as more and more of the street culture they have created, under incredible stress to provide a means of survival, is being criminalized (and callously commercialized). To be a man of color of a certain economic class and milieu is equivalent in the public eye to being a criminal.

Prison itself, with its unacceptably large percentage of men and women of color, is being transformed by the street values and street needs of a younger generation of prisoners to mirror the conditions of urban war zones and accommodate a fluid population who know their lives will involve inevitable shuttling between prison and the street. Gang affiliation, drug dealing, the dictates of gang leaders, have replaced the traditional mechanisms that once socialized inmates. Respect for older, wiser heads, the humbling, sobering rites of initiation into a stable prison hierarchy, have lost their power to reinforce the scanty official impetus toward rehabilitation that prison offers. The prison is the street, the street is prison.

If we expand our notion of prison to include the total institution of poverty, enlarge it to embrace metaphorical fetters such as glass ceilings that limit upward mobility for executives of color, two facts become apparent: There is a persistence of racialized thinking that contradicts lip service to a free, democratic society; and for people of color, doing time is only one among many forms of imprisonment legitimized by the concept of race.

The horrors of the prison system, the horrors of racism, depend upon the public's willed ignorance. Both flourish in the darkness of denial. As long as the one-way street of racial integration and the corrosive notion of a melting pot confuse our thinking about national identity and destiny, we'll continue to grope in darkness. We need to be honest with ourselves. Who we are, what kind of country we wish to become, are at issue when we talk about prisons.

PETER ANNIN, "INSIDE THE NEW ALCATRAZ"

Driving up the main road you pass a work camp, a medium-security facility and a maximum-security facility, all part of the big federal corrections complex outside Florence, Colo. Then you come to the place that is, literally and figuratively, the end of the line—the new Alcatraz, the toughest federal penitentiary in America. This is the Administrative Maximum Facility, also known as ADX. Inmates call it "the Big One" or the "Hellhole of the Rockies."

Since it opened in 1994, ADX has held the unique mission of confining "the worst of the worst"—400-plus inmates from all across the federal prison system, men so dangerous no other pen can hold them. Some, like terrorist Ramzi Yousef, mastermind of the World Trade Center bombing, were sent to ADX because authorities feared their supporters might try to rescue them: among other security features, the prison is specifically designed to thwart an attack from outside. Other cons were transferred there because they killed or assaulted guards or inmates. The cells . . . look like they were designed for Hannibal Lecter. All furniture is concrete, to prevent occupants from making weapons out of bed frames or other metal parts, and each cell has a special vestibule where the inmate is shackled, hands behind his back, when he is being taken elsewhere in the prison. Solitary confinement is the norm: 40 percent of the cons stay in their cells 22 hours a day, and another 33 percent, the hardest of the hard core, are locked down 23 hours a day. They get out only for an hour of exercise—which they take all alone, in a room that looks like an undersize racquetball court. "It's not a prison where you have to worry about getting raped," one visitor says.

The triangular main building is like something out of M. C. Escher—full of angles and obstructions that aren't quite what they seem. The entry is underground, through a heavily guarded tunnel. Cells have slit windows that show only a sliver of sky. That makes it hard for inmates or visitors to tell precisely where they are within the prison building, which complicates planning rescues or escapes. But it also makes ADX one of the most psychologically debilitating places on earth. "Lock yourself in your bathroom for the next four years and tell me how it affects your mind," says Raymond Luc Levasseur, a veteran of the '70s radical underground who is serving 45 years for a series of bombings. "It begins to erode the five senses. It's dehumanizing."

Who's who at ADX is usually secret—another security precaution. But the names of high-profile inmates sometimes leak out. NEWSWEEK has learned that Oklahoma City bomber Timothy McVeigh and Ted Kaczynski, the Unabomber, share the same cellblock (and round-the-clock video surveillance) with Ramzi Yousef. Terry Nichols, McVeigh's accomplice, may be transferred to the prison soon. Gang leader Luis Felipe, head of New York's Latin Kings, is already there. Felipe, who was convicted of ordering at least six murders while serving time in a New York state prison, is prohibited from having any visitors other than his lawyer, Lawrence Feitell. According to Feitell, Felipe has broken down from the stress of his isolation. He has difficulty sleeping and eating and suffers from shakes or tremors, Feitell said; Prozac hasn't helped. "He falls into fits of weeping. He's written letters to the judge begging for some form of human contact," Feitell says. "The kind of mind it would take to create a place like that is beyond me."

The credit belongs to Norman Carlson. Director of the U.S. Bureau of Prisons until

Originally printed in *Newsweek*, July 13, 1998, 35.

1987, Carlson says ADX is a direct response to the sharp increase in "violent and preda-tory" inmates during the 1970s and '80s, particularly at the federal pen in Marion, Ill. Twenty inmates were murdered in 18 years at Marion—and on Oct. 22, 1983, two guards were stabbed to death by "two members of the Aryan Brotherhood who were just trying to outdo each other," Carlson says. The whole prison went on permanent, 23-hour lock-down and the "supermax" concept was born. Following the Feds' example, more than 30 states now have supermax pens.

This trend disturbs prison-rights activists, who argue that supermax prisons are a form of "cruel and unusual" punishment prohibited by the Constitution. "There has al-ways been solitary confinement in this country," says Jamie Fellner of Human Rights Watch. "The difference is the length of time. We're not talking about putting someone in the hole for 15 days. We're talking about 15 years or life." But the federal courts have up-held the practice of 23-hour lockdowns, and that means ADX and the supermax concept are here to stay. Says architect John Quest, who designed the brick-and-concrete struc-ture: "This building shows that prisons don't have to be ugly to be secure." The view from inside isn't nearly so pretty.

CHAPTER 8

Monuments and Memory: Building and Protecting the American Past

"A society first of all needs to find landmarks," the sociologist Maurcie Halbwachs wrote in the 1930s. Halbwachs was no sentimental lover of old buildings; rather, he argued that landmarks were essential to perpetuating the "collective memory" that knit a society together. Not only did he believe that collective memories were "socially" constructed, they were also literally constructed. Memory was built into the physical landscape and recalled individuals' encounters with buildings, natural sites, and whole regions. Landscape and memory are codependent; memories are impossible without physical landscapes and structures to store and serve as touchstones for the work of recollection.

Writing about the ways in which the past plays into the development of American architecture may seem a dead-end pursuit. After all, a powerful stereotype of American life has been that Americans care little about their own past; it holds little power over the way Americans act or how the nation builds cities and designs buildings. Henry James perhaps said it best when he returned from Europe in 1904. Although he was speaking of New York City, it could have been the entire country to which he would apply his words: "Crowned not only with no history, but with no credible possibility of time for history," the United States was defined less by stable traditions than by the "dreadful chill of change." Indeed, if one of the primary ways people have linked themselves, however weakly or fleetingly, to the past has been through attachments to relatively stable landscapes, America offered a difficult landscape for memory. The rapidity with which the United States built and rebuilt itself in its first two hundred years made this connection highly problematic at times. While many, especially at the turn of the twentieth century, agreed with James, many others looked at James's criticism with delight: the United States would indeed have no history and would escape what Friedrich Nietzsche called the "cancerous growth of history on life." In the United States, the past would not be an anchor weighing down future generations, as it had in Europe.

This chapter argues with James and with this powerful cultural stereotype. Americans have not been an ahistorical people. All people in all places make their way in the world with some nod to the past and with an eye to the future. We want to argue that, in fact, in few places has the tension between looking backward and looking forward been greater than in the United States, a new world born of old worlds. Few nations have possessed as intense a desire to escape the sins and failures of the rest of the world and to establish roots in the interest of creating a new set of traditions.

The paradoxes of American attitudes toward the past are many. America was the "new world," a place where regeneration was possible. At the same time, it was a nation with as diverse and as long a history as any nation, with the collective histories of the Native Americans—who had imagined both specific sites of remembrance and a broader sacred landscape built into the land—Spanish invaders, French traders, and German immigrants embedded into the land. Furthermore, the very diversity of American life and the fluidity

8.1. Maxwell Street, Chicago, 1999. Courtesy of Iguana Photo, www.iguanaphoto.com. The historic preservation movement, which dates back to well before the turn of the twentieth century, became a national movement in the wake of the destruction of Pennsylvania Station and the subsequent passing of the 1966 National Landmarks Preservation Law. But for much of the subsequent thirty years, the movement focused on sites of the elite. Even today, as the preservation has been broadened to include slave quarters and immigrant tenements, many places that have played a crucial part in the development of American life—such as Maxwell Street in Chicago, where the urban blues were born—have been destined for destruction.

of it, with waves of immigrants arriving in the hundreds of thousands yearly, regularly infused the country and its built environment with new traditions. In rebuilding San Francisco's Chinatown in the wake of the 1906 earthquake, residents chose to decorate plain buildings in the elaborate style of northern Chinese temples, not because this was their true heritage (it generally was not) but because it helped to created a cohesive community and was an "exotic" lure for visitors. Shotgun houses in Louisiana and throughout the South are derived from African traditions transferred across the Atlantic to the Carribbean and on to the United States, kept alive by African-American builders.

Still we should be clear: those with the great influence over what traditions were built into and onto the land were those in the positions of economic and political power: for much of American history, Anglo-Saxon, Protestant, and white. The dominant narrative of American history was usually reinforced by the way history was written into the landscape.

There are two ways this has been done that we will consider here. One has been the preservation of buildings, or particular places, in ways that freeze them and put them off-limits to the processes of change that other places undergo. The other is to build or erect some kind of monument designed to evoke specific memories of specific events. Both have served powerfully to crown the American landscape with a sense of history.

James might have found the United States a country without history, but both Nathaniel Hawthorne and Ralph Waldo Emerson, writing in the antebellum period, disagreed. Emerson complained in 1836 about his "retrospective" age and wondered why Americans chose to build "sepulchers to the fathers." Indeed, there are numerous instances of early preservation and memorial efforts, including the successful effort to save Independence Hall from demolition (1811), the founding of the New-York Historical Society (an institution dedicated to saving art and objects of early America) in 1804, and the preservation of colonial-era homes. Furthermore, under the influence of Thomas Jefferson, Greek and Roman Revival architecture found a welcome home, for a brief time in private homes, and a more long-lasting one in public and educational institutions. Finally, in an almost manic way, American builders in the years before the Civil War sampled architectural styles of the world, building in styles as wide-ranging as Egyptian, "Persian," Gothic, and Romanesque. In the midst of this, Hawthorne mused: "The present is burdened too much with the past."

It was during the latter half of the nineteenth century that Americans developed a distinctive historical consciousness. That consciousness was born out of the crucible of the Civil War and the transformation of American life by immigration and by industrialization. This new historical sense drove the efforts of historic preservation.

When Abraham Lincoln appealed to the "mystic chords of memory" in his first inaugural in 1861 he sought to remind Americans divided sharply, and soon violently, by region of their national allegiances and heritage. This sentiment was the animating force behind historical interests of the late nineteenth century: to create a common heritage in the face of increasing divisions in American life, by race, class, and ethnicity. Inscribing history into the built environment—through the adaptation of historical styles, the creation of monuments and memorials, and the preservation of historic buildings—would help to quell nascent furies and unify the nation. Or so it was hoped.

While Americans had sampled a variety of historical styles as they built their homes and institutions in the antebellum era, that historicism was nothing like the obsession with all things colonial that overtook American architecture in the wake of the Civil War and especially after the 1876 Centennial Exhibition in Philadelphia. The struggle to preserve Mt. Vernon, which is rightly seen as a turning point in American attitudes toward their physical past, grew directly out of an effort to seek unity between North and South before and after the Civil War.

The succeeding decades saw the development of an organized, institutionalized preservation movement, even though a crucial actor—the federal government—remained largely removed from the undertaking. The majority of preservation efforts at the turn of the century were directed at saving homes and public buildings considered important for their Revolutionary War associations, or ones that had particular architectural merit. Especially important, in the minds of late-nineteenth-century elites, was that the immigrants from southern and eastern Europe who were rushing to the United States be Americanized. Historic buildings could speak to immigrants, unschooled in the governing myths of the nation.

In the South, the memorializing instinct was especially powerful. After the tragic end of Reconstruction, Southern white leaders manipulated the design of homes, war monuments, and public buildings to win the war for the memory of the Civil War. In that narrative, which anchored the Jim Crow South for nearly a century, the Civil War had not been about slavery but about a sincere battle over a vision of government, a battle between white brothers. The landscape of the "Lost Cause"—the network of Civil War memorials and faux antebellum plantations—helped to win that war. When Margaret Mitchell wrote *Gone with the Wind* in 1936 she drew inspiration from a landscape that was littered with monuments to the war and buildings as often as not built after the Civil War but designed to look like they were built in the antebellum era. Whatever the regional differences, the early preservation movement was important in establishing the ethos of historic preservation, in establishing key organizations, and in linking preservation, planning, and social reform to larger cultural concerns.

One consequence of this nascent preservation movement was to launch a renewed interest in historical styles. Merging new interest in preservation with historical research, the Colonial Revival exploded and still echoes in American design. (The form of every other new suburban home built in the United States is testament to the lasting influence of this revival.) The Colonial Revival was joined with a renewed interest in the classical vocabulary, especially examples from the Renaissance. Led by the firm of McKim, Mead, and White, which built such buildings as the Boston Public Library and New York's Pennsylvania Station, American architects studied and adapted the great buildings of the classical era.

The reformers associated with Progressive Era in the late nineteenth and early twentieth centuries wanted to bring the tools of modern social science to bear on social problems. Yet they too turned to the past as a way of achieving some of their goals. In an approach that one historian has called "nostalgic modernism," Progressive Era reformers looked to the past pragmatically as a sourcebook for creating better citizens, better cities, and better buildings.

Progressive reformers recognized that the rapid destruction and rebuilding of American cities and towns, which they themselves promoted, threatened to create a society with few reminders of the past. In each of the issues they confronted—zoning, planning, slum clearance, preservation—the question of how to protect and perpetuate the best buildings and architectural values of the past was central. While Progressives took the preservation movement further than it had ever come, however, they also enshrined a new notion about how historic buildings would fit within the city. A few "gems" would be preserved, usually surrounded by a green park, amid the rapidly changing city. The sanctity of a few key buildings would be protected, but so would private real estate's prerogative of developing the vast majority of the rest of the city. This "masterpiece theory," championed by preservationists in the postwar era, came to dominate ideas about the physical past in the city.

American immersion in the past reached a culmination of sorts in the 1920s and 1930s. In the 1920s, the past became a refuge from the relentless change of the modern world; in the 1930s, the past served as an escape from the crushing trauma of the Depression.

The two greatest private efforts, John D. Rockefeller's Colonial Williamsburg and Henry Ford's Greenfield Village, both represented the fruition of years of development among the "history industry" composed of museums and preservation organizations, local history writers and historicist architects. Neither was built by antiquarians but rather by captains of the present and future—American industrial entrepreneurs. Both were extensive recreations of the past according to careful research and reconstruction—this was a scientific approach to rebuilding the past. Finally, each represented a sweeping effort to celebrate a common national past by wiping away the contradictions and inequities that characterized American life. Slavery disappeared from Williamsburg; labor strife and religious prejudice were absent from Henry Ford's small town.

Over the longer run, the involvement of the federal government in the construction of a national memorial landscape was of greater significance. The federal government launched a series of efforts to recover and document aspects of America's physical past. The Historic Sites Act in 1935 committed the federal government for the first time to obtaining and preserving key places in American history. (The Antiquities Act of 1906 had established the idea of national historical landmarks and helped to save a number of ancient Native American sites, but it did not have the force or scope of the 1935 law.) Less glamorous but equally important was the creation of the Historic American Building Survey (HABS) in 1933 (the Historic American Engineering Record was added in 1969), which was charged with documenting in great detail important works of American architecture.

It was not simply the force of the federal government in preservation activities that was revolutionary, it was also the democratizing instinct inherent in these efforts. The HABS mission statement, for example, was unequivocal: *"the survey shall cover structures of all types from the smallest utilitarian structures to the largest and most monumental."* For the first time, vernacular structures and the architecture of minorities and Native Americans found their way into government documents as places of national historic importance. In the 1930s, the history in America's landscape became somewhat more democratic.

Though Americans emerged from the Second World War full of confidence and hubris and as great promoters of modern architecture, the movement for historic preservation also flourished in the 1950s and 1960s. Driven by the ravages of urban renewal, in places like Philadelphia's Society Hill preservation prevailed over demolition. Although the impact of the demolition of Pennsylvania Station between 1963 and 1966 has been exaggerated, the loss of that building led directly to the creation of New York's Landmarks Preservation Commission and, somewhat less directly, to the passing of the 1966 National Preservation Act, establishing the National Register of Historic Places and each of the state preservation agencies. This watershed moment in the history of preservation put the federal government firmly behind the struggle to restrict the development of property in the interest of history. Although the right of communities to insist on the preservation of significant structures was challenged, most notably in the 1978 Penn Central case (involving Grand Central Station in New York City), the law held and has served as the anchor for a growing preservation movement.

The social movements of the 1960s transformed virtually every aspect of American culture, including the way historians conceived of the narrative of American history, and who should be included in it. Workers, immigrants and ethnic minorities, slaves, and women all found themselves as part of American history in a way they had not been before. It took some years, however, for historic preservation to catch up with this "new social history." Preservation remained the purview of elites, with buildings of traditional historic importance and high architectural merit still dominating the National Register and local landmark lists. Old plantations (turned into museums) in the South as often as not hid the story of slavery. In Atlanta, despite the presence of the Martin Luther King, Jr.,

National Historic Site, the places of civil rights protest have been covered over, more often than not, for parking. In Chicago, the birthplace of the Chicago blues, Maxwell Street was left to deteriorate so that finally the University of Illinois in Chicago could demolish it and build parking lots and dormitories. A concerted effort to include a greater range of histories was slow in coming. Indeed, at the end of the millennium it was a process still only at its beginning.

At the beginning of the new millennium, the paradoxes of America's relationship to its many pasts were as many as, though very different from, those at the start of the new nation. What prevailed and has grown since the century's end is the role of history and historic places as a commodity. Increasingly, historic places and objects are not treated as sites removed from the market but as quite valuable within the market. Although many would struggle mightily to remove the past from the world of buying and selling, in fact the past became a product like others. Colonial-style mansions are a good selling point in America's gated communities. The National Trust for Historic Preservation markets a line of paints that are, somehow, "historic" in appearance. The Disney company manufactured a small southern town (not far from its manufactured world of Disneyworld) and called it Celebration. In Atlanta, the Post Apartment Company invented a history for its brand-new faux-urban development. The past is everywhere, to be consumed and profited from, if not actually learned from. As a fortune in a fortune cookie notes: "The greatest profit [*sic*] of the future is the past."

Americans seem to yearn for the past even as they grow more distant from it. The dream of recreating—whether in a museum or with house paint—a simpler, less complicated time is a nostalgic one, born of legitimate dissatisfaction with the way we seem to be at once drowning in the past and also somehow unmoored from it. Lewis Mumford, the greatest historian of cities and sharpest architectural critic of the twentieth century, wrote in his monumental *The City in History* that the goal of citybuilding was, or should be, to "make time visible." More than ever, Americans seem to be struggling to figure out a healthy way of doing just this.

100

JOSEPH SANSOM,
"DESCRIPTION OF AN INDIAN MOUND," 1822

As white settlers flooded into the trans-Appalachian region in the early national period they were bewildered to discover evidence of previous occupation. The Ohio and Mississippi Valleys were dotted with man-made mounds, some only small hillocks, others quite elaborate representations of birds, snakes, and other figures. Who built them and what had become of those builders remained a puzzling question through much of the nineteenth century. These mounds also became casualties of agricultural expansion and town development, often destroyed completely or partially by farmers and builders. Here Joseph Sansom, writing from Ohio, urges that this particular mound be spared that fate. This letter may well be the first recorded example of the conflict between road building and historic preservation.

About ten miles from the town of Newark, in the State of Ohio, upon the head waters of the river Scioto, is a regular mound of stone, which has not been hitherto noticed in print, as far as I know.... It may be referred, with probability, to the same period of aboriginal polity and comparative civilization, which cannot be satisfactorily applied to the rude ancestors of the present race of Indians, inhabiting the actual territory of the United States of America.

This immense pile of stone, the construction of which (like that of Egyptian Pyramids) must have commanded the labour of a numerous people, under the control of an absolute chieftain, very different from the lax authority, and parental domination of the native Sachems of the present race, is not less than two hundred feet diameter, and may be little short of fifty in height. The large and mossy stones, with which it is composed, though without the use of cement, are artificially, as well as laboriously, put together, as appears on examining the sides of a circular aperture, which has been made for discovery, in the centre of a flat space of twenty or thirty feet diameter, on the summit of the mound. And the stones which form the outer coat of the semi-globular cone appear to have been originally matched or jointed, with their flattest sides outward, for the purpose of forming a regular swell, which might be ascended on all sides, without difficulty or danger; though they have since been much broken up and, displaced, by accident or design.

The interstices between the angles of the stones having admitted; in the lapse of ages, of soil enough to support a scanty growth of slender starving trees, and where the mound rises, conically from the surface of a hard stony knoll, a coat of fine peat, turf, has formed a sort of matted appendage to the monument, which with the gray moss that has gathered on the parts, which have never been disturbed, give to this unique object a most interesting air of antiquity.

The stony and barren tract on which it stands, scarcely admitting the growth of trees, even under our vernal sun, and exhibiting no remains of contemporaneous occupation, was probably a place of occasional resort, allotted for the assembling of public councils. Perhaps it might have been intended to perpetuate the memory of some national era; as no bones have been found to indicate a burying place.

This venerable mound being by far the noblest monument of antiquity now extant in North America not excepting the Mexican Empire, it is devoutly to be hoped that

Originally printed in *Port Folio*, 1822.

8.2. Cliff dwelling, Colorado. The Historic American Buildings Survey, 1968. Americans who searched for architectural styles that would give America a national credibility on the international scene eagerly exploited the exotic built environment of Native Americans. Here, they argued, was America's connection to ancient times. And here were artifacts and buildings dating back to the time of the cathedrals in Europe, or even the temples in Rome. So it should not seem ironic at all that some of the very first preservation endeavors were around ancient Indian sites, including the cliff dwellings of the West.

Congress, will forbid the contractors for the continuation of the national turnpike, which will run within a few miles of it, from making use of its materials for paving stones, which may easily be found elsewhere; leaving this magnificent proof of aboriginal skill and application, for the contemplation of the latest posterity.

101

S., EXCERPT FROM
"CHURCH ARCHITECTURE IN NEW-YORK," 1847

This document poses a different but equally perplexing issue confronted by Americans in the first century of the new nation: how, if at all, it should adapt historical styles. The author walks the line between scolding Americans for adapting the Gothic style and revering the "original" and "authentic" Gothic church buildings in Britain. The irony, only appreciated in hindsight, is that those "authentic" parish churches in British villages were about to be transformed. In the latter half of the nineteenth century, amid the Victorian period, small churches were transformed under the urging of such theorists as Ruskin and Pugin to make them more "picturesque" and less rough-hewn, more as people of the Victorian era would like those churches to have looked. In the first half of the nineteenth century American builders spun through a dizzying array of European styles, adapted to

Originally printed in *United States Magazine and Democratic Review*, vol. 20, 1847.

be made more cheaply and with abundant American materials. Greek and Roman models proved most sturdy, but Gothic, French Renaissance, Egyptian, and even "Persian" were all sampled and displayed in homes and public buildings.

Since my arrival in New-York, I have, according to my usual rule of following the custom of the country, been very constantly going to church; and for the same reason, constantly going about from one church to another, I find that all of them, the modern ones that is, are Gothic, or what is so styled by courtesy—and the fashion, though now some years old, is as universal as ever—indeed, no fashionable neighborhood can be considered complete, without its be-pinnacled and be-buttressed mass of brown freestone. Certainly, we Americans, like Prince Hal, "have damnable iteration." Trinity, (I suppose it may fairly be christened "old Trinity" again, being in the fourth or fifth year of its age,) has become "the fruitful parent of a hundred more," all claiming to be Gothic, though Vandalic would often be the fitter term—on all of which I have been casting a critical eye of late, and about which I want to say a word or two.

Now don't be alarmed; I am not going to bore you about trefoils and quatrefoils, labels and lancets, spandrels and gargoyles. Time enough for minute criticism some indefinite number of years hence; when our general ideas of art shall be sound and true, we can afford to attend to details; but at present I only want you to notice, with me, the one grand defect—vice, I might fairly call it—which runs through nearly all our modern attempts at Gothic churches. It is an ambitious straining after effect, not warranted by the space or means at command; a copying of large models in little, combining a showy outside with meanness behind the scenes—stone fronts ending in brick-work; that peculiarly New-York style of building, of which our City-Hall furnished the model, and which Stewart's brick-sided palace so successfully illustrates. Trinity is, on the whole, solid and truthful; the Church of the Holy Communion, Sixth Avenue, graceful and unpretending; but these are almost the only exceptions to this general character. This shabby-genteel sort of *veneering* is bad enough at all times, but nowhere does it so grate on the feelings, as in a house dedicated to Him who is truth itself; and one can't but fancy it must be up-hill work to worship in spirit and in truth in a building, at once pretentious and shabby, lofty in design and diminutive in proportions—"frogs trying to look ox-like." This is the difficulty with all of them; they are small copies of large models—regular miniature cathedrals. Now, churches of like pretensions in Europe, have a length of from 250 to 400 feet, sometimes nearly 500, and are wide and high in proportion; but our churches, not over half, sometimes not a quarter their size, must have all the members of their larger brethren; the same aspiring portal, the same massive tower, or sky-piercing spire, the same number of buttresses and windows. A stately pile looks well in the design, and makes a showy engraving; nay, even when you look at the building itself, the first effect is rather good—the eye glances up the side, along six, eight, or ten mullioned windows, with their lattices, as many as Notre Dame in Paris with its 400 feet of length, and graced with a corresponding forest of pinnacles—but the very next moment the want of depth is evident; you see that the windows are reduced in size, and crowded into half the space they should occupy. The stage-trick is now evident; you discover that you have been taken in, and the littleness of everything comes out all the stronger. It is impossible to give the idea of great size in 50 by 100; least of all can it be done by trying to squeeze a church into that space which ought to occupy three times as much. Gothic is nothing without solidity and amplitude; in our churches all this is lost, by putting half a dozen windows where there should be only half as many. The compartments, bays they are called, are quite too small, and there is absolutely no space between the windows— only mere piers—and the church is like a Broadway store, all openings. This is unavoidable, if we will persist in copying the most ambitious churches of Europe "in little." To "cut our coat according to our cloth," is in all cases good taste as well as good sense. We should choose those humbler, though equally beautiful models, which are within our ground-room and building-funds.

Another thing very noticeable is, that every church of every denomination is now-a-days Gothicized. "It was always yet the trick of our English nation, if they have a good thing, to make it too common." I want to know why we do this; why every place of worship, Episcopal, Presbyterian, Congregational, and what not, put up, in this democratic land, in this nineteenth century, must be Gothic and *moyen âge*? What business have so many imitation mediaeval cathedrals, standing alone and forlorn among houses, streets, and people, all of yesterday? In the midst of all this, you set up a building in the style of a remote age, without precedent or model, among us, wanting all its natural accessories— the gray moss of centuries, the clothing ivy, the irregular antique street, the humble hovel, the cloister pale, the stately palace, the dignity of age, the splendor of rank, the pomp of an Establishment—all, things unknown and foreign to us—(perhaps there are those among you who wouldn't object if some, at any rate, of them were not?) These things are gone, and for ever—lucky that we have something better in their place. In Europe, a bit of even modern Gothic is felt to be in good keeping; for it has all around it companions and predecessors of every age, and all precedent and tradition, all scenery and associations, harmonize with it. In that soil it grows indigenous; here, it is at best but a forced and feeble plant. Don't understand me as saying a word against Gothic architecture in itself. I have spent too much time in studying out its noblest specimens to have any such feelings. But it is the very strength of my love that makes me lift up my voice against the way it is caricatured among us. Everything is against it here, and makes it a thing without sentiment and without poetry, a hollow mockery of the past. Our very climate is against it. It depends for much of its effect on a play of light and shade, which is seldom met with under our brilliant American skies. Gothic is the poetry of shade, our climate of light, and you cannot have both together. To counteract the glare without, we are forced to make gloom within, and turn our churches into dull masses of darkness or sickly yellow. Every painter will tell you that it is as idle to look for that constantly varying play of light and shade, those exquisitely broken effects, which in European churches make the artist's heart dance with delight, under the flood of light of our American sky, as it is to look for the twilight gleams of romance and poetry, which light up the darkness of the middle ages so beautifully, under the broad, all-pervading, life-giving sun-light of democracy.

Then again the history, the associations and the details of the Gothic style, make it the exclusive property of certain forms of religious belief, and out of their hands it has no place nor fitness. It was *Catholic* faith and *Catholic* art that reared those giant piles, monuments as imperishable and as inimitable of the religion of Rome, as are her aqueducts and amphitheatres of her Pagan greatness. They were built for *Catholic* worship, and in that worship every part has its proper use, and for any other purpose, both the parts and the whole are meaningless. The vast expanse of the nave for the kneeling multitude, unpolluted by those wooden sentry boxes in which Protestant exclusiveness delights to lock itself up—the marble floor, paved with the monuments of grim knight and bearded bishop—the soldier and the priest of the cross resting side by side in its shadow—the side chapels and altars for private and particular devotion, the Lady chapel as the apsis; graceful as the worship to which it is devoted; the high altar at which the daily sacrifice is offered up, the pictures and statuary, ornaments worthy of such a fabric, making it the treasure-house of art as well as the shrine of faith; all these things, and many more I omit, are Catholic, and Catholic only, and they all enter into the perfect idea of a Gothic cathedral. Denounce their religion as much as you please—I have not a word to say for it; but at any rate Gothic architecture is their property, and theirs only, and you cannot share it with them.

What a difference, indeed, between our modern Protestant efforts in the Gothic line, and the models we pretend to follow! To build the one, the Hirams of the day met together from east and west, and sat long in high debate, ere they settled on the plan of a building, the completion of which their own eyes were never to behold. They built for all time; and age after age added its share to the glorious pile, till it reached its perfect development. For the other, all that is needed is a copy of Britton or Pugin, and to look out to have the job done as cheap as may be. And how paltry the result! How unidea'd, how wanting in poetry, in richness, in ornament? True, we clap on a profusion of pinnacles, and here and there a plaster finial or so *purpureus pannus,* showing the nakedness they seek to hide....

If we must have Gothic churches, however, and I suppose we must, till the fashion changes, let us build them on a moderate scale, one fairly within our means, and which we can consequently carry out fully and fairly.—No necessity for always copying the largest and most expensive churches in Europe.

Understand me, Mr. Editor, I don't find fault with our architects. They must work "to order," like any other artist. It galls them, I know, to feel their genius cabined, cribbed, confined by the exigencies of our unformed taste and Protestant prudishness; but what can they do? The architect must think of the figures of arithmetic as well as of those of art; and a too honest love for the latter may materially damage the amount of the former. He must *work down* to the level of his employers, and his only hope is to raise the general standard of taste as high as his own. When this happens, we shall no longer see our toil and outlay ending in amorphous incongruities, which, though they make the ignorant smile, make the judicious grieve....

I don't know which would be the severer criticism on them—to say what they are or what they are not. At the same time, a decided improvement is on the whole to be seen in our later as compared to the earlier Gothic of a few years ago. Unluckily, failures in buildings are not covered by the ground, as they are in medicine. We must find our consolation in the fact, that we are thus furnished with capital specimens of what to avoid, though it costs a good deal to get up such a rich series as we can now boast of—so complete a museum of architectural deformities.

In this desert, how refreshing is the one green spot—how pleasant to find one church we can praise without ifs and buts. I mean, of course, that built by Mrs. Rogers, in the Sixth Avenue. It is no would-be metropolitan, but an unpretending, simply beautiful parish church—such as you find by dozens yet in the "rural districts" of England. The same quiet elegance reigns within and without; it is *totus teres,* and almost alone in being so. I am glad to see this,—not only for its own sake, but as a promise of better things for the future; and since I saw it, begin to hope that we may before long build as good churches as we did a century ago. As it is, if a foreigner of taste were to ask to be shown our best churches, I should certainly give Grace and Calvary a wide berth, and ask him as a favor to shut his eyes to everything between the Church of the Holy Communion and St. Paul's.

102

ANONYMOUS, "WASHINGTON'S EXAMPLES," 1866

The effort to save Mt. Vernon, George Washington's home, is often treated as the starting-point of the historic preservation movement in the United States. Though there were numerous earlier efforts to preserve important buildings of the young nation, such as the fight over Independence Hall in 1811, the successful effort to preserve Mt. Vernon crystallized a nascent worship of the Revolutionary generation and solidified some of the ideas that would animate preservation over the next century. What should also be clear from the effort to save Mt. Vernon is that protection of the past was always immersed in present-day politics. In the case of Mt. Vernon, the effort to preserve the house was seen as a way of finding a common cultural purpose between North and South starting before the Civil War and continuing into the Reconstruction era of the 1860s and 1870s.

The birthday of Washington has, this year, been observed with more than the usual expression of interest. As time rolls on, the worth of his great examples in public life shines out from the night of the past and the clouds of the present with clearer and holier luster, as the star of hope for our Republic. His name is the national watchword, and never spoken but with reverence and honor.

And yet Washington's greatest worth was not in his public example. We must set his private life before Young America, and keep in the hearts of the people the love of his private virtues. This is the lamp of goodness which, like the sacred fire on the altar, should be always burning in the homes of our land. And women must watch this light. It is their duty.

It seems but a fitting tribute to the Christian virtues of this *Husband and Wife,* that the HOME, where they lived and died, and the TOMB, where they rest together in the blessed hope of a glorious resurrection, should be watched over by the guardian care of Woman.

This sacred charge the Women of America have now in trust. The Homestead of Mount Vernon (200 acres), the Home and the Tomb of Washington and his wife, are made sure as a perpetual inheritance of the People of the United States, because the title-deeds are sure to the "Mount Vernon Ladies' Association of the Union," which has purchased and paid for this holiest place in uninspired history.

Would this guardianship of woman be fitting over the tomb of any other celebrated hero? Could women sympathize with the warrior's fame of Alexander, Caesar, Napoleon? Or in any greatness won by Force, Fraud, Selfishness and Sin?

Bear in mind that whatever crushes out moral power destroys the Christian virtues; and these are chiefly what are termed *feminine virtues.*

Man's despotic power has always wronged and degraded women. To honor the tombs of such heroes would seem unnatural and awful; as though we should imagine the women of Bethlehem carrying sweet spices to embalm the body of Herod.

Washington only, among the world's Heroes, deserves the homage of women; to him only has it been given. This is his highest distinction among warriors, and should be held up as the crowning glory of our free land. In the heart of the "Model Republic" there is a domain consecrated to Peace, Goodness, and Christian Love, where War, Covetousness, and Disunion can never come.

Originally printed in *Godey's Lady's Book,* April 1866.

"The Mount Vernon Ladies' Association of the Union" holds right and rule over this Washington domain. The sacred trust has not been invaded by a hostile footstep during the long four years of the late terrible war. The thunder storms of battle have been heard on every side; yet Peace, like a brooding dove, has kept her nest there, sacred as that of the swallows in the House of the Lord; while women have watched over the dust of Washington! ...

[The MVLA h]as been, as it were, hidden from the public eye by the overshadowing events of the last five years. Yet its light has been faithfully tended; and now its friends trust that Mount Vernon will soon become the brightest spot in our Country's love.

There is to be a Report on this subject by the Regent; but a few words here may be interesting to our readers who have not been familiar with the past history of the Association. Families who have the Lady's Book from 1855 to 1861 on hand, will find in those volumes records of the manner in which efforts to raise funds for the purchase of the Mount Vernon estate were begun and managed.

The women of the South came up first to the rescue of the Home and Tomb of Washington from the covetousness of speculation; the women of the North responded warmly, joining hearts and hands with the South in the efforts to raise funds for the purchase of Mount Vernon.

They succeeded. The Estate was bought, paid for, and the ladies took quiet possession before the agitation that brought on the last civil war had become alarming. It was a matter of serious importance for the neutrality of the place that the owners were the ladies of the United States; this, added to the inherent reverence of almost every American, indeed, of foreigners as well, for the Grave of Washington, has preserved it from the perils of war.

103

CHARLES ELIOT NORTON, EXCERPT FROM "THE LACK OF OLD HOMES IN AMERICA," 1889

Many Americans, especially over the course of the nineteenth century, lamented that the United States had no history, and more, that unlike the European landscape, dotted with the physical evidence of the past, everything in America seemed new. In this sense, Harvard professor Charles Eliot Norton, among the most influential writers and critics on matters of aesthetics, bangs an old drum in this essay and sounds a note of nostalgic elitism doing so. What he points to particularly is the transience of America's population, and the lack of connection with the built environment across even a few generations. New houses might be more convenient, he acknowledges, but old homes foster a link with the past that is just as important.

Of the twenty houses built more than fifty years ago nearest my own, only one is lived in by the family by which it was originally occupied, while most of the others have had

Originally printed in *Scribner's Magazine* 5 (May 1889): 636–40.

numerous successive owners or tenants. Of my own friends near my own age there are but two or three anywhere who live in the houses which their fathers occupied before them. This lack of hereditary homes . . . is a novel and significant feature of American society. In its effect on the disposition of the people and on the quality of our civilization it has not received the attention it deserves. . . .

The active employments, the animated life, and high wages of manufacturing towns have competed with the more fertile fields of the West to depopulate the quiet villages of New England.

Moreover, while new cities in the West have been building, the old cities on the seaboard have been rebuilding. In Boston and New York, for example, scarcely a house remains that was a home at the beginning of the century, and of the few of this sort that may still exist very few, if any, are occupied by persons of the same social position, and hardly a single one by persons of the same family that dwelt in it fifty years ago. . . .

In the older parts of the country, the pleasant, old-fashioned virtue of neighborliness does not flourish as it once did. Railroads and other modern improvements have weakened the bonds that used to unite men in a genuine community. The village, in becoming more dependent on the city, has lost in self-reliance, in interest to its own people, and in local pride. . . . The railroad train brings the city newspaper and the outer world, opens the way to a larger, less concentrated, less friendly and domestic life; it brings strangers, it carries away neighbors, it empties homes. . . .

An old home acquires power over the heart with course of time; it comes by degrees to touch the imagination with a sense of life inherent in itself. . . . Birth and death, joy and sorrow, hope and disappointment—all that men endure and enjoy, give to it a constantly increasing sanctity, and a power to affect the hearts of those who dwell within it. Memory awakes imagination. . . .

In our country, barren as it is of historic objects that appeal to the imagination and arouse the poetic associations that give depth and charm to life, such a home is even more precious than in lands where works abound that recall the past by transmitting its image to our eyes. . . .

The time is still far distant before the influences which have made the American restless and home-changing will lose their force, and their effect upon the national character grows stronger with each generation that is exposed to them. They tend not only to produce uniformity and monotony, but to weaken the force of other influences of a different order that have been among the most powerful in shaping the moral nature of the English race. Sentiments which have been the most deeply rooted in the hearts of our forefathers . . . only flourish where their roots can strike deep into the past. Never has there been seen on the face of the world such a multitude of new houses, comfortable, convenient, excellent for the passing day; but in no civilized country are there so few old homes.

104

ANONYMOUS, EXCERPT FROM "A GREAT BATTLE PARK," 1895

The waning years of the nineteenth century saw a flurry of efforts to memorialize the Civil War, without a doubt the single most significant event of the era. These included erecting monuments in small towns and big cities, and culminated, in a way, in 1913 when the remaining veterans of the Confederate and Union armies who had fought at Gettysburg reunited to shake hands with one another. Part of this memorializing effort included setting aside the sites of those battles as preserved—almost sacred—ground. Here, reporting on the preservation of Chickamauga in Tennessee, this anonymous writer provides his criteria for how such sites ought to be preserved.

This week will witness the dedication, with imposing ceremonies, of the great national park, which includes the battlefield of Chickamauga, with parts of Missionary Ridge, Lookout Mountain and other places made memorable by that long struggle which, in the magnitude of the forces engaged, the number of lives sacrificed and the importance of the results which depended upon it, ranks among the great battles not only of our Civil War, but of the world. The field of Chickamauga embraces fifteen square miles, much of which is in forest, and, besides this, the Government has acquired and improved in a most substantial manner scores of miles of road by which the armies marched to the field or left it. The city of Chattanooga, too, which, with its surroundings, made one great battlefield, has made liberal grants of land for the erection of monuments and built a great central drive to the park, along Bragg's line of battle on the crest of Missionary Ridge and through the field of Chickamauga to a point twenty miles away.

Of course, this is not intended as a pleasure-ground. What has been attempted is a restoration of the country to the condition at the time when the battles were fought, with the placing of such monuments and tablets at critical points [to] indicate the battle lines and movements of the various bodies of troops throughout the whole series of engagements. Tall observation-towers are to be erected from which the mountain ranges and the rivers can be seen at a glance, so that the strategy of each army can be studied and the history of every operation on these famous fields can be accurately seen. When all is completed it will be possible for the visitor to gain a clear idea of the great military movements across the broad river, among the forests and on the mountain sides. Nowhere else in the world is there an object-lesson approaching this in magnitude of completeness of treatment. . . .

[I]t is stated that 106 monuments and 150 granite markers are to be finished and set up before the dedication, besides 129 of these memorials already in place. What we desire especially to call attention to here, however, is an editorial note in the same magazine in reference to the service which art can render in celebrating the heroes of those days of flame. Upon this hallowed ground something more than historic accuracy is needed, and the appeal to the imagination ought to be made as distinct and powerful as possible. Of course, no art can make Lookout Mountain or Missionary Ridge more impressive than they are, but memorial structures can be erected here which will distract the attention by their obtrusiveness, and if they lack dignity or propriety they will help to belittle

Originally printed in *Garden and Forest* 8 (September 18, 1895): 371.

the legitimate impressions which the spectacle ought to create. It is truly said in the article alluded to that "there are few pieces of good sculpture on the battlefield of Gettysburg besides the beautiful and appropriate Celtic cross which marks the position of the body of Irish troops. There are a few unobtrusive pieces of natural rock which fittingly express the willing sacrifice or unyielding valor, but, for the most part, that beautiful chosen valley of the nation's salvation has become, through lack of coördination in plan and good taste in execution, an unsightly collection of tombstones." As the fields of Antietam and Shiloh are now coming under Government control, these great battlefields should not be allowed to become mere cemeteries, and without a protest. To this end certain practical rules are laid down which deserve careful consideration. These are so sound and so judiciously set forth that we reproduce them in full:

1. Every commission should avail itself of the advice of the best landscape-architects, so that park-like effects may be attained as far as may be consonant with the more practical objects of the reservation.
2. Lines of battle should be marked clearly, but unpretentiously, with a low uniform stone, and the whole plan should be worked out artistically before large monuments are erected.
3. The commission should have the advice of a competent board of sculptors, and should be guided by them in the acceptance of plans for monuments.
4. The monuments, to be of artistic excellence, must be few; and to this end the unit of celebration, so to speak, should be the corps. The sense of historical perspective is lost by allowing each regiment to determine the proportions and character of the memorial.

One can hardly hope that the 385 monuments and markers already, or soon to be, in place in Chickamauga are all worthy of the heroic deeds they commemorate, and it is not reassuring to be told that 3,500 acres of forest have been cleared of underbrush and smaller timber so that carriages may be driven through every portion of the park. But every thoughtful person will approve the suggestion that no work of this sort be done in future without "a severe artistic supervision, such as made the Court of Honor of the Columbian Exposition the admiration of the world."

105

PARK PRESSEY, EXCERPT FROM "PRESERVING THE LANDMARKS," 1914

The Progressive Era coincided with several movements among artists, critics, and aesthetes who reacted against the modern industrial world in a variety of ways. One way in

Originally printed in *House Beautiful* 36 (September 1914): 97–100.

which this impulse manifested itself was in a rush to preserve the buildings of America's colonial past. Park Pressey makes the case for preserving seventeenth- and eighteenth-century houses in this essay. He reports happily on a growing number of organizations dedicated to this task and on a few successful preservation efforts. The sorts of things he believes ought to be preserved, however, reveal his attitudes about just what history Americans ought to revere.

"Destroy not the ancient landmark" is a very old injunction, but one likely to be little heeded in a new country. Older nations, settled in their ways, take pride in their historic treasures. Their castle ruins are sacred to the memory of monarch or nobleman; their ancient buildings are shrines to which travelers are urged to come and worship. Each community has its particular attraction for filling the visitor with awe and veneration—and for enticing away his money. But in America we are so accustomed to constant change and improvement that an old building is likely to be considered an impediment to progress rather than an object of affection.

Until recent years it was only accident or lack of enterprise that allowed any building to stand long enough to become historic. And when one did gain distinction through age or associations, no special effort was made to keep it for coming generations. Even such a priceless gem as the Hancock mansion in Boston was lost forever when a little effort might have saved it. This beautiful home of the President of the Second Continental Congress, first signer of the Declaration of Independence, and first Governor of the Commonwealth of Massachusetts, was offered to the state for the mere valuation of the land on which it stood, but sufficient interest could not be aroused to secure its purchase. And the Barker house at Pembroke, Mass., said to have been the oldest house in New England twenty years ago, was allowed to fall to pieces.

Within a decade there has been a decided awakening in this country. We are now coming to realize that there are, right at home, just as quaint bits of architecture, just as sacred shrines to departed heroes, as we journey abroad to see, and that these are worthy of care and preservation.

From old homesteads erected by Pilgrims and Puritans have gone out families that are now scattered all over the country, and these descendants have come to see the value of preserving the old rooftrees. The Fairbanks, Alden, and Manning families have done an excellent service by making possible the continuance in the family name of buildings which, in more than two hundred years, have never left the possession of the direct line. And the Howland and Wyman descendants have rendered about equal service in restoring to family ownership old houses that had been allowed to pass into other hands. . . .

Historical and patriotic societies, too, have done much in the way of saving buildings rich in historic associations: The Colonial Dames secured, and spent considerable sums of money in repairing, the "Dorothy Q" house in Quincy, home of the Dorothy Quincy made famous by Holmes's poem to his great-grandmother, and of that other Dorothy equally renowned as the wife of John Hancock. The Ipswich Historical Society restored to its old-time form the ancient Whipple house, which has existed almost from the beginning of the Massachusetts Bay Colony. The home of Deane Winthrop, son of the Colonial governor, owes its restoration to the Winthrop Improvement Society. The "Parson Capen Garrison," raised "July ye 8, 1683," and one of the finest examples of overhanging second story and gables with "drops, brackets, and verger boards," is now saved to lovers of the Dutch style in early New England architecture, through the efforts of the Topsfield Historical Society.

Special organizations, also, have come into existence when imminent danger has threatened the loss of some object of historic interest. The Paul Revere Memorial Association rescued from Italian fruit sellers and cigar makers the old home in Boston of the hero of the ride to Lexington, and spent several thousand dollars in its renovation. The Daniel Webster Birthplace Association has put back to its original condition, insofar as that was possible, the little one-story house among the hills of New Hampshire where that state's most prominent son first saw the light. And the Royall house in Medford, finest survivor of all the mansions of its day, has become the property of the Royall House Association.

Then, too, private enterprise has had its part in dedicating homes of long ago to the use of generations yet to come. It was owing to the wisdom of one of Salem's most public spirited women that the "House of the Seven Gables" was thoroughly repaired and restored to its condition in the years before it was shorn of its distinguishing features. The owner then established within it a neighborhood settlement, with classes in useful arts as well as opportunities for social enjoyment. . . .

Other instances might be given of efforts to save, here and there, a particularly desirable house; but many buildings, equally interesting, disappeared because no one made it his business to look out for them. The old home of the Mathers on Hanover Street in Boston, built about 1677, and the Sueton-Grant house at Newport, R.I., were torn down within the past few years, for just that reason. There was need of some concerted action to secure from destruction "the finest of New England's old buildings," wherever located, and whenever special effort was required.

106

HELEN BURNS, EXCERPT FROM "COLONIAL WILLIAMSBURG," 1940

Of all the historic preservation projects undertaken in the United States, Williamsburg, Virginia, remains the most extensive, ambitious, and in some ways controversial. Begun in the late 1920s, and funded by members of the Rockefeller family, the goal of Williamsburg is to recreate, as completely as possible, the city as it appeared in the mid-eighteenth century. To do this, some buildings have been restored with painstaking archival and archaeological research, while others have been demolished because in their newness they were deemed to be anachronistic. But from the outset, Williamsburg chose to preserve and present a particular view of eighteenth-century life. Absent until quite recently has been any attempt to deal with issues of eighteenth-century social inequality, or even slavery, upon which Williamsburg and eighteenth-century Virginia were built. These oversights seem not to bother Helen Burns, who found in the elegance of eighteenth-century Williams-

Originally printed in *Living Age* 398 (1940): 279–83.

burg a welcome antidote to twentieth-century European fascism and the American Depression.

The agonized poet who pleaded for time to turn backward on its flight must have felt something akin to the way many Americans feel today, distracted by the speed and noise of a fiendish age, baffled and in doubt as to whither the world and the nation are drifting, beset by fears of war and the fate of democracy.

In Williamsburg, once the capital and metropolis of aristocratic Colonial Virginia, one really can retard the clock and step back more than 300 years into the pages of the first chapter of America's history. Here, through painstaking work of exact restoration, through the interest of John D. Rockefeller, Jr., a magnificent task of reconstruction as an essentially educational undertaking, Williamsburg today is almost exactly what it was in the mid-eighteenth century, when a group of young bloods whose names were George Washington, Patrick Henry, Thomas Jefferson and Francis Lightfoot Lee dined and drank in the tap-room of the Raleigh Tavern. There, over their tankards, they plotted and schemed for the overthrow of the Royal rule in the colonies unmindful, perhaps, that the Governor himself, unprepared for unexpected guests at the Palace, was entertaining in the next room. . . .

Although most of the residents of Williamsburg today dress no differently than the residents of any other American city, and the students of the College of William and Mary resemble those of every typical campus in the country, the attendants who preside over the restored buildings, dress for their roles—the gaolers appear much as they did in 1704, when the Public Gaol received and held the worst criminals and offenders in Virginia during the seventy-five years that institution served as a place of detention for debtors, lunatics and military prisoners of the American Revolution; hostesses at the Raleigh Tavern, where Phi Beta Kappa was born, are attired in the manner befitting the Colonial women who served the gentry of Virginia; and at the Governor's Palace the same motif adds to the illusion of the grandeur of the King's Viceroys in the Colony.

Americans, seeking a reinterpretation of their former Government and a revaluation of democracy, may well step back onto the soil of Tidewater Virginia, where the spirit of America was born and cradled and which now is a perfect mecca for Americans in these dictator-ridden days of doubt. . . .

The restored city of Williamsburg is a classical gem of Colonial days and its restoration is one of the greatest contributions to the study of American history. Up to the present, 68 Colonial buildings have been restored, 139 have been rebuilt, 514 modern buildings have been torn down and 33 stores and shops of purely colonial type have been erected to provide a suitable business district—one of the national chain stores is housed in a structure in which even George Washington would feel at home!—while a great many magnificent old gardens have been restored, particularly those behind the Governor's Palace. The people of Williamsburg live in the town's restored buildings and beautiful homes, devoting a great portion of their time, interest and labor to turning back the pages of history and assisting in the work of making Williamsburg today exactly as their forefathers knew it.

Of particular interest is the restored Capitol which gives the visitor the feeling of stepping back into the days of old when the aristocrats, in their silks and satins, occupied special galleries in the General Court, and peered down upon the "common people" seated on hard benches to receive a justice which was usually severe and necessarily quick, because the Gaol was too small to accommodate all miscreants. . . .

When the restoration of the Capitol began in 1928, Colonial Williamsburg, Incorporated, was confronted with a difficult problem: two Capitol buildings had stood successively on the old foundations, which had been kept intact by the Association for the Preservation of Virginia Antiquities. Of these, the first building was historically significant in itself, and was the more interesting architecturally. The second building was undistinguished architecturally, but had greater historical interest. The first building was selected for reconstruction however, both because of its architectural significance and because voluminous and contemporary records available permitted an accurate and detailed restoration, whereas such information was lacking in the case of the second building.

By consulting the records of the Assembly, the work of restoration began with archaeological investigation of the colonial foundations which were very nearly intact and which evidenced the alterations which had been made after a fire razed the original building in 1747. While this work was in progress, researchers sought out all available references to the building, compiling specific documentary and pictorial data pertaining to the first building's architecture, furnishings and surroundings. So detailed were the contemporary accounts and descriptions of the building that it is believed that the reconstructed Capitol may be accepted as the exact counterpart of the original which was completed on the same foundation in 1705. Furthermore, Williamsburgers feel that, should Patrick Henry walk into the building in which he so often spoke, he would not know the difference today. . . .

Perhaps the most magnificent building of Colonial America, is the Governor's Palace which, from 1705, paralleled the distinguished life of the community which it predominated, standing as a more or less convivial symbol of royal authority and prestige. It was the residence of one of the most remarkable succession of able men that ever governed a British colony—Alexander Spotswood, Hugh Drysdale, William Gooch, Robert Dinwiddie, Francis Fanquier, Norborne Berkeley (Baron de Botetourt), and, at the end, John Murray, the Earl of Dunmore. For five years after the outbreak of the Revolution, the building served as the executive mansion of the Virginia Commonwealth and domiciled Patrick Henry and Thomas Jefferson. Finally, after the removal of the seat of Government to Richmond, the Palace served as a hospital for the wounded of General Washington's army at Yorktown. While serving as a military hospital, the Palace was destroyed by fire in December 1781. . . .

The Palace was the center of social life of the Colony and to be entertained there was the near equivalent of acceptance at Court in England. But the cost of entertainment was a serious drain on the finances of the governors themselves who feted anywhere from fifty to one hundred guests several days a week at dinners alone during the time when the Assembly was in session.

When the problem of rebuilding the Palace was undertaken in 1930 there was a vast amount of information available as a basis for accurate reconstruction. For instance, a copperplate engraving showing the principal front of the building as it appeared in 1732, was found at Oxford, England; a floor plan of the principal building, drawn by Thomas Jefferson in 1779, was located through the Massachusetts Historical Society; and another map, showing the arrangement of the principal buildings, was in the possession of the College of William and Mary. Besides, the journals of the House of Burgesses and other records contained frequent intimate reference to the Palace. . . .

The reconstructed Palace, now standing on the original foundation, is one of the most extensive single Colonial restorations ever undertaken. The lavish furnishings in the Palace itself are as accurate a duplication as possible, even including wall-paper, pianos and knick-knacks. . . .

While British rule in America began at Jamestown, it ended only about twenty miles from there—at Yorktown, where Cornwallis surrendered to Washington, closing the American Revolution and assuring the Colonies of their independence. Thus, the Colonial National Historical Park, embracing a part of Jamestown, nearly all of Yorktown and a connecting parkway is termed the "Alpha and Omega of British rule in America." Almost between the two towns is Williamsburg, which stands as a lesson "that the future may learn from the past." No wonder this small area in tidewater Virginia is the new national mecca for Americans, this year bent on "Seeing America First."

107

LEWIS MUMFORD, "THE DISAPPEARANCE OF PENNSYLVANIA STATION," 1958

Still considered one of the greatest crimes against architecture in the history of the United States, the demolition of Pennsylvania Station in New York City is fairly credited with if not launching, then powerfully fueling a growing preservation movement in New York and in the nation. From its demise came, very directly, the New York City Landmarks Commission in 1965, and the following year, the National Historic Preservation Act. In this piece, written five years before the start of the demolition of Penn Station (which took several excruciating years), Lewis Mumford decries the destruction already taking place: the transformation of the interior of the great space, modeled on the Baths of Caracalla in Rome. For many preservationists it was this dedication to authenticity and integrity of structures that would anchor the movement for preservation. It would also reinforce the bias to preserve only great works of architecture and not vernacular architecture.

For perhaps two years, I have watched, with silent misgiving, the reorganization of the interior of Pennsylvania Station. As the extent of the demolition grew, my bewilderment grew with it. I hardly believe that any rational purpose could justify the devastation that was being worked, and as the bottoms of the row of great stone columns that run from north to south across the station were chipped away and covered with a light-hued plastic, my bewilderment became incredulity. So I waited, hoping that some brilliant stroke of planning, beyond any notions I could form from the unfinished work, would turn the phantasmagoria my eyes beheld into a benign dream. But now that the scheme had taken shape, it is plain that I waited in vain. As things are going, I fully expect that Jules Guerin's begrimed mural maps, which adorn the walls above the concourse and which were once, not unjustly, described as one of the few examples of successful mural art in

Originally published in *The New Yorker* 34 (June 7, 1958): 106–11.

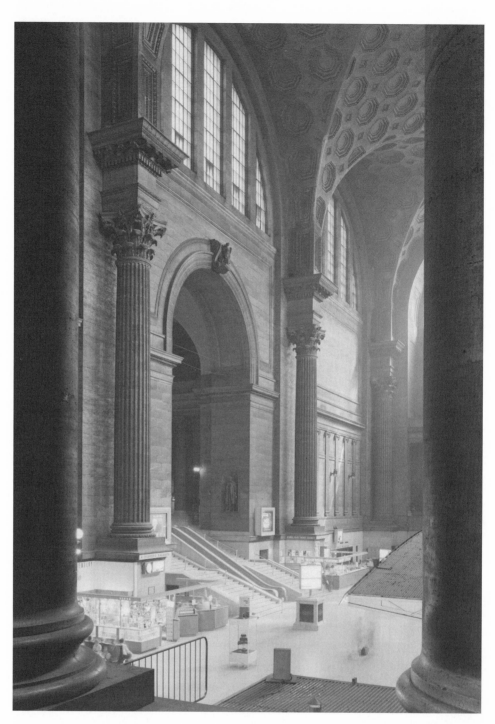

8.3. Pennsylvania Station, New York. The Historic American Buildings Survey, 1962. Railroad stations were often among the most magnificent, not to mention the most frequented, buildings in cities great and small. None was more magnificent than the Pennsylvania Railroad's New York City terminal. The demolition of Penn Station still constitutes one of the greatest crimes against architecture ever committed, and it helped galvanize the historic preservation movement.

the country, will give way to colossal color transparencies or winking whiskey ads. The only consolation is that nothing more that can be done to the station will do any further harm to it. As in nuclear war, after complete destruction has been achieved, one cannot increase the damage by doubling the destructive forces.

The Pennsylvania Station, now half a century old, was the collaborative product of Alexander Johnston Cassatt, the Pennsylvania Railroads president, and Charles Follen McKim of McKim, Mead & White, who got the commission in 1902 and finished the job in 1910, after four years of building. The purpose Mr. Cassatt had in mind was to provide a magnificent, monumental structure that would serve the railroad well and embellish the city. "Certain preliminary matters had to be settled with President Cassatt before McKim could begin to think of the design," Charles Moore, McKim's biographer, notes. "The company had a notion of utilizing the very valuable air space above the station by building a hotel. Mr. McKim argued that the great Pennsylvania Railroad owed the metropolis a thoroughly and distinctly monumental gateway." And professional and civic pride won out over cupidity. But, unfortunately, the spirit of adventure had gone out of American architecture. Except for Louis Sullivan, Frank Lloyd Wright, and a handful of their followers, no one any longer had the courage or the imagination to create new forms native to our own culture and the century. So the station was cast in the classic form of the Roman baths of Caracalla; indeed, McKim had intuitively prepared himself for this commission, in 1901, by assembling a gang of workmen in those very baths, so that he could study the esthetic effect of the huge scale of the structure on the crowds passing under its arches. The punctuating beat of the rows of vast classic columns, without and within, of Pennsylvania Station turned out to be the dying note of the classic revival that had begun in 1893 with the Chicago World's Fair. But though the classic forms were symbolically dead and functionally meretricious, McKim's handling of the main elements of the design for the station was superb. The basic practical problem, created by the fact that the railway tracks, in order to pass under the East and Hudson Rivers on their way out of town, were far below ground, has, it is true, never been properly solved. Above the track level is a second level, along which one makes one's way from the trains to the subway lines on Seventh and Eighth Avenues; above this is a third level, containing the concourse and the ticket offices, and flanked by the taxicab ramps. Even this level is well below ground, and it is reached from east, west, north, and south by broad stairways from the streets surrounding the station. The ambiguity of the many exits from the trains, some leading to the second level and some to the third, is baffling to anyone attempting to meet a person arriving on a train, and creates a certain degree of confusion for the traveller seeking a taxi or a subway. Even worse, the inadequacy of the escalator system handicaps the passenger with heavy baggage much more today than it did in those fabled days when porters were numerous and did not become invisible when a train arrived. In these respects, the Thirtieth Street Station in Philadelphia and the Union Station in Washington, even with their two levels of railway tracks are more satisfactory, despite the fact that the system of widely space doubled exits in the Philadelphia station makes meeting an incoming passenger difficult without prearrangement.

But, apart from these vexatious lapses, the general plan of Pennsylvania Station had a noble simplicity that helped it to work well. A broad, unobstructed corridor, running from east to west, was the visible expression of the station's axis, from Seventh Avenue clear through to Eighth Avenue. McKim made good use of his eight-acre site, which covered two entire blocks, by providing a sunken entrance, at the concourse level, for vehicles on both the north and the south sides of the station—far more adequate than the accommodations at Grand Central. If one approached the station by car, one had to walk but a short distance to the ticket windows and the trains. The ticket offices, the big waiting rooms, and the ample concourse, capable of embracing the largest holiday crowds, were at right angles to the axis and flanked the broad corridor. McKim, wishing to keep the axis and corridor clear, even placed the information booth in a northern corner, in a niche formed by the men's waiting room and some of the ticket booths, but wiser heads soon moved this important facility to the center of the ticket hall, so that passengers could approach it from the four points of the compass.

McKim's plan had a crystal clarity that gave the circulation the effortless inevitability of a gravity-flow system, with pools of open space to slow down or rest in when one left the main currents. Movement is the essence of transportation, and movement is what McKim's plan magnificently provided for. Amplifying this spaciousness were the great columns and high ceilings of both the main entrance corridor (leading west from Seventh Avenue and lined with shops and restaurants) and the ticket hall, waiting rooms, and concourse—the scale gigantic, the effect not only imposing but soothing and reassuring, as if a load were taken off one's chest. In this terminal, meant to encompass crowds, there was no sense of crowding; the ticket hall was as long as the nave of St. Peter's. The shopworn tags of McKim's classic decoration receded from consciousness, and what remained was a beautiful ordering of space, whose proportions veiled the appropriate decorative pomp and nullified the occasional irritations of the ascent from or descent to the trains. Even the fifty-year accumulation of grime on the travertine walls of the interior has not robbed this building of its essential grandeur, which now suggests the musty subterranean passages in the contemporary remains of a Roman bath. There is never too much of that grand Roman quality in a modern city. It comes from a princely sense of magnificence, a willingness to spend munificently on a purely esthetic pleasure, instead of squeezing out the last penny of dividends. American railroad stations as late as twenty-five years ago compared favorably with those of England and the Continent, because of their interior serenity and dignity as well as the fact that they were then altogether free of advertisements—a point the European traveller often remarked on with surprise, as a pleasing contradiction in the land of the almighty dollar.

No one now entering Pennsylvania Station for the first time could, without clairvoyance, imagine how good it used to be, in comparison to the almost indescribable botch that has been made of it. To take the most favorable view of the new era, let us enter the main approach, from Seventh Avenue—the only element left that faintly resembles the original design. But the spaciousness of the corridor, with its long view, has been diminished by a series of centrally placed advertisements—a large aluminum-framed glass box for posters; then that standard fixture of today's railroad station, a rubber-tired confection from Detroit suggesting to the guileless traveller the superior claims of private motor transportation; then another poster box, holding an illuminated color photograph of a steak dinner. These nagging intrusions are only a modest beginning; in time, the top of this great, barrel-vaulted corridor will probably, like the concourse, be punctuated with transparencies and flying signs.

Happily, these obstacles serve an esthetic function; they soften the shock that one encounters at the head of the stairs to the main floor. There one discovers that almost the whole interior arrangement has been swept away. The broad east-west corridor has vanished, and in its place a huge plastic crescent canopy, brittle, fragile, and luminous, opens out, fanlike, across one's view—a canopy slanting upward at an awkward angle and suspended in midair by wires from the sturdy-looking stone columns of the original design: in all, a masterpiece of architectural and visual incongruity. This vast arched canopy drenches the space below it with diffused fluorescent light, illuminating a semicircle of ticket counters and, behind them, clerks at ranks of desks. The semicircle completely blocks the main channel of circulation to the concourse; moreover, it conceals the bottom half of the great window that once marked the western end of the station's axis. The counters of the ticket office are laid out in saw-tooth indentations—open and without grillwork, like the ones in the newer banks—and a closed-circuit television set beside each counter presents the intending traveller with a visual summary of the accommodations available for the next week or so on whatever train he has in mind. This saw-toothed arrangement and the abandonment of the framed booth are the only elements in the design for which the most charitable observer can say a good word: let the reader linger over this moment of praise. The rest of this new office is a symposium of errors. To provide enough space in the rear for the booking clerks, once housed in the innards of the station, the designer wiped out both waiting rooms, for which a wholly inadequate substitute has been provided by a few benches on the concourse. To reach these, and the trains, one must walk all the way around the ticket counters. And the large central information booth has disappeared, to be replaced by a tiny counter tucked away north of the stairs from the Seventh Avenue entrance in such a fashion that people making inquiry at it obstruct one exit to the subways. "Meet me at the information booth" is now, at any busy hour, a useless suggestion. "Meet me at Travelers Aid" would be more to the point. To conceal the information booth so neatly and to block so effectively an exit, is a feat that only emphasises the quality of this renovation—its exquisite precision in matching bad esthetics to a bad plan.

But these are minor matters; the great treason to McKim's original design, and the overpowering blunder, is the conception of these misplaced ticket counters, with their background of ticket clerks busily acting their parts under television's myriad eyes. If treated rationally and straightforwardly, the change-over to open counters with television equipment and doubled space for ticket selling could have been accomplished without destroying a single important feature of the whole station. But rational considerations of fitness, function, and form, with a view to the ultimate human decencies, seem as unimportant in the reconstruction of Pennsylvania Station as they do to some of our designers of motorcars. One suspects that the subversion of McKim's masterly plan was due simply to the desire to make the whole design an immense advertising display, and, in fact, this design now centers on the suspended canopy, which not merely provides a ceiling of light for the office space below but juts out many feet beyond the counters, as if it had the function it might serve in the open air—of offering shelter against rain. The purpose of such a design, psychologically speaking, is possibly to convince the railroad user either that the Pennsylvania Railroad has gone modern and that the old station can be as pinched for space, as generally commonplace, as a bus terminal, or else that it can be as aerodynamic in form as an airport terminal. The effort to shorten the time needed to make reservations is a laudable one, though it may be doubted whether electronic feathers will do much to improve a system whose worst bottleneck is not communications but wholesale advance bookings by business corporations (often far in excess of their needs), which create the difficulty of allotting too few spaces to too many. But let us nevertheless assume that the new installation provides handsome gains in efficiency.

These gains must be weighed against serious losses of efficiency at other points. There is no reason, for instance, that the booking clerks should occupy the space once given over to waiting rooms. As a result of this pointless dramatization of the process of ticket selling, the waiting passengers are now squeezed onto a few benches, many of them a constant obstacle to passenger circulation.

What on earth were the railroad men in charge really attempting to achieve? And why is the result such a disaster? Did the people who once announced that they were planning to convert the station property into a great skyscraper market and Fun Fair decide, finding themselves temporarily thwarted in that scheme, to turn their energies to destroying the station from the inside, in order to provide a better justification for their plans? Or did the management see pictures of the new Rome station and decide that it would be nice to have a station equally up-to-date, and even more flashily so? But they forgot that though the Rome booking hall is in effect a canopy, it is a free-standing structure poised dynamically on its own base, serving not as a piece of phony stage decoration but as a shelter for its activities. To transport the idea of a canopy into Pennsylvania Station, whose overwhelming quality, esthetically, depends upon its free command of space, was to nullify not merely its rational plan but its height, its dignity, and its tranquil beauty. If the planners had cut the height of the main level in two by inserting another floor above it, they could not have debased the original design more effectively than they have by introducing that mask of light, suspended by wires. This glaring device was not necessitated by the television system of communication. The special merit of such a system is that the headquarters of the operation can be miles away from the place where the information registers. To disrupt the whole flow of traffic through the station so as to put the system on display is a miscarriage of the display motive.

Behind this design, one must assume, was the notion that has made automobile manufacturers add airplane fins to their earth-bound products. This shows a loss of faith in their trade, on the part of railroad men, that may hasten the demise of the railways. If they had sufficient pride in their own method of transportation, they would emphasize the things that make it different from air or motor transportation—its freedom from tension and danger, the fact that planes stack up interminably over airports in poor weather, the fact that a motor expressway, according to surveys, can handle only four thousand people an hour, while a railroad line can handle forty thousand people an hour. This capacity for coping quickly with crowds that would clog the best highway facilities for hours is the special achievement of the railroad. What the railroad does superbly the motor expressway does badly, and planes, even though they travel at supersonic speed, cannot do at all. This was boldly dramatized by McKim in the great vomitoria he designed to handle the crowds in Pennsylvania Station. Everything that clutters up a railroad terminal either physically or visually must accordingly be rated as bad design, and, ultimately, because of its retarding effect on convenience and comfort, as bad publicity, too.

Some of the engineering ingenuity that was spent in devising the vast electronic juke box of Pennsylvania Station might well have gone into repairing the crucial error in McKim's design—the failure to carry the system of circulation into its final stage; that is, an adequate method of passing immediately to and from the trains. As it is, a beautiful trip out of town can be soured in a few minutes by the poverty of mechanical means for changing levels and for transporting hand baggage. Moving platforms, escalators, lightweight two-wheeled luggage trucks, like the carts at a supermarket; identification signs for baggage lockers, so that one might recognize at a distance where one left one's bags, just by looking at the color of one's key; a well-identified enclosure for meeting—such highly desirable improvements as these are untouched by the present innovations.

The lack of improvements in these essential matters is a symptom of the bureaucratic fossilization in railroading, and that backwardness cannot be overcome by jazzing up the ticket service. If the Pennsylvania Railroad had given thought to these inefficiencies and discomforts and inconveniences, it would have treated the improvement of the ticket services with the same sharp eye on the business of railroading, and with the same readiness to keep the original design quietly up-to-date, without sacrificing the qualities in it that are timeless. Such a thorough renovation might be even more expensive than the present disarrangement, but it would pay off by improving every aspect of the service, instead of simply faking a loudly "modern" setting in the hope that the passenger will forget the many ancient coaches and Pullman cars, with their shabby upholstery, that are still in service.

But no sort of renovation of Pennsylvania Station makes sense until the railroad is ready to commission the one operation that would really cause it to look fresh and bright without benefit of fluorescent lighting—a complete cleansing of its soiled interior. The plaster has begun to crack and peel in the Seventh Avenue corridor; the mural maps are almost invisible; and, as if to accentuate the dirt, the thrifty management has merely scoured the columns and walls to a height of ten feet, making the worst of a bad job. As for the vast blaze of light from the low ceiling in the renovated portions, its chief effect at night is to make the train hall look as though it were under an air-raid blackout. If it was sad that Alexander Cassatt should have died in 1906, without seeing his great station erected, it was a mercy that he did not live until 1958, to witness its bungling destruction. It would take even mightier powers than these old railroad titans wielded to undo this damage.

108

RUSSELL KIRK, "DESTROYING THE PAST BY 'DEVELOPMENT,' " 1965

Historic preservation is usually seen as a movement of the enlightened wealthy, who shared a liberal belief that the government must intervene in the real estate market to protect historic places. But here, Russell Kirk, a longtime columnist for the *National Review*, William F. Buckley's journal for the conservative movement, supports preservation from a more conservative angle. He taps into resentment against the excessive concentration of power in big corporations that, he argues, are happy to wipe away historic places to make way for new, more profitable plants and office buildings. He supports the preservation movement's belief that buildings hold moral values in their walls and links to an earlier, and presumably, more virtuous time. While he recognizes the contradictions in

Originally printed in *National Review* 17 (April 6, 1965): 285. © 1965 by National Review, Inc., 215 Lexington Avenue, New York, NY 10016. Reprinted by permission.

his thinking—"few people are more reluctant than this writer to interfere with private property and free enterprise"—he sees the long-term need for protecting the past. Preservation, at least in some quarters, transcended ideology.

Few corners of the world are exempt from a raging destruction of historic and beautiful buildings. The principal cause of this devastation is greed: the avarice of "developers," contractors, architects, land speculators, political contact-men, faceless mercantile corporations, and their hangers-on.

The great cities of America are fast losing whatever character and charm they still retain before such pressures. Though the public is virtually voiceless and leaderless when some "developing" energumen decides he can make money by cutting vast swathes through an organic community, the agents of devastation are well organized, well financed (often by federal subsidies), reinforced by public-relations staffs, and possessed of strong political influence. They usually win, naturally.

Just now, the scheme for smashing the lower Manhattan expressway through the most interesting part of New York City is sufficient illustration. Its backers, and most of the politicians, defend their monstrosity by the argument that it would "create thousands of jobs." On such logic, we ought to pull down the whole of New York and build anew, since that undertaking would "create millions of jobs." What happens to whole communities, the evangels of bulldozer "progress" prefer to ignore. One prays that the public opposition, led by the redoubtable Mrs. Rosemary McGarth, may make Mayor Wagner think twice before he openly approves the malign folly.

San Francisco is confronted by the prospect of having a freeway (built to "standard specifications") thrust through Golden Gate Park! Temporarily, this madness has been blocked; but those who would profit by the contracts are persistent.

Everywhere I roam, similar forces are at their ugly work—a destruction often more shocking even than our American bulldozery, because other lands have more and finer things to destroy. The world may become one enormous sprawl of shoddy modernity. The Communist Chinese eradicate the wonderful ancient quarters of Peking, to build the collectivist "progressive" slums of the future; the Western democracies are almost as determined, apparently, to reject the beauty and the neighborliness of our civilized inheritance.

Stellenbosch, in the Cape, is South Africa's Williamsburg. Yet Stellenbosch's charming common, with its old churches, curious powder-magazine, and historic houses, is to be overshadowed by an incongruous fourteen-story monster. At one corner of this great square, an "O. K. Bazaar," a chain store, has intruded its vulgarity, occupying the site of the old stone mill. The civic authorities of Johannesburg have tried to pull down the old fort, built in the Boer War, but happily have been prevented by the Historic Monuments people. . . .

Readers of this page may recall my article, three years ago, called "Dreamthorp and Linlithgow." Since then, the town council of Britain's little ancient Linlithgow have been steadily at work, thoughtfully reducing that beautiful burgh to architectural boredom. The latest atrocity is a plan to demolish the Golden Cross Inn and the other building at the gates of the royal palace, since a "working party" of commercial developers wants a contract for a dismal modern row there. As Mr. Moultrie Kelsall, the author of *A Future for the Past,* writes in *The Scotsman:*

The plain fact of the matter is that these buildings are to be destroyed, not because there is any serious difficulty about saving them but because some of the people concerned have a strong interest in removing them, and nobody else is apparently prepared to put the very strong case for retaining them. In other words, the dice have been loaded against the old buildings from the start.

York—which has probably more of its medieval character remaining than has any other English city, and where the Civic Trust fights hard to retain civic beauty and historic buildings—now is menaced by really incredible proposals for commercialized vandalism. Dr. Patrick Nuttgens, head of the Institute of Advanced Architectural Studies at the University of York, recently resigned from the panel of architects advising York Corporation, "in growing frustration and despair at the callous disregard for the visible history of this city."

In Sweden, nearly all of the seventeenth-century city of Stockholm, on its islands, is being torn down in the craze for novelty and the thirst for profits. In Spain, laws meant to protect the Spanish architectural heritage are administered, too often, by local functionaries whose pockets can be lined. Only France—where hundreds of cities and towns are controlled under a program of preservation—labors diligently to keep the glory of the past.

Few people are more reluctant than this writer to interfere with private property and free enterprise. Yet no man, and no corporation, has a vested right to make a town and a country ugly and monotonous, or to annihilate the past for immediate profit. The time has come when governmental powers must be employed to save what remains for us of our visible heritage.

Everyone with any affection for the continuity of culture, or with any concern for posterity, ought to work for local ordinances, state legislation, and—where appropriate—federal regulations to check this lucrative onslaught against good architecture, true community, and the memorials of a nation's development. The Romans, according to Tacitus, created a wilderness, and called it peace; we moderns, decreeing flashy commercialism, call that wilderness "renewal" and "progress."

109

HERBERT J. GANS, EXCERPT FROM "PRESERVING EVERYONE'S NOO YAWK," 1975; AND ADA LOUISE HUXTABLE, EXCERPT FROM "PRESERVING NOO YAWK LANDMARKS," 1975

This public exchange between Herbert Gans, a sociologist and social theorist, and Ada Louise Huxtable, architectural critic and member of the *New York Times* editorial board, sketches as succinctly as any the contours of the debate over historic preservation and the new social history of the 1960s and 1970s. Whose history should be preserved and why? Who gets to make those decisions? Gans attacks not simply the New York City Landmarks Preservation Commission but what he sees as the whole thrust of the historic preservation movement, of movements of elites to preserve elite history. Huxtable counters both by pointing out that Gans has some of the history wrong, but also with a defense of the importance of preserving "great" architecture.

HERBERT J. GANS, EXCERPT FROM "PRESERVING EVERYONE'S NOO YAWK"

Every time the Landmarks Preservation Commission designates a landmark, the outside of which must be retained in its present state, the commission rewrites New York City's architectural history. Since it tends to designate the stately mansions of the rich and buildings designed by famous architects, the commission mainly preserves the élite portion of the architectural past. It allows popular architecture to disappear, notably the homes of ordinary New Yorkers, and structures designed by anonymous builders without architectural training.

The landmark policy distorts the real past, exaggerates affluence and grandeur, and denigrates the present. When only the most prominent old buildings are protected, the new must look worse than the old. The policy is undemocratic, for it implies that the only city history worth protecting is that of the élite. . . .

To be sure, the commission's practice only follows the élitism of most public cultural policy, which routinely discriminates against the popular; it is also similar to typical museum practices, which save and exhibit mainly the art of the rich and famous.

In a democratic society, landmarks policy should serve a more representative purpose. The commission should be protecting some typical and atypical buildings erected by and for all the city's people. It should designate a sampling of popular residential architecture, for example the incredible variety of small rowhouse designs to be found especially in Brooklyn, and of office buildings and factories. It should also preserve some of the 19th-century tenements that still stand in lower Manhattan and elsewhere.

These should not only become landmarks; some should be restored to their original condition and others should be preserved as they are today, in their dilapidated, stinking state.

Aside from their historical value, these slums provide . . . evidence of how many people still have to call them home in 1975—which might help to get rid of such buildings.

Finally, the commission should designate some of the special buildings that served ordinary New Yorkers: a 19th-century vaudeville theater, a public bathhouse, and some taverns, for example. Indeed, these should be made into museums, to leave a permanent record of how most New Yorkers lived, worked and played in the past. . . .

My proposal may be questioned on several grounds. Why, for example, make landmarks of buildings that are still plentiful? A good point, except that bit by bit, the popular architecture of the past is being demolished. Then, aren't most New Yorkers more interested in looking at old élite architecture than at its popular equivalent? No one knows, but they have never been given a choice, or even consulted on landmarks policy.

But wouldn't the designation of popular architecture encourage the preservation of

Originally printed in *New York Times*, January 28, 1975, 33. By permission of Herbert Gans, Robert S Lynd Professor of Sociology at Columbia University, and author of *People, Plans and Policies*, Columbia University Press, 1991.

the ordinary and ugly? I believe that history should always include both the ordinary and the extraordinary, and whether buildings are beautiful or ugly is a personal judgment that should not be left solely to professional estheticians. . . .

The popular museums I have proposed are entitled to the same public funds as museums that collected the élite past, for fairness alone demands that ordinary people, who pay most of the taxes, should be able to protect their past the same way.

ADA LOUISE HUXTABLE, EXCERPT FROM "PRESERVING NOO YAWK LANDMARKS"

The Landmarks Preservation Commission has recently and wrongly been accused—in an article on this by Prof. Herbert Gans—of espousing the undemocratic designation of élite and stately buildings by and for the rich and famous, while allowing popular architecture to disappear.

The truth is quite different. Of the approximately 450 buildings that have been designated in New York, some are undoubtedly élite and stately; indeed we are fortunate to have a few in that category. But 26 historic districts have also been listed, containing about 11,000 buildings, the overwhelming majority of which are popular or vernacular. (The word democratic is to be avoided. The romantic fallacy of esthetic virtue comes off better in Ruskin.)

These districts consist of houses, warehouses, lofts and modest commercial structures, and at least 2,000 of one of Prof. Gans's most-wanted items—the tenement. "The small rowhouse designs to be found especially in Brooklyn" that he admires and seems to believe have also been bypassed are designated in Boerum Hill, Carroll Gardens and Park Slope among others, with perhaps a dozen variations from the Bronx and Harlem and Queens.

The 27th historic district designation, for a section of workers' houses in the Steinway area of Queens, was turned down by the Board of Estimate recently because the people who lived in them didn't want them listed. (That was probably democratic.)

Professor Gans asks for a public bathhouse. The one at East 23rd Street and Asser Levy Place in Manhattan is a landmark. He mentions taverns. The Old Stone Jug and others in historic districts are protected. First Houses, the first low-income public housing in the country has received designation.

The reality is that architectural historians and professional preservationists are passionately dedicated to the popular and the vernacular; these are probably today's largest areas of documentation research. Neighborhood preservation, where the whole is often more important than its anonymous parts and the emphasis is on the synthesis of sociology and style, is a joint preoccupation of preservationists, planners and scholars. Industrial archaeology (factories and industrial buildings of all kinds) is a booming new field. So much of man's life and taste and achievement is written in these structures; the point is not only to study but to save them.

However, to stigmatize major architectural monuments as products of the rich, and attention to them as elitist cultural policy, is a perverse and unserviceable distortion of history. The art historian who does this is playing a false and dangerous game.

These buildings are a primary and irreplaceable part of the story of civilization. Esthetic singularity is as important as vernacular expression. Money frequently made superb

Originally printed in *New York Times*, February 4, 1975.

examples of the art of architecture possible, and there were, fortunately, great architects to design and build great buildings. There will probably never be enough money, or craft, or the cultural moment, to create such things again. And because their restoration and re-use are formidably difficult and costly and their land values usually high, these are the hardest buildings to preserve. So "élite" them not; they need all the help they can get.

"The ordinary and the extraordinary" is the proper range of history, according to Professor Gans. In this he is totally correct. That includes the buildings of the rich and the poor, of the famous and the anonymous, of the masses and the aristocracy. It treats of the beautiful and the ugly—the evaluation changes with the eye of each generation making nonsense of the question he raises about "who is to judge beauty"—in the full range of Establishment and vernacular worlds....

The point to be made is that history, and particularly the history of building, is in-clusive. It is a tangible record of the nature of our lives, ideals, pleasures and aspirations, the conditions of our compromises, failures and defeats, our sense of community and worth. And that is art and history in the most comprehensive sense.

110

PAUL GOLDBERGER, "THE VIETNAM MEMORIAL," 1982

Maya Lin's Vietnam Veterans Memorial was one of the most controversial and influential works of architecture in the last quarter of the twentieth century. Not only did it bring to the fore all the submerged fury and anguish about the Vietnam War, but it also offered a radical departure in how we think about monuments and memorials. Taking inspiration from innovative "counter-monuments" to the Holocaust in Germany and Israel of the 1960s and 1970s, Lin rejected the overtly nationalistic monuments that had so decisively defined the art of memorials to that point. Her austere, even quiet, slabs of polished gran-ite pointing to the Lincoln and Washington monuments spoke of the tragedy and horror of war without turning the dead—who should be the true objects of remembrance in a memorial—into tools of a patriotic purpose. The level of anger on the part of Vietnam veterans toward the monument—one called it the "black gash of shame"—quieted quickly when the monument was completed and its power was evident to all.

When a plan by Maya Yang Lin, a twenty-year-old Yale architecture student, was selected last year as the winner of a nationwide competition to find a design for the Vietnam Vet-erans Memorial on the Mall near the Lincoln Memorial in Washington, it was hailed by the architectural press with words such as "stunning," "dignified," and "eminently right."

The reaction was less enthusiastic from Vietnam veterans themselves, some of whom found the proposed memorial rather more cool and abstract than they would

8.4. Vietnam Veterans Memorial, Washington, D.C. Courtesy of Iguana Photo, www.iguanaphoto.com. The Vietnam Veterans Memorial, designed by a twenty-year-old Chinese-American woman, Maya Lin, was the subject of one of the largest competitions in the history of architecture, with thousands submitting their entries to a blind jury. Lin's design provoked an equally large and controversial debate over its appropriateness. Once built, however, it was beloved by most who visited it, and it transformed the very idea of the modern monument. In one sharp-angled gesture, Lin challenged a century of columns, statues, and plaques that had dotted the American landscape since the Civil War.

have liked. Nonetheless, Miss Lin's scheme, which is neither a building nor a sculpture but, rather, a pair of 200-foot-long black granite walls that join to form a V and embrace a gently sloping plot of ground between them, was approved rapidly by the Department of the Interior, the Fine Arts Commission, and other public agencies that have jurisdiction over what is built in official Washington.

Construction began last March. Next week, however, the Fine Arts Commission will hold a public hearing to consider a revised design for the memorial, despite the fact that by now the granite walls—on which are carved the names of all 57,692 Americans who were killed in Vietnam from 1963 to 1973—are nearly complete. Opposition to the scheme from Vietnam veterans, which was muted when Miss Lin's design was first announced, later grew so intense as to lead to the unusual step of a proposed design change in midconstruction.

The hearing is scheduled for October 13, and the battle lines have already been drawn fairly sharply. On one side, defending the changes, will be the Vietnam Veterans Memorial Fund, the organization that sponsored the architectural competition and had committed itself to building the winning scheme, as well as the advisory committee of Vietnam veterans who were among the more outspoken critics of the original design.

On the other side is not only Miss Lin, the designer, but the American Institute of Architects, which has taken a strong public position in defense of the original design and which sees the move to change the memorial as a threat to the integrity of the system of architectural competitions in general. Robert M. Lawrence, the institute's president, wrote this summer to J. Carter Brown, chairman of the Fine Arts Commission. "What we have here is nothing less than a breach of faith. The effort to compromise the design breaks faith with the designer who won the competition and all those who participated in this competition."

What has provoked the heated emotions, however, is less the integrity of architectural competition than the specifics of Miss Lin's design. To many of the Vietnam veterans, her scheme was too abstract to reflect the emotion that the Vietnam War symbolized to them, and too lacking in the symbols of heroism that more conventional monuments contain. They saw in the simple granite walls on which the names of the dead are inscribed not merely a means of honoring the dead, but a way of declaring that the Vietnam War was in some way different from past wars—from wars such as World War II, whose heroism could be symbolized in such a vibrant and active memorial as the Iwo Jima Monument just across the Potomac River, which contains a statue of marines struggling to raise the American flag.

The changes in the Vietnam Memorial, therefore, have all been in the direction of making it less of an abstraction and more realistic. When the Vietnam Veterans Memorial Fund decided some months ago to give in to criticism of the design from Vietnam veterans, it named an advisory committee consisting entirely of Vietnam veterans, in contrast to the jury of internationally known architects and design professionals who had selected Miss Lin's design. That committee selected Frederick Hart, a thirty-eight-year-old sculptor who had been a partner in a losing entry in the original competition, and commissioned him to create a realistic sculpture to act as the memorial's new centerpiece.

What Mr. Hart has created is an 8-foot-tall statue of three armed soldiers, one black and two white, which would be placed within the triangular piece of land between Miss Lin's granite walls. The revision of the design also includes a 50-foot-tall flagpole outside the granite walls, and thus it will change the view of the observer who is looking at the memorial in any direction.

Mr. Hart claims that his statue will "preserve and enhance" Miss Lin's design, and will "interact with the wall to form a unified totality." Miss Lin, however, disagrees and in a letter to the Memorial Fund on September 20 she called the changes an "intrusion" that "destroys the meaning of the design."

Ironically, it is the very strength of the original design—its ability to be interpreted in a variety of ways—that is making for the current controversy. Miss Lin's original scheme is, in a sense, a tabula rasa, a blank slate—not a room, not a building, not a plaza, not a park, not a conventional memorial at all. It is a place of reflection, where the gradually sloping land, the thousands of carved names on sombre granite, and the view of the buildings of official Washington in the distance should combine to create an understated, yet powerful presence.

It is a subtle design, like every great memorial capable of being given different meanings by each of us. The anguish of the Vietnam War is present here, but not in a way that does any dishonor to veterans. To call this memorial a "black gash of shame," as Tom Carhart, a Vietnam veteran who was another losing entrant in the competition, has said, is to miss its point entirely, and to fail to see that this design gives every indication of being a place of extreme dignity that honors the veterans who served in Vietnam with more poignancy, surely, than any ordinary monument ever could.

The Lin design is discreet and quiet, and perhaps this is what bothers its opponents the most. It is certainly what bothers Mr. Carhart, whose own design was described as "a statue of an officer offering a dead soldier heavenward." By commissioning the Hart sculpture and the flagpole, the Vietnam Veterans Memorial Fund seems intent on converting a superb design into something that speaks of heroism and of absolute moral certainty. But there can be no such literalism and no such certainty where Vietnam is concerned; to try to represent a period of anguish and complexity in our history with a simple statue of armed soldiers is to misunderstand all that has happened, and to suggest that no lessons have been learned at all from the experience of Vietnam.

The Vietnam Veterans Memorial, as it now nears completion, could be one of the most important works of contemporary architecture in official Washington—and perhaps the only one that will provide a contemplative space equal to any in the past. The insertion of statues and a flagpole not only destroys the abstract beauty of that mystical, inside-outside kind of space that Maya Yang Lin has created; it also tries to shift this memorial away from its focus on the dead, and toward a kind of literal interpretation of heroism and patriotism that ultimately treats the war dead in only the most simplistic of terms.

For in the original design, the dead are remembered as individuals through the moving list of their names carved against the granite. It is the presence of the names, one after the other, that speaks. But if the statues are added, they will overpower the space and change the mood altogether. A symbol of loss, which Miss Lin's design is, will become instead a symbol of war. The names of the dead and hushed granite wall will become merely a background for something else, and the chance for a very special kind of honor—and for a very special kind of architecture—will be lost.

The Fine Arts Commission did approve the addition of the Hart sculpture and flagpole, although at greater distance from the main portion of the memorial than originally proposed. By the spring of 1983, however, these elements still had not been added, and the final outcome was uncertain.

111

PHIL PATTON, EXCERPT FROM
"THE HOUSE THAT RUTH'S FATHER BUILT," 1991

The twentieth century saw the arrival of mass spectator sports, most especially baseball and football, and the building of new stadiums in which to play the games. The century closed with a flurry of new stadiums for professional baseball, football, basketball, and hockey teams. Ironically, baseball teams in the 1990s found themselves playing in new facilities designed to look remarkably like those from the beginning of the century, most of which had been unceremoniously torn down a generation earlier. The first of these "retro"-style ball parks, and still arguably the most successful from the point of view of design and urbanism, was Baltimore's Camden Yards, described here by Phil Patton. It proved such a hit that it spawned many imitators, including parks in Cleveland, Denver, and Philadelphia. While the new ballparks traded on a nostalgia for summers gone by, they were built primarily to generate greater revenues through higher ticket prices, luxury sky boxes, and the like. Babe Ruth's father might recognize the old fashioned form of the new Camden Yards, but the new-fangled ticket prices would have made his head spin.

At Oakwood Sod Farm, outside of Salisbury, Maryland, the grass on which the Baltimore Orioles will play next year is growing this year. Before it is transplanted to Baltimore's new Camden Yards ball park, whose girders are now springing up at their own seemingly photosynthetic speed from an old rail yard downtown, the expanse of Midnight, Touchdown, and Eclipse bluegrasses will have spent longer maturing than most players these days spend in the minors.

The stadium, due to open next spring, gets back to baseball fundamentals—and not only by offering natural turf. It has been designed to restore the feel of an old-time *ball park*—the Orioles even insist on the term. There are no spiraling concrete ramps here, but towers of stairs. The field is sunk below street level as it was at The Polo Grounds, and the trusswork of its steel superstructure rises above a base of arched brick and stair towers topped with pitched roofs, like little houses. Sure, you have wider seats and aisles than in days of yore, a video board and private suites, but there's a little roof over the upper deck and an asymmetry to fit the site: 319' on the line to the right, 335' to left, 410' at the deepest point, in left center. The stadium is smaller than Memorial Stadium, where parking was a chronic problem, but the seats are closer to the action. Foul territory is reduced, and the bullpen is raised so fans can see who is warming up. . . .

Retro is the latest thing in stadiums: It's the *Field of Dreams* look. The leader of the movement is HOK Sports Facilities Group, which also did Pilot Field for the Buffalo Bisons of the American Association in a similar style. Eli Jacobs, the Orioles' owner, believes Ebbets Field was one of the greatest parks ever, and so the team, which a couple of years ago replaced the cartoon bird on its cap with a specimen worthy of Roger Tory Peterson, is aiming to build a park that looks the way a baseball park is supposed to look.

No wonder you hear stadium planners sounding like Stephen Jay Gould writing about baseball in *The New York Review of Books,* talking, as does the Orioles' Janet Marie Smith, about "contextual sensitivity" and "immediate recognizability."

Originally printed in *Esquire,* April 1991.

Smith and other Orioles planners looked at postcards of vanished stadiums, such as Shibe in Philadelphia. They toured older stadiums. What these had in common, they found, was that they were built for baseball only, were downtown, and occupied a single block of irregular shape. Building the stadium to fit the configuration of a block, Smith can argue, like some sort of semiologist, "means the game is taking on the character of the community it is in."

One would worry, after all that, that the sense of history being produced here could end up as slick and glib as in Baltimore's Rouse-developed Harborplace, where tradition is used to provide an enveloping theme for your basic upmarket shopping mall. But the stadium project's saving grace is its site, which includes one of the oldest railroad stations in the country, and a great old brick Baltimore & Ohio warehouse, a thousand feet long, both of which will be incorporated into the facility.

There is genuine baseball history here, too. The turf that is now growing will end up on the ground where Babe Ruth's dad sold booze. In short left-center stood one of the several taverns the family ran until one bar fight too many carried off the patriarch—a hard blow against a curb, a fractured skull.

The Ruth saloon was hardly a fitting place to raise a boy. That's why the Babe, who at age seven began chewing tobacco and exhibiting a marked disinclination for public education, was sent off to St. Mary's Industrial School. Under the tutelage of a Xaverian brother named Mathias, he became the best pitcher in town, star of the Orioles of the International League, who sold his contract to the Red Sox, who sold it to the Yankees.

But on school vacations and even after he made it to the Bigs, Ruth returned to the tavern off-season to help Mom in the kitchen—her famous soup was a dime a bowl—and Dad at the bar—beer was a nickel a bottle.

Before construction began, the Maryland Stadium Authority hired archaeologists to excavate the place, in consultation with the Babe's ninety-year-old sister, Mamie Moberly. They found bones from Mom Ruth's soup and broken beer bottles. They even dug up the family privy.

Some local buffs want to name the stadium after Ruth. They may be right. While the Babe never played major-league ball there, and while he may have consecrated the grounds at Yankee Stadium and cursed the turf at Fenway, only in Baltimore did he literally dispense spirits in the outfield.

112

ANN CARRNS, "HOW A BRAND-NEW DEVELOPMENT
CAME BY ITS RICH HISTORY," 1998

If anything is clear about the way Americans have engaged in the protection of the past, it is that the past has proved to be a valuable commodity for those in the real estate business.

Originally printed in *Wall Street Journal*, February 18, 1998, B1.

The ongoing effort to use history to sell a building, or a city, or a new development received its latest iteration in the invented history created for a new apartment complex by staff at the Post Apartment Company, one of the largest of such developers in the South and West. Here at Riverside, Georgia (the name of the development, not a real city), the developers wrote and published a "history" of a town that never existed until they developed plans for it in the late 1990s. The development, taking some of the New Urbanist ideas to their logical extreme, has been designed not only to make historical references but to create an ensemble of buildings that look as if they might have grown up naturally over time. This is Williamsburg for the twenty-first century.

The village of Riverside, Ga., has a colorful history. Just look at the sepia photographs showing the town in the 19th century, or read excerpts from period novels lauding the settlement's cosmopolitan flair. You'll discover that the town was used as a Union garrison during the War Between the States. And that its historic buildings are being painstakingly renovated, in the tradition of town father Waymon Paulk.

The only hitch is that Mr. Paulk is fictional, and Riverside didn't exist until this year. The account of the 19th century Riverside is a clever fabrication, created to promote a new housing and commercial development of Post Properties Inc., one of the South's largest apartment developers. The story "is a figment of our imagination," acknowledges the company's chairman, John Williams.

The appeal of "neotraditional" communities like Walt Disney Co.'s Celebration in Celebration, Fla., which evoke nostalgia for days gone by, is well-established. Now, Post is taking this "theming" concept one step further by making up a detailed history for Riverside. It's an effort to create overnight what has evolved over hundreds of years in many other cities: A past.

Developers see this latest twist as harmless fun. But it makes some historians uneasy. "It's another example of the trivialization of the attempt to understand our past," says Dan Carter, a professor of Southern history at Emory University in Atlanta. "When you make up history, you don't have to deal with the real thing."

Riverside's master planner, influential Miami architect Andres Duany, praises Post for being innovative but also questions the wisdom of manufacturing a past for the town. "The project's real history—the process that created it—is interesting enough. You don't need to make it up," he says.

But Mr. Williams, who is fond of teasing credulous visitors by telling them his company was founded by cereal magnate, C.W. Post (another fib), relishes the chance to spin a yarn. "Did you know there used to be an old village here?" he asks, pointing to a model of the project with a grin. "And a ferry crossing, down here at the river."

The idea of Riverside was hatched more than two years ago, when Post embraced "new urbanism," which holds that neighborhood design should allow people to live near their work, interact better with their neighbors and get around more on foot. Post decided to unveil its new approach with a $115 million showcase development—to include offices and shops, as well as more than 500 apartments—at a wooded spot on the Chattahoochee River in northwest Atlanta. The site will also house Post's new corporate headquarters.

Post executives, at Mr. Duany's suggestion, visited Princeton, N.J., and Manhattan's Upper West Side to inspect streets that welcome pedestrians. And Mr. Duany himself drove around Atlanta snapping hundreds of pictures of buildings he admired. Then, architects and Post executives critiqued various combinations of their favorite styles during an intense, week-long brainstorming session. The result: A town square framed by three "vintage" structures, including one office building and two apartment blocks.

The seed of the town's apocryphal history was planted during a presentation by Rafael Garcia of Niles Bolton Associates Inc., one of the architects who designed Riverside's apartments. Mr. Garcia says the challenge was to create a place that "looked like it's evolved over a period of time, even though it's absolutely new."

To inspire his team, Mr. Garcia penned a narrative that provided a "unifying thread" pulling Riverside's various elements together. He imagined a settlement founded at a ferry crossing before the Civil War and rebuilt during the decades between Reconstruction and World War I.

He peppered the account with fanciful details. In one incident he conjured up, a building that had housed small mills and workshops—and a secret arsenal during the war—collapsed during renovations. Fortunately, according to the story, no one was injured, and the building was replaced by a nine-story commercial building after the turn of the century. "You have to have a happy ending," jokes Mr. Garcia.

Mr. Garcia illustrated his memo with pen-and-ink drawings of 19th- and early 20th-century buildings culled from architecture texts. Some of the story's details are quiet plausible, as there were indeed two well-known ferry crossings on the Chattahoochee. "I'm kind of a history buff, but I didn't try very hard to make it authentic," he recalls, noting that at the time, the memo was solely for internal use.

But that quickly changed when Post executives saw the document and recognized its potential as a marketing tool. "I sent it right to John Williams, because I knew he'd like it," says Katharine Kelley, senior vice president of Post's development division.

Thus began the metamorphosis of Mr. Garcia's memo into an advertising campaign featuring a mock historian's treatise, "Historical Notes on Riverside." Ads published in local newspapers feature tintypes of purported town denizens accompanied by "quotes" that closely resemble documentary film-maker Ken Burns's technique of excerpting period correspondence to tell the story of the Civil War and other historical eras. "You'll find no better place for whatever your occupation than Riverside," fictional engineer Josiah Mink writes in a "letter" to his brother.

"During those years, I often thought back to the gentle peace I discovered at Riverside, and I vowed to settle there after the war," reads a plaudit attributed to Randall Gray Cartwright, M.D., in "Memoirs of a General Practitioner (1873)."

One ad depicts a dapper gentleman in a bowler hat identified as "philanthropist" Edwin G. Post, said to have donated a fountain to the town. Another photo shows the frame of a post-and-beam building accompanied by the caption, "Princeton during the 1890 remodeling." The Princeton, one of the project's apartment blocks, is said to be the village's "oldest surviving structure." (The second apartment block is named the Pittman, after Mr. Williams's grandmother.)

Fine print at the bottom of the ad informs readers that the story of Riverside is "a whimsical account of how the town could have been developed, and is not factual." Says Mr. Williams: "We'd love for that history to be true. But we didn't have that history here, so we're creating our own."

The nine-story Riverside office building resembles an existing mill building in a neglected south Atlanta neighborhood that another developer is restoring as loft apartments. "I'm more of a purist, and I like the real thing," says Louis Brown, president of Aberhold Properties Inc., which is renovating the massive Fulton Cotton Mill. But Mr.

Brown says he sympathizes with Post's approach: "You've got to have something that differentiates your project from every other Plain Jane development with no theme."

Fictional history aside, Riverside appears poised to become a big hit. Two months before the first building is scheduled to be completed, all of Riverside's retail space is leased, and 65 people have inquired about renting the apartments, which are expected to command premium rents.

Bob Anderson, a recently retired Price Waterhouse partner, plans to rent a large apartment and office space at Riverside. He says he heard about the project by word of mouth and paid scant attention to the ads. He likes the development because he will be able to walk to his new office and "it will look like it's been there for a long time."

113

TRACIE ROZHON, EXCERPT FROM "OLD BALTIMORE ROW HOUSES FALL BEFORE THE WRECKING BALL," 1999

Row houses defined Baltimore for several generations of its residents. Small and compact, they were built to house the inhabitants of a growing city. One hundred years later, Baltimore finds itself with a shrinking population and growing abandonment. In this essay, reporter Tracie Rozhon looks at the city's plan to demolish thousands of now-empty row houses. While finding the solution to Baltimore's problems in "the wrecking ball" sounds much like the urban renewal strategies of the 1950s, or even the Progressive Era, this essay also describes just how complicated it is for cities to regenerate themselves. Is it worth preserving a city if no one lives there anymore?

Teresa Oliver remembers when her block of North Castle Street was tidy and picturesque, its handsome brick houses lined up in an unbroken row, their marble steps gleaming from a combination of soft soap and hard scrubbing. In the evenings, their work done, families sat out on the sidewalks in webbed folding chairs with their beers, laughing while their children played around them.

But that was almost 20 years ago. Now, the chairs and families are gone. Three days after her reminiscence, Mrs. Oliver was gone, too, because the city plans to tear down all the row houses on her east-side block.

"This used to be, well, just a real solid neighborhood," she said.

So did the blocks along Edmondson Avenue, on the west side of town, where dozens of three-story row houses have been knocked into rubble. Windows of abandoned houses that still stand are stoppered with plywood or nothing; lace curtains fly in tatters. Marble steps lie broken.

Baltimore has declared war on huge swaths of its formerly treasured row houses, whose distinctive architecture has sheltered waves of immigrants and the city's working-

Originally printed in *New York Times*, July 13, 1999, A1.

8.5. Baltimore row houses. The Historic American Buildings Survey, 1968. Row houses, modest single-family homes built all in a row, housed thousands of Baltimore's working people and lay at the heart of many of its neighborhoods. With the postindustrial collapse of many of these neighborhoods, thousands of row houses were abandoned and have fallen into disrepair. Baltimore—like Philadelphia and Detroit—has been tearing them down at a great rate, ignoring the question of what will replace them.

class for over a century, but which city officials now describe as derelict. More than 4,000 row houses have been bulldozed in the last three years, virtually all in poor neighborhoods, part of the city administration's mission to remove unsafe urban eyesores. Thousands more have been abandoned and will be demolished. The city has no comprehensive plan to replace them and is not yet sure what it will do with the empty land.

Census tracts show about 66,000 houses in the center city. If demolition continues as planned, the city will have torn down 20 percent of them by the year 2004, in what preservationists assert is a disorganized rush to destruction and city officials describe as an urgent necessity.

Preservationists like Richard Moe, president of the National Trust for Historic Preservation, shudder at the prospect.

"The destruction of these historic row houses will result in a loss of a major part of Baltimore's identity, its greatest asset," Mr. Moe said. The designated houses are usually vacant and always rundown, preservationists say, sometimes serving as crack houses and headquarters for drug dealers.

"We asked the communities what is your worst problem—and we've tried to respond with the wrecking ball," said Daniel P. Henson 3d, the City Housing Commissioner. "I want to get rid of 11,000 of the worst between now and 2003."

The style of Baltimore's row houses—stretching north and south, east and west in seemingly unbroken patterns—has been toasted by Frances Trollope and H. L. Mencken, commemorated in film by Alfred Hitchcock and John Waters and relished by millions who gazed down at their flat roofs from the Boston-Washington trains.

Vincent Scully, professor emeritus of architecture at Yale, praised the form of Baltimore's row houses, "their doors and windows showing the scale of human use."

Built for newly arriving Poles, Italians and Irish in the mid- and late-19th century, these narrow houses remained largely undisturbed while glossy tourist hotels and a model baseball stadium were erected down by the harbor, where an increasing number of visitors flock to see the Orioles and enjoy the paddle-it-yourself harbor skiffs.

But Baltimore, like many older cities,—Philadelphia, Detroit and St. Louis, among them—has been losing population at an alarming rate. Mayor Kurt L. Schmoke said the population drain had resulted in thousands of abandoned houses; estimates range as high as 40,000.

About 1,000 city residents a month are moving out, notably black workers moving to the suburbs in Baltimore County, following the white exodus in the 1960's and 70's to the land of horse farms and better schools. From 1980 to 1990, 76,000 people migrated to the county and of those, 57,000 were black.

In a trend urbanists refer to as "undercrowding," Baltimore City's population plummeted to about 657,000 in 1997 from 950,000 in 1960, according to city planning documents. . . .

"This year, we'll have a net loss of about 6,000 people," said Commissioner Henson, who grew up in a West Baltimore row house but 20 years ago moved his family to a house with a lawn and a pool near the county line.

Common Problem But More Profound

Baltimore's problems, while common to other American cities, are more pronounced, said Douglas Rae, a professor of urban management at Yale who coined the term "undercrowding."

"Baltimore's very heavy reliance on row houses sets it apart," Professor Rae said. "Also the scale of the population loss is larger. And finally, the intensive suburban development in the county is more extreme than most other cities facing undercrowding."

The poor, inner-city neighborhoods began to deteriorate visibly in the late 1970's. Rows of houses started to show their age and a few were boarded up.

But since then the changes have accelerated. Mr. Hensen said that by the early 80's, sizable chunks of West Baltimore and East Baltimore and parts of North-Central Baltimore near Johns Hopkins Hospital had lost much of their sense of neighborhood. . . .

But officials are not thinking about restoring the old row houses; they are mostly thinking of tearing them down. Today, whole blocks lie in rubble.

Officials contend that not enough people are moving to Baltimore, and those who are—"urbanites or empty nesters," Mr. Henson said—do not want an antique row house unless it is near the harbor.

In the last five years, the price of restored row houses in waterfront manufacturing areas has tripled or quadrupled. Canton, once a seedy warehouse area east of the glamorous harborside renewal, now has row houses priced as high as $150,000—compared with the virtually valueless houses in West Baltimore and parts of East Baltimore. . . .

Another deterrent to rehabilitation of the old houses has been the expense: $85,000 to $100,000 for each full-scale renovation. An average mid-block row house costs up to $30,000 to demolish, which includes shoring up the survivors on either side with cinder block and mortar.

City Handed Tool to Speed Process

This spring, the Schmoke administration got what it was seeking from the State Legislature: a speeded-up demolition process under which the city can get approval from a judge to demolish a block when 70 percent of its housing is vacant, rather than wait for the block to empty. . . .

The administration is reaching out for solutions for hard-hit neighborhoods. Early this year, the city and the Historic East Baltimore Community Action Coalition picked an area near Johns Hopkins Hospital and held a design competition.

One of the two winning entries, from Glatting Jackson, an architectural firm in Orlando, Fla., proposed lining the old alley streets with new garage buildings, with apartments overhead. The other entry, by A. Nelessen of Princeton, N.J., called for 50 percent of the narrow houses to be renovated, with some joined together to make loft-like spaces. Houses also incorporated garages, that symbol of suburbia.

"If you want to compete with the suburbs, you have to offer amenities like garages," said Rob Inerfeld, program coordinator for the Neighborhood Design Center, a sponsor of the competition. "When most of Baltimore was built, people didn't drive."

To William Rees Morrish, director of the Design Center for American Landscape at the University of Minnesota, and a juror for Baltimore's design competition, the row-house problem is an ecological one.

"Animals, when their shells grow obsolete, they shed the shell and move on," he said. "Many row houses have reached the point where they're falling down and the city has to move on."

But even Mr. Henson, the aggressive campaigner for demolition, is a little sad to see so many houses being ripped apart.

How does he feel when he drives through his old neighborhood in West Baltimore and sees the rubble and ruin?

"It makes me feel so bad, I want to cry," the Commissioner said.

114

HERBERT MUSCHAMP, "NEW WAR MEMORIAL IS SHRINE TO
SENTIMENT," 2001

The movement begun—or at least expressed most powerfully—with Maya Lin's Vietnam
Veterans Memorial may have been stalled or even reversed with the victory of tradition-
alists in the design of the Second World War veterans memorial to be built between the
Washington and Lincoln memorials. Sentiment and nostalgia, Herbert Muschamp argues,
won out over the more difficult, but arguably more meaningful, emotions called on by
Maya Lin in her nearby Vietnam memorial. The memorial, Muschamp charges, "represents
our yearning for the timeless and eternal to distract us from the relative and the complex." The battle also brought into the fore the debate over public places. As the number
and importance of public spaces has diminished in the United States, the battles over true
public spaces—and the mall in Washington evokes deep-seated patriotism in even the
most skeptical of citizens—have grown more heated.

Three works of architecture in postwar Washington have challenged the status quo: I. M.
Pei's East Wing of the National Gallery, Maya Lin's Vietnam Veterans Memorial and
James Ingo Freed's United States Holocaust Memorial Museum. They owe their distinction to the skill with which they honor the Enlightenment concept of clear geometric
form while rejecting the ornamental particularities of neo-Classical style.

Mr. Pei introduced geometric abstraction and asymmetry into an illustrational
backdrop of classical order. Ms. Lin opposed the horizontal contour of a sunken black
chevron against a city of white columns. Mr. Freed, in the most astonishing inversion of
the city's classical harmony, turned his stone facade into a sinister symbol of the totalitarian state. All three designs developed abstract geometry into complex formal vocabu-
laries. The forms enabled them to express complex ideas. As a result, they honored
the Enlightenment tradition of daring to know. They renewed the meaning of the neo-
Classical buildings around them.

By contrast, Friedrich St. Florian's design for the National World War II Memorial
diminishes the substance of its architectural context. The design does not dare to know.
It is, instead, a shrine to the idea of not knowing or, more precisely, of forgetting. It
erases the historical relationship of World War II to ourselves. It puts sentiment in the
place where knowledge ought to be.

An aura of inevitability surrounded the memorial even before the legislation to
build it had been signed. It is the aura we have come to associate with certain Hollywood
movies—"Pearl Harbor" being the most recent example—whose commercial success is
virtually guaranteed even if critical esteem eludes them.

As designed by Mr. St. Florian, the Rhode Island architect, the memorial reproduces
a style of architecture associated with the World War II period and the decade preceding
it. Sometimes called modern classical, the style was frequently used by architects for federal buildings in Washington and elsewhere. Columns and pilasters are more massive
than the classical orders, typically rectangular rather than round. Friezes, lettering and
articulation of the volume substitute for antique refinements like fluting and scrolls.

Originally printed in *New York Times* June 7, 2001.

The project, whose construction may be speeded by legislation that President Bush signed last week, will occupy 7.4 acres on the Mall. The bulk of this is properly described as landscape, rather than architectural, design. It incorporates the area now occupied by the Rainbow Pool, at the eastern end of the Reflecting Pool between the Washington Monument and Lincoln Memorial.

The pool will be restored and enclosed by two hemicircles of steles. The 56 granite pillars 17 feet tall represent each state, territory and the District of Columbia during that war period. Arched pavilions 43 feet high on the north and south ends of the plaza will be dedicated to the Atlantic and Pacific theaters of the war. The design's best feature is its sensitivity to the site. Scale notwithstanding, the memorial is not the visual obstruction many have feared. The remodeled Reflecting Pool, which has been in a state of decrepitude for years, will enhance, not diminish, the existing vistas. The hemicircular arrangement enables the steles to be partly screened by trees.

Still, the design is seriously flawed. Its classical vocabulary does not create the transcendent framework that the sponsors (the American Battle Monuments Commission and an advisory board) seem to have in mind. Rather, the forms employed are charged with historical and ideological content that contradicts this apparent intention.

Some critics have compared St. Florian's design to the work of Albert Speer, Hitler's armaments minister. A trained architect, Speer was chosen by the Führer to redesign Berlin as Germania, the colossally scaled capital of the Thousand Year Reich. The comparison is overwrought. The memorial's modern classical style was favored by Mussolini, Roosevelt, Stalin and other government leaders in the 1930's. Examples of this style can be found all over Washington and in many other cities with federal courthouses, post offices and other government buildings designed in the 1930's and 40's. In that limited sense, St. Florian's design is true to the events it commemorates.

But the design also reveals the hazard of relying on period styles to evoke memories of past events. Those who expect memorials to deepen historical awareness will be disappointed by the design. Theoretically, the memorial has been conceived to honor those who fought in service of democracy. In fact, the style chosen recalls a period gripped by the widespread fear that democracy was doomed.

In the United States, this fear was held alike by left and right wings of the political spectrum. Democracy, so the reasoning went, equaled individualism, and unbridled individualism had precipitated the catastrophe of the Depression. Only strong centralized government, whether socialist or fascist, could lead the country out of the mess. Political extremes met in the bombastic form of massive granite facades, square pilasters, eagles and other motifs from the repertory of ancient Rome.

This is an astonishing message to reiterate at a time that professes opposition to Big Government. Though the message may be unintentional, the design nonetheless displays a profound sense of historical amnesia. There is a difference between architecture and propaganda, even if Washington is a city where the distinction is easily blurred. The memorial's design can't be accurately appraised without venturing into the fog. Washington's core formal concept—its neo-Classical plan and architectural aesthetic—is symbolically sound. Architects of the Enlightenment saw neo-Classicism as a reaction to rococo excess. The relative clarity of the style's geometrical forms represented scientific reason. It suited the idea of a nation governed by laws, not men.

But Enlightenment architects also believed that art and architecture adhered to universal laws. It was the job of the academies to discover and enforce them. It turns out, however, that the culture of a modern democracy thrives on challenging this belief. Our political system is great because it enables authority to be challenged. Washington is relatively insubstantial architecturally because it does not. The city's Fine Arts Commission, the agency charged with regulating architectural aesthetics, is more or less in the business of preventing such challenges from materializing where they might distract visiting schoolchildren from the overwhelming impression of authority.

In recent years, "World War II" has come to epitomize the use and misuse of historical memory. Tom Brokaw's best-selling books, Steven Spielberg's blockbuster movies, a forthcoming 10-part HBO miniseries "based on the true story of the men of Easy Company" and other offerings have simultaneously increased historical awareness and substituted emotional manipulation for it.

However sincere the intentions of individual writers, filmmakers and producers of commercial spinoffs, the cause of remembering the war has also served the objective of forgetting the unfolding of history before and since. Before Vietnam, before Watergate, before the cultural distortions of the cold war, there was an age of moral certainty, a time innocent of complexity, irony or ambiguity. This time can be bracketed between the years 1939 and 1945.

But this view of the war years is rooted in the moral uncertainties of our own day. So is the World War II Memorial's design. It represents our yearning for the timeless and eternal to distract us from the relative and the complex. After the failures of the so-called American Century, that yearning is understandable and even heroic, up to a point. If the soldiers who fought in the war aren't entitled to such sentiments, who is?

But the yearning for a transcendent meaning raises new complexities in turn. When Washington was conceived, it was possible to imagine a nation that would stand outside history, including its own. It would adhere to the Enlightenment belief in natural law. That belief, along with its architectural representation, remains valid in the case of government institutions.

In the case of historical memory, it is inadequate. We do not honor history by seeking to transcend it. Nor do we transcend it by copying period styles. The sponsors of the St. Florian design want it both ways. They ask us to accept that a period style can remember and transcend simultaneously. Instead, these goals neutralize each other. At best, the result represents a failure of historical imagination. This failure condemns a potential work of architecture to a level of well-designed propaganda.

Mr. St. Florian's design looks like a monument. It looks like history. It was probably chosen on account of its generic appearance. And in a city whose public architecture often resembles a revolving rack of postcards, well-designed propaganda may well pass for authenticity itself.

This may be a case where people will want to decide for themselves where their sentiments about the war lie. That is because the official World War II Memorial gives the impression of being foisted upon us, like it or not. The impression is not entirely false. It stems from the embattled condition of public space in the era of privatization. Isn't this the heart of the problem? For all its claims to moral certainty, the memorial is mired in our present-day confusion over the rights and responsibilities of government in the management of public space. . . .

In the United States, public space is rapidly becoming a subsidiary of the entertainment industry. Television occupies a vast majority of the social realm once defined by streets, town halls, public squares. Computers take up an increasing share of the rest.

Then come shopping malls, business improvement districts, theme parks, multiplexes and Indian casinos. There's a bit left over for sidewalks, but perhaps not for long. It's too expensive to police them. They've got to pay their way. Eventually someone will patrol them with surveillance cameras and market the videos on reality pay TV.

The World War II Memorial can be seen as a monument to the military-entertainment industry complex, our new enforcers of the global Pax American Pop Culture. It is a Spielberg production featuring Tom Hanks in a cast of all-star unknown soldiers. Naturally, the design looks authentic. It's a special effect. A digitized backdrop, like the Colosseum in "Gladiator." Mr. St. Florian's simulated national monument is perfect, down to every period detail.

No one can say that this project is out of step with our recent political life. It is faithful to Ronald Reagan, who confused making combat training movies with actually seeing wartime action. To George Bush senior, the president who defeated the "Vietnam syndrome" with the televised Operation Desert Storm. And to Bill Clinton, the maestro of public emoting, choking back tears on Normandy Beach.

The National Mall, however, is not the place for a permanent movie set, nor should the public be treated like a captive audience. If you don't like "Pearl Harbor," you can always walk out. If the buzz around "Saving Private Ryan" or "Schindler's List" strikes you as manipulative and overblown, you can stay away from the multiplex. These options will not be available for visitors to the Mall. You liked the movie. You'll love the building. It will outlive you, anyhow.

THEMATIC INDEX

We have organized the chapters of this book along the themes we believe to be the central ones in understanding Americans and their relationship to the built environment. However, a number of other themes appear repeatedly in documents across the chapters; these themes can be found through the use of this index. Numerals refer to documents.

African-Americans, 46, 64, 99

American homes and housing, 10, 33, 45, 49, 52, 64, 77–79, 80, 85, 90, 96, 97, 102, 103, 112, 113

Architecture: of commerce, 13, 30, 50, 65, 69, 74; of entertainment and sport, 28, 73, 74, 111; and religion, 6, 19, 44, 59, 87, 88, 90, 101

Industrialization, 34, 92

Institutions and public buildings, 2, 5, 15, 25, 36, 39, 41, 62, 87, 89, 94, 99, 102, 107

Major cities: Chicago, 7, 61, 69; New York, 13, 14, 66–68, 71, 75, 101, 109; Philadelphia, 55, 56; Washington, D.C., 5, 57, 110, 114

Native Americans, 29, 32, 42, 100

Regions: Northeast, 30, 31, 34, 43, 44, 55; South, 36, 37, 47, 104, 106, 112; Midwest, 29, 38, 61, 69; West, 32, 49, 51, 53, 54, 60, 73, 74, 85

Urban planning, 22, 24, 56–58, 61, 66, 70, 77, 86, 93, 98, 113

Women and the built environment, 21, 69, 70, 80, 84, 110

Working-class neighborhoods and architecture, 59, 63, 64, 69, 72, 91, 96, 97, 109

ACKNOWLEDGMENTS

This project began a long time ago. It started on the streets of New Haven, Connecticut, when we were inspired by our professors and by the city around us to see the story of America as it was written in the built environment. It continued to percolate during our years in graduate school together in Philadelphia, by way of New York and Providence and Berlin and London. In the classes we took and taught, we regularly left the classroom to see what we could learn and teach about American history from the built environment of that place. This book has come, finally, to fruition as we have settled into academic careers, other projects behind us, and fulfilled the promise we made to do this book on the streets of Philadelphia.

Across this distance of time and space we have accumulated countless debts, to teachers, students, colleagues, friends, family. To all of you, we extend our thanks and the promise to reciprocate should you ever ask.

This project began in earnest with the help of graduate student David Madden, and it could not have happened without his able work and his equally astute observations. He was succeeded by other assistants, including Il-Song Park, Shane Hankins, Jill Ogline, and Jill Stover, all of whom kept this anthology moving, even when its editors flagged.

Thanks too to all the undergraduates who had to endure our walking tours and who forced us to think more deeply about how to understand and teach the built environment, though many of them simply wanted to get in out of the cold.

This volume has been mightily improved due to the help we have received from wonderful scholars around the country, including Daniel Bluestone, David Brownlee, Dolores Hayden, Greg Hise, Paula Lupkin, James O'Gorman, John Reps, Andrew Shanken, George Thomas, Dell Upton, Ted Wolner, and Gwendolyn Wright. John Tully and Brad Austin of the Goldberg Center in the History Department at Ohio State University came to our technical rescue, enduring Steve's questions, problems, and ineptitude with unfailing good humor. They are gentlemen and scholars both. In the eleventh hour, Geoff Smith of Ohio State's Special Collections department and Susan Wyngaard of the Fine Arts Library bailed us out of bibliographic jams.

Grants from the Graham Foundation for Advanced Studies in the Fine Arts and from the Furthermore program of the J. M. Kaplan Fund enabled us to include images and texts in this book that would have otherwise been beyond our reach and helped keep the cost of this book manageable.

We owe a special debt to our editor, Robert Lockhart, of the University of Pennsylvania Press not simply for shepherding this unruly beast along but for the enthusiasm with which he embraced it from the very outset. Without that, our manuscript might well have moldered in the proverbial desk drawer. His colleague Erica Ginsburg deserves particular thanks for minding the details and for dealing with two editors not very good at doing that.

Finally, there are those who lived with this more than they ought to have, who cleared out space for us to finish it, and who did so with love and generosity. The Coppingers and Teresa Jones and DeWitt Thompson gave up a big dining room table for weeks at a time in an old farm house on the side of a hill in Montague, Massachusetts.

Over the years this has been in the works, many Conns and Pages cheered us when cheering was needed most.

And to Eve and Angela—this book is a small offering for everything we owe to you both.